THIRD EDITION

THE SOCIOLOGY OF EDUCATION

A Systematic Analysis

JEANNE H. BALLANTINE

Wright State University

PRENTICE HALL, Englewood Cliffs, N.J. 07632

Library of Congress Cataloging-in-Publication Data

Ballantine, Jeanne H.
  The sociology of education : a systematic analysis / by Jeanne H.
Ballantine—3rd ed.

  Includes bibliographical references and index.
1. Educational sociology. I. Title.
LC191.B254 1993
370.19—dc20   92-36233
ISBN 0-13-819095-X   CIP

Acquisitions editor: Nancy Roberts
Editorial/production supervision and interior design: Barbara Reilly
Copy editor: Eleanor Walter
Editorial assistant: Pat Naturale
Cover design: Ray Lundgren Graphics, Ltd.
Cover photo: Alan McEvoy
Prepress buyer: Kelly Behr
Manufacturing buyer: Mary Ann Gloriande

We gratefully acknowledge the following sources for permission to reprint the photos
that appear in this text on the pages listed: Alan McEvoy, Wittenberg University (pp. 13,
30, 89, 119, 149, 230, 260, 295, 389, 397); UNESCO/Paul Almasy, p. 186; UNESCO/
Louis Duré, p. 331 (top); UNESCO/Dominique Roger, p. 331 (bottom).

*To my parents,
Peggy and Dan Hazen*

Printed in the United States of America
10 9 8 7 6 5 4 3 2 1

ISBN   0-13-819095-X

Prentice-Hall International (UK) Limited, *London*
Prentice-Hall of Australia Pty. Limited, *Sydney*
Prentice-Hall Canada Inc., *Toronto*
Prentice-Hall Hispanoamericana, S.A., *Mexico*
Prentice-Hall of India Private Limited, *New Delhi*
Prentice-Hall of Japan, Inc., *Tokyo*
Simon & Schuster Asia Pte. Ltd., *Singapore*
Editora Prentice-Hall do Brasil, Ltda., *Rio de Janeiro*

CONTENTS

PREFACE   *xi*

1   *SOCIOLOGY OF EDUCATION*
A Unique Perspective on Schools   *1*

The Field of Sociology of Education   **2**
What sociologists study   2
Why study sociology of education?   3
Kinds of questions asked by sociologists of education   4
Theoretical Approaches and the Development of Sociology
of Education   **5**
Functionalist theory   6
Conflict theory   9
Interaction theories   11
Other recent theories in the sociology of education   11
American sociology of education   12
The Open Systems Approach   **13**
Research Methods in Sociology of Education   **20**
Sociology of Education in the Next Century   **21**
Organization of the Book   **22**
Summary   **22**

Studies in sociology of education   23
Putting sociology to work   24
Notes   24

2   CONFLICTING FUNCTIONS AND PROCESSES
What Makes the System Work   27

Conflicting Functions of Education   27
The Importance of Processes in Systems   29
The Function of Socialization: Who Gets Ahead in the Process?   29
The early childhood education controversy   30
Role of the media in socialization   35
Political socialization   36
**The Function of Cultural Transmission and Process
of Passing On Culture   38**
Some factors affecting learning   39
How to pass on culture   40
What culture to pass on   41
**The Function of Social Control and Personal Development:
Preparing the Individual for Society   50**
Discipline in schools   50
Students' rights   53
The Function of Selection and Allocation: The Sorting Process   54
The testing game   54
Studies related to IQ testing and environmental influences   57
Achievement tests   57
**The Function of Change and Innovation: The Process
of Looking to the Future   58**
Summary   59
Putting sociology to work   61
Notes   61

3   EDUCATION AND THE PROCESS
OF STRATIFICATION   68

The Crisis in Schooling   68
Education and stratification in America   68
The Process of Stratification: Is Inequality Inevitable?   70
Determinants of social class   71
Major explanations of stratification   74
Stratification and Equality of Educational Opportunity   79
The meaning of "equality of educational opportunity"   79

Social class reproduction: the debate over public versus private schools 79
The controversial issue of "choice" 81
Ability grouping and teacher expectations 83
Families and schools: home environment effects on educational achievement and stratification 89
Financing schools in the United States 95
Summary 96
Putting sociology to work 97
Notes 97

4 SEX, RACE, AND ATTEMPTS TO ACHIEVE EQUALITY OF EDUCATIONAL OPPORTUNITY 103

Sex and Equality of Educational Opportunity 103
Sex role socialization 104
Sex differences in the educational system 105
School achievement: the case of math and science 110
"Biological destiny" 111
Combatting sexism in educational systems 112
Race and Attempts to Rectify Inequalities in Educational Opportunity 112
Trends in public school enrollments 113
At-risk students 114
Research on equality of educational opportunity 116
The battle over desegregation 117
Court cases on desegregation 118
The big yellow school bus: attempts to desegregate by busing 120
Effects of busing to desegregate schools 121
Integration Attempts 126
Educational Experience of Other Minorities in the United States 128
Hispanic students 128
Immigrants 130
Asian-American students 130
Native American students 131
Special education students 132
Gifted students 134
Improving Schools for Minority Students 136
Summary 138
Putting sociology to work 139
Notes 140

5   THE SCHOOL AS AN ORGANIZATION   146

Social System of the School   147
Goals of the School System   148
  Societal and community goals   149
  School goals   151
  Individual goals   151
School Functions: The Purposes of the School   152
  Diverse functions   152
  Unanticipated consequences of functions   152
  Conflicting goals and functions   153
The School as an Organization   154
  The school as a bureaucracy   154
  Characteristics of bureaucracy   155
  Development of schools as bureaucracies   159
  Problems in educational bureaucracies   160
  Schools as "loosely coupled organizations"   162
Centralized versus Decentralized Decision Making:
    The Fight Over Control of Schools   163
  Centralization of decision making   163
  Decentralization   164
Professionals in the Educational System   165
Summary   167
  Putting sociology to work   168
Notes   168

6   FORMAL SCHOOL STATUSES AND ROLES
    "The Way It Spozed to Be"   171

The Meaning of Roles   171
  Status and roles in the system   171
  The school organization and roles   172
  Role expectations and conflict   172
  Perspectives on roles   173
Roles in Schools   173
  School boards: liaison between school and community   173
  Superintendent: manager of the school system   177
  The principal: school boss-in-the-middle   180
  Teachers: the front line   184
  Students: the core of the school   195
  Support roles in the school: behind the scenes   208
Summary   211
  Putting Sociology to Work   212
Notes   212

7   THE INFORMAL SYSTEM AND THE "HIDDEN CURRICULUM"
What Really Happens in School   218

The Open Systems Approach and the Informal System   219
The Hidden Curriculum   220
  Reproduction theory and the informal system   221
The Educational "Climate" and School Effectiveness   222
  The value climate   222
  The school climate and effective schools   227
  Effective schools: what works?   228
  Classroom climate   229
Power Dynamics and Roles in the Informal System   236
  Theoretical explanations of power dynamics
    in the classroom   236
  Students and the informal system   237
  Teacher strategies and the informal system   243
Summary   245
  Putting sociology to work   246
Notes   247

8   THE EDUCATIONAL SYSTEM AND THE ENVIRONMENT
A Symbiotic Relationship   251

The Environment and the Education System   252
  Types of environments   253
**The School Systems' Environments: Interdependence
    Between Institutions**   254
  Home and family influences on school   255
  The institution of religion: separation of church and state   256
  The economics of education: financing schools   258
  The political and legal institution   264
  Communities and their schools   267
Summary   268
  Putting sociology to work   269
Notes   269

9   THE SYSTEM OF HIGHER EDUCATION   272

History and Development of Higher Education   273
  Historical functions of higher education   273
  Trends in development of higher education   274
Theoretical Approaches to Higher Education   277
  The expansion of higher education   277
  Access to higher education   278

Stratification and equal opportunity in higher education   278
Elite versus public colleges   280
Admissions and the courts   280
Characteristics of Higher Education in the United States   281
Growth of higher education   283
The "body-count game" and the credential crisis   283
Functions of the Higher Education System   284
The university as a community   284
The function of research   285
The function of teaching   285
The function of service   285
The function of the "national security state"   285
Conflicts over the university's function   286
The academic function of universities versus big business   286
What type of curriculum   287
Higher Education as an Organization   288
Higher education structure and the bureaucratic model:
   does it work?   288
Roles in Higher Education   291
Roles in higher education: the clients   291
Gender and race in higher education   293
The graying of college graduates   297
Roles in higher education: the faculty   301
Faculty issues in higher education   303
Roles in higher education: administrators   306
Environmental Pressures on Higher Education   306
Government influence on funding of higher education   307
The courts and affirmative action   310
Environmental feedback and organizational change   311
Outcomes of Higher Education   312
Higher education: attitudes, values, and behaviors   312
The value of a higher education   313
Problems and Reform in Higher Education   314
Summary   317
Putting sociology to work   319
Notes   319

10   EDUCATION SYSTEMS AROUND THE WORLD
A Comparative View   326

Cross-Cultural Educational Studies   328
Comparative education as a field of study   328
Comparative education and the systems approach   329

Approaches to Cross-Cultural Studies of Educational Systems   329
   Comparative international studies of achievement   330
**Theoretical Perspectives and Typologies
   in Comparative Education   332**
   Modernization and human capital perspectives   332
   "Legitimation of knowledge" perspective   333
   Rich versus poor: an educational typology   334
   National structures of educational systems and curricula:
     comparative variables   336
**Cross-Cultural Approaches to Educational Systems: World
   and Institutional Interdependence   337**
   World system analysis   337
   Education and economic institutions   338
   Stages of economic development and educational change   339
   Education and political-economic institutional systems   340
   Education and the institution of religion   343
   Family, social class, and education   343
   Higher education around the world   345
Case Studies of Educational Systems   345
   Education in Britain   346
   Education in the People's Republic of China   352
   History of education in colonial Africa   355
Summary   360
   Putting sociology to work   361
Notes   361

11   EDUCATION MOVEMENTS AND REFORM   366

The Nature of Educational Movements   369
Educational Movements Throughout History   371
   Early European education: purpose and function
     for society   371
   Educational movements in the United States   372
Alternative Education and Related Movements   375
   The development of free schools   376
   English primary schools   377
   Impact of the alternative education movement   378
   Open classrooms   378
Back to Basics and Accountability   380
   Private schools   382
   Accountability movements   383
   The testing controversy and back to basics   385
   Effective schools and educational reform   386
   Structural and curricular changes in the schools   386

The "Choice" movement   387
"Multiculturalism" and "Political correctness"   387
Technology and the classroom   388
Other movements, reforms, and fads   389
Summary   390
Putting sociology to work   391
Notes   392

12   CHANGE AND PLANNING IN EDUCATIONAL
       SYSTEMS   395

The Dynamics of Change   396
Change and levels of analysis   397
Sources of change   399
Perspectives on Change   400
Structural-functional approach to change   400
Conflict approach to change   401
Open systems approach to change   404
Bringing About Change   405
Individuals in the system   405
Change at the school level   406
Strategies for School Change   406
Types of strategies   407
Obstacles and resistance to implementation of change   409
**The Sociologist's Role in Educational Change
    and Policy Formation   410**
Summary   411
Putting sociology to work   413
Notes   413

Epilogue   SCHOOLS IN THE EARLY TWENTY-FIRST
           CENTURY   415

Demographic Trends   415
Family and Social Trends   416
Schools in the Early Twenty-First Century   418
Reform and Policy in Educational Systems   419
Goals for the Year 2000   421
Some Things We Have Learned   422
Notes   422

INDEX   424

PREFACE

This book attempts to capture the scope and usefulness of the sociology of education. It emphasizes the diversity of theoretical approaches and issues in the field and the application of this knowledge to the understanding of education and schooling. Education is changing rapidly; it is no easy task to present the excitement of a dynamic field with diverse and disparate topics. To present the material to students in a meaningful way, a unifying framework—an open systems approach—is used. It is meant to provide coherent structure, not to detract from the theory and empirical content of sociology of education.

After teaching sociology of education to many undergraduate and graduate students and using a variety of materials, I was concerned that the materials available, though excellent in quality, were not reaching my undergraduate students who were from sociology, education, and other majors. The level of many texts was too advanced, the themes of some books made their coverage or approach limited, or the books presented research in such depth that they were boring or beyond the grasp of undergraduates. During my work with the Project on Teaching Undergraduate Sociology, I focused on presentation of materials to undergraduates, and I have attempted to translate these ideas to this text. The book is best suited for sociology of education and social foundations of education courses at the undergraduate or beginning graduate level.

Several goals guided the writing:

1. To make the book comprehensible and useful to students. Realizing that most students are interested in how the field can help them deal with issues they will face, I emphasized usefulness of findings. Choices had to be made concerning

which studies and topics to cover. Those chosen should have high interest for students and help them as they interface with school systems.

2. To present material in a coherent framework. The instructor has leeway within the open systems approach to add topics, drop sections of the text, and rearrange order of topics without losing the continuity and integration present in this framework.

3. To present diverse theoretical approaches in sociology of education. Several valuable perspectives exist today; the book gives examples throughout of theories as they approach issues in the field.

4. To include as major sections several topics that have not been singled out by many authors but that are important current or emerging topics and of interest to students. Separate chapters have been devoted to higher education, informal education ["climate" and the "hidden curriculum"], the school's environment, and educational movements and alternatives.

5. To indicate how change takes place and what role sociologists play. With the increasing emphasis on applied sociology, more courses are including information on applied aspects of topics covered. This is the focus of the final chapter but is covered throughout.

6. To stimulate students to become involved with educational systems where they can put to use the knowledge available in textbooks. This text can be used to stimulate discussion and allow other topics of interest to be introduced into the course in a logical way. Useful features of the book to enhance the teaching effectiveness include projects at the end of each chapter, the coverage of issues, and the instructor's manual complete with classroom teaching aids, techniques, and test questions.

The book does not attempt to use one theoretical approach to the exclusion of others. Rather, it focuses on the value of several approaches and their different emphases in dealing with the same issue. Because the book is meant as an overview, it surveys the field rather than providing comprehensive coverage of few topics. This allows instructors flexibility to expand where desired.

The third edition provides an update of issues and data, as well as revisions in theories where new trends or developments have occurred.

Thanks go to many people: for suggestions on early drafts of the first edition, to Peggy Hazen, Paul Klohr, Alan McEvoy, Reece McGee, Matthew Melko, Darryl Poole, Ted Wagenaar, and colleagues at Bulmershe College of Higher Education in England. For a review of the manuscript, to Sandra Damico, University of Florida, and Nolan Armstrong, Northern Illinois University. For helping on research, to Mary French and to Harden Ballantine, Ed.D., for the section on alternatives in education. For providing the materials and atmosphere for producing the end product, to Antioch University Library, University of Reading (England) Library, and the University of London and Bodleian libraries.

A special thanks to the supportive group at Prentice Hall, especially Nancy Roberts and Barbara Reilly who provided expert editorial assistance.

Finally, interest in this field is constantly stimulated by the diverse and ever-changing experiences of my children as they pass through the stages of schooling and share their experiences, and by Hardy, whose knowledge and creative ideas in the field of education gave original impetus and continuing support and encouragement to this work.

1

SOCIOLOGY OF EDUCATION
A Unique Perspective
on Schools

Education begins the day we are born, and ends the day we die. Found in every society, it comes in many forms, ranging from the "school of hard knocks" or learning by experience to formal institutional learning, from industrial to nonindustrial communities, from rural to urban settings, and from age group to age group.

Remember your first day in the formal school setting? You had anticipated that day for some time. You met the teacher who would serve as a surrogate parent for the year, and children you would get to know whether you liked them or not. Education was a given, a compulsory part of growing up. Going to college was "what people do after high school." But for many people in the world, education is a privilege available only to a select group. One-quarter of primary-age children in the world are not even in school, and 40 percent of young women in Africa and southern and western Asia are illiterate.[1]

Sociologists are interested in learning experiences of all types, formal and informal. This fits into their broader focus on group life. The purpose of this introductory chapter is to acquaint you with the unique perspective of the sociology of education: the questions it addresses, the theoretical approaches it uses, the methods employed to study educational systems, and the open systems approach used in this book.

THE FIELD OF SOCIOLOGY OF EDUCATION

Educational issues face us constantly as students, parents, and members of a community. Consider the following examples.

When Should a Child Start School?   Some argue that children should be removed from a total home environment at an early age and exposed to other children, stimulation, and ideas. Others feel that removing children from the home deprives them of a secure early childhood environment and even weakens the family. It is an emotional issue that reaches around the world. What are the results of early childhood educational policies?

Should Minimum Competency in Key Subjects such as Reading and Math Be Required for High School Graduation?   In many countries and some cities and states in the United States students are required to take reading exams in order to enter high school and be graduated from it. Some educators argue that required competency tests will force teachers to teach for the tests; others state that schools should be held responsible for the academic competence of students who move through the system, and tests are one way to accomplish this. What are some implications of requiring tests?

How Should Education Be Funded?   Many countries have centralized funding and decision making. However, across the United States taxpayers are defeating school levies, and some schools are being forced to curtail programs because there is no money. Is this a protest against the job schools are doing? Is it a demand for the development of other funding sources? Is it a bid for more community control?

What Type of Teachers and Classroom Environments Provide the Best Learning Experience for Children?   Educators debate lecture versus experiential learning, and discussion versus individualized instruction. Studies of effective teaching strategies can help educators carry out their roles.

Sociological research knowledge sheds light on these and other issues, and thus helps teachers, citizens, and policymakers with the decision-making process. The first step in understanding the institution of education is to discuss its meaning and lay the theoretical groundwork.

What Sociologists Study

Sociologists study people in group situations. Within this broad framework are many specialties; these can be divided into studies of institutions in society, studies of processes, and studies of other group-related situations. The *structure* of society is represented by six major institutions that constitute subject areas in sociology: family, religion, education, politics, economics, and health. Formal, complex organizations such as schools are part of the institutional structure of society. *Processes,* which are the action part of society, bring the structure alive.

Through the process of socialization people learn roles expected of them; the process of stratification determines where people fit into the social structure and their resultant lifestyle; change is an ever-present process that is constantly affecting our lives. All of us are being educated, both formally in a school setting and informally by our family, peers, media, and other influences on our lives. Not all children in the world receive formal school education, but they are trained in some way for adult roles they will hold.

The institution of education interacts and is interdependent with each of the other institutions listed above. For instance, the family's attitudes toward education will affect the child's response in school. Other examples throughout the book will make this apparent, as will the open systems model diagram (Figure 1-2).

Why Study Sociology of Education?

There are several answers to this question. Someday you may be a professional in the field of education or in a related field; you *will* be a taxpayer, if you aren't already; you may be a parent with children in the school system; right now you are a student involved in higher or continuing education. If you are a sociology major, you are studying education as one of the major institutions of society; if you are an education major, sociology can give you a new perspective on your field. You may be at college in pursuit of knowledge; or it may be that this course is required, or you need the credit, or the teacher is supposed to be good, or it fits into your schedule. Let's consider these reasons further.

Teachers and Other Professionals.   In 1990, of all college graduates, 104,715, or 10 percent, were graduated in the field of education,[2] and many hold teaching positions. Many other college graduates will teach in their respective academic fields or become involved with policy matters in the schools. Professionals in such fields as social work and business have regular contact with schools when dealing with clients and employees.

Taxpayers.   Taxpayers finance schools at the elementary, secondary, and higher education levels. Almost 100 percent of the bills for physical plants, materials, salaries, and other essentials come from tax monies. In 1989, revenues for schools, a large amount of which is from sales, income, and property taxes, come from three sources: 6.2 percent from federal government, 47.7 percent from states, and 46.1 percent from local funds.[3] (Of course, there are variations within and between states.) Sociology helps taxpayers know about the school system.

Parents.   Forty percent of our population are in the primary parenting years of 18 to 44;[4] the average size of families in 1984 was 2.7 members, meaning that the average family has one child.[5] According to the Gallup polls on adult attitudes toward education, adults expect schools to teach basic skills, discipline children, and instill values and a sense of responsibility. The concerns of the American public regarding schools have shown a high level of consistency from year to year (Table 1-1). It is interesting to note that the integration/segregation/busing category drops to number 9 in the 1991 listing. Parents need to make decisions related to children's education; understanding of school systems can be gained from a study of the sociology of education.

Students.   College attracts a wide variety of students with numerous motivations and goals for their educational experience. Understanding your own and others' goals will help you get the most from your educational experience.

For sociology majors, sociology of education provides a unique look at the social variables that affect the education systems and illustrates the interdependence among the major institutions in society. For education majors, new insights can be gained by looking into the dynamic interaction both within the institution and between the institution of education and others in society. These insights should give education majors greater ability to deal with complex organizational and interpersonal issues that confront teachers and administrators.

Other Reasons.   Knowledge for the sake of knowledge—learning what there is to learn—is another reason to study sociology of education. Other prime motivators for taking such a course may be busy schedules; the goal of "getting through college"; and such practical considerations as class time, required courses, and necessary credits.

Kinds of Questions Asked by Sociologists of Education

This topic is best dealt with by looking through the whole book, but the following sampling of questions that have been considered by researchers in the field will give an idea of the wide range of possible subject matter:

1. How does the physical setup and program of an educational organization affect such variables as learning, communication between faculty and students, and the subject areas taught?
2. How effective are different teaching techniques, styles of learning, and classroom organizations in teaching students of various types and ability levels?
3. What are some community influences on the school, and how do these affect decision making in schools, especially as it relates to socialization of the young?
4. How does professionalization of teachers and teacher militancy affect the school system? Do teacher proficiency exams increase teaching quality?
5. How do issues such as equal opportunity and integration affect schools? Can minority students learn better in an integrated school?
6. Are some students overeducated for the employment opportunities that are available?
7. How does education affect income potential?

Multitudes of questions arise, and many of them are being studied around the world. Sociology of education books and courses are organized around the key topics discussed throughout this text.

TABLE 1-1   Concerns Regarding Schools

1975	1981	1991
1. Lack of discipline	1. Lack of discipline	1. Use of drugs
2. Integration/segregation/ busing	2. Use of drugs	2. Lack of discipline
3. Lack of proper financial support	3. Poor curriculum/poor standards	3. Lack of proper financial support
4. Difficulty of getting "good" teachers	4. Lack of proper financial support	4. Difficulty of getting "good" teachers
5. Size of school/classes	5. Difficulty of getting "good" teachers[a]	5. Poor curriculum/poor standards
	6. Integration/busing[a]	6. Large schools/ overcrowding
		7. Parents' lack of interest
		8. Pupils' lack of interest/ truancy
		9. Integration/busing
		10. Low teacher pay

[a]Items 5 and 6 were tied.

Elam, Stanley M., Lowell C. Rose, and Alec M. Gallup, "The 23rd Annual Gallup Poll of the Public's Attitudes Toward the Public Schools," Phi Delta Kappan, *September 1991, p. 55.*

THEORETICAL APPROACHES AND THE DEVELOPMENT OF SOCIOLOGY OF EDUCATION

Sociology of education is a fairly recent field of inquiry. In the past half-century, emphasis has been given to education as a unique institution and objective field of study. During this period, studies have focused on social issues in which education plays a part, such as the role of schools in providing opportunities for the poor to raise their economic status, conflicting value systems that threaten the environment,[6] assimilation of immigrants, or the role of education in promoting inequality.

In this century, work in the sociology of education can be divided into studies that describe large systems (education as one part of the whole interdependent society), studies that deal with specific institutions of education or parts of systems, and studies of interaction in educational settings.

Theoretical perspectives are used by scientists to provide logical explanations for why things happen the way they do. Starting the study of a subject with a theoretical perspective provides a guide, a particular conception of how the social world works. Of course, a point of view also influences what the researcher sees and how it is interpreted.

Just as we have various interpretations of events in our everyday lives, so too there are several sociological perspectives on why things happen the way they do in society. These theories sometimes result in different emphases or interpretations of the same information or data. Just as each individual interprets situations differently depending on his or her background, theorists focus on different key aspects of a research problem.

A theoretical approach helps to determine the questions to be asked by researchers and the way to organize research in order to get answers. Some-times elements of several theories are combined. Below, key aspects of three important theories are discussed. Sociologists using each theoretical approach have made major contributions in the field of sociology of education, and you will be meeting many of them as you proceed through the text.

The first two approaches focus on differing views of the way society works. The third deals with interactions in social situations. These three approaches also focus on different "levels of analysis": the functional and conflict approaches tend to deal with macro-level view of social relations and the culture of the school (that is, large-scale societal and cultural systems), whereas the interaction approach focuses on small-scale interaction between individuals and small groups.

An aspect of educational systems that is not stressed in these approaches is the school as an open system dealing with pressures from the environment. The open systems approach, which is the framework for this book, is explained at the end of this chapter.

Functionalist Theory

One major theoretical approach in sociology is *functionalism,* also referred to as structural-functionalism, consensus, or equilibrium theory. A sociologist using this approach starts with the assumption that society and institutions within society, such as education, are made up of interdependent parts all working together, each contributing some necessary activity to the functioning of the whole society. This approach is often likened to the biological functioning of the human body: Each part plays a role in the total system and all are dependent on each other for survival. Just as the heart or brain is necessary for the survival of a human being, an educational system is necessary for the survival of society.

Reviewing past work in sociology of education helps us formulate a theoretical and practical base on which to build; it also helps provide a historical perspective on the field. While many philosophers, educators, and other social scientists contributed their insights on education to sociological knowledge, early sociologists provided the first scientific treatments of education as a social institution.

Durkheim's Contributions to Functionalism.   Emile Durkheim (1858–1917) set the stage for the conservative functional approach to education. A professor of pedagogy at the Sorbonne in Paris before sociology was "admitted" as a major field, he is generally considered to be the first person to recommend that a sociological approach be used in the study of education. He was awarded the Sorbonne's professorship of sociology, combined with education, a post he held in 1906 and for most of the years until his death in 1917. Thus, sociology came into France as a part of education. Since Durkheim taught all students graduating in education, many were exposed to his ideas.

Durkheim was employed to lecture primarily in education, but his sociological approach was his unique contribution. His ideas centered around the relationship between society and its institutions, all of which he saw as being interdependent. Many of the issues about which Durkheim spoke in the late 1800s are as real today as they were then: the needs of different segments of society in relation to education, discipline in the schools, the role of schools in preparing young people for society. Most important, Durkheim attempted to understand why education took the forms it did, rather than judging those forms, as had been done so often.

Durkheim's major works in the field of sociology of education were published in collections entitled *Moral Education,*[7] *The Evolution of Educational Thought,*[8] and *Education and Sociology.* In these works, he outlined both a definition of education and the concerns of sociology as he saw them, thus defining the field for future sociologists. He wrote:

> Education is the influence exercised by adult generations on those that are not yet ready for social life. Its object is to arouse and to develop in the child a certain number of physical, intellectual and moral states which are demanded of him by both the political society as a whole and the special milieu for which he is specifically destined. . . .[9]

Durkheim observed that education has taken very different forms at different times and places, showing that we cannot separate the educational system from the society, for they reflect each other. In *The Evolution of Educational Thought,* he describes the history of education in France, combining ideas from some of his other works in a historical-sociological analysis of the institution of education. Always he stresses that in every time and place education is closely related to other institutions and to current values and beliefs.

In another major work, *Moral Education,* Durkheim outlines his beliefs about the function of schools and their relationship to society. Moral values are, for Durkheim, the foundation of the social order, and society is perpetuated through its educational institutions. Any change in society reflects a change in education, and vice versa; in fact, education is an active part of the process of change. In this work, he analyzes classrooms as "small societies," agents of socialization. The school serves as an intermediary between the affective morality of the family and the rigorous morality of life in society. Discipline is the morality of the classroom, and without it the class is like a mob.

Some aspects of education that are of great concern today—the function of selection and allocation of adult roles; the gap between societal expectations of schools and actual school performance—were not dealt with by Durkheim. He was concerned primarily with value transmission for stability of society and did not consider the possible conflict between this stable view and the values and skills necessary for changing, emerging industrial societies. He argued also that education should be under the control of the state, free from special-interest groups; yet most governments are subject to influence from interest groups and to trends and pressures affecting society. Pressures from the school's environment in the areas of curriculum content, for instance, are very real.

Durkheim outlined certain areas that he felt were important for sociologists as researchers to address, including the functions of education, the relationships of education to societal change, cross-cultural research, and the social system of the school and classroom.[10] His writings and guidelines for further research provided a useful beginning for the field; they also serve as a measuring stick for how far we have come. Durkheim set the stage for the current functionalist theoretical approach to education. Themes of his general writing are reflected in his concerns about consensus, conflict, and structure in education.[11]

Functional Theory Today.   A primary function of schools is the passing on of the knowledge and behaviors necessary to maintain order in society. Since children learn to be social beings and develop appropriate social values through contact with others, schools are an important training ground. Following Durkheim, sociologists see the transmission of moral and occupational education, discipline, and values as necessary for the survival of society.

Functional theorists conceive of institutions as parts or components of total societies or social systems. The parts of the system are discussed in terms of their *functions,* or purposes in the whole system. The degree of interdependence among parts in the system relates to the degree of *integration* among these parts; all parts complement each other, and the assumption is that a smooth-running, stable system is well integrated. Shared values, or consensus, among members are important components of the system, as these help keep it in balance.

Functional theorists tend to focus their research on questions concerning the structure and functioning of organizations. For instance, sociologists using this theoretical approach to study educational systems would be likely to focus attention on the structural parts of the organization, such as subsystems and positions within the structure, and on how they are functioning to achieve certain goals. Sociologists who research and interpret events from this theoretical perspective see as central the functions of education for society.

The problem most often seen by critics of this approach is that it fails to recognize the number of divergent interests, ideologies, and conflicting interest groups. In heterogeneous societies, each subgroup may have its own agenda for the schools—an agenda to further its own interests.

A second problem is that it is difficult to analyze individual interactions, such as the classroom dynamics of teacher-student or student-student interactions, from this perspective. A related criticism is that the functionalist approach does not deal with the "content" of the educational process:[12] what is taught and how it is taught. Individuals do not just carry out roles within the structure; they create and modify them.

In addition, there is a built-in assumption that change, when it does occur, is slow and deliberate and does not upset the balance of the system—which simply is not true in all situations. The assumption of change as a "chain reaction" is implied, but does not necessarily reflect the reality of stable societies or rapidly changing societies.

In a now-classic analysis,[13] Jean Floud and A. H. Halsey suggest that little advance had been made in the field since the studies of Durkheim and Max Weber (whose theories are discussed below). They argue that the dominant theoretical approach of structural-functionalism has not been capable of moving the field ahead because of its status quo orientation in a society faced with constant change. "Structural-functionalism, it is suggested, tends to play down problems of social change, and is therefore . . . unsuitable for the analysis of modern industrial societies."[14] In part as a reaction to these shortcomings, conflict theory began to take a prominent role in the field.

Both functional and conflict theories attempt to explain how education contributes to the maintenance of the status quo in society. However, neither focuses on the individual, the individual's "definition of the situation," or interactions in the educational system, as does the third theory to be discussed.

Conflict Theory

In contrast to the functional approach is the *conflict theory* approach, which assumes a tension in society and its parts created by the competing interests of individuals and groups. Variations of this approach stem from the writings of Karl Marx and Max Weber. Society's competing groups, the "haves" and the "have-nots," are seen as being in a constant state of tension, leading to the possibility of struggle. The "haves" control power, wealth, material goods, privilege, and influence, the "have-nots" constantly present a challenge as they seek a larger share of society's wealth. This struggle for power helps determine the structure and functioning of organizations and the hierarchy that evolves as a result of power relations. The "haves" often use coercive power and manipulation to hold society together, but change is seen as inevitable and sometimes rapid, as the conflicts of interest lead to the overthrow of existing power structures.

Weber's Contributions to the Sociology of Education.   Max Weber (1864–1920) presented a particular brand of conflict theory. Weber contributed less directly than Durkheim to the sociology of education, and provided a less systematic treatment of education. His work in related fields of sociology, however, has contributed to our understanding of many aspects of education. He is noted for his work on bureaucracy and for the concept of status group relationships. In fact, he writes that the "main activity of schools is to teach particular 'status cultures,' both in and outside the classroom."[15] Power relationships and the conflicting interests of individuals and groups in society influence educational systems, for it is the interests and purposes of the dominant groups in society that shape the schools. Weber's unique approach combined the study of the macro-school organization with an interpretive view of who or what brings about a situation and how we interpret or define these situations.

Within the school there are "insiders" whose status culture, as Weber sees it, is reinforced, and "outsiders" who face barriers. Transpose these ideas to school systems today as they deal with poor and minority students and the relevance of Weber's brand of conflict theory becomes evident. His theory deals with conflict, domination, and groups struggling for wealth, power, and status in society. These groups differ in property ownership; cultural status, such as ethnic group; or power derived from positions in government or other organizations. Education is used as one means to attain these ends. Relating this to Marx's writings on conflict theory, education produces a disciplined labor force for military, political, or other areas of control and exploitation by the elite.

Weber's writings, using cross-cultural examples and exploring preindustrial and modern times, shed light on the role of education in different types of societies and at various time periods.[16] In preindustrial times, education served the primary purpose of a differentiating agency that trained people to fit into a way of life and a particular "station" in society. With industrialism, however, new pressures faced education from upwardly mobile members of society vying for higher positions in the economic system. Educational institutions became increasingly important in training people for new roles in society.

Weber described a trend toward the rational organization of bureaucracy in modern society, noting that one characteristic of modern bureaucratic organization is its rational-expert leadership. The leaders are selected on the basis of examinations, which single out those who best fits jobs at different levels of the bureaucracy. Today, charismatic leaders and those born into positions of power are less dominant in many institutions, including education, than are competent, professional experts whose merit is measured by examination.[17]

In his essay "The Rationalization of Education and Training,"[18] Weber points out that rational education develops the "specialist type of man" versus the older type of "cultivated man," described in his discussion of education systems in early China. Again we see the relevance of Weber's writings: Today's institutions of higher education are debating the value of vocationally oriented education versus education for the well-rounded person.

Conflict Theory Today.   Weber and Marx set the stage for branches of conflict theory held by theorists today. Research from the conflict theorists' perspective tends to focus on those tensions created by power and conflict that ultimately cause change in the system. Some conflict theorists see mass education as a tool of capitalist society, controlling entrance into higher levels of education through the selection and allocation function and manipulating the public.[19] Applying this idea at the school and classroom level, Willard Waller states that schools are in a state of constant disequilibrium; teachers are threatened with the loss of their jobs because of lack of discipline; and authority is constantly being threatened by students, parents, school boards, and alumni who represent other, often competing, interest groups in the system.[20]

Cultural reproduction and resistance theories argue, very generally, that those who dominate capitalistic systems mold individuals to suit their own purposes. Theorists study the cultural processes by which students learn knowledge and what knowledge is transmitted. Resistance to this control has also been the topic of many recent studies.[21] These will be discussed in some detail in later chapters.

This approach implies a volatile system, with the ever-present possibility of major disruption. The approach can be very useful in attempting to explain situations where conflict exists; however, critics argue that the connection between curriculum and capitalism has not been clearly laid out and little empirical data has been presented to substantiate the claims.[22] Also, this theory does not offer useful explanations concerning the balance or equilibrium that does exist between segments of a system or the interactions between members of the system.

Interaction Theories

A third theoretical approach in sociology focuses on individuals in interaction with each other. Individuals sharing a culture are likely to interpret and define many social situations in similar ways because of their similar socialization, experiences, and expectations. Hence, common norms evolve to guide behavior. However, differences also exist based on individual experiences, social class, and status.

The *interaction theory* approach has been used increasingly since World War II, and emphasizes social-psychological questions. Sociologists of education using this approach are likely to focus on interactions between groups—peers, teacher-student, teacher-principal; on student attitudes and achievement; on student values; on students' self-concepts and their effect on aspirations; and on socioeconomic status as it relates to student achievement.

Two interaction theories useful in sociology of education are labeling theory and exchange theory. If Johnny is told repeatedly that he is dumb and will amount to little, he may incorporate this "label" as part of his self-concept and behave as the label suggests. There is evidence that students behave well or badly depending on teacher expectations. *Labeling theory* is discussed further in other sections of the book.

Exchange theory is based on the assumption that there are costs and rewards involved in our interactions; reciprocal interactions bind individuals and groups with obligations—for example, student learns and teacher is rewarded. Rewarding behavior is likely to be continued. These interaction theories are useful to us in understanding the dynamics of the classroom.

Other Recent Theories in the Sociology of Education

A "new" sociology of education has been a focus of attention of many British sociologists since the early 1970s and has supporters in the United States and elsewhere. In reaction to "macrocosmic" approaches, which put little emphasis on interaction, these theorists base their ideas on symbolic interaction, ethnomethodology, and phenomenology, arguing that an alternative approach to sociology of education is needed if we are to understand educational systems.

These theorists stress the need to understand our commonsense views of reality—how we come to view the events and situations around us and react to them as we do. Applied to education, this has taken the form of studying interaction processes in classrooms, the management and use of knowledge, the question of what it is to be "educated," curriculum content, and so forth. (Some examples of work using this approach will be cited in Chapter 6.)

The work of two proponents of this approach, Basil Bernstein and Pierre Bourdieu,[23] seems to show a synthesis of macro- and microcosmic approaches rather than a totally new approach.[24,25] Bernstein argues that the structural class and power relations of the system (the "macrocosmic" levels of analysis) and the interactional educational processes of the school (the "microcosmic" levels) need to be integrated.[26] One effort at integration is seen in his work on the speech patterns that, he argues, perpetuate one's social class. One's family class position determines this pattern, which, in turn, affects one's position in society—as exemplified by the poorer academic performance of working-class children. He also points out the need to evaluate the effect of class bias in teaching and educational ideology on students' performance. Bernstein's later work focuses on curriculum and the pedagogy used to transmit knowledge. Curriculum—what is taught—defines "valid knowledge," and how it is transmitted has consequences for different groups of students based on social class and power relations. His attempts to link the societal, institutional, interactional, and intrapsychic realms have moved the field closer to an integration. However, more empirical testing is necessary, and applications to educational practice and policy need to be carried out.[27,28]

American Sociology of Education

In American sociology of education there was an early motivation to reform society. Lester Frank Ward, one of the six founding fathers of American sociology and first president of the American Sociological Association, argued in 1883 that education is a principal source of human progress and agent of change that can foster moral commitment and cognitive development to better society.[29] The field was referred to as *educational sociology*, and focused on practical issues and the formulation of policy and recommendations. The name *sociology of education* was introduced in the late 1920s by Robert Angell.[30] Angell and others saw educational institutions as sources for scientific data; they felt that sociology could not and should not promise to produce answers or suggest changes to solve school problems. However, today there is a need for sociologists with both emphases: one group to carry out objective research and one to work with schools in interpreting and implementing scientific findings. The latter group needs to have special training in scientific methodology, as well as practical knowledge of the functioning of schools.

This book deals both with theoretical studies of schools and with the practical application of theory in schools and classrooms.[31] The latter aspect is important since most of you will be using this knowledge in your roles as parents or professionals. Sociology can have practical applications and an impact on policy rather than remaining abstract and theoretical.

Many children attended one-room schoolhouses during the early days of American education.

THE OPEN SYSTEMS APPROACH

By now it is clear that a number of theoretical approaches are used to study the institution of education. Each provides valuable insights into a complex system. How are we to order this complexity and make it understandable?

Some sociologists favor one theoretical approach for all of their work; others select an approach to fit the problem. Our goal is to understand the educational system and the contribution that each approach can make to that understanding. For this reason this book is organized around a systems model of education. Using this model, we can break this complex system into its component parts for study. One theoretical approach may be more applicable than another for the study of certain parts of the system or of educational problems that arise in the system. It makes it possible for us to see the interconnections between parts and theories. Let us now move to an explanation of the model.

If we want to understand an educational system as a whole, integrated, dynamic entity, we are faced with a problem. Most research studies focus on parts of the whole system, and most theoretical approaches have specific foci. An open systems approach is not a panacea for all the problems we face when trying to get the total picture, but it can help us conceptualize a whole system and understand how the small pieces fit together, and which pieces do not fit. A model provides a useful way of visualizing the many elements in the system; it helps order observations and data, and represents a generalized picture of complex interacting elements and sets of relationships.[32] The model given below does not refer to one particular organization or theoretical approach, but rather gives us a framework to consider the common characteristics of many educational settings.

While this model indicates the component parts of a total system, it does not imply that one theory is better than another for explaining situations or events in the system. Neither does it suggest which is the best methodology to use in studying any part of the system. It does allow us to visualize the parts we may read about or study in relation to the whole system—to see where they fit and what relationship they bear to the whole.

In describing a systems model, Marvin Olsen has said:

> It is not a particular kind of social organization. It is an analytical model that can be applied to any instance of the process of social organization, from families to nation. . . . Nor is [it] a substantive theory—though it is sometimes spoken of as a theory in sociological literature. This model is a highly general, content-free conceptual framework within which any number of different substantive theories of social organization can be constructed.[33]

Figure 1-1 shows the basic components of any social system. We will discuss the parts by following five steps. An example for each step, taken from an educational setting (Figure 1-2) is included to help clarify the content of each part of the system.

Step 1. Focus your attention on the center box, the *organization.* This refers to the center of activity and the central concern for the researcher. This box can represent a society (such as the United States), an institution (such as education or family), an organization (such as a particular school or church), or a subsystem (such as a classroom). For purposes of discussion, we shall refer to this as "the organization." It is in the organization that action takes place, illustrating that the organization is more than structure, positions, roles, and

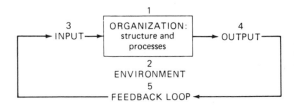

FIGURE 1-1
Systems model.

Source: Adapted from Ludwig Von Bertalanfly, "General Systems Theory—A Critical Review," *General Systems,* Vol. 7, 1962, pp. 1–20.

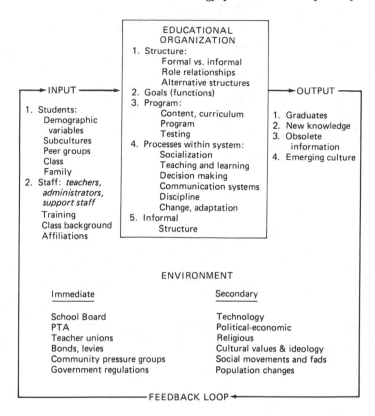

FIGURE 1-2   Systems model of education.

functions. Within the organizational boundaries is a *structure* consisting of parts and subparts, positions and roles. Although we speak of the organization as though it were a living entity, we are really referring to the personnel who carry out the activities of the organization and make decisions about organizational action. The *processes* in the system bring the organization alive. Decision making by key personnel, communication between members of the organization, socialization into positions in the organization—these are among the many activities that are constantly taking place.

Some theoretical approaches emphasize only this internal organizational analysis, but these processes do not take place in a vacuum. The decision makers holding positions and carrying out roles in the organization are constantly responding to demands from both inside and outside the organization. The boundaries of the organization are not solid, but rather remain flexible and pliable in most systems to allow system needs to be met. We call this "open boundaries" or an *open system.*

The formal relationships within educational organizations are only part of the picture. Capturing the informal relationships in the school—who eats

---

EXAMPLE: AN OPEN SYSTEM ORGANIZATION

"High School" was filmed to "show it like it is." Frederick Wiseman moved his film crew into a high school and shot reels of film. Later, in the editing process, he put together scenes representing life in the high school. The film showed *roles:* teachers were interesting, boring, humiliating, supportive, threatening when dealing with students. Students were attentive, bored, hostile, compliant. Administrators mediated, scolded, doled out punishments. This probably sounds familiar—we have all been through similar experiences. We have all been key functionaries, going through *manifest processes* of teaching, learning, decision making, communicating, and disciplining; we have also experienced the *latent processes* of rebelling and participating in a peer subculture.

Wiseman also looked at the *subparts* or smaller divisions of the high school *structure.* The film contains scenes showing individual classrooms; the principal as he was dealing with parents; the assistant principal's office, where disciplinary matters were being handled; the hallway; the gym; cooking class; the lunchroom.

---

lunch with whom, who cuts classes, what subtle cues teachers transmit to students, what is the gossip in the teachers' lounge—can tell us as much about its functioning as observing formal roles and structure.

Step 2.   An open system implies that there is interaction between the organization and the environment outside the organization.

Focus now on the *environment.* This includes everything that surrounds the organization and influences it in some way. Typically, the environment includes other surrounding systems. For a country, these would be all other countries of the world; for an organization, they would be other competing or cooperating organizations. In addition, there is the *technological environment,* with new developments that affect the operation of the system; the *political environment,* which affects the system through legal controls; the *economic environment,* from which the system gets its financing; the *surrounding community* and its prevailing attitudes; the values, norms, and changes in society, which are often reflected in *social movements* or *fads; population changes;* and so forth.

For each organization, the crucial environment will differ and can change over time, depending on issues facing the school. Importance, however, does not. The organization depends on the environment for meeting many of its resource requirements and for obtaining information.

Each school and school district faces a different set of challenges from the environment. There are necessary and desired interactions with the environment, and some that are not so pleasant. The interaction of the school with the environment takes place in our systems model in the form of inputs and outputs.

EXAMPLE: THE ENVIRONMENT

Imagine that you are the principal of the local elementary school. Your responsibilities involve maintaining a smoothly running school and meeting the goals of educating the children. Some of the factors with which you must contend are predictable; others are not. Here are some examples from a week in your life.

1. A school board meeting is coming up for which you must prepare a budget report justifying the expense for a new series of second-grade readers.
2. The PTA has asked you to speak on the counseling program in the school.
3. You have received notification from Washington that the school must develop a plan to mainstream some of the community's disabled students and train teachers to deal with them in the classroom.
4. Contract negotiations are coming up with the teachers' union, and you must justify the school's needs in several areas, such as in-service training that requires teachers to stay after school.
5. A bond levy will be on the next ballot, asking the voters for funds to buy new playground equipment and library resources. To get the bond passed will require lobbying in the community.
6. A group of citizens is asking for a conference to discuss the Title IX legislation related to sexism in the schools, and what steps are being taken to eliminate sexism at your school.
7. A new reading program has been developed, using sophisticated equipment. You must consider whether the expenditure would be worth the potential improvement.
8. Some parents in the community are concerned about Christmas carols being sung in classes and the Christmas tree in the school lobby. A decision must be made as to whether to eliminate these religious symbols.
9. You have received the projections for population trends in the community for the next ten years. They show a likely decline in elementary school enrollment. You need to plan a strategy to deal with this probability.
10. The state legislature passes numerous bills related to education, some of which are directly relevant. You must keep up with this information.

Source: Excerpts from interviews with principals conducted by author.

Step 3. The organization receives *input* from the environment in such forms as information, raw materials, students, personnel, finances, and new ideas. Furthermore, the persons who are members of an organization all belong to other organizations in the environment and bring into the organization influences from the outside environment.

Some of the environmental inputs are mandatory for the organization's survival; others vary in degree of importance. For most organizations, some inputs are undesirable, but unavoidable; new legal restrictions, competition, or financial pressures. The organization can exert some control over the inputs. For instance, schools have selection processes for new teachers, text-

---

EXAMPLE: INPUT

In universities, students are key participants. You fill out forms to enter the system, wait in line to sign up for classes and pay tuition, come to class to take notes and exams, obtain credits, and are graduated. In systems terms, you are *inputs* into the system, and *outputs* upon graduation. And you are "processed" through the system. In the process you wait in lines to become inputs, and suffer humiliation and sometimes defeat in being processed by the system—but also are rewarded for academic efforts.

You bring to the system your personality, your contributions, your money, *and* your problems. For instance, a number of students attending universities are parents. When the public schools are not in session, they are faced with the problem of child care. At these times, the number of individuals in the university classroom may increase, with little persons accompanying their parents, or may decrease, because of child-care problems.

The school system includes personnel who act as buffers. For instance, a class is closed. You really need that class at that time. Instructor's permission is required to let you in, but the instructor is nowhere to be found. The departmental secretary takes your name and assures you that the instructor will be in touch with you if you are permitted to enter the class. There is an effective buffer.

---

books, and other curricular materials. Certain positions in the organization are held by personnel who act as *buffers* or liaisons between the organization and its environment. The secretary who answers the phone, for example, has a major protection and controlling function, and the social worker and counselor are links with the environment.

Step 4.   *Output* refers to the material items and the nonmaterial ideas that leave the organization: completed products, such as research findings; graduates; wastes; information; evolving culture; new technology. There may be personnel in *boundary-spanning* positions, bridging the gap between organi-

---

EXAMPLE: OUTPUT

A ceremony with full academic regalia and a sheepskin (or more likely an engraved paper) marks the passage from the school organization to the environment. Graduates are a clear example of a university's output or product, which also includes books and articles written by faculty reporting research findings; new ideas and evolving culture that affect our lifestyle and values; jargon; and major league football and baseball players.

There are also "negative" outputs—students who drop out or fail, faculty members who do not receive tenure, students who graduate but are unable to find jobs in the tightening job market. These can be seen as system failures.

zation and environment. Personnel with responsibility for selling the organization's product, whether they work in a manufacturing organization or in a placement office for college graduates, serve this function.

Step 5.   A key aspect of a systems model is the process of *feedback*. This step implies an organization constantly adapting to changes and demands in the environment as a result of new information it receives. For instance, the organizational personnel compare the current state of affairs with desired goals and environmental feedback to determine new courses of action. The positive or negative feedback requires different responses.

The basic model (Figure 1-2) can serve us in many ways. It is used as a framework for organizing content in this book. But, as conceived by some of its early proponents, it is more inclusive and flexible, and it can help promote interdisciplinary study. Consider, for example, Kenneth Boulding's statement:

> . . . an interdisciplinary movement has been abroad for some time. The first signs of this are usually the development of hybrid disciplines. . . . It is one of the main objectives of General Systems Theory to develop these generalized areas, and by developing a framework of general theory to enable one specialist to catch relevant communications from others.[34]

Sociology of education cannot be discussed within the fields of education and sociology alone. Examples of related fields are numerous: economics and school financing; political science, power, and policy issues; the family and the child; church-state separation controversies; health fields and medical care for children; humanities and the arts; and the school's role in early childhood training.

Several social scientists[35] have pointed to the value of an open systems approach in organizational analysis. David Easton, for example, writes: "A

EXAMPLE: FEEDBACK

The university graduates education majors who obtain teaching jobs in the community. But the graduates have weak skills in dealing with minority students and their families. Not only are the schools dissatisfied, but the students are frustrated. This message reaches the university and plans are begun to modify the curriculum. Included in the modified curriculum are both course work and practical experience in urban schools and with minority students. The feedback has indicated need for change and decisions have been made within the organization to bring about the needed change.

We can now picture a full cycle of continuous activity. The processes never cease. We can only study an organization or some aspect of it at a given moment in time, for new events will bring constant modification of that organization. Most organizations, however, develop sufficient stability and adapt to environmental demand well enough so that change is slow and deliberate.

systems analysis promises a more expansive, more inclusive, and more flexible theoretical structure than is available even in a thoroughly self-conscious and well-developed equilibrium approach."[36] For our purposes, this approach not only serves the functions noted above, but helps give unity to a complex field. Each chapter in the book describes some part or process in the educational system.

RESEARCH METHODS IN SOCIOLOGY OF EDUCATION

A theory is used to give direction to research studies, determine data and materials to be collected, and guide interpretations of data. However, a theory is only a guideline. Content must be added. Using scientific and objective techniques, data must be collected in order to test the usefulness and accuracy of theoretical explanations of events.

A sociologist is a scientist and therefore employs the scientific method in studying issues and problems. Some sociologists focus their attention on the institution of education and issues related to it. Their research techniques are essentially the same as those used by sociologists studying other areas.

Prior to 1950, few studies of education used objective standards and measures. Most frequently, anecdotes and value judgments were used to illustrate and support arguments.[37] More recently, the emphasis in published literature has been on empirical studies. Several research methods are now used in sociology of education: participant observation, surveys, secondary analysis, controlled laboratory studies, and case studies. To decide which technique to use, the researcher must define the problem to be studied and determine the possible sources of information related to the problem. Then the researcher selects the population or group to be studied and determines whether to study all or part of the population. The researcher may want to talk directly with the persons in the group to be studied, observe them at some task, obtain statistical information such as test scores, or use a combination of these and other techniques.

Several recent works rely heavily on observation in schools. Two examples are Lubeck's *Sandbox Society*[38] and Metz's *Classrooms and Corridors*.[39] In each, observation in classrooms produced data to study research questions. Philip Jackson also relied heavily on systematic classroom observation in writing *Life in Classrooms*.[40] Observations of activities in several elementary classrooms over time and studies done by other researchers were the foundation for his well-known book. Ethnographic researchers consider how students and teachers construct the classroom social situation. Observation, sometimes through videotapes, is used to understand the way classrooms work.

Another famous study used controlled classroom settings. Robert Rosenthal and Lenore Jacobson studied the effects of teacher expectations on student performance through "manipulating the classroom situation, by assigning some of the children to a special treatment which was not accorded to their classmates."[41] This experiment comes close to being a controlled laboratory experiment with a minimum of influence from external sources; yet it is difficult to rule out all of the influences from outside the classroom that might have affected the study results.

In yet another well-known study, James Coleman and others[42] surveyed approximately 5 percent of the schools in the United States to ascertain the degree of equality of educational opportunity. In this massive study, students at five grade levels were given standardized tests. Additional information about the students and schools was collected by survey and secondary analysis. Further examples of research techniques will be mentioned as we discuss various studies.

At times it is useful to combine methodological techniques in order to obtain the most accurate picture of what we are studying. Coleman, for instance, was criticized for not using observation or other techniques to describe the operations that went on in the schools he surveyed.

SOCIOLOGY OF EDUCATION IN THE NEXT CENTURY

When several prominent sociologists of education were asked about their predictions for the field in the years ahead, most predicted that the problems facing American schools would see little improvement in the near future.

The student population is changing dramatically. Thus, U.S. schools soon will be dealing with the most diverse group of students ever. "By 2000, more than ten states will have [a majority of their] student populations who trace their ancestry to Africa, the Hispanic world, the Pacific Islands, Arabia, or somewhere other than white Europe. The Los Angeles public schools already teach children who speak at least 81 languages other than English at home. Economic inequalities in our society are widening."[43,44]

The problems that face our schools reflect the problems in our society. The number of children living in poverty and "at-risk" educationally is increasing rapidly, especially in urban areas. Books such as Kozol's *Savage Inequalities*[45] document the inequalities between rich and poor school districts.

The sociologists interviewed suggest that sociological theories and methods will make a major contribution to understanding the societal forces and school dynamics that underlie the problems schools will face; this knowledge is essential to tackle the problems of the twenty-first century.

Schools are often expected to be the unifier of a fragmented society and to produce competent adults who can perform their roles well. To understand how and to what extent this is possible, sociologists of education can contribute knowledge on school, classroom, and family social systems; on the factors contributing to inequality; on nonacademic factors that affect children's learning and achievement; and on many other areas of concern to educational systems. For instance, it is difficult to produce competent adults from abused or neglected children. Longitudinal research (research conducted on a group of students over time), ethnographies, and statistical data sets are among the major methods that will provide the data for analysis of schools.[46]

ORGANIZATION OF THE BOOK

Each chapter in the book describes some part of the system of education. As you read, be aware of which part is being discussed, and by the end of the book you should have a fairly complete picture of the total education system. The order of chapters can be changed and still fit into the total model. Theoretical approaches discussed in this chapter are related to practical issues throughout the book. In addition, you can enhance your effectiveness in dealing with schools by learning to "do" sociology, learning about the methodology used, and becoming knowledgeable producers and consumers. At the end of each chapter you will find a chapter summary and suggested projects related to each topic. You are encouraged to try to make the subject more useful to yourself by doing these projects. For instance, after reading this chapter, ask yourself what questions you feel sociology of education should address. Keep these in mind as you read. You might also consider doing further research or projects on the questions you raise.

We are now ready to enter the school. The scene is an active, dynamic one. Let us take a closer look at some of the processes taking place.

SUMMARY

In this chapter we have discussed the perspective of sociology of education.

I. The Field of Sociology of Education

Sociologists study group life. One of the institutions in society is education: As a part of group life it is of interest to sociologists. All of us are involved with educational systems during our lives, and education interacts with and is interdependent with other institutions in society.

We study sociology of education because it is or will be relevant to roles we play as taxpayers, parents, professionals, and students.

Researchers in sociology of education have focused on numerous areas of study: the socialization process; the relationship between education and stratification; control of education; and so forth.

The functions or purposes of education are the same in each society but are carried out differently. They include learning to be a productive member of society; passing on culture; selecting, training, and placement of individuals in society; change and innovation; and social and personal development. These functions are not always carried out smoothly and may be points of conflicts in school policies.

II. Theoretical Approaches and the Development of Sociology of Education

Sociology of education is a fairly recent field, much of the literature having been developed in the past half-century. However, it has roots in European sociology.

In recent years, the field has moved from practical to more theoretical emphases, although both are still found.

Three types of studies dominate sociology of education: large systems, specific institutions, and interaction in educational settings. Each focuses on a different level of analysis and uses different methods for research.

Theory provides guidelines for studies. Dominant theories are as follows:

- *Functionalist theory* views the education system as an integral, interrelated part of the whole societal system, carrying out certain necessary functions for the survival of society. Systems are held together by shared values. Durkheim first applied the sociological perspective and methods to the study of education.
- *Conflict theory* assumes that tension exists in society because of competing interest groups. The "haves" control the power and resources, and thus the educational systems—including access to higher levels of education. There is the ever-present possibility of struggle. Weber's contributions, less directly in the field of education than Durkheim's, were in the areas of organization and training members for society.
- *Interaction theory* focuses on individuals and how they form interpretations of the world around them. Labeling and exchange theory are two types of interaction theory. Recent perspectives include the "new" sociology of education, which is related to interaction theory and claims to be an alternative approach to the macrocosmic theories.

III. The Open Systems Approach

This book is organized around the open systems model presented in Figure 1-1. Each part of the system is discussed: the organization, its environment, inputs and outputs, and feedback. Using this approach allows us to visualize the whole system, each subpart in relation to the whole, and the environment surrounding the system. Models help us picture the relationship between parts.

IV. Research Methods in Sociology of Education

Sociological methods used to study educational systems include observations, surveys, the use of existing data such as test scores, controlled laboratory experiments, and case studies. Any of these methods, or a combination of methods, can be used—depending on the theory and level of analysis used—to collect data to help answer questions within a theoretical framework.

STUDIES IN SOCIOLOGY OF EDUCATION

The following are examples of research questions that have been asked in recent studies:

- Is college a route for getting ahead in society?
- How are social class and school achievement related?
- Why do girls take fewer math and science courses than boys?
- Do schools make a difference in our earning power?
- What teaching styles are most effective?
- Should non-native-language speakers learn in their own language or in English?

- What differences do teacher expectations of students make?
- What is the importance of the "informal" system of schools?
- What effects does TV watching have on educational achievement?

PUTTING SOCIOLOGY TO WORK

1. Evaluate your own motivations for your education and for taking this course. Understanding your goals can help you get the most from this course and help you meet your educational needs (refer to page 3).

2. Write down some questions you have concerning schools, and relate them to questions asked by functionalists, indicated on pages 6–9.

3. From the brief descriptions of contributions made by Emile Durkheim and Max Weber, describe those issues facing education today that relate to aspects of their writings.

4. View the film "High School." Diagram this school using the elements of a systems model. Indicate roles people play and processes being carried out. Compare this with your own high school experience (refer to page 14).

5. What are some questions concerning education that come to mind when using functional theory? conflict theory? interaction theory?

6. Citing an example, explain how the open systems approach can help us conceptualize a whole working organization.

7. Consider the questions asked in relation to each theoretical perspective (project 5). What method(s) could be used to help you answer each question?

8. The projects in this chapter give you the framework for developing a research project of your own: a theoretical perspective, a research question, a methodology. Plan a research project based on a question of interest to you.

NOTES

[1] United Nations, *The World's Women: 1970–1990* (New York: United Nations, 1991).

[2] *The Chronicle of Higher Education Almanac* (Washington, D.C.: U.S. Dept. of Education, August 26, 1992).

[3] National Center for Education Statistics, *Digest of Education Statistics: 1991*, Washington, D.C.: U.S. Department of Education, November 1991, p. 147.

[4] *Projections of the Total Population by Sex and Age: 1985 to 2000* (Washington, D.C.: U.S. Department of Commerce, Bureau of the Census, 1986).

[5] *Statistical Abstracts of the United States, 1980* (Washington, D.C.: U.S. Department of Commerce, Bureau of the Census, 1980), Table 62, p. 45.

[6] Schumacher, E. F., *Small Is Beautiful: Economics as If People Mattered* (New York: Harper & Row, 1973).

[7] Durkheim, Emile, *Moral Education* (trans. Everett K. Wilson and Herman Schnurer) (Glencoe, Ill.: Free Press, 1961).

[8] Durkheim, Emile, *The Evolution of Educational Thought* (trans. Peter Collins) (London: Routledge & Kegan Paul, 1977).

[9] Durkheim, Emile, *Education and Sociology* (trans. Sherwood D. Fox) (Glencoe, Ill.: Free Press, 1956), p. 28.

[10] Brookover, Wilbur B., and Edsel L. Erickson, *Sociology of Education* (Homewood, Ill.: Dorsey Press, 1975), pp. 4–5.

[11] Saha, Lawrence J., "Durkheim's Sociology of Education: A Critical Reassessment," paper presented at American Sociological Association meetings, Atlanta, August 1988.

[12] Karabel, Jerome, and A. H. Halsey, *Power and Ideology in Education* (New York: Oxford University Press, 1977), p. 11.

[13] Floud, Jean, and A. H. Halsey, "The Sociology of Education: A Trend Report and Bibliography," *Current Sociology,* Vol. 7, 1958, pp. 165–235.

[14] *Ibid.*

[15] Collins, Randall, "Functional and Conflict Theories of Educational Stratification," *American Sociological Review,* Vol. 36, 1971, pp. 1002–19.

[16] Weber, Max, "The Chinese Literati," in H. H. Gerth and C. Wright Mills (eds. and trans.), *From Max Weber: Essays in Sociology* (New York: Oxford University Press, 1958), pp. 422–33.

[17] Weber, Max, "The Three Types of Legitimate Rule," in Amitai Etzioni (ed.), *Complex Organizations: A Sociological Reader* (New York: Holt, Rinehart and Winston, 1961).

[18] Gerth, H. H., and C. Wright Mills (eds. and trans.), *From Max Weber: Essays in Sociology* (New York: Oxford University Press, 1946), pp. 240–43.

[19] Bowles, Samuel, "Unequal Education and the Reproduction of the Social Division of Labor," in Martin Carnoy (ed.), *Schooling in a Corporate Society* (New York: David McKay, 1972), pp. 36–64.

[20] Waller, Willard, *The Sociology of Teaching* (New York: Wiley, 1965), pp. 8–9; and Willower, Donald J., and William Lowe Boyd (ed.), *Willard Waller on Education and Schools* (Berkeley, Calif.: McCutchan, 1989).

[21] Liston, Daniel P., *Capitalist Schools: Explanation and Ethics in Radical Studies of Schooling* (New York and London: Routledge, 1988).

[22] Anyon, Jeanne, "Social Class and School Knowledge," *Curriculum Inquiry,* Vol. 11, 1981, pp. 3–42.

[23] Karabel and Halsey, *Power and Ideology,* p. 60.

[24] Bernstein, Basil, *Class, Codes and Control,* Vol. 3 (London: Routledge & Kegan Paul, 1975).

[25] Bourdieu, Pierre, "Cultural Reproduction and Social Reproduction," in Richard Brown (ed.), *Knowledge, Education, and Cultural Change* (London: Tavistock, 1973), pp. 71–112.

[26] Bernstein, Basil, "Sociology and the Sociology of Education: A Brief Account," in John Rex (ed.), *Approaches to Sociology* (London: Routledge & Kegan Paul, 1974), pp. 145–59.

[27] Sadovnik, Alan R., "Basil Bernstein's Theory of Pedagogic Practice: A Structuralist Approach," *Sociology of Education,* Vol. 64, 1991, pp. 48–63.

[28] Bernstein, Basil, *Class, Codes and Control,* Vol. 3 (London: Routledge & Kegan Paul, 1975), and *The Structuring of Pedagogic Discourse,* Vol. 4 (1990).

[29] Bidwell, Charles E., "The Sociology of the School and Classroom," paper presented at American Sociological Association meetings, Boston, August 1979.

[30] Angell, Robert, "Science, Sociology, and Education," *Journal of Educational Sociology,* Vol. 1, 1928, pp. 406–13.

[31] Parsons, Talcott, "The School Class as a Social System: Some of Its Functions in American Society," *Harvard Educational Review,* Vol. 29, No. 4, 1959, p. 299.

[32] Griffiths, D., "Systems Theory and School Districts," *Ontario Journal of Educational Research,* Vol. 8, 1965, p. 24.

[33] Olsen, Marvin, *The Process of Social Organization: Power in Social Systems,* 2nd ed. (New York: Holt, Rinehart and Winston, 1978), p. 228.

[34] Boulding, Kenneth E., "GST—The Skeleton of Science," *Management Science,* Vol. 2, 1956, pp. 197–208.

[35] Scott, W. G., "Organization Theory: An Overview and an Appraisal," in J. A. Litterer (ed.), *Organization: Structure and Behavior* (New York: Wiley, 1963).

[36] Easton, David, *A Systems Analysis of Political Life* (New York: Wiley, 1965), p. 20.

[37] Conrad, Richard, "A Systematic Analysis of Current Researches in the Sociology of Education," *American Sociological Review,* Vol. 17, 1952, pp. 350–55.

[38] Lubeck, Sally, *Sandbox Society: Early Education in Black and White America* (London: Falmer, 1985).

[39] Metz, Mary H., *Classrooms and Corridors: The Crisis of Authority in Desegregated Secondary Schools* (Berkeley: University of California Press, 1978).

[40] Jackson, Philip, *Life in Classrooms* (New York: Holt, Rinehart and Winston, 1968).

[41] Rosenthal, Robert, and Lenore Jacobson, *Pygmalion in the Classroom* (New York: Holt, Rinehart and Winston, 1968).

[42] Coleman, James, *et al., Equality of Educational Opportunity* (Washington, D.C.: U.S. Department of Education, 1966).

[43] *Sociology of Education Newsletter,* ASA Section on Sociology of Education, Winter 1992, pp. 4–6.

[44] Natriello, A., E. McDill, and A. Pallas, *Schooling Disadvantaged Children: Racing Against Catastrophe* (New York: Teachers College Press, 1990).

[45] Kozol, Jonathan, *Savage Inequalities: Children in America's Schools* (New York: Crown, 1991).

[46] *Sociology of Education Newsletter,* winter, 1992, comments by James E. Coleman, Caroline Hodges Persell, Karl Alexander, and Maureen T. Hallinan, pp. 4–6.

2

CONFLICTING FUNCTIONS AND PROCESSES
What Makes the System Work

This chapter is about controversies in schools. Surrounding each function of education are debates on power, access, and knowledge. Schools exist within a larger framework of society. They are "part of the economic, political, and cultural spheres. . . . The dynamics which make up these spheres also interact in everyday activities in schools."[1] Therefore, controversies in the society at large become part of the school. After a general introduction concerning the conflicting nature of functions and the importance of processes in educational systems, we look at selected issues and controversies related to each function of education.

CONFLICTING FUNCTIONS OF EDUCATION

In any society, children must be taught the ways of the group and skills necessary for society and the individual to survive. The basic functions or purposes of education are the same in most societies, but the importance of these functions and the means of achieving them vary greatly among societies and even among groups or social classes within each society. For instance, the degree of industrialization of the society will affect the content and the form of the educational process. The form of the political system will affect the content and control of the educational process. The expectations of the family in socializing the child to be a productive member of society will affect the type of educational content. Here we can see the interdependence of parts in society.

Function 1. Socialization: Learning to Be Productive Members of Society and the Passing On of Culture.   Each new generation of children learns the rights and wrongs, values and roles of the society into which it is born. In learning their role, children are socialized or taught how to meet the expectations placed upon them. Educational systems *socialize* students to become members of society, to play meaningful roles in the complex network of interdependent positions. Some critics, however, argue that students have different experiences in the school system, depending on their social class, racial or ethnic background, neighborhood in which they live, and other variables that influence their education.

Function 2. Transmission of Culture.   Similarly, the *transmission of culture* is often controversial, each group wanting its programs, curricula, or values promulgated. In addition, different groups of students are taught different norms, skills, values, and knowledge. Thus, a student destined for a leadership or elite position may acquire a different set of skills and knowledge base than one who will enter the blue-collar work force.

Function 3. Social Control and Personal Development.   *Social control* is, similarly, controversial. Discipline differs by social class, racial-ethnic group, and sex, even though the offense may be the same. Controversies surround search and seizure, and rights of students. Do school officials have the right to "protect students" by searching for weapons or drugs, especially when these searches may disproportionately affect some groups of students?

Function 4. Selecting, Training, and Placement of Individuals in Society.   This is probably the most controversial function. Critics argue that we are "reproducing" social classes and maintaining the social hierarchy by educational policies and practices that select some students for higher tracks. Yet some policies, such as testing, give the "appearance" of equality.

The access that students have to technology will influence their chances to compete in the future. Knowledge of computers and other high-tech machines gives some students an edge on leadership positions because these students possess the skills needed in the future. Thus, the question of what the balance is between ascribed and achieved characteristics in the determination of someone's future educational and occupational success is sometimes raised.[2] Chapters 3 and 4 focus on this function.

Function 5. Change and Innovation.   *Change and innovation* is an expected function of education, yet institutions often resist change that affects routine work tasks. Education is no exception.

THE IMPORTANCE OF PROCESSES IN SYSTEMS

Have you ever tried to describe your day using action verbs? Today I *got up, dressed, ate* my breakfast, *put on* my coat, *walked* to school, *entered* the classroom, *sat* at my desk, *opened* my book, *read* it, *wrote* names as the teacher *communicated,* and *learned* about educational systems. The italicized verbs describe processes, the action part of your day. Learning, teaching, socializing, disciplining, selecting, innovating, decision making, changing—these are only a few of the processes that make up the action part of the system of education. The education system is a stable and relatively permanent structure. Processes are the action part of the system, what is happening.

Nothing is ever fixed or final. People, things, and organizations are always becoming something new through the process of change. Always we grow older, learn new behavior, and adjust to changes in the world around us. Educational systems affect our change process, and in turn are affected by processes in their environments, or surroundings.

Structure refers to parts of the educational system that can be described and diagrammed: roles, social classes, organizations, institutions, societies. People in the structure act. They bring the structure alive, make it move. Their acts are processes. People bring their own personalities and interpretations to situations, and act accordingly. Structure and action cannot be separated. There would be no processes without structure, and structure would be meaningless without processes. We are not simply social classes or roles; we are what results from those structural parts and the processes that make them work.

Implicit in an open systems approach are the processes that make any system a dynamic, working unit. Some processes are found in almost every organization—interaction, decision making, conflict, cooperation. Others are predominant in particular systems. These processes make the system work and give it life, but they can also produce controversy, as we shall see.

Processes also provide a link between the organization, such as an education system, and the environment. The process of communication, for instance, links the school with parents, community leaders, and state legislators.

THE FUNCTION OF SOCIALIZATION: WHO GETS AHEAD IN THE PROCESS?

According to functional theory, a society, in order to survive, must train its members to be productive and to carry out required roles. However, there is disagreement on how, when, and for whom training should take place. Criticisms of the process of socialization have covered a range of topics. Here we focus on three: early childhood education, the role of the media in socialization, and political socialization.

The Early Childhood Education Controversy

From the moment we are born, the socialization process is part of our lives; its influence is felt through the family, school, religious institution, and workplace. Learning to become a member of society has both formal, planned components and informal aspects.

The family is the primary context within which the child receives initial socialization. Variations in the process of early childhood socialization are tremendous, dependent on society, social class, and family background. As children grow, they come into contact with socialization agents outside the home: relatives, neighbors, church, nursery school, playmates. But there is little preparation for the major transition to the formal institution of the school.

Over half the nations of the world have some formal early childhood education for 3- to 5-year-olds. In some countries, such as China and Israel, care is begun shortly after birth and is sometimes mandatory.

For years, bills have been introduced in the U.S. Congress proposing legislation to support early childhood education, reflecting pressure on government and work institutions from women's groups. So far, most of that legislation has gone down to defeat despite the growing number of working mothers with young children under 5 needing day care. The movement against day care comes mainly from those who consider it a threat to the family and to the maternal role.[3]

A recent Gallup poll of public attitudes shows that 55 percent favor public preschools for 3- and 4-year-old children, and 40 percent oppose the

Children gain group experiences through early childhood education.

idea.[4] More and more school districts are offering classes for 4-year-olds. Where finding adequate child care is difficult, public schools are being pressured to fill a need.[5]

Yet early childhood education is distrusted by some because many programs are aimed at particular classes and racial groups. While stated intentions are to give these children advantages, this "special attention" has also been interpreted as a technique to perpetuate a class structure and train compliant members of society.

Early childhood education takes on special significance because children are developing their self-concept and social awareness. Issues that surround early socialization include where cognitive development should take place—home or school; at what ages children should enter formal school; benefits of preschool for children of working parent(s) or for those living in poverty; and the role of preschool and kindergarten programs in the socialization of children.

In the 1960s and early 1970s, researchers and educators began taking early childhood education seriously. Two major types of research emerged with regard to early childhood education. Research related to Head Start programs attempts to measure the effects of the program on poor children deprived of some important early experiences; day-care research attempts to evaluate whether any harm results from alternatives to home care. In the latter case, there have been five principal research concerns: damage to the infant-mother attachment; retardation of cognitive development; lack of self-control, aggressiveness, or passivity; too great a reliance on peers or unsatisfactory later peer relationships; and usurpation of the mother's responsibility for the child.[6] It is not our task to examine in detail the research in each of these areas, but Peters reports that the concerns now appear to be unfounded.

The greatest return on investment, according to one assessment of early childhood education, comes from providing preschool education for 3- and 4-year-olds from low-income families, children who are at special risk of failure. From studies of mental and physical development, we know that infants show learning at two-and-a-half months, if not earlier;[7] and the brain has spurts of growth, one of which extends from the ages of 2 to 4. In fact, 50 percent of general intelligence develops between birth and 4 years of age. As early as 10 to 18 months of age, children show differences in competence that relate to types of interactions with their mothers.[8]

Some evidence shows that infants' intellectual development is adversely affected if both parents work during the first year of life, but can be enhanced by mothers who work outside the home thereafter. Therefore, many advocate more generous maternity/paternity leave, a practice more common in some European countries than in the United States.[9]

Poverty is deeply rooted in institutions, embedded in the economic system and technological development of a country. Disaffection from school of "at-risk" children can begin as early as nursery school.[10] A substantial number of 3-year-olds from poor families are nine months or more behind in language and intellectual development by the time they start nursery school. To prevent these losses, some propose training programs for new parents to get children off to a good start in life.[11,12]

Intervention programs in the preschool years cut human and financial costs later; parents' active involvement in the preschool education of their children is also stressed.[13] Preschool education is positively related to higher graduation and employment rates and lower welfare, detention, and arrest rates; this results in overall reduced rates for special schooling and other social programs.[14]

One program that has continued to garner support from Washington despite slashes in other education programs is Head Start. That program's 1993 budget increase is the largest annual amount ever—$600 million, a 27-percent increase. Rationale for its continued support is that it strengthens families and communities. However, this budget is still $5 billion short of what is needed to serve all eligible children (Figure 2-1). Although 621,000 children now participate in Head Start, 1.8 million are eligible.[15]

The Head Start program operates on the assumption that educational differentials between groups can be reduced by increased attention. A summary study of 28 Head Start evaluations found little that was encouraging about the short-term effects of Head Start programs, but found positive long-term effects, most notably the higher rate of high school graduation for Head Start students.[16–19]

A. H. Halsey reviewed the progress of Head Start children upon entry into school. Table 2-1 indicates some of the findings. Note particularly the fourth column, "reduction in failure," which is estimated at 36.4 percent for those attending Head Start programs. Halsey feels that applying reverse discrimination in the preschool years will have positive effects on attainment and achievement in primary and secondary education, especially as "preschool mediates family and peer group influences." Having no follow-through experiences for children after Head Start and other preschool enrichment programs may reduce the effectiveness of early childhood education. This is

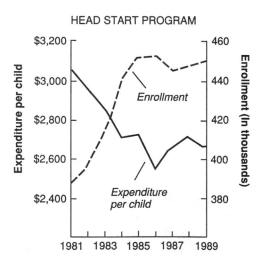

HEAD START PROGRAM

FIGURE 2-1

"Shortchanged." Money for Head Start, as with other federal programs in the '80s, did not keep up with demand.

Source: High/Scope Educational Research Foundation; reprinted in "Shortchanged," *Newsweek Special Issue,* Fall/Winter, 1990, p. 79.

TABLE 2-1   Long-Term Effects of Head Start[a]

Head Start Project	Failure Rate of Project Children (%)	Failure Rate of Control Children (%)	Reduction in Failure by Attending Project (%)	Total
Good experimental design				
Gordon	39.1	61.5	36.0	82
Gray	55.6	73.7	24.6	55
Palmer	24.1	44.7	46.1	221
Weikart	17.2	38.5	55.3	123
Median	31.6	53.1	41.1	481
Quasi-experimental design				
Beller	48.6	53.1	8.5	69
Levenstein	22.1	43.5	49.2	127
Miller	20.6	11.1	—	125
Zigler	26.6	32.3	17.6	144
Overall median	25.4	44.1	36.4	920

[a]Failure is defined as being placed in special education classes, and/or retained in grade, and/or dropped out of school. Reduction is % control minus % project, divided by % control. Children's data were collected in different grades. The design of the Miller project permits no "reduction" conclusion. The numbers in the total are of project children plus control children.

Source: Halsey, A. H., "Education Can Compensate," *New Society,* January 24, 1980, pp. 172–73.

especially true for young males; however, positive alterations in parent-child interactions, a goal of Head Start, can reduce delinquency and increase school achievement.[20,21]

Those favoring early childhood education have several arguments:

1. Early childhood education provides valuable learning experiences not available at home.
2. Young children need to interact with children and with adults other than their parents.
3. Parents and siblings are not always the best or most capable handlers of children.
4. For many families, day care is necessary as both parents must work; in case of single-parent families, the only alternative may be welfare.
5. A good day-care center is often preferable to leaving a child with relatives or neighbors.

Another study showed that for 3,000 mostly black and poor children, the lasting effects of preschool education were manifested primarily in five areas:

1. . . . [T]he beneficiaries are less likely to be assigned later to special or remedial classes.
2. There has been the same lasting effect with respect to drop out from school and . . . retention in grade (fewer being held back to repeat a year's work because of poor performance).
3. Achievement in mathematics at age 10 (fourth grade) is significantly improved by preschooling. The evidence also suggests a trend toward better scores on reading tests at the same age.

4. Children from poor families who went to preschool programs scored higher than the "control" children on the Stanford Binet IQ test for up to three years afterwards. In some projects, this superiority was maintained. . . .
5. Preschool children retain more "achievement orientation," and their mothers tend to develop higher vocational aspirations for them than mothers have for themselves.[22]

Thus, whereas early evidence seemed negative, studies on Head Start and other preschool programs are now showing that long-term effects exist and are positive.

Two recent studies have reviewed the literature on the effects of early childhood education and come up with similar results. One concludes:

> If children are placed in a decent program after two years of age, effects, if any, are likely to be positive. Children's development of social and intellectual skills is likely to be advanced, and there are no apparent detrimental effects on their emotions. Developmental acceleration is especially likely in programs that offer systematic educational activities and opportunities for social interaction and exploration of materials.[23]

Claire Etaugh indicates that one can safely conclude ". . . that high-quality nonmaternal care does not appear to have harmful effects on the preschool child's maternal attachment, intellectual development, social-emotional behavior, or physical health."[24]

It should be noted that the child's readiness to enter a school situation and learn are crucial components of a successful socialization experience. If a child enters school feeling optimistic, curious, and happy, the experience is likely to be positive. Studies reveal that children who were not ready for first-grade experience, however, continued to have academic difficulty in elementary school. In general, early childhood education programs, especially Head Start, do show success on a number of indices, including dropout prevention.[25]

For many children, school starts with kindergarten. Note in the following excerpt how formal, institutional socialization begins:

> The unique job of the kindergarten in the educational division of labor seems (rather) to be teaching children the student role. The student role is the repertoire of behavior and attitudes regarded by educators as appropriate to children in school. Observation in the kindergartens of the Wilbur Wright School revealed a great variety of activities through which children are shown and then drilled in the behavior and attitudes defined as appropriate for school and thereby induced to learn the role of student.[26]

Kindergartens began in 1855 as child-centered programs for 5-year-olds. In recent years, some major shifts occurred in kindergarten curriculum, making it more like a downward extension of primary education with emphasis on achievement and learning goals. This has created controversy among educators. Pressure to increase academics for kindergartners is considered by some educators to be a major contributor to failure and frustration among children.[27] Yet even parents are pushing for more academics, and testing for readiness for first grade often includes math and reading skills.[28] Because kindergarten has taken on more serious "work," readiness for the academic work of kindergarten has become an issue for parents and teachers.[29]

Early childhood education as a function of socialization is likely to become less controversial in the United States and around the world as economic development takes root and more women struggle to attain full economic and political citizenship in the world economy. Change in women's status will lead to the development and utilization of child-care facilities.[30] Evidence indicates that in Third World countries, children and families benefit from early intervention that brings them information, health care, and other supports. Early education also helps poor children with the transition to schooling.[31]

Role of the Media in Socialization

Other socialization agencies complement or compete with the school for the attention of students. The media is one such agency. When TV first became widespread in the 1950s, many thought that it would solve educational problems and bring education to millions around the world. To some extent this has been realized. TV satellites beam a variety of programs to many nations, ranging from basic literacy training to advanced college courses; thus education becomes accessible to a wider population and spreads culture and ideas. However, the controversy is this: Do the educational benefits of TV outweigh the negative outcomes? Many concerns focus on school achievement and amount of TV watching, TV's possible distortion of information, and TV's effects on negative behaviors, such as aggression and suicidal tendencies.

The evidence regarding TV watching and school achievement is mixed; more TV means less time for other activities, such as reading and homework. On average, there is little clear evidence that TV watching lowers achievement *unless* it is excessive.[32] Although TV viewing may be satisfying different needs than those satisfied by reading and other activities, reading for pleasure is more beneficial to achievement.[33] And, interestingly, a recent survey of students indicates that 40 percent prefer reading to TV, yet most spend twice as much time watching TV as they do reading.

Achievement can encourage selective TV watching, with other variables, such as race, sex, parental education level, educational resources, and intelligence, playing a role in behavior regarding TV.[34] For those concerned about the amount of viewing, it may be encouraging to know that the national poll on "TV watching as the favorite pastime of Americans" was down from 46 percent in 1966 and 1974 to 33 percent in 1986.[35]

Teachers complain that the TV generation expects to be entertained in school or they turn off. Data to support this were reported in a California Department of Education survey: "[T]elevision viewing adversely affects student performance on achievement tests. . . . A negative relationship was found between the amount of time students indicated they spent watching television and the scores they attained.[36] The concern that we become mesmerized by the tube has led some critics to question whether we are critical enough in our TV watching, whether we accept simplistic explanations without careful consideration.

Perhaps the most serious controversy centers around the *behavioral effects* of TV watching. The concern is that TV socializes children into antisocial, aggressive behaviors. One hypothesis that has been tested in many experiments links watching TV violence to aggressive behavior; *experimental* results carried out in laboratory settings generally show a small, consistent positive correlation between viewing violence and aggressiveness, but there is little evidence that this carries over to *natural settings* outside the laboratory.[37] There is some evidence from studies of TV shows concerning suicides that there is an increase in suicidal behavior in the week or two weeks following the shows.[38,39] However, these "copycat" suicides are among students who are already at risk. "There is no clear evidence that highly publicized suicides increase the suicide rate."[40]

Clear evidence regarding the *impact* of TV on socialization and learning comes into two areas: First, parental involvement in children's TV watching has a powerful effect on its impact. Concerning elementary school children, the Singers conclude that the child's cognitive and behavioral tendencies are correlated with several aspects of family patterns. Two of these especially relevant to TV are parents who play an active role in helping children understand the world around them, including what they see on TV, and parents who "watch less television themselves and who hold a less 'mean and scary' view of their environment."[41] The second evidence on impact comes from studies of children's educational television, such as "3-2-1-Contact," "Sesame Street," and "Square I," which generally show positive outcomes for children who watch.[42]

In 1990, Congress passed the Children's Television Act with the goal of making TV programming more educational and discouraging commercial TV that promotes existing toys.[43] Because of pressure from lobbying groups such as Action for Children's Television (ACT), changes are occurring. PBS is starting new educational series such as "Futures," which deals with math applications. In addition, Children's Television Workshop (the producers of "Sesame Street") is making specific episodes available to teachers through an index system. Educational video games are also being developed.

Following the lead of the TV generation, over 3,000 schools have subscribed to "Channel One," a news show for school children, getting the "free" loan of equipment and satellite dishes that come with the deal. The controversy surrounds the 12-minute news show, which comes with two minutes of commercials for such products as M & Ms, Cheetos, and Gillette razors. The "donors" of the equipment require that children watch these advertiser-sponsored newscasts in exchange for having use of the free TV, videocassette recorder, and dish. Critics feel that this is unfair socialization of a captive audience of children.[44] Evidence is still coming in; meanwhile, the controversy and tension between the educational and entertainment roles of TV will not go away.

Political Socialization

Schools teach us political roles: for instance, honoring the monarchy, obeying the military or police state, or expressing views and voting. While the context of teaching varies with the historical-political conditions,[45] the content of political socialization is usually systematically planned to teach information, attitudes, and values. Washburn[46] outlines five types of manifest and latent political content:

1. *National loyalty.* This is the we/they, "my country is best" phenomenon.
2. *Political authority.* This functions to teach children that obedience, respect, even idealizing of the political system and leaders are proper. It may involve the beliefs "what the government does is best" and "its laws are fair."
3. *Concerning citizenship.* Young children see good citizens as good persons—those who obey laws, vote, pay taxes, and carry out whatever obligations their country deems important.
4. *Facts of political life.* This includes a knowledge of history and governmental structure. Students in the United States generally have low fact knowledge.[47]
5. *Democracy.* In the United States, schools have been moderately successful in teaching the values of majority rule, participation, and the importance of the vote. However, the abstract concepts of criticism and free speech are more difficult to teach.

Recent concerns among U.S. educators regarding the lack of knowledge about citizenship, national and global affairs, and civic values are confirmed by a nationwide survey and by interviews of 15- to 24-year-olds; for teens, civic responsibility is a low priority next to achieving career success and having a good time. Ralph Lauren is more familiar to them than Martin Luther King. Only 24 percent of those surveyed indicated that they saw "helping their community" as important. In a study comparing seniors in German and American high schools, both groups show positive orientations toward democracy, but American students in particular do not show much trust in politicians or other citizens.[48]

What can we do about citizenship training? Students need more direction on *how* to be good citizens. Civics curricula are receiving more attention now.[49] In fact, the latest figures show that 25 percent of private and 4 percent of public high schools require students to do community service in order to graduate. Colleges are also developing such requirements.[50]

Political socialization is influenced by students' social class and curriculum track. Middle-class college-bound students are more likely to participate in school activities and politics, and in later political activities. However, students in urban settings are likely to participate in collective action.[51]

Whether items of political socialization are taught explicitly as part of the curriculum or as implicit, latent functions in the "hidden curriculum" of schools, political socialization takes place in every school system. Conflict theorists argue that political socialization corresponds to the dominance, subordination, and motivation that students will have in society. They learn to accept their positions and the degree of "powerlessness" they will have; even the school structure reinforces their positions in society.[52,53]

THE FUNCTION OF CULTURAL TRANSMISSION
AND PROCESS OF PASSING ON CULTURE

"The educational foundations of our society are presently being eroded by a rising tide of mediocrity that threatens our very future as a Nation and a people. What was unimaginable a generation ago has begun to occur—others are matching and surpassing our educational attainments. . . . [W]e have, in effect, been committing an act of unthinking, unilateral educational disarmament."[54] This statement and the report *A Nation at Risk* opened a floodgate of questioning and self-criticism.

With these hard words to the American people came concern about the "cultural literacy" and illiteracy of the United States. Are young people learning the very core of knowledge that holds a nation together with a common thread—that information which is understood and shared by all? Some argue that this knowledge core has slipped in several ways.[55] A test developed under the National Endowment for the Humanities shows shallow learning of literary and historical knowledge, according to Diane Ravitch, who analyzed the preliminary results.[56]

Imagine going into a store and not being able to read the labels on the cans. Illiteracy among young people and adults is a skill problem that many of those affected try to hide, but it is estimated that there are 27 million functionally illiterate adults who cannot read simple instructions, and 47 million more who cannot read well. Six percent of people in the early 20s read below the fourth-grade level, and 5 percent cannot perform such routine and uncomplicated tasks as filling out a job application or totaling two entries on a bank-deposit slip.[57] Illiteracy affects women in poverty disproportionately. Increased attention to this problem in the media, and adult education classes, may help some who are occupationally and culturally handicapped.

Educators are looking at why nine out of ten children who start first grade in the bottom reading group stay there throughout elementary school. Currently there is a hodgepodge of programs for teaching reading. For some children, new and coordinated approaches to reading may be key. Some are advocating a return to phonics-based reading for low-income children instead of the whole-language approach, which works better with at-home support. Others argue that the money spent on intensive, personalized education early on more than pays off later.[58]

For older students, educators are trying everything from tying drivers' licenses to academic performance and skills and staying in school, to offering literacy training in alternative locations such as work settings.

The number of college freshmen who are unprepared for college-level work is also alarming. Data show that 16 percent are in remedial reading, 21 percent are in remedial writing, and 25 percent are in remedial mathematics courses, and enrollments in these courses have been on the increase. Studies also show that scientific illiteracy is widespread.[59]

Some Factors Affecting Learning

Learning as a process is influenced not only by the teacher, the techniques used, the classroom setting, and the formal or informal material to be taught, but by the child's ability, motivation, interest in the subject matter, readiness to learn, retentiveness, values and attitudes, relationship with the teacher, feelings about self, relationships with peers, and background experiences. Also of importance are the environmental pressures for learning, the time allotted for learning, family support for learning, and the atmosphere of the school and classroom. Children's learning experiences differ as a result of such variables as race, sex, and class. Thus, it is superficial to explain learning differences between children by one primary factor, such as intelligence.

Because of concerns about dropping achievement test scores and the back-to-basics movement, high school curricula have undergone some significant changes. There is particular pressure in the areas of math and science, where educators feel that the United States is losing whatever competitive edge it may have had, especially in high-tech areas. "The low level of scientific and technological literacy in our society is deplorable, and the trickle of talent flowing into careers in engineering, mathematics, and the sciences . . . is deeply disturbing."[60] So begins the National Science Foundation's evaluation of science and math curricula in the United States. The report points out that all segments of the community must be involved in remedying the situation, but puts special emphasis on teachers at all levels to improve curricula and motivate students.

Complaints about math and science education are exemplified by the following findings from recent studies: We spend too much time reviewing old math material,[61] with the result that students are testing below grade level, according to the National Assessment of Educational Progress (NAEP) tests. The United States spends relatively little money on math and science education compared with many other countries, though it professes to feel that they are crucial to today's technological world.[62,63] Women are less likely to view themselves as competent in math and, thus, may avoid math courses.[64] These are only a few of the factors that affect math and science education. Some universities are providing special programs for younger students to encourage them in these fields. Some businesses are even promising high school graduates free college educations for staying in school.

Other reports have followed *A Nation at Risk,* and we discuss these throughout the book; some are sponsored by foundations, others by government agencies or academicians. Some suggest tighter control over curriculum and requirements and changes in teacher education so that teachers specialize in an area of expertise. Unfortunately, in a five-year follow-up to *A Nation at Risk,* Secretary of Education William Bennett argued that little progress has been made toward suggested improvements.

How to Pass On Culture

The debate over *how* to pass on culture covers issues from what materials, textbooks, and technology to use, to the philosophy of effective teaching. Arguments over philosophy of education pit the "back to basics" advocates, who stress basic skills, against the "progressive" educators, who argue that education must be relevant to the surrounding environment and future social participation of students.

For much of the history of formal education, children have been taught those things that were regarded as important for the community and for the children's survival in it. John Dewey made a great impact on education with the idea that learning could be more effective if made relevant to the lives of children. Dewey's progressivism contended that schools were irrelevant to the daily lives of most children, and therefore an alienating experience; techniques of memorization and authoritarian atmospheres were not conducive to learning. He proposed using the children's experience and involving them actively in the learning process. His extensive writings have been interpreted, misinterpreted, and modified, but they have influenced all movements in education since the turn of the century. Going beyond Dewey's ideas are child-centered curricula that focus on learner needs and interests, are highly flexible, provide many options to the learner, and involve learners in planning their own curricula around their needs. Free and alternative schools have adopted some of these ideas.

Recent movements to improve the passing on of culture have included "writing-across-the-curriculum," computers in the classroom, accountability and assessment, and critical thinking; that is, reflective and reasonable thinking that is focused on deciding what to believe or do. Some of these ideas result from social forces such as declines in achievement test scores and criticisms of schools, and the lack of correspondence between demands to think more maturely and what the school program teaches. The idea of critical thinking contrasts with educational styles that concentrate only on facts. Related to Bloom's taxonomy and "higher order thinking skills," critical thinking requires one to support conclusions and request evidence from others before accepting their conclusions.[65]

Some teachers do include elements of critical thinking in their teaching, but it is more often found in classrooms of college-bound or brighter students, not where such thought processes would lead to change in the system through which minority children are taught. All students need to be able to express their thoughts cogently in oral and written form, and to evaluate their value stances on issues. Training in critical thinking aids in these processes, but is not equally available to all.

The publication of "public and private school differences" by James Coleman caused a flood of studies on what makes students in some schools higher achievers than others. One factor suggested was homework assigned. As a result of this and other reports urging stricter homework policies, the Chicago public schools, among others, instituted policies that all students would get homework, from 15 minutes in kindergarten up to two-and-a-half hours in high school.[66]

However, more homework is not necessarily better for all students, and *too* much can be counterproductive. It appears that there is a difference in the effectiveness of homework related to tracks and characteristics of students. For instance, low-ability students doing ten hours of homework a week had as good grades as high-ability students doing little homework.[67] Homework is particularly useful for slower students to compensate for their deficiencies.

Recent reports on the status of education in the United States have recommended longer school days and years, tougher graduation standards, and more homework; as a result, changes are taking place in districts across the country. In late 1987, U.S. Secretary of Education William Bennett recommended a basic curriculum for American high schools. The plan included specific course descriptions and the numbers of years that courses should be taken. He argued that many high schools lack a basic core curriculum. Critics point out that his core is comparable to the college preparatory track in most schools, does not allow for regional differences, and may cause higher dropout rates. The "Proposed Course of Study" is shown in Box 2-1. In 1991, President Bush advocated his *America 2000* program for schools, which stressed, among other things, national standardized testing.

What Culture to Pass On

Another debate related to cultural transmission focuses on *what* is taught in schools. What culture *is* transmitted and what *should be* transmitted? Who should decide these difficult questions? What should be the goals of the curriculum? In every society there are expectations, usually unwritten, concerning what a successful adult should be able to do, and related ideas about what "products" schools should turn out. An assumption built into the curriculum is that there are desired changes to be made in the students' existing knowledge by the introduction of new ideas, by the correction of misconceptions, or by additions to existing knowledge. The curriculum provides for instruction in areas seen as desirable, through "planned experiences."

What Should Be Taught? What *is* being taught in the formal curriculum can be fairly easily and accurately determined, though the range is great. A look at curriculum plans and textbooks is a start. Generally, curriculum plans in primary schools focus on developing basic skills; secondary schools refine these skills and add content. Math, language skills, science, art and music, social science, physical education, and history are common components of secondary school curricula. The transmission of specific content such as sex education has been the subject of controversy in many communities because questions of responsibility and control of knowledge by family or education systems enter in.

Functional theorists see schools as transmitting those parts of the culture necessary to perform successfully in the adult world. Schools provide a transi-

BOX 2-1   *PROPOSED HIGH SCHOOL COURSE OF STUDY, RECOMMENDED BY FORMER EDUCATION SECRETARY WILLIAM J. BENNETT IN 1987.*

- *English*—Four years, broken into the following two-semester courses, all with regular writing assignments:

    "Introduction to Literature" for freshmen, "confined to recognized masterworks of Western literature" such as "a few books of Homer's *Odyssey*, parts of the Bible, sonnets and plays of Shakespeare, *Huckleberry Finn* and a Dickens novel."

    American literature in tenth grade, including works by such authors as Hawthorne, Poe, Whitman, Melville, Dickinson, Faulkner, Hemingway, Frost, Ellison, and Robert Penn Warren.

    British literature for juniors, from Chaucer to Milton to T.S. Eliot to Shaw. Bennett had considered offering English electives in eleventh grade, but scrapped them in the final version of his report.

    Introduction to world literature for seniors, including translations of Greek and Roman classics, Dante, Cervantes, Dostoevsky, Zola, Mann, and Ibsen, and "depending on the instructor's knowledge and interest, a small number of works from Japan, China, the Near East, Africa or Latin America."

- *Social Studies*—Three years, including: Western civilization in ninth grade, American history in tenth grade, and "Principles of American Democracy" in the first semester of eleventh grade and "American Democracy and the World" in the second semester.

- *Math*—Three years, from the following one-year courses: Algebra I; Geometry; Algebra II and Trigonometry; introductory and advanced Calculus. Students could also take one-semester courses in statistics and pre-calculus. Bennett said, "We seem possessed by the false notion that many students have an incurable math phobia or disability."

- *Science*—Three years, from the following one-year courses: astronomy/geology; biology; chemistry; physics; and "Principles of Technology."

- *Foreign Language*—Two years of a single foreign language. The choice of languages "is clearly a matter for local decision."

- *Physical education*—Two years of physical education/health for freshmen and sophomores, with a quarter of the time devoted to health (including nutrition and first-aid techniques such as cardiopulmonary resuscitation and the Heimlich maneuver), drug, and sex education. Students would be taught "the facts of life . . . in an open, serious and moral context, emphasizing restraint and the importance of the family."

- *Fine arts*—One-semester courses in art history and music history.

Source: "Bennett's Report Suggests Curriculum for High Schools," *Dayton Daily News*, December 30, 1987, p. 4.

tion from the warm, protective, accepting environment of the home to the competitive, performance-oriented atmosphere of the work world. Children learn that the same rules are supposed to apply to all. In this way schools are seen as serving a crucial function of preparing young people for society.[68,69]

Conflict theorists view the cultural transmission of these values and norms as serving the needs of a capitalist society rather than those of individuals, who are dehumanized and alienated by the process.[70] However, Christopher Hurn[71] points out that schools are seldom completely effective in transmitting these cultural values, as exemplified by the disruptions and rebellions in many schools. Hurn also suggests that schools may not be "teaching" these norms as a formal part of the curriculum or because the community expects such teaching. Rather, these norms may have evolved as a way to operate because such behaviors "work" in the school setting; they become part of the hidden curriculum.

What is being taught reflects forces both within and outside the school. Internal educational forces are those that have direct influence on the curriculum and processes of the school. For example, teachers may express preferences for certain materials and classroom organization and reject others, and the structure, composition, hierarchy, philosophy, principal, and architecture of any one school influence the curriculum content within that school.

In addition to the internal education forces affecting curriculum, there are many environmental factors. Recall the systems model. The environment includes all those factors outside the school that influence what happens within it. Consider the following:

1. Local, state, and federal regulations stipulate certain curricular requirements. For instance, a state board of education may require that a certain amount of state history be taken before students can be graduated. The federal government may require that a certain curricular content be included as a stipulation for receiving federal money.
2. Accrediting agencies reflect state or regional decision making concerning school standards, and may specify required aspects of curriculum.
3. Testing services that develop achievement tests for different grade levels and for college entrance do much to influence knowledge material taught. Some states require skills tests for graduation from high school.

Curriculum content is influenced by certain concerns and trends in society. Career education, women's studies, minority studies (African-American, Chicano, Native American, Appalachian, Chinese), multicultural and bilingual education, environmental studies, urban studies, and drug and sex education are among the subjects that have been introduced into curricula as a result of societal trends.

The call for curricula that fairly represent the history and current status of minorities in the United States has led to the multicultural education movement. Teaching race, class, and gender issues is a theme receiving increasing attention.[72] Some advocate courses on specific minority topics; others push for an accurate portrayal of minority history and contributions. Still others advocate global studies to familiarize students with the broader world issues that affect them.[73] Sociologists are uniquely qualified to develop cross-cultural models for curricula that take into consideration micro- and macroexplanations of societies and change.[74] Attempts to pluralize the curriculum have also met with criticism from those who oppose reducing or eliminating teaching of traditional "Western culture," which has been at the core of most courses of study in U.S. high schools and colleges.[75] Recommendations to change minority education stress the need for reform from preschool to graduate school.[76] These ideas may prove passing fads, or be integrated into the curriculum, or remain distinct fields of study. In any case, those with power in society generally make educational decisions.

Who Should Make Decisions Concerning Curriculum Content?   Many groups vie for decision-making responsibility, and many have an influence on decisions. We have mentioned environmental influences on curricular decisions. Because educators have been professionally trained to deal with matters related to education and the curriculum, they naturally prefer to keep decision making in the schools, removed from external politics and other pressures. Educators have used various techniques to maintain control of education decisions and keep schools independent of external influences; controlling information about what is going on within the school, releasing selected positive information, and assigning sympathetic community members to committees are examples.

"Academic freedom" refers to attempts by schools and colleges to minimize the control and influence primarily from the external environment. Schools can maintain this autonomy to the extent that their program and staff remain uncontroversial. However, should controversy arise, autonomy may be threatened. Education is an open system and therefore subject to pressures and scrutiny.

In heterogeneous societies without centrally run educational systems, curriculum planners face pressures from many diverse individuals and groups. In centrally run state systems, decisions are more protected from public scrutiny and challenges. The United States is an example of a heterogeneous society and federally decentralized system; below we discuss briefly three areas of curriculum decision making that have created heated controversy in many communities and that reflect this diversity: sex and drug education, creationism, and censorship of textbooks.

Sex and Drug Education.   Schools as condom dispensaries? A few years ago this idea was unthinkable, but with the threat of AIDS confronting more and more teens, "condom sense is common sense." School boards across the country attack the issue of "what culture should be taught." A growing number of urban school systems, including New York, Philadelphia, and Los Angeles, are making condoms available in attempts to prevent teen pregnancy, venereal disease, and AIDS.

Sex and AIDS education are also on the increase, despite objections from some parents and community groups. They argue that discussion of these topics belongs in the home and that schools should discourage sexual activity, not encourage it through classes and the distribution of condoms.

A study by the Alan Guttmacher Institute shows major changes in teenage sexual activity, which increased greatly throughout the 1980s, especially for young women. "The percentage of girls age 15 to 19 who reported having sex jumped from 47.1 percent in 1982 to 53.2 percent in 1988. Many had multiple partners. The largest increase was among white girls, with rates for black girls staying at about 60 percent. The gap between lower- and middle-income girls is narrowing, but lower-income youth still report more sexual activity. An increasing number are using contraceptives, now approximately 65 percent. This accounts for teen pregnancies staying about the same."[77]

The public's top concern with schools is drugs.[78] Therefore, there is less controversy about school involvement in drug education and prevention. The most successful programs seem to be well-publicized no-drug policies that also offer help to kids in trouble; these programs begin drug education as early as kindergarten, and involve the whole community in working against drugs (see Box 2-2).

For many teens, the preferred drug is alcohol (see Table 2-2).[79] Messages passed on through our culture about usage comes from parents, advertising, and peers. Many underage drinkers are children of alcoholic parents, estimated at up to 15 million persons under 18 in the United States.[80] These children are at higher risk for being abused, attempting suicide, running away, delinquency, and poor school achievement.

Drug Abuse.   The problem of drug abuse among students as well as others was brought into the limelight with the death of a prominent college basketball star, Len Bias, from a drug overdose, and reports of extensive misuse among athletes. William Bennett, secretary of education under the Reagan administration, declared a "war on drugs." In some districts, this has included searches and urine tests for drug use, practices that have met with court challenges. A U.S. Department of Education report, *Schools Without Drugs,*[81] made a number of recommendations to attack the problem, including a controversial plan to divert $100 million from other higher-education programs to fight the problem (Box 2-3).

University of Washington researchers point to a number of childhood predictors of drug or alcohol abuse:

- family history of alcoholism,
- family history of criminality,
- poor parental child-raising practices, such as lax supervision and constant criticism,
- parental drug use or permissive attitudes toward drugs,
- early antisocial behavior in school, especially aggressiveness,
- alienation and low commitment to getting an education,
- academic failure in mid- to late elementary school,
- socializing with friends who take drugs, and
- first use of drugs before age 15.[82]

If intervention deals with the causes in addition to the actual abuse, results will be more effective.

Substance abuse and other problems point again to the controversy—the role of schools versus families in educating students about problem areas. Should the schools offer drug and alcohol counseling and rehabilitation; sex and AIDS education, pregnancy counseling, testing, and contraceptives; and

BOX 2-2   *WHAT CAN WE DO? A PLAN FOR ACHIEVING SCHOOLS WITHOUT DRUGS*

Parents

1. Teach standards of right and wrong, and demonstrate these standards through personal example.
2. Help children resist peer pressure to use drugs by supervising their activities, knowing who their friends are, and talking with them about their interests and problems.
3. Be knowledgeable about drugs and signs of drug use. When symptoms are observed, respond promptly.

Schools

4. Determine the extent and character of drug use and establish a means of monitoring that use regularly.
5. Establish clear and specific rules regarding drug use that include strong corrective actions.
6. Enforce established policies against drug use fairly and consistently. Implement security measures to eliminate drugs on school premises and at school functions.
7. Implement a comprehensive drug prevention curriculum for kindergarten through grade 12, teaching that drug use is wrong and harmful and supporting and strengthening resistance to drugs.
8. Reach out to the community for support and assistance in making the school's antidrug policy and program work. Develop collaborative arrangements in which school personnel, parents, school boards, law enforcement officers, treatment organizations, and private groups can work together to provide necessary resources.

Students

9. Learn about the effects of drug use, the reasons why drugs are harmful, and ways to resist pressures to try drugs.
10. Use an understanding of the danger posed by drugs to help other students avoid them. Encourage other students to resist drugs, persuade those using drugs to seek help, and report those selling drugs to parents and the school principal.

Communities

11. Help schools fight drugs by providing them with the expertise and financial resources of community groups and agencies.
12. Involve local law enforcement agencies in all aspects of drug prevention: assessment, enforcement, and education. The police and courts should have well-established and mutually supportive relationships with the schools.

Source: U.S. Department of Education, *What Works: Schools Without Drugs,* 1987, p. ix.

TABLE 2-2   Alcohol Use by High School Seniors, 1982–1991

	PERCENTAGE OF HIGH SCHOOL SENIORS REPORTING USE		
Years	Consumed in last 30 days	Heavy drinking in last two weeks	Total
1982	29	41	70
1983	27	41	68
1984	27	39	66
1985	28	37	65
1986	29	37	66
1987	29	38	67
1988	29	35	64
1989	28	33	61
1990	26	32	58
1991	26	30	56

suicide-prevention programs? Or should these "personal and moral matters" be left to families? The Surgeon General of the United States leaves no doubt as to his office's position: Explicit sex education in schools is essential to prevent the spread of AIDS.

Creationism versus Secularism.   A Tennessee court battle opened July 14, 1986, to national headlines that referred to it as "Scopes II" (a reference to the famous case of 1925, in which a biology teacher named John Scopes was tried for teaching Darwinian theory in a public school in Tennessee).[83] It pitted fundamentalist Christians against "secular humanists." The fundamentalists, represented by Vicki Frost, objected to many ideas in basic textbooks, such as pictures of a boy cooking. She and others argue that secular humanism has destroyed values and caused children to act like animals, and that religious truth should prevail. Secular humanists fought back, arguing that *no one* has absolute truth and that moral laws are human-made, not God-given. In this case, the parents won the first round and gained the right to teach their children reading at home.[84]

Several states have considered laws related to the teaching of evolution in schools. For instance, Georgia, Iowa, Florida, and Tennessee have considered legislation to drop the teaching of biology in schools. Georgia Bill 690 requires equal time for teaching evolution and for teaching fundamentalist views about the creation of the world. In California in 1981, the Superior Court heard a case brought by Segraves, also labeled by the press "Scopes II." Segraves, founder of the Creation Science Research Center, argued that the state of California "had violated the religious freedom of his children by teaching evolution as fact."[85] The judge's decision held that the state does not violate rights by teaching evolution, but that it should be taught as a theory, not as dogma.

In a number of states, fundamentalists are pushing for the teaching of "scientific creationism," as it is called, as well as evolution.[86] Some creation educators argue that contemporary theology of creation also includes social, ecological and nuclear issues and values for survival.[87] A 1989 U.S. federal

BOX 2-3   *THE LITTLE RED BOOK: SCHOOLS WITHOUT DRUGS*

Entitled *Schools Without Drugs,* literally tens of thousands of free copies of this handbook have been distributed in the past several months. Neatly timed to coincide with passage of the "Drug-Free Schools and Communities Act," the "little red book" is likely to become an important reference for schools seeking funds for developing substance-abuse prevention programs.

Although only 79 pages long, the book is filled with ideas, strategies, and references to guide schools and communities in establishing a drug-free environment. The goals of the book are laudable:

- To completely eliminate all drug and alcohol abuse in the school-age population.
- To develop appropriate role models for children and to help them resist peer pressure to experiment with drugs.
- To implement a comprehensive drug-prevention curriculum in schools, and to establish corrective policies regarding users.
- To involve entire communities in prevention efforts.
- To teach students to maintain sound personal health, to respect laws and rules prohibiting drugs, and to promote the positive, drug-free aspects of student life.

Perhaps the main strength of the handbook is that it provides practical strategies for working toward accomplishing these goals. Included are a number of example programs used in various schools, which the book represents as successful models.

Source: McEvoy, Alan W., "Children of Alcoholics and Addicts," *School Intervention Report,* June–July 1990, Vol. 3, No. 6, p. 1.

court rejected a teacher's claim to the right to teach creation, arguing that "the First Amendment is not a teacher license for uncontrolled expression at variance with established curricular content." The judge argued that teaching creationism violates separation of church and state; an appeal of this decision may reach the Supreme Court.[88] A dozen states have introduced legislation requiring textbooks and science courses to include the creationist viewpoint. The creationists use data from the sciences to support their ideas, but many scientists argue that their "facts" are faulty or unproven. In a Little Rock, Arkansas, case in January 1982, a federal judge struck down the state's creationism law, ruling that it violated First Amendment separation of church and state. "It was simply and purely an effort to introduce the biblical version of creation into the public school curricula. . . . It explains nothing and refers to no scientific fact or theory," the judge argued. The issue will see more action in the courts for some time to come.

Censorship of Textbooks and Library Books.   Obscenity, sex, nudity, political or economic "bias," profanity, slang or questionable English, racism or racial hatred, antireligious or anti-American ideas—all have been reasons for censoring text and library books in schools. Such books as *The Wizard of Oz, Rumplestiltskin, The Diary of Anne Frank, Madame Bovary, Soul on Ice, Grapes of*

Wrath, Shakespeare's *Hamlet, Huckleberry Finn,* Chaucer's *The Miller's Tale,* and Aristophanes' *Lysistrata* have been on the "hit list" of organizations attempting to ban books. Several well-known children's book authors, including Judy Blume and Norma Klein, have the distinction of being "most banned."[89] "The books that have been challenged most frequently in recent years include John Steinbeck's *Of Mice and Men;* J. D. Salinger's *The Catcher in the Rye;* Stephen King's *Cujo;* Harper Lee's *To Kill a Mockingbird;* Judy Blume's *Deenie, Forever, Blubber,* and *Then Again Maybe I Won't.* The most frequently mentioned objections to these books are their vulgar language, profanity, and sexual content. Other targeted books and the reasons given for the challenge include: *The Diary of Anne Frank* (a passage that suggests that all religions are equally valuable); *Cinderella, The Wizard of Oz, Macbeth* (depictions of good witches and references to the occult); *Romeo and Juliet* (romanticization of suicide); *Ordinary People* by Judith Guest (depressing and obscene); and Alice Walker's *The Color Purple* (troubling ideas about race relations and human sexuality)."[90] The question is whether concerned parents have the right to have certain materials removed from classes and school libraries. The Supreme Court ruled that school "boards may not remove books from school library shelves simply because they dislike the ideas contained in these books."[91] Rather, they must establish and follow reasonable procedures before removing controversial books.[92]

Controversies over library books and class texts have torn communities apart. A recent example is Yucaipa, California, a small town of orange groves and ranch homes.[93] The controversy is over a K–6 reading series called *Impressions,* which includes selections of children's literature by C.S. Lewis, Laura Ingalls Wilder, Lewis Carroll, and Martin Luther King, as well as other classic children's readings.[94]

Some social analysts describe the controversies as rooted in the "politics of lifestyle."[95] For example, the ultra-fundamentalists (fundamentalists with a political agenda) "seek to have prayer included in the curriculum of the public schools, because it is a symbolic reaffirmation of their religious values and belief system."[96,97] Books provide symbolic victories in status politics. The struggle is to regain what was lost in the social revolution of the 1960s.[98]

Most educators claim that censorship threatens academic freedom; groups calling for removal argue that they are protecting their children from "secularism," obscenity, and other negative influences. Court rulings have varied, but the balance of cases are coming down on the side of academic freedom.

Cultural politics is also involved in text selections. State-level text selection involving citizens and interest groups allows the public's competing interests to be represented, but the pressure on school professionals, many of whom are turning toward texts with packaged materials, is somewhat limited.[99] Texas and California, the largest buyers of texts, are having a major influence on what types of textbooks are produced. The two states constitute about one-fifth of the textbook publishers' market, giving them major influence in what texts will cover, including controversial topics like evolution.[100]

Schools are one place where individuals and communities can dig in and take a stand; events in other institutions may seem uncontrollable. The key point is that decision making about curriculum content represents broader issues about power and control of people's lives, what happens to their children, and changes in their communities. Much of the impetus for resisting change in curricula comes from rural and small-town areas, where residents see pressure from a rapidly changing, urbanized world threatening many of their long-held beliefs and values. Cultural transmission is not a straightforward process but one that reflects the dynamic and heterogeneous viewpoints of a pluralistic society.

THE FUNCTION OF SOCIAL CONTROL AND PERSONAL DEVELOPMENT: PREPARING THE INDIVIDUAL FOR SOCIETY

Community members expect students to learn the skills necessary to become productive, law-abiding citizens. According to functional theory, students are expected to learn, through formal or informal means, such values as discipline, respect, obedience, punctuality, and perseverance. These are seen as essential to survival in the work force and in school. Schools are expected to instill values related to social control and individual development. In this way society's problems can be reduced because individuals will be trained to fit into society in acceptable ways. Conflict theorists have a different view of social control, however. They contend that schools are the tool of capitalist societies—controlling, training, sorting human beings for places in the societal system and perpetuating unequal class systems.

Schools have varying ways of passing on the skills of social control. They range from authoritarian to humanistic methods. The process of discipline is the major method of enforcing control in schools. The means for achieving social control *within* the school and for preparing disciplined workers creates dilemmas and controversies for schools as well as for society. Two interrelated issues illustrate this point: discipline and students' rights.

Discipline in Schools

A picture of an authoritarian school or classroom might look something like this: It would have strict disciplinary rules, stress orderliness, make clear who is running the school or class, and mete out swift and consistent punishment. A "hard-line" approach was used in one New York City high school, where the principal held the belief "that a child's right to an education is terminated at the point where the child interferes with the rights of other children to have one."[101] Translated into practice, this meant that teachers should not tolerate disorder. There was no attempt to focus on individual students' problems at home, or to make the school into a "media center, playground, or psychiatric clinic" to meet student or parent desires. The emphasis was on strict enforcement of controlled group interaction, which facilitated orderly classroom learning. This technique resulted in a formal atmosphere in the school and classroom with regard to discipline and learning, and the rigid expectations were clear.

The humanistic school classroom, on the other hand, would stress humaneness and respect for all, involve students in the school community and in running the school, stress helping students to make decisions and act in a responsible manner, and have rules that set only "necessary" limits. An example of the "humanistic approach" is found in a high school system in a midwestern city that employed a counselor, social worker, and psychologist, in addition to specialists in academic areas. This team worked with classroom teachers to help children who had problems, trying to discover the roots of the problem and provide services to deal with them. The philosophy behind this approach was that the child whose basic needs for love, belonging, security, even food were not being met could not begin to learn effectively; thus, attacking these problems was the first step toward the child's experiencing success in school.

Between these extremes is a continuum of approaches to discipline. At the authoritarian end of the continuum is corporal punishment, which has been used since schooling began, and has had a significant place in American schools. In 1975, the Supreme Court gave its approval to "reasonable" corporal punishment for children as young as 4 years for any "alleged misconduct in school." As of May 1990, 31 states allowed corporal punishment to some degree.[102] Attempts to pass legislation banning corporal punishment in British schools have met with mixed results, but by 1985, 18 local education authorities were allowing parents to indicate if they wish their children not to be "caned."[103,104] In Sweden, corporal punishment is banned in both schools and homes. In the United States, the National PTA is fighting against "child abuse" in the form of corporal punishment.[105]

Students in high schools and middle schools in some localities are angry and defiant. Some schools have become repressive places with strict discipline and guards in the halls, at times resembling armed camps.

The Youth Risk Behavior Survey finds that 20 percent of high school students carry weapons and 5 percent carry a firearm at least once a month. Male students, especially blacks and Hispanics, are far more likely to carry weapons, with 40 percent carrying a weapon monthly.[106] Sometimes serious crimes and injuries occur, as students are stealing gold jewelry, leather jackets, money, and other valuables from other students, and will kill if necessary. Some urban schools have gone so far as to install metal detectors.[107]

Discipline is a prime concern of parents and teachers alike, and during the past ten years it has ranked consistently at or near the top, along with drugs, in the Gallup poll of major problems facing education.[108] In a comparison of teachers' perceptions of disruptive student behavior in 1983 and 1987, 28 percent felt it was about the same, 44 percent felt it was somewhat to much more, and 27 percent felt it was less.[109]

Some sociologists see discipline problems as representing power struggles between students and adults in a system where students are powerless and often rebel against the authoritarian rules restricting their thoughts and behaviors. These sociologists contend that unless the coercive, alienating power structure surrounding students is radically altered, discipline will always remain a problem.

One controversy centers around the type of discipline in schools. The use of "authoritarian techniques" with corporal punishment and suspensions is favored by recent U.S. federal administrations to protect the rights of teachers and students to safe educational environments. Some research indicates that strict discipline is a key component for achievement in low-income city schools.[110] "Humanistic approaches" oppose strict discipline except in extreme cases, arguing that delinquent behavior has causes such as aversive school and home environments and pain-avoidance behavior.[111]

Various studies show the results of physical punishment as ranging from "ineffective" as a control mechanism to a breeder of violence. A British study found corporal punishment to be worse than ineffective; it contributed directly to misbehavior and juvenile delinquency outside of school.[112] Psychologists point to the ineffectiveness of negative reinforcement, such as corporal punishment, in bringing about desired changes in behavior. Some educators indicate that corporal punishment dehumanizes the school, that it is inappropriate for the school environment, and that it increases disruptive, rebellious behavior and hinders learning. The students who receive the most corporal punishment are those who are already disenchanted with school. Critics of such punishment claim that it not only serves to discourage students from making an effort to succeed, but labels them negatively among teachers. The point is that teachers and schools can *teach* violence by condoning and using physical force.

Evaluation of one policy, school suspension, shows that African-American male students in the United States are in many cases disproportionately suspended. Although this may solve the immediate goals of removing the problem and punishing the students, it can create long-term problems that cost society: reducing black male chances for productive lives; limiting educational opportunity; increasing dropout rates; and causing reliance on welfare services, incarceration in prisons, and commitment to mental hospitals.[113]

- *Non-interventionist* strategies share a belief in students' ability to solve their own problems if given support by the teacher. Techniques range from Gordon's "Teacher Effectiveness Training," in which active listening (listening to the other person's concerns) is stressed, to "Values Clarification" and the exploration of personal values.

- *Interactionalists* believe that teachers should limit students' behavior to choices within socially approved rules and regulations. For example, Dreikurs points out that misbehavior is caused by misdirected goals (need for attention, power, revenge, or feelings of helplessness), and once the teacher has found the goal, students can be encouraged to redirect behavior to meet that goal.

- *Interventionists* argue that classroom management involves setting clear standards of behavior and using appropriate positive and negative reinforcers. Behavior modification falls under this category; reinforcers are used to encourage or discourage student behavior.

- *The eclectic* approach adheres to no one explanation for how students grow, learn, or behave and uses a variety of tools.[114]

The technique used in a classroom affects the atmosphere and student-teacher interactions. More systematic research into power structures, discipline techniques, and their results is needed.

All human beings have certain basic needs—food, shelter, love and affection, respect, trust, knowledge, and truth.[115] If basic underlying needs are not met, children may exhibit disruptive behavior. For instance, if children come to school hungry or lacking affection at home, they are more likely to be disruptive in school. Teachers do not always have the time, energy, or interest to deal with these problems directly and instead resort to techniques of discipline or control such as corporal punishment, expulsion (ten days or more) or suspension (ten days or less), detention, transfer to another class or school, loss of privileges, drugs to calm children, or special-education classes.

Students' Rights

Power conflicts and inconsistencies in the process of discipline were major factors when the issue of students' rights arose in the late 1960s. Parents, citizens' groups, and students became concerned about the lack of constitutionally guaranteed rights for students as compared with other members of society. Since minority-group students were especially subject to arbitrary disciplinary measures, it was argued that schools were passing on racism and classism, making sure that some students would not do well in school or get good jobs. In this way, it was claimed, schools were serving the middle classes well. Few schools had due process procedures and many students were suspended for long periods of time, a practice that punished them dually because they also got further behind in their work. School systems had long been oblivious by habit or neglect to constitutional rights relating to students. Areas of controversy include First Amendment rights—free speech, freedom of the press, freedom of assembly.[116] In 1965, the U.S. Court of Appeals heard a case involving students suspended for wearing buttons with a political message. Since that time, the courts have ruled on a number of cases involving freedom of speech, the press, and assembly. In *Goss v. Lopez* (1975),[117] procedural requirements for short-term (ten days or less) suspensions under the Fourteenth Amendment due process clauses were established. Students must be given oral or written notice of charges, and if the charges are denied by the student, explanation of evidence and opportunity to present student's side must be granted.

Another key case involves freedom of speech and the press. In *Hazelwood School District v. Kuhlmeier* (1988),[118] the court ruled that school administrators have the right to censor school newspapers. This ruling has led to many cases of censorship and even affects districts' decisions to ban books.[119,120] Personal rights relating to dress, hair length and style, and other matters have also been contested. Court rulings on cases in this area have produced mixed results.

Other issues have come up with regard to Fourth Amendment rights to search students. Statistics show that the increase of violence in schools during the late 1970s and early 1980s seems to have leveled off, but reports of weapons being brought to schools and shootings continue to make news headlines. Inner-city schools sometimes take on a "survival atmosphere" rather than an achievement and learning climate.[121] The question involves the extent to which school authorities have the right to search students when there is suspicion of breaking school laws, or to carry out random "shakedowns" looking for weapons, drugs, and alcohol.

In an "easing" of the Fourth Amendment, the Supreme Court found in *New Jersey v. T.L.O.* (Case 83-712) that public school officials, acting alone and on their own authority, are not required to obtain a warrant prior to conducting a search of a student when "there are reasonable grounds for suspecting that the search will turn up evidence that the student has violated or is violating either the law or rules of the school."[122] Lower-court rulings in California hold schools liable for unsafe "campuses," and several schools around the country have periodic shakedowns for weapons and have installed metal detectors at some schools. However, "sweep" searches have been challenged by the ACLU and other civil rights advocates. Attempts to control the use of drugs through searches and urine tests have also been controversial, with charges of "invasion of privacy."

Some administrators and teachers express the following dilemma: How can schools teach and maintain social control in an obligatory, compulsory situation and at the same time honor the individual rights guaranteed by the Constitution? Many students do not share the schools' values, yet community members expect schools to instill cultural values and develop disciplined young people. Part of the dilemma stems from the fact that students' and children's rights do not always coincide with the views or wishes of parents, institutions, policies, and legislation on the issues. Who has the right to decide these issues?[123]

Schools have moved a long way from the repressive times when children were "seen but not heard," and discipline was unquestioned and authoritarian. Most schools have developed policies for dealing with students' rights. But the problem of social control has deep roots that relate to the class structure of society, which is discussed in the next chapter.

THE FUNCTION OF SELECTION AND ALLOCATION: THE SORTING PROCESS

What is the best way to determine whether you or the next person gets the best college placement, admission into your field, and the highest-paying and most prestigious job? This issue is discussed in detail in Chapters 3 and 4; here we consider one method used by most industrial countries—testing. The controversy lies in the role that exams play in placement, and whether they are fair to all students.

The Testing Game

Many modern industrial societies emphasize achievement and merit. In these test-oriented societies, it is beneficial to be skilled at test taking. We will be faced with intelligence quotient (IQ) tests, aptitude tests, achievement tests, career-interest inventories, psychological tests, Civil Service tests, SAT, ACT, Miller's Analogy test, Graduate Record Examination, job-aptitude tests, and so on. Schools use exams at various checkpoints to track or stream students and to ensure that students are achieving at grade level, since schools are held accountable by the community for their activities. Many states now require examinations for graduation from high school, and students must take the Scholastic Aptitude Test (SAT) or American College Testing Program (ACT) for college entrance. Tests are a part of our lives, helping educators and others to select and allocate according to ability. Are some groups at an advantage in the testing process?

The use of IQ test scores has been controversial for years. Alfred Binet first developed intelligence tests in France to diagnose mental retardation and areas of individual difficulty or weakness. Binet felt that an individual's intelligence was not a fixed quality, but could be increased with expert training. It was not his idea to use the test for mass placements, but this soon became common. U.S. Army recruits were given intelligence tests and were classified as alpha (literate) or beta (illiterate) in order to sort and select them for various roles in the armed service. Concerns about IQ testing intensified when schools also began to use the tests for sorting purposes. This practice has come under attack, but many school districts still use IQ tests to help with general placement of children. In the 1970s, debate intensified with the publication of several articles on the nature and use of IQ tests. Several concerns have been raised about the nature of intelligence tests:

1. What are we really measuring?
2. To what extent do genetic or environmental factors influence test results?
3. Can we develop a culture-free test?

The first problem deals with the nature of intelligence. Jot down some characteristics that make someone you know seem intelligent. Compare your ideas of intelligence with someone else's. Probably you have some overlap and some differences in your definitions. The same problem exists for social scientists trying to pinpoint what we really mean by intelligence; there is not complete agreement on what innate qualities to look for or how to find them.

As many as 23 different mental abilities have been included in definitions of intelligence—among them, "verbal fluency, spatial perception, analogical reasoning, series and sequence manipulation, memory, and creativity.[124] In attempting to define intelligence we are not referring to a simple quantity, but to a complex system of reasoning.[125] Howard Gardner refers to "multiple intelligences."[126] Robert Sternberg argues that intelligence refers to "an information processing framework," which "deals with what happens to information from the time we perceive it until the time we act upon it. Some people have proven to be less adept than others at different stages in processing. . . ."[127]

Philip Mason[128] has set forth a view of intelligence as divided into three parts:

- innate, inherited intelligence,
- environmentally influenced intelligence, and
- measured IQ (some undetermined combination).

Not only are we unable to measure all three parts, but we cannot be sure of the exact combination of factors that make up intelligence.

The second problem deals with the controversy over genetic and environmental determinants of intelligence. In 1969, Arthur Jensen made the following statement: "What IQ tests measure is 80% inherited, 20% cultural."[129] This statement and the general content of his article in the *Harvard Educational Review* generated a controversy that continues to this day. Jensen and others such as Richard J. Hernstein[130] theorize that IQ differences between socioeconomic, social, and ethnic groups are due primarily to genetic factors. This assumes that intelligence is understood, definable, and testable, and that we have a test that can measure intelligence accurately. These factors are questionable. If one could assume IQ tests to be valid and intelligence to be inherited, some feel that the distribution of positions in society could be justified on the basis of intelligence groups—the argument being that some are more able than others. Some individuals may indeed be more able, but we must be sure that we can determine this accurately before pigeonholing the population on the basis of a test.

Different authors have proposed varying relationships between intelligence and environment, but as Christopher Jencks pointed out in a debate on the topic,[131] we don't even have an adequate definition of environment and all its components. Nor can we measure the influence of genes on the environment or that of the environment on genes.

The third problem with using intelligence tests to classify members of society deals with whether it is possible to devise tests that are free of cultural bias—class, ethnicity, regionalism, and the other variables that make our nation and school systems so diverse. Consider the following situation. Children are asked to draw a horse. Who do you think would draw the "best" horse? Native American children living in rural areas do best at this task because of their familiarity with the subject.

In one attempt to develop a culture-free test, Jane Mercer[132] devised a technique called SOMPA (System of Multi-Cultural Pluralistic Assessment), which allows comparison of an individual's test scores with those of other children from similar socioeconomic backgrounds. It provides a means for compensating for test bias. When sociocultural factors were held constant, there were no measurable intellectual differences between racial and ethnic groups.

One environmental factor that affects intelligence tests is the region of the country from which a person comes. In IQ tests administered to army recruits after World War I, researchers noted that army recruits did *not* follow the stereotypic pattern of blacks scoring lower than whites, but that region made a significant difference in their scores. Northern whites scored highest, followed in descending order by northern blacks, southern whites, and southern blacks.[133]

Several other variables affect test scores: the race of the person in charge of the testing situation, the sex of the test-taker, the motivation of the test-taker, how the test-taker is feeling on the day of the test—even whether the individual had a good breakfast. You probably remember feeling nervous on testing days. Some children do better under stress, some do worse, and some just give up in the face of a threatening or difficult situation. Individual factors of this type can affect test scores significantly.

Studies Related to IQ Testing and Environmental Influences

In order to examine environmental influence on IQ, several studies have been conducted with children who were orphans or born to low-IQ mothers.[134-136]

For example, Rick Heber[137] and his co-workers set up a "total immersion intervention" project for an experimental group of children whose mothers were regarded as mentally retarded. The children and parents were placed in enrichment programs, children were tested to ascertain the results, and results were compared with a control group of similar children who were not receiving the intervention. The results were impressive. By age 6, the experimental group had an average IQ of 121, while the control group's average IQ was 87.

Such studies point to the problem of ranking or classifying people on the basis of scores that are unreliable or changeable and that are influenced by environmental circumstances. They also suggest that intelligence—as typically measured—is not a fixed, inherited attribute, but a variable depending on stimulation and on cultural and environmental factors.

Achievement Tests

The scene of a student waiting by the mailbox in anticipation, dreading to open "the envelope," is familiar around the world. That envelope holds the answer to the future of many young people—scores on achievement tests. Those numbers determine for many students their entrance to or rejection by universities. Those scores are important—and controversial—because they tap the core of *how* we evaluate and place people.

In the United States two national achievement tests are given to college-bound high school students: the ACT and the SAT. Scholastic Aptitude Test scores rose in 1991 for the first time since 1987, up one point in verbal skills and two points in math.[138] However, scores of minority students are still significantly lower than those of whites. Some educators criticize the tests, arguing that they do not test classroom reality, but that they are tending to shape what happens in the classroom. The Educational Testing Service, authors of the SAT and achievement tests, have developed revised tests that they say are more closely tied to classroom experiences.[139]

Test-makers will continue to improve the validity of their tests; educators will continue to question the relationship between curricular materials and test items; parents and students will share concerns about the meaning of tests for life chances; and minority advocates will keep a watchful eye on tests for bias. However, in meritocracies some forms of testing, however imperfect, are likely to continue.

THE FUNCTION OF CHANGE AND INNOVATION:
THE PROCESS
OF LOOKING TO THE FUTURE

Schools provide a link with the future; it is through research and teaching the next generation new knowledge that societies move forward. Universities are generally on the cutting edge of research, passing this knowledge on to students. Although few deny the inevitability of change, questions arise as to how change takes place and who controls change.

One thing we know is that those who possess technological skills and knowledge for the twenty-first century, and who know how to get information important to functioning in the future, will rise in the hierarchy. Can schools teach and implement new technology? Are these tools equally available to all?

In the mid-1980s, then–U.S. Secretary of Education Terrel H. Bell formed the National Task Force on Educational Technology to look into appropriate integration of technology to improve schools. The task force concluded that technology can aid individual students in receiving the education that each person needs by individualizing instruction. This proposal, they felt, would be cost-effective by reducing the need for special classes for students.[140] Yet some argue that the use being made of computers in classrooms (Figure 2-2) is often not productive for future needs.[141]

Computer technology is subject to the whims of unstable economies. The "Massachusetts Miracle," touted by journals on electronic wonders in the classroom as one of the most advanced plans for computer education,[142] went bust with the economic slump and declining federal dollars; preparation of works for the "information age" has taken a back seat to more pressing economic needs. To keep our "human capital" competitive internationally, technological knowledge is crucial.[143]

Inequalities enter the classrooms of urban and suburban schools, even when both have computers: Urban schools are so busy playing catch-up that computers are used more for computer-based drill—seen as good preparation for standardized tests—than for analysis, writing, and problem solving. Elite private schools, for instance, use innovation in the form of microcomputers as one way to add to their cultural capital, which leads to cultural reproduction.[144] The "technological gender gap" also concerns many educators: Female and male high school students have different attitudes, behaviors, and skills, and if those differences are not addressed, the gap could leave many women without skills needed to pursue technological careers. Suggestions to remedy the gap range from integrating computers across the curriculum to eliminating sexist stereotypes from computer software.[145]

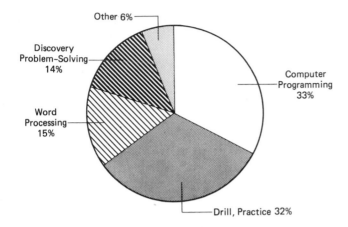

FIGURE 2-2   Classroom use of computer time. Two-thirds of computer time goes into programming and drill and practice, activities of disputed educational value. Word processing is performed less but is more useful.

Source: "Something Doesn't Quite Compute," *U.S. News & World Report*, November 10, 1986, p. 78.

Computers may have a dramatic impact on the way we learn, from home teaching through terminals hooked to teachers, to audioteleconferencing with distant experts. However, any change results in social transformations as well, and the information age is ushering in new technology that will force changes in social structures. These changes may be resisted unless the key participants have motivations or incentives for changing.

For integrated learning systems and computer-managed instruction (CMI) to be effective, classroom teachers must see benefits to changing their teaching patterns.[146] Teachers who have a professional identity are likely to want to adopt new practices such as computer integration. To the extent that change and innovation are seen as possible, supported, and part of the normative structure of professionals in a school system, teachers are more likely to adopt the innovations.[147]

Any educational issue we choose to investigate is likely to fall into one of the functions of education. Those discussed here are a few examples. We move now to a discussion of the school function of selection and allocation, which takes place through the process of stratification.

SUMMARY

In this chapter we have considered the five primary functions of education and processes that make the system function.

I. Conflicting Functions of Education

To illustrate the dynamic nature of systems, examples of controversies surrounding each function are discussed.

II. The Importance of Processes in Systems

Processes are the action part of systems; they link the system parts and the system with the environment.

III. The Function of Socialization: Who Gets Ahead in the Process?

Three controversies are discussed here:

1. *The early childhood education controversy*—Controversies surround who should provide early care, and the long-term results of early care. Research finds that there are some long-term positive effects of programs on poor children, and no deleterious effects of early childhood education on other children.
2. *Role of the media in socialization*—Controversies surround the role of media in education or entertaining, and the possible negative results of television watching. Excessive TV watching lowers achievement, but the effects of TV violence on aggression are less clear. Suicide rates do go up after shows concerning suicide have aired. There is clear evidence regarding the effect of parental involvement in TV decisions, and the positive effects of educational TV for children.
3. *Political socialization*—schools play a role in teaching children their political roles in society.

IV. The Function of Cultural Transmission and Process of Passing On Culture

Concern has risen over poor skills of students, as shown by low standardized test scores and cultural illiteracy. Some advocate much stricter core curricula to correct deficiencies. What to teach and who should decide are also controversial questions, especially in heterogeneous societies. Three areas are used to exemplify the controversies: drug and sex education, creationism versus secularism, and censorship of textbooks.

V. The Function of Social Control and Personal Development: Preparing the Individual for Society

Two issues that point to the attempt by schools to maintain social control are discipline and students' rights. Controversies center around what type of discipline to use, and whether students have the same rights under law as adults, such as free speech and freedom from search and seizure.

VI. The Function of Selection and Allocation: The Sorting Process

How individuals are placed in society is the key controversy here. Because testing is used extensively for placement in schooling and jobs, the fairness of this procedure is discussed. (This function is discussed extensively in Chapters 3 and 4.)

VII. The Function of Change and Innovation: The Process of Looking to the Future

Who has access to the technological training necessary to advance in society is one issue raised here. To the extent that certain students have more access than others, they may have an edge in future placements.

PUTTING SOCIOLOGY TO WORK

1.   Discuss the main processes involved in your role as a student.
2.   What controversy over curriculum content has been present in a town with which you are familiar? What sociological factors underlie this controversy?
3.   Visit a nursery school and observe. What types of socialization experiences are the children having that might differ from home experiences?
4.   Discuss with some parents of young children and with teachers of young children their feelings about early childhood education.
5.   Interview fundamentalist religious leaders about their views concerning the school curriculum. What changes or additions, if any, would they like to see? If there are fundamentalist church schools in your area, try to visit, observe, and learn about their program.
6.   Discuss with school board members and school administrators the pressure groups that influence their decision making, on what issues, and using what tactics.
7.   Discuss with several teachers the techniques they feel are most effective in helping children learn, and discipline techniques they use in the classroom.
8.   What are the biggest discipline problems facing schools in your area? Visit a school in a different type of community and find out the same information. What are the reasons for the similarities or differences in discipline problems? This may involve learning how the school deals with discipline.
9.   Interview students of different ages to learn their views about discipline and students' rights.

NOTES ————————————————————

[1] Apple, Michael W., and Lois Weis, "Seeing Education Relationally: The Stratification of Culture and People in the Sociology of School Knowledge," *Journal of Education*, Vol. 168, No. 1, 1986.

[2] *Ibid.*, p. 14.

[3] Peters, Donald L., "Social Science and Social Policy and the Care of Young Children: Head Start and After," *Journal of Applied Developmental Psychology*, Vol. 1, 1980, p. 22.

[4] Elam, Stanley M., Lowell C. Rose, and Alec M. Gallup, "The 23rd Annual Gallup Poll of the Public's Attitudes Toward the Public Schools," *Phi Delta Kappan*, September 1991.

[5] Mitchell, Anne, Michelle Seligson, and Fern Marx, *Early Childhood Programs and the Public Schools: Between Promise and Practice* (Dover, Mass.: Auburn House, 1990).

[6] Peters, "Social Science," p. 22.

[7] Raymond, Chris, "Pioneering Research Challenges Accepted Notions Concerning the Cognitive Abilities of Infants," *The Chronicle of Higher Education*, January 23, 1991, p. A5.

[8] Soderman, Anne K., "Schooling All 4-Year Olds: An Idea Full of Promise, Fraught with Pitfalls," *Education Week*, March 14, 1984, p. 19.

⁹ Raymond, "Pioneering Research."

¹⁰ Barrett, Gill, *Disaffection from School? The Early Years* (London and Phila., Pa.: Falmer Press, 1989).

¹¹ Reynolds, Arthur J., "Early Schooling of Children at Risk," *American Educational Research Journal*, Vol. 28, No. 2, Summer 1991, pp. 392–422.

¹² White, Burton L., "Early Childhood Education: A Candid Appraisal," *Principal*, May 1991, pp. 9–11.

¹³ Materials from National PTA, Chicago.

¹⁴ Schweinhart, I. J., and Weikart, D. P., *Young Children Grow Up: The Effects of the Perry Preschool Program on Youths Through Age 15* (Ypsilanti, Mich.: The High/Scope Press, 1980).

¹⁵ Pitsch, Mark, "President's 1993 Budget Will Include $600 Million Increase for Head Start," *Education Week*, January 29, 1992, p.1.

¹⁶ Peters, "Social Science," p. 14.

¹⁷ Deutscher, Irwin, and David M. Bass, "The Long-Term Effects of Head Start: An Examination of Twenty Years of Evaluation Research," paper presented at American Sociological Association meetings, 1986, p. 20.

¹⁸ Lazar, I., and R. Darlington, "Lasting Effects of Early Education: A Report from the Consortium for Longitudinal Studies," *Monographs of the Society for Research in Child Development*, Vol. 47, pp. 2–3 (Serial No. 195).

¹⁹ McKey, Ruth Hubbell, *et al.*, "The Impact of Head Start on Children, Families, and Communities," Final Report of the Head Start Evaluation, Synthesis and Utilization Project (Washington, D.C.: Administration for Children, Youth, and Families, June 1985), p. 20.

²⁰ Evans, Ellis D., "Longitudinal Follow-Up Assessment of Differential Preschool Experiences for Low Income Minority Group Children," *Journal of Educational Research*, Vol. 78, No. 4, 1985, p. 201.

²¹ Peters, "Social Science," p. 24.

²² Halsey, A.H., "Education Can Compensate," *New Society*, January 24, 1980, pp. 172–73.

²³ Clarke-Stewart, A., and Fein, G. G., "Early Childhood Programs," in M. M. Haith and J. J. Campos (eds.), *Infancy and Developmental Psychobiology*, Vol. 2 of P. H. Mussen (ed.), *Handbook of Child Psychology*, 4th ed. (New York: Wiley, 1983), p. 980.

²⁴ Etaugh, Claire, "Effects of Nonmaternal Care on Children," *American Psychologist*, Vol. 35, 1980, pp. 309–19.

²⁵ Honig, Alice Sterling, "Longitudinal Effects of Quality Preschool Programs," *Day Care and Early Education*, Vol. 17, No. 2, Winter 1989, pp. 35–38.

²⁶ Gracey, Harry L., "Learning the Student Role: Kindergarten as Academic Boot Camp," in Dennis Wrong and Harry L. Gracey (eds.), *Readings in Introductory Sociology* (New York: Macmillan, 1967).

²⁷ Peck, J., G. McCaig, and M. Sapp, *Kindergarten Policies: What Works Best for Children?* (Washington, D.C.: National Association for the Education of Young Children, 1988).

²⁸ Bergan, John R., *et al.*, "Effects of a Measurement and Planning System on Kindergartners' Cognitive Development and Educational Programming," *American Educational Research Journal*, Vol. 28, No. 3, Fall 1991, pp. 683–714.

²⁹ Holloman, Susanne T., "Retention and Redshirting: The Dark Side of Kindergarten," *Principal*, May 1990, pp. 13–25.

³⁰ O'Connor, Sorca, "Women's Labor Force Participation and Preschool Enrollment: A Cross-National Perspective, 1965–1980," *Sociology of Education*, January 1988.

³¹ Halpern, Robert, "Effects of Early Childhood Intervention on Primary School Progress in Latin America," *Comparative Education Review*, Vol. 30, No. 3, 1986, pp. 193–216.

³² Fetler, Mark, "California Surveys of Home Television Viewing and School Achievement," *Educational Media International*, No. 4, 1984, pp. 22–25.

³³ Neuman, Susan B., "Television and Reading: A Research Synthesis," paper presented at American Educational Research Association meetings, April 1986.

³⁴ Gaddy, Gary D., "Television's Impact on High School Achievement," *Public Opinion Quarterly*, Vol. 50, 1986, pp. 340–59.

[35] "TV Remains Our Favorite Pastime, but Other Diversions Grow," *Gallup Report, #248*, May 1986, pp. 7–8.

[36] "California Survey Links TV Viewing, Poor Test Scores," *Education Times*, November 24, 1980, p. 7.

[37] Freedman, Jonathan L., "Effect of Television Violence on Aggressiveness," *Psychological Bulletin*, Vol. 96, No. 2, 1984, pp. 227–46.

[38] Phillips, David P., and Lundie L. Carstensen, "Clustering of Teenage Suicides after Television News Stories about Suicide," *New England Journal of Medicine*, September 11, 1986, pp. 685–689.

[39] Gould, Madelyn S., and David Shaffer, "The Impact of Suicide in Television Movies: Evidence of Imitation," *New England Journal of Medicine*, September 11, 1986, pp. 690–694.

[40] McEvoy, Alan, and Jeff Brookings, "Does Talking About It Make It Happen?" *School Intervention Report*, Vol. 1, No. 1, September 1987, p. 4.

[41] Singer, Dorothy G., and Jerome L. Singer, "Parents as Mediators of the Child's Television Environment," *Educational Media International*, Vol. 4, 1984, pp. 7–11.

[42] Chen, Milton, *A Review of Research on the Educational Potential of 3-2-1-Contact: A Children's TV Series* (Washington, D.C.: U.S. Department of Education, January 1984).

[43] Walsh, Mark, "New Federal Rules for Children's Television Draw Fire," *Education Week*, November 21, 1990, p. 4.

[44] "Schools Tune In to the Latest in Educational Television," *American School Board Journal*, September 1990, pp. A6–9; "Here Comes 'McSchool,' " *American School Board Journal*, September 1991, pp. 30–31.

[45] Travers, E. F., "The Role of the School in Political Socialization Reconsidered: Evidence from 1970 and 1979," *Youth and Society*, Vol. 14, 1983, pp. 475–500.

[46] Washburn, Philo, "The Public School as an Agent of Political Socialization," *Quarterly Journal of Ideology*, Vol. 10, No. 2, 1986, pp. 24–35.

[47] Sigel, R. A., and M. B. Hoskin, *The Political Involvement of Adolescents* (New Brunswick, N.J.: Rutgers University Press, 1981).

[48] Hastings, William L., and Kenneth A. Payne, "Democratic Orientations Among High School Seniors in the United States and Germany," *Social Education*, November/December 1990, pp. 458–65.

[49] Viadero, Debra, "Two Groups Unveil Detailed Plan for Civics Education," *Education Week*, October 2, 1991, p. 13.

[50] Harrington-Lueker, Donna, "Earning an 'A' in Idealism," *The American School Board Journal*, March 1990, pp. 34–37.

[51] Paulsen, Ronnelle, "Education, Social Class, and Participation in Collective Action," *Sociology of Education*, Vol. 64, April 1991, pp. 96–110.

[52] Bowles, Samuel, and Herbert Gintis, *Schooling in Capitalist America: Education and the Contradictions of Economic Life* (New York: Basic Books, 1976).

[53] Aggerton, Peter J., and Geoff Whitty, "Rebels Without a Cause? Socialization and Subcultural Style Among the Children of the New Middle Class," *Sociology of Education*, Vol. 58, No. 1, 1985, pp. 60–72.

[54] Bell, Terrel, National Commission on Excellence in Education, April 1983 report, *A Nation at Risk*, p. 5.

[55] Hirsch, E. D., *Cultural Literacy: What Every American Needs to Know* (Boston: Houghton Mifflin, 1987), p. 152.

[56] "Ravitch: Test Shows 'Cultural Illiteracy,' " *Education Week*, December 4, 1985, p. 4.

[57] Otto, Jean H., "Citizenship Literacy: No Longer a Luxury," *Social Education*, October 1990, p. 360.

[58] McGill-Franzen, Anne, and Richard L. Allington, "Every Child's Right: Literacy," *The Reading Teacher*, Vol. 45, No. 2, October 1991.

[59] National Center for Education Statistics, 1983–84 Academic Year: from "Many Freshmen in Remedial Classes," *Education Week*, February 13, 1985, p. 11.

[60] National Science Foundation, *America's Academic Future*, January 1992, pp. 1–4.

[61] Usiskin, Zalman, "School Mathematics Project," University of Chicago, paper presented at ASCD, 1990.

[62] National Assessment of Educational Progress, report released June 6, 1990.

[63] Carnegie Commission on Science, Technology, and Government, "In the National Interest: The Federal Government in the Reform of K–12 Math and Science Education," 1991.

[64] Stipek, Deborah J., and J. Heidi Gralinski, "Gender Differences in Children's Achievement-Related Beliefs and Emotional Responses to Success and Failure in Mathematics," *Journal of Educational Psychology*, Vol. 83, No. 3, September 1991, pp. 361–70.

[65] Furst, Robert H., "Bloom's Taxonomy of Educational Objectives for the Cognitive Domain," *Review of Educational Research*, Vol. 51, 1981, pp. 441–53.

[66] Snider, William, "Chicago Board Adopts Strict Homework Policy," *Education Week*, June 11, 1986, p. 4.

[67] Epstein, Joyce L., "Homework Practices, Achievements, and Behaviors of Elementary School Students," working paper, Center for Social Organization of Schools (Baltimore: Johns Hopkins University, 1983).

[68] Parsons, Talcott, "The School Class as a Social System," *Harvard Educational Review*, Vol. 29, 1959, pp. 297–318.

[69] Dreeben, Robert, *On What Is Learned in School* (Reading, Mass.: Addison-Wesley, 1968).

[70] Bowles, Samuel, and Herbert Gintis, *Schooling in Capitalist America* (New York: Basic Books, 1976).

[71] Hurn Christopher J., *The Limits and Possibilities of Schooling* (Boston: Allyn and Bacon, 1978).

[72] King, Edith W., *Teaching Ethnic and Gender Awareness*, 2nd ed. (Dubuque, Iowa: Kendall/Hunt Publishing Co., 1990).

[73] Sobol, Thomas, "Understanding Diversity," *Educational Leadership*, November 1990, p. 27.

[74] Zakharieva, Mariana, "Studying Innovations in Education: Internationalization of Approaches," *Current Sociology*, Vol. 39, No. 1, Spring 1991, p. 119.

[75] Hilliard, Asa G., "Why We Must Pluralize the Curriculum," *Educational Leadership*, December 1991/January 1992, p. 13.

[76] The Carnegie Corporation, "Education That Works: An Action Plan for the Education of Minorities," 1990.

[77] *Family Planning Perspectives*, September/October 1990.

[78] Elam, *et al.*, "The 23rd Annual Gallup Poll," p. 55.

[79] "Alcohol Use by High School Seniors," *NIDA High School Senior Survey*, 1991 (in *Education Week*, February 5, 1992, p. 10).

[80] McEvoy, Alan, "Children of Alcoholics and Addicts," *School Intervention Report*, Vol. 3, No. 6, June–July 1990, p. 1.

[81] Hertling, James, "Bennett Declares War on Drugs in School," *Education Week*, March 5, 1986, p. 10.

[82] "Drug Education Gets an F," *U.S. News & World Report*, October 13, 1986, p. 63.

[83] "A Reprise of Scopes," *Newsweek*, July 28, 1986, p. 18.

[84] "Tennessee Parents Win Textbook Suit," *Education Week*, October 29, 1986, p. 1.

[85] " 'Scopes II' in California," *Newsweek*, March 16, 1981, p. 53.

[86] "New Battle Over Teaching of Evolution," *U.S. News & World Report*, June 9, 1980, p. 82.

[87] Hill, Brennan R., "Creation Education: An Overview of Contemporary Theology Education," *Religious Education*, Vol. 85, No. 3, Summer 1990, pp. 382–400.

[88] Armstrong, Liz Schevtchuk, "Federal Court Rejects Teacher's Claim of Right to Teach Theory of Creation," *Education Week*, Vol. 10, No. 12, November 21, 1990, p. 9.

[89] People for the American Way, "Most Frequently Challenged Books, 1982–1987," *Education Week*, September 16, 1987, p. 3.

90 Bjorklun, Eugene C., "School Book Censorship and the First Amendment," *The Educational Forum*, Vol. 55, No. 1, Fall 1990, pp. 37–38.

91 Fischer, Louis, David Schimmel, and Cynthia Kelly, *Teachers and the Law*, 2nd ed. (New York: Longman, 1987) p. 33.

92 *Board of Education, Island Trees Union Free School District No. 26 v. Pico*, 457 U.S. at p. 880, 102 S.Ct. at p. 2814.

93 Warren, Jenifer, "Schoolbook Furor Rends Rural Town," *Los Angeles Times*, August 20, 1990, p. A3.

94 Harrington-Lueker, "Earning an 'A' in Idealism," p. 18.

95 Page, Ann L., and Donald A. Clelland, "The Kanawha County Textbook Controversy: A Study of the Politics of Life Style Concern," *Social Forces*, Vol. 57, 1978, pp. 265–81.

96 Provenzo, Eugene F., *Religious Fundamentalism and American Education: The Battle for the Public Schools* (Albany: SUNY Press, 1990) p. 88.

97 Rose, Susan D., *Keeping Them Out of the Hands of Satan: Evangelical Schooling in America* (New York: Routledge, 1989) p. 203.

98 Bjorklun, Eugene C., "School Book Censorship and the First Amendment," *The Educational Forum*, Vol. 55, No. 1, Fall 1990, p. 37.

99 Wong, Sandra L., "Evaluating the Content of Textbooks: Public Interests and Professional Authority," *Sociology of Education*, Vol. 64, January 1991, pp. 11–18.

100 "California and Texas Enter Textbook Deal," *The American School Board Journal*, August 1991, p. 11.

101 Postman, Neil, "Order in the Classroom," *The Atlantic*, October 1979, pp. 35–38.

102 "The Debate on Corporal Punishment Goes Nationwide," *The American School Board Journal*, May 1990, p. 12.

103 Hearn, Jeff, "Progress Towards the Abolition of Corporal Punishment," *Forum for the Discussion of New Trends in Education*, Vol. 27, Spring 1985.

104 Garner, Richard, "More Backing for Cane Ban," *Times Educational Supplement*, March 14, 1980, p. 7.

105 "The Debate on Corporal Punishment," p. 12.

106 *Youth Risk Behavior Survey* (Atlanta: U.S. Centers for Disease Control, 1991).

107 "Metal Detectors Work, Says UFT," *American Teacher*, Vol. 74, No. 5, February 1990, p. 1.

108 Gallup, George, Elam, *et al.*, "23rd Annual Gallup Poll."

109 National Center for Education Statistics, *Digest of Education Statistics 1991* (Washington, D.C.: U.S. Department of Education, November 1991), Table 140, p. 135.

110 Wynne, Edward, "Discipline in a Good School," *Society*, Vol. 27, May/June 1990, pp. 98–101.

111 Agnew, Robert, "A Revised Strain Theory of Delinquency," *Social Forces*, Vol. 64, September 1985, pp. 151–57.

112 Kujoth, Jean S. (ed.), *The Teacher and Social Discipline* (Metuchen, N.J.: Scarecrow Press, 1970).

113 Taylor, Maurice C., and Gerald A. Foster, "Bad Boys and School Suspensions: Public Policy Implications for Black Males," *Sociological Inquiry*, Vol. 56, Fall 1986, pp. 498–506.

114 Glickman, C., and R. Tamashiro, "Clarifying Teachers' Beliefs About Discipline," *Educational Leadership*, Vol. 37, 1980, pp. 463–64. Reprinted with permission of the Association for Supervision and Curriculum Development. Copyright © 1980 by the Association for Supervision and Curriculum Development. All rights reserved.

115 Maslow, Abraham H., *Toward a Psychology of Being* (New York: Van Nostrand Reinhold, 1962).

116 Glasser, Ira, "School for Scandal: The Bill of Rights and Public Education," *Phi Delta Kappan*, December 1969, pp. 190–94.

117 *Goss v. Lopez* (1975), Record Group 267, Records of the U.S. Supreme Court.

118 *Hazelwood School District v. Kuhlmeier* (1988), 484 U.S. 260.

[119] Repa, Barbara Kate, "The First Amendment Finds a New Battleground: The Classroom," *Social Education*, October 1990, p. 335.

[120] Shoop, Robert J., "A Free Student Press Fosters Responsibility," *Educational Leadership*, November 1990, p. 69.

[121] National Center for Education Statistics, "Incidents of Student Infractions," *Digest of Education Statistics 1991* (U.S. Dept. of Education, 1991), p. 134.

[122] "Court Upholds 'Reasonable' Searches of Students," *Education Week*, January 23, 1985.

[123] Thomas, Arthur E., "Community Power and Students' Rights," *Harvard Educational Review*, Vol. 42, 1972, pp. 173–216.

[124] Rice, Berkeley, "Brave New World of Intelligence Testing," *Psychology Today*, September 1979, pp. 27–30.

[125] *Psychology Today*, September 1979 (issue devoted to discussion of intelligence and its testing).

[126] Gardner, Howard, "The Theory of Multiple Intelligences," *Annual Dyslexia*, Vol. 37, 1987, pp. 19–35.

[127] Sternberg, Robert, "Stalking the IQ Quirk," *Psychology Today*, September 1979, pp. 42–54.

[128] Mason, Philip, *Race Relations* (London: Oxford University Press, 1970), pp. 40–43.

[129] Jensen, Arthur, R., "How Much Can We Boost IQ and Scholastic Achievement?" *Harvard Educational Review*, Vol. 30, 1969, pp. 1–123.

[130] Hernstein, Richard, "In Defense of Intelligence Tests," *Commentary*, February 1980, pp. 40–51.

[131] Jencks, Christopher, "Heredity-Environment Debate," paper presented at American Sociological Association meetings, Boston, August 1979.

[132] Mercer, Jane R., *Labeling the Mentally Retarded: Clinical and Social System Perspectives on Mental Retardation* (Berkeley: University of California Press, 1973).

[133] Hoult, Thomas F., *Sociology for a New Day*, 2nd ed. (New York: Random House, 1979), p. 14.

[134] Skeels, Harold M., "Some Iowa Studies of the Mental Growth of Children in Relation to Differentials of the Environment: A Summary," in *Thirty-ninth Yearbook of the National Society for the Study of Education*, Part II, *Intelligence: Its Nature and Nurture* (Bloomington, Ill.: Public Publishing, 1940), pp. 281–308.

[135] Skeels, Harold M., "Adult Status of Children with Contrasting Early Life Experiences," *Monographs of the Society for Research in Child Development*, Vol. 31, No. 3, 1966.

[136] Spitz, Rene A., "Hospitalism: An Inquiry into the Genesis of Psychiatric Conditions in Early Childhood," in Anna Freud, *et al.* (eds.), *The Psychoanalytic Study of the Child* (New York: International Universities Press, 1945).

[137] Heber, Rick F., "Sociocultural Mental Retardation—A Longitudinal Study," cited in Hoult, *Sociology for a New Day*, p. 15.

[138] "SAT Scores Showing Slight Gain," *Dayton Daily News*, August 27, 1992, p. 1.

[139] Patterson, Janice, H., "Minorities Gain, but Gaps Remain," *Peabody Journal of Education*, Winter 1991, pp. 72–88.

[140] *Transforming American Education: Reducing the Risk to the Nation* (Washington, D.C.: National Task Force on Educational Technology, 1986).

[141] "The Electronic School," supplement to *The American School Board Journal*, October 1991.

[142] Levinson, David L., "Structuring Education for the 'Information Age': High Technology's Influence upon Higher Educational Policy in Massachusetts," paper presented at the 85th Annual Meeting of the American Sociological Association, Washington, D.C., August 1990.

[143] Marshall, Gail, "Drill Won't Do," *The American School Board Journal*, July 1990, p. 21.

[144] Persell, Caroline Hodges, and Peter W. Cookson, "Microcomputers and Elite Boarding Schools: Educational Innovation and Social Reproduction," *Sociology of Education*, Vol. 60, April 1987, pp. 123–34.

[145] Perelman, Lewis J., "Learning Our Lesson: Why School Is Out," *The Futurist,* March/April 1986, pp. 13–16.

[146] Trotter, Andrew, "Computer Learning," *American School Board Journal,* July 1990, pp. 12–13.

[147] Kelly, Thomas F., "Effective Schools and Computers," *Principal,* Vol. 10, No. 3, January 1991, p. 53.

3

EDUCATION
AND THE PROCESS
OF STRATIFICATION

THE CRISIS IN SCHOOLING

Schools are an easy target for criticism, anger, and hostility. Within the school walls lies the key to our futures; most people believe that schooling is directly linked to occupational and financial success. Because schools are accessible targets, parents, educators, students, and policymakers voice their concerns in public forums and at the ballot box.

There is general agreement that schools should produce individuals who can function in society, but *how and why* is controversial. Schools carry out their tasks of transmitting basic skills as formerly, but now we have higher expectations of what schools can and should do. For instance, by increasing access to education, Americans have tried to control poverty and social ills.[1]

In this chapter we consider several issues related to selection and placement of students, and the process of stratification. One of those issues is the very meaning of the term "equality of educational opportunity." Other issues relate to variables that cause different school outcomes for children and adults; public or private schools, ability grouping, home and community environments, teacher and student expectations, and other variables.

Education and Stratification in America

There is a crisis, according to a number of educational critics,[2] because of changes in the educational environment, and hopes for schools that are not being met. The old Horatio Alger success stories just do not seem to be coming true any more and the image of the "land of opportunity" is fading. Until recently, Americans believed that education could do everything. We pictured immigrants coming from societies where poverty and caste were inherited, rising in the social structure, and being given a chance to reach their full potential. In 1848, Horace Mann, father of public education in the United States, wrote "Education, beyond all other devices of human origin, is the great equalizer of the conditions of men—the balance wheel of the social machinery."[3] But things have not worked out quite that way.

In the early history of the United States, essential skills were passed from generation to generation through the family. With the growth of industry, new and more formal mechanisms to transmit knowledge were necessary, and this function was gradually transferred from family to school. Schools had the responsibility to prepare workers for industry and to assimilate immigrant subcultures into the mainstream. Some early schools, including those for children working in factories, used the "monitorial system"; here, minimal learning was provided in reading, writing, math, and citizenship by monitors trained under teachers. These schools gave way to the "common schools," espoused by Mann, with an attempt to create a common identity and unifying force in the United States. At first they were open to all white children; later, segregated schools were provided for blacks. Some children rose in the social structure as a result of education, but others, including Native Americans and freed slaves, suffered. Some immigrant groups, not satisfied with the public school education, formed their own schools to serve their own needs.

As industry and formal schooling expanded, the division of labor between those who controlled capital and decision making and those who were controlled began to be formalized and to result in inequalities. Private schools were established for elites, ensuring a continuation of their privileged positions. Mass education was encouraged to provide workers with necessary skills, including punctuality, obedience to authority, and accountability. Many felt that education for factory work provided hope for a better life, and indeed, that hope was realized for many. However, education also served to help perpetuate class distinctions between capitalists and the working class. "Sanctions, tracking and leveling, economics, power, sorting and selection, and dependency"—these school policies generally favor advantaged students.[4]

Many subcultural groups today wish to maintain their ethnic identities; minority-group pressures have changed the emphasis over time from assimilationist goals to respect for and preservation of minority identities while providing access to social, economic, and political institutions. As we shall see, this model has met with mixed results and the controversies over access continue.

Mass education has spread around the world in the past two centuries until today about 75 percent of primary-age children have some type of formal schooling. Worldwide access to secondary education has also increased, but small numbers attend. The fact is that for most people around the world, "education may be the most important element of their social status, and their educational background will have a greater direct impact on their overall life chances than any other element but nationality."[5]

Variables such as sex, race, and family status have substantial effects on occupation, income, and poverty. It has been suggested that improvements in the educational standing of various groups in the United States would lead to social equality; in fact, there has been a reduction in equality of income. Twenty-three percent of all children under 6 were poor, and there have been alarming trends in black teenage unemployment and a lowering of the average black family income despite advances in education. In other words, economic inequality has increased despite greater educational opportunities for many children.[6]

Society requires a cadre of trained workers to "keep the wheels of industry turning." Many levels and types of training are necessary, requiring a selection and allocation process that begins at school. The school system is thus expected to raise everyone's chances for a better life, to provide equality of opportunity, and to select those who are most qualified for the most powerful and prestigious positions in society. The inherent contradiction inevitably leads to some dissatisfaction. Schooling helps some children move up; it locks others into low-level positions in society.[7,8]

In order to deal with the complex relationships between the process of stratification and education, we need to address a number of interrelated topics. Several key questions will provide the underlying framework for this chapter and Chapter 4:

1. What role does stratification play in the societal system?
2. What roles does education play in social stratification?
3. What are some key variables, both in and outside the schools, that affect stratification?
4. Can education lead to equal opportunity for members of society?

THE PROCESS OF STRATIFICATION: IS INEQUALITY INEVITABLE?

Most of us have a general idea about the meaning of stratification: It refers to our position in society. In the United States, an "open class" system predominates. The majority of us would probably answer "middle class" if asked our position in society. "Middle class" implies that our family has an "average" lifestyle—house, car, a white-collar wage earner. This contrasts with caste or estate systems, in which structured inequality is built into the society—individuals are born into their permanent, ascribed positions.

From our open class system perspective, stratification is seen as an interwoven part of the whole societal fabric or system. We cannot isolate one institution, such as education, from the whole system and understand the phenomenon of stratification. While our focus will be on education, we will bring aspects of family, politics, and economics into our discussion. Figure 3-1 indicates the interrelationships between the process of stratification and the educational system. Note the stratification of groups within the school, among those who enter the school as teachers and students, and in the community.

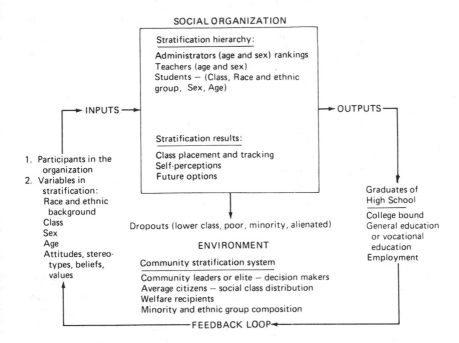

FIGURE 3-1   Stratification and the educational system.

Determinants of Social Class

Sociologists have studied stratification, defining the meaning of social class and discussing its significance and implications for individuals in society. Class has been described by Weber[9] as a multidimensional concept that is determined by three major variables: wealth, power, and prestige. *Wealth* refers to one's property, capital, and income. The striking fact about the United States is that three-quarters of the wealth is owned by one-twentieth of the population,[10] leaving a tremendous gulf between rich and poor. Most segments of society have raised their standard of living in recent years, but the relative distribution of wealth has remained nearly the same. The small group at the top of the hierarchy generally perpetuates itself through inherited wealth or high-paying positions.

Power implies the ability to make major decisions or to influence others to act to one's benefit. Much power has become concentrated in the upper levels of government and business. C. Wright Mills[11] argues that the "power elite" that dominates society and controls decision making is composed of members of the economic, political, and military elite. Others argue that interest groups such as unions vie with each other for power. In either case, the average person has little power in decision making.

Occupation is a main factor in one's *prestige*. Education affects occupational status, and income is closely associated with it. Various occupations have different amounts of prestige, including the ability to influence others.

The class system in the United States has been described by different sociologists. In the 1920s the Lynds[12] were among the first to study the relationship between social class and educational achievement. Through an indepth analysis of a small midwestern city in the United States referred to as "Middletown," the Lynds concluded that working-class children do not have many of the verbal and behavioral skills and traits that are prerequisite to success in the classroom. In a number of community studies conducted by Warner[13] in the United States, schools sorted students based on their potential for upward mobility. Lower-class children are often regarded as not capable. Other studies have replicated the social class–educational achievement relationship and confirmed these findings.

Table 3-1 shows one of the many typologies of social class in the United States, indicating the relationship between class and education. Thus, educational achievement is highly correlated with social class; students from lower classes have a much lower likelihood of going on to college than those of higher classes, even though they may have high ability.

One's position in the class stratification system implies a certain lifestyle, membership in certain groups, political affiliations, attitudes toward life chances, health, child-rearing patterns, and many other aspects of life. From an early age, we are socialized to be members of a social class and to develop strong loyalties to the values of our class, including its attitudes toward education.

In the United States, the expectation is that we can improve our life position with good education and hard work, that all members of society have an equal opportunity to experience upward mobility. Those with higher levels of education have more chances at a better job and salary, but the question remains: Who gets the higher levels of education?

In 1989 men with eight years or less of education received a median annual income for full-time year-round work of $17,555; women received $12,188. With four years of high school, these figures jumped to $26,609 for men and $17,528 for women. With four years of college the figures are

TABLE 3-1   Social Class Typology

Class and Percentage of Total Population	Education	Education of Children
Upper class (1–3%)	Liberal arts at elite schools	College education by right for both sexes
Upper-middle (10–15%)	Graduate training	Educational system biased in their favor
Lower-middle (30–35%)	High school Some college	Greater chance of college than working-class child
Working (40–45%)	Grade school Some high school	Educational system biased against them; tendency toward vocational programs
Lower (20–25%)	Illiteracy, especially functional illiteracy	Little interest in education; high dropout rates

Source: Daniel W. Rossides, *Social Stratification: The American Class System in Comparative Perspective* (Englewood Cliffs, N.J.: Prentice Hall, 1990), pp. 406–8.

$38,565 for men and $26,709 for women. Additional degrees command higher incomes.[14] From 1986 to 1990 "the earnings disadvantage of not finishing high school was about 27 percent for white and black males between 25 and 34 years old." For females it was 39 and 42 percent, respectively.[15] Education plays a role in sorting people into occupational categories according to abilities. However, many less tangible factors enter into this sorting process. These include the following:

1. differences in the level and quality of education available in the country, region, or community in which one lives,
2. differential access to educational facilities according to one's social class status, religion, race, and ethnic origins, and
3. differences in one's motivations, values, and attitudes; differences in the willingness and ability of one's parents and significant others to provide the financial and psychological supports necessary for the maximization of talent potentials.[16]

The status attainment model (see Figure 3-2), shows six major ascribed and achieved variables that affect one's educational and occupational positions:

1. father's and mother's education, father's occupation, family income,
2. ability, measured by achievement or IQ test (academic aptitude),
3. academic performance,
4. significant others' performance,
5. educational/occupational aspirations, and
6. educational attainment's direct influence on occupational attainment.

FIGURE 3-2   The process of status attainment in the United States.

Source: From Beeghley, Leonard, *The Structure of Social Stratification in the United States.* Copyright © 1989 by Allyn and Bacon. Reprinted with permission.

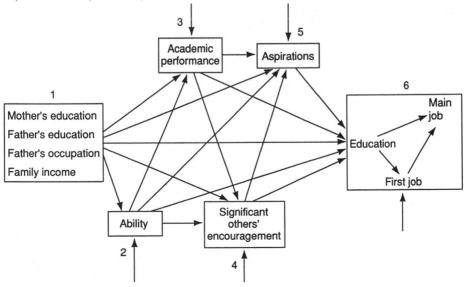

If we do not have other favorable factors in our lives, schooling alone is likely to make little difference to our economic and social success in society.

Major Explanations of Stratification

We all have ideas about how society should work and why some people succeed in society while others do not. Social scientists have explanations as well. From our systems perspective, we get a general framework for viewing stratification. Schools alone cannot cause or cure problems resulting from the stratification system, since they are but one part of a total, integrated system. Thus, to understand the role of schools in the process of stratification one must view interrelationships among schools, family, politics, religion, economics, and other integral parts of society. This will be the major emphasis of our discussion of stratification, as presented by classical theorists in sociology.

Two opposing theories of stratification are most often used to explain the unequal class system in our society: the functionalist (consensus) theory and the conflict theory. Our discussion here cannot do justice to the volumes of detailed analysis related to these complex theories; one's theoretical perspective influences policy decisions affecting school reforms and allocation of resources, benefiting students unequally—gifted, at-risk, special-education, low or high socioeconomic level, minorities, urban, rural.[17] We can give an idea of some of the important issues surrounding these and related theories of stratification.

Functionalist (Consensus) Theory of Stratification.   According to this perspective, each part of society is related to each other part in the total society. In order to maintain a working balance between the parts, the system has certain requirements and agreed-upon rules. From this starting point, functional theorists explain the inevitability of inequality and the role education plays in the process of stratification. A major function of schools is to develop, sort, and select individuals by ability levels to fill hierarchical positions; functionalists argue that this is a rational process based on the merit of individuals. By following the argument of Kingsley Davis and Wilbert Moore in a classic article on stratification,[18] the role of education in the stratification process becomes clearer:

1. People are induced to do what society needs done, motivated to fulfill roles by extrinsic rewards (money, prestige).
2. The importance of a particular role and scarcity of qualified persons to fill the role determine the prestige ranking of positions. For instance, doctors are seen as more important than bartenders, and have more prestige and higher pay.
3. Those positions that are most complex and important and require the most talent and training—that is, education—are the most highly rewarded.

Presumably, then, the more schooling one has completed, the more productive and valuable one is to society. Hence, a stratification system evolves, with some inevitably attaining more education and higher positions than others.

Another well-known theorist, Talcott Parsons, has laid the groundwork for much of functionalist theory. Parsons argues that society has shared norms and values by which to judge or evaluate its members. Those who come closest to meeting the established needs and values of society are likely to have higher status and occupational prestige.[19] Inequality, then, is inevitable, according to Parsons. Some will always be at the top because of their value to society; others will fall to the bottom. The question for Parsons becomes not whether inequality need exist, but rather how much inequality is justifiable. There is no easy answer to such a question, although he contends that some inequality is useful in motivating members of society to work hard, get ahead, and fill the positions necessary to keep society running.

The selection process that will eventually determine occupational status begins in school, where functionalists argue that students are placed more according to individual abilities than to group differences such as race and sex. Some functionalists point out opportunities that exist for working-class students to achieve mobility through school achievement. They argue that the system is flexible, allowing opportunity for most American students to attend college. They stress the improvements in educational achievement levels of the poor, minorities, and women as evidence that abilities are taking precedence over race and sex. Robert Hauser and David Featherman, in an analysis of male students, found that members of minority groups were completing more years of schooling; this, they feel, indicates that inequality in education is declining.[20]

The functionalist view of society has not only many proponents, but also many critics. Criticisms fall into several categories, but of primary concern to us are the ideological critiques:

1. Functional or consensus theory presents a conservative view; many argue that it supports existing systems and the dominant power group, whether good or bad, and preserves the social order. Rather than finding a way out of wars, inequality, and scarcity, it is committed to "making things work."[21]

2. The implication that people must meet the needs of the system, rather than vice versa, is seen by some critics as false and misleading. Similarly, *functions* of education may represent powerful individuals or groups pursuing their own interests.[22]

3. To assume that we can locate the most talented and motivated individuals through the schools or other institutions is questionable, especially when we look at statistics as to who is successful in society. The socioeconomic status of the student is an important determinant of college graduation. Consistently, higher-status students complete college at a greater rate than lower-status students.[23]

4. To assume that extrinsic rewards such as wealth and prestige are primary motivators for individuals to train for certain occupations may be false. Individuals may have other motivations, such as humanitarian goals, for entering certain occupations. In addition, not all talented individuals who wish to become doctors or lawyers may have the opportunity to pursue those careers.

We turn now to contrasting views of the education system.

Conflict, Neo-Marxist, and Reproduction Theories of Stratification.   Conflict theorists see the stratification system and equality of opportunity from a different perspective. They believe that problems in the educational system stem from the conflicts in the society as a whole. Education is but one part of a system that is based on "haves" and "have-nots." Karl Marx, father of conflict theory, felt that educational systems perpetuate the existing class structure. When the type of education and knowledge available to various groups of people is controlled, their access to positions in society is controlled. Thus, the education system is doing its part to perpetuate the existing class system; to prepare children for their roles in the capitalistic, technological society, controlled by the dominant groups in society.

Members of social classes share socialization, which leads to traits such as common language, values, lifestyle, manners, and interests. These "status groups" distinguish themselves from others in terms of categories of *moral evaluation*—honor, taste, breeding, respectability, propriety, cultivation, good fellows, plain folk.[24] Each group struggles for a greater share of those parts of society that make up "the good life"—wealth, power, and prestige—and it is because of this competition that conflicts exist. Some look to education to reduce inequalities, but according to conflict theorists education in fact serves to reproduce the inequalities based on power, income, and social status.[25] The values, rules, and institutions of society reflect the interests of the dominant groups, the ruling class; this is seen in the institution of education in the way resources are distributed.[26] Thus, education is no exception.

Samuel Bowles, outlining the role of education from the conflict perspective, contends

> (1) that schools have evolved in the U.S. not as part of a pursuit of equality, but rather to meet the needs of capitalist employers for a disciplined and skilled labor force, and to provide a mechanism for social control in the interests of political stability; (2) that as the economic importance of skilled and well-educated labor has grown, inequalities in the school system have become increasingly important in reproducing the class structure from one generation to the next; (3) that the U.S. school system is pervaded by class inequalities, which have shown little sign of diminishing over the last half-century; and (4) that the evidently unequal control over school boards and other decision-making bodies in education does not provide a sufficient explanation of the persistence and pervasiveness of inequalities in the school system.[27]

Origins of inequality are found in the class structure, capitalism, and modernity,[28] and education reflects this. Inequality is part of the capitalist system, likely to persist as long as capitalism itself. Conflict theorists argue that while statistics show a narrowing of the educational gap between groups, this has not been translated into a more equal sharing of society's wealth. "Research has documented repeatedly that the dollar value of education depends, in part, on the labor supply characteristics of workers such as their age, gender, race and social class." However, the characteristics of the particular urban community and the economic structure in which individuals live also affects their job opportunities and thus the value of their education. For instance, white male college graduates benefit in types of economic sectors that disadvantage equally educated females.[29]

Schools have come under increasing attack by frustrated minority groups hoping to improve their lot. A great variety of new approaches and special programs to improve opportunities have been initiated through education systems. Conflict theorists argue that other, more extensive, alterations in the fabric of societal order will be necessary to attack the underlying causes of inequality.

In recent decades a new group of theorists called reproductionists, revisionists, and neo-Marxists have developed explanations of stratification. Stemming from the idea that the upper-middle class "conspires" to perpetuate their own class interests by limiting access to educational opportunities for other groups, these theorists argue that the underclasses are channeled into poor secondary schools, community colleges, vocational schools, and lower-level jobs.

Bowles and Gintis, quoted above, argue that schools are agencies for "reproducing" the social relations of production necessary to keep capitalistic systems working. "The social relations of schooling and of family life correspond to the social relations of production, allowing some students more 'cultural capital' to be successful both in school and after, while others lack this advantage. They are reproduced in the schools in a way that tends to reproduce the social class structure later." This is referred to as the "correspondence principle."

There is some empirical evidence to support the idea that classes are reproduced.[30] In a study of American educational structures and reproduction of the "mental-manual" division of labor (or intellectual, white-collar class versus the working class), Colclough and Beck[31] found that between 56 and 76 percent of male students reproduced their class status when looking at three key determinants of reproduction (discussed later); public versus private schooling, socioeconomic community of the schools, and curriculum tracking within the schools. "Curriculum tracking was shown to be the critical determinant of reproduction." The authors found that "students from manual class backgrounds are over twice as likely to be placed in a vocational track" and from there are channeled into manual class jobs.

In the late 1960s and early 1970s sociologists in Europe were exploring the effect that the cultural form and content inside schools had on stratification and reproduction.[32] Young's *Knowledge and Control* (1971),[33] followed by works of Bernstein, Bourdieu, Passeron, and others (1977), argued that "the organization of knowledge, the form of its transmission, and the assessment of its acquisition are crucial factors in the cultural reproduction of class relationships in industrial societies."

Some lower-class students *do* resist the tendencies toward class reproduction and learn to think independently, even to recognize their disadvantages. Willis describes the school counterculture of working-class boys in England, which rejected the dominant values and norms of the educational process.[34] However, Willis's counterculture boys are only a few; many working-class students conform to the norms and try to make the system work for them. The lower and upper extremes of the stratification system are most locked in; some individuals in the middle classes are mobile.

Viewed from an international perspective, some have argued that schooling in the United States has a limited degree of stratification compared with other countries, especially Europe. Rubinson argues that political forces in the United States have acted to limit the extent to which political decisions influence schools. Thus, class analysis is important but does not necessarily determine schooling.[35]

Lower-class, minority, and female students in the United States fall disproportionately at the bottom of the economic hierarchy. These three groups—class, race, and sex—are those on which we focus throughout our discussion of equal educational opportunity here and in the next chapter. Sex and race are discussed extensively in the next chapter.

Social class background can aid or hinder students. Schools have a middle-class "bias" and are more closely aligned with the values and behavior patterns of middle-class children. A student's social class is determined by the home environment and is reflected in school grades, achievement, intelligence test scores, course failure, truancy, suspension, the high school curriculum pursued, and future educational plans. One school district has begun placing students in schools to achieve socioeconomic balance.[36] Class is not the only variable affecting achievement, and within each class there is wide variation, but there is definitely a significant relationship between class and achievement.

The sex difference favors girls initially, but reverses later. Girls achieve grades as high as and higher than those of boys through high school. On standardized achievement tests, boys score higher than girls in some areas, such as math and science, and girls score higher in reading and writing. More girls graduate from high school, but about equal numbers of males and females go on to postsecondary education. It is there that males move ahead, obtaining more years of schooling and higher degrees.

Other discussions of inequalities in education and society have concerned who has *access* to education, the *content* of education, and the *outcomes* of the educational process in terms of power, prestige, and income.[37] These "new left" conflict theorists argue that it is the long-term results of education that in part determine class structure. Other modern theorists argue that *power* and *coercion* are more important determinants of inequality than economics and social class. An altogether different approach to inequality, phenomenology, is concerned with the *content* of the education process and the passing on of information that can perpetuate the class system. Clearly, many factors contribute to the stratification into unequal class systems. Our task in the remainder of this chapter is to explore in more detail the role of education in the stratification process.

STRATIFICATION AND EQUALITY OF EDUCATIONAL OPPORTUNITY

Equal opportunity exists when all people, even those without status, wealth, or membership in a privileged group, have an equal chance of achieving a high socioeconomic status in society regardless of their sex, minority status, or social class. This requires removing obstacles to individual achievement, such as prejudice, ignorance, and treatable impairments.[38]

The Meaning of "Equality of Educational Opportunity"

James Coleman explores the concepts of equality and inequality, considering two opposing theories. One states that inequalities are justified only if they provide advantage to the unprivileged in society or if they benefit all. The other states that each person is entitled to what she or he has justly earned. Contrasting these two extremes points to the dilemma of two sets of values in American society—equal access or individual freedom, the state's right to impose equality versus the individual's right to choose his or her own school. This conflict is exemplified in the disputes over busing. Over time, the equality of educational opportunity has changed in meaning from equal school resources to equal outputs.

In practice, each society places before its children the opportunities deemed appropriate and valuable in that society, and attempts to give children an equal chance to compete within that framework. Some children's talents may go unappreciated in any particular society. In the United States and other heterogeneous societies there are many value systems competing; those who feel underrepresented argue that the schools are not giving them a fair shot at success within their framework of values.

Conflicts arise over differential treatment in school and unequal *outcomes* of the education process in terms of wealth, occupational status, and opportunities.[39] Given that students have different abilities and needs, can some type of equality of outcome be expected? What if unequal outcomes break down along racial, ethnic, social class, or gender lines? Even more controversial are proposals that argue that life chances are unfair to some, and that to ensure "equality of results," society should distribute jobs and wealth. These proposals range from progressive income taxes to curb extreme poverty and wealth to total restructuring of the economic system of society. Coleman concludes that equal treatment of students alone cannot produce equal outcomes.[40]

Social Class Reproduction: The Debate over Public versus Private Schools

Students who get the best educations are more likely to be selected for the preferred jobs in society. How to get that "best" education is the question. Those who can afford to go to elite private schools pay for the special "status rights" and social networks that allow for the "passage of privilege,"[41] and hope that this will maintain their privileged position or help them obtain a better position. Elite secondary schools socialize students into elite peer groups that form their adult primary groups and perpetuate status.[42] The selection of single-sex private or religious schooling is based largely on family tradition.[43]

In 1982, Coleman and colleagues published another controversial study, entitled *Public and Private Schools*.[44] In the study, 58,728 sophomores and seniors in 1,016 public, private, and parochial high schools around the country were tested. Major findings, which have stimulated the controversies surrounding the study, indicate that, controlling for family background, students in private schools (mostly Catholic) achieve at a higher level than do those in public schools; private schools tend to have smaller classes and more involvement of students; private schools provide more disciplined, orderly, and safe environments and have school climates more conducive to achievement; more homework is required in private schools and they have better attendance records. All of these findings combine to produce higher academic achievement.[45]

Coleman states: "The evidence is strong that the Catholic schools function much closer to the American ideal of the 'common school,' educating children from different backgrounds alike, than do the public schools."[46] Additional findings show that Catholic schools produce positive effects on verbal and math achievement from grades 10 to 12 in high school, with an advantage of one-half to one year over other students. These findings are greatest for minority and low-socioeconomic-group students.

Findings on achievement of minority students show that racially mixed groups of students in Catholic and other private schools achieve at a higher level in vocabulary and mathematics than do students in public schools.[47,48] Catholic schools do well in the inner city: Students there receive higher test scores than do students in public inner-city high schools, have less gang involvement and fewer discipline and dropout problems, take more advanced courses, and have more parental involvement.[49] Students in private schools for African-Americans receive more college preparatory courses and have better test scores.[50]

The main criticisms of Coleman's study fall into three categories: methodological problems, accuracy of interpretations and alternative findings, and policy implications of the findings. Critiques of the methodology generally present alternative statistical methods or models for analyzing the data.[51]

Reanalysis of data by a number of researchers has challenged the major finding—that Catholic private schools are superior. Controlling for background variables such as class and race, critics argue that there is not a significant difference between public and Catholic schools in academic achievement.

Just what *is* a significant difference in achievement is also in question. Some argue that where findings show a one-half- to one-year difference, this is not large enough to claim that private schools are significantly superior.[52]

Research questioning the role of private schools, concerned with the role they play in the perpetuation of elites, is being conducted in many foreign countries. Findings from the Netherlands generally uphold Coleman; private schools do have higher-achieving students.[53] A concern in some European nations is that where the government helps fund private schools they may also be helping to perpetuate the elite status of those who are accepted and can afford to go to private schools.[54]

Advocates of federal support for private education in the form of vouchers, tuition tax credits, or other federal aid are using Coleman's findings and recommendations to bolster their claims. Others, however, contend that federal support would increase religious and racial segregation of schools. James Catterall and Henry Levin[55] analyzed the tax credit policy suggestion and estimate that "an extremely small number of poor and minority children would be enticed into private schools."

Alternative interpretations suggest other policies. James McPartland and Edward McDill,[56] arguing that student body composition accounts for school effectiveness, suggest that policy be concerned with "allocation practices determining student body enrollments"; busing has been one such practice.

Despite the controversies over Coleman's findings on academic achievement and access to the best educations, several messages seem clear from the data:

> What it does show is that good schools have an orderly climate, disciplinary policies that students and administrators believe to be fair and effective, high enrollment in academic courses, regular assignments of homework, and lower incidence of student absenteeism, class-cutting, and other misbehavior. These conditions are found more often in private than public schools.[57]

The debate over fair access to education and how to improve public schools to provide equal opportunity will continue.

The Controversial Issue of "Choice"

If public schools are found to be wanting, or if private schools receive federal funding, are we undermining a basic institution in society, the mass public school? Some argue that we are. In response to this, some politicians and educational leaders are advocating "choice"—allowing parents to select between schools. In May 1991, President Bush unveiled a plan, *America 2000: Excellence in Education Act,* that could shift millions of taxpayer dollars into private schools. Thus, choice is becoming a main strategy for reform and restructuring. Most often the plans involve giving families a voucher for each student and allowing them to select between schools, including private schools.[58,59]

When a Gallup poll asked for public attitudes toward school choice, 50 percent favored the idea, with strongest support coming from minorities and inner-city dwellers.[60] Proponents argue that competition between schools for students will improve school quality. Choice helps increase accountability and gives parents and students more sense of ownership over schools. And in fact, choice seems to have worked in some districts (Box 3-1).[61] Other districts are initiating such plans.[62,63,64]

BOX 3-1   *BEFORE AND AFTER CHOICE*

The Richmond Unified School District:

- 50 schools, including 37 K–6 elementary schools
- 30,000 students, of whom 37 percent are black, 33 percent white, 13 percent Hispanic, and 11 percent Asian-American
- 2,900 employees

Before Choice, 1987–88:

- The dropout rate was 35 percent.
- Suspensions totaled 27,000 days for the year.
- The system was $4.2 million in the red.
- Parents lacked confidence in the schools.

Since Choice Was Implemented:

- 46 schools have converted.
- California Assessment Program test scores have risen in every grade.
- Suspensions have been cut by half.
- Total absence rates declined by 18 percent at high school level and almost 5 percent in elementary schools.
- Enrollment figures are up, including 400 students regained from private schools.
- The district has won a total of $7 million in state and private-sector competitive grants.
- PTA meeting attendance has risen substantially.

The Choice Menu:

- Basic curriculum includes reading and language arts, mathematics, sciences, and history and social studies.
- Specialty programs at the elementary level include classical studies, futures studies, gifted and talented programs, international studies, Montessori method, university laboratory, and whole-language studies.
- Specialty programs at the secondary level include applied arts and sciences, classical studies, math/science/technology, university laboratory, and visual/ performing arts and humanities.

Source: Guiton, Bonnie, "Choice in Education: A Consumer Issue," *Principal,* March 1990, p. 34.

In a controversial discussion of the choice issue, Chubb and Moe question whether school systems should be subjected to individual choice and market forces. The researchers focused on school practices and achievement differences between public and private school students, and from their results come down on the side of choice.[65] They argue that most school systems have become so politically and bureaucratically complex that elements that make for high achievement, including autonomy and professionalism of school staff, are limited. Under a free market system, educators could design any programs they think could compete successfully for students.

Opponents decry the potential decline in numbers and quality of the common school, or public school, pointing out that only the least capable students will be left, accentuating the problem for ill-prepared students; the best teachers will be drained off to better schools. *American 2000* does not address problems of school funding, an acute problem for inner-city schools; of poverty which faces many students who have little choice of school; or of multicultural issues. School choice would likely increase religious and social segregation along race and class lines. They point out disparities between public and private school students now and argue that little will change without fundamental restructuring of the system (Figure 3-3).[66,67,68]

Ability Grouping and Teacher Expectations

Most highly industrialized societies claim to be *meritocracies,* societies that attempt to place and advance individuals based on their merits. Yet few achieve a perfect match between abilities and responsibilities. "Observed distribution of the labor force is and has been far from the meritocratic ideal with respect to status mobility, status determination, and status inequality."[69]

Testing, discussed in Chapter 2, is one method used to determine education and job placement, yet many hold strong sentiments against the use of standardized tests for placement and see poor, nonwhite, disabled, and female students as at a disadvantage. In the rush to make schools and teachers accountable, many states and districts instituted placement exams; yet studies

FIGURE 3-3   Distribution of public and private elementary and secondary students, by family income, October 1990.

Source: U.S. Department of Commerce, Bureau of the Census; reprinted in Snyder, Thomas D., "Trends in Education," *Principal,* September 1991, p. 8.

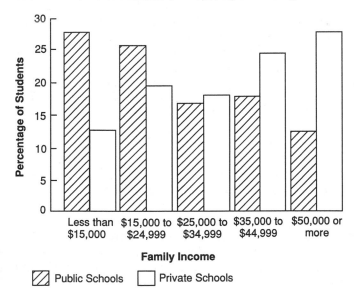

show that critical thinking and other creative techniques of teaching that may be most helpful to poorer students are used less often as teachers attempt to prepare students for standardized tests.[70]

Ability Grouping.   Ability grouping is a common practice in schools around the world because it is easier to teach a group of like-ability students. Different tracking patterns emerge under different organizational structures, depending on the structural constraints and the school's atmosphere or "culture." An example of a structural constraint would be students demanding to be placed in a particular track.[71,72] Groupings are usually based on reading and math and assume different levels within the same curriculum.[73]

Most schools studied using national data sets have similar tracking systems and sequencing of courses in math;[74] there is more variation in science sequencing. By eighth grade, students' science grouping affected their future science curriculum.[75] Placement in science and math often go together. Unfortunately, not all students are placed on the basis of careful evaluation of their interests and abilities. A study of inner-city urban schools found many factors operating in the placement of students—filling study halls or low enrollment classes, filling remedial courses so that funding would continue to come to the school, and staff preferences for course assignments.[76]

Proposals for reform from such organizations as the National Academy of Sciences call for complete restructuring of the math and science curricula on a national level; these proposals are receiving serious consideration by governmental committees and national educational organizations.

Movement from one track to another is usually downward, based primarily on achievement. However, a student's socioeconomic level does affect assignments, with higher-socioeconomic-level students disproportionately in college tracks.[77]

National sequencing of courses is less common in the United States than in many other countries because of local control and no national tests. However, standards set by teachers' organizations and college entrance requirements have some influence on sequencing of courses and tracking of students.[78] Japan, which values group conformity, is one of the few societies with heterogeneous grouping in schools, treating all students alike by age cohorts. Japanese parents and teachers expect each child to achieve in school, and believe that all can, although some may need to work harder than others. On the other hand, an underlying assumption in American education, despite the efforts toward equality, is that some will fail. Elites, according to Oakes, are unlikely to change basic structures that work for their class interests. Thus, reforms have benefited many but have not changed their relative educational and economic position. Proposed reforms will work primarily to the advantage of children with "superior abilities."[79]

Ability grouping often begins in elementary school and continues through high school as students are "tracked" into curricular models. The problem is to determine who gets placed where; too often, placement correlates directly with the child's background, language skills, appearance, and other socioeconomic variables.[80,81]

Seventy-seven percent of the school districts in the United States use ability grouping, despite the fact that the Supreme Court's 1967 ruling in *Hobson v. Hansen* in Washington, D.C., stated that separation of students into fast and slow tracks resulted in unconstitutional segregation of minority and nonminority students. Yet many teachers argue that finding the best "fit" between students and teachers increases classroom effectiveness and that grouping students makes it possible to teach them more effectively at their own levels.

Students in different ability groupings have quite different school experiences. These in turn affect their life chances, self-concepts, motivations, IQ and achievement levels, and other aspects of school and work experiences. Of the three major ways in which reproductionist theorists argue that classes are reproduced (public versus private schooling, socioeconomic class composition of school communities, and ability grouping of students), research shows tracking to be the most important mechanism in the reproduction process. Colclough and Beck[82] show that students from manual class backgrounds are over twice as likely to be placed in a vocational track as are other students. Table 3-2 shows the importance of each of these factors in the reproduction of class.

Thus, we know that ability is not a perfect predictor of placement in

TABLE 3-2   Social Class and Schooling Structures

Schooling Structure	Mental Class	Manual Class	Overall
I. School type			
Public schools			
Percent students recruited from	33.37	66.63	—
Percent class membership reproduced	52.92	70.85	64.87
Private schools			
Percent students recruited from	43.93	56.07	—
Percent class membership reproduced	62.02	53.94	57.49
II. School community			
High-minority communities			
Percent students recruited from	26.59	73.41	—
Percent class membership reproduced	45.27	71.13	64.25
Low-minority communities			
Percent students recruited from	36.29	63.71	—
Percent class membership reproduced	55.33	70.72	65.14
III. Curriculum track			
General track			
Percent students recruited from	26.96	73.04	—
Percent class membership reproduced	33.41	81.91	68.83
Vocational track			
Percent students recruited from	19.70	80.30	—
Percent class membership reproduced	16.67	90.27	75.77
College-bound track			
Percent students recruited from	45.63	54.37	—
Percent class membership reproduced	69.32	44.95	56.07

Source: Colclough and Beck, "The American Educational Structure," p. 469.

ability groupings. Characteristics including socioeconomic status (SES) of students and community, race, percentage of minority students in the school, the proportion of students in the school in an academic track, and the method for assigning tracks—self-selection versus assignment—are influential in a student's placement. Consider Table 3-3; the higher the SES, the more likely students will be in academic tracks.[83] Placements tend to be fairly stable over the year. We know that students placed in high-ability groups are taught more and at a faster pace than are those in low-ability groups.[84]

Anyon compared the socioeconomic composition of schools with the work tasks of students in these schools by studying five elementary schools with very different compositions based on parents' occupations: two working-class, one mixed (middle-class), one "affluent professional," and one executive elite. The school patterns train students for their respective social classes. In working-class schools, children follow procedures—usually mechanical, rote behavior. In the middle-class school, getting the right answer and following directions is important, but some choice is possible. In the "affluent professional" school, stress is on independent creative activity in which students express and apply ideas and concepts. In the "executive elite" school, develop-

TABLE 3-3 Sophomore Curriculum Track Location by Measured Test Performance and Socioeconomic Origin, by Race[a]

	LOW PERFORMANCE			*MIDDLE PERFORMANCE*			*HIGH PERFORMANCE*		
	Low SES	*Middle SES*	*High SES*	*Low SES*	*Middle SES*	*High SES*	*Low SES*	*Middle SES*	*High SES*
Hispanic									
Academic	11.1	13.3	9.9	24.8	25.0	46.7	53.6	44.0	72.3
General	47.8	48.1	37.2	56.9	55.9	40.7	41.5	49.4	21.3
Vocational	41.1	38.7	52.8	18.3	19.1	12.6	4.8	6.6	6.4
Total	100.0	100.0	100.0	100.0	100.0	100.0	100.0	100.0	100.0
N	193	158	17	154	176	32	17	32	30
Black									
Academic	10.5	23.7	29.4	32.9	43.4	52.5	46.7	60.2	81.2
General	47.1	33.7	28.9	41.3	35.3	36.1	49.6	27.3	16.9
Vocational	42.3	42.6	41.7	25.8	21.3	11.4	3.7	12.5	1.9
Total	100.0	100.0	100.0	100.0	100.0	100.0	100.0	100.0	100.0
N	415	337	51	250	267	68	30	46	30
White									
Academic	5.0	9.2	17.2	17.5	26.5	39.3	54.7	53.7	69.5
General	58.5	60.8	58.5	57.9	52.5	49.3	34.7	35.8	26.7
Vocational	36.5	29.9	24.3	24.3	21.0	11.4	10.6	10.5	3.7
Total	100.0	100.0	100.0	100.0	100.0	100.0	100.0	100.0	100.0
N	637	776	187	1,075	2,947	1,248	252	1,577	1,415

[a]Low performance indicates the lowest quartile on BYTEST, the composite measure of sophomore test scores; middle performance indicates the average of scores in the second and third quartiles; high performance indicates the highest quartile on BYTEST. Totals are rounded to 100.0.

Source: Vanfossen, Beth E., James D. Jones, and Joan Z. Spade, "Curriculum Tracking and Status Maintenance," *Sociology of Education,* Vol. 60, April 1987, pp. 104–22.

ing analytical intellectual ability, learning to reason, and producing quality academic products are important. Conceptualizing rules by which elements fit together is a key goal.[85]

Tracking has other consequences for students who develop "student cultures" within each track. These cultures add to the perpetuation of attitudes and behaviors that reproduce social class. In Israel, a multiethnic society, students from the same ethnic groups have tended to group together. Vocational education has come under question because it reproduces the same class of students in the same occupations, reproducing subordinate social classes.[86]

Many writers have commented on the effects of grouping. A summary of findings follows.

1. Lower-ability groupings tend to include a disproportionate number of lower-class and minority children; this stratification influences educational attainment and is likely to affect the students' later job attainments and earnings.

2. Children from low socioeconomic backgrounds are more likely to be placed in low-ability groups because of low test scores, which some argue do not measure ability accurately.[87] In addition, they are often stigmatized, and scores keep falling in relation to other groups.

3. Each school has its own stratification system dependent on students coming into the system, but children in any given grouping tend to be more homogeneous in terms of socioeconomic status and race than are children in the school as a whole. In other words, groupings within the school are highly related to the background of the students. Once students are labeled and grouped, there is less chance of their moving from one category to another.

4. Students in upper-ability groupings are disproportionately of higher socioeconomic status, are more motivated, and have higher achievement, class rank, and test scores, all of which give them a better start after high school. Teachers give more feedback and praise to high-ability groups and plan more creative activities for them. For the lower-ability groupings, the opposite is true. This same distinction by class status holds at junior and community colleges in the vocational versus academic tracks.

5. Summaries of research on the effects of ability grouping indicate that the practice benefits gifted students and those placed in high tracks. Lower-ability groups receive less teacher attention and poorer instruction, setting them farther behind in the quest for equal opportunity. Ability groups often reinforce race and class segregation and stereotypes, and lower the aspirations and self-esteem of lower-group students.[88] Cross-cultural data from Israel give support to mixed groupings because they have less negative impact.[89]

6. Most problematic is the conflicting evidence on the effects of grouping. In a review of 29 studies on the effects of ability grouping, Slavin finds little evidence of beneficial effects.[90] However, he does not address institutional and curricular differences in students' experiences, but mainly uses test scores.

    Some studies show no justification for the use of tracking and question programs that "pull out" students from regular classes, such as Chapter I.[91] Most damning is a recent study showing minority students' disproportionate placement in low-ability math and science classes with the least-qualified teachers and less access to computers, science equipment, and quality textbooks. Students in low-ability groups lose ground and perform poorly on reading and math achievement tests.[92]

Are there solutions to the problem of homogeneous versus heterogeneous grouping? Most suggestions focus on restructuring classroom groupings: Students work together in many subjects but are grouped in reading, language arts, and math. Low achievers are not stigmatized or made to feel they are "dummies." Low achievers are few in the class, so that the teacher can give them needed help. Success, experts argue, is dependent on small student-to-teacher ratios and effective teachers.[93,94]

Some elementary schools in Britain and the United States have attempted alternatives to grouping, making constructive use of the diverse abilities and backgrounds of the students. In these schools, children work at their own levels of ability in reading and math. The teacher gives the class lessons on particular topics suitable for the range of abilities, and works with individual children or with small groups, sometimes with the help of an aide. Cooperative relationships between children are encouraged—for example, children who understand a math concept may be assigned to help teach others. This fosters not only cooperation but also feelings of self-worth. It also avoids some of the problems associated with labeling.

Teacher Expectations and Student Achievement.   Teacher expectations are influenced by various factors, including records of the students' previous work and test scores; the student's dress, name, physical appearance, attractiveness, race, sex, language, and accent; the parents' occupations; and the way the student responds to the teacher. Teacher expectations are manifested in the teachers' behavior toward and treatment of individual children and their grouping of the children in the classroom situations. Children pick up the subtle cues; the "self-fulfilling prophecy" can cause them to believe that they have certain abilities and can influence future behaviors.

Many teachers in schools with low-achieving students become discouraged about the children's ability to learn. Their expectations for student learning are reduced, creating that self-fulfilling prophecy in which teachers expect less and students give less.

Students are influenced by their teachers' expectations and internalize them. Even though some students have given up on education, they dislike teachers who do not carry out the illusion of believing in education. Positive teacher attitudes and approaches toward learning are necessary if students are to believe that they can achieve; some inner-city schools that have rigorous expectations have raised levels of achievement significantly.[95] What difference do teacher expectations of students make in student performance?

In a pioneering study,[96] Robert Rosenthal and Lenore Jacobson tested the effects of teacher expectations on interactions, achievement levels, and intelligence of students in a San Francisco elementary school with a high percentage of lower-class and Mexican students. This study gave support to their hypothesis that once a child is labeled by the teacher and others, a "self-fulfilling prophecy" operates: The teacher expects certain behaviors from the child and the child responds to the expectations. Once this pattern is established, it is hard to alter.

Teacher expectations affect student performance.

Criticisms of their study have focused on its methodological weaknesses and have pointed out that their findings apply mainly to lower grades. Multiple factors enter into teacher interactions with students; nonetheless, they pioneered in an important area of research that has provided valuable insights on teacher-student dynamics.

Teachers manipulate the classroom situation so as to affect student performance through ability grouping and creating other groups within the classroom. An example of this is seen in an experiment conducted by a classroom teacher in Iowa. She was concerned that her students really understand the impact of discrimination, so she set up an experiment, the results of which surprised even her. She divided the children in her all-white class into two groups, blue- and brown-eyed. For the first day, one group was given privileges and made to feel superior. The situation was reversed the next day. The children took their roles very seriously, with the superior ones taking delight in putting down the inferior ones and in excelling in their own work. The inferior for the day were outperformed. Labels can affect the self-concept of students and their treatment by others, even in such a short-term experiment.[97]

Families and Schools: Home Environment Effects on Educational Achievement and Stratification

I once knew a school social worker who had in her district an elementary school that served a poverty-stricken area. She told of children whose parents could not care for them because of their working hours or illness, and of young children who took care of younger siblings. She told of children who had cola and potato chips for breakfast; of children who came to school in winter with holes in their shoes and wet feet; and of children who had unexplained bruises and even rat bites. Children facing such environmental hardships do not have the support system necessary to do well in school. The film *Inside/Out*[98] also documents the educational problems faced by children in difficult family situations.

We all have solutions to the problem—so why doesn't someone *do* something? Children's positions in school and society are determined in large part by their family background. Coleman,[99] Jencks,[100] and Moynihan find that one-half to two-thirds of student achievement variance is directly related to home variables such as socioeconomic level.[101] Family "processes" are a better predictor of positive achievement and grades than all other variables.[102]

Some home environment factors that influence student achievement include social class of family, early home environment, parenting style, "type" of mother-child interaction, effect of the mother working, parent involvement in school decisions and activities, family and student aspirations, and number of children in the family.[103]

An underlying question here is how schools can meet every child's needs. We know that schools use social constructs, with organization and language that are more familiar to middle- and upper-class children. These children are more likely to have home experiences with the values, attitudes, and training in cognitive skills that will help them adapt to school demands.

During the early formative years, children learn languages, values, and an orientation toward the world. Let us follow two 5-year-old children of equal ability into school. Joey comes from a working-class family, Billy from a middle-class family. Why is it likely from the outset that Joey will achieve at a lower level than Billy? We must be ever cautious of generalizing from two cases, and we must be aware that there are many variations in patterns of child-rearing; yet research in the United States and Britain has identified some common class-related child-rearing patterns, and these give Joey and Billy different tools with which to approach the school experience.

The early home learning environment of children is crucial; Bloom estimates that 80 percent of our potential intelligence is developed by age 8. Stimulating environments can help recover lost potential, but the process becomes more difficult.[104]

Joey and Billy's differences fall into several categories: learning right and wrong, attitudes and values, language ability and cognitive skills, family structure, and parent-child interaction. When Joey misbehaves, his parents are quick to discipline him. The most common punishments are threats about consequences of his actions or withdrawal of privileges or belting him with a strap. Billy is also disciplined, but the method is very different. His parents use reasoning, guilt, and shame to instill right and wrong values. These different patterns are discussed in research by Gerkas,[105] who summarizes a large number of studies on socialization differences by class. Joey's socialization may be useful training for living in a sometimes dangerous environment, but it does not help him meet certain demands of the classroom situation, such as creative or independent thinking.

Although most parents place a high value on the education and achievement of their children, their methods of encouraging education are different. Working-class parents expect their children to "behave" in school, stressing conformity and obedience to authority, necessary for working-class jobs. Socialization of middle-class children stresses independence and self-direction, important in carrying out white-collar jobs.

Parenting styles also affect student achievement. Authoritarian and permissive parenting styles (very rigid or very lax) are negatively associated with student achievement, whereas an authoritative style (guidance with reasoning) is positively related to achievement. "Children who live with single parents or step-parents receive less parental encouragement and attention with respect to educational activities than children who live with both biological parents." These children report lower educational expectations, less monitoring of school work, and overall less supervision than children from intact families. Strength of the attachment to step-parents is also a factor in the equation.[106] Children who are left to make their own educational plans and decisions, where parents have little involvement, are more likely to be dropouts.[107] These findings are confirmed by a study in the Netherlands which reported that the negative effects of the single-parent family have increased in the 1980s.[108]

Joey and Billy are likely to develop different language patterns. Both speak English, but middle-class children learn formal or elaborated language in addition to "public" language used in everyday conversing by both children. The more restricted "public" language limits the child's ability to conceptualize new ideas and concepts. Formal language allows Billy to deal with more complex ideas and feelings.[109]

Family and student aspirations for the future are another aspect of the influence of class, racial, or ethnic background. Parents who set high standards and have high aspirations for their children are more likely to have high-achieving children. James Coleman and colleagues found that black and white seniors had comparable aspirations; it was in taking the necessary steps to carry out their goals that the difference lay. Black students felt that they had less control over their environment and left their fate to luck and chance.[110] From Coleman's research in *Equality of Educational Opportunity* (the Coleman Report), the most extensive study done in the field of education, comes evidence that the effects of the home environment far outweigh the effects of the school program on achievement. Educational and social class background is the most important factor in determining differences between students. Next most important is the school composition—the backgrounds of other children in the same school.

Another extensive study, by Christopher Jencks and others,[111] reached the same general conclusion: Family characteristics are the main variable in a student's school environment. In fact, Jencks's findings indicate that family background accounts for more than one-half of the variation in educational attainment. Regardless of the measure used—occupation, income, parent education—family socioeconomic status is a powerful predictor of school performance.

Children succeed in large part because of their family background and what parents do to support their children in their education. Parenting styles and parental expectations play a crucial role in setting the child's educational agenda. Guidelines about after-school and weekend activities, television watching, homework, and other school-related decisions give the child structure.[112]

One of the most important ingredients in a child's success in school is the degree of parental involvement in the educational process of the child. Questions concern what parental activities help or harm a child's school achievement. Involvement of parents is shaped by their social and financial resources, their opportunities to be involved, and their own orientation toward education (Figure 3-4).[113,114]

Parents' involvement in the educational process also differs by social class. A great deal of research has focused on the "cultural capital" that children bring to school from their family life. Some of this facilitates school learning, some does not.[115] In fact, social class position can become a form of "cultural capital" leading to different schooling experiences. The cultural capital of middle- and upper-class children provides useful resources for educational experiences, whereas that of the lower classes provides resources not valued by dominant social institutions such as education.[116]

Middle-class families tend to have more educational materials in the

FIGURE 3-4   Factors affecting parental influence on children's achievement and behavior.

Source: Schneider, Barbara, *Parents, Their Children and Schools* (Boulder, Colo.: Westview Press, forthcoming), p. 35.

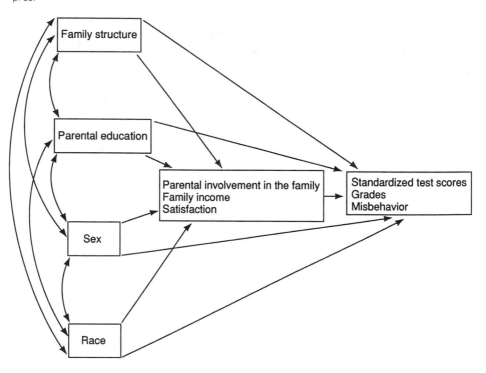

home—books, newspapers, magazines. "Students who read a lot at home show larger gains on reading achievement tests." Their parents read, visit the library, and participate in school activities.[117] They also visit more museums and attend concerts; all of these are activities that reinforce values of education.

Higher-class parents are active in managing their children's education at home and at school, whereas lower-class parents do what the schools ask but little more. Both sets of parents hold similar educational values, and parents are treated the same by the school. However, higher-class parents have more "cultural capital," and if they use it, their children benefit.

Parents of working-class children are less comfortable dealing with schools and teachers than those of higher-class students, who feel more comfortable communicating with teachers and are more involved with school activities.[118]

Children from one-parent households have lower grades, lower test scores, and higher dropout rates than those from two-parent households; these results are also influenced by the race or ethnicity of the family, the educational level of the parent(s), and low level of involvement by or absence of a parent. Unless there is significant parent support and supervision, these factors are correlated with children being tardy or absent from school, not doing homework, not having contact with their parents, and engaging in frequent dating.[119,120] However, single parents who do become involved in their children's education can compensate for the problems mentioned above. New policies can provide for the involvement of families in schools.[121,122] Recent findings indicate that mothers who work part-time tend to be very involved with their children's education, and children perform at a higher rate. Full-time work affects after-school supervised time for the child; it is here that differences exist (Box 3-2).[123]

Studies of mothers' interactions with their young children delve further into the process of different language and value transmission. Burton White and his associates at Harvard University evaluated the influence that different "types" of mothers have on their children.[124] A part of their study involves use by mothers of the physical environment of the home. Women were divided into type A and type C mothers. A mothers allowed children more freedom of movement and encouraged independence, whereas C mothers kept their children confined for long periods to protect them and avoid clutter. A mothers spent more time talking to their children, responding to and encouraging the child's initiatives. C mothers were less patient with their children's demands and used TV more often to occupy them. The findings seem to indicate that children raised by type A mothers will have an advantage intellectually and in attitudes toward learning.

Other evidence shows the involvement of mothers in the schooling process. For instance, eighth-grade-educated mothers discuss similar strategies for encouraging their children's school achievement, but their use and implementation of these strategies differed by their socioeconomic level. College-educated mothers "managed" their children's high school schedule by selecting college preparatory courses. High-socioeconomic-background children do better in the school system partly because their parents have better manage-

BOX 3-2 *DEMOGRAPHICS OF MODERN U.S. FAMILIES*

Traditional families with two married parents accounted for only 56 percent of all households in 1989—a decline of 71 percent since 1970. In only one in five families does the mother stay home. Eight of ten 5-year-olds have been in day care. Although the number of divorces stabilized at approximately 1.2 million per year in the 1980s, divorce rates have consistently been highest for those under 30—the group most likely to have school-age children.

Half of all children—and five out of six black children—will spend at least six years living with a single parent, most often the mother. Even when divorced mothers remarry, approximately half experience a second family disruption before their children reach 16.

Additional one-parent families are created through teenage pregnancies. The pregnancy rate for female adolescents age 15 to 19 rose from 96.2 per 1,000 in 1973 to 111.2 in 1980 before declining slightly. But increasing sexual activity of girls 14 and younger is reflected in pregnancy rates that rose from 13.5 per 1,000 in 1973 to 16.6 in 1983.

Most teenage mothers are neither emotionally nor financially equipped to deal with the demands of parenthood, usually in the absence of teenage fathers, and the immediate consequences are likely to be reduced education . . . and long-term socioeconomic disadvantages for their children.

Source: Rubin, Linda S., and Sherry B. Borgers, "The Changing Family: Implications for Education," *Principal,* September 1991, pp. 11–12.

ment skills.[125] In fact, some middle-class parents may try to "control" schools and take action if a child is having problems, whereas lower-class parents feel helpless and alienated in their interactions with schools.

A question of concern to many families is the effect of working mothers on the achievement of children. Study results are mixed, and many other variables enter into the question, such as the number of hours worked and intensity of the work, care of children, and the socioeconomic level of the family. Summarizing the major findings, we can say that black, single, working mothers have a positive effect on the achievement of black elementary school children. Working mothers from black two-parent families have little effect on children's achievement; however, there is mixed evidence about the effect of white working mothers from two-parent families on achievement of their elementary and high school children's math and reading achievement.[126] One major study finds a negative effect, while another points out that there are mitigating variables, such as smaller families and time spent with each child, that lessen the negative effect. As can be imagined, this is a sensitive area for many working mothers, and the data are still coming in.[127]

The number of children in the family is another variable that affects school experience, especially the years of schooling that a child completes. About 60 percent of adults surveyed in the United States felt that two children is the ideal number, but 35 percent favored three or more children.[128] We know that boys who come from families with a small number of siblings have more mobility; that is, more often complete more years of schooling than did their fathers. The more siblings in a family, the more diluted the parents' attention and material resources.[129]

Children from small-sibling families "gain many advantages of a personal nature, including markedly higher verbal ability, motivation to perform in school, a preference for 'intellectual' extracurricular activities, a family setting that is typically conducive to study and academic pursuits, and encouragement to go to college." Those from large-sibling families, "on average, have lower verbal IQs, perform less well in school, engage less in intellectual extracurricular activities and more in sports and community activities, are less likely to be encouraged to go to college, and, as a consequence, are more dependent on being shored up by familial status if they are to graduate from high school."[130]

Schools have a role to play in making it possible to involve parents. Not all schools are welcoming; teachers are overworked and parents add one more layer to the work load.[131] Some parents expect too much from teachers or are downright abusive.[132] However, there are constructive ways to involve parents both in the education of their own children and in the school program.[133]

Financing Schools in the United States

Wealthy school districts attract the best-educated and more experienced teachers. They can offer higher salaries, superior facilities and materials, support staff to handle problems, and a potentially achievement-oriented group of students. Poorer and minority schools get new, inexperienced teachers. There is also a tendency for minority teachers to be concentrated in *schools* with heavy concentrations of minority students, depriving all districts of an integrated teaching staff.

This imbalance has stimulated several court cases concerning equal financing of education. In the 1974 landmark *Serrano v. Priest* case, the California Supreme Court ruled that forcing school districts to rely heavily on local property taxes created sharp inequalities between state districts. In 1976, California was ordered to reduce the gap between districts substantially by 1980. Many other state courts considered cases on finances, one of which was heard by the Supreme Court. In *San Antonio Independent School District v. Rodriguez*, the Supreme Court left decisions regarding property tax funding of schools up to each state. Property tax is still the most substantial part of local school funding, but often not the most equitable way of collecting funds for education. School spending per student can be up to four times greater in wealthy districts than in poor ones. Property taxes are highest in cities, causing middle classes to leave and businesses to locate elsewhere, resulting in a small tax base. Urban students often require different types of programs—bilingual, vocational, compensatory, or special education—all of which cost additional money. On average, local districts provide about 46.1 percent of school revenues as a percentage of GNP and revenue sources for schools, states provide 47.7 percent, and federal sources 6.2 percent. Most federal support was for special programs, such as compensatory education.[134]

States help support education through income tax, sales tax, and lotteries. On the average, per pupil expenditures in the U.S. were $4,639 in 1989, but this ranges from $2,579 in Utah to $7,850 in Washington, D.C. and $7,663 in New York State.[135] The U.S. federal government holds a big stick over local and state education by threatening to withdraw funding for special programs if districts do not comply with federal laws barring racial bias in programs of instruction such as Title IV of the Civil Rights Act of 1964.

Educators will continue to struggle over ways to involve all children fully in the educational process. For some, this means finding ways to alter the disadvantages of "cultural capital" brought to school by lower-class children. For others it means restructuring the system so that all children have a place, regardless of family background and financing factors. In the next chapter, we discuss the effect of educational policies on specific groups of students.

SUMMARY

Schools are the target for the frustrations of many groups; they represent at the same time a means to get ahead and an institution that is holding some students back.

I. The Crisis in Schooling

According to many experts, there is a crisis in schooling. Both the public and educators are concerned about evidence indicating the failure of schools to meet expectations. However, it is also true that we expect schools to solve some problems that have their roots in the structure of societal institutions. This chapter addressed the stratification system, its role in education and society, and equality of educational opportunity.

II. The Process of Stratification: Is Inequality Inevitable?

Stratification, a process that is interlaced through the whole societal structure, refers to our position in society. Our social class, the structure of American stratification, is determined by several variables, including wealth, power, and prestige. Educational attainment is closely associated with these variables. In addition, education is used to sort people into future societal roles. Thus people look to education to improve their status in society.

There are two major theoretical explanations of stratification systems. Functional theorists see inequality as inevitable, and education as playing a role in selecting and training people for unequal positions in society. The question is this: How much inequality should be tolerated? Among the criticisms of functional theory is the charge that, by assuming inequality, it assumes perpetuation of the status quo.

Conflict theorists disagree with the assumption that inequality is inevitable. They argue that it is perpetuated by those in power, the "haves." We are distinguished by status groups, with the dominant group controlling. Conflict theorists hold that education alone cannot solve the problems of inequality in society, but that it will take a restructuring of the whole society to bring about change.

III. Stratification and Equality of Educational Opportunity

Equality of opportunity refers to all people having an equal chance of achieving a high socioeconomic status in society, regardless of sex, race, or class. Related to schools, it refers to equal facilities, financing, and availability. Problems arise over different treatment and outcomes—the fact that certain groups come out consistently on the bottom.

Social classes are "reproduced" through several mechanisms, such as elite and private schools, tracking and ability grouping, teacher expectations, and home environment. For instance, certain school policies can influence groups negatively. Testing tends to favor middle-class white students; ability grouping falls along race and class lines. Teacher behaviors and expectations can also affect student achievement. Some research points to the importance of early childhood and home environment in educational achievement. All of these factors can influence the child's achievement and attainment in school.

Many ideas have been proposed to bring about change, including legislation, changing the financing of schools, and compensatory education.

PUTTING SOCIOLOGY TO WORK

1. What evidence, if any, do you see in your community for "the crisis in schooling"?
2. Do you have evidence that your social class, race, subculture, or sex has affected your educational experience? Document. Talk with others about their experiences.
3. Describe examples of differences in educational achievement by race, sex, or class from data available for your community or for other communities. How would a structural-functionalist explain these differences? a conflict theorist?
4. Talk to teachers or school officials about school policies that influence stratification: testing, ability grouping, teacher expectations. Ask about the influence of the home environment on children's school performance.

NOTES

[1] Beck, E. M., and Glenna Colclough, "Schooling and Capitalism: The Effect of Urban Economic Structure on the Value of Education," in George Farkas and Paula England (eds.), *Industries, Firms and Jobs: Sociological and Economic Approaches* (New York: Plenum Press, 1987).

[2] Young, Robert E., *A Critical Theory of Education: Habermas and Our Children's Future* (New York: Teacher's College Press, 1990).

[3] Mann, Horace, *The Twelfth Annual Report*, 1848, in *Life and Works of Horace Mann* (New York: C. T. Dillingham, 1891), vol. IV.

[4] Calabrese, Raymond, "Public School Policies and Minority Students," *The Journal of Educational Thought*, Vol. 23, 1989, p. 187.

[5] Boli, John, Francisco O. Ramirez, and John W. Meyer, "Explaining the Origins and Expansion of Mass Education," *Comparative Education Review*, Vol. 29, No. 2, 1985, p. 145.

[6] *Five Million Children: A Statistical Profile of Our Poorest Young Citizens* (Washington, D.C.: National Center for Children in Poverty, 1990).

[7] Kozol, Jonathan, *Savage Inequalities: Children in America's Schools* (New York: Crown Publishers, 1991).

[8] *Learning to Fail: Case Studies of Students at Risk* (Bloomington, Ind.: Phi Delta Kappa, 1991).

[9] Gerth, H. H., and C. Wright Mills (eds. and trans.), *From Max Weber: Essays in Sociology* (New York: Oxford University Press, 1958), pp. 180–84.

[10] Gilbert, Dennis, and Joseph A. Kahl, *The American Class Structure* (Homewood, Ill.: Dorsey Press, 1982), p. 106.

[11] Mills, C. Wright, *The Power Elite* (New York: Oxford University Press, 1956).

[12] Lynd, Robert S., and Helen M. Lynd, *Middletown: A Study of American Culture* (New York: Harcourt Brace & World, 1929).

[13] Warner, W. Lloyd, Robert J. Havighurst, and Martin R. Loeb, *Who Shall Be Educated?* (New York: Harper & Row, 1944).

[14] National Center for Education Statistics, *Digest of Education Statistics: 1991* (Washington, D.C.: U.S. Department of Education, November 1991), Tables 357–58.

[15] National Center for Education Statistics, *The Condition of Education: 1992* (Washington, D.C.: U.S. Department of Education, June 1992), p. 84.

[16] Sewell, William H., and Vimal P. Shah, "Socioeconomic Status, Intelligence, and the Attainment of Higher Education," *Sociology of Education*, Vol. 40, 1967, pp. 1–23.

[17] Scheurich, James Joseph, and Michael Imber, "Educational Reforms Can Reproduce Societal Inequalities: A Case Study," *Educational Administration Quarterly*, Vol. 27, No. 3, 1991, pp. 297–320.

[18] Davis, Kingsley, and Wilbert Moore, "Some Principles of Stratification," *American Sociological Review*, Vol. 10, 1945, pp. 242–49.

[19] Parsons, Talcott, "Equality and Inequality in Modern Society, or Social Stratification Revisited," in Edward O. Lauman (ed.), *Social Stratification* (New York: Bobbs-Merrill, 1970), pp. 13–72.

[20] Hauser, Robert M., and David L. Featherman, "Equality of Schooling: Trends and Prospects," *Sociology of Education*, Vol. 49, 1976, pp. 99–120.

[21] Gouldner, Alvin, *The Coming Crisis of Western Sociology* (New York: Avon Books, 1971).

[22] Levitas, Maurice, *Marxist Perspectives in the Sociology of Education* (London: Routledge & Kegan Paul, 1974), p. 165.

[23] Sewell and Shah, "Socioeconomic Status."

[24] Collins, Randall, *Conflict Sociology* (New York: Academic Press, 1975).

[25] Carnoy, Martin, *Education as Cultural Imperialism* (London: Longman, 1974), p. 4.

[26] Scheurich and Imber, "Educational Reforms."

[27] Bowles, Samuel, "Unequal Education and the Reproduction of the Social Division of Labor," in Jerome Karabel and A. H. Halsey (eds.), *Power and Ideology in Education* (New York: Oxford University Press, 1977), p. 137.

[28] Young, *A Critical Theory of Education.*

[29] Beck and Colclough, "Schooling and Capitalism."

[30] Snipp, C. Matthew, "Men's Education and the Reproduction of Social Class: Schooling and Credentials," paper presented at American Sociological Association meetings, Washington, D.C., 1985.

[31] Colclough, Glenna, and E. M. Beck, "The American Educational Structure and the Reproduction of Social Class," *Sociological Inquiry*, Vol. 56, No. 4, Fall 1986, pp. 456–73.

[32] Apple, Michael W., and Lois Weis, "Seeing Education Relationally: The Stratification of Culture and People in the Sociology of School Knowledge," *Journal of Education*, Vol. 168, No. 1, 1986, pp. 19–20.

[33] Young, Michael F. D. (ed.), *Knowledge and Control* (West Drayton, Middlesex, England: Collier Macmillan, 1971).

[34] Willis, Paul, *Learning to Labor: How Working Class Kids Get Working Class Jobs* (Aldershot, Hampshire, England: Saxon House, 1979).

[35] Rubinson, Richard, "Class Formation, Politics, and Institutions: Schooling in the United States," *American Journal of Sociology*, Vol. 92, No. 3, 1986, pp. 519–48.

[36] Schmidt, Peter, "District Proposes Assigning Pupils Based on Income," *Education Week*, October 30, 1991, p. 1.

[37] Byrne, David, Bill Williamson, and Barbara Fletcher, *The Poverty of Education: A Study in the Politics of Opportunity* (Oxford, England: Martin Robertson, 1975).

[38] Gardner, John W., *Excellence* (New York: Harper & Row, 1984), p. 46.

[39] Brookover, Wilbur B., and Edsel L. Erickson, *Sociology of Education* (Homewood, Ill.: Dorsey Press, 1975), pp. 108–9.

[40] Coleman, James S., *Equality and Achievement in Education* (Boulder, Colo.: Westview Press, 1990).

[41] Persell, Caroline Hodges, and Peter W. Cookson, Jr., "Chartering and Bartering: Elite Education and Social Reproduction," *Social Problems*, Vol. 33, No. 2, December 1985.

[42] Cookson, Peter W., and Caroline H. Persell, "English and American Residential Secondary Schools: A Comparative Study of the Reproduction of Social Elites," *Comparative Education Review*, August 1985, pp. 283–84.

[43] Lee, Valerie E., and Helen M. Marx, "Who Goes Where? Choice of Single-Sex and Coeducational Independent Secondary Schools," *Sociology of Education*, Vol. 65, July 1992, pp. 226–53.

[44] Coleman, James S., Thomas Hoffer, and Sally Kilgore, *Public and Private Schools*, Report to the National Center for Education Statistics (Chicago: National Opinion Research Center, 1981).

[45] Hoffer, Thomas, Andrew M. Greeley, and James S. Coleman, "Achievement Growth in Public and Catholic Schools," *Sociology of Education*, Vol. 58, April 1985, pp. 74–97.

[46] Coleman, "The Concept of Equality."

[47] Greeley, Andrew M., *Catholic High Schools and Minority Students* (New Brunswick, N.J.: Transaction Books, 1982).

[48] Bryk, Anthony, *et al.*, *Effective Catholic Schools: An Exploration* (Washington, D.C.: National Catholic Education Association, 1984).

[49] "Of More Than Parochial Interest," *U.S. News and World Report*, May 22, 1989, p. 61.

[50] Walsh, Mark, "Students at Private Schools for Blacks Post Above-Average Scores, Study Finds," *Education Week*, October 16, 1991.

[51] Noell, Jay, "Public and Catholic Schools: A Reanalysis of Public and Private Schools," *Sociology of Education*, Vol. 55, No. 2/3, 1982, pp. 123–32.

[52] Alexander, Karl L., and A. M. Pallas, "Private Schools and Public Policy: New Evidence on Cognitive Achievement in Public and Private Schools," *Sociology of Education*, Vol. 56, 1983, pp. 170–82; "In Defense of 'Private Schools and Public Policy': Reply to Kilgore," *Sociology of Education*, January 1984, pp. 56–58; "School Sector and Cognitive Performance: When Is a Little a Little?" *Sociology of Education*, Vol. 58, April 1985, pp. 115–28.

[53] Van Laarhoven, P., B. Bakker, J. Dronkers, and H. Schijf, "Achievement in Public and Private Secondary Education in the Netherlands," paper presented at American Sociological Association meetings, Chicago, 1987.

[54] Teese, Richard, "Private Schools in France: Evolution of a System," *Comparative Education Review*, May 1986, pp. 247–59.

[55] Catterall, James, and Henry M. Levin, "Public and Private Schools: Evidence on Tuition Tax Credits," *Sociology of Education*, Vol. 55, No. 2/3, 1982, pp. 144–51.

[56] McPartland, James M., and Edward L. McDill, "Control and Differentiation in the Structure of American Education," *Sociology of Education*, Vol. 55, No. 2/3, 1982, pp. 77–78.

[57] Ravitch, Dianne, "What Makes a Good School?" *Society*, January/February 1982, pp. 10–11.

[58] Rose, Mike, "Private School Choice: Empty Promises?" *American Teacher*, November 1991, pp. 8–9.

[59] Toch, Thomas, "Public Schools of Choice," *The American School Board Journal,* July 1991, p. 18.

[60] Elam, Stanley M., Lowell C. Rose, and Alec M. Gallup, "The 23rd Annual Gallup Poll of the Public's Attitudes Toward the Public Schools," *Phi Delta Kappan,* September 1991, p. 47.

[61] Roe, Ellen, "Striving in Seattle," *The American School Board Journal,* February 1990, p. 26.

[62] Young, Timothy W., *Public Alternative Education: Options and Choice for Today's Schools* (New York: Teachers College Press, 1990).

[63] Devins, Neal E. (ed.), *Public Values, Private Schools* (London: Falmer Press, 1989).

[64] Viadero, Debra, "Pennsylvania Senate Approves Sweeping School-Choice Plan," *Education Week,* December 4, 1991, p. 17.

[65] Chubb, John E., and Terry M. Moe, *Politics, Markets and America's Schools* (Washington, D.C.: The Brookings Institution, 1990).

[66] Bastian, Ann, *Unwrapping the Package: Some Thoughts on School Choice* (New York: New World Foundation, 1989).

[67] Lieberman, Myron, *Privatization and Educational Choice* (New York: St. Martin's Press, 1990).

[68] Rothman, Robert, "Paper Launches Academic Attack on Chubb-Moe Book on Education," *Education Week,* November 14, 1990, p. 1.

[69] Krauze, Tadeusz, and Kadimierz M. Slomczynski, "How Far to Meritocracy? Empirical Tests of a Controversial Thesis," *Social Forces,* Vol. 63, No. 3, 1985, pp. 623–42.

[70] Ennis, Robert H., "A Logical Basis for Measuring Critical Thinking Skills," *Educational Leadership,* Vol. 43, No. 2, 1985, pp. 45–48.

[71] *Ibid.*

[72] Kilgore, Sally B., "The Organizational Context of Tracking in Schools," *American Sociological Review,* Vol. 56, No. 2, April 1991, pp. 201–2.

[73] Brookover and Erickson, *Sociology of Education,* p. 129.

[74] Hoffer, Thomas B., and David H. Kamens, "Tracking and Inequality Revisited: Secondary School Course Sequences and the Effects of Social Class on Educational Opportunities," paper presented at American Sociological Association, Pittsburgh, Pa., August 1992.

[75] Schiller, Kathryn S. and David Stevenson, "Sequences of Opportunities for Learning Mathematics," paper presented at American Sociological Association, Pittsburgh, Pa., August 1992.

[76] Riehl, Carolyn, Gary Natriello, and Aaron M. Pallas, "Losing Track: The Dynamics of Student Assignment Processes in High School," paper presented at American Sociological Association, Pittsburgh, Pa., August 1992.

[77] Lucas, Samuel R., "Secondary School Track Rigidity in the United States: Existence, Extension, and Equity," paper presented at American Sociological Association, Pittsburgh, Pa., August 1992.

[78] Op Cit., Schiller

[79] Oakes, Jeannie, "Tracking, Inequality, and the Rhetoric of Reform: Why Schools Don't Change," *Journal of Education,* Vol. 168, No. 1, 1986, pp. 60–80.

[80] Weaver, Rosa Lee, "Separate Is Not Equal," *Principal,* Vol. 69, May 1990, p. 40.

[81] Oakes, Jeannie, *Multiplying Inequalities: The Effects of Race, Social Class, and Tracking on Opportunities to Learn Mathematics and Science* (Santa Monica, Calif.: The Rand Corporation, 1990).

[82] Colclough and Beck, "The American Educational Structure," p. 469.

[83] Jones, James D., Beth E. Vanfossen, and Joan Z. Spade, "Curriculum Placement: Individual and School Effects Using the High School and Beyond Data," paper presented at American Sociological Association meetings, August 1985.

[84] Hallinan, Maureen T., and Aage B. Sorensen, "Student Characteristics and Assignment to Ability Groups: Two Conceptual Formulations," *The Sociological Quarterly,* Vol. 27, No. 1, 1986, pp. 1–13.

[85] Anyon, J., "Social Class and the Hidden Curriculum of Work," *Journal of Education,* Vol. 162, pp. 67–92.

[86] Yogev, Abreham, and Hanna Avalon, "Vocational Education and Social Reproduction: Students' Allocation to Curricular Program in Israeli Vocational High Schools," paper presented at American Sociological Association meetings, Chicago, August 1987.

[87] Weaver, "Separate Is Not Equal," p. 42.

[88] Raze, Nasus, *Overview of Research on Ability Grouping* (Redwood City, Calif.: San Mateo County Office of Education, November 1984).

[89] Dar, Yehezkel, and Nura Resh, "Classroom Intellectual Composition and Academic Achievement," *American Educational Research Journal,* Vol. 23, No. 3, 1986, pp. 357–74.

[90] Slavin, Robert E., "Achievement Effects of Ability Grouping in Secondary Schools: A Best-Evidence Synthesis," *Review of Educational Research,* Vol. 60, No. 3, Fall 1990, pp. 471–99.

[91] Oakes, "Multiplying Inequalities."

[92] Hallinan, Maureen T., "The Effects of Ability Grouping in Secondary Schools: A Response to Slavin's Best-Evidence Synthesis," *Review of Educational Research,* Vol. 60, No. 3, Fall 1990, pp. 501–4.

[93] Gamoran, Adam, "Instructional and Institutional Effects of Ability Grouping," *Sociology of Education,* Vol. 59, October 1986, pp. 185–98.

[94] Levine, D. U., and J. Stark, "Instructional and Organizational Arrangements That Improve Achievement in Inner City Schools," *Educational Leadership,* Vol. 40, pp. 41–46.

[95] Good, T. L., "Teacher Expectations and Student Perceptions: A Decade of Research," *Educational Leadership,* Vol. 38, pp. 415–22.

[96] Rosenthal, Robert, and Lenore Jacobson, *Pygmalian in the Classroom* (New York: Holt, Rinehart and Winston, 1968).

[97] Peters, William, *A Class Divided* (New York: Doubleday, 1971).

[98] *Inside/Out: Saving Our Upper Urban Schools,* film, producer Jack Robertson, 1970.

[99] Coleman, James S., Ernest Q. Campbell, *et al., Equality of Educational Opportunity* (Washington, D.C.: U.S. Department of Education, 1966), Chapter 3.

[100] Jencks, Christopher, *et al., Inequality: A Reassessment of the Effects of Family and Schooling in America* (New York: Basic Books, 1972).

[101] Greenwood, Gordon E., and Catherine W. Hickman, "Research and Practice in Parent Involvement: Implications for Teacher Education," *The Elementary School Journal,* Vol. 91, No. 3, 1991, p. 287.

[102] Dornbusch, Sanford M., and Philip L. Ritter, "Home-School Processes in Diverse Ethnic Groups, Social Classes and Family Structures," (forthcoming chapter), in press.

[103] Rubin, Linda J., and Sherry B. Borgers, "The Changing Family: Implications for Education," *Principal,* September 1991, pp. 11–12.

[104] Bloom, Benjamin S., *All Our Children Learning* (New York: McGraw-Hill, 1981).

[105] Gerkas, "The Influence of Social Class on Socialization," in Wesley R. Burr, *et al.* (eds.), *Contemporary Theories about the Family* (New York: Free Press, 1979).

[106] Astone, Nan Marie, and Sara S. McLanahan, "Family Structure, Parental Practices and High School Completion," *American Sociological Review,* Vol. 56, No. 3, June 1991, pp. 318–19.

[107] Rumberger, Russell W., "Family Influences on Dropout Behavior in One California High School," *Sociology of Education,* Vol. 63, October 1990, pp. 283–99.

[108] Dronkers, Jaap, "The Changing Effects of Single-parent Families on the Educational Attainment of their Children in an European Welfare State," presented at spring 1992 meetings of Social Stratification and Mobility, International Sociological Association, Trento, Italy.

[109] Bernstein, Basil, "Codes, Modalities and the Process of Cultural Reproduction: A Model," *Language and Society,* December 1981.

[110] Coleman, *et al., Equality of Educational Opportunity.*

[111] Jencks, *et al., Inequality.*

[112] Dornbusch, S.M., *et al.,* "The Relation of Parenting Style to Adolescent School Performance," *Child Development,* Vol. 58, pp. 1244–57.

[113] Lee, Seh-Ahn, "Family Structure Effects on Student Outcomes," *Resources and Actions: Parents, Their Children and Schools,* Report to National Science Foundation and National Center for Educational Statistics, August 1991.

[114] Schneider, Barbara, *Parents, Their Children and Schools,* (Boulder, Colo.: Westview Press, forthcoming).

[115] Bourdieu Pierre, "Cultural Reproduction and Social Reproduction," in J. Karabel and A. H. Halsey (eds.), *Power and Ideology in Education* (New York: Oxford University Press, 1977), pp. 487–511.

[116] Lareau, Annette, "Social Class Differences in Family-School Relationships: The Importance of Cultural Capital," paper presented at American Sociological Association meetings, August 1985.

[117] Anderson, Richard C., *et al., Becoming a Nation of Readers: The Report of the Commission on Reading* (Washington, D.C.: National Institute of Education, National Academy of Education, 1985).

[118] Lareau, Annette, *Home Advantage: Social Class and Parental Intervention in Elementary Education* (London: Falmer Press, 1989).

[119] Mulkey, Lynn M., Robert L. Crain, and Alexander J.C. Harrington, "One-Parent Households and Achievement: Economic and Behavioral Explanations of a Small Effect," *Sociology of Education,* Vol. 65, January 1992, pp. 48–65.

[120] Pallas, Aaron M., "The Changing Nature of the Disadvantaged Population: Current Dimensions and Future Trends," *Educational Researcher,* June/July 1989, pp. 16–22.

[121] Lee, "Family Structure Effects," p. 35.

[122] Pallas, "The Changing Nature."

[123] Muller, Chandra, "Maternal Employment, Parent Involvement, and Academic Achievement: An Analysis of Family Resources Available to the Child," in *Resources and Actions: Parents, Their Children and Schools,* Report to the National Science Foundation and National Center for Education Statistics, August 1991.

[124] White, Burton L., "Growing Up Competent: How Families Make the Difference," *Carnegie Quarterly,* Summer 1973, pp. 6–8.

[125] Baker, David P., and David L. Stevenson, "Mothers' Strategies for Children's School Achievement: Managing the Transition to High School," *Sociology of Education,* Vol. 59, July 1986, pp. 156–66.

[126] Milne, Ann M., David E. Myers, Alvin S. Rosenthal, and Alan Ginsburg, "Single Parents, Working Mothers, and the Educational Achievement of School Children," *Sociology of Education,* Vol. 59, July 1986, pp. 125–39.

[127] Heyns, Barbara, and Sophia Catsambis, "Mother's Employment and Children's Achievement: A Critique," *Sociology of Education,* Vol. 59, July 1986, pp. 140–51.

[128] *Gallup Report 248,* May 1986.

[129] Blake, Judith, "Number of Siblings and Educational Mobility," *American Sociological Review,* Vol. 50, 1985, pp. 84–94.

[130] Blake, Judith, "Sibship Size and Educational Stratification: Reply to Mare and Chen," *American Sociological Review,* Vol. 51, 1986, p. 416.

[131] Dornbusch, Sanford M., and Philip L. Ritter, "Home-School Processes in Diverse Ethnic Groups, Social Classes and Family Structures," in Sandra Christenson and Jane C. Conoley (eds) *Home-School Collaboration* (Washington, D.C.: National Association of School Psychologists), in press.

[132] Ostrander, Kenneth H., and Katherine Ostrom, "Attitudes Underlying the Politics of Parent Involvement," *National Forum of Applied Educational Research Journal,* Vol. 3, No. 2, 1990–91, p. 37.

[133] Epstein, Joyce L., and Susan L. Dauber, "School Programs and Teacher Practices of Parent Involvement in Inner-City Elementary and Middle Schools," *The Elementary School Journal,* Vol. 91, No. 3, 1991, p. 289.

[134] National Center for Educational Statistics, "School Revenues," *The Condition of Education* (Washington, D.C.: U.S. Department of Education, June 1992), p. 335.

[135] National Center for Educational Statistics, *Digest of Education Statistics 1991* (Washington, D.C.: U.S. Department of Education, November 1991), p. 157.

4

SEX, RACE, AND ATTEMPTS TO ACHIEVE EQUALITY OF EDUCATIONAL OPPORTUNITY

Black and white, female and male, Hindu and Moslem, rich and poor—such dichotomies in our ascribed status also imply different points on the continuum of educational experiences and outcomes. The positions that individuals hold in the societal and educational system are influenced by their race, sex, cultural background, and social class. These background factors affect the stratification within educational systems and society as a whole; the dynamics of systems cannot be understood without regard for such factors. In this chapter we focus first on the experiences of females and males in the educational system, and how this influences the status and role of men and women in society. (A distinction is made in most discussions between "sex," which generally refers to biological aspects of an individual, and "gender," which refers to sociocultural aspects that determine appropriate behavior patterns. Here we use the term "sex" and "sex roles" to refer to both biological and sociocultural aspects.) In the second section we look at some attempts to rectify the unequal treatment of racial, ethnic, and other minorities in the educational system, and results of these attempts.

SEX AND EQUALITY OF EDUCATIONAL OPPORTUNITY

Why is it that girls and boys who go into the same schools and classroom systems come out with different experiences, interests, achievement levels, and expectations?[1] Scientific research addresses these and other questions about the differences in the school experiences of boys and girls. Theoretical explanations of the different educational experience focus on socialization, the role of societal systems, and "biological destiny."

Sex Role Socialization

The socialization process begins the day we are born and ends the day we die. Informal education is continuous throughout life; formal education is restricted to certain periods. Girls and boys have different socialization experiences from birth, and by the time they enter nursery school, most children already have a good idea of their gender identity from parents, siblings, TV, and other "socialization agents."

The socialization function takes place in schools while students spend more than six hours a day in classes and school-related activities. Teachers and schools become important sources of information on sex-appropriate behavior; children learn by observing and imitating adult roles, including the roles of teachers and administrators. They observe the ratio of males to females and the authority structure in the educational hierarchy. They learn their own sex-appropriate behavior through positive and negative sanctions, as well as through textbooks.

Children's toys play a major role in sex socialization as well. "Boys' toys"—chemistry sets, doctor kits, telescopes, microscopes—encourage manipulation of the environment and are generally more career-oriented and more expensive than "girls' toys."[2] Parents are generally very conscious of buying sex-appropriate toys for their children. Toy choices carry over to children's play; by the time young children reach nursery school they have already learned to play with sex-appropriate toys.[3]

Sexism in textbooks has received a great deal of attention. Books are a major source of messages about sex roles. Among the best known of the many studies done on readers and storybooks are those by a group based in Princeton, New Jersey, called Women on Words and Images.[4] They have evaluated sexism in children's readers and have updated their findings as new editions from 18 major textbook companies are released. Content analysis of texts looks at the sex of the main character, illustrations, positive and negative images of men and women, stereotypes, and many other factors related to the portrayal of sex roles in the societal system. Recent analyses show improvements, but imbalances still favor males in rate of portrayal and types of roles assigned.[5]

Recent studies reveal that science, social studies, and even math books depict girls and women in stereotypic sex roles. For instance, math problems involving girls often show them jumping rope, buying clothes, sewing, cooking, or calculating the grocery bill,[6] limited views of what girls see as viable options and uses for their studies. These socialization experiences influence what boys and girls learn about their roles and what they see as possible roles as they grow to adulthood.

Differences in behaviors begin early, when children as young as three-and-a-half start to influence their peers. Girls tend to be ignored and often stop trying. Girls form intimate "chumships," while boys relate through groups organized around activities. Even speech patterns differ, with boys using speech for egoistic purposes and girls for social binding.[7]

Sex Differences in the Educational System

Some argue that if women want to get ahead, all they have to do is work hard like anyone else who "makes it" in society. This is an appealing argument to some, but it ignores historical factors, stereotyping, and the interaction among various segments of society.

The sex role distinction in education is not of recent origin. The Puritans in the United States discouraged literacy for women, except to ensure salvation through reading the Bible. After the American Revolution, it became a responsibility of women to teach young children and pass on moral standards; thus a limited amount of education became acceptable, perhaps even encouraged, in a male-dominated society. This attitude is illustrated in the following quotation from a school observer in the 1880s:

> We noticed the boys all writing, but none of the girls; turning to our friend Tullis for an explanation, he said it was not safe for girls to learn to write, as it would culminate in love-letter writing, clandestine engagements and elopements. He said women were allowed to study arithmetic, though, for Miss Polly Caldwell studied as far as long division, and Mrs. Kyle, while a widow, got as far as reduction. He says Polly Caldwell was a weaver, and required the aid of figures to make her calculations for warping.[8]

Oberlin was the first U.S. college, in 1833, to open its doors officially to women, but their education was restricted to domestic subjects. With the development of women's colleges in the mid–nineteenth century came women reformers and women professionals. Since that time, the picture has been one of steady advancement for women in education, with both all-female and coeducational schools and entry into a wide range of professions. In recent years many of even the staunchest male institutions have become coeducational.

Societal systems are dependent on schools to pass along crucial beliefs and values—among them, sex role behaviors and expectations. In part, this occurs formally through courses and texts used in the curriculum or through the structure that assigns privileges and tasks by sex. But many of society's expectations are passed on through the informal or "hidden" curriculum (discussed in Chapter 7), including materials, activities, differential treatment, and counseling. Sex roles in schools mirror those in society.[9] Our behavior and our expectations for each sex, from child-rearing activities to school expectations, are greatly affected by sexual stereotypes. Stereotypes about male and female characteristics are fairly consistently held by members of our society: Girls are docile, gentle, cooperative, affectionate, nurturant; boys are aggressive, curious, competitive, ambitious.

Evidence of these stereotypes is apparent around the world. Statistics on literacy rates for men and women exemplify the different societal expectations for the sexes (Figures 4-1 and 4-2). Without education, women cannot participate fully in the economic and political spheres of society, yet access to

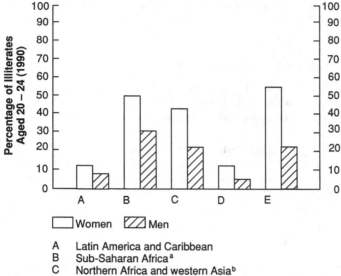

Women   Men

A   Latin America and Caribbean
B   Sub-Saharan Africa[a]
C   Northern Africa and western Asia[b]
D   Eastern and southeastern Asia
E   Southern Asia

FIGURE 4-1   Illiteracy rates are still much higher for young women than men. The widest gaps between women and men are in Africa and southern and western Asia.

Note: Based on total population of women and men aged 20–24 years in each region.

[a]Includes Sudan; excludes South Africa.

[b]Includes Somalia and Mauritania; excludes Cyprus, Israel, and Turkey.

Source: The World's Women 1970–1990: Trends and Statistics (New York: United Nations, 1991), p. 46.

literacy and education remains a major problem for the bulk of the world's population. The impact of educational systems on sex role learning is shown in the following examples.

Sex Role Composition of Schools.   Major sex composition differences remain in the structure of educational systems. For instance, in the United States, 70 percent of public school teachers were women[10]; 86 percent of the elementary school teachers are female, while only 56 percent of high school teachers are female. Moving on up the ladder, 22 percent of the assistant principals, 14 percent of principals, and only 1 percent of superintendants are women. The pattern of "the higher, the fewer" continues at the university level. Why have these inequalities come about? Socialization affects attitudes; structural barriers limit access. And the educational system is slow to change. For instance, socialization has influenced women not to seek administrative responsibilities; interpersonal barriers confront aspiring women when they face the dominant power structure; organizational and institutional barriers

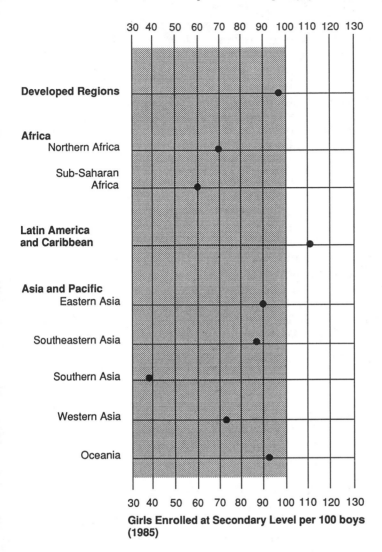

FIGURE 4-2   Girls' secondary enrollment still lags behind boys' in much of Africa and Asia.

Source: Prepared by the Statistical Office of the United Nations Secretariat from UNESCO, *Statistical Yearbook* (Paris, various years); reprinted in *The World's Women 1970–1990: Trends and Statistics* (New York: United Nations, 1991), p. 47.

occur during recruitment, selection, placement, evaluation, and other processes. Thus, at several levels women face obstacles to achieving higher positions in the structure.

Single-sex high schools and universities have been dwindling since the 1960s, yet some research shows that they can provide support by separating the academic and social concerns of adolescence, especially for girls. In academic achievement, achievement gains, educational aspirations, sex role stereotyping, and attitudes related to academics, single-sex schools had some advantages. Women who have attended single-sex schools do better in later life, whereas males do more talking in mixed classrooms.[11] At the higher educational level also, debate about the value of single-sex education continues; faculty members take male contributions to classroom discussions more seriously than those of females, and permit males to dominate.[12] When all-women Mills College in California decided to admit men, storms of protest at the possibility of integrating with men arose. In this instance, the wishes of the students prevailed. Without the social distractions of a coeducational institution and with norms of academic focus, encouragement to excel is stronger at single-sex institutions.[13]

Activities in Schools. Activities of persons in contact with children—parents, classroom teachers, administrators, and other school decision makers—must also be taken into account. In elementary school the child is most likely to have a female teacher. While most classrooms are coeducational, many activities within the classroom are sex-linked. Further, girls do not receive the same attention boys do; boys are encouraged to solve problems while girls are given the answers. Thus, teacher actions reinforce sex stereotypes. Girls are often asked to water the plants and boys to clean the blackboards. Children line up for activities by sex. Even in discipline and amount of teacher time spent with children, there are sex differences; studies find that boys receive more and harsher discipline, but also more teacher time and praise. Teacher expectations enter into differential treatment of students by sex as well as by class and race.

Activities reflect stereotypic attitudes, as exemplified by Lever's study of fifth grade out-of-school and playground activities.[14] Lever's data revealed six differences in the play patterns of boys and girls:

1. boys play outdoors far more than girls,
2. boys more often play in larger groups,
3. boys' play occurs in more age-heterogeneous groups,
4. boys' play occurs in less sex-segregated groups (that is, girls were more often found playing predominantly male games than boys playing girls' games),
5. boys' games last longer than girls' games, and
6. boys play competitive games more often than girls.

"The lessons learned on the playground stand a boy in good stead when he is later working his way through the corporate world. . . ."[15]

Sex Role Stereotypes. Society's stereotypes of male/female behavior are set fairly early in a child's life. By adolescence, girls are struggling to resist the loss of psychological strengths and to speak up as they felt free to do in earlier years, with schools playing a crucial role in passing on cultural stereotypes.

Schools tend to reward autonomy rather than encouraging relationships. Girls begin to hesitate to say certain things because the "perfect girl" avoids being mean and bossy.[16,17]

Ruth Hartley's classic study of 8- to 11-year-old boys found greater pressure for conformity on boys than on girls. Boys felt that they should be able to "fight in case a bully comes along, run fast, play rough games, take care of themselves, and know what girls don't know." Boys are "noisy, get dirty, mess up the house, get into more trouble than girls do, and are not to be crybabies." When asked what men should be, they replied: "strong, able to protect women and children in emergencies, able to fix things, able to get money to support their families, and be in charge of things."[18] Although these stereotypes of sex role behavior are changing, their legacy puts a heavy burden on children. Girls' self-esteem is tied to grades much more than is boys' self-esteem.[19] When girls make course decisions in junior high and high school, their sex role stereotypes can influence their choices. For instance, working-class girls' choices of business courses reproduce their class and gender status. These girls are aware and self-directed, making realistic choices that from their experience they feel are most likely to lead to jobs and other goals.[20]

Achievement and Motivation.   "Girls face pervasive barriers to achievement throughout their precollegiate schooling and are 'systematically discouraged' from pursuing studies that would enhance their prospects for well-paying jobs. . . ."[21] Though girls achieve higher grades throughout their public school education, 'they have been systematically tracked toward traditional, sex-segregated jobs, and away from areas of study that lead to high-paying jobs in science, technology, and engineering."[22] On standardized test measures of achievement, however, the male/female scores depend on the content of the tests; girls tend to do better in reading, writing, and literature, boys in math and science. However, composite SAT and ACT scores are higher for males. High school females received somewhat higher science grades than males but males tended to take more optional math and science courses than females.

Girls often surpass boys in elementary school in performance and achievement, and through high school in grades achieved. But, usually in middle school, changes caused by the onset of adolescence and girls' perceptions of who they are and how they should behave begin to affect their career choices. By the time girls are seniors, their plans and values for future participation in the work force closely parallel the actual sex differences in occupations. These plans and values seem to reflect "what is deemed acceptable and feasible in today's world of work.[23]

Women face challenges in adult life as well, often not receiving respect for intellectual achievements. For instance, African-American intellectuals, especially women, are caught in a bind, living in a basically "anti-intellectual society." They often feel that their intellectual work is seen as less valuable than that of activists,[24] though their contributions lay the groundwork for activism. "Be smart, but not too smart—and always expect confrontation with harsh realities," is the advice of one woman.

School Achievement: The Case of Math and Science

Why do boys outscore girls on math achievements? This question is of particular interest because of concerns about equal opportunity for women and the loss of valuable human resources that occurs when some fail to achieve at a high level in mathematics.

Girls are slightly more likely to be in eighth-grade algebra than boys, but are less likely to persist through 12th-grade calculus and trigonometry.[25] In science, boys outnumber girls in chemistry two to one, and in physics five to one.[26]

Though much has been made of the difference in math scores between girls and boys on standardized tests, these differences are not significant and need to be considered in light of social and cultural factors that bar girls from participation in achievement in math and science.[27] Cross-cultural studies of differences in parental support, teacher expectations, study habits, and values and beliefs that affect achievement indicate that girls in some countries excel in math. Though researchers have looked for biological explanations for differences in math achievement, "no biological explanation is required for Asian-American women's relatively higher representation in science and engineering positions (5%) than the general work force (2%) in the United States."[28]

If disproportionately smaller numbers of women pursue math, science, and technical careers, they will be left farther behind in a world that increasingly values and rewards these skills. In the United States, this problem has stimulated a number of federally funded projects to ascertain the causes. The problem of gender inequities in math and science is international, however. Where women have lower status, the gender achievement differential in math and science is also greater.[29]

Most research discounts a biological explanation for male-female differences, pointing to evidence that overall school math performance differences are very small and exist mainly among higher-ability students.[30] These are directly related to course-taking, career expectations, and social behavior such as "sophomore math performance, number and level of mathematics courses taken, and absence of serious sophomore dating behavior." Whether students take math courses is in turn related to college and career plans, and girls tend to take fewer. This may be because they realized the difficulty of women working in some fields, or the effects of sex role stereotypes about occupations.[31]

Tests of visual and verbal abilities using children from age 2 on show little sex difference until adolescence, and these differences vary across cultures, with some showing no sex differences. Therefore, cultural variations must be considered part of the equation.[32]

Parental support and involvement influence attitudes toward math and science and curricular choices in the United States and other countries.[33] Parents with higher socioeconomic status are more likely to be "active managers" of their daughters' school course selections.[34] These girls tend to have more advanced coursework, which in turn contributes to social class reproduction.[35]

There are few differences in the enrollment in mathematics courses, but more males are enrolled in related computer science and science courses that utilize the math knowledge. Women tend to see less use or need for math. Achievement is similar if male and female students take the same amount of math, but at the advanced level results are less clear and males seem to have an advantage. Those talented math students, both male and female, have favorable attitudes and take more science, the exception being physics, in which more boys are enrolled. Girls may take less science or drop it because they find it "dull."[36] Teachers tend to expect boys to be better problem solvers and often ask them more high-level questions than girls. High-achieving girls receive less attention than boys. A simple summary states that "males tend to attribute successes to internal causes and failure to external or unstable causes. Females tend to attribute success to external or unstable causes and failure to internal causes."

Most researchers theorize that the differences in mathematical ability result from socialization and experiences of boys and girls. These experiences start as early as primary school. White males have been encouraged to be independent thinkers and can develop creative ways of dealing with mathematics rather than following rigid norms of math formulas.[37]

Math lessons in a Japanese school encouraged children to think through the problem rather than give the answer. Comparative data show that female and minority students in the United States tend not to think through a problem in other than a set formula or procedure.

Attempts to narrow the gap between the mathematical performance of boys and girls has resulted in a plethora of innovative programs for teaching math and for attacking the problem from the attitudinal and organizational levels. If the socialization experience of students and school structural elements regarding math are altered in positive ways, we may see changes.

"Biological Destiny"

Is there evidence that inborn characteristics are at the root of differences in educational experiences of girls and boys? Studies of sociobiologists and other researchers fall into several categories: boys' adjustment to early years of schooling; girls' math and science ability; biological learning styles of each sex; and general intelligence of each sex. The problem with biological explanations is that they seldom consider the strong influence of cultural expectations and environmental constraints on students and are therefore incomplete explanations taken alone; evidence is still inadequate to draw conclusions about what role biology plays in sex differences in learning and achievement. The following summarizes some directions in biological research:

1. Boys are disadvantaged in grade school because they are more active and do not have the physical ability to sit still and learn to read and write. Therefore, they have more discipline problems and are less well adjusted in early school years. Boys learn better by manipulation of objects.[38]

2. Studies concerning verbal and visual-spatial abilities consider chromosome differences, serum uric acid, hormone differences, brain functioning and lateralization

differences, and other biological factors. Although these are not necessarily independent of each other, there is evidence only in brain lateralization. Boys tend to use both brain hemispheres for spatial and mathematical reasoning, while girls concentrate in the left hemisphere. They may have more right-hemisphere concentration than boys in developing verbal skills. Hormones may interact with brain functioning to cause some differences that appear at adolescence.[39]

In a study of superior young math students, boys outnumbered girls by 13 to one. The researchers conclude that male ability in spatial tasks is related to their superior performance;[40,41] although this finding is controversial, again because it puts little emphasis on cultural factors.

3. General intelligence studies conclude that there is no overall difference between the sexes, but that there is a wider spread of intelligence for boys, with more falling at the bottom or top of the spectrum.

Combatting Sexism in Educational Systems

Evidence indicates that subtle and blatant sexism occurs at all levels of the educational system. There is no one solution for eradicating it, but steps are being taken at various levels of the system to lessen its effects.

1. In teacher education, awareness of stereotypes and practices that commonly operate in the classroom can make teachers more sensitive to the formal and informal curriculum that perpetuates such practices. Simple changes in classroom practices are the easiest to tackle. Teacher education texts have had an almost total lack of information on sex equity in education, according to a content analysis of 24 widely used books. "Most of the texts characterized by these omissions (of sexism) were in methods of teaching mathematics and science, the very areas in which girls are most likely to experience difficulties."[42]

2. The Title IX program, an example of federal concern, covers admissions quotas by sex, different course offerings by sex, and athletic programs. Regulations for schools include analysis of existing programs and equal treatment of all students in courses, financial aid, counseling, services, and employment. Title IX has affected sports facilities, physical education equipment, and course offering, which must be equivalent for men and women. It has led to test cases regarding women students playing on formerly all-male teams. However, a 1984 high court ruling limited it to programs and activities rather than institutions violating Title IX, a ruling which has limited its impact.[43]

Every institution in society has been affected by the changing roles of men and women. The changes are occurring rapidly and we have not yet seen their end effect on education, other institutions, or equality of opportunity for women.

RACE AND ATTEMPTS TO RECTIFY INEQUALITIES IN EDUCATIONAL OPPORTUNITY

The issue of equality of educational opportunity lays in the lap of society the problems of disadvantage, poverty, and discrimination, with the clear implication that society plays a key role in these problems and that it is society's job to do something to correct the injustices suffered by racial minorities. Educational disadvantage stems from formal schooling, family, and community sources, not under the control of any individual student. "At-risk" students in this category have insufficient educational experiences in one or more of these areas.[44] There are demands for equal school facilities, experienced and trained teachers, and per-pupil expenditures; for an integrated racial composition; and for preferential treatment, such as affirmative action, to make up for past inequities.[45]

Trends in Public School Enrollments

Dramatic shifts in public school enrollments are underway. In most states the number of white students will shrink, while African-American and other minority students will increase. In 1990, minority children made up 29 percent of elementary school enrollment, with African-American, 16 percent, and Hispanic, 11 percent (Table 4-1). By 1995, the picture will look quite different from what it did in the 1980s and earlier (Figure 4-3). In 1986, 22 percent of the graduates were minority, and by 1995 that number will be at least 28 percent. Some estimate the number as high as 37.5 percent, with Hispanics making up 14 percent.[46] The District of Columbia will have 98 percent minority graduates, and California, Hawaii, Mississippi, and New Mexico are predicted to have minority students be the majority by 1995.

The fastest growth is in the Asian and Pacific Islander population, rising 58 percent in less than ten years because of immigration and high birth rates among some groups. Hispanics will have the largest increase in graduates, up 52 percent from 1986. African-Americans and white will decline in numbers.

One concern is that the growing groups do not graduate at the same rate

TABLE 4-1   Percentage of Public School Enrollment by Ethnicity: 1976 to 1996

	1966	1976	1986	1996
Total Number	43,039[a]	43,714[a]	41,156[a]	43,775[a,b]
		Percent		
White	80.2	76.0	70.4	62.5[c]
Total Minority	19.8	24.0	29.6	37.5[c]
Black	14.3	15.5	16.1	17.6[c]
Hispanic	4.6	6.4	9.9	14.0[c]
Asian	0.4	1.2	2.8	4.4[c]
American Indian	0.5	0.8	0.9	1.0[c]

[a]Number in thousands.

[b]Based on U.S. government projections that extend to 1997.

[c]Based on extrapolation of U.S. data and population reference data by author (Bouvier & Davis, 1982; Ornstein, 1984).

Source: From *The Condition of Education 1989*, Vol. 1 (Washington, D.C.: U.S. Government Printing Office, 1989), pp. 110–11; *Digest of Education Statistics 1976* (Washington, D.C.: U.S. Government Printing Office, 1977), p. 40; and *Projections of Educational Statistics to 2000* (Washington, D.C.: U.S. Government Printing Office, 1989), p. 5; reprinted in Snyder, Thomas D., "Trends in Education," *Principal*, Vol. 71, No. 1, September 1991, pp. 6–9.

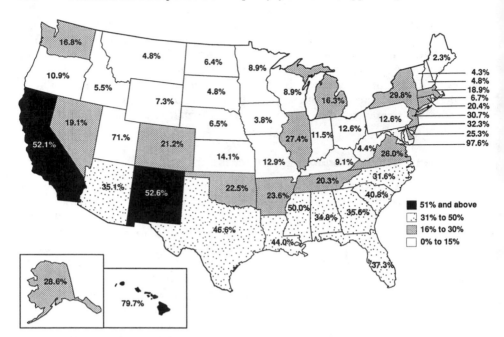

FIGURE 4-3   Minority public high school graduates, 1995 (projections, by state, of proportions of graduates who are minority-group members).

Source: Western Interstate Commission for Higher Education, 1991; reprinted in "Minority Public High School Graduates, 1995," *The Chronicle of Higher Education,* September 18, 1991, p. A40.

as whites and are often not prepared for the work force. The dropout rate for Native Americans from high school is 27 percent; for Asians, 2 percent; for African-Americans, 11 percent; for Hispanics, 18 percent; and for whites, 8 percent (see Box 4-1).[47]

At-Risk Students

The term "underclass" was coined by Gunnar Myrdal, a Swedish observer of American society. The term was brought into current usage by William Julius Wilson. Most researchers define this group as "people who share some basic traits: poverty, poor education and health, unstable family life, and antisocial behavior such as drugs and crime."[48] It has also usually come to refer to minorities. However, not all agree with the concept and its implications of "blaming the victim" for the problem; "underclass" has become a political policy issue. Herbert Gans describes it this way: "On the right and the left, the former arguing that underclass behavior is the product of the unwillingness of the black poor to adhere to the American work ethic, among other cultural deficiencies, and the latter claiming that the underclass is the consequence of changes in the industrial economy."[49] One study of Hispanic populations points out that, despite poverty and deprivation, Hispanics do not

BOX 4-1 *HIGH SCHOOL ATTAINMENT*

Western states tend to have the highest percentage of adults aged 25 and older who are high school graduates, according to a survey by the U.S. Census Bureau.

The report, based on 1989 data, includes for the first time high school and college completion rates for all states and many large metropolitan areas.

The 10 states with the highest reported high school completion rates (ranging from 83.2 percent to 88.2 percent) in 1989 were Utah, Washington, Alaska, Wyoming, Minnesota, Nevada, Oregon, Montana, Iowa, and Colorado. Alabama (63.2 percent) had the lowest rate.

The metropolitan area with the highest high school completion rate was Seattle-Tacoma, Washington, with 90.3 percent. The lowest rate was in San Antonio, with 68.5 percent.

The data showed that, overall, whites had the highest completion rate (78.4 percent), followed by Asian, Pacific Islander, and Native American groups (76.1 percent), blacks (64.6 percent), and Hispanics (50.9 percent).

The highest college completion rate was in the Washington, D.C., metropolitan area, with 41.2 percent.

The high school and college completion rates for young adults (those aged 25 to 29) were not significantly different from those recorded in the mid-1970s, the bureau said.

Census bureau officials cautioned that the data are from a survey, not the 1990 census, and are more susceptible to error.

Copies of "Educational Attainment in the United States: March 1989 and 1988" are available for $5.50 each from the Superintendent of Documents, U.S. Government Printing Office, Washington, DC 20402. The stock number is 803-005-00051-6.

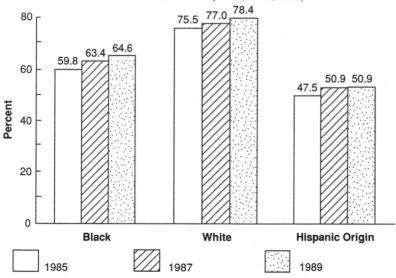

HIGH SCHOOL COMPLETION RATES FOR AMERICANS
AGED 25 AND OLDER (1985, 1987, 1989)

Source: U.S. Census Bureau; reprinted in "High School Attainment," *Education Week,* November 20, 1991, p. 3.

have many of the traits associated with "underclass," such as poor health indicators and family breakdown.[50]

Research on Equality of Educational Opportunity

While literature related to equality abounds, two studies stand out because of their comprehensive data collection, analysis, and contribution to understanding inequality: the Coleman Report[51] and Jencks's study of inequality.[52]

The Coleman Report.   The best-known study of desegregation is the Coleman Report. The Department of Health, Education, and Welfare hired Coleman and his associates to do a study ten years after the *Brown* decision was handed down to determine the state of affairs in education. Coleman's findings turned up both some expected results and some quite unexpected ones. Indeed, the report proved highly controversial, partly because it challenged some strongly held but untested assumptions about schools and education.

The purpose of the study was to evaluate opportunities and performance of minority students compared with white students. Coleman's survey extended to about 5 percent of the schools in the United States and covered 645,000 students at five grade levels. The children were given tests of several types; information about the children's backgrounds and attitudes was collected; and school administrators filled out questionnaires about their schools. Coleman's findings revealed a number of interesting points.

1. Minority students (except for Asian Americans) scored lower on tests at each level of schooling than did white students, and this disparity increased from the first to 12th grades. Coleman attributed the disadvantage of minority students to a combination of out-of-school factors, many of which center in the family: poverty, parents' education, and other environmental factors.
2. The majority of children at the time of the report attended segregated schools. Teachers also tended to teach children of their own race.
3. The socioeconomic makeup of the school, the home background, and the background of other students in the school were factors that made the biggest difference in students' school achievement levels. This was a surprising finding and led to the recommendation that schools be integrated, in order to have a racial-class mix of students.
4. Curriculum and facilities made little difference in student achievement levels— another surprising finding. In fact, school facilities turned out to differ very little across predominantly black or white schools.
5. White children had somewhat greater access to physics, chemistry, language labs, textbooks, college curricula, and better-qualified and higher-paid teachers, but the differences were not very great.

These findings have been tested and retested by researchers, and while there are variations in the results, Coleman's general conclusions have been upheld. It was these findings that led to Coleman's recommendation that one way to improve the academic achievement of poor and minority children would be to integrate the schools, putting minority children with white children to produce a climate for achievement and to provide educational role models. The study provided the impetus for increased efforts to desegregate, especially through the use of busing.

Jencks's Study of Inequality.   Another famous and often quoted study questions the use of schools to attain equal opportunity in society. In their report, Christopher Jencks and his colleagues reanalyze the Coleman data plus many other data sets and argue that no evidence suggests that school reform can bring about significant social changes outside schools:

> [T]he evidence suggests that equalizing educational opportunity would do very little to make adults more equal. If all elementary schools were equally effective, cognitive inequality among sixth-graders would decline less than three percent . . . cognitive inequality among twelfth-graders would hardly decline at all, and disparities in their eventual attainment would decline less than one percent. Eliminating all economic and academic obstacles to college attendance might somewhat reduce disparities in educational attainment, but the change would not be large.[53]

Jencks points out that experience over the past 25 years suggests that even when the educational attainment gap between minorities and whites is narrowed, economic inequality among adults continues to exist.

Jencks concludes that schools can do little to change people's status in society after graduation. Even school reform and compensatory education programs are not seen as effective in substantially changing the differences between adults. These conclusions both startled and angered educators and others; it is not pleasant to hear that schools make little difference. In this study, Jencks does not deny that schools are important for everyone—he did say that they cannot solve society's problems. He also concludes, as did Coleman, that the school achievement of children is dependent on one major factor—their families. Family background and attitudes toward education are primary determinants of school experience. Jencks argues that since schools cannot achieve an egalitarian society and economic equality, we must redistribute income by changing the economic institution into a more socialistic system.

While the tests and retests of Coleman's and Jencks's conclusions come up with varied results, most uphold the importance of students' families and the backgrounds of peers. The significance of school "climate" is discussed in Chapter 7.

In further analysis of data, Jencks reports that family background accounts for about 48 percent of one's occupational status and 15 to 35 percent of income differences between individuals. Amount of education and family status are closely associated.[54]

The Battle Over Desegregation

Poverty and racism have been ugly realities in the history of the United States. Kidnappings, lynchings, mob violence, and abuse could not stop the protests against unfair treatment of large segments of the population. These problems were reflected in the school system and every other part of society. The schools developed as segregated institutions in much of the country.

When discussing desegration, people often use two terms interchangeably; however, their meanings are technically different. *"Desegregation* of schools refers to enrollment patterns wherein students of different racial groups attend the same schools, and students are not separated in racially isolated schools or classrooms. *Integration* refers to situations in which students of different racial groups not only attend schools together, but effective steps have been taken to . . . overcome the disadvantages of minority students and develop positive interracial relationships.[55]

Concerned over the controversy about the importance and value of desegregation, a number of scholars including Gary A. Orfield presented a summary statement of social science research over the past 20 years. The findings fall into four areas and show the following:

1. The desegregation of a school district can positively influence residential integration in the community.
2. Desegregation is associated with moderate academic gains for minority-group students and does no harm to white students.
3. Desegregation plans work best when they cover as many grades as possible, when they encompass as large a geographic area as possible, and when they stick to clearly defined goals over the long haul.
4. Effective desegregation is linked to other types of educational reform.[56]

Court Cases on Desegregation

In 1954, the Supreme Court pronounced its landmark "separate is not equal" decision in the *Brown v. Board of Education* case, a ruling that has been seen as a blessing by some and a curse by others. Has it made any difference in the education or social status of minority groups in our society? Ten years after the *Brown* decision, the courts still had made no rulings on what desegregation meant. Therefore in 1964, the Civil Rights Act ruled that delays in desegregation were no longer tolerable. In order to achieve equality of opportunity desegregation was ordered. However, patterns of enforcement have varied, and the rulings in test cases—from the Supreme Court down to district courts—have been inconsistent. The picture remains muddled.

Since the 1954 "separate is not equal" Supreme Court ruling, and the order to change with all deliberate speed, courts at every level have been busy interpreting the ruling for their districts. Landmark cases from the Supreme Court have sometimes clarified requirements, but not always.

The most recent requests from lower courts and school districts have asked the high court to clarify *when* districts can return to local control following court-supervised desegregation plans. Cases in Kansas City, St. Louis, and Oklahoma City have been heard. In the *Board of Education of Oklahoma City Public Schools v. Dowell* (58 USLW 3536), the 10th Circuit Court of Appeals said that court oversight of city schools should continue until the school district could show that ending busing would not resegregate schools. This ruling conflicted with a Norfolk, Virginia, ruling that schools could end mandatory busing to desegregate until cities could prove this would lead to resegregation. Oklahoma City had tried various plans, including one in which children from kindergarten to fourth grade could attend neighborhood schools. This resulted in 33 of 64 elementary schools being at least 90 percent minority or white, the key percentage for considering a school segregated. The Supreme Court ruled that "desegregation should be kept in place,"[57] a response that has not clarified the situation for many other districts.

In a 1992 Supreme Court ruling on a Georgia case, *Freeman v. Pitts* (Case No. 89-1290), local districts can gain control over some aspects of their operations, such as assignment of students, even though they may not have fully complied with other ordered changes. "Returning schools to the control of local authorities at the earliest practicable date is essential to restore their true accountability in our governmental system" was the conclusion of the judge writing the decision.[58] In another case affecting higher education, the U.S. Supreme Court specified how states must demonstrate that they have removed segregation. This ruling affects 19 Southern and border states.[59]

Extent of the Desegregation-Integration Problem. Social scientists have conducted well over a hundred studies of busing and desegregation, with research focused on several primary questions:

1. Is busing accomplishing its goals of integrating schools, improving the quality of education for minority children, and improving relations between the races?
2. Is busing causing neighborhoods to become more segregated owing to "white flight" from the affected school districts?
3. What are the effects of integration on children's achievement and self-concept?
4. Are attempts at desegregation through busing failing and schools becoming resegregated?

The Big Yellow School Bus has become for many a symbol of conflict.

5. Can busing help accomplish the ultimate goals—equality of opportunity in society? Or are we piling our societal racial problems on a yellow school bus and shutting the door?

Almost three decades have passed since the U.S. Supreme Court rejected voluntary desegregation and required cities to initiate desegregation plans, but the national debate about busing continues. The pattern of segregation is like a patchwork quilt: Some areas have successfully desegregated, while others remain almost exclusively black or white.

Efforts to desegregate can be divided into four periods: first, the 1954 Supreme Court decision; second, the 1968 ruling requiring southern rural schools to adopt desegregation plans; third, in 1973, when desegregation moved from the south to the north and west when Denver was required to rectify segregation; and fourth, the current court cases that are rescinding mandatory busing in some cities. Minority schools are those that have 90 percent or more minority students, and in 1980 one-third of black students attended such schools. "Predominantly" minority schools are those in which 50 percent or more of the students are from minority groups.[60]

The Coleman Report documented the extent of segregation in the nation's public schools and the benefits to children where integration had occurred. With these data, pro-integration forces stepped up efforts to force integration, bringing numerous cases before the courts.

By the mid-1980s there seemed to be a slow but steady reversal of years of desegregation efforts. Still the subject of controversy in both black and white communities, court cases in many cities were in limbo. Polls show opposition to busing declining,[61] but plans ranged from abandoning busing in the elementary grades in Norfolk and Oklahoma City, to increasing efforts to integrate through magnet school programs as in Tampa, Florida, and other areas. Jefferson County in Louisville, Kentucky, even adopted a plan to pay those who volunteer to be bused out of their neighborhoods, so as to keep the plan "voluntary."[62]

In some inner cities, education officials, resigned to the growing segregation of schools, have tried to ameliorate the problem by instigating new, innovative programs for their minority constituents. This has led some to dispute whether "better but segregated" is just a return to "separate but equal."[63]

The Big Yellow School Bus: Attempts to Desegregate by Busing

Busing has been with us for years, bringing children to schools from outlying areas and carrying white and black children past each other's neighborhoods to segregated schools. But used as a tool to implement integration, buses became symbols of a social problem that tore some cities apart throughout the 1970s and that is still an emotional issue today.

However, as the controversy over busing intensified and social scientific studies of the effects of busing began accumulating, the picture was far from clear. To confuse matters further, Coleman came out with the following pronouncement:

> The goals of desegregation have been forgotten in the mad rush to implement what was seen as the Supreme Court's mandate. Those goals had to do with making it possible for every child to attend the school he (or she) wanted to independent of the fact that race precludes [the students] living in a particular area. That doesn't require all schools be racially balanced.[64]

Coleman's "reversal," which some saw as a backing away from the implications of his original 1966 study findings, caused a great deal of controversy and stimulated a flurry of new studies. Social scientists, some of whom had significant impact on the 1954 "separate is not equal" decision, have produced conflicting study results on the effects of busing on segregation. That water is muddy.

Effects of Busing to Desegregate Schools

What happens when minorities and whites go to school together? Are students helped or hurt? Studies have considered the interpersonal relations; the self-esteem of students; the academic achievement and social roles of both black and white students; and "white flight" and the effects on the communities involved. Volumes of information have been collected on each of these; a few examples follow.

Interracial Relations.   In a study of black-white contact in school, Martin Patchen pointed out that peer attitudes and goals are important in promoting interracial friendships. In addition, he found the following:

1. Similarity of values and school behavior between black and white students seem more important for social relations than similarity of socioeconomic status.
2. The friendliest interracial attitudes and behaviors were found among those who attended classes with a black majority.
3. Black students' academic outcomes were affected little by whether they were friends with white schoolmates or by characteristics of white peers, a finding which contradicts Coleman's study finding on the importance of peer characteristics.
4. Academic outcomes tended to be poor for black and white students when they attended classes which did not have a white majority.
5. Academic standards of teachers were more crucial for students' efforts and achievement than the racial composition of the classrooms.[65]

The results of this study have implications for promoting good social relations and high academic achievement in mixed schools.

Self-Esteem, Self-Concept and Achievement.   Self-esteem is important to achievement in school. Black children have been of concern to psychologists for many years because measurements of racial preference have shown that they lack a positive sense of racial identity and self-esteem. In a recent replication of studies conducted since the 1940s, questions about black or white doll preference were asked. "Pick the nice, bad, pretty doll, and the one you'd most like to play with." Sixty-five percent of the African-American children and 75 percent of the white children preferred the white doll.[66]

Studies have found that black students have self-concepts that are the same as or higher than those of white students, except in integrated school settings. Here, black students tend to have lower self-confidence, self-esteem, and levels of aspiration than blacks' in less integrated schools, even though they do better, go to college more often, and are more successful in finding jobs and receiving higher incomes. Desegregation's effects on race relations is problematic since "resegregation" is common in "desegregated classrooms," and lower self-esteem continues.[67]

Student Goals, Aspirations, and Future Prospects. African-American students' educational aspirations surpass those of whites; fewer black students wanted to end their education with high school. Yet there may be a "lack of realism in aspiration," especially among black students whose responses deviate most from actual rates of college-going and completion of high school.[68] Other recent studies confirm the high aspirations of black students. Alejandro Portes and Kenneth Wilson counter the idea of "lack of realism" with the interpretation that the high aspiration of blacks may be responsible for the narrowing educational gap between blacks and whites, and will continue to be useful to blacks in making advancement.[69]

The effect of desegregation on aspirations and achievement has been another area of concern for researchers, especially since there was a decline in African-American college entry from 1977 to 1986 compared with whites. Plans to complete four-year college programs increased for both African-American and white students, but actualization of plans decreased for African-Americans.[70]

The norms that dominate a school influence what students see as possible. Thus, black students in desegregated schools, especially males, have a higher likelihood of attending college and completing more years of schooling than do those from segregated schools. This is probably related to the aspiration and achievement levels at the schools and to opportunities available. Blacks who attend desegregated high schools also get better jobs than those from segregated high schools, and see more chances for promotion.[71]

Concerned with the public policy implications of research on desegregation through busing, the National Institute of Education contracted with seven leading social scientists who had done work in the field and who had found results on various sides of the issue of desegregation and academic achievement. This was especially interesting since the 1977 *Milliken v. Bradley* Supreme Court decision changed the emphasis from desegregation to the performance of African-Americans. The major conclusion summarizing their study stated the following: "Desegregation has small positive effects on black student achievement in reading and no effects on black achievement in mathematics"[72]

In summary, desegregation very seldom lowers the achievement of minorities and quite often raises it. Also, there is virtually no evidence that desegregation lowers the achievement levels of whites. Achievement gains for racial minorities, according to Weinberg,[73] seem most likely when the following conditions are met:

1. There is relatively little racial hostility among students.
2. Teachers and administrators understand and accept minority students, and these characteristics are encouraged by effective in-service programs if necessary.
3. The majority of students in any given classroom are from middle- or upper-level socioeconomic classes.
4. Desegregation occurs within the classroom, not just at the schoolwide level.
5. Rigid ability grouping and tracking do not occur.
6. The community is not inflamed by racial conflict.

Schools transmit status. In research on black females in desegregated classrooms, Linda Grant[74] studied how academic and social roles are passed on through face-to-face interactions. A combination of factors contribute to their place, including teachers' evaluations and behaviors toward students, students' orientations toward teachers, and peer interactions. African-American girls are usually academically at the top in black schools but not in mixed schools, where the balance is on social skills. Their social roles tend to be those of serving others and "maintaining peaceable ties among diverse persons."

The results of numerous studies indicate that achieving the goals of integration and positive race relations will not be easy, but lessons from successful programs provide models for reaching goals. Key in these programs are good human relations within classrooms, in cooperative learning, and in extracurricular activities; fair enforcement of clear rules; and positive involvement of parents and other community members.[75]

"White Flight."   While citizens and policymakers were arguing over the effects of busing, social scientists began debating "white flight." Was busing or the threat of busing causing cities to become more segregated than before because of whites moving out of the cities to avoid school integration?

In 1975, James Coleman released some results of a new study. In it, Coleman concluded that school desegregation contributed to "white flight" from big cities and was fostering resegregation of urban districts. Whites were leaving large and middle-sized cities with high proportions of African-Americans. Coleman and his supporters now seemed to be suggesting less integration and more segregation to remedy "white flight."

Table 4-2 illustrates the change in percentage of minority students in major city schools between 1968 and 1998 (projected). Studies since Coleman's have pointed out other important variables related to "white flight" that account for much of the decline of white population in large urban areas:

1. higher birthrate of minority families, resulting in more school-aged children,
2. economic and class differences in upward mobility to suburbs,
3. new minority families moving into urban areas,

TABLE 4-2 Minority Student Enrollment of the 25 Largest City School Systems: 1968–1998

City	1968 Student Enrollment	1968 Percent Minority	1978 Student Enrollment	1978 Percent Minority	1988 Student Enrollment	1988 Percent Minority	1998 Student[c] Enrollment	1998 Percent[d] Minority
New York City	1,063,787	54.2[c]	998,947	71.3	960,000	79.0	935,000	85
Los Angeles	653,549	42.6[c]	556,236	70.3	594,802	84.4	635,000	92
Chicago	582,274	61.5[c]	494,888	78.5	410,230	87.6	355,000	94
Philadelphia	282,617	61.0	244,723	69.0	191,141	76.5	160,000	81
Detroit	296,097	61.2	220,657	85.8	175,469	95.5	135,000	98
Houston	246,098	46.2	142,553	70.6	190,381	84.5	235,000	94
Dade County (Miami)	232,465	41.3	229,254	62.2	251,100	68.0	275,000	79
Baltimore	192,171	65.1	149,465	77.6	107,250	83.0	90,000	88
Dallas	159,924	38.4	133,289	66.2	131,582	81.8	145,000	91
Cleveland	156,054	57.9	103,627	67.6	73,350	76.0	60,000	85
Washington, D.C.	148,725	93.5	108,903	96.0	88,631	96.5	75,000	99
Milwaukee	130,445	23.9	95,502	49.4[a]	88,832	68.3	80,000	80
San Diego	128,914	21.7	115,007	38.3	117,057	58.6	125,000	70
Memphis	125,813	53.6	113,108	74.0	103,099	78.0	93,000	82
St. Louis	115,582	63.5	72,515	74.8	47,117[e]	80.7	40,000	88
Atlanta	111,227	61.7	76,625	90.5	61,718	93.4	55,000	96

New Orleans	110,783	67.1	88,714	85.8	85,113	92.7	75,000	96
Columbus	110,699	26.0	82,691	36.8	65,160	50.4	55,000	60
Indianapolis	108,587	33.7	73,569	48.2[a]	50,143[e]	50.6	40,000	55
Denver	96,577	33.4	68,830	55.6	58,626	64.8	50,000	72
Boston	94,174	27.1	71,303	60.4	54,765[e]	75.5	45,000	85
Ft. Worth	86,528	32.7	68,224	52.6	68,410	64.4	75,000	74
Albuquerque	79,669	37.7	81,913	46.7[a]	84,783	51.0	85,000	55
San Antonio	79,353	72.9	63,214	87.1	61,246	93.1	70,000	96
Newark	75,960	81.8	65,575	90.7	49,728[e]	92.3	40,000	95
Totals	5,468,072	51.9[b]	4,519,334	71.3[b]	3,863,027	85.8[b]	4,028,000[c]	87.2[b]

[a] By 1980, these school systems (Milwaukee, Albuquerque, and Indianapolis) were more than 50% minority.

[b] Weighted percentage minority based on total population.

[c] Projections include a slight increase in student enrollments, most of it in California and Texas.

[d] Projections are conservative for minority enrollments, based on 50% or less of the growth rate between 1978 and 1988. The assumption is that most white flight has already occurred; however, immigration trends and family size of minorities will affect school enrollments.

[e] From 1968 to 1978 the 25 city school districts were the largest city districts nationwide. By 1988–89, Mobile (69,000), Nashville (63,000), Fresno (65,500), and Tucson (57,000) had replaced St. Louis, Newark, Indianapolis, and Boston in the top 25 list.

Source: Allan C. Ornstein, "Urban Demographics for the 1980s," Education and Urban Society, August 1984, pp. 477–96; reprinted in Ornstein, Allan C., "The Relationship of the School Organization to Minority Students," Peabody Journal of Education, Vol. 66, No. 4, Summer 1991.

4. discrimination against minorities in suburban housing, and
5. differences in "white instability" related to percentage of black concentration.

A recent national study evaluating the impact of school desegregation programs on white public-school enrollment trends finds that, comparing districts that desegregated with those that did not, desegregation enrollment trends are the same. Prior to desegregation enrollments declined, and the largest decline occurred during the year of actual desegregation and increased racial contact. Districts with more than one-third black enrollment experienced twice as much enrollment loss.[76] Specific district-level characteristics associated with reduced white school enrollments include the proportion of African-American pupils in the district, implementation of minor desegregation programs, and substantial proportions of Hispanic pupils.[77] Otherwise, there is little evidence that desegregation promotes resegregation.[78]

Though busing remains controversial, the results seem to weigh in on the positive side if measured in terms of benefit to the most people.

INTEGRATION ATTEMPTS

In addition to busing, other steps have been undertaken to achieve equality. The best known of these are the federally sponsored compensatory education programs. The Elementary and Secondary Education Act was passed in 1965 with the expressed goal of improving the education of poor and minority children. Initially, $1 billion was appropriated, and the figure has continued to grow. Compensatory education programs, funded primarily by federal government agencies, have included programs from preschool to higher education; the following describes several of these programs.

1. *Early childhood education.* Head Start and Follow-Through are the most common programs under this category. Whereas Head Start attempts to help disadvantaged children achieve "readiness" for the first grade, Follow-Through concentrates on sustaining readiness and supplementing in the early grades whatever gains are made by the children who have had a year's experience in Head Start. Only 48 percent of those eligible are enrolled in Head Start.[79]
2. *Bilingual education.* Emphasis and content of these programs vary, but they commonly focus on children whose mother tongue is not English. Spanish-speaking children are the major target groups in these programs. Debate surrounding bilingual education centers in part on the best way to integrate non-English-speakers into American society.[80] How people attain literacy in a second language is influenced by their culture and the social context in which the language training takes place. Effective programs will take this into consideration in developing methods of instruction.[81] One concern among those teaching English as a second language is how long federal funds should support children in bilingual programs; the current limit is five years, but many argue that more time is needed to integrate students into regular classes.[82]
3. *Guidance and counseling programs.* Various social, psychological, and vocational services have been provided for the disadvantaged. Social workers and commu-

nity aides have been involved to help bridge the gap between the school and home.

4. *Higher education.* Special programs in this area include the following: (a) identifying students of college potential early in the secondary schools and enriching their program; (b) accepting special provisions and lower academic requirements for college admission; (c) using admission criteria that allow open enrollment, whereby every high school graduate has the opportunity to attend a two-year or four-year college, thus favoring low academic achievers who might not otherwise be granted admission; (d) transition programs to increase the probability of success for disadvantaged youth once admitted into college; and (e) special scholarships, loans, and jobs based solely on financial need and minority status.[83]

Other programs help schools revise curricula, pay for instructional materials, hire auxiliary personnel for tutoring, and provide adult education programs.

There are other less tangible results of compensatory education. Upward Bound projects provide academic training for high school students with college potential. Statistics have provided mixed results on achievement, but young blacks and whites who have never before met children of the other race live and study together, play together, and make new friendships. The overall atmosphere is cooperative. Many of these programs are held on college campuses where the students not only experience a campus atmosphere but also live in dormitories away from home. These are students who might not have seen college life as a possibility before this experience.

Early evaluation of compensatory education programs showed few long-range academic gains. However, changes in the programs showed more positive results in the 1980s, and we can conclude that compensatory education can have successful results. School achievement in early grades is up for Head Start children, and some programs have long-lasting effects. Factors such as frequent monitoring of students, more time on tasks, and parental involvement were found to be related to success.

On the pessimistic side, some believe that compensatory educational experiences provide a drop in the bucket toward societal change, insufficient to counteract the existing differences. Schools reflect and reinforce prejudices of the outside world, which cannot be equalized by special programs, improved teacher quality, or other patchwork remedies. According to some conflict theorists, increasing resources cannot equalize the inequality built into societies:

> The solution may be to change schooling for all children and to create an educational process that does not preconceive social roles or even clearly define what or how a child must learn. This process would require new kinds of tests to measure results and a different kind of teacher to produce them. Education of this type could allow a child's own stereotypes of himself and others to be destroyed and be replaced by personal relationships. The alternative strategy, then, creates equality among groups of children, by believing that all children are equally acceptable.[84]

Debate over whether all-minority schools with "Afro-centric" curricula have positive or negative outcomes will continue. Some inner-city minority schools offer curricula with African-American cultural content; Milwaukee has been a leader in this area.[85] The structure of schools, hierarchical role structure, student-teacher relations, and student role perception would need to be altered. Whether leaders of societies are willing to make radical changes is questionable.

EDUCATIONAL EXPERIENCE OF OTHER MINORITIES IN THE UNITED STATES

We have spoken so far of minorities in general terms, lumping all groups together, but focusing mainly on African-Americans. There are, however, unique differences in the problems facing specific groups. Children of migrant farm workers have little chance of receiving a consistent or continuous education, though mobile school programs have been set up to move from camp to camp with the migrants. Children whose mother tongue is not English suffer from that "handicap" in the middle-class American school. Special attention is given to this problem in areas with a concentration of non-English-speaking groups—for instance, schools with heavy concentrations of Mexican-Americans and Puerto Rican–Americans often have bilingual facilities. Influxes of Southeast Asian and Cuban refugees are creating a need for special language and culture programs. The adjustment and assimilation process seems to be rapid in communities with lower concentrations of a particular immigrant group, and where communities help with language and cultural adjustment for the newcomers—Laotians, Cambodians, Vietnamese, and others.

Hispanic Students

Today close to half of America's population growth comes from immigration, primarily of Hispanics and Asians. Hispanics are the fastest-growing ethnic group in the United States, increasing from 4.6 percent of public school enrollment in 1966 to an estimated 14 percent in 1996, and 20 percent (projected) by the year 2030. The average age of Hispanics is much younger than whites because of high birth rates and youth immigration. One in three Hispanics is under age 15.[86] Thus, their numbers in schools are large and increasing. Although Spanish-speaking residents are often grouped under the label "Hispanic," there are differences between the groups, with Cubans and other Latin Americans faring well in school compared to whites, and Puerto Ricans and Mexicans faring generally less well.[87]

Two factors stand out concerning Hispanics and schools. First is the issue of increasingly segregated schools, and second is bilingual education. Schools used to be responsive to pressure groups, including immigrants, when authority structures were decentralized and there was more local control; however, where centralization of schools is dominant, there is less flexibility in meeting the special needs of ethnic groups.[88]

Segregation of Hispanic students rose dramatically from 1970 to 1986 from 55 to 70 percent attending predominantly minority schools, and from 23 to 33 percent attending schools that were 90 to 100 percent Hispanic (Table 4-3).[89] The size of the Hispanic student body has increased from one-twentieth to one-tenth of all students in the United States. With the increase in numbers has come an increase in segregation in most states. Forty-four percent of the nation's Hispanic students are in the west, accounting for one-fifth of the students.

The gradually increasing segregation is a result of several factors: As the number of Hispanics in an area grows, their percentage in school grows; many are concentrated in urban areas that are losing white population. Language and cultural barriers may limit interaction with others and encourage concentrations.

Only 30 percent of Hispanic children attend preschool, compared with 40 percent of African-American preschool-aged children and 50 percent of whites. High school dropout rates are more than double that of other groups.[90]

Behaviors that increased the chances of dropping out include cutting classes, suspensions, early dating, being older than classmates, and being female. School factors such as counseling, tracking, changing schools and residential mobility are also important.[91] The causes differed by Hispanic group. However, Mexican-Americans born and raised in the United States often fare as well as their classmates from other backgrounds.[92]

We know that factors such as family background and school culture affect student achievement in schools. Hispanic high school seniors were older than white classmates; received lower grades; were less involved in high school activities; and reported worries over money, family situations, and lack of support for their education.[93] The emphasis on conformity—that is, "parents are to be obeyed and have the right answer"—in families has been found to influence schooling and is associated with lower grades. This pattern has been found in Hispanic families, especially for female students.[94]

TABLE 4-3   Percentage of Hispanic Students in Predominantly Minority and 90 to 100 Percent Minority Schools, 1968–1986

Year	Predominantly Minority	90–100% Minority
1968	54.8	23.1
1970	55.8	23.0
1972	56.6	23.3
1974	57.9	23.9
1976	60.8	24.8
1978	63.1	25.9
1980	68.1	28.8
1986	70	33

Source: Orfield, Gary, *Public School Desegregation in the United States, 1968–1980* (Washington, C.D.: Joint Center for Political Studies, 1983), p. 4. U.S. Department of Education data.

Bilingual Education.   This concentration of Hispanics means that many children are surrounded by Spanish in their schools as well as their homes. The controversial issue of bilingual education has been debated for a number of years, not only for Hispanics but for other minorities as well. Should state and federal governments provide special funds to teach minority children in their own tongues? Will teaching in native tongues help or disadvantage minority children?

Many argue that to teach children in their mother tongues hurts them in the competitive system, and that English facility is crucial to get ahead; but others argue that children are disadvantaged by being taught in a language they do not know, that they wish to retain their cultural language, and that they resent being considered unacceptable the way they are.

Federal funds are being granted primarily to programs that try to "mainstream" bilingual students; some limit special language classes to five years. Yet some studies show that language-minority students instructed in the minority language perform as well in English academic skills as do comparable students instructed totally in English.[95]

Immigrants

Immigration accounts for one-fifth of the population growth in the last decade in the United States.[96] In recent years, the proportion of immigrants from Asia has been close to 50 percent; from Latin America, 35 percent; and from Europe, 10 percent. The 1990 immigration law not only increases by 40 percent those permitted to enter, but allows more Europeans and Africans to enter. This means more and diverse students and faculty from abroad will be entering the U.S. educational system.[97]

Several issues become important in the new immigration wave. Each skilled immigrant who enters a new country is creating a "brain drain" in the country of origin. New immigrants have new and different needs, as we shall see below; schools are often forced to take into account different value systems and behavior patterns.[98] Language barriers create challenges for school districts, and the issue of illegal immigrants raises questions about the rights of this group.[99]

Asian-American Students

The list of Asian-American cultures and languages is huge, making categorization difficult. These immigrants, many political refugees from war-torn lands, range in background from preliterate hill tribes whose children have never held a pencil to children of professional Asians.[100] Over 800,000 Southeast Asian refugees—Vietnamese, Cambodians, Laotians, Hmong— have come to the United States since 1975. They now number over 1 million. California has 40 percent of this population. Because their values differ from Americans' in some key areas that affect education, it is important for educators to be aware of these differences and work with them. For instance, "filial piety," unquestioning loyalty and obedience to parents and other authority figures, means that some parents do not attempt to see teachers; yet it is important to have parental involvement to help children. Several factors are directly related to parent involvement: level of literacy, educational level, and perceptions of what the school expects.[101]

Many Asians come from large, tightly-knit kin groups; the largest groups are Indochinese and Filipino, and of these the Vietnamese children are most successful.[102] Because education is highly valued in many Asian cultures, especially those with a Confucian base, students are cooperative and teachers are held in high esteem. The general attitude is that Asian students are good students, and schools with high percentages of Asian students are good.

Despite language barriers, Asian students as a group outscore other minorities, and sometimes Caucasian students, on standardized examinations.[103] For instance, the average reported math score for Asian-Americans was 16.6, compared with the next highest for whites, 15.5. Language skill scores were high despite the language barrier for many—25.2 for Asian-Americans, compared with 27.8 for whites, and 18.5 for Native Americans.

In one study, Asian students took more courses in foreign languages, mathematics, and natural science than did other students. Asian-American students are also overrepresented in college-preparatory programs and in gifted and talented programs in high schools.

Explanations for the high educational achievement of Chinese-Americans in particular are largely related to the group's traditional family values and views on education, but also to the high aspirations of many Chinese families, especially small-business owners who see education as a channel of intergenerational mobility.[104]

Recent studies, however, are showing that with successive generations in American society, this achievement differential is coming more in line with white student achievement, rather than exceeding it. This may be caused in part by successive strains on the close-knit family and community, and integration into the dominant peer-group value system.

Native American Students

The case of Native Americans is unique. When colonists first settled in the United States, Native Americans spoke over 2,000 different languages, 300 of which are still spoken today. At first, missionaries provided education, but by 1890s education was under government control.[105] The government and churches saw it as their duty to "civilize the Indian population," to eliminate their linguistic and cultural differences. In the early nineteenth century Congress appropriated monies for a "civilization fund." Boarding schools were established to remove children from tribal and family influences and assimilate them into American culture. In 1928, the "Meriam Report"[106] questioned government's "respect for rights of the Indian . . . as a human being living in a free country," criticizing the government policy of boarding schools where 40 percent of Indian children were enrolled. Today, 83 percent of the 300,000 Native American students are in public schools, many in major cities. Others are in tribally contracted schools. Parental involvement is low in non-

Indian-controlled schools, absenteeism is high, and the dropout rate for high school students is 50 percent. Of the 25 percent of high school graduates who go on to attend college, 65 percent leave without degrees.[107]

In order to improve Native American education and create effective schools, educators need to be sensitive to the needs of these children, plan appropriate student-centered curricula, hold high expectations, and maintain good home/school relations. Box 4-2 describes the clash of cultures experienced by Native American children in the traditional school setting. To counter such problems, Choctaw Indians have been given complete control of education programs on a Mississippi reservation, and have built a new, modern school. The result of this local autonomy from the Bureau of Indian Affairs is that education programs are geared toward the needs of the community; more students are attending and staying in school longer.[108]

Gradually policies changed; schools became day schools and bilingual Native American teachers were employed. In 1968, President Johnson urged putting control of Indian schools into Indian hands. For the most part this shift has taken place and it seems unlikely that control will again revert to the Bureau of Indian Affairs.[109]

Special Education Students

Which children can attend regular classrooms, and which should be separated for part or all of their education? This question of school and classroom organization and where handicapped students fit into this environment has stimulated both commentaries and research.

The era of the special education student began with the 1975 passage by Congress of PL 94-142, the Education for All Handicapped Children Act. It stated that all handicapped children must be educated in the "least restrictive environment" possible. More recently, PL 99-457 has been added, requiring school districts to educate all disabled children between the ages of 3 and 21. The interpretation of these laws and how to carry out their intentions have varied greatly, but they brought to the attention of educators and the public the importance of considering each child's special needs and then to design programs suited to them.[110] In order to be classified as disabled, the child must have a health condition or impairment (1) that limits the ability of the child to perform a major life activity, (2) for an extended period of time.

Conditions include learning disabilities; speech, hearing, orthopedic, and visual disabilities; mental retardation; serious emotional disturbance; and other forms of disability.[111] A trend is for fewer students to be classified as mentally retarded, more as learning disabled.[112]

Under the Education for All Handicapped Children Act (PL 94-142), about 4.6 million children from birth through age 21 were served in the 1988–89 school year; most were between 6 and 17. About 30 percent are in regular classes, 38 percent are in resource rooms for special help at least part of the day, and 7 percent are in separate buildings. Services are provided for a variety of students (Figure 4-4). About twice as much money is spent to educate a disabled child as before PL 94-142, yet many are not receiving special

BOX 4-2   *AN INDIAN FATHER'S PLEA*
        by Robert Lake (Medicine Grizzlybear)

Dear Teacher,
I would like to introduce you to my son, Wind-Wolf. He is probably what you would consider a typical Indian kid. He was born and raised on the reservation. He has black hair, dark brown eyes, and an olive complexion. And, like so many Indian children his age, he is shy and quiet in the classroom. He is 5 years old, in kindergarten, and I can't understand why you have already labeled him a "slow learner."

He has already been through quite an education compared with his peers in Western society. He was bonded to his mother and to the Mother Earth in a traditional native childbirth ceremony. And he has been continuously cared for by his mother, father, sisters, cousins, aunts, uncles, grandparents, and extended tribal family since this ceremony.

The traditional Indian baby basket became his "turtle's shell" and served as the first seat for his classroom. It is the same kind of basket our people have used for thousands of years. It is specially designed to provide the child with the kind of knowledge and experience he will need to survive in his culture and environment.

Wind-Wolf was strapped in snugly with a deliberate restriction on his arms and legs. Although Western society may argue this hinders motor-skill development and abstract reasoning, we believe it forces the child to first develop his intuitive faculties, rational intellect, symbolic thinking, and five senses. Wind-Wolf was with his mother constantly, closely bonded physically, as she carried him on her back or held him while breast-feeding. She carried him everywhere she went, and every night he slept with both parents. Because of this, Wind-Wolf's educational setting was not only a "secure" environment, but it was also very colorful, complicated, sensitive, and diverse.

As he grew older, Wind-Wold began to crawl out of the baby basket, develop his motor skills, and explore the world around him. When frightened or sleepy he could always return to the basket, as a turtle withdraws into its shell. Such an inward journey allows one to reflect in privacy on what he has learned and to carry the new knowledge deeply into the unconscious and the soul. Shapes, sizes, colors, texture, sound, smell, feeling, taste, and the learning process are therefore functionally integrated—the physical and spiritual, matter and energy, and conscious and unconscious, individual and social.

It takes a long time to absorb and reflect on these kinds of experiences, so maybe that is why you think my Indian child is a slow learner. His aunts and grandmothers taught him to count and know his numbers while they sorted materials for making abstract designs in native baskets. And he was taught to learn mathematics by counting the sticks we use in our traditional native hand game. So he may be slow in grasping the methods and tools you use in your classroom, ones quite familiar to his white peers, but I hope you will be patient with him. It takes time to adjust to a new cultural system and learn new things. He is not culturally "disadvantaged," but he is culturally "different."

Source: Lake, Robert, "An Indian Father's Plea," *Teacher Magazine,* Vol. 2, September 1990, pp. 48–53. Reprinted with permission from *Teacher Magazine.*

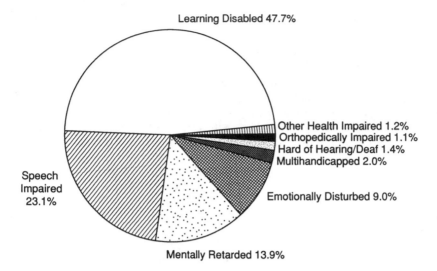

FIGURE 4-4   Students, aged 6–21, receiving services in 1988–89.

Source: "Students, Age 6–21, Receiving Services in 1988–1989," *Teaching Exceptional Children,* Summer 1990, p. 71. Copyright 1990 by the Council for Exceptional Children. Reprinted by permission.

education even now. Part of the problem is assessment: determining whether a child is categorized as learning disabled or if he or she has some other problem.

Most research results show that integration of as many special education students as possible has positive results; students have peer models from whom to learn social skills and competencies.[113] Integrating special education students into classrooms provides models and expectations that are powerful influences on children.

However, low self-esteem is a concern when mainstreaming special education students. Some studies indicate that special education students have lower self-concepts in relation to academic achievement in regular classes than in separate classes.[114] The effects of labeling students for special placement can influence peer-group relations, but the research has not clearly documented whether separate placement or mainstreaming has any detrimental effects.

Of major concern is the number of minority students labeled retarded or learning disabled. It is estimated that 300 percent more Hispanics are represented in this group than the average. Clearly, careful and fair assessment is in order.

Gifted Students

Few think of gifted students as disadvantaged, but if their talents are not being developed, we may argue that they are in a disadvantaged position. Societies need to develop and utilize the talents of their most gifted members, but this presents dilemmas and controversies in democracies: To single out some students for special treatment or training is to give advantage to some and create an elite intelligentsia; yet if ability is considered regardless of other factors, such as family position, we are developing and utilizing needed resources.

Controversy continues when schools consider which students to place in gifted programs. Congressional act PL 95-561 defined "gifted" as including general intellectual ability, specific academic aptitude, creative or productive thinking, leadership, and the visual and performing arts. But who is gifted is actually defined by each program that singles out children for special treatment, and herein lies the controversy (see Box 4-3). Low test scores and institutional discrimination may hide the talents of some students, especially minority students.

We know that gifted students benefit from homogeneous ability grouping. But in the process some students are labeled "better" than others, and a self-fulfilling prophecy can result in which there is added stress and pressure to succeed and play a "significant" role in society.

Although there is lack of agreement on one strategy, many feel that individualized instruction combined with some joint classroom activities with other students may best serve both groups.

Separating students from their peers does occur when students are tracked, sent to special programs or classes, or "pulled out" of classrooms for any purpose. Most useful to gifted and other students are programs that support a variety of learning styles.[115]

BOX 4-3   *THE CASE OF A "DULL" GENIUS*

Perhaps a good place to begin is with the case of a boy who was a slow developer, particularly with respect to language. He did not begin to talk until after his second birthday, and language difficulties persisted for him into adulthood. He did poorly in school; his temper tantrums proved highly disruptive to the classroom. Both his parents and his teachers thought him dull, and neither envisioned much of a future for him.

Finally, however, when he was 14, his parents happened upon a different kind of school pursuing a more holistic approach to education, and a less exclusively linguistically oriented one. The boy blossomed and his world changed. His name was Albert Einstein. His later writings suggest what may well have been the key problem: Even as an adult, Einstein continued—unlike most of us—to think in visual images rather than in words. Thus, he might understandably have found classrooms dealing only in words very hard to handle. (It may be worth noting, however, that the apparent language deficiency that handicapped him as a pupil may have empowered him as a creative genius. It has been said that Einstein's ability to depart from traditional physics may well have been associated with his independence from its concepts, as he dealt instead with visual images.)

Source: Raywid, Mary Anne, "Separate Classes for the Gifted? A Skeptical Look," *Educational Perspectives*, Vol. 26, No. 1, 1989, p. 44.

IMPROVING SCHOOLS FOR MINORITY STUDENTS

The U.S. educational system is built on the premise that *all* should be educated. This responsibility has been entrusted to the federal government, to take an active role in ensuring rights for minorities including African-Americans, Hispanics, immigrants from other countries, women, and other disadvantaged groups.[116] Though there is an impatience to reform education, any new programs need to take all students into account; thus, reforms must come from old and new ideas, from the powerful and not so powerful in society, from the various groups who will be affected.[117] Real change in the situation of minority students will not come about without individual and structural changes involving education, family, and other groups that act to empower minority students rather than disenfranchise them. However, this is a formidable task considering our reluctance to change power relations in society. Many programs only perpetuate the structure as it is and produce little change, in part because they deal only with part of the situation.

Cummins[118] proposes that changing the patterns of interaction in schools to reverse those that prevail in society will help minority students succeed. This involves cultural and linguistic integration into schools, participation of community members in the educational process, appropriate pedagogy, and proper assessment of minority students. Change is needed in the attitudes and orientations of educators who interact on a daily basis with minority students; otherwise, schools will continue to reproduce power relations that characterize the wider society. This is the challenge faced by schools.

Some general conclusions and recommendations that stem from the research, especially that related to "at-risk" students, include the following:

1. Use early intervention strategies to produce the best results.
2. Increase the amount of time students spend "on task" to increase opportunities for learning.
3. Tailor curricula to needs of individual students and work with small groups to increase learning.
4. Have high expectations of students and avoid remedial education, which alienates students and leads to dropping out.
5. Change record-keeping procedures for dropouts, including summer dropouts, so that records of the problem are more accurate.
6. Provide day care for student-parents.
7. Mainsteam potential dropouts and avoid labeling and isolating these students.
8. Be cautious about using vocational education as a holding ground for poor students.
9. Reduce the size of schools to increase interaction.
10. Use mixed-grade classes and cooperative learning in early grades, which can be more effective than traditional methods to increase achievement.[119]

Many researchers and policymakers are experimenting with program ideas such as multicultural education programs, school climates that reduce prejudice, and community and career involvement programs.

Multicultural Education Programs.   These programs help students develop more accurate and sophisticated concepts about the variety of cultural groups that make up American society. Most often proposals involve changing the curriculum, especially social studies and English courses, to represent diversity.[120]

Effective Schools.   Such environments create both positive academic achievement and school climate, and raise students' self-esteem, reduce student alienation and delinquency, encourage interracial friendships, and integrate teaching of racial equality into the school curriculum.[121]

All students are highly involved in extracurricular activities, and teachers display behaviors that favor racial integration and prejudice reduction. Crain suggests what schools can do to improve their social climates:

1. Use in-service training to focus on the central role of the teacher in influencing prejudice reduction and better intergroup relations.
2. Obtain human relations materials for both teaching staff and students.
3. Increase times spent teaching minority groups about their traditions, customs, and history, but not create separate minority-studies classes.
4. Establish human relations committees to deal with school ethnic and racial issues.
5. Involve more students in extracurricular activities.
6. Increase the size of physical education programs.
7. Increase the size of drama, music, and art programs in the school.
8. Hire a person to obtain and distribute instructional materials to other teachers and staff and to develop an audiovisual resources program.[122]

Some argue that the "effective schools movement" helps suburban but not inner-city students because of structural differences between the different schools.[123] However, the ideas of raising expectations and involving parents, which go along with the movement, can only help all students.

Choice Programs.   President Bush's plan for revitalizing education allows parents to choose the kind of school that meets their needs. In theory, this should provide competition and improve schools. However, there are many problems with the concept, as outlined elsewhere.

Cooperative Learning.   This technique involves groups of four to six heterogeneous members who work together toward achieving a goal. This idea stems from the work of Slavin and others at the Center for Social Organization of Schools at Johns Hopkins University.[124] Findings show that cooperative learning positively affects student relationships and achievement.

Attitudes of Schools and Teachers.   Among the many recent reports on how to improve schools is one called *What Works*. It documents a number of findings from research that might result, in the authors' opinions, in effective schools. The general conclusions support our discussion here concerning the need for improving the achievement and attitudes toward minority students. Teachers must communicate high expectations to all of their students; schools need strong educational leadership that emphasizes academic achievement; and parents need to be involved in the education of their children.[125]

Community Involvement. This addresses the need to approach school reform from many angles. Schools alone cannot change the situation for minority students. Involvement of parents and business are two methods of changing the situation. In 1981, a New York City businessman promised sixth graders from his alma mater financial support to attend college if they finished high school. Instead of up to 75 percent dropping out, as was the norm, 83 percent finished high school and many have gone on to college. This one case started a national business-school liaison, the "I Have a Dream Foundation," to help 10,000 children pursue higher education.[126]

Although we may not agree with all of these recommendations, those cited above point again to the importance of considering all aspects of the system in order to bring about change.

The process of stratification pervades education systems both as a reflection of the stratification patterns in the society and its institutions, and as a mechanism to reinforce and perpetuate those patterns within society. From children's homes, neighborhoods, and peer groups to the political and economic systems, children are socialized to play their roles in society and to occupy a place in the societal system. Issues of equal opportunity have been raised, especially by those who feel that they are receiving unfair treatment and unequal chance for the rewards society can offer. Education is a target for these criticisms because of its perceived importance in providing opportunities for a better life. The open systems perspective reminds us that problems of equality go far beyond the effect of schools alone. Schools may be the nursery of integration, but equal access to housing, equal pay for equal work, employment opportunities, and many other areas must also be considered in the fight for equality of opportunity.

In summary, education is still a route to social mobility for many students, but for those locked into minority schools and neighborhoods and those who suffer from other disadvantages, achievement is more of a challenge.

SUMMARY

In this chapter we have continued our discussion of the process of stratification in education and society. The focus was on the problem of sex inequality in schools, followed by discussions of attempts to rectify sexism. Problems facing minority groups in American education included discussions of African-Americans, Native Americans, Hispanics, and Asian-Americans.

I. Sex and Equality of Educational Opportunity

Girls and boys have different school experiences, partly because of differences in expectations, encouragement, and treatment. The sex role socialization process begins at birth, influencing what children feel is appropriate to their sex. Male-female achievement is affected by parental expectations; books, texts, and other materials; TV and media; toys; achievement motivation; sex role models; teacher stereotypes and expectations; and peer group pressures. The reasons for differences in math achievement are discussed, concluding that there is little evidence for biological explanations of differences. Efforts that combat the negative effects of sexism, such as Title IX programs, were discussed.

II. Race and Attempts to Rectify Inequalities in Educational Opportunity

Do schools make a difference? Findings related to this question indicate a complex interaction between family and schools that affects equal opportunity.

Because of inequalities in educational opportunities for minorities, the political and legal systems have intervened. Numerous court cases have ordered school districts to desegregate through busing children. Attempts to bus, the effects of busing and "white flight," self-concept, and achievement were discussed.

III. Integration Attempts

The attempt to rectify inequality through compensatory education programs was described and evaluated.

IV. Educational Experience of Other Minorities in the United States

Hispanic students are the fastest-growing and most segregated group in schools, and also come from many different backgrounds. Whether to teach these students in English or their native language is a controversial subject; which will give them greater opportunity in the future?

Asian-American students do best of the minority groups, whereas Native Americans have perhaps the most difficult time. Other groups, such as special education students, are discussed briefly.

V. Improving Schools for Minority Students

Several programs that attempt to change the situation for minority students are discussed: changing patterns of interaction in schools, multicultural education programs, school climate, and community involvement are examples.

PUTTING SOCIOLOGY TO WORK

1. At your local library randomly select a sample of children's books. Tabulate the following:

	Male	Female
1. Number of stories where main character is:	_____	_____
2. Number of illustrations of:	_____	_____
3. Number of times children are shown:		
a. in active play	_____	_____
b. using initiative	_____	_____

      c. displaying independence   _____ _____
      d. solving problems   _____ _____
      e. earning money   _____ _____
      f. receiving recognition   _____ _____
      g. being inventive   _____ _____
      h. involved in sports   _____ _____
      i. fearful or helpless   _____ _____
      j. receiving help   _____ _____

2. Interview a group of eighth-grade girls, then boys, about their aspirations, future career plans, and high school curriculum plans. Compare these aspirations.

3. Talk with students who are being bused in order to desegregate schools. What are their experiences and feelings both about busing and about its effects on the school, academic work, their own attitudes, and friendships or peer group relations?

4. What are the admissions policies with regard to race and sex for professional schools (medical, law, nursing, dental) in your area?

NOTES

[1] Renzetti, Claire M., and Daniel J. Curran, *Women, Men and Society,* 2nd ed. (Boston: Allyn and Bacon, 1992), Chapter 5.

[2] Richmond-Abbott, Marie, *Masculine and Feminine: Gender Roles over the Life Cycle,* 2nd ed. (New York: McGraw-Hill, 1992), p. 87.

[3] O'Brien, Marion, and Aletha C. Huston, "Development of Sex-Typed Play Behavior in Toddlers," *Developmental Psychology,* Vol. 21, No. 5, 1985, pp. 866–71.

[4] "Dick and Jane as Victims," slide presentation and booklet (Princeton, N.J.: Women on Words and Images, 1988).

[5] Purcell, P., and L. Steward, "Dick and Jane in 1989," *Sex Roles,* Vol. 22, 1990, pp. 177–85.

[6] Richmond-Abbott, *Masculine and Feminine,* pp. 87, 116.

[7] Tavris, Carol, "Boys Trample Girls' Turf," *Los Angeles Times,* May 7, 1990, p. B5.

[8] *History of Miami County, Ohio, 1880* (Chicago: W. H. Beers; reproduction by Unigraphic, Inc., Evansville, Ind., 1973).

[9] Delamont, Sara, *Sex Roles and the Schools* (London: Methuen, 1980).

[10] National Center for Education Statistics, *Digest of Educational Statistics, 1990* (Washington, D.C.: U.S. Department of Education, 1991).

[11] Tannen, Deborah, *You Just Don't Understand: Women and Men in Conversation* (New York: Ballantine Books, 1991); "Teachers' Classroom Strategies Should Recognize That Men and Women Use Language Differently," *The Chronicle of Higher Education,* June 19, 1991, pp. B2–3.

[12] Fiske, Edward B., "Gender Issues in the College Classroom," in Rothenberg, Paula S., ed. *Race, Class, and Gender in the United States,* 2nd ed. (New York: St. Martin's Press, 1992), pp. 52–53.

[13] Lee, Valerie E., and Anthony S. Bryk, "Effects of Single-Sex Secondary Schools on Student Achievement and Attitudes," *Journal of Educational Psychology,* Vol. 78, No. 5, 1986, pp. 381–95.

[14] Lever, J., "Sex Differences in the Complexity of Children's Play and Games," *American Sociological Review,* Vol. 43, 1978, pp. 471–83.

[15] Harragan, Betty, *Games Mother Never Taught You* (New York: Warner, 1977), p. 33.

[16] Richmond-Abbott, *Masculine and Feminine,* p. 74.

[17] "Scholar Whose Ideas of Female Psychology Stir Debate Modifies Theories, Extends Studies to Young Girls" (interview with Carol Gilligan), *The Chronicle of Higher Education,* May 23, 1990, pp. A6, 9.

[18] Harley, Ruth, "Sex-Role Pressures and the Socialization of the Male Child," *Psychological Reports*, No. 5, 1959, pp. 457–68.

[19] Busching, William A., and Michael Farrell, "Gender Differences in the Relationship between Self-Esteem and Grades," paper presented at American Sociological Association meetings, Atlanta, August 1988.

[20] Gaskell, Jane, "Course Enrollment in the High School: The Perspective of Working-Class Females," *Sociology of Education*, Vol. 58, January 1985, pp. 48–59.

[21] American Association of University Women, "The A.A.U.W. Report: How Schools Shortchange Girls" (Annapolis, Md.: A.A.U.W., 1991).

[22] Lawton, Millicent, "Schools' 'Glass Ceiling' Imperils Girls, Study Says," *Education Week*, February 12, 1992, p. 17.

[23] Herzog, A. Regula, "High-School Seniors' Occupational Plans and Values: Trends in Sex Differences 1976 Through 1980," *Sociology of Education*, Vol. 55, 1982, p. 11.

[24] Hooks, Bell, and Cornel West, *Breaking Bread: Insurgent Black Intellectual Life* (Boston: South End Press, 1991), Chapter 9.

[25] National Research Council, *Everybody Counts: A Report to the Nation on the Future of Mathematics Education* (Washington, D.C.: National Academy Press), 1989.

[26] Campbell, Patricia B., "So What Do We Do with the Poor, Non-White Female? Issues of Gender, Race, and Social Class in Mathematics and Equity," *Peabody Journal of Education*, Vol. 66, No. 2, Winter 1989, pp. 95–112.

[27] Wright, Randall L., "Tearing Down the Wall Between Girls and Science," *Principal*, Vol. 71, No. 1, September 1991, pp. 47–48.

[28] Bellisari, Anna, "Male Superiority in Mathematical Aptitude: An Artifact," *Human Organization*, Vol. 48, No. 3, Fall 1989, pp. 273–79.

[29] Baker, David P., and Deborah Perkins Jones, "Creating Gender Differences: A Cross-National Assessment of Gender Inequality and Sex-Differences in Mathematics Performance," unpublished manuscript, 1991.

[30] Moore, Elsie G. J., and A. Wade Smith, "Sex and Race Differences in Mathematics Aptitude: Effects of Schooling," *Sociological Perspectives*, Vol. 29, No. 1, 1986, pp. 77–100.

[31] Vanfossen, Beth E., "Sex Differences in Mathematics Performance: Continuing Evidence," paper presented at American Sociological Association meetings, Chicago, 1987.

[32] Renzetti, Claire M., and Daniel J. Curran, *Women, Men, and Society*, 2nd ed. (Boston: Allyn and Bacon, pp. 23–24).

[33] Tocci, Cynthia M., and George Engelhard, Jr., "Achievement, Parental Support, and Gender Differences in Attitudes Toward Mathematics," *Journal of Educational Research*, Vol. 84, No. 5, May/June 1991, p. 280.

[34] Useem, Elizabeth L., "Student Selection into Course Sequences in Mathematics: The Impact of Parental Involvement and School Policies," *The Journal of Research on Adolescence*, Vol. 1, No. 1, 1991.

[35] Useem, Elizabeth L., "Social Class and Ability Group Placement in Mathematics in the Transition to Seventh Grade: The Role of Parental Involvement," paper presented at American Educational Research Association meetings, Boston, April 1990.

[36] Fennema, Elizabeth, and G. C. Leder (eds.), *Mathematics and Gender* (New York: Teachers College Press, 1990).

[37] Grieb, Aimee, and Jack Easley, "A Primary School Impediment to Mathematical Equity: Case Studies of Rule-Dependent Socialization," *Advances in Motivation and Achievement: Women in Science*, Vol. 2 (Greenwich, Conn.: JAI Press, 1984), pp. 317–62.

[38] Stake, Jayne E., and Jonathan F. Katz, "Teacher-Pupil Relationships in the Elementary School Classroom: Teacher-Gender and Pupil-Gender Differences," *American Educational Research Journal*, Fall 1982, p. 465–71.

[39] Sherman, Julia, "Effects of Biological Factors on Sex-Related Differences in Mathematics Achievement," in L. H. Fox and E. Fennema (eds.), *Women in Mathematics: Research Perspectives for Change* (Washington: D.C.: National Institute of Education, 1977), pp. 181–82.

[40] Benbow, Camilla Persson, and Julian C. Stanley, "Sex Differences in Mathematical Reasoning Ability: More Facts," *Science,* December 2, 1983, pp. 1029–31.

[41] Benbow, Camilla Persson, and Lola L. Minor, "Mathematically Talented Males and Females and Achievement in the High School Sciences," *American Educational Research Journal,* Vol. 23, No. 3, 1986, pp. 425–36.

[42] Sadker, Myra Pollack, and David Miller Sadker, "Sexism in Teacher-Education Texts," *Harvard Educational Review,* Vol. 50. 1980, pp. 36–46.

[43] Mickelson, Roslyn Arlin, and Stephen Samuel Smith, "Education and the Struggle against Race, Class, and Gender Inequality," in Margaret L. Anderson and Patricia Hill Collins, *Race, Class, and Gender: An Anthology* (Belmont, CA.: Wadsworth Publishing Company, 1992), pp. 365–66.

[44] McDill, Edward L., Gary Natriello, Aaron M. Pallas, "The Changing Nature of the Disadvantaged Population: Implications for American Education," paper presented at American Sociological Association meetings, Atlanta, August 1988, p. 5.

[45] Coleman, James S., *Equality and Achievement in Education* (Boulder, Colo.: Westview Press, 1990).

[46] Ornstein, Allan C., "Enrollment Trends in Big-City Schools," *Peabody Journal of Education,* Vol. 66, No. 4, Summer 1991, pp. 65–67.

[47] Zuniga, Robin Etter, "The Road to College: Educational Progress by Race and Ethnicity," study sponsored by Western Interstate Commission for Higher Education and The College Board (Boulder, Colo.: Wiche Publications, 1991).

[48] Wilson, William Julius, *The Truly Disadvantaged: The Inner City, The Underclass, and Public Policy* (Chicago: University of Chicago Press, 1987).

[49] Winkler, Karen J., "Researcher's Examination of California's Poor Latino Population Prompts Debate over the Traditional Definitions of the Underclass," *The Chronicle of Higher Education,* October 10, 1990, p. A5.

[50] *Ibid.*, p. A8.

[51] Coleman, James S., *et al., Equality of Educational Opportunity* (Washington, D.C.: U.S. Department of Education, 1966), p. 54.

[52] Jencks, Christopher, *et al., Inequality: A Reassessment of the Effects of Family and Schooling in America* (New York: Basic Books, 1972).

[53] Aronson, Ronald, "Is Busing the Real Issue?" *Dissent,* Vol. 25, 1978, p. 409.

[54] Jencks, Christopher, *et al., Who Gets Ahead? The Determinants of Economic Success in America* (New York: Basic Books, 1979).

[55] Ornstein, Allan C., and Daniel U. Levine, *An Introduction to the Foundations of Education,* 3rd ed. (Boston: Houghton Mifflin, 1985), p. 398.

[56] Orfield, Gary A., *et al.,* "Status of School Desegregation: The Next Generation," Report to the National School Board Association (Alexandria, VA.: National School Board Association, 1992).

[57] "Court Eases Restrictions on Schools," *Springfield News and Sun,* April 1, 1992, p. 1.

[58] Walsh, Mark, "High Court Eases Federal Guidelines for Desegregation," *Education Week,* April 8, 1992, p. 1.

[59] Jaschik, Scott, "High-Court Ruling Transforms Battles over Desegregation at Colleges in 19 States," *The Chronicle of Higher Education,* July 8, 1992, p. A16.

[60] Orfield, Gary, *Public School Desegregation in the United States, 1968–1980* (Washington, D.C.: Joint Center for Political Studies, 1983), p. 4. U.S. Department of Education data.

[61] Snider, William, "Opposition to Busing Declines, Poll Finds," *Education Week,* January 21, 1987, p. 6.

[62] *Education Week,* October 23, 1991, p. 1.

[63] "Busing—The Next Phase," *Newsweek,* November 17, 1986, p. 60.

[64] Green, Robert L., and Thomas F. Pettigrew, "Urban Desegregation and White Flight: A Response to Coleman," *Phi Delta Kappan,* February 1976, pp. 399–402.

[65] Patchen, Martin, *Black-White Contact in Schools: Its Social and Academic Effects* (West Lafayette, Ind.: Purdue University Press, 1982). Reprinted from *U.S. News & World Report*. Copyright 1978, U.S. News & World Report, Inc.

[66] Talan, Jamie, "After 40 Years, Black Kids Still Lack Strong Racial Identity," *Dayton Daily News*, September 6, 1987, p. 11-E.

[67] Wortman, Paul M., *School Desegregation and Black Achievement: An Integrative Review* (Ann Arbor: University of Michigan Press, 1983), p. 113.

[68] Coleman, *et al., Equality*, pp. 280–81.

[69] Portes, Alejandro, and Kenneth L. Wilson, "Black-White Differences in Educational Attainment," *American Sociological Review*, Vol. 41, 1976, pp. 414–31.

[70] Hauser, Robert M., and Douglas K. Anderson, "Post–High School Plans and Aspirations of Black and White High School Seniors: 1976–1986," *Sociology of Education*, Vol. 64, No. 4, October 1991, p. 272.

[71] McPartland, James M., Russell L. Dawkins, Jomills H. Braddock II, Robert L. Crain, and Jack Strauss, "Three Reports: Effects of Employer Job Placement Decisions, and School Desegregation on Minority and Female Hiring and Occupational Attainment," Report 359, Center for Social Organization of Schools (Baltimore: Johns Hopkins University, July 1985).

[72] *Ibid.*

[73] Weinberg, Mayer, "The Relationship Between School Desegregation and Academic Achievement," *Law and Contemporary Problems*, Vol. 34, p. 269.

[74] Grant, Linda, "Black Females' 'Place' in Desegregated Classrooms," *Sociology of Education*, Vol. 57, April 1984, pp. 98–111.

[75] Crain, Robert L., Rita E. Mahard, and Rita E. Narot, *Making Desegregation Work* (Cambridge, Mass.: Ballinger, 1982).

[76] Wilson, Franklin D., "The Impact of School Desegregation Programs on White Public School Enrollment, 1968–1976," *Sociology of Education*, Vol. 58, July 1985, pp. 137–53.

[77] Ornstein, "Enrollment Trends," p. 66.

[78] Smock, Pamela J., and Franklin D. Wilson, "Desegregation and the Stability of White Enrollments: A School-Level Analysis, 1968–1984," *Sociology of Education*, Vol. 64, October 1991, pp. 278–92.

[79] Waldman, Steven, "The Stingy Politics of Head Start," *Newsweek*, Special Issue, Education: A Consumer's Handbook, Fall/Winter 1990–91, pp. 78–79.

[80] McGroarty, Mary, "The Societal Context of Bilingual Education," *Educational Researcher*, Vol. 21, No. 2, pp. 7–9.

[81] Ferdman, Bernardo M., "Literacy and Cultural Identity," *Harvard Educational Review*, Vol. 60, No. 2, May 1990, p. 201.

[82] Schmidt, Peter, "Department to Reconsider Controversial Bilingual-Ed Rules," *Education Week*, February 5, 1992, p. 21.

[83] Ornstein, Allan *Foundations of Education*, 3rd ed. (Boston: Houghton Mifflin, 1985), pp. 546–48.

[84] Carnoy, Martin, "Is Compensatory Education Possible?" in M. Carnoy, (ed.), *Schooling in a Corporate Society* (New York: David McKay, 1975), pp. 188–89.

[85] Scherer, Marge, "School Snapshot: Focus on African-American Culture," *Educational Leadership*, Vol. 49, No. 4, December 1991/January 1992, p. 17.

[86] Haycock, Kati, and Luis Duany, "Developing the Potential of Latino Students," *Principal*, Vol. 70, No. 3, January 1991, pp. 25–27.

[87] Velez, William, "Why Hispanic Students Fail: Factors Affecting Attrition in High Schools," in Jeanne H. Ballantine, *Schools and Society: A Unified Reader*, 2nd ed. (Mountain View, Calif.: Mayfield Publishing Co., 1989), pp. 380–88.

[88] Fernandez, Ricardo R., and William Velez, "Race, Color, and Language: Changing Schools in Urban America," in Joan W. Moore and Lionel W. Maldonado (eds.), *Urban Affairs Annual Review*, Vol. XXIX (Beverly Hills, Calif.: Sage Publications, June 1985).

[89] Haycock, "Developing the Potential of Latino Students," p. 25.

144   *Sex, Race, and Attempts to Achieve Equality of Educational Opportunity*

National Council of La Raza, "The State of Hispanic Americans 1991: An Overview," National Council of La Raza, 1991.

Velez, William, "High School Attrition Among Hispanic and Non-Hispanic White Youths," *Sociology of Education*, Vol. 62, No. 2, April 1989, pp. 119–33.

"New Findings on Dropout Rates of Mexican-Americans," *Education Week*, January 29, 1986, p. 2.

Cortese, Anthony J., "Family, Culture, and Society: Educational Policy Implications for Mexican-Americans," paper presented at American Sociological Association meetings, Atlanta, August 1988, pp. 4–5.

Valenzuela, Angela, and Sanford M. Dombusch, "Emphasis on Conformity in the Family: The Case of Latinos in the Schools," paper presented at American Sociological Association meetings, Chicago, August 1987.

Cummins, Jim, "Empowering Minority Students: A Framework for Intervention," *Harvard Educational Review*, Vol. 56, No. 1, 1986, pp. 18–35.

Stewart, David W., *Immigration and Education: The Crisis and the Opportunities* (New York: The Free Press/Macmillan Publishing Co., 1992).

Harrington-Lueker, Donna, "Demography as Destiny: Immigration and Schools," *The American School Board Journal*, Vol. 177, May 1990, pp. 16–20.

Stewart, *Immigration and Education*, p. 23.

Suarez-Orozco, Marcelo M., *Central American Refugees and U.S. High Schools: A Psychosocial Study of Motivation and Achievement* (Stanford, Calif.: Stanford University Press, 1989).

Gifford, Bernard R., and Paula Gillett, "Teaching in a Great Age of Immigration," *Social Education*, Vol. 5, No. 3, 1986, pp. 184–88.

Morrow, Robert D., "The Challenge of Southeast Asian Parental Involvement," *Principal*, Vol. 70, No. 3, January 1991, p. 20.

Rumbaut, Ruben G., and Kenji Ima, "The Adaptation of Southeast Asian Refugee Youth: A Comparative Study," Office of Refugee Settlement, U.S. Department of Health and Human Services, December 1987.

So, Alvin Y., "The Math/Reading Gap among Asian American Students: A Function of Nativity, Mother Tongue and SES," *Sociology and Social Research: An International Journal*, Vol. 70, No. 1, 1986, pp. 76–77.

Sanchirico, Andrew, "The Importance of Small-Business Ownership in Chinese-American Educational Achievement," *Sociology of Education*, Vol. 64, October 1991, pp. 293–304.

Chavers, Dean, "Indian Education: Dealing with a Disaster," *Principal*, Vol. 70, No. 3, January 1991, pp. 28–29.

Report of Board of Indian Commissions to Secretary of Interior, 1928, iii + 41p.

Gipp, Gerald E., and Sandra J. Fox, "Promoting Cultural Relevance in American Indian Education," *National Forum*, Vol. 71, Spring 1991, pp. 2–4.

Walker, Reagan, "School Built by Mississippi Indian Tribe 'Breaks New Ground'," *Education Week*, Vol. 10, No. 8, October 24, 1990, p. 11.

Final Report of the Commission on the Higher Education of Minorities (Los Angeles: Higher Education Research Institute, 1982).

Summary of Data on Handicapped Children and Youth, Human Service Research Institute for U.S. Department of Education, December 1985.

Special Education: A Decade of Growth," *Education Week*, November 13, 1985, p. 16.

American Freshman: National Norms for 1986 (Los Angeles: Higher Education Research Institute, 1986).

Wang, Margaret C., Maynard C. Reynolds, and Herbert J. Walberg, "Rethinking Special Education," *Educational Leadership*, September 1986, pp. 26–31.

Ayres, Robert, Eric Cooley, and Cory Dunn, "Self-Concept, Attribution, and Persistence in Learning-Disabled Students," *The Journal of School Psychology*, Vol. 28, No. 2, Summer 1990, pp. 153–62.

Raywid, Mary Anne, "Separate Classes for the Gifted? A Skeptical Look," *Educational Perspectives*, Vol. 26, No. 1, 1989, p. 44.

[116] Willie, Charles V., and Inabeth Miller, *Social Goals and Educational Reform* (New York: Greenwood Press, 1988), Chapter 1.

[117] Coleman, James S., *Equality and Achievement in Education* (Boulder, Colo.: Westview Press, 1990).

[118] Cummins, Jim, "Empowering Minority Students: A Framework for Intervention," *Harvard Educational Review,* Vol. 56, No. 1, 1986, pp. 18–33.

[119] Rodgers, Harrell R., Jr., *Beyond Welfare: New Approaches to the Problem of Poverty in America* (New York: M.E. Sharpe, 1988).

[120] King, Edith W., *Teaching Ethnic and Gender Awareness* (Dubuque, Iowa: Kendall/Hunt, 1990).

[121] Crain, Robert L., Rita E. Mahard, and Ruth E. Narot, *Making Desegregation Work: How Schools Create Social Climates* (Cambridge, Mass.: Ballinger, 1982).

[122] King, Edith W., "Recent Experimental Strategies for Prejudice Reduction in American Schools and Classrooms," *Journal of Curriculum Studies,* Vol. 18, No. 3, 1986, pp. 331–38.

[123] Hammack, Floyd M., "From Grade to Grade: Promotion Policies and At-Risk Youth," in Joan Lakebrink (ed.), *Children at Risk* (Springfield, Ill.: Thomas, 1990).

[124] Slavin, Robert, *Cooperative Learning* (New York: Longman, 1983).

[125] *What Works: Research about Teaching and Learning* (Washington, D.C.: U.S. Department of Education, 1986).

[126] Sommerfeld, Meg, "Asked to 'Dream,' Student Beat the Odds," *Education Week,* April 8, 1992, p. 1.

5

THE SCHOOL
AS AN
ORGANIZATION

It is Monday morning at 8:45. We are entering high school. Sounds of loud voices, banging lockers, and running feet greet us as the big, heavy doors slam behind us. A loud bell clangs through the chaos and students begin disappearing behind closing doors along the corridor. And so another day begins. Each student knows his or her proper place in the system. If a later student enters, disrupting the routine, the school personnel will attempt to socialize this disruptive student into proper behavior and instill the value of punctuality.

There are many ways of looking at the school as an organization; in the following chapter we focus on the role structure of the school, and in Chapter 7 on its informal organization—classroom interactions, teaching and learning processes, and school climate. Here we look at the important structural components of the system, and analyze aspects of the school as a bureaucracy.

Although each school has its own culture and subcultures, complete with legends, heroes, stories, rituals, and ceremonies,[1] certain organizational facts are relevant to any discussion of schools. For instance, the size of a school is correlated with the type of organizational structure and degree of bureaucratization—the larger the school, the higher the degree. The region of the country and a school's setting affect the degree of centralization—many rural schools tend to become more centralized because the area covered is more sparsely populated; community residents in urban school districts often push toward decentralization because of the diverse needs of large populations. The community's class and racial composition influence

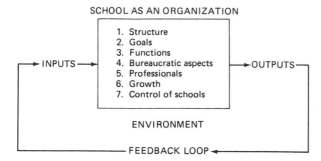

FIGURE 5-1 Open system model of educational organizations.

the school structure and climate, and private or religious schools are affected by other unique variables.

In considering the social structure of the school as an organization, our open system boundaries fall around the school and classroom (Figure 5-1). While the internal structure of the school system is our focus, we must keep in mind that the system is shaped and changed through interaction with the environment. Schools cannot exist independently of the purposes they serve for other structures in society.[2] For instance, when we discuss school goals we are really discussing what is expected of schools by their environments and how that is reflected in school goals. We separate out the school as an organization for analytical purposes only, to understand the whole educational system.

SOCIAL SYSTEM OF THE SCHOOL

According to the functionalist approach, the school system is composed of many distinct subsystems or parts, each with goals; together these parts make up a functioning whole (Figure 5-2). If one of these parts experiences problems or breakdown or does not carry out its functions, other interdependent parts are affected. Each part is dependent on the others for smooth operation, for the materials or resources it needs to function, and even for its existence. As you read, picture a school with which you are familiar.

1. As we enter the school we are directed to the *office*. Here a member of the school staff, usually the secretary, greets us and ascertains our business. The office and its staff act as buffers to protect the rest of the school from interruptions in routine.
2. *Classrooms* take up most of the physical structure of the school; within the classroom, teacher and students are the main occupants. However, the order of the classroom—including seating arrangement, work groups, location, style of leadership, class size, and the types of students—affects the relationships between position holders, and the consequent roles they play. These in turn affect the

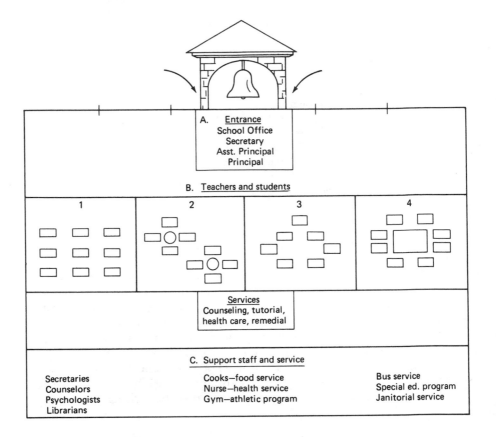

FIGURE 5-2   School system structure and roles.

activities taking place within the classroom. Each classroom has a distinct climate and social structure.

3. *Support services* are necessary for classrooms to function; standard services include food, janitorial, and emergency health services. In addition, most schools have facilities for counseling, special services such as psychological testing or tutoring help, bus service, and library service. This total school system exists in a larger societal context, including the local community with its social class and minority-group compositions and interest groups; the regional setting; the state government with its board of education, legislative bodies, rules, and regulations; and the federal government with its federal regulations and funding. A school system—people, buildings, classrooms, textbooks, and equipment—becomes what it is through interaction with the environment.

GOALS OF THE SCHOOL SYSTEM

Formal goals serve several purposes for social systems. They provide guide-lines for activities of the system and focus the activities of members; they imply social acceptance of the stated purposes and of means to achieve them; and they legitimate the activities of the system. However, there is not always consensus on what goals should receive highest priority or how they should be achieved. Witness the controversies over school curricula: Some adults are concerned that schools are not putting enough emphasis on basic skills, and that too many "frills" (art and music, for example) are included in the program. Others argue that children need exposure to a broad curriculum. Schools are also under pressure from many community members to take on ever greater roles, especially in social service areas such as child-care provision and intervention in personal and family problems.

Thus, goals are constantly being "negotiated" and reconsidered dependent upon the interests of the powerful and the needs of the system. We now consider briefly some goal expectations of various societal sectors that influence official school goals.

Societal and Community Goals

Each society has certain goals for its educational system that, ideally, are put into practice in the schools and classrooms. In homogeneous societies there is often consensus on key goals, and national education programs determine uniform curriculum and materials. But heterogeneous societies have constituencies with competing goals. Functional theorists hold that these goals give direction to the school, helping it to function smoothly and to support the societal system. Conflict theorists argue that these are goals of the dominant

Many educational goals—order, discipline, respect—are carried out within the classroom.

power groups in society, that they represent only one segment of society, and that there are competing and contradictory goals held by other groups in society.

Over time, goals change. The early sociologist Emile Durkheim spoke of the "social organization of the school classroom that fosters the moral habits that bind the national society together."[3] Contemporary writers following Durkheim's lead argue that "the key to schools lies in their moral dimension. Moral qualities are taught not only explicitly in the formal curriculum, but also implicitly in the procedure used, teachers' attitudes, and other nuances in the school."[4] However, the emphasis on *what* morals should be taught changes over time.

The diversity of goals and expectations in the United States is exemplified by the fact that there is little consensus among those who have vested interests in schools—students, social scientists, educators, parents, and politicians, to name a few. This diversity of goals presents a dilemma for school districts beholden to their constituencies.

Each new national administration presents its goals for education. "America 2000: An Education Strategy"[5] is President Bush's plan, drafted by Secretary of Education Lamar Alexander. It calls for six national education goals:

1. Ensure that every child starts school ready to learn.
2. Raise the national high school graduation rate to 90 percent.
3. Ensure that students leaving grades 4, 8, and 12 can show competence in core subjects (English, math, science, history, geography).
4. Make our students first in the world in math and science.
5. Ensure that all our adults are literate and have the skills needed to compete in a global economy and exercise rights of citizenship.
6. Free schools of drugs and violence to encourage learning.

Some of the plans to reach the goals include merit pay for teachers, alternative certification, a longer school year, improved adult literacy programs, choice plans for parents and students, use of federal incentives such as rewards, and national standards and exams. Some schools will be granted money to develop exemplary school programs[6]; however, assessment procedures to determine success of new programs are still in the development stages.

Other plans for reform also receive national attention. Theodore Sizer has influenced education reformers with his call for fewer subjects taught in greater depth and diplomas given only after mastery of certain subjects. "Teachers would teach fewer subjects than they do now, and teach them in greater depth. Students would be active learners. . . ."[7] John Goodlad, another visionary, has stimulated reform at teachers' colleges as well.[8]

Individual communities' expectations of their schools are likely to be far more specific than the general goals of society. For instance, schools in old, small towns in rural areas such as that described in *Elmtown's Youth*[9] are likely to stress hard work, moral orientation, and other major American values.[10] The dominant community members (business leaders, politicians) control school board elections and screen out teachers who might try to change things. Urban schools, because of the heterogeneous population served, have less consensus on academic goals, and spend more energy on "goals" of discipline and control. Suburban schools are likely to focus on success and achievement. Emblems, mottoes, and student handbooks stating very general goals are redefined and operationalized constantly to meet community needs and expectations. It is precisely because of the constant pressures for change that goal statements are kept on a broad and widely acceptable level. This avoids clashes between schools and government, community, family, and other groups. However, vague, general goal statements also mean that schools are vulnerable to influence and pressure from many conflicting interest groups.

School Goals

A broad and generally accepted model for most schools' formal goal statements was developed in 1918 by the National Education Association's Commission on the Reorganization of Secondary Education.[11] It recommended that secondary education should: "Develop in each individual the knowledge, interests, ideals, habits and powers whereby he will find his place and use that place to shape both himself and society toward ever nobler ends." While dated, this statement reflects some basic American values, which ideally should be reflected in local schools: good citizenship, or fitting into society; and individuality, or making one's own way through acceptable means. In reality, these goals are not working for some groups in American society; equal opportunity is far from reality, as we discussed in Chapters 3 and 4.

The stated goals are often different from the operational procedures, which outline what is to happen and what programs are to be carried out in each school. These procedures focus on curricular content, classroom style, and organizational structure to accomplish the stated goals. It is in the school that stated goals must be translated into action; in this process conflicts over purpose and interpretation can arise.

Subsystems within the community and school may have *informal unstated goals* that differ from and perhaps even contradict the stated formal school goals. For instance, teachers may seek to buffer themselves from the community to protect their professional autonomy, while the school may profess an open-door policy toward parents and community members and at the same time put up protective barriers to maintain the school's operational goals and control over the academic program.

Individual Goals

Members of the organization holding different roles are also likely to have different goals. For instance, administrators and teachers desire high-quality education, but they also have personal motivations such as the need for money, prestige, and knowledge. For students school is obligatory; they are required to attend. Their goals will vary depending on individual motivations, ranging from dropping out at 16 to attending college. Parents' goals are sometimes in conflict with school policies, as we shall see.

SCHOOL FUNCTIONS: THE PURPOSES OF THE SCHOOL

The goals just discussed reflect many of the functions or purposes that education serves in society, and that help the society survive. Several manifest (obvious and stated) functions apply to all school systems in industrialized societies, and are often made explicit in goal statements.

Diverse Functions

Since schools include many diverse functions reflecting competing interest groups in communities, it is useful to look at these functions of schooling from differing perspectives within the system—those of society, community, family, and individual student.

For *society,* important school functions are to socialize the young to carry out needed adult roles; keep the young occupied; delay entry to job market; help perpetuate society; socialize into particular societal values, traditions, beliefs; develop skills needed to live in society—reading, writing, responsibility; and select and allocate the young to needed roles, from professionals to laborers.

For the *community and family,* the functions of schools that are seen as important are to formalize socialization experience, especially in formal learning; facilitate peer interaction; structure socialization experience; help meet family goals for successful children; give child more options in the competitive marketplace; and produce young people who will fit into the community.

Individual groups or families in a community may differ on goals because of social class, religious affiliation, or minority status. For individual *students,* school provides an opportunity to get together with peers and engage in sports and other activities. Student attitudes toward and cooperation with adults help socialize them into having acceptable attitudes and behaviors, and provide skills and knowledge for them to fit into society's competitive bureaucracies.

Although these functions overlap, it is also apparent that conflicts may arise between the different groups over the importance of various functions in the school setting.

Unanticipated Consequences of Functions

Each of the functions listed may have both positive and negative outcomes; the intended purpose is not always the only result or even the main result of the process of education. For instance, schools bring age peers together in the classroom and for other school-related activities. This bringing together enables friendship groups or cliques to develop and the youth subculture to flourish; these groups in turn may profoundly influence the school, as we shall see in Chapter 7. Delaying young people's entry into the job market may serve the purpose of keeping more adults employed while the students receive more education, but may also cause strain when overeducated, unemployed young people do reach the job market.

Conflicting Goals and Functions

Controversies occur between community members and the school over issues such as curriculum and school structure. Many families desire to have children learn, but *not* be exposed to ideas that contradict the families' values and teaching. For example, school personnel may consider sex education important for teenagers; some families object to the school's taking over this educational task. The court cases brought by religious groups such as the Amish and fundamentalist Christians are further examples of community-school conflicts.

What to do with early adolescents? This is the question underlying debate about the virtues of middle school structures versus junior high or other organizations. The middle school model—typically grades 6, 7, and 8 or 7 and 8—is winning out and growing in popularity. This period serves as a transition from the nurturing elementary school years to the all-important high school years.[12] It is during the early adolescent period that some students exhibit behaviors that begin a cycle of academic failure and dropping out of school.[13]

Promising programs for middle schools share several features: individualized instruction, evaluation techniques to determine progress, flexible temporary student groupings to avoid labeling of students, attention to different styles of learning, family involvement, student responsibility for learning, extra staff and resources, and staff development.[14] "They are organized in ways that correspond as much as possible to the distinct developmental needs of youngsters between the ages of 10 and 15."[15]

The Carnegie Task Force on Education of Young Adolescents produced a report, *Turning Points: Preparing American Youth for the 21st Century.* Its recommendations address the mismatch between the intellectual and emotional needs of 10- to 15-year-olds and the organization and curriculum of middle grades; for instance, they suggest building on the preoccupation with social relations by forming small work groups, and having an adult available to talk with individual students.[16] The director of the middle school programs at Johns Hopkins University Center for Research on Elementary and Middle Schools suggests a transition team to give guidance and control in moving from elementary to high school.[17]

Individual students face conflicts also. Formal schooling may broaden opportunities and career options, but also narrow freedom to choose what to learn and how to act. Students may gain security and a sense of belonging from peer groups or "youth subcultures" with their own special values; but at the same time these groups' values may contradict school academic programs and family goals such as achievement, successs and conformity.

School goals and functions are carried out within a formal structure. Our next step in understanding the organization is to look at the elements making up the school system.

THE SCHOOL AS AN ORGANIZATION

Sally Joseph is a fifth-grade teacher, popular among students and parents because of the results she achieves in reading and math and her ability to relate to children in her classes. Ms. Joseph has relative autonomy in leading her classroom. How she organizes and presents her materials is primarily her decision, within the parameters of her physical space and the broad goals outlined by the school district. Yet she functions within a larger organizational system that presents her with both opportunities and constraints. Traditionally, sociologists have viewed the situation within which Ms. Joseph works as a bureaucracy, but pointed out the limitations of this model for educational organizations; what works in formal bureaucracies such as business organizations may be dysfunctional in schools. Another recent model views educational systems as "loosely coupled" organizations. We shall look briefly at both of these models for viewing school structures.

The School as a Bureaucracy

Bureaucracy! How often we throw up our hands in disgust at the red tape, forms, impersonal attitudes, and coldness of bureaucracies. How infuriating to be treated as a number! But behind the stereotypic face of bureaucracy are millions of individuals with histories and feelings and experiences like ours. What is it that makes us bristle at the idea of bureaucracy? Bureaucracy is a rational, efficient way of completing tasks and rewarding individuals based on their contributions. However, it can also represent an inefficient, cumbersome organization unresponsive to human needs, as you have perhaps experienced as you waited in line to accomplish some task, such as registering, paying fees, or renewing a drivers license.

By dividing organizations into formal and informal parts (discussed in Chapter 7), we can better understand the working bureaucracy and the way it relates to schools. Although we may complain, bureaucracy serves a vital function in our society. A system based on nepotism and favoritism rather than selection and promotion based on merit, for example, would be certain to raise cries of unfairness and discrimination, and be dysfunctional for society.

A note of caution is necessary in discussing schools as bureaucracies, because schools are unique organizations. As Christopher Hurn indicates, schools are distinctive because they are expected to transmit values, ideals, and shared knowledge; foster cognitive and emotional growth; and sort and select students into different categories—college material, promising, bright, and so forth—with consequences for future adult status. Organizationally, schools are divided into classrooms, the day into periods, and students into groups by grades or performance on examinations.[18] Other bureaucracies have different purposes and structures.

Characteristics of Bureaucracy

The bureaucratic form of organization became prominent in Western Europe and the United States during the Industrial Revolution, primarily because it was seen as the most efficient and rational form for organizations with goals of high productivity and efficiency.

Max Weber, whose ideas were discussed briefly in Chapter 1, described the elements that make up a bureaucratic organization.[19] His typology of characteristics is what is called an "ideal type"; no real organization is going to match these characteristics completely, but it gives a set of characteristics against which to compare real organizations. The italicized points in the following five statements are Weber's characteristics; these are followed by an explanation of their relation to schools, as outlined by David Goslin:

1. an increasingly fine *division of labor*, both at the administrative and teaching levels, together with a concern for allocating personnel to those positions for which they are best suited and a formalization of *recruitment and promotion policies;*
2. the development of an *administrative hierarchy* incorporating a specified chain of command and designated channels of communications;
3. the gradual accumulation of *specific rules of procedure* that cover everything from counseling and guidance to school-wide or system-wide testing programs and requirements concerning topics to be covered in many subjects such as history, civics, and social studies;
4. a de-emphasis of personal relationship between students and teachers and between teachers and administrators, and a consequent reorientation towards more *formalized and affectively neutral role relationships;* and finally
5. an emphasis on the *rationality* of the total organization and the processes going on within the organization. In general, the movement, particularly at the secondary school level, has been in the direction of the rational bureaucratic organization that is typified by most government agencies and many business and industrial firms.[20]
6. In addition to these characteristics discussed by Goslin is Weber's point that *the positions individuals hold in the organization belong to the organization.*

Let us look at each of Weber's characteristics more closely.

Division of Labor, Recruitment, and Promotion Policies. *Division of labor.* Each of us has specific tasks on the job and at home. We become specialists. With busy schedules, efficiency is higher if we each know the tasks for which we are responsible and become adept at carrying these out. One problem that can result from a high degree of specialization is boredom—consider the assembly-line worker who faces eight hours daily at a single monotonous task. However, for a teacher, each student and class is different and challenging, and there is constant updating of material and techniques, and learning new knowledge. This relieves boredom, but the intensity can also cause burnout, a problem discussed in Chapter 6.

Hiring and firing based on competence and skill. The following is taken from a teacher job description of a large school district:

Duties of teachers. Teachers shall take charge of the division of classes assigned to them by the principal. They shall be held responsible for the instruction, progress and discipline of their classes and shall devote themselves exclusively to their duties during school hours. Teachers shall render such assistance in the educational program in and about the buildings as the principal may direct, including parent-interviews, pupil-counseling, corridor, lunchroom, and playground supervision, and attendance at professional staff meetings.[21]

With extensive certification regulations and testing, personnel policies, hiring committees and procedures, and equal opportunity regulations, school personnel must fit pretty clearly into the positions to be filled. Training institutions become important for preparing individuals with the skills and attitudes necessary for the job. Colleges of education are usually accredited by state and regional organizations. They are required to teach the needed job skills and must be run in accordance with federal and state regulations governing education. The colleges also serve as screening points; those who can fit into the system and abide by rules are likely to be passed on to school systems with high recommendations.

Promotion and salary based on merit.   Salary schedules and criteria for promotion are usually formulated by the superintendent's office and approved by the school board. These two are closely linked to the individual's level of education and number of years of service.

Hierarchical System of Authority.   You need spend little time in the halls of learning to know who is boss and who is being bossed. The hierarchy of authority in any bureaucracy can be diagrammed, and most schools fit into the model shown in Figure 5-3. The hierarchy has implications for communication channels in schools. Depending on the position in the hierarchy, a person will receive and give out varying numbers and types of messages. Consider your college classrooms: There is a variety of teaching style, class size, and information flow. One typical pattern is a downward flow of communication from instructor to student. Some educators have suggested that modifying the one-way flow and encouraging more interaction would lessen the alienation created in a large bureaucracy. More teachers would become "facilitators" in the learning process instead of "directors" or one-way communicators.

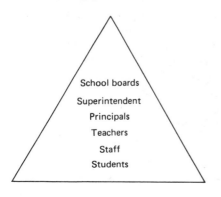

FIGURE 5-3
Hierarchical system of authority in schools.

Part of the individual's responsibilities in the hierarchy involve reciprocal relationships; that is, relating to others in the organization. This is illustrated in the use of names: Teachers call their peers and students by first names, but the reverse is seldom true. The hierarchical differences are acknowledged in the formal title. The formal organization hierarchy chart alone cannot provide an accurate picture of where authority and power lie and how they are used, but it can give a picture of structure and formal relations.

Rules, Regulations, and Procedures.   School begins at 8:40 A.M. Late students must report to the office for a tardy slip. At 8:50 A.M. students move to class period 1. . . . This is the routine set up by rules, but in addition there are rules covering most forms of behavior in the school, including dress, restroom behavior, cafeteria time, recess, after-school activities, bus behavior, and on and on.

Each individual is socialized into the system's rules and regulations. Often these rules are formalized in an orientation program for new students or written in a student or teacher handbook. Most of the expectations, however, are passed on informally through observation, discussion, and ridicule, or by more severe sanctions if rules are violated. Part of our anxiety about entering new situations is the fear of violating the rules, making faux pas, and being singled out for ridicule. Most of us wish to avoid such embarrassment, so we do our utmost to conform.

Bel Kaufman, in her amusing but sobering account of the bureaucracy, provides us with vivid examples of rules and regulations. In Box 5-1 the tasks to be accomplished by the teacher during the homeroom period are outlined.

Formalized and affectively neutral role relationships. Those individuals holding a certain position in the bureaucratic organization are treated alike in a formal, "neutral" manner; at least, that is the way it is supposed to be to avoid favoritism. The following example will sound familiar. The school is giving standardized examinations. All the children will sit in rows in the auditorium, where they are handed a test book and told to "Begin," "Stop," "Now turn the page," "Close your test booklet," and "Pass it to the right."

Exceptions to the rule may cause problems for bureaucracies. Efficiency is based on an assumption of sameness, and each exception takes time and energy from the organizational routine. If an individual is treated "differently" there may be charges of preferential treatment, prejudice, or discrimination. Formalized, impersonal treatment pervades many aspects of our school systems, but where human relations are involved formal relations are constantly being challenged, as we discuss in Chapter 7. Human beings do not fit into simple boxes.

Rationality of the Total Organization.   The tendency in organizational administrations is to seek more efficient means of carrying out functions. Schools are no exception in the attempt to achieve greater efficiency; as the size of schools has grown, so have formalization, specialization, and centralization. However, there are attempts in many districts to decentralize.

BOX 5-1   *PROGRAM FOR TODAY'S HOMEROOM PERIOD*
          (Check Off Each Item Before Leaving Building Today)

- Make out Delaney cards and seating plan
- Take attendance
- Fill out attendance sheets
- Send out absentee cards
- Make out transcripts for transfers
- Make out 3 sets of students' program cards (yellow) from master program card (blue), alphabetize and send to 201
- Make out 5 copies of teacher's program card (white) and send to 211
- Sign transportation cards
- Requisition supplies
- Assign lockers and send names and numbers to 201
- Fill out age-level reports
- Announce and post assembly schedule and assign rows in auditorium
- Announce and post fire, shelter and dispersal drills regulations
- Check last term's book and dental blacklists
- Check library blacklist
- Fill out condition of room report
- Elect class officers
- Urge joining C.O. and begin collecting money
- Appoint room decorations monitor and begin decorating room
- Salute flag (only for non-assembly or Y2 sections)
- Point out the nature and function of homeroom: literally, a room that is a home, where students will find a friendly atmosphere and guidance

Teachers with extra time are to report to the office to assist with activities which demand attention.

Source: *Up the Down Staircase* by Bel Kaufman. © 1964 by Bel Kaufman. Published by Prentice-Hall, Inc., Englewood Cliffs, NJ 07632.

Positions Belong to the Organization.   The retirement dinner was crowded with well-wishers; she has been a popular teacher, well-liked by colleagues and students. She will leave, but the position will be refilled. Next fall a new, younger teacher will fill it, bringing a new personality and different talents to the job.

One thing is clear: The job description belongs to the organization, and carries with it the rights and responsibilities of the position. Each individual hired to fill a role will do so in a unique way, interjecting his or her own personality and experience into the job. We know that Mrs. Jones has a reputation for being a strong disciplinarian, Mr. Smith for being good at teaching math concepts, and so forth. Yet each holds a position with the same job description.

The holder of the position has authority or legitimacy over others only in areas related to the job. Authority is one type of power that gives the role-holder the right to make decisions and exert influence and control in specified areas. In school systems legitimacy is granted on the basis of expertise and position in the hierarchy. Should a teacher overstep the power vested in the position, the teacher's legitimacy could be challenged. For instance, your teacher or professor cannot require you to get a good night's rest, eat a good breakfast, or even spend a certain number of hours outside school working on school-related activities.

When a teacher retires, resigns, or is fired, the replacement assumes the same responsibilities, and allegiance is given to the new position-holder. Personal reasons for allegiance may vary—respect for authority or for the person's expertise, or knowledge that the person holds power in the form of job security, money, or responsibility for giving grades. But the position remains the same.

Professionals are generally highly trained and have more autonomy and freedom in the way they execute their roles than do those lower in the hierarchy. How much freedom they have depends on their reciprocal roles and the setting in which they are working, as discussed in Chapter 6.

Part of learning our roles in an organization involves understanding the reciprocal roles. Symbolic interaction theory explains the process that is constantly taking place in our adjustment to situations as "taking the role of the other." This helps us learn our own roles and their limitations *and* anticipate the mind set of the reciprocal role-holders so that we can understand and meet their expectations. This process is discussed further in Chapter 7.

Development of Schools as Bureaucracies

In the nineteenth century, schools were scattered throughout the country; their size depended on location, but most were small compared with today's inner-city and consolidated rural schools.

> By 1865 systems of common schooling had been established throughout the northern, midwestern and western states. . . . The common schools of the period varied in terms of size, organization and curricula depending on their location. In rural areas, where the majority of Americans lived, one would most likely find the one- or two-room schoolhouse in which a pupil's progress was marked not by annual movement from one grade to the next but by his completion of one text and beginning of the next in the series. Only in larger towns and cities had grading been introduced.[22]

The movement to mass secondary schooling forced a change in early high schools to more modern models. The main changes included the bureaucratization of public education and the move from the innovative structures of individual schools to strong, centralized structures and administration in which teachers had little power.[23]

Since the turn of the century, schools have become larger and increasingly bureaucratic, exhibiting many characteristics close to those presented in Weber's "ideal type" bureaucracy. A result of the changing size of school populations and movement to urban centers has been the centralization and bureaucratization of schools.

In the period from 1938 to the 1980s these small, informal systems were transformed into large, professionally run bureaucratic organizations. In 1940 there were on average 2,437 school districts per state, compared with 318 in 1980, showing enormous consolidation. In 1946 there were 3,841 schools per state, whereas in 1980 the average was 1,736. The average district in 1940 has 216 students, compared with 2,646 in 1980. In the 1940s lay control of schools was strong and few districts could afford superintendents. These moves toward consolidation of school districts resulted in part from modernizing state bureaucracies that pushed for change.[24]

Today there is more than one administrator for every ten teachers, and in some districts less than half of the employees are teachers. The main role of many administrators is to respond to higher administrative levels in the state or federal governments. For enrollments in elementary and secondary schools from 1970 to 2000 see Figure 5-4.

In recent years a number of researchers have pointed out both academic and personal value in small schools; they tend to be more personal and students are more involved in activities. A small but consistent relationship exists between size and disorder as well; small schools are safer, have greater communication and performance feedback, and have more individuals involved in decision making.[25]

Problems in Educational Bureaucracies

Any time we attempt to put people into neat categories to maximize efficiency in an organization, there will be some who do not fit the categories. A further problem is that its very structure as a bureaucracy may cause a school to experience difficulties. Consider the following types of problems:

FIGURE 5-4   Trends in public elementary and secondary school enrollments, 1970–2000.

Source: U.S. Department of Education, National Center for Education Statistics, 1990.

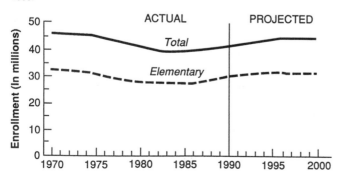

1. Huge enrollments make test scores—rather than in-depth knowledge of a student's family, background, problems, motivations, and other personal characteristics—the major criteria for screening and placement of students, and thus the determinants of their future.

2. The impersonal nature of teacher-student relationships means that students, particularly the disadvantaged, cannot receive the counseling and support, or the exposure to "acceptable" role models that they need to develop a positive self-image.

3. Official rules tend to overcontrol the behavior of school personnel and are difficult to circumvent when problems arise.

4. Teachers and students often feel powerless to change school conditions and so become apathetic about solving problems.

5. Teachers, and particularly administrators, can develop bureaucratic personalities, becoming insecure, overly protective of their jobs, narrowly specialized, less and less concerned with teaching, and inflexible in their daily behavior.[26]

For students who conform to bureaucratic expectations, life in school is most probably rewarding. However, for many students school bureaucracy presents a bewildering and alienating maze through which they must struggle.

Our negative feelings toward bureaucracy come into play as the system gets larger and we are caught up in the rules and regulations and treated as a number being processed. The following extract from *110 Livingston Street* describes the morass in the impersonal system:

> The New York City school system is typical of what social scientists call a "sick bureaucracy"—a term for organizations whose traditions, structure, and operations subvert their stated missions and prevent any flexible accommodation to changing client demands. It has all those characteristics that every large bureaucratic organization has, but they have been instituted and followed to such a degree that they no longer serve their original purpose. Such characteristics as (1) overcentralization, the development of many levels in the chain of command, and an upward orientation of anxious subordinates; (2) vertical and horizontal fragmentation, isolating units from one another and limiting communication and coordination of functions; (3) the consequent development of chauvinism within particular units, reflected in actions to protect and expand their power; (4) the exercise of strong, informal pressure from peers within units to conform to their codes, geared toward political protection and expansion and ignoring the organization's wider goals; (5) compulsive rule following and rule enforcing; (6) the rebellion of lower-level supervisors against headquarters directives; alternating at times with overconformity, as they develop concerns about ratings and promotions; (7) increasing insulation from clients, as internal politics and personal career interests override interests in serving various publics; and (8) the tendency to make decisions in committees, making it difficult to pinpoint responsibility and authority, are the institution's main pathologies.[27]

The larger the system and the more entrenched the bureaucracy, the more there is resistance to change, as illustrated in the description of New York City's school system. A teacher facing 30 or more students each period, six periods a day, is unlikely to recognize an individual student's problem and take time and energy to deal with it. And that individual student may retreat further and further into the faceless mass at the high school, where 5,000 bodies are processed through the system. Various solutions to the impersonal bureaucracy have been proposed: decentralization of decision making; curricular changes; personalizing instruction; and having students more involved in community settings.

Schools as "Loosely Coupled Organizations"

Organizations in which activities and decisions made at one level are not necessarily reflected at other levels have been called "loosely coupled" organizations.[28] School districts have been characterized as having ambiguous goals, unclear "technology," and shifting and uncertain participation, thus making clear decisions to specific problems difficult.[29] Part of this problem comes from the autonomy and physical separation of levels of hierarchy in educational systems. Teachers such as Sally Joseph in our opening example are spatially isolated and professionally autonomous in classrooms.[30] Many teachers who desire autonomy support this situation; actions of administrators may also facilitate teacher autonomy by granting them control over organization of the classroom. Viewing schools as "loosely coupled" may be closer to the reality faced by teachers than trying to understand their behavior and feelings of control over decision making through more traditional theories that focus on bureaucracy, control mechanisms of schools, or environment pressures.[31]

Intervention in classroom teaching may become virtually impossible; therefore, decisions made at administrative levels have little impact on classrooms, and what goes on in classrooms is removed from the school's formal hierarchy, according to this model. Recent research suggests that many administrators spend little time on instructional matters. The dilemma for schools and their administrators is central coordination of educational activities when teachers are largely autonomous.

However, schools are more tightly controlled in some areas. Where administrations control the availability and use of resources, such as funds for materials, units of the educational system may be more dependent on each other. How tightly or loosely coupled the system is also varies by grade and subject matter.[32] The pressure from communities for accountability of school systems and teachers may result in more centralized control, but that raises questions of professional autonomy of teachers, decision-making power, and control.

One example of a loosely coupled educational system can be seen in large metropolitan districts with multiple layers of administration. In contrast, private schools in the United States, such as preparatory and Catholic schools, are more tightly coupled with administrations that are less complex; the result of the latter in most cases is more curricular coherence.[33] Teachers have more sense of control over classroom practice in Catholic schools, which leads to higher levels of satisfaction.[34]

CENTRALIZED VERSUS DECENTRALIZED DECISION MAKING: THE FIGHT OVER CONTROL OF SCHOOLS

In every system there are centers of power where decision making takes place. In the social system of the school, the locus of power has been in contention over the years. The question is whether power should be concentrated in one central place or be distributed among parts of a system—who should make decisions for whom, and at what level.

Centralization of Decision Making

The degree to which decision making is centralized varies with the degree of homogeneity of the people involved in the system and their goals for the system. Centralization of different degrees can be found at the national, state, or local level. Certainly control of the purse strings is one key determinant of the locus of power. For instance, the federal government has garnered increased control in education in recent years by determining areas of national concern and allocating funds for education in those areas.

When federal funds are provided for new programs, new administrators are hired to take on program responsibilities. This increases local educational bureaucracy and administrative expenditures, but without integration of the administrative unit. This phenomenon of increased administrative size without integration has been called "fragmented centralization."[35] More recently, federal grant programs were filtered through state departments of education when the Reagan administration greatly reduced the role of the U.S. federal government in direct funding to districts.

Funds were allocated for accelerated science and math programs in the "Sputnik Era" of the 1950s, when the U.S. government was concerned that the Soviet Union was gaining a technological lead in the space program. More recently, laws have been passed requiring that all disabled children have access to education. However, centralized power and decision making in education are not necessarily representative of the interests and concerns of the local community.

State initiatives in educational reform are now moving to the foreground, spurred on by federal and private foundation commission reports lamenting the condition of education. State boards and commissions of education are recommending new policies at an unprecedented rate: tougher graduation standards, textbook and curricular revisions, longer school days and years, and many other reforms.

Many of these new state initiatives are aimed at the very core of the instructional process—what is taught, how, and by whom—reducing the autonomy and decision making of local boards, administrators, and teachers. However, state representatives argue that until the local units and professional organizations take leadership, someone else must.

Elected or appointed boards of education have the ultimate decision-making power—on paper. In reality, as school districts have become larger and more centralized—and as the issues have become complex, requiring trained experts—school boards have tended to leave issues of educational policy to the school administrators, giving them rubber-stamp approval. They have retained for themselves the role of mediators between the schools and the community. In this way, professional educators have gained more autonomy over policy issues.

Another contender in the "control of education" contest is private organizations such as foundations and industries, which are becoming increasingly involved in educational practice and policy. Some predict that school boards will contract out for more services in coming years, negotiating with the company that can provide the most for the least. This is most likely to occur, and already does, in noninstructional areas such as food and janitorial services, but could also move into instructional services.[36] One example is that of private-company reading programs that promise to raise reading levels of children. In some areas businesses are providing financial support for programs, teacher training, and special programs for children. Privatization could leave the school board more time to deal with educational issues, but it also gives other organizations influence in school decision making and signifies another level of educational control.

Large school districts such as New York City have had major disputes over control of local schools, with concerned local citizens wanting control of staff hiring and firing, building maintenance, construction plans, curriculum and book selection, and budgets.

Decentralization

In Chicago, parents made a grass-roots push for site-based management that resulted in the School Reform Act. Decentralization has different meanings to different people. Often referred to as site-based management, and popular in discussions of educational reform, the idea "involves shifting the initiative in public education from school boards, superintendents, and central administrative offices to individual schools." The idea is to give local schools more responsibility for school operation.[37]

Decentralization is an ambiguous word. Some view decentralization simply as an administrative device—as a shift in administration from the national to the state or city governments, or from central city administrative offices to the local schools. Others insist that decentralization plans should embody a design for meaningful shifts in power from central agencies to local communities, not merely administrative adjustments, and that plans should go beyond education to other crucial areas such as health. Advocates of local control maintain that only such plans can temper the central bureaucratic monopoly on power and decision making.

In a study of major urban and suburban school systems, researchers drew five conclusions about site-based management:

1. Though site-based management focuses on individual schools, it is in fact a reform of the entire school system.
2. Site-based management will lead to real changes at the school level only if it is a school system's basic reform strategy, not just one among several.
3. Site-managed schools are likely to evolve over time and develop distinctive characters, goals, and operating styles.
4. A system of distinctive site-managed schools requires rethinking accountability.
5. The ultimate accountability mechanism for a system of distinctive site-managed schools is parental choice.[38]

Systems moving toward site-based management need to have the support of school boards, teachers' unions, business and community leaders, and parents.

While the power struggles continue, some parents are expressing their concern about the direction of the schools by withdrawing their children altogether and placing them in private schools. Some proposals for alternative structures of education have been realized in New York and elsewhere in the form of alternative and free schools. Parent and student input into decision making is built into the structure of these schools. Critics such as Ivan Illich[39] have recommended total restructuring or "deschooling" of education, as we know it today, in order to change the locus of power. (These alternatives are discussed in Chapter 11, which is concerned with educational alternatives and movements.)

One thing is clear: The issues that fuel locus-of-control fires are still hot. The issue of school control concerns more than just the control of education; for minority groups, it reflects issues of control over life chances.

PROFESSIONALS IN THE EDUCATION SYSTEM

Professionals are characterized by several factors: specialized competences having an intellectual component; strong commitment to a career based on a special competence; monopoly over service offered because of special competence; influence and responsibility in the use of that special competence; and a service orientation to clients. Certain occupations, such as law and medicine, fall clearly into the category of professions.

Because of professionals' commitment to their fellow professionals in the area of expertise, and to their professional organizations, conflict can arise between the principles governing bureaucracies and those governing professionals. Thus, professionals often have a hard time adjusting to bureaucratic structures.

The school system presents a unique situation. Teachers—who make up the majority of staff members—are "marginal professionals," or what has been referred to as "semiprofessionals." They share this not-quite-professional status with nurses, social workers, and librarians, among others. These semiprofessions have some common characteristics: They involve nurturing, helping, and supporting. They also have a preponderance of females. For instance, in 1961, 69 percent of public elementary and secondary schoolteachers in the United States were female; in 1971, 66 percent; and in 1981 and 1983, 67 percent.[40] While more males are entering teaching each year, many are skimmed off for administration, and move into positions of power. Even at secondary school levels, teaching has been characterized as a "feminine role," though there is more of a balance between male and female teachers.

Strong arguments have been made that only predominantly male occupations receive professional status and that predominantly female occupations have failed to do so because of a male political and economic elite that keeps job status and pay of teachers and other semiprofessionals down, and leaves them little autonomy within the bureaucratic system.[41]

Teachers have made claims for professional status in order to gain higher prestige and pay, but they have not yet developed the "teacher subculture" (unity as a group) to claim full professional status.[42] This difficulty stems from several factors related to the nature of teaching. First, teaching was not considered to be "regular" employment in this country until the mid-nineteenth century; it acquired serious occupational status with the advent of free, public education, and the founding, in 1857, of the professional organization, the National Teachers Association (now the National Education Association). However, teachers are still employed by bureaucracies, under the direction of principals, superintendents, and boards of education; this they have generally not contested. Direction, then, comes from the bureaucracy rather than the professional organizations.

Another factor making professional status unclear is the question of membership. Professions have clear qualifications and boundaries for membership, whereas membership in the teaching occupation is much less clearly defined.

Professions have high prestige in occupational rankings. However, teaching is not at the top. In data comparing 60 countries with the United States on occupational prestige rankings, high school teachers ranked 64 and 63.1 out of 90, respectively.[43] National Opinion Research Center data indicate that occupational rankings in general have changed little since the 1920s, when data began to be collected.[44] Nevertheless, teaching is still one of the highest-prestige occupations readily available to women.

While most professions operate on a "fee-for-service" basis, teachers provide a service and cannot afford to lose clients. A further distinction is that professionals have expert training and a command of knowledge not generally possessed by lay persons, and are scrutinized by colleagues, whereas teachers do not possess unique knowledge (though their skills are specialized) and are scrutinized and regulated by the bureaucracy and lay public. To put it bluntly, the knowledge and skills of professionals are seen as vital, but "no one ever died of a split infinitive."[45]

In total bureaucratic settings, teachers must contend with close supervisions, emphasis on rules, and centralization of decision making. These factors of standardization and centralization are alienating to those who want to be considered and treated as professionals. The desire for professional status and frustration in trying to gain recognition, prestige, autonomy, and higher salaries in the bureaucratic setting has led to reform movements, militancy, and unionization, which will be discussed in Chapter 6.

SUMMARY

In this chapter we have discussed the school as an organization, focusing on formal aspects of the internal functioning of schools. In our systems model, the organization represents the actual school or system being considered. For analytical purposes, the focus here is on the internal organization more than on the interaction of the organization with its environment. However, when discussing goals and centralized versus decentralized decision making, the influence of the environment cannot be ignored. The following outline summarizes major topics covered.

I. Social System of the School

The relation of the organization to the systems model was discussed, summarizing structural components of the system such as classrooms and positions.

II. Goals of the School System

School goals serve multiple purposes in helping define the system's activities. Goals are not the product of isolated education systems, but reflect the concerns of the larger society, the community, participants in the school, and individuals.

III. School Functions: The Purpose of the School

Societies have several manifest functions for schools that relate to perpetuation of society. Communities refine these functions to represent their particular needs. Because there are sometimes diverse needs within a community or society, agreement on goals may be difficult to reach and conflict may erupt. Goals also serve certain latent functions—functions that are not stated.

IV. The School as an Organization

Two models of schools organizations are discussed: bureaucracy and loosely coupled. Characteristics of bureaucracy as outlined by Max Weber were discussed:

1. division of labor, recruitment, and promotion policies,
2. hierarchical system of authority,
3. rules, regulations, and procedures,
4. holders of similar positions treated the same, and
5. rationality of the organization.

Problems in using a bureaucratic model in education settings were outlined, and the relationship between growth and bureaucracy was discussed. Loosely coupled organizations reflect activities and decisions that are made at one level, but not necessarily carried out at other levels. Because teachers have autonomy, this model may come close to fitting many schools.

V. Centralized versus Decentralized Decision Making: The Fight over Control of Schools

With the growth of schools has come more centralized decision making. However, challenges from local residents of huge bureaucratic systems have forced school officials to heed demands for greater local representation. One movement for decentralization is site-based management. Another is "choice," discussed in Chapter 3.

VI. Professionals in the Educational System

Professionals present unique challenges for organizations. The semiprofessional status of teaching, male-female composition of the occupation, and conflicts between teachers and the bureaucratic organization were discussed.

PUTTING SOCIOLOGY TO WORK

1. Visit a high school—the one you attended, if possible. In your field notes, indicate examples of Weber's characteristics of bureaucracies and decision-making patterns in the school and classroom.
2. Imagine you are from another culture; describe the school you visit as if you had no familiarity with it. Note the norms (rules, behavior patterns, communication patterns, and so forth) and functioning of the organization.
3. What are your most memorable school experiences? How do they relate to the material in this chapter? (For example, what were your positions in the structure?)
4. Compare your goals for high school when you were a student with your goals for high schools now. What were your goals for college while in high school? Have they changed?
5. Analyze the communication flow in your college classes over a set period of time.

NOTES

[1] Owens, Robert G., "American High School as a Clan: Dynamics of Organization and Leadership," paper presented at American Educational Research Association meetings, Chicago, April 4, 1985.

[2] Katz, F. E., "The School as a Complex Social Organization," *Harvard Educational Review,* Vol. 34, 1964, pp. 428–55.

[3] Durkheim, Emile, *Moral Education* (Glencoe, Ill.: Free Press, 1961).

[4] Corwin, Ronald G., *Education in Crisis: A Sociological Analysis of Schools and Universities in Transition* (New York: Wiley, 1974), p. 13.

[5] *American 2000: An Education Strategy* (Washington, D.C.: U.S. Department of Education, 1991).

[6] Lewis Anne C., "Washington News," *Education Digest*, Vol. 57, No. 4, December 1991, pp. 56–59.

[7] Sizer, Theodore R., *Horace's Compromise:The Dilemma of the American High School* (Boston: Houghton Mifflin, 1985).

[8] Goodlad, John, *A Place Called School* (New York: McGraw-Hill, 1984).

[9] Hollingshead, A. B., *Elmtown's Youth* and *Elmtown Revisited* (New York: Wiley, 1975).

[10] Williams, Robin, *American Society: A Sociological Interpretation* (New York: Alfred A. Knopf, 1970).

[11] Schwartz, Audrey James, *The Schools and Socialization* (New York: Harper & Row, 1975), pp. 108–9.

[12] Vassallo, Philip, "Muddle in the Middle," *The American School Board Journal*, September 1990, p. 26.

[13] Eccles, Jacquelynne S., and Sarah Lord, "What Are We Doing to Early Adolescents? The Impact of Educational Contexts on Early Adolescents," *American Journal of Education*, Vol. 99, No. 4, August 1991, p. 521.

[14] Epstein, Joyce, and Karen Salinas, "New Directions in the Middle Grades," *Childhood Education*, Annual Theme 1991, p. 285.

[15] George, Paul S., et al., *The Middle School and Beyond* (Alexandria, Va.: Association for Supervision and Curriculum Development, 1992), p. 38.

[16] Carnegie Task Force on Education of Young Adolescents. *Turning Points: Preparing American Youth for the 21st Century* (Washington, D.C.: Carnegie Council on Adolescent Development, 1989).

[17] MacIver, Douglas J., and Joyce L. Epstein, "Responsive Education in the Middle Grades: Teacher Teams, Advisory Groups, Remedial Instruction, School Transition Programs, and Report Card Entries," Report No. 46 (Baltimore: Center for Research on Elementary and Middle Schools, The Johns Hopkins University, February 1990).

[18] Hurn, Christopher J., *The Limits and Possibilities of Schooling: An Introduction to Sociology of Education* (Boston: Allyn and Bacon, 1978), p. 218.

[19] Weber, Max, *The Theory of Social and Economic Organization* [Talcott Parsons (ed.), translated by A. M. Henderson and Talcott Parsons] (Glencoe, Ill.: Free Press, 1947).

[20] Goslin, David A., *The School in Contemporary Society* (Glenview, Ill., Scott, Foresman, 1965), p. 133.

[21] Teacher job description, Board of Education, Dayton, Ohio.

[22] Binder, Frederick M., *The Age of the Common School, 1830–1865* (New York: Wiley, 1974), pp. 94–95.

[23] Labaree, David F., *The Making of an American High School: The Credentials Market and the Central High School of Philadelphia* (New Haven, Conn.: Yale University Press, 1988.)

[24] Strang, David, "The Administrative Transformation of American Education: District Consolidation 1938–1980," unpublished manuscript.

[25] *The Safe Schools Study* (Washington, D.C.: National Institute of Education, 1978); and Gottfredson, Denise C., *School Size and School Disorder* (Washington, D.C.: National Institute of Education, February 1986), Government Printing Office Vol. 21, No. 2.

[26] Smith, Ronald W., and Frederick W. Preston, *Sociology: An Introduction*, 2nd ed. (New York: St. Martin's Press, 1982), pp. 395–96.

[27] Rogers, David, *110 Livingston Street: Politics and Bureaucracy in the New York City School System* (New York: Vintage Books, 1969), p. 267.

[28] Weick, Karl E., "Educational Organizations as Loosely Coupled Systems," *Administrative Science Quarterly*, Vol. 21, 1976, pp. 1–19.

[29] Cohen, Michael D., *et al.*, "A Garbage Can Model of Organizational Choice," *Administrative Science Quarterly*, Vol. 17, 1972, pp. 1–25.

[30] Bidwell, Charles E., "The School as a Formal Organization," in James G. March (ed.), *Handbook of Organizations* (Skokie, Ill.: Rand McNally, 1965), pp. 972–1018; and Gamoran, Adam, and Robert Dreeban, "Coupling and Control in Educational Organizations," in Ballan-

tine, Jeanne H., *Schools and Society: A Unified Reader,* 2nd ed. (Mountain View, Calif.: Mayfield, 1989), pp. 119–38.

[31] Leiter, Jeffrey, "The Organizational Context of Teachers' Perceived Control over Decision Making," *Sociological Focus,* Vol. 19, August 1986, pp. 263–83.

[32] Gamoran and Dreeben, "Coupling and Control."

[33] Scott, W. Richard, and John W. Meyer, *Environmental Linkages and Organizational Complexity: Public and Private Schools,* Project Report 84-A16, Institute for Research on Educational Finance and Governance (Stanford, Calif.: Stanford University, July 1984).

[34] Lee, Valerie E., Robert F. Dedrick, and Julia B. Smith, "The Effect of the Social Organization of Schools on Teachers' Efficacy and Satisfaction," *Sociology of Education,* Vol. 64, July 1991, pp. 190–208.

[35] Meyer, John W., W. Richard Scott, and David Strang, *Centralization, Fragmentation, and School District Complexity,* Stanford Policy Institute (Stanford, Calif.: Stanford University, February 1986).

[36] Lieberman, Myron, "Privatization and Public Education," *Phi Delta Kappan,* June 1986, pp. 731–34.

[37] Rist, Marilee C., "Chicago Decentralizes," *The American School Board Journal,* September 1990, p. 21.

[38] Hill, Paul T., and Josephine Bonan, "Site-based Management: Decentralization and Accountability," *Decentralization and Accountability in Public Education* (Santa Monica, Calif.: The Rand Corporation, 1991).

[39] Illich, Ivan, *Deschooling Society* (New York: Harper & Row, 1971).

[40] *The Condition of Education: A Statistical Report* (Washington, D.C.: U.S. Department of Education, 1985), p. 154.

[41] Theodore, Athena (ed.), *The Professional Woman* (Cambridge, Mass.: Schenkman, 1971), p. 4.

[42] Lortie, Dan, "The Partial Professionalization of Elementary Teaching," in Amitai Etzioni (ed.), *The Semi-professions and Their Organization* (Glencoe, Ill.: Free Press, 1969), pp. 15–30.

[43] Tremain, Donald, *Occupational Prestige in Comparative Perspective* (New York: Academic Press, 1977).

[44] National Opinion Research Center, *General Social Surveys, 1972–1983,* Cumulative Codebook (Chicago: National Opinion Research Center, 1983).

[45] Lortie, "The Partial Professionalization of Elementary Teaching."

6

FORMAL SCHOOL STATUSES AND ROLES
"The Way It Spozed to Be"

For each of us there is a degree of discontinuity in the status we hold. We have a high status in one social setting—parent, oldest sibling, supervisor over other workers, president of a club—and low status in other social settings—patient, student, low-guy-on-the-totem-pole at the neighborhood gym.

THE MEANING OF ROLES

Try to recall your experience as a student in elementary and high school. Not only did your status and role change as you progressed through the system, but in some classroom situations your status was higher than in others. Perhaps you won the English composition competition but were unskilled in math; you may have been the fastest runner on the playground but could not spell "whether."

Status and Roles in the System

This section on status and role structure in the organization is a continuation of our discussion of the internal organizational structure of the total system (Figure 6-1). Every organization is made up of an interrelated set of statuses or positions that members of the system occupy. They are needed to carry out duties and meet the goals of the system. Implicit in each position is a set of responsibilities or parts to be played that the individual holding that

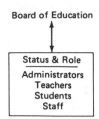

Board of Education

Status & Role

Administrators
Teachers
Students
Staff

FIGURE 6-1
Hierarchy of positions.

position is expected to carry out; these activities make up the role.[1] Sometimes the specific requirements of the position are written out; these represent the ideal for that position. Sometimes positions are only roughly defined, allowing considerable room to determine one's own role behavior. Often, there is a great deal of flexibility in role performance, especially as one moves up in the hierarchy and gains seniority. All individuals bring their own experiences and personalities into the position. Principal A is not identical to principal B, although the job descriptions may be the same.

Role expectations held by those outside the role affect the selection of persons for particular positions. Choices may reflect prevailing stereotypes or norms, such as those that encourage selecting women for elementary-level teaching positions, or selecting males for administrative positions.

The School Organization and Roles

The organizational settings in which we play our roles define and limit ways we behave. For example, David Rogers describes the types of pressures toward centralization in the New York City system: "to guarantee uniform standards across the city, to preserve professional autonomy from outside political interference at the local level, to prevent ethnic separation, and to maintain headquarters control over field officials."[2] As a result of such organizational trends, decision making and autonomy in carrying out one's role are affected. "Most decisions on such matters as curriculum, staffing, budgeting, supplies, construction, and maintenance are made by professionals at central headquarters, several layers removed from the schools themselves."[3]

Centralization is but one organizational factor that affects role performance. However, teachers in autonomous classrooms have a great deal of flexibility in how to implement programs. Among the other factors are rules, especially rigid ones that work against what one sees as important.

Role Expectations and Conflict

Schools function smoothly when people agree on role expectations; however, when they disagree, conflicts arise. A key problem here is that the goals of education are often ambiguous, even contradictory, and not universally shared; this causes confusion in role expectations.

In Chapter 5 we discussed conflicting goals held by various members of the education system. Role expectations also vary depending on one's position in the organization. Role conflict occurs for individuals when their own role expectations are in conflict or cannot be met—for instance, when students must study for exams and carry out family responsibilities—or when one's expectations are in conflict with those of other members of the system—for instance, when teachers differ with parents over course content or discipline techniques. This may happen when definitions of the position and the function the position plays toward meeting system goals differ between members of the organization.

Perspectives on Roles

How roles should be viewed is debatable. From the functionalist perspective, role expectations as defined by the organization are seen as benefiting all by helping to maintain the system. If individuals carry out their roles, the organization functions smoothly. Teachers fill the expectations of their job contract and position description. However, this is not always simple. From the conflict perspective, roles held by some are seen as putting them in advantageous positions for obtaining the scarce resources of society, such as prestige and salary. The more authority there is in a role, the greater the possibility of conflict between that role and roles of those with less authority. For instance, persons in the teacher role have the authority to dominate those in the student role. Conflict theorists might argue that this domination is achieved in subtle ways through the socialization process, which forces students into a subordinate role. Each theoretical approach is useful for analysis and explanation of some situations. In this chapter we focus on the ideal-typical role types, while recognizing that there is great variation in role expectation and performance, depending on the position held in the system and the theoretical approach one uses.

ROLES IN SCHOOLS

Roles locate us in relation to others who hold reciprocal positions, for no role exists in a vacuum. Following the role hierarchy we can now look at the role responsibilities of each of these position-holders and evaluate their relationship to one another.

School Boards: Liaison Between School and Community

It was an exciting meeting! Half the town turned out to express views and hear discussion on the issue of a sex education course in the local middle school. The seventh graders were being shown anatomy videos and contraceptives, and a large group of parents disapproved, arguing that these matters should be dealt with in the home. Other parents took the position that teenagers need all the information they can get, especially with the rising rate of teenage pregnancy. Since the topic is not dealt with in many homes, they felt schools should cover it. Such a situation is typical of the conflicting pressures facing school boards around the country.

Role of the Local School Board.   Theoretically, local school boards have a tremendous amount of power awarded to them by the state. This power stems from the tradition in our country of democratic lay control over schools. It may be known as a board of regents, a board of education, a board of trustees, a board of directors, or a school board. Whatever the label, nearly every school at every level, public or private, has its board.

The National School Boards Association compiled the following list of formal duties representing the legal role of school boards:

1. hiring superintendent, principals, and teachers,
2. determining teachers' salaries and contracts,
3. providing transportation for students,
4. determining the size of the school budgets,
5. deciding the length of the school term,
6. building new schools and facilities,
7. changing school attendance boundaries,
8. selecting textbooks and subjects to be taught, and
9. maintaining school discipline.

In reality, once the board has selected the superintendent, it generally exerts little control over the administration or teaching, but concerns itself with school policy matters.

State boards of education, often appointed by state governors and subject to the approval of legislators, oversee state standards and district policies, especially where state monies are concerned. In recent cases of bankruptcy of large school districts, state boards of education have played major roles in devising new financing plans. While decisions over curriculum are primarily a local matter, states may wield considerable influence in decisions on expenditures and methods for financing schools.

Elected versus Appointed School Boards.   In the United States each state's law determines how board members are to be selected and delegates certain powers to local school boards. Neo-Marxists Samuel Bowles and Herbert Gintis argue that schools serve the interests of those who dominate the economy in a capitalist system.[4] Appointed school board members are more likely than elected members to represent bourgeois interests of those in power, and the potential for conflict with other community interest groups is great.

The New York City Board of Education was a case in point: The appointed board was not very responsive to external political pressures from community groups. In 1969, Rogers saw "the main disadvantage of the system [as being] the privacy with which the board operates, in isolation from large elements of the population and from the city government, and the limited provisions from outside review and control."[5] For instance, in Ocean Hill–Brownsville, one of three experimental decentralization districts in New York City, the appointed school board acted as a buffer for the school administration; was not representative of the diverse communities in the large district; and, according to some, was insensitive to community problems and needs. Today, in New York City, largely thanks to community pressure groups that demanded control of schools, there are 32 community boards *elected* by their districts under a system of decentralization. In Massachusetts the governor has signed into law a bill that allows Boston's mayor to appoint a seven-member panel, a move being challenged by legal groups. Ohio's governor is seeking the same authority.[6]

Composition and Expectations of School Boards.   Boards are composed predominantly of married, white, professional males with graduate degrees; 41 to 50 years of age; and with children in school. Females make up 33.8 percent of board members nationally; African-Americans, 4.6 percent; and Hispanics, 1.4 percent.

Not all agree with conflict theorists that this means that minority views are not represented or influential in decision making. Members of the community likely to serve on the volunteer school boards generally have a genuine interest in the education system, and represent a cross-section of community interests, yet they usually have little orientation or training for their job.

Community members have certain expectations of school boards members. While these may differ depending on the individual's position in the community structure, six role expectations stand out: promote public interest in education; defend community values; hear complaints and grievances; supervise school personnel; conserve resources; and promote individual rights and interests within the school (for one perspective, see Box 6-1).[7]

When the priorities of school board members and the public are compared, the discrepancies represent the boards' concerns with managerial problems and different community and parent concerns.

Factors Affecting Board Decisions.   The most troublesome issues facing board members, according to a national survey, are money issues, such as facilities that need to be renovated, and state mandates. In a classic article, Norman Kerr[8] reported influences that act upon school board members in their attempts to carry out prescribed goals. The following excerpt indicates some of the complex factors affecting a board member's actions.

> The community's demand for representation (1) is an obvious feature of the American school system. . . . The community's ignorance about schools (2) no doubt lies behind the candidates' ignorance, since the latter are more or less typical members of the community with respect to their amount of information. . . . The ignorance of the community about the school board's job promotes the board's alienation from it. . . . Under certain conditions the chief contribution of school boards to the continuance of our educational system is their legitimation of the schools' policies, rather than their representation of the community.[9]

Boards may become mired in controversial issues that prevent them from dealing with long-term planning and policy issues.

BOX 6-1   *SCHOOL BUDGETS AND NATIONAL PRIORITIES*

[I have] the budget report for next year. The bottom line: approximately a million in the red. Just about the cost of one of those Patriot missiles, I reflect. Calculating quickly, I realize that every time one of them exploded, we blew away, in effect, another 43 school teaching positions or another 1,500 classroom computers or another 25 or 30 college educations.

Somehow I find myself wondering what I'd say if I had Secretary of Defense Dick Cheney's ear for a few minutes to present a school board member's ideal budget. Here's the list I come up with—just for our 8,300-student, K–12 district:

- Merge interactive video learning technologies with computer labs in our 16 schools: $120,000.
- Install fully equipped science labs in all 16 high schools: $70,000.
- Hire 40 counselors to track, monitor, and advise every child, K–12: $1.25 million.
- Set up a central computer program for tracking every child, K–12, so kids can't fall through the cracks: $200,000.
- Build a new school to eliminate overcrowding: $5 million.
- Offer every hungry kid a hot breakfast and lunch: $100,000.
- Provide after-school tutoring: $45,000.
- Reduce class sizes by hiring 50 new teachers: $1.5 million.
- Give every teacher a $1,000 tuition grant for professional development: $530,000.
- Grant sabbaticals to prevent burnout and ensure teacher renewal: $1.9 million.
- Expand travel budgets so half of our teachers can attend two professional conferences: $530,000.

"Mr. Secretary," I would say, "this comes to a grand total of $11.2 million. If I have my figures right, sir, this is approximately 1/47th the cost of just one Stealth bomber."

But reality, of course, comes crashing back.

Source: Nolen, Donald M., "Smart Bombs or Smart People?" *The American School Board Journal*, September 1991, p. 52.

Boards are limited in their effectiveness and influence in part because they are caught in the middle between the demands of electors or appointers and the needs of the school. As shown by the example concerning sex education, given at the beginning of the section, some issues faced by school boards are specific, perhaps isolated concerns, causing brief episodes of conflict. Most of the boards' decision making, however, is routine, and interactions are primarily with the PTA, administration, and teachers. School boards cannot be expected to command the knowledge of the professional educators—superintendents, principals, and teachers—and this fact alone limits their decision-making capabilities and control. In fact, boards often rely on the knowledge and expertise of professional educators when making decisions.

School boards have reciprocal relationships with other role-holders in the system. The most direct link is through the superintendent they hire. In selecting this key administrator, boards find communication skills most important.[10] This relationship has been compared to a marriage, and for the most part the partnership is a happy one, with board members supportive of superintendents. However, breaks do occur, primarily because of loss of confidence and faith, and evidence of mismanagement of finances.[11]

This interdependence between roles also affects decision making. Boards receive carefully selected information on issues from teachers and administrators; some issues may be filtered out and never reach the board. Effective superintendents have developed good communication and trust, and possess knowledge that no board member can fully master; by controlling information, they have great influence over board decisions.

Superintendent: Manager of the School System

The office was large. A long table covered with computer printouts and charts took up one side of the room, and a rather large desk faced by two easy chairs stood on the other side. Books on administration matters, teaching, and curriculum were shelved around the walls. As I entered, the superintendent jumped up, looking relieved to take his eyes off the figures for a few minutes and discuss his role. The responsibilities of a superintendent of a small school district include a large number of routine roles: issuing budget reports; engaging in staff negotiations; answering mail and phone calls; meeting with principals, staff, and others; carrying out routine "blessings" on projects; giving symbolic gestures of support and approval; preparing reports for the board, the state, and the federal government; keeping up with new regulations; responding to questions; making staff recommendations. These tasks take up the bulk of time. If time remains, matters such as long-term planning and curriculum evaluation can be considered.

Crises interrupt the normal flow of work, making it difficult to plan a firm schedule. An unexpected shortage of heating fuel, for example, can make it suddenly necessary to arrange for double sessions. Successful superintendents juggle their various constituencies—community groups, the school board, principals, teachers, and staff—with skill. In large districts the responsibilities of the role may be divided between several assistant superintendents, each of whom specializes in an aspect of the role such as curriculum, public relations, and staffing.

Superintendents are usually white males, mostly in mid-career. Of the nation's 15,557 superintendents, 96 percent are men, mostly white, though two-thirds of public school teachers are women.[12] "Sex—more than age, experience, background, or competence—determines the role an individual will hold in education."[13]

Large urban school districts are finding it increasingly difficult to attract superintendent candidates. Why? Some reasons include problems with hostile boards, shabby treatment, negative publicity, graft and corruption, conflicting expectations, and rigid requirements for the job.

The Advent of Administration.   Until the late nineteenth century, boards were responsible for running the schools. With smaller districts and fewer compulsory years of schooling, this was possible. As school systems became increasingly large and complex, a force of trained, full-time professionals took over the day-to-day running of the schools; school boards relied on these hired agents, delegating significant power to them.[14]

The number and specialization of administrators depends largely on the size and complexity of the system. Small districts may have one superintendent who is a generalist, as in the example above; large districts need specialized managerial expertise in such areas as business, legal matters, personnel, public relations, and data processing operations.[15]

Today administrative structures vary directly with the size of the system. The hierarchical design of the huge New York City system is shown in Figure 6-2. It is difficult to give a single description of the responsibilities of an administrator in such a complex system.

Power of the Superintendent.   The actual power of the superintendent to make decisions for the system is related to such diverse factors as the type of community in which the position is held; the school board; baby booms, which cause expanding student populations; teacher strikes; demands by teachers, students, and community for more power and autonomy in decision making; federal guidelines and control; and court orders.[16]

In attempts to exercise power, the superintendent may be faced with conflicting demands from the school board, teachers, and other constituencies. For example, pressures may be brought to bear on superintendents to cut costs radically at the same time that the teachers are demanding higher salaries. The most serious conflicts arise over external policy issues such as school closings and facility construction, whereas the least opposition occurs on internal issues where superintendents have the most technical expertise on matters confined to the school system.[17]

Often the outcome of power conflicts depends on the superintendent's style. Being politically suave in dealing with the board and public and using expertise to its greatest advantage puts the superintendent in a powerful position. As Willard Waller suggests:

> . . . [W]e must conclude that it is a difference in [superintendents'] personal techniques which accounts for this [ability to deal with the school board.] . . . that ability to dominate a school board pleasantly is a greater factor in determining personal advancement in this walk of life than the ability to administer a school system of students and teachers.[18]

Regardless of the distribution and degree of power, the role of superintendent has become a firmly established and essential part of most districts.

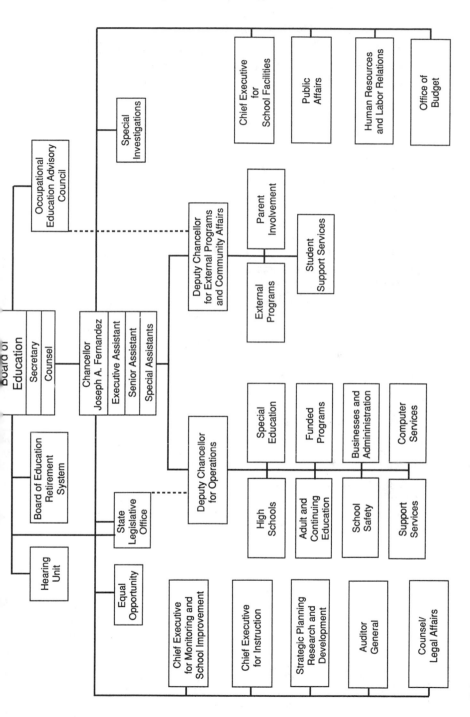

FIGURE 6-2 New York City Public Schools: Table of organization.

Source: New York City Public Schools, Table of Organization, 1991.

179

The Principal: School Boss-in-the-Middle

Principals are managers and coordinators. Their roles include supporting teachers, disciplining students, counseling students and teachers, managing the budget, scheduling classes, and handling the myriad problems that arise each day.

Role of the Principal.   A careful look at these roles shows that most, by definition, involve interaction with another individual:

> There are many in the school system who play roles complementary to that of the principal. These include teachers, supervisors, and the like. The principal cannot perform his own roles without giving some consideration to how his performance might affect or infringe upon the roles of others. In essence, then, these others play an important part in the definition and delineation of his role.[19]

Principals have more direct contact with the public than do superintendents. They hold a position in the middle, and the interests presented to them are often conflicting. They are the bosses of their schools, and as such must make recommendations on hiring and firing of teachers, *and* must give moral support to their teachers. Handling such potentially conflicting responsibilities is not easy. Principals must deal with professionals and technical experts in education, parents and community members, superintendents, and students.

Principals can exert control over the teaching staff by rewarding cooperative teachers and causing less desirable situations for less cooperative ones through such mechanisms as classroom placements, assignments of unruly students, and undesirable scheduling. The principal's expectations of teachers strongly influence their morale, performance, and self-concept; teachers indicate that they are more satisfied with principals who make clear what is expected and reward good work.[20] Nevertheless, teachers claim professional status and the need for autonomy. They expect the principal to stand up for them in situations where their authority is challenged, and sometimes use their collective power to make this clear to the principal,[21] as in cases where grievances are filed or strikes occur.

When we hear little from the principals' offices, things are probably going smoothly. They are busy managing their schools; facilitating the processes taking place; dealing with daily routine, teacher needs, and student concerns; and maintaining good relationships with groups outside the school. Many variables affect the role and expectations of a principal—size of the school and district, a rural or big-city location, and the social class background of the children attending the school. Here is a small-town elementary school principal describing a typical day:

> My day starts before the school opens. I check to make sure the building is in order and teachers in place. When possible, I like to be in the halls to greet students as they come in; seeing them gives me a lift.
> Many of my interactions with teachers take place in the halls where we ex-

change a few words about an issue or problems. Most problems for teachers can
be solved in this way. Of course, we have team leaders' meetings too.

Only severe discipline problems come to me. Most are handled in the classroom. But if students are damaging property or endangering other children or
fighting, then I see them.

There are always the routine things to do—reports, curriculum matters, budgeting, and so forth. But when a parent comes in, I drop everything, if possible,
to see that parent.

I think some people feel we sit behind a desk and shuffle papers, but that's
only the tip of the iceberg. I have a daily plan, but more often than not things
come up which need immediate intervention.[22]

The principals of middle schools or junior high schools face a different
type of situation than elementary principals. Students in the junior high age
group have been described as a "jumble of hormones." They are trying to "get
it all together," and each child copes in a different way. Discipline may become
more of an issue at this level, and kids may be less manageable within the
classroom, thus involving the principal and assistant principal more often.

High school principals have the additional role of preparing students for
the transition to college and the work world. High school principals and
school districts are being held accountable for the students they pass from
grade to grade and graduate. Several legal suits have been brought against
school systems on the grounds that they graduate students who cannot read or
write at a 12th-grade or even tenth-grade level. Competency testing of students and testing of new teachers is also being carried out in some states and
school districts. These issues are discussed further in Chapter 11. Also of
particular concern for high school principals are curriculum and counseling.
Yet some suggest that expecting principals to be effective managers and instructional leaders is unrealistic, and that these tasks should not fall to the
same person.[23]

School administrators spend part of each day dealing with the unexpected; this includes disasters such as bus accidents, suicides or murders,
natural disasters such as tornadoes, bomb threats, and weapons. Having a
plan in place to deal with tragedy is the recommendation of *When Disaster
Strikes*. Combining knowledge from the social sciences to deal with problems
can prevent more damage. Knowing what to expect in the way of reactions
and grief and having the mechanisms in place are important steps.[24]

Over one-fifth of students indicate that they do not feel safe at school,
usually because of threats from bullies and weapons,[25] and many others are
afraid of attack going to and from school, usually from street gangs.

Surprisingly, there have been few studies of the principal, but those that
have been done provide us with information on the characteristics of principals. Table 6-1 shows the results of one study.

Female administrators, though few in number, bring different leadership, communication, and decision-making styles and skills to school leadership.[26] They spend more time on instructional leadership activities such as
"interacting with teachers as a resource provider, instructional resource, com-

TABLE 6-1   Principals in Public Schools

Selected Characteristics	Total[1]	PERCENT OF PRINCIPALS, BY HIGHEST DEGREE EARNED[2]				AVERAGE YEARS OF EXPERIENCE		
		Bachelor's	Master's	Education Specialist	Doctor's & First Professional	As a Principal	Other School Position	As a Teacher
Sex								
Men	58,585	1.9	55.7	34.3	8.2	11.2	3.6	9.0
Women	19,118	3.9	46.6	37.8	11.3	6.1	4.0	12.3
Race/ethnicity								
White[3]	69,048	2.5	53.7	35.0	8.6	10.1	3.6	9.6
Black[3]	6,696	(5)	51.4	36.9	11.5	8.8	4.8	11.8
Hispanic[4]	2,483	(5)	54.2	30.2	(5)	6.6	5.4	9.8
Asian or Pacific Islander	434	(5)	52.8	33.4	(5)	7.7	4.5	10.8
American Indian or Alaskan native[3]	821	(5)	51.2	(5)	(5)	9.9	4.6	9.1
Age								
Under 40	14,430	3.6	54.7	33.7	(5)	4.3	2.5	7.8
40 to 44	17,755	2.0	49.0	39.7	9.2	6.8	3.7	9.2
45 to 49	16,408	0.0	52.8	35.8	9.6	10.0	4.0	10.3
50 to 54	14,936	2.2	56.6	33.2	7.9	13.2	4.3	10.6
55 or over	13,891	2.7	55.9	31.7	9.6	16.5	4.1	11.4
Total	**77,890**	**2.4**	**53.4**	**35.1**	**8.9**	**10.0**	**3.8**	**9.8**

Note: Details may not add to 100 percent because of rounding and survey item nonresponse.

[1] Total differs from data appearing in other tables because of varying survey processing procedures and time period coverages.

[2] Percentages for those with less than a bachelor's degree are not shown.

[3] Includes persons of Hispanic origin.

[4] Persons of Hispanic origin may be of any race.

[5] Too few sample cases (fewer than 30) for a reliable estimate.

Source: National Center for Education Statistics; reprinted in *Education Week,* February 5, 1992, p. 7.

municator, and visible presence."[27] Female principals spend 38.4 percent of their time on instructional leadership, while males spend 21.8 percent.[28,29]

This style of leadership is compatible with the characteristics of effective leadership behavior in schools:

- Emphasize achievement and convey to teachers their commitment to fostering academic success.
- Set instructional strategies and accept responsibility for facilitating their accomplishment.
- Provide an orderly atmosphere and ensure that the school's climate is conducive to learning.
- Frequently evaluate student progress in light of performance expectations.
- Coordinate instructional programs consistent with the overall goals of the program and the school.
- Support teachers with regard to staff development.[30]

"The ideal principal must now cultivate all the virtues that have always been expected of the ideal woman,"[31] but also act with assertiveness, strength, controlled emotions, and independence. This requires women in leadership positions to practice androgynous behavior, drawing on stereotyped male and female behaviors that meet the needs of the situation.[32]

Female administrators do not always receive the same treatment as their male counterparts. In a study of independent school salary schedules, women heads of schools received 15 percent less than the average salary earned by men. In addition, their benefits, such as free housing, pensions, and other factors, did not measure up to those of men in the same positions (see Table 6-2 for salaries of school personnel in general).[33]

The Principal's Power and Effect on Change in the School. Principals and other administrators have power to influence school effectiveness through their leadership and interactions. Jean Wellisch found that, in schools that succeeded in raising student achievement, the administrators:

- were more concerned with instruction,
- communicated their views about instruction,
- took responsibility for decisions relating to instruction,
- coordinated instructional programs, and
- emphasized academic standards.[34]

In the successful schools, principals met with teachers regularly, asked for suggestions in curriculum, and gave teachers information concerning effectiveness. Principals rarely act alone. Those concerned with effective schools argue that principals should spend up to 75 percent of their time improving instruction, but this seldom happens with the many responsibilities that face the principal.[35]

Teachers' primary responsibility is in the classroom; they feel less successful in their efforts at schoolwide decision making, which intensifies teachers'

TABLE 6-2   Average of Salaries Paid Personnel in Selected
Professional Positions in All Reporting School
Systems, 1990–91

Position	Average Annual Salary
Superintendents (contract salary)	$79,874
Assistant superintendents	66,553
Subject area supervisors	48,366
Principals	
Elementary school	51,453
Middle school	55,083
High school	59,106
Assistant principals	
Elementary school	43,548
Middle school	46,981
High school	49,009
Classroom teachers	32,915

Source: Robinson, Glen, and Melinda Brown, "Principals' Salaries and
Benefits, 1990–1991," *Principal,* May 1991, Table 1, p. 53.

autonomous "culture of teaching" and acts as an obstacle to change and innovation proposed by principals.[36]

While the principal has the power to run the school, he or she is also
constrained by the environment: the superintendent and board, teacher
unions, student demands, and state and local regulations. Principals are involved in decision making in many areas but share the responsibility with
those holding reciprocal roles.

Teachers: The Front Line

Looking back at our school days, the persons we remember most fondly
or with the greatest dislike are teachers. Occasionally a principal makes an
imprint in our memory, or a counselor influences our decisions. But the
teacher is the one with whom we have the most contact, and his or her classroom is where we lay ourselves open for scrutiny, praise, and criticism. Often
not even our parents spend as much time with us and understand our capabilities as well as our teachers do.

Why Teachers Teach.   Why do teachers choose to become teachers? Most
teachers indicated one or more of the following reasons: the desire to work
with young people and impart knowledge; love of children; desire to do
something valuable for society; interest and excitement about teaching and
subject-matter field; security and financial rewards; and short working days
and long vacations.[37]

Characteristics of Teachers.   Approximately 2,700,000 Americans are
employed as professional educators in American primary and secondary
schools. Characteristics of teachers are outlined in Table 6-3. These individu-

TABLE 6-3 Selected Characteristics of Teachers, School Year 1987–88

| | TEACHERS | | | |
| | Public School | Percent of Total | Private School | Percent of Total |
Characteristics				
Sex				
Male	681,161	29.3	66,785	21.7
Female	1,631,168	70.2	239,975	78.1
Not reported	10,875	0.5	370	0.1
Race/ethnicity				
American Indian, Alaskan native	24,670	1.1	2,827	0.9
Asian or Pacific Islander	21,307	0.9	3,987	1.3
Black	190,018	8.2	7,165	2.3
White	2,050,400	88.3	288,432	93.9
Not reported	36,810	1.6	4,719	1.5
Ethnic origin*				
Hispanic	67,084	2.9	8,569	2.8
Non-Hispanic	2,207,746	95.0	292,566	95.3
Not reported	48,374	2.1	5,995	2.0
Age				
Under 40	1,124,105	48.4	170,130	55.4
40 to 49	752,301	32.4	83,021	27.0
50 or older	416,857	17.9	49,378	16.1
Not reported	29,941	1.3	4,601	1.5
Total	2,323,204	100.0	307,131	100.0

* Hispanics and non-Hispanics may be of any race.

Note: Columns may not add to totals due to rounding or item nonresponse. Cell entries may be underestimated due to item nonresponse.

Source: U.S. Department of Education, National Center for Education Statistics, Schools and Staffing Survey, *Characteristics of Public and Private School Teachers, 1987–88*, 1990; and The Teaching Force, Fall 1970–92, *Education Week*, September 23, 1992, p. 7.

als have chosen to devote their skills and energy to transforming American young people into educated adults.

An individual writing "teacher" in the occupation blank on a form would generally fall into the category "middle class." Teaching has been seen by many as an easy route to upward mobility from lower classes; not only is the cost of training for this profession lower than for many others, but the occupation is a familiar one. We all "understand" teachers.

In the 1960s there was a shortage of teachers brought about by the rapid increase in the number of school-aged children from the baby boom. When teacher shortages occur, they are often accompanied by a drop in ability level of new teachers, as measured by standardized tests.[38] However, as the 1970s came to an end, over 600,000 teachers were labeled "surplus" and most could not find jobs. The predicted job market low passed in 1983, and the situation for teachers is improving. By the mid-1980s shortages existed in mathematics, physics, chemistry, computer programming, and some fields of education. It is

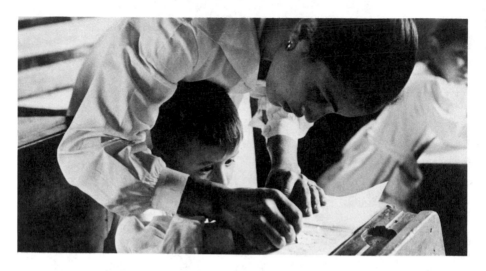

The teacher role involves close work with students.

expected that more than 200,000 new teachers will be needed each year between 1990 and 2000;[39] the Department of Education predicted shortfalls of 394,000 teachers between 1985 and 1993 (Figure 6-3).

However, not all agree with this dire assessment, pointing out the reservoir of unemployed teachers, certified during the slump, estimated at 636,000; the increase in applicants to teachers' colleges; and the rising salaries of starting teachers, which will attract some professionals from other fields. Supply and demand forces, it is argued, will balance the equation. One of the most difficult tasks for school administrators is to predict the population fluctuations in their districts and prepare for them.

At one time teaching was one of the few career paths accessible to highly qualified women and minorities. In 1970, 36 percent of women college graduates were headed for teaching; by 1980, that number was only 18 percent.[40] With the widening career opportunities come fewer entering the teaching profession and a loss of one more talent pool.[41] For instance, among teachers who scored in the top 10 percent on the National Teacher Examination in North Carolina, two-thirds had left teaching within seven years.

It is no secret that there is a heavy preponderance of women in teaching's lower levels—both grade level and professional rank. This fact has not been overlooked by researchers or feminists. In elementary schools, 86.2 percent of teachers are female and 13.8 percent are male. Forty-two percent of the male teachers and 18 percent of the female teachers teach at the senior high school level.[42] In high schools, 44 percent of teachers are male and 56 percent female. Between 80 and 90 percent of primary school teachers are female, a figure that has held steady since the early 1900s. The figure for secondary school female teachers has fluctuated from 47 to 65 percent in the same period.

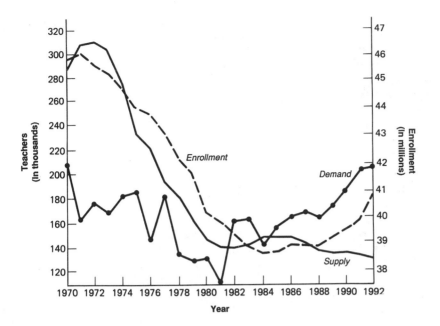

FIGURE 6-3   Supply and demand for teachers, 1970–92.

Sources: U.S. Department of Education, National Center for Education Statistics, *Statistics of Public Elementary and Secondary School Systems,* various years; *Projections of Education Statistics to 1992–93,* 1985; and *The Condition of Education 1985,* 1985.

Overall, about 75 percent of all public school teachers in 1988 were female.[43] Males predominate as school administrators and superintendents.

Women who do move into administration do so slowly, spending many more years in the classroom than men. There appear to be two overlapping reasons for this imbalance: convenience and discrimination. For women, teaching has been more available and acceptable than other professions; the accessibility of education is greater than many other fields; time and cost of getting a degree are less in education than in some other fields; the hours, vacations, and schedule are compatible with home and children; the job can be pursued in many locations; and for many, the "nurturing" experience coincides with life experiences. Discrimination is a factor in the imbalance because many other career paths are closed to women at the training or entrance level. Men have a greater variety of career opportunities available; many male teachers make the teaching career decision after realizing that other goals are unattainable. Yet as more jobs become available, fewer highly qualified women and minorities choose education.

Of all teachers, unmarried women have the lowest turnover rates and spend the most time on the job. The trend for married women teachers is to stay on the job rather than to view it as temporary employment before starting a family.[44] Commitment to teaching may be low if teaching is seen as merely a stepping stone to educational administration, which brings higher salaries, more power, and more prestige. When teachers do leave their jobs, the majority assume other teaching positions.[45]

Teachers' career cycles typically follow three stages: *survival* in the new setting and discovery of new challenges; *stabilization* through the middle years; and *disengagement* from their strong investment in teaching as their careers come to an end. Teachers' commitment differs depending on the career stage, with mid-career teachers having lower commitment to their jobs.[46]

Today, 50 percent of teachers are 40 years or over, and the teaching force is aging.[47] There are certainly advantages to having a high concentration of older teachers. They have much teaching experience and consider themselves professionals. Collectively, they belong to more professional organizations and have more ties in the community than younger teachers. But there are disadvantages, too: Some tenured teachers are not competent, but must be kept on; older teachers are more expensive to the system; their presence prevents younger teachers from filling a percentage of the teacher slots. Young teachers bring new teaching ideas and new developments in the discipline to their first jobs, helping to keep older colleagues in touch with their fields. Thus, a two-way socialization takes place between older and younger teachers.[48]

Whether or not they have tenure, teachers can be fired only with good and just cause. Such causes, though difficult to prove, generally include imcompetence (knowledge of subject matter, teaching methods); immorality (lying, falsification of records, misappropriation of funds, and cheating); drug abuse; critical and derogatory statements about the employer; and profane language.

Role Expectations for Teachers.   Teachers are primary socializers of children; that is, they play an important role in teaching the child how to be a member of society. The primary reciprocal role for the teacher is that with the student.[49] It is an involuntary relationship for both. The teacher holds power and has several means of exerting it: adult authority, grades, punishments such as detention or humiliation—and also affective behavior, praise, reinforcement, and personal contact. The question of how to socialize young people most effectively in the schools is, according to some, the most pressing issue schools face.

Teachers are expected to teach children the three R's, manage and facilitate classrooms, provide an atmosphere conducive to maximum learning, and in general be gatekeepers who control the flow of activity and students.

As socializers, teachers are in very visible roles, expected to set good moral examples for students. Yet what is defined as "good" is often controversial. For example, some court cases challenge teachers' negative influence on their students because of their dress, appearance, alcohol or drug charges outside of school, sexual orientation, or unseemly behavior with students.

Accountability and Testing: Pressure from the Community. Peter Doe has graduated from high school, unable to read.

> In an historic case in California, Peter W. Doe (pseudonym for the student filing the case) charged the Galileo High School with negligence, misrepresentation, and breach of statutory duty. He sued "the city's school district for $1 million because he still reads and writes at the fifth-grade level, leaving him unqualified for any employment other than the most demeaning, unskilled, low-paid manual labor."[50]

His mother claimed that teachers had told her Peter was making adequate progress, with no indication that special help was needed.

Teachers are conveyers of knowledge and skills, yet we hear about students such as Peter Doe who are graduated without basic skills—and the public is angry. The many recent court cases attest to the fact that teachers are under increasing pressure from parents, community members, and students to produce results, often meaning higher student scores on standardized tests.

Teacher Preparation. The reality of facing that first class full of children challenges every beginning teacher. Some feel that their teacher training did not adequately prepare them for the job ahead.[51] In fact, revamping teacher education programs is on the minds of many teaching colleges. Dissatisfaction with schools has forced educators to examine the total system, including teacher education. Evaluating curricula and redesigning content to address current concerns includes everything from classroom management practices, to multicultural and global education, to special training for teaching in the middle grades, to improving the quality of math and science education, to working with differences in male/female learning styles.[52,53,54]

Interest in careers in teaching has dropped steadily since the 1970s, but is now rising slightly.[55] However, it is hardly enough to meet the impending teacher shortage as larger cohorts of students enter the system. School districts are resorting to several techniques to meet the need; one is to retool current teachers who are in fields with less demand, training them in other areas. Another is "alternative credentialing," to attract qualified individuals working in other areas into teaching.[56] In most cases, pedagogical training is provided when the person begins teaching. The public favors hiring these individuals for their subject area expertise, especially if they have shown talent for teaching.[57]

To improve teachers' effectiveness, especially in content areas, some educators propose a universal master's degree. However, having a master's has not been shown to make significant improvements in teaching.[58]

Testing and Licensing. In an effort to raise standards, approximately 45 states now require tests for licensure of teacher candidates; many require teachers to pass minimum competency tests. The National Teacher Examinations are used in 32 states.[59] What is tested and the basic purpose for the tests vary:[60]

What Is Tested?	For What Purpose?	By Whom?
Basic skills	Entry to teacher education	State Department
Reading	Initial certification	of Education
Writing	Recertification	Universities
Mathematics	Career ladder	Professional
Professional knowledge	advancement	organizations
Child development	Professional	
School resources	recognition	
School law		
Methods of teaching		
Subject area specialty		
Minimum competence		
Mastery		

According to the legal system, states may use several criteria to judge the competency of teachers, as long as these criteria are directly related to the job.[61]

Because teachers are concerned about how test scores of their pupils affect their own job standing, many teach to the tests and reduce content outside of that narrow range.[62]

The National Teacher Examinations are used by many school districts, but a number of competing testing companies offer their wares, and some states have developed their own tests. The two national teachers' unions, the National Education Association and the American Federation of Teachers, support teacher tests.

As a result of a major recommendation in its commission report, the Carnegie Forum set up a panel on teacher certification with the purpose of setting professional standards. Leaders of both of the major teachers' unions are members.[63,64]

Controversy over testing and licensing of teachers continues, with some arguing that skills tests may not be valid, are not the only measure of competent teachers, and may discriminate against minority teachers. Others point out that it is harmful to children to have teachers in the classroom who lack basic skills. Court cases challenging the fairness of state testing have been brought forth in several states.

National Reports and Teaching.   The concern with dropping student achievement scores, rising dropout rates, poor placement of American students on international exams, and other problems have set off the alarm bells in the Department of Education and in private foundations and organizations devoted to the betterment of education. In the 1980s a spate of reports were produced, dealing with the "crisis in education" and making some radical suggestions for change. *Beyond the Commission Reports: The Coming Crisis in Teaching* starts out with the following job description of a typical secondary school teacher:

WANTED

College graduate with academic major (master's degree preferred). Excellent communication and leadership skills required. Challenging opportunity to serve 150 clients daily, developing up to five different products each day to meet their needs. This diversified job also allows employee to exercise typing, clerical, law enforcement, and social work skills between assignments and after hours. Adaptability helpful, since suppliers cannot always deliver goods and support services on time. Typical work week 47 hours. Special nature of work precludes fringe benefits such as lunch and coffee breaks, but work has many intrinsic rewards. Starting salary $22,830.[65]

The report argues that before the United States can upgrade educational programs and curricula, it must make teaching a more attractive profession; as older, experienced teachers retire and gifted young ones leave for other professions, the qualifications of the teaching force are dwindling.

The report argues that with the upcoming shortage of teachers we will have to "scrape the bottom of the barrel" unless we raise standards and salaries. The catch-22 is that as educational administrations have to dictate policy to control the quality of education, fewer professional teachers will be attracted to education. Good teachers want autonomy and need competitive pay and working conditions; yet 10 to 50 percent of teachers' time is spent on noninstructional duties: record keeping; monitoring playgrounds, lunchrooms, and hallways; making copies. The report has a number of suggestions for improvement that have been highly praised by educators:

- Create a national board for professional teaching standards.
- Restructure schools to provide a professional environment for teachers.
- Restructure the teaching force, and introduce a new category of lead teachers.
- Require a bachelor's degree in the arts and sciences as a prerequisite for the professional study of teaching.
- Develop a new professional curriculum in graduate schools of education leading to a master in teaching degree.
- Mobilize the nation's resources to prepare minority youngsters for teaching careers.
- Relate incentives for teachers to schoolwide student performance, and provide schools with the technology, services, and staff essential to teacher productivity.
- Make teachers' salaries and career opportunities competitive with those in other professions.[66]

The main message is that teachers need more pay, more respect, more professional treatment, and more opportunity for advancement if we are to attract and keep high-quality individuals in the field.

Other Reports and Recommendations.   Merit, incentive, or performance-based pay has been proposed as a way to reward teacher excellence, and many administrators are moving to implement such plans. A majority of the public favors such plans, and over half the states in the United States are considering or have pilot projects on merit pay. However, some argue that these plans lower teacher morale, create dissension, make the situation competitive, and are impossible to administer. Surveys show teachers as a group opposed to merit pay; they would rather see the money go into reducing class sizes, developing teachers' skills, and expanding career opportunities.[67]

What Works: Research About Teaching and Learning makes a series of recommendations for improving the education of young children; these involve cooperative efforts on the part of parents, classroom teachers, and the schools. Teachers are given findings from research about the teaching of specific subjects such as reading and writing, and are advised to set and communicate high standards, explain and demonstrate what is expected, assign meaningful homework, help students develop study skills, and carry out a number of other recommendations aimed at improving education.[68]

Bad conditions in schools need to be rectified before real change can occur. Private and parochial schools, which have less money for salaries, structure the system so that teachers have more freedom and fewer bureaucratic rules, allowing professionals to flourish and share a mission in a team atmosphere. Public schools, because of their level in the hierarchy and bureaucracy, must be routinized, standardized, and regulated. Parents and children provide the controls through choice of schools and the use of vouchers.[69]

The National Commission on Excellence in Teacher Education focused on two general recommendations: that all teachers be required to take a competency exam, and that teacher-preparation programs be improved and extended to five years—in particular that teachers be required to obtain a degree in a particular content area and then take teacher training. While these recommendations appeal to many, there is fear that a five-year program would discourage some potential teachers.

Carrying Out the Role.   There are many different types of classrooms and schools, reflecting the varying philosophies about the best style of teaching. At one extreme is the teacher-directed classroom, where the primary goals are order, quiet, and discipline. The teacher has a daily lesson plan geared toward helping all children progress at the same rate and in an expected manner through the material. At the other extreme is the student-centered class, where the teacher reacts to the children's individual needs. The free exchange often seems to produce a less "orderly" class. These classes reflect different assumptions about the purpose of the classroom and the learning styles of children.

Philip Jackson estimates that teachers have 1,000 interchanges a day in their roles as managers of the classroom.[70] The teacher is a gatekeeper who controls the flow of activity and students, grants privileges, gives special resources, acts as timekeeper, is traffic manager, and spends a great deal of time "in neutral." Teachers, administrators, and the public may agree in principle as to the teacher's role, but the way the teacher carries out the role to achieve end goals may cause conflict among the various constituencies.

Sam Sieber and David Wilder[71] found that mothers generally prefer teachers to be content-oriented. (Teachers see themselves as discovery-oriented.)

Furthermore, there are variations between social class levels: Working-class mothers show preference for more control and authoritarian styles than do middle-class mothers. As professionals, most teachers seek autonomy to manage the classroom as they see best and as best suits their styles and personalities.

Teacher Stress and Burnout. Teacher stress and burnout affect up to one-third of public school teachers in urban areas. They often feel that their work is meaningless and that they are powerless to effect changes in their situations. A number of factors contribute to the problem: Some are characteristics of teachers, others are located in the school structure and culture, and still others are found in societal pressures. For instance, the level of burnout rises with age and years of experience in teaching, peaks at ages 41 through 45, and then declines. Teachers with higher levels of education, and therefore higher career expectations, experienced more frustration.[72] The following is a list of characteristics identified in a study of teacher burnout.

Specifically, the report indicated that burnout was more common among teachers who:
1. were under 30 years of age;
2. were white and from middle-class backgrounds;
3. were inexperienced, having taught for fewer than five years;
4. were racially isolated, teaching in schools where most of the student body is of another race than their own;
5. felt that members of their own race have been targets of discrimination at their school;
6. preferred not to be assigned to the school at which they teach;
7. believed that fate or luck controls their destinies and, hence, their future is out of their hands; and
8. disagreed with their principals on the appropriate role for a campus administrator.

The research revealed that the best single predictor of the likelihood that a teacher would plan to quit teaching was a sense of burnout. Teachers who wanted to quit also fit the characteristics of the teachers who were burned out.[73]

Teachers in some urban school settings feel physically and emotionally victimized, situations that increase stress and burnout.

Three general conclusions can be drawn from the research:
1. Teacher entrapment and burnout are much more prevalent in urban public schools than is teacher turnover, despite the fact that schools have emphasized turnover as their chief personnel problem.
2. Supportive school principals can do much to break the functional link between stress and burnout, and hence entrapment.
3. Burnout per se has a negligible effect upon student learning outcomes, except when bright students are involved.[74]

School culture and structural variables that cause teachers to burn out and quit are equally important.[75] Highly organized schools may not provide the flexibility teachers need to be spontaneous and initiate new ideas. Teachers need to feel that they have some control over the environment, and that they have some say in school policies. Effective teachers have a sense of control over their classrooms; they minimize lost class time and reduce interruptions by being good managers and enforcing necessary rules.

The social and political changes from the 1960s through the 1990s stimulated criticisms of teachers and schools along with expectations that went beyond the role of the school. Hence, many teachers felt "dissatisfied, stressed, worn out, frenetic, overcommitted, and underchallenged; they are leaving the field."[76] It is estimated that some 300 task force reports have been issued since *A Nation at Risk* appeared in 1983. Plans have been offered for everything from revising teacher training, recruitment procedures and certification requirements, to recreating and restructuring public schools. Though some reforms call for more teacher autonomy, change can leave teachers in a state of uncertainty and affect morale negatively. Relationships with principals, with other teachers, and with parents would change with proposed reforms.[77]

Are there solutions? Studies suggest two tentative ideas: First, teachers need to feel a sense of control over their domain, that they can be creative and spontaneous; second, supportive principals are a key factor in reducing stress and burnout.[78]

Teacher Autonomy and Unions.

When a group is faced with threats from its environment—low prestige and low salaries; poor working conditions; lack of autonomy and professionalism they seek; physical threats; hurt pride because of difficulty dealing with some students; and criticisms from angry minorities, parents, and administrators—there are bound to be reactions: stress, burnout, and dropping out.

As a group, teachers may form a subculture—often unconsciously—to insulate themselves from pressures of their environment. Mary Metz[79] reports on a faculty subculture that first developed in response to difficult relations with a deprived, angry black student body; when the school was transformed into a magnet school for the gifted and talented, the subculture persisted as teachers faced criticisms from parents and administrators. This teacher subculture formed a social shared basis for agreement on more specific beliefs and actions, and for protecting teachers' pride in the face of strong hierarchical administration. Male and female teachers responded differently to the threat to autonomy, with males relying more on the subculture.

Many teachers join unions. "Teachers have turned to the National Education Association or American Federation of Teachers and their affiliates in large numbers because, lacking the former deep identification with school and community, they can identify with their group, and be helped by it."[80] At a recent convention, the National Education Association (NEA) endorsed a "children's bill of rights," asking the federal government to provide children with adequate nutrition; housing; health care; high-quality education; and safety from abuse, violence, and discrimination. The American Federation of Teachers (AFT) criticized President Bush's "America 2000" plan, especially the idea of private school choice, and advocated a restructuring of schools that would help them compete in the world.[81] In recent years, unions have been advocating a new form of collective bargaining that would be less confrontational and would involve teachers as part of a team in formulating educational policy.[82]

Recommendations to Improve the Role of Teacher.   "I like the kids; I like the job; I like the satisfaction I get from the work. But I feel I'm not doing something which is really valued by society. Look at our pay scale and the lack of autonomy we as professionals have. So I don't know what the future holds for me or for the profession."[83]

Teachers have traditionally been seen as dedicated, low-paid public servants who give more than they receive. As they change this image to that of an assertive group with collective power, demanding a greater share, teachers are more likely to come under public scrutiny,[84] as they have over the question of accountability. The public has been generally unsympathetic to teacher strikes.

Task forces and commission reports have made suggestions for sweeping changes, some of which are discussed above. But how do teachers feel about their circumstances? In a survey of 2,223 teachers in 29 states using the NSSE Teacher Opinion Survey, most teachers expressed "fair satisfaction" with their jobs. They would like to see schools more involved in career selection and vocational education, and drug and sex education; they want more say over their own in-service training and policy matters; and they desire more opportunities to enhance their professional development, such as extended contracts, sabbatical leaves, grants for further education, and professional development. Such programs would enhance teachers' self-esteem and reduce the stress that causes turnover and burnout. In addition, teachers call for more effective leadership, better relations with the community, and more contact with parents.[85,86]

In 1979 Houston, Texas, began giving incentive pay to teachers in several categories: for teaching in high-priority schools; for teaching subjects in which there was a staff shortage; for good attendance; for professional training; for student gains on standardized tests; and for teaching at an experimental school. According to officials, the results have been positive. Teachers gained from $300 to $3,500, and there were improvements in most areas of concern. Teachers and administrators alike benefited from the plan.[87]

It is clear that there are areas of agreement between teachers and others on how to improve teachers and the teaching profession. All of these recommendations cost money, and until the financing of education at the local, state, and national levels is overhauled, these ideas are likely to remain on paper.

Teachers work with students daily and have certain expectations of the student role. This reciprocal role relationship is our next topic.

Students: The Core of the School

I chatted with a group of fourth-grade boys[88] about their school experiences. There was no question about their knowing what is expected of them by the adult world and why they go to school. They all chimed in that they must learn to read and write to survive in today's world, that they couldn't get a job if their skills weren't developed. What does it mean to be a good or bad kid in school? Again, they did not need to stop and think. A good kid is one who turns in assignments on time, listens and pays attention in class, and doesn't mess around. Bad kids are disruptive, sometimes mean and aggressive, and don't really care about learning. Is it hard to be a good kid in school? When the teachers are picky or in a bad mood, it is; but most of the time it's not, if you want to be good. I had a feeling of *déjà vu;* things hadn't changed much since I was in school. The continuity in expectations is remarkable.

Characteristics of Students.   Students come in many sizes, shapes, intellectual capacities, and motivation levels. They can be active learners, passive attendees, or disruptive troublemakers. Estimates indicate that most children in the world between the ages of 6 to 9 attend school all or part of the time, but after about third grade the picture is spotty. Attendance is near 100 percent in industrialized nations, but much lower in less developed countries, as we shall see in Chapter 10 (See Box 6-2).

The number of students in U.S. public schools dropped during the 1970s, but private and parochial school enrollments were gradually increasing at the secondary level. Projections to the year 1992 show further sharp declines after 1989. "The decrease in the number of high school graduates for the past several years reflects the fact that fewer children were born in the mid-1960s than in the late 1950s and early 1960s." The low point was between 1973 and 1976. By the mid-1990s, a new wave of larger graduating classes should again raise the numbers (Figure 6-4).[89]

High school students are taking more courses (seven per year) than they did in 1972–73, but spending less time on work for these classes. The largest increase in courses taken was in math and science, but social studies and English also increased. Only foreign language dropped.[90] This trend toward more academic courses being offered and taken may reflect the pessimistic predictions of early commission reports arguing that we needed to upgrade our programs.

By the year 2000, minority students will be a majority in ten states. These students need minority role models and bridges between the middle-class culture of the school and minority subcultures.[91] However, the number of minority teachers declined from 12.5 percent in 1980 to 5 percent in 1992.[92] Estimates indicate that the number of minority students could be as high as 39 percent by 2020, but minority teachers would still constitute only 5 percent of the teaching force.[93] Techniques for increasing the number of minority teachers must approach the problem at many levels, from individual incentives to teacher college programs, to state and national policies.[94]

Expectations for the Student Role.   In most public school systems, role expectations for students are standardized by grade. Elaborate plans outline where a student should stand academically at what point. In some open classroom situations or free schools this is not stated as explicitly. Formal student

BOX 6-2   *SCHOOL ENROLLMENTS, 1991–92*

Total enrollment in the nation's elementary and secondary schools in 1991–92 was estimated at 47 million, including pre-kindergarten students, according to early estimates from the U.S. Education Department's National Center for Education Statistics.

Of that total, 41.8 million students were attending public schools, compared with 41.2 million the year before. Private school enrollment was estimated at 5.2 million. Public school enrollment has increased some 1.8 million since 1987, while private school enrollment has remained fairly steady, the center reports.

The center estimates that 2.8 million teachers work in the nation's schools, 2.4 million of them in the public sector. Based on its early data, the pupil-to-teacher ratios for pre-kindergarten through grade 12 are 17.2 for public schools and 14.6 for private schools.

An estimated 2.5 million students graduated from high school in the 1990–91 school year, the center reports, and another 2.5 million were expected to graduate in 1991–92.

The center estimates that the cost of public education in 1991–92 was $5,097 per student.

Early Estimates of Key School Statistics: 1991–92

| | | | GRADUATES | |
	Students	*Teachers*	*1990–91*	*1991–92*
All schools	47,032,084	2,785,646	2,510,625	2,485,349
Public schools	41,838,871	2,431,008	2,263,482	2,250,894
Private schools	5,193,213	354,638	247,143	234,455

Source: National Center for Education Statistics; reprinted in *Education Week,* February 5, 1992, p. 3.

roles—club officer; athletic team member; or (at the lower grades) trash emptier, board eraser, or traffic guard—are found in most schools, but these roles do not capture the flavor and variety of the classroom and student roles.

In describing the role of students in the school we must consider what is called "student culture." We were all a part of it once, but memories fade and times change, keeping the student culture apart from the world of adults. Students are at the bottom of the role hierarchy with a power structure looming over their heads; while they are a numerical majority in the system, they are a distinct minority in decision making. Often students are spoken of as an almost alien group—the enemy; the group to be "subdued," disciplined, or conquered by the school staff. The student subculture determines for many young people the acceptable behaviors for peer survival, behaviors that are often at odds with adult expectations. Two examples of student subcultures are seen in the following studies of "jocks" and "burnouts" and of athletes and nonathletes.

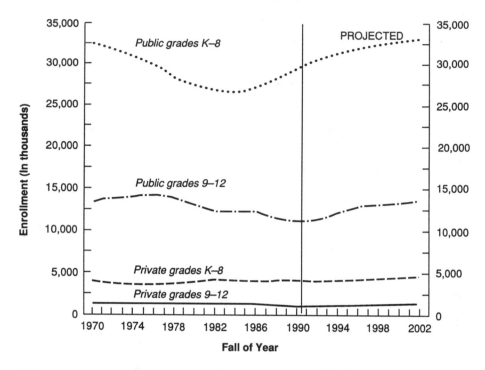

FIGURE 6-4   Changes in public school enrollments with projections.
Source: "Changes in Public School Enrollments with Projections," *The Education Digest*, Ann Arbor, Mich., October 1990.

Class reproduction can occur through adolescent peer groups. "Jocks," college-bound middle-class students, have an investment in the school system, whereas "burnouts," working-class students who often feel hostile or alienated in the school environment, are stigmatized in schools. Working-class students engage in behaviors that will prevent them from succeeding in high school.[95]

Research comparing the academic achievement of athletes with other students shows little difference between athletes and nonathletes in reading and writing skills, but vocabulary comprehension is lower in athletes across sports.[96] Scholar-athletes and pure scholars have higher self-esteem, extracurricular involvement, and leadership ability than do pure athletes or students who are neither scholars nor athletes.[97]

Another variable that affects the student role is gender. Even such subtleties as language usage can have an impact on the student experience. If teachers are aware of the different uses of language, they may be able to use this knowledge more effectively in teaching girls and boys. According to a study of student language usage, girls tell secrets to their best friends, while boys have activities in larger groups and develop hierarchies of status. Boys are more comfortable in putting themselves forward and are more willing to "argue," whereas girls resist "hostile" discussions. Because of such differences, some argue that single-sex education may lead to more positive social and academic outcomes for female students.[98]

Conflicting Expectations for the Student Role. The school is expected to socialize children to be successful members of society; this implies academic and social skill development for students in the school. However, students may have another agenda, centered around peer group involvement and acceptance. Willard Waller points out this conflict between adult and student values very aptly. His analysis describes a basic function of schools, cultural transmission:

> Certain cultural conflicts are at the center of the life of the school. . . . A conflict arises between teachers and students because teachers represent the culture of the wider group and students are impregnated with the culture of the local community. . . . A second and more universal conflict between students and teachers arises from the fact that teachers are adults and students are not, so that teachers are the bearers of the culture of the society of adults, and try to impose that culture upon students, whereas students represent the indigenous culture of the group of children.[99]

The school expects "successful" students to carry out two components of achievement at the elementary level, according to Talcott Parsons. The first is "cognitive" learning of information—skills, frames of reference, and factual information about the world. The second is a "moral" component, including responsible citizenship, respect, consideration, cooperation, work habits, leadership, and initiative.[100] To the extent that student peer groups rebel against these goals, division and conflict are created.

Adolescent employment also creates conflicting expectations; adolescents supply labor as workers in fast-food restaurants, as newspaper carriers, and in many other positions in evenings and on weekends. Work experience is valuable training for adult roles, especially in responsibility, punctuality, working for a boss, following orders, handling money, and demonstrating whatever skills may be acquired. On the other hand, work takes time from studies, extracurricular activities, peer associations, and "growing up." Some students must work to help their families, but fewer than one in ten donate part or all of their earnings to help support their families. If adolescents work limited hours at times that do not interfere substantially with other activities, there are benefits from the experience. Almost one in three high school students worked in 1990, and African-American students were less than half as likely as white students to work (Figure 6-5).

Students who work part-time may select jobs that fit their personal orientation; for instance, internally oriented students generally select less stressful jobs. Students often develop feelings of "mastery" and self-confidence through their jobs, especially if they see their jobs as providing opportunities for future advancement.[101]

However, dropping out of high school is also related to the number of hours a student works during high school, and the motivation for work; some students work more hours than allowed by law. Students who are motivated to

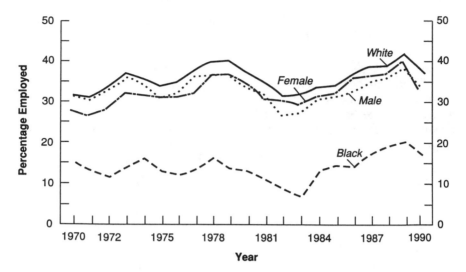

FIGURE 6-5   Percentage of high school students 16 to 24 years old who were employed, 1970–90.

Source: U.S. Department of Labor, Bureau of Labor Statistics, *Labor Force Statistics Derived from the Current Population Survey: 1940–1987, Employment and Earnings,* and unpublished tabulations.

save money for college are more likely to finish high school and attend college.[102] However, other students work because they need the money; one-half of all Hispanic students dropped out of school in the 1980s to help their families, but most ended up in deeper poverty. Only 51 percent of Hispanic dropouts over 25 had finished high school, compared with 78 percent non-Hispanic.[103]

Learning the Student Role.   School deals with the intellectual abilities of the child; in contrast, the family deals with the whole child. Preschool programs and kindergarten introduce the child to the institution of education and have been described as "academic boot camp."[104]

Each year in most classrooms a new crop of students must be socialized into the rules of the elementary school classroom. This can be a time-consuming process. Students preparing to enter a new classroom or school are concerned about making mistakes in front of their peers or getting in trouble because they have not yet learned their role expectations. Most children want to fit in. Much of the students' role learning ties in with the social control function of education—learning how to adjust, take orders, and obey. To become a "good" student means to follow the school's routine and rules.

Students are the most transient members of the system. The school system is geared toward facilitating the successful movement of students through the system. Movement requires progress, which in turn requires control and cooperation. Because students are not in school by choice, most schools find it necessary to keep them in line by using incentives such as positive reinforcement and interesting subjects, or punishment such as extra work, detentions, and suspensions, and by giving grades in order for students to accomplish their goals.

Each year's crop of students becomes a "class" and is processed through the system as a group, or cohort. Picture a giant sieve with layers. Students are put in the top and pass through the layers, which have succeedingly smaller holes. Those who fail to pass through a level are retained or drop out of the sorting and selecting process. At the bottom of the sieve comes graduation.

If students with common experiences and values are placed according to ability levels, their labels—brains, jocks, losers—may affect their role patterns. The fact that students are placed in different tracks also points to the extent of variation in the education experience. The courses students pursue are generally influenced by and selected on the basis of their future plans for either further schooling or work. In several European countries—Germany and England, for example—tracking or "streaming" becomes increasingly rigid as students move through the system. Exams at several school levels in Germany, at age 16 in England, and for university entrance in Japan and many other countries have a major impact on determining a student's future educational opportunities. Scholastic Aptitude Tests or other exams are required by many U.S. colleges and universities.

Students have views on their own educational roles. The National Center for Educational Statistics sponsored national longitudinal studies in 1972, 1980, and 1984. In a 1984 follow-up study of the 1980 graduates, some of the goals they held as seniors had changed. For instance, marriage, family, and having children had much higher priority, whereas success in work and having lots of money had decreased in importance relative to other life goals.[105]

Student Coping Mechanisms and Failure.   Students use different coping mechanisms to get through the levels of the system. Varying roles are adopted—the leader, the clown, the bully. Playing these roles requires adapting to the demands of differing situations.

> Thus the leader may remain a leader, but he must adapt his leadership to the (usually) superior force of the teacher, which he may do through alliance, opposition, rivalry, or other means. The clown is still a clown, but his buffoonery must be disguised, it may become covert, or it may adopt a mien of innocence and pose as blundering stupidity.[106]

Waller points out that an effective teacher recognizes student roles, manipulates them, and uses them effectively. Teachers speak differently to students for whom they have high expectations and low expectations. Students can pick up cues about how teachers feel about them.[107] Students may also attempt to sabotage the teaching effort by maintaining an emotional detachment from what is happening in the classroom, devaluing what is taking place, cheating, daydreaming, or acting bored.[108]

Students may choose apathy to protect themselves against total failure in a competition they cannot win. Their sense of self-worth is threatened, thus reducing their desire to try to achieve.[109] Until these students see the possibility of success from effort, they are unlikely to put forth that effort.

Why should we care? The loss in human potential is tremendous. "Our society is aging and the number of children and youths in relation to other age groups in the population is declining. If current trends continue, a disproportionate number of our young will grow up poor, undereducated, and untrained at the very time that our society will need all of our young to be healthy, educated, and productive."[110]

Dropouts.   Alienation is a sense of powerlessness, normlessness, meaninglessness, isolation, or self-estrangement. In schools its roots are inherent in the formal, impersonal bureaucratic educational system. However, complete overhaul of this structure would be necessary to prevent the feelings that drive some students to drop out of the system.[111]

Dropouts are individuals who

1.   were enrolled in school at some time during the previous year,
2.   were not enrolled at the beginning of the current school year,
3.   have not graduated from high school or an approved educational program, and
4.   have *not* transferred or been suspended or are temporarily absent.[112]

"The at-risk student with little promise of success in the greater society becomes a part of an underclass culture, and early pregnancy may be an adaptive behavior for members of this culture."[113] Sheri is a high school dropout and an unwed mother, a double stigma. Her intentions were to finish high school while her baby attended day care; then she could get a good job to support the baby. But when winter came and the baby got sick, she could not get to school regularly and dropped out.

Juan's family moved to a large city from his native Puerto Rico when he was in elementary school. He worked part-time while attending high school because his family needed the money. With the language barrier, need for immediate cash, and little support from home, he dropped out to work longer hours at his menial job.

Who drops out? One in four students will not graduate from high school. Where ethnic diversity is greatest, retention rates are lowest. African-Americans and Latino students feel more alienated, with a higher sense of powerlessness and isolation than Caucasians; this is especially influential in dropout decisions for males. Dropouts are disproportionately male, older than average (two or more years behind grade level), burdened with low grades and behavior problems, minorities, from low-income families with low educational attainment, and given little educational encouragement. It is these individuals who make up the reserve labor force in capitalistic systems. About one-fourth of the female and close to 30 percent of the male dropouts between 16 and 24 years old were unemployed in 1989.[114]

The dropout problem is growing worse in many major U.S. cities, where the average rate is over 40 percent; in New York City the rate is around 50 percent. However, in the nation as a whole the rate has leveled and is declining slightly (Figure 6-6). Box 6-3 shows some characteristics of those who are "at risk" to leave school.

What causes some to drop out? "Many youngsters arrive in school homeless, sick, hungry, and destitute—plagued by problems that often make staying and succeeding in school virtually impossible."[115] Students also come to school with varying coping strategies. Those with positive attitudes are likely to be high achievers. Those who are defensive or have low self-esteem or other problems often need help to succeed. While schools cannot solve society's problems, they can collaborate with other human service agencies to meet student needs.

However, some schools are so poor and crowded that they cannot begin to offer in-school support, much less coordinate with other agencies. Kozol describes differences in two Chicago-area schools—one wealthy, one poor. The wealthy school has an average class size of 24 children; 15 in classes for slow learners. The poor school has remedial classes with 39; classes for the "gifted" with 36. Each student at the wealthy school has an adviser assigned; at the poor school, one guidance counselor advises 420 children.[116]

Some students have personal problems. Others cannot cope with the requirements of the compulsory, rigid, formal, education system, which has no room for misfits, and drop out when they reach legal age.[117]

FIGURE 6-6   Dropout rates by race/ethnicity and sex, 1970–88 (3-year average).

Note: Dropout rates for whites and Hispanics have leveled off since 1988, and have dropped slightly for African-Americans.

Source: U.S. Department of Education, National Center for Education Statistics, *Dropout Rates in the United States;* High School and Beyond survey; U.S. Department of Commerce, Bureau of the Census, October Current Population Survey, reprinted in *The Condition of Education* (Washington, D.C.: Department of Education, 1992), p. 59.

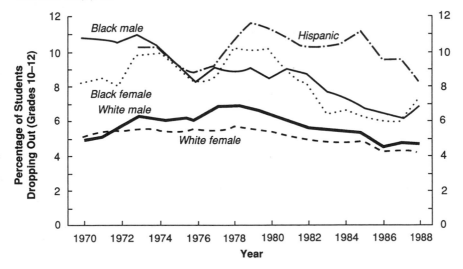

BOX 6-3   *YOUTH "AT RISK" (YOUTH: 2000 DEMOGRAPHICS)*

What Do the Data Tell Us About "At Risk" Youth?

- The number of high school dropouts, already about a million a year nation-ally, will increase.
- One of every four ninth graders will not graduate from high school. For minorities and the poor, the rates are higher.
- One out of eight 17-year-olds is functionally illiterate.
- A growing percentage of new entrants into the labor market between 1986 and 2000 will likely be black, Hispanic, immigrants, from single-parent families or poor.
- Scarcely more than half of your black males aged 16 to 19 are in the labor force; less than one-third are employed; and one-fourth have never been employed.
- The pregnancy rate for young women is increasing significantly; four in ten teenage girls will become pregnant before the age of 20. Half of all teen mothers will never complete high school; most do not marry.
- Teenage pregnancies cost the nation over $16 billion a year in welfare costs alone.
- An increasing number of children are growing up in poverty. One out of four children under the age of 6 is poor; for black children, the rate is one in two; for Hispanic children, it's one in three. Ninety percent of the increase in child poverty is related to the increase in single-parent families. Three-quarters of all single mothers under age 25 live in poverty.
- The economic implications for the skilled work force and military are enormous. The technology will be in place, but there will not be enough workers to run it.

Source: "Youth: 2000 Conference," Executive Summary, February 1987, sponsored by Miami Valley Regional Planning Commission, Dayton, Ohio.

Problems faced by students range from family breakups to neighbor-hood dangers from gangs and drugs. Consider the following problems that affect children's ability to function in school:

1. *"Crack babies,"* their numbers estimated at between 50,000 and 200,000, are now arriving at the school door. While many are not brain-damaged, they do require special structuring of the classroom with few distractions, a stable environment, and a feeling of safety. Because many were born prematurely with low birth weight and small head size, they do poorly on developmental tests and have less ability to concentrate. "They are kids wired for 110 volts, living in a 220-volt world."[118]

2. *Homeless children,* estimated at over 500,000 and growing, have special educa-tional and social needs. Until they have proper food and shelter, they are unlikely to be able to learn. The McKinney Homeless Assistance Act (P.L. 100-77), passed in July 1987, created a structure for programs to give homeless children educa-tional rights. Runaways constitute a special problem for educational authorities, since they are often fleeing from what authority represents.[119]

TABLE 6-4 Reasons Cited by 1980 Sophomore Dropouts for Leaving High School Before Graduation, by Sex and Race/Ethnicity, Spring 1982

Reasons[a]	Total	MALE			FEMALE		
		Total	White[b]	Minority[c]	Total	White[b]	Minority[c]
School-related							
School was not for me	33.1%	34.8%	45.6%	14.8%	31.1%	34.1%	24.9%
Had poor grades	33.0	35.9	38.4	31.2	29.7	30.0	30.0
Couldn't get along with teachers	15.5	20.6	19.8	22.0	9.5	10.2	8.1
Expelled or suspended	9.5	13.0	12.3	14.3	5.3	6.3	3.2
Didn't get into desired program	6.1	7.5	4.7	12.8	4.5	4.2	5.0
School grounds too dangerous	2.3	2.7	2.9	2.2	1.7	1.1	3.1
Family-related							
Married or planned to get married	17.8	6.9	7.6	5.5	30.7	36.4	19.2
Had to support family	11.1	13.6	9.3	21.5	8.3	7.1	10.6
Was pregnant	10.9	—	—	—	23.4	20.5	29.2
Peer-related							
Couldn't get along with students	5.6	5.4	4.7	6.6	5.9	6.0	5.7
Friends were dropping out	4.6	6.5	6.7	6.0	2.4	2.7	1.7
Health-related							
Illness or disability	5.5	4.6	4.6	4.7	6.5	5.3	9.0
Other							
Offered job and chose to work	19.5	26.9	28.4	24.1	10.7	9.7	12.8
Wanted to travel	6.8	7.0	7.3	6.5	6.5	8.5	2.4
Wanted to enter military	4.3	7.2	6.7	8.3	.8	.6	1.1
Moved too far from school	3.6	2.2	2.2	2.2	5.3	5.2	5.5
Sample size	2,289	1,188	648	537	1,101	615	486

[a] Students might report more then one reason.

[b] Includes Asian-Americans, only 18 in number, because they responded with similar reasons for dropping out.

[c] Includes Hispanics, blacks, and American Indians/Alaskan natives.

Source: "High School Dropouts: Descriptive Information from High School and Beyond," U.S. Department of Education, National Center for Educational Statistics, Bulletin NCES 83 221b, November 1983.

3. *Teenage pregnancy* often prevents young mothers from finishing school. This problem is most prevalent in the inner city. Early intervention to provide sex education, parenting training, child care, and easy access to education are necessary. Many programs are being targeted to inner-city schools.[120]
4. *Gang violence* is a threat to neighborhoods and schools. Armed, angry, and impulsive, these hostile youths have little regard for others. Social ills are directly related to kids' joining gangs. They are often territorial. Methods of dealing with gangs are discussed in Chapter 2.[121]

Dropouts face a grim future. They are more likely to be on welfare and to have dependent children;[122] a disproportionate number of dropouts end up in the nation's jails and prisons and are four times as likely to engage in unlawful behavior; dropouts have difficulty competing in the labor market; they lack skills for today's jobs, have less knowledge for daily living, and have low self-esteem. But most important is the human cost of individuals who cannot compete in the world.

In a comparison of the cognitive development of school and nonschool populations, researchers found that those students who stay in school are at an advantage, particularly in specific competency areas as measured by tests, and minority students benefited the most from staying in school.[123] Most dropouts were already lagging behind before they dropped out. Unfortunately, some proposals to raise standards in schools (such as requiring graduation examinations), if implemented, could also increase the dropout rates of marginal students.

Fortunately, some dropouts end up completing their high school degrees. Of the 16 percent of sophomore 1980 dropouts, 40 percent returned by 1984 to complete their degrees.[124] Schools may also need to rethink how they deal with "at-risk" students; increased resources, more flexible time requirements, altered suspension policies, and special counseling services are but a few areas of concern.[125]

To prevent students from dropping out, programs that focus on the most vulnerable populations, try to reduce causes of apathy and alienation, raise self-esteem and success of students, and begin early in students' careers are important. Most experts advise identifying at-risk students early and intervening quickly. Unfortunately, too many schools use strategies (such as suspensions) that reduce expectations and stigmatize students. The students who are suspended are often the at-risk students. Many intervention programs have been proposed and some have been tested at the elementary and middle school grades. Accelerated academics, alternative schools, and Saturday and after-school programs are some of the academic approaches used. Laws to deny driver's licenses to students in academic difficulty or to those who drop out of school before age 18 are being passed in a number of states. Getting parents involved in programs to keep students in school and holding parents accountable for students who do not attend school are other strategies. Finally, for those students who do drop out, an increasing number of programs for completing high school are available.

One program developed by sociologists, which combines knowledge from the numerous studies on dropouts, is called Project RAISE. It involves at-risk middle school students in one-on-one mentoring using outside adults. During the two years the program has been in operation, students improved in attendance and in report card grades in English; but this program alone is not enough to remove the years that led up to the risk of dropping out.[126]

Schools contribute to the dropout process—or, as some have referred to it, the "pushout" process—by giving signals that the schools cannot deal with certain students. Detentions, suspensions, expulsions, and no school support system are recipes for creating dropouts.[127] Retained students lose achievement and have higher dropout rates as well. It is estimated that 2.6 million students are retained at a cost of $10 billion. These students are often young males with low socioeconomic status, poor self-esteem, and low motivation, a description that matches that of the typical dropout.[128]

Criticisms of the Student Role. Several problems seem to be inherent in the student role: labeling students, attitudes toward failure, treating all students alike, and tracking students for their future roles in society.

Students are generally well aware of where they stand academically. They have been labeled by teachers and other students from their earliest days in school. In one second-grade classroom the teacher divided the children into reading groups—the rocket ships, jet airplanes, and Piper cubs. There was no doubt in those children's minds as to where they stood! Even the type of subjects taken by older students encourage role definitions; there are "dumbbell" courses and "elite" ones. These placements and labels can have a permanent, sometimes detrimental, effect on a student's self-perception.

Attitudes toward student learning differ across cultures. The Japanese have few student "failures," in part because they do not define students as failures. If a student is not succeeding, parents and teachers expect him or her to work harder to accomplish what is expected. Instead of assuming that some students cannot do the work, the assumption is that all (except those with a disability) can pass if they put in enough time and effort. This corresponds with the findings on effective schools in the United States, which hold high academic expectations for students and teachers.

According to anthropologist Jules Henry and other critics of schools, students are put in a position that compromises their integrity; they must "give the teacher what she wants." Henry elaborates the reason for this in his book *Culture Against Man:*

> American classrooms, like educational institutions anywhere, express the values, preoccupations, and fears found in the culture as a whole. School has no choice; it must train the children to fit the culture as it is. School can give training in skills; it cannot teach creativity. . . . Schools deal with masses of children, and can manage therefore only by reducing them all to a common definition.[129]

Thus, students are not encouraged to be creative, but only to toe the line, according to Henry.

Many educators have raised criticisms about the student role that concern the core of society itself. Bowles and Gintis argued that the roles of students in schools prepare them for the unequal stratification system in society at large. Students divided into tracks conform to different behavioral norms. "Vocational and general tracks emphasize rule-following and close supervision, while the college track tends toward a more open atmosphere emphasizing the internalization of norms." These differences in social relationships reflect students' social backgrounds and likely future economic positions:

> Thus blacks and other minorities are concentrated in schools whose repressive, arbitrary, generally chaotic internal order, coercive authority structures, and minimal possibilities for advancement mirror the characteristics of inferior job situations. Similarly, predominantly working-class schools tend to emphasize behavioral control and rule-following, while schools in well-to-do suburbs employ relatively open systems that favor greater student participation, less direct supervision, more student electives, and, in general, a value system stressing internalized standards of control.[130]

According to this perspective, docility, lack of creativity, and conformity are the goals being met by schools.

The view of the student role has not changed significantly in most school settings, even with educational movements advocating more rights, power, equal opportunity, and freedom for students. Students are the clients of education, yet they have almost no control over the service rendered. Do students have the right to determine what they learn and how they should learn it? Radical educators such as Illich and Kozol argue that this is a basic right that is being denied to students for reasons other than sound pedagogy. This idea is discussed further in Chapter 11.

Support Roles in the School: Behind the Scenes

School Staff: Guardians of the Gateway.   Most schools have a supporting staff of both professional specialists and service workers. Upon entering the school, our first contact is usually with an office worker behind a counter who serves the important functions of "buffering" and "filtering" in dealing with the community. The irate parent comes in demanding to see the principal immediately; the text salespersons would like to speak to someone "in charge." The office worker must determine the appropriate place for the complaint or request, screen out unnecessary interruptions of school personnel, and match the visitor with the appropriate person.

Office workers also have control over such key information as the contents of files. For example, if the vice-principal needs information on the arrangement made with the food distributor for deliveries, he or she relies on the office worker to locate the material. Teachers and students are also dependent on office workers for many services and information. In this respect the person holding the role may wield a great deal of influence.

Other important support roles include librarians, special education teachers, paraprofessionals, food service workers, bus drivers, and nurses. One important role is often overlooked: Janitors are in a unique position. While they hold little formal power in the hierarchy, they may be extremely influential members of the community in which a school is located. They have an insider's view about the running of the school, a vantage point almost no others, often not even the principals, have. While many janitors are neutral entities, some have used the position in a political way, as exemplified in the following excerpt from Waller:[131]

> [T]he janitor is always a member of the local community, whereas teachers belong rather to the outside world. . . . The janitor is important, too, as a talebearer. Often he regards himself as an official lookout for the community; it is his role to see what he can and to report what he observes to his friends and connections by way of gossip.

Another crucial role in schools is carried out by paraprofessionals—individuals with less than a four-year college degree. While they do not have total control of a classroom, they do carry out numerous tasks in classrooms and schools. The largest number work with special education programs, including remedial and bilingual classes.[132]

The role of school nurses has changed dramatically, from giving bandages and immunizations to handling medications for chronically ill students, dealing with abuse, and working with other social problems that affect health services.[133] Sometimes this involves coordinating social services to get children the help they need.[134]

To meet the impending teacher shortage in some subjects, school districts are resorting to several techniques. One is to retool current teachers who are in fields with surplus personnel to teach in other areas. Another is "alternative credentialing"—attracting qualified individuals working in other areas into teaching. In most cases, pedagogical training is provided. The public favors hiring people who have expertise and show talent for teaching.[135]

Counselors: The Selection and Allocation Function.   As high schools have become larger and more diverse in programs and courses offered, their personnel have become more specialized. Counselors are hired by many school systems, mostly to deal with students at the high school level. They usually have degrees in school counseling and have often had teaching experience. From the American School Counselor Association (ASCA) comes a policy statement that includes a clear definition of the formal role of the counselor:

> The pervasive role of counselors must derive from their unique ability to serve pupil needs by:
> a. assisting pupils to understand themselves and their social and psychological world;
> b. helping pupils accept their aptitudes, abilities, interests, and opportunities for self-fulfillment;
> c. helping pupils develop decision-making competency;
> d. helping all staff members to understand individual pupils by providing material, information, and evaluations;
> e. assisting parents to understand the developmental needs and progress of their children;

      f.   developing and/or using community resources for meeting the unusual or extreme needs of pupils.[136]

Counselors have a great deal of power in determining what happens to each student—a "gatekeeping" role. With all the student records at hand, they can guide students into courses and programs to meet students' and society's needs. The counselor can make lifetime decisions for young people. Counselors use not only the objective criteria of grades and test scores, but also their impressions of the students, often formed in brief encounters spread over several years. Labels students attain from teachers and peers can influence the counselor's impressions. Factors such as the student's class background, dress, and manner of speaking influence the counselor's opinions of what the student can do and recommendations for future plans. A dilemma is present for the counselor who is expected to keep "societal" goals in mind, get to know students well enough to plan their futures, and work with students and parents to achieve what are sometimes unrealistic goals.

    Special Support Roles.   Because of growing concern in the nation in the 1970s over the apparent decline of basic skills, Title I (Elementary and Secondary Education Act) was passed to provide supplementary monies to districts for additional personnel and special programs. Schools can hire specialists in reading, mathematics, and sometimes preschool education, to work with children who score below third-grade level on standardized tests. In addition, needy children in Title I programs are offered some auxiliary services such as food, medicine, dental services, and clothing.

    The national report *A Nation at Risk* recommended use of "the voluntary efforts of individuals, businesses, and civic groups to cooperate in strengthening educational programs."[137] Operation Rescue, administered by the Washington, D.C., Urban League and the public schools uses residents, businesses, organizations, and churches to tutor first- through third-grade students who are having trouble with basic skills. "Rather than 10,000 students failing, over 7,000 students graduated to the next grade level, due in part to the one-on-one or small group tutorial assistance they had received through Operation Rescue."[138] The program incorporates recommendations of the report *Schools That Work.*[139]

    Reports of schools with volunteer programs abound. With shortages of funds and personnel, extra hands to do special tasks can be invaluable. Retired teachers and other professionals, community citizens with skills, parents, business members, substitute teachers, even upper-level students or college students volunteer to tutor; aid teachers or substitute in classes; give lessons on specific topics; help in the office, library, or other areas; chaperone; and run after-school programs in sports or other special-interest activities. Some programs utilize community resources to place students for internships, and in other communities businesses provide personnel and resources to the schools for special programs.

    Alumni are the biggest school boosters and the strongest school critics. They provide financial support, especially at the college level, and are often community members in their high school home towns, attending sporting events and volunteering help in various capacities.

However, alumni can be a hindrance in efforts to change. A prestigious preparatory school set quotas for accepting a percentage of minority students each year; it then considered becoming coeducational. Protests and loss of alumni support—including financial help—followed these moves.

How individuals carry out roles varies greatly. In our next chapter we consider the informal aspects of the educational system and how roles actually work.

SUMMARY

No system can work without individuals who fill the necessary roles, which in turn make the system alive. While the major obligations for most positions are usually clearly defined, individuals bring unique sets of characteristics, training, abilities, and background experiences with them when playing their roles. Hence, no one description can capture the richness and variety that enter into the system of roles.

I. The Meaning of Roles

Roles refer to the parts individuals play in the social system. In school organizations roles include administrators, teachers, students, and support staff. Conflicts may arise from incompatible demands on those holding particular roles. Reciprocal roles in the education system illustrate the interdependence of parts; for instance, without students other roles in the education system would be nonexistent. Those taking on a role are usually socialized rather rapidly into that role; few can tolerate the uncertainty of an ill-defined role, and few want to face the ridicule or punishment likely to follow defiance of role expectations. Hence, the school system has a built-in guarantee that most neophytes will fit in nicely and without disruption. This is one reason why change in the system is often slow.

II. Roles in Schools

School boards consist of lay community members who have varying degrees of control over school personnel, budget, and policy; these may be points of tension.

Superintendents are the overall managers of schools. They provide the liaison between the schools, the board, and the community.

Principals are bosses of individual schools, but their authority lies between that of the superintendent and the teachers. This often requires them to play a balancing act to keep both satisfied.

Teachers are on the front line, running the classrooms. The conflict between their desire for autonomy and pressures from the environment can lead to tensions. Recently, there have been controversies over teacher accountability, testing of teachers, and teacher training. Several national U.S. commission reports have addressed the problem of how to improve teaching.

Students often have a different agenda from that of the adults who teach them. Students come from many backgrounds with many motivations. Some co-operate with the school system, others are alienated and rebel, even drop out.

A number of other support roles exist in schools, each playing an important role in the overall functioning of the school.

PUTTING SOCIOLOGY TO WORK

1. Imagine yourself in the various roles of a specific school system. Compare your role behavior in each role.
2. Try to recall the highlights of your education at different levels in your role as a student. What were different role expectations at different levels?
3. Observe the people in a school. Note the differing roles and the reciprocal relationships.
4. View the documentary film "High School" and try to identify some of the formal school roles you see individuals performing. Describe the reciprocal role relationships.
5. Examine several of the "Problems in Teaching Series"[140] films of teaching anecdotes, and identify the roles the teacher, students, and administrators are taking or might take in performing their formal roles.

NOTES

[1] Linton, Ralph, *The Study of Man* (New York: Appleton-Century-Crofts, 1936).

[2] Rogers, David, *110 Livingston Street: Politics and Bureaucracy in the New York City School System* (New York: Vintage Books, 1969), p. 272.

[3] *Ibid.*, p. 271.

[4] Bowles, Samuel, and Herbert Gintis, *Schooling in Capitalist America* (New York: Basic Books, 1976).

[5] Rogers, *110 Livingston Street*, p. 212.

[6] Freeman, Jesse L., Kenneth E. Underwood, and Jim C. Fortune, "What Boards Value," *The American School Board Journal*, January 1991, pp. 32–39.

[7] Goldhammer, Keith, *The School Board* (New York: Center for Applied Research in Education, 1964), pp. 11–14.

[8] Kerr, Norman D., "The School Board as an Agency of Legitimation," *Sociology of Education*, Vol. 38, 1964, pp. 34–59.

[9] *Ibid.*, p. 59.

[10] Anderson, Robert E., and Jean S. Lavid, "Factors School Boards Use When Selecting a Superintendent," *Spectrum: Education Research Service*, Summer 1985, pp. 21–25.

[11] Yock, Carla, et al., "Happily Ever After," *The American School Board Journal*, January 1990, pp. 28–33.

[12] "Where Are All the Women Superintendents?" *The American School Board Journal*, September 1990, p. 8.

[13] Whitaker, Kathryn S., and Kenneth Lane, "What Is 'a Woman's Place' in Educational Administration?" *The School Administrator*, February 1990, pp. 8–12.

[14] Bendiner, Robert, *The Politics of Schools: A Crisis in Self-Government* (New York: Harper & Row, 1969).

[15] Goldhammer, Keith, "Roles of the American School Superintendent," 1954–1974, p. 157.

[16] *Ibid.*

[17] Hentges, Joseph T., "The Politics of Superintendent–School Board Linkages: A Study of Power, Participation, and Control," *Journal of School Research and Information*, Vol. 4, No. 3, 1986, pp. 23–32.

[18] Waller, Willard, *The Sociology of Teaching* (New York: Russell & Russell, 1961; repro. of 1932 edition), p. 94.

[19] Goldman, Samuel, *The School Principal* (New York: Center for Applied Research in Education, 1966), p. 14.

[20] Blase, Joseph, Charles Dedrick, and Marlene Strathe, "Leadership Behavior of School Principals in Relation to Teacher Stress, Satisfaction, and Performance," *Journal of Humanistic Education and Development*, Vol. 24, June 1986, pp. 159–70.

[21] Becker, Howard S., "The Teacher in the Authority System of the Public Schools," *Journal of Educational Sociology*, Vol. 27, 1973, pp. 128–41.

[22] Interview with elementary school principal by the author.

[23] Rallis, Sharon F., and Martha C. Highsmith, "The Myth of the 'Great Principal,' " *Phi Delta Kappan*, December 1986, pp. 300–304.

[24] McEvoy, Alan W., *When Disaster Strikes* (Holmes Beach, Fla.: Learning Publications, 1992).

[25] *Ibid.*

[26] Gross, Neal, and Anne E. Trask, *The Sex Factor and the Management of Schools* (Ann Arbor: University of Michigan Press, 1991).

[27] Andrews, Richard L., and Margaret R. Basom, "Instructional Leadership: Are Women Principals Better?" *Principal*, Vol. 70, No. 2, November 1990, p. 38.

[28] Shakeshaft, Carol, *Women in Educational Administration* (Newbury Park, Calif.: Sage Publications, 1987).

[29] Smith, Wilma, and Richard Andrews, *Instructional Leadership: How Principals Make a Difference* (Alexandria, Va.: ASCD Press, 1989).

[30] Shakeshaft, Carol, "The Female World of School Administrators," *Educational Horizons*, Vol. 44, Spring 1986, pp. 117–22.

[31] *Ibid.*, p. 119.

[32] Kerickson, H. Lynn, "Conflict and the Female Principal," *Phi Delta Kappan*, December 1985, pp. 288–91.

[33] Rodman, Blake, "For Women at the Top: Less Money, Fewer Prerequisites," *Education Week*, March 20, 1985, p. 14.

[34] Wellisch, Jean B., et al., "School Management and Organization in Successful Schools," *Sociology of Education*, Vol. 51, 1978, pp. 211–26.

[35] Roe, William H., and Thelbert L. Drake, *The Principalship*, 2nd ed. (New York: Macmillan, 1980).

[36] Hargreaves, Andy, "Experience Counts, Theory Doesn't: How Teachers Talk About Their Work," *Sociology of Education*, Vol. 57, October 1984, pp. 244–53.

[37] NEA, *Status of American Public Teachers, 1975–76* (Washington, D.C.: National Education Association, 1976); Bartholomew, Bernard, *Nationwide Teacher Opinion Poll—1981* (Washington, D.C.: National Education Association, 1981).

[38] *A Nation Prepared: Teachers for the 21st Century* (New York: Carnegie Forum on Education and the Economy, May 1986), pp. 28–29.

[39] U.S. Department of Education, National Center for Education Statistics, *The Condition of Education*, 1990, p. 28.

[40] Reid, Bill, and Edith King, "Selling Teaching," *Education*, Vol. 167, January 1986, p. 18.

[41] *A Nation Prepared*, p. 30.

[42] *Statistical Abstracts of the United States*, 107th ed. (Washington, D.C.: U.S. Department of Commerce, Bureau of the Census, 1987).

[43] Huberman, Michael, "The Professional Life Cycle of Teachers," *Teachers College Record*, Vol. 91, No. 1, Fall 1989, pp. 31–57.

[44] Lortie, Dan C., *Schoolteacher: A Sociological Study* (Chicago: University of Chicago Press, 1975), pp. 86–90.

[45] Langlois, Donald E., and Charlotte Rappe Zales, "Anatomy of a Top Teacher," *The American School Board Journal,* August 1991, pp. 44–46.

[46] Rosenholtz, Susan J., and Carl Simpson, "Workplace Conditions and the Rise and Fall of Teachers' Commitment," *Sociology of Education,* Vol. 63, No. 4, October 1990, pp. 241–57.

[47] U.S. Department of Education, *The Condition of Education,* p. 96.

[48] Goldman, Paul, "Occupational versus Organizational Socialization of High School Teachers: Theoretical and Policy Issues," paper presented at American Sociological Association meetings, Chicago, 1987.

[49] Brophy, Jere E., and Thomas L. Good, *Teacher-Student Relationships: Causes and Consequences* (New York: Holt, Rinehart and Winston, 1974).

[50] "California Student Sues School: Poor Reader Fault of System," *Library Journal,* Vol. 98, 1973, p. 206.

[51] Louis Harris and associates, *"The First Year: New Teachers' Expectations and Ideals"* from Teacher Survey (Boston: Massachusetts Teachers' Association, 1991).

[52] Trent, William, "Race and Ethnicity in the Teacher Education Curriculum," *Teachers College Record,* Vol. 91, No. 3, Spring 1990, p. 361.

[53] Bruce, Michael G., et. al., "Developing a Global Perspective: Strategies for Teacher Education Programs," *Journal of Teacher Education,* Vol. 42, No. 1, January/February 1991, pp. 21–27.

[54] *Science and Math Teacher Preparation* (Washington, D.C.: U.S. Department of Education, National Center for Education Statistics, 1991).

[55] Clarridge, Pamela Brown, "Multiple Perspectives on the Classroom Performance of Certified and Uncertified Teachers," *Journal of Teacher Education,* Vol. 41, No. 4, September/October 1990, pp. 15–25.

[56] "Alternatives, Yes; Lower Standards, No: Minimum Standards for Alternative Teacher Certification Programs" (Reston, Va.: Association of Teacher Educators, 1989).

[57] Elam, Stanley M., Lowell C. Rose, and Alec M. Gallup, "The 23rd Annual Gallup Poll of the Public's Attitudes Toward the Public Schools," *Phi Delta Kappan,* September 1991, p. 51.

[58] Knapp, John L., et. al., "Should a Master's Degree Be Required of All Teachers?" *Journal of Teacher Education,* Vol. 41, No. 2, March/April 1991, pp. 27–37.

[59] Anrig, Gregory R., "New Directions for Certifying Teachers," *NASSP Bulletin,* April 1990, pp. 58–62.

[60] Hardy, Roy A., "Teacher and Administrator Testing: Status and Trends," *Journal of School Research and Information,* Vol. 4, No. 4, 1986, p. 5.

[61] Wolf, W. C., Jr., and Matthew W. McDonough, Jr., "Issues, Legal Precedents, and Psychometric Developments Related to Testing Teachers," *National Forum of Applied Educational Research Journal,* Vol. 2, No. 1, 1989–90.

[62] Smith, Mary Lee, "Put to the Test: Effects of External Testing on Teachers," *Educational Researcher,* Vol. 20, No. 5, June/July 1991, p. 8.

[63] Haberman, Martin, "Licensing Teachers: Lessons from Other Professions," *Phi Delta Kappan,* June 1986, pp. 719–22.

[64] "Carnegie Forum Sets Panel on Teacher Certification," *Education Week,* September 10, 1986, p. 7.

[65] Adapted from Darling-Hammond, Linda, *Beyond the Commission Reports: The Coming Crisis in Teaching* (Santa Monica, Calif.: Rand Corporation, July 1984), p. 1.

[66] *A Nation Prepared.*

[67] Olson, Lynn, "Performance Pay: New Round for an Old Debate," *Education Week,* March 12, 1986, p. 1ff.

[68] *What Works: Research About Teaching and Learning* (Washington, D.C.: U.S. Department of Education, January 1986).

[69] Chubb, John E., and Terry M. Moe, *Politics, Markets and the Organization of Schools* (Washington, D.C.: Brookings Institution, 1986).

[70] Jackson, Philip W., *Life in Classrooms* (New York: Holt, Rinehart and Winston, 1968), pp. 11–12.

[71] Sieber, Sam D., and David E. Wilder, "Teaching Styles: Parental Preferences and Professional Role Definitions," *Sociology of Education*, Vol. 40, 1967, pp. 302–15.

[72] Friedman, Isaac A., "High- and Low-Burnout Schools: School Culture Aspects of Teacher Burnout," *Journal of Educational Research*, Vol. 84, No. 6, July/August 1991, pp. 325–31.

[73] Dworkin, Anthony Gary, *When Teachers Give Up: Teacher Burnout, Teacher Turnover and Their Impact on Children* (Austin: University of Texas, 1985), p. 9.

[74] Dworkin, Anthony Gary, and C. Allen Haney, "Fear, Victimization, and Stress Among Urban Public School Teachers," *Journal of Organizational Behavior*, Vol. 9, 1988, pp. 159–71.

[75] LeCompte, Margaret, and Anthony Gary Dworkin, *Giving Up in School* (Newbury Park, Calif.: Sage, 1992).

[76] Farber, Barry A., *Crisis in Education: Stress and Burnout in the American Teacher* (San Francisco: Jossey-Bass, 1991), p. 280.

[77] Dworkin, Anthony Gary, and Merric Lee Townsend, "Teacher Burnout in the Face of Reform: Some Caveats in Breaking the Mold," in Bruce Anthony Jones and Kathryn M. Borman (eds), *Breaking the Mold: Alternative Structures for American Schools* (Norwood, N.J.: Ablex, in press).

[78] Dworkin, Anthony Gary, *et al.*, "Stress and Illness Behavior Among Urban Public School Teachers," *Educational Administration Quarterly*, Vol. 26, No. 1, February 1990, pp. 60–72.

[79] Metz, Mary Haywood, "Faculty Culture: A Case Study," paper presented at American Sociological Association meetings, San Antonio, Texas, August 1984.

[80] Brenton, Myron, *What's Happened to Teacher?* (New York: Coward, McCann, and Creohegan, 1969), pp. 116–26.

[81] Natale, Jo Anna, "NEA: Toward a More Perfect Union," *The American School Board Journal*, September 1991, pp. 46–49.

[82] Bacharach, Samuel B., *et al.*, "School Management and Teacher Unions: The Capacity for Cooperation in an Age of Reform," *Teachers College Record*, Vol. 91, No. 1, Fall 1989, p. 97.

[83] Interview with teacher by the author.

[84] Goodman, Ellen, "Fewer and Fewer Are Content to Be 'Just' a Teacher," *Dayton Journal Herald*, October 22, 1979.

[85] Engelking, Jeri L., "Teacher Job Satisfaction and Dissatisfaction," *Journal of School Research and Information*, Winter 1986, pp. 33–37.

[86] Chase, Clinton I., "Two Thousand Teachers View Their Profession," *Journal of Educational Research*, Vol. 79, No. 1, 1985, pp. 12–18.

[87] Say, Elaine, and Leslie Miller, "The Second Mile Plan: Incentive Pay for Houston Teachers," *Phi Delta Kappan*, December 1982, pp. 270–71.

[88] Interview with fourth-grade boys by author.

[89] "High School Graduates: Past and Projected," *American Education* (Washington, D.C.: U.S. Department of Education, May 1984), pp. 28–29.

[90] "Offerings and Enrollments in Public High Schools," *American Education*, Vol. 21, No. 1, pp. 28–33.

[91] Irvine, Jacqueline Jordan, "Beyond Role Models: An Examination of Cultural Influences on the Pedagogical Perspectives of Black Teachers," *Peabody Journal of Education*, Vol. 66, No. 4, Summer 1989, p. 51.

[92] Justiz, Manuel J., and Marilyn C. Kameen, "Increasing the Representation of Minorities in the Teaching Profession," *Peabody Journal of Education*, Vol. 66, No. 1, Fall 1988, p. 91.

[93] Irvine, "Beyond Role Models," p. 51.

[94] Education Commission of the States, "New Strategies for Producing Minority Teachers" (Denver: Education Commission of the States, 1990).

[95] Eckert, Penelope, *Jocks and Burnouts: Social Categories and Identity in High School* (New York: Teachers College Press, 1989).

[96] Kohl, Patricia T., Wilbert M. Leonard II, William Rau, and Donna Taylor, "Vocabulary and Academic Interest Differences of Athletes and Nonathletes," *Journal of Sports Behavior*, 1990, pp. 71–83.

[97] Snyder, Eldon E., and Elmer Spreitzer, "Social Psychological Concomitants of Adolescents' Role Identities as Scholars and Athletes: A Longitudinal Analysis," paper presented at the American Sociological Association meetings, Cincinnati, Ohio, August 1991.

[98] Riordan, Cornelius, *Girls and Boys in School: Together or Separate?* (New York: Teachers College Press, 1990).

[99] Waller, *Sociology of Teaching*, p. 104.

[100] Parsons, Talcott, "The School Class as a Social System: Some of Its Functions in American Society," *Harvard Educational Review*, Vol. 29, 1959, pp. 222–23.

[101] Marsh, Herbert W., "Employment During High School: Character Building or a Subversion of Academic Goals?" *Sociology of Education*, Vol. 64, July 1991, pp. 172–89.

[102] National Council of La Raza, "The Decade of the Hispanic: A Sobering Economic Retrospective" (Washington, D.C.: National Council of La Raza, 1991).

[103] Finch, Michael D., *et al.*, "Work Experience and Control Orientation in Adolescence," *American Sociological Review*, Vol. 56, No. 5, October 1991, pp. 606–7.

[104] Gracey, Harry L., "Learning the Student Role: Kindergarten as Academic Boot Camp," in Dennis Wrong and Harry L. Gracey (eds.), *Readings in Introductory Sociology* (New York: Macmillan, 1967).

[105] *Four Years After High School: A Capsule Description of 1980 Seniors,* Office of Educational Research and Improvement, Center for Statistics (Washington, D.C.: U.S. Department of Education, August 1986), p. 40.

[106] Waller, *Sociology of Teaching*, pp. 332–33.

[107] Babad, Elisha, Frank Bernieri, and Robert Rosenthal, "Students as Judges of Teachers' Verbal and Nonverbal Behavior," *American Educational Research Journal*, Vol. 28, No. 1, Spring 1991, pp. 211–34.

[108] Jackson, *Life in Classrooms*, p. 27.

[109] Raffini, James P., "Student Apathy: A Motivational Dilemma," *Educational Leadership*, September 1986, pp. 53–55.

[110] Children's Defense Fund, *A Children's Defense Fund Budget* (Washington, D.C.: Children's Defense Fund, 1988 and 1990).

[111] Young, Thomas J., "Alienation in Contemporary Education: A Social Psychological Perspective," *Contemporary Education*, Vol. 56, No. 3, 1985, pp. 143–47.

[112] National Center for Education Statistics, *National Dropout Statistics Field Test Evaluation* (U.S. Department of Education, January 1992), p. xi.

[113] Farrell, Edwin, *Hanging In and Dropping Out: Voices of At-Risk High School Students* (New York: Teachers College Press, 1990), p. 80.

[114] Digest of Education Statistics 1991, p. 382.

[115] DeRidder, Lawrence M., "How Suspension and Expulsion Contribute to Dropping Out," *Educational Horizons,* Spring 1990, pp. 153–57.

[116] Kozol, Jonathan, *Savage Inequalities: Children in America's Schools* (New York: Crown, 1991), p. 66.

[117] Strother, Deborah Burnett, "Dropping Out," *Phi Delta Kappan*, December 1986, p. 325.

[118] Wehling, Cindy, "The Crack Kids Are Coming," *Principal*, May 1991, p. 12.

[119] Welker, Robert, "Educating Homeless Children," *School Intervention Report,* August/September 1990, pp. 1–2.

[120] Scott-Jones, Diane, "Educational Levels of Adolescent Childbearers at First and Second Births," *American Journal of Education*, August 1991, p. 461.

[121] McEvoy, Alan, "Confronting Gangs," *School Intervention Report*, February/March 1990, p. 1.

[122] Olsen, Laurie, and Melinda Moore, *Voices from the Classroom: Students and Teachers Speak Out on the Quality of Our Schools,* (Oakland, Calif.: Citizens Policy Center, 1982).

[123] Alexander, Karl L., Gary Natriello, and Aaron M. Pallas, "For Whom the School Bell Tolls: The Impact of Dropping Out on Cognitive Performance," *American Sociological Review*, Vol. 50, June 1985, pp. 409–20.

[124] *The Condition of Education,* (Washington, D.C.: Center for Education Statistics, U.S. Department of Education, 1987).

[125] Interview with Dr. Edward McDill in *School Intervention Report,* Vol. 1, No. 5, February 1988, p. 7.

[126] McPartland, James M., and Saundra Murray Nettles, "Using Community Adults as Advocates or Mentors for At-Risk Middle School Students: A Two-Year Evaluation of Project RAISE," *American Journal of Education,* Vol. 99, No. 4, August 1991, p. 568.

[127] Herbert, Victor, "School-Based Collaborations in Dropout Prevention," *NASSP Bulletin,* September 1989, p. 84.

[128] Nason, R. Beth, "Retaining Children: Is It the Right Decision?" *Childhood Education,* Annual Theme 1991, pp. 300–304.

[129] Henry, Jules, *Culture Against Man* (New York: Vintage Books, 1963), pp. 287, 320–21.

[130] Bowles and Gintis, *Schooling in Capitalist America,* p. 132.

[131] Waller, *Sociology of Teaching,* p. 80.

[132] Blalock, Ginger, "Paraprofessionals: Critical Team Members in Our Special Education Programs," *Intervention in School and Clinic,* Vol. 26, No. 4, March 1991, pp. 200–214.

[133] Mehl, Robert A., "The School Nurse: Beyond the Band-Aids," *Principal,* Vol. 70, No. 2, November 1990, p. 22.

[134] Nebgen, Mary, "Knitting Up the Safety Net," *The American School Board Journal,* November 1991, p. 51.

[135] Elam, Stanley M., Lowell C. Rose, and Alec M. Gallup, "The 23rd Annual Gallup Poll of the Public's Attitudes Toward the Public Schools," *Phi Delta Kappan,* September 1991, p. 51.

[136] Bernard, Harold W., and Daniel W. Fullmer, *Principles of Guidance,* 2nd ed. (New York: Thomas Y. Crowell, 1977), pp. 134–35.

[137] National Commission on Education, *A Nation at Risk* (Washington, D.C.: U.S. Department of Education, 1983).

[138] Epperson, Audrey I., "The Community Partnership: Operation Rescue," *Journal of Negro Education,* Vol. 60, No. 3, 1991.

[139] U.S. Department of Education, *Schools That Work: Educating Disadvantaged Children* (Washington, D.C.: U.S. Department of Education, 1989).

[140] Science Research Associates (subsidiary of IBM), Chicago, film series, "Problems in Teaching Series."

7

THE INFORMAL SYSTEM AND THE "HIDDEN CURRICULUM" What Really Happens in School

Each of us is faced with conflicting emotions as we enter the classroom. Remember the first day in a new school year or new school? These memories are vivid and lasting because we invest a tremendous amount of time and energy in schooling. During our time as students, we spend over a thousand hours each year in school.[1] Probably our clearest memories of school are the high and low points, not the daily routine. Ask your friends what they remember about early school experiences and you will hear about winning the spelling bee; standing in front of the class to recite a poem; getting detention for nothing; searching for the hamster that got loose in the school and missing math period; falling on the playground and getting stitches; starring in the school play and forgetting the lines. These highs and lows help make up our feelings about schools, and are part of the informal system.

We tend to define ourselves in relation to those around us in school—our peers and teachers. We are tested, rewarded, accused, cajoled, punished; favored, ridiculed, praised, made fun of. And possibly, we fail. John Holt discusses this topic and in doing so points out some of the variables that shape children's school experiences:

> They are afraid, above all else, of failing, of disappointing or displeasing the many anxious adults around them, whose limitless hopes and expectations for them hang over their heads like a cloud. They are bored because the things they are told to do in school are so trivial, so dull, and make such limited and narrow demands on the wide spectrum of their intelligence, capabilities, and talents.

They are confused because most of the torrent of words that pours over them in school makes little or no sense. It often flatly contradicts other things they have been told, and hardly ever has any relation to what they really know—to the rough model of reality that they carry around in their minds.[2]

Our feelings about school are affected by the teacher, by the atmosphere of the classroom, by events taking place outside the school, and by our own perceptions. Yet most of us have not given much thought to our feelings about school. Social scientists and educators have not paid much attention to this topic until recently. Judging by the scarcity of studies, students' feelings about school would appear to be of little concern; after all, kids must go to school, so why question how they feel about it? What good would it do anyway? Schools have functions to perform and they cannot always be to the liking of students, who probably do not know anyway what is important to learn.

In this chapter we look at several aspects of the informal system of schools, those unplanned experiences that happen apart from or as a result of the formal, planned curriculum of schools. The informal system covers topics ranging from coping strategies of individual students and teachers at the micro level of analysis to the structure and culture of schools at the macro level. Because the informal system permeates every aspect of education, we can only give examples of what this system is and how it works.

THE OPEN SYSTEMS APPROACH AND THE INFORMAL SYSTEM

The internal system of the school has both a formal part, consisting of roles and structure, and an informal aspect. Consider the model shown in Figure 7-1, and note the interaction between the internal system and environment, discussed further in Chapter 8. Our topics in this chapter cover several aspects of the informal system: the hidden curriculum and reproduction theories,

FIGURE 7-1   The open system of schools.

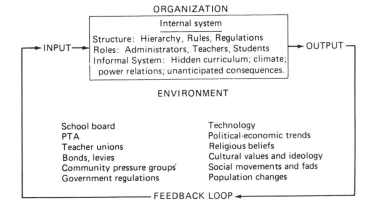

pedagogical "codes," educational climate and effective schools, peer cultures and peer group influences, the school as an informal agent of socialization, power dynamics in the school, and student and teacher coping mechanisms.

THE HIDDEN CURRICULUM

Under the organized, structured curriculum lies another, the three R's: rules, routines, and regulations of the "hidden curriculum," as demonstrated in the syllabus outlined in Table 7-1. Most of us have had similar questions as we entered each new class and evaluated each new teacher. "The hidden curriculum is what is taught by school, not by any teacher. However enlightened the staff, however progressive the curriculum, however community-oriented the school, something is coming across to the pupils which need never be spoken. . . . They are picking up an approach to living, and an attitude in learning."[3]

The name *hidden curriculum* was coined by Benson Snyder[4] in 1971, but the concept has been used for many years by educators, sociologists, and psychologists in describing the informal system of schools. Snyder refers to the "implicit demands (as opposed to the explicit obligations of the 'visible curriculum') that are found in every learning institution and which students have to find out and respond to in order to survive within it."

Many alternative adjectives exist for the "hidden" curriculum: unwritten, unstudied, tacit, latent, unnoticed, and paracurriculum. In David Hargreaves's[5] analysis of the research done on the "paracurriculum," he finds two major categories: (1) the social-psychological aspects of the paracurriculum from functionalist-conservative or radical-conflict points of view; and (2) the

TABLE 7-1   Syllabus for Course 101

Actual or Visible Curriculum	*Hidden Curriculum*
Instructor: Name	*Instructor:* How is the instructor really referred to?
Texts: Names	*Texts:* Do we really have to have them and read them?
Course topics: Listed	*Course topics:* What is the instructor really going to teach? What is he or she really interested in?

Requirements:
  Readings
	Requirements:
	  What do I really have to do to get by?

Projects	Will it help if I speak up in class?
Exams	Will it help if I go see the instructor?
Bibliography	*Bibliography:* Am I really supposed to use this?

sociological aspects from a functionalist-conservative account or the more radical-conflict position. We will refer to these perspectives in our discussion of the informal system.

From the systems perspective, the hidden curriculum is one part of the total system, and we can understand it only by understanding the context in which it exists. Therefore, we now review some of the elements that make up the informal system.

Reproduction Theory and the Informal System

To conflict theorists, the social control function of the hidden curriculum reproduces the social class of students;[6] for instance, working-class students learn to cope with boredom in schools, which enables them to endure a life of boredom on the job. Hargreaves points out the effects of the hidden curriculum on different students; working-class students learn that they are "written off" in the educational system.[7]

The hidden curriculum contains a social and economic agenda that is responsible for separating social classes, giving elites more freedom and opportunity, and training nonelites to accept their lot as punctual workers. Most students learn to accept that their political-economic system is best, whatever their position within it.[8]

However, some students oppose this "informal reproduction process" with resistance behaviors, some of which become ritualized. McLaren describes behaviors that contest "the legitimacy, power, and significance of school culture in general and instruction in particular." The "class clown," for instance, can often penetrate the orderly classroom and formal expectations by deconstructing the familiar through "sarcastic comments, a trickster-like prankishness, parody, and burlesque."[9]

Anyon documents the differences in school experiences and expectations by describing five elementary schools in contrasting communities, from working-class to professional and executive elite schools. Although many outward similarities exist, the hidden curriculum in each school addresses the "needs" of the social class represented by the majority of students in the school.

1. The working-class schools stressed following the steps of a procedure, mechanically, by rote, with little decision making, choice, or explanation why it was done a particular way. Grading is based on following procedures.
2. The middle-class school stressed getting the right answer. There is some figuring, choice, and decision making; for instance, asking the children how they got an answer.
3. The affluent professional school stressed creative activity carried out independently, with students asked to express and apply ideas and concepts, and think about the ideas.
4. The executive elite school stressed developing one's analytical intellectual powers, reason through problems, conceptualize rules by which elements may fit together in systems and apply these to solving problems. Included here is successful presentation of self.[10]

Anyon points out that these aspects of the hidden curriculum are preparing the students for their future productive roles in society. The working class is being prepared for future wage labor that is mechanical and routine, the middle class for bureaucratic relation to capital, the professionals for instrumental and expressive roles that involve substantial negotiation, and the elite for "knowledge of and practice in manipulating the socially legitimate tools of analysis of systems." In conclusion, "the 'hidden curriculum' of school work is tacit preparation for relating to the process of production in a particular way." Where students are tracked in class-heterogeneous schools, the same process can take place.

An ethnographic study by Lubeck[11] documents the importance of the *use* of time and space structures to transmit adult values. The differences between the Head Start and other child-care settings she studied illustrate the importance of these values for reproducing class. In Head Start settings serving low-income children, time and space tended to be more rigidly structured for the children than in other centers, where children had some control.

Students develop coping mechanisms or strategies for survival within the structure of contradictions—delays while much of the day is spent waiting to hurry up, and denials when students are told the many things they cannot do. Students try to find the approved responses among the mixed messages; successful students become adept at beating the system.[12]

THE EDUCATIONAL "CLIMATE" AND SCHOOL EFFECTIVENESS

Let us enter the school again as we did when we discussed the formal school system. However, this time we are looking for the informal aspects of the system. We can observe only a handful, but these few will provide examples of the informal system within schools.

Some elements of the informal system are fairly easily observed: the school's architecture, open versus closed classrooms, ability grouping, age grading, team teaching. Many of these are discussed elsewhere in the text. Others are not so easily observed. Here we are particularly interested in the educational "climate" or "culture" as it affects what happens in schools and classrooms and as it contributes to effective schools. Factors both inside and outside the school influence the value climate, our first topic.

The Value Climate

What affects students' motivations, aspirations, and achievement? Why are some schools more productive than others? Do peers have more influence over students than teachers and parents? It is difficult to unravel this interlocking group of questions, for the variables are closely interrelated and no single one can provide an answer. Each major research project concerned with the value climate has included slightly different research questions, variables, methods, and settings, resulting in conclusions that are often diverse and even contradictory. While this is a field in the process of development and change, the studies cited here show the relationship of value climate to home environment, self-concept, achievement, and teacher expectations, and illustrate some of the major interests and findings in the field to the present time.

Influences of Home Environment, Race, and Socioeconomic Status on School Value Climate.   Students come in many types. Some are rich; some poor. Some come from families that stress education; some do not. Some are highly motivated toward educational attainment; some are not. The school system must accept the variety of students and make them fit into the school system, preparing them to fit into future roles in society. A school's value climate results from the combination of students' race, family background, and socioeconomic status (SES); that is, the composition of the school's student body. The effect of home on school climate became a widely researched topic, especially following Coleman's 1966 study, *Equality of Educational Opportunity*.[13] This study, discussed in Chapter 4, concluded that the effects of the home environment were more significant in students' achievement than effects of the school program. The family's educational and social background was most important, followed by the backgrounds of other children in the school. Some follow-up studies, such as that by Jencks[14] and the Plowden Report from Britain, confirmed the prime importance of home background for school success. From Coleman's findings came the recommendation to integrate the schools so that lower-class students, who were disproportionately black and minority, would share an education with middle-class students, and thus be in an atmosphere or "value climate" more favorable to achievement. More recent research by Coleman and his associates[15] indicates that private schools provide superior education to public schools because the value climate in many private schools is more conducive to learning. Components that influence value climate include principal leadership, staff cooperation, student behavior, teacher control over school and classroom policy, and teacher morale.[16]

Both the idea that schools make little difference in the achievement of children and the finding that private schools provide superior education have been challenged in a number of studies. The "Wisconsin Social-Psychological Model of Status Attainment," a longitudinal study originally developed in 1957 and repeated since then, has provided a useful analytical model for many researchers. In a revised model, the authors found that "socioeconomic status has no effect on high school performance independent of measured ability, and on education and occupational aspirations, and via these aspirations, on educational attainment and occupational achievement."[17] Sewell and Hauser also report that *ability* has direct effects on high school performance, regardless of socioeconomic status. The importance of SES variables on attainment comes from the encouragement received from significant others and from educational aspirations.

Other studies find that achievement and school value climate are affected by the student body's composition, particularly race and socioeconomic status, and the neighborhood in which students live. For instance, attitudes of African-American adolescents toward education reflect multidimensional influences. They express high regard for education, though performance may be poor. This attitude-achievement dilemma reflects the dominant ideology in U.S. society that education is desirable. However, concrete attitudes come from life experience, and educational achievement may not be fairly rewarded by the opportunity structure.[18,19]

A study of neighborhood effects on a school district in Scotland found that deprived home and neighborhood environments influence educational attainment negatively. The importance lies in taking into account the wider socioeconomic structure outside the school and including the home when formulating policies to deal with school performance.[20]

By changing the school composition, the value climate can be altered, and achievement raised. Other findings indicate that lower-class students achieve at a higher level in racially mixed schools, while integration does not adversely affect the middle-class students.

One attempt to improve the motivation and achievement level of children in a lower-class, low-achieving school showed dramatic results. The school was located in an area of high unemployment in England where some parents were barely literate. Teachers visited the homes of students, asking parents to spend a few minutes each day listening to their children read. Most parents cooperated, and many became involved in improving their own skills. Reading in the school improved significantly, showing that developing a link between school and home may work to the benefit of all.

School Value Climate and Self-Concept.   Self-concept refers to the way individuals view themselves in particular roles, and varies depending on each different role being considered. This view determines to a large extent how people perform in given roles. In Chapters 3 and 4 we discussed self-concept by sex, race, and class as it affects aspirations and achievement of students. Self-concept has several dimensions—what individuals expect of themselves, how they feel about their ability to carry out a role, and the value they place in the role.

To carry out a role, individuals must feel that they can be successful. Therefore, students must believe that they can be high achievers in order to try to be so. This evaluation of our beliefs in ability can be altered depending on the perceived costs, rewards, and motivations involved. Evaluation of academic performance is approached differently by high- and low-achieving students; students who are low achievers tend to avoid being evaluated as students and attempt to withdraw self-investment from the student role.[21]

Wilbur Brookover and colleagues[22] show that "self-concept of academic ability is significantly correlated with academic performance." Labeling and conditioning influence the way we see our abilities in any area. If many students in a school have low achievement expectations, this influences the school's achievement level. Manipulating school variables may improve students' chances of academic success. School value climate, background experiences, peer-group relationships, and other factors in students' careers influence academic self-concept, and vice versa. Thus, the recommendation in the effective schools literature is to raise students' self-concept *and* academic expectations.

School Value Climate and Student Achievement. Schools reward incompetence. So argues Jackson,[23] pointing out that the average student spends 20 hours a week on courses, does little to no homework, and plays dumb. The reward for success in school is more hard work, so why try? Here we look at school effects on student achievement.

Wilbur Brookover and his colleagues[24] set about to test Coleman and Jencks's findings that the home environment supersedes school influence in students' school achievement. In ongoing research on school climate and performance, they administered questionnaires to students and teachers. Results showed that academic value climate of school for elementary students is affected by four types of perceptions:

1. student perceptions of the present "evaluations/expectations" of "others" (parents, teachers, friends) in their school and social system,
2. student perceptions of the future "evaluations/expectations" of "others" in their school and social system,
3. student perceptions about the level of feelings of futility permeating the social system of the school, and
4. student perceptions of those academic norms stressing academic achievement that exist in their school and social system.[25]

The most important variable by far was the students' reported sense of futility—their feelings of hopelessness and their sense that teachers do not care about their academic achievement. The role of teachers' and classmates' attitudes in establishing these feelings is obviously an important part of the school climate.

In a more recent study, Brookover and colleagues[26] considered the effects of school social structure and social climate on student achievement. *Student achievement* was measured by reading and writing competencies, academic self-concept, and self-reliance. The *school social structure* was measured by teacher satisfaction with the school structure, parental involvement, differentiation in student programs, principals' reports of time devoted to instruction, and student mobility in school. The *school climate* was measured by student perceptions, teacher perceptions, and principal perceptions. More than 85 percent of the variance in student attainment was explained by the combination of the above variables. In a summary of findings, which compared improving and declining schools, Brookover and colleagues found the following: The staff of improving schools place more emphasis on accomplishing basic reading and mathematics objectives; they believe *all* students can master basic objectives and they hold high expectations; they assume responsibility for learning and accept being held accountable. Principals in improving schools are instructional leaders and disciplinarians. In short, Brookover argues that schools can and *do* make a difference.

Brookover and colleagues also report on a recent attempt to put the concept of "school climate" into practice. In a pragmatic program in the Chicago public school system, using variables mentioned to alter school climate, school achievement levels were raised significantly.

Edward McDill and Leo Rigsby have also been working on the question of educational climate and productivity for a number of years. They identified six dimensions of school climate:

1. the value placed on academics by students,
2. the degree to which acquisition of knowledge and learning is valued,
3. the degree to which intellectual criteria versus other criteria are emphasized for status,
4. the emphasis placed on science in the school,
5. emphasis on art, humanities, social studies, and social issues, and
6. academically oriented students' status system and extracurricular activities.[27]

They found a positive relationship between high rankings on the six dimensions, high mathematical achievement, and socioeconomic status (SES). Each climate dimension except number four was more strongly related to achievement than was SES. In short, climate dimensions were better indicators of academic achievement in mathematics than SES.

According to Alexander and McDill,[28] the curriculum in which a high school student was enrolled affected the student's values and attitudes. Students who followed an academic, college preparatory curriculum were more likely to be high achievers; this placement also affected class rank, math achievement, self-concept, values and attitudes, and other factors.

Many recent commission reports encourage teachers to set high academic standards and assign more well-constructed homework with grades and meaningful comments. In fact, there is a relationship between the two; research indicates that achievement and test scores improve with increased time spent outside the classroom. "High [achievement performance] standards set by teachers, parents, and peers also generate greater effort on homework." However, higher standards are set by teachers and peers for high-ability students who can handle a challenge. Parents are more likely to set higher standards for lower-ability students less able to deal with the challenge. This difference may result from teachers' expectations of high-ability students and parents' response to their student's poor performance.[29,30]

The findings of a recent English study are similar to the results of Brookover, McDill, and others who have looked at the question, "Do schools make a difference?" The researchers studied 12 inner-city London secondary schools, which showed great variation on between-school differences in student behavior and attainment. School variations remained fairly constant over time, even when controlling for students' family background and personal characteristics. Examination results, behavior, and degree of delinquency were closely related in successful schools, but not related to school size, physical aspects of the building, or administrative structure.

Outcomes were related to school characteristics as social institutions—"academic emphasis, teacher action in lessons, the availability of incentives and rewards, good conditions for pupils, and the extent to which children were able to take responsibility." These factors could all be influenced by staff.

Abilities of children also affected outcomes. The combined factors created "a particular ethos, or set of values, attitudes, and behaviors which (will) become characteristic of the school as a whole. This is the school value climate. Behaviors and attitudes are shaped by school experience, and these in turn shape outcomes of schools."[31]

In a recent summary of findings of effective and ineffective schools, Ronald Edmonds[32] testified before Congress that the behavior of schools is critical in determining the quality of education. "Effective schools share a 'climate' in which it is incumbent on all personnel to be instructionally effective for all pupils."

Whatever the academic norms of a school, students tend to conform. Where academic achievement is rewarded by faculty and peers, students tend to achieve better.[33] School climate explains much of the difference in levels of school achievement, differences sometimes attributed to race, SES, and home effects.[34]

Value Climate Related to Teacher and Student Expectations. Within schools, groups of student peers can be identified by their cohesiveness; along with that cohesiveness goes a set of expectations, values, and aspirations. Willis[35] describes how boys in an all-male comprehensive secondary school in England were divided into the "lads," who "worked the system" to gain control over their time, and the "ear 'oles," (earholes) who complied with authority and the expectations of the school. Lads were learning to belong to the working class by rejecting the mental work of the school; they were reinforcing and reproducing their status. The culture lads reproduced for themselves was actually their realistic assessment of chances within the school and social class context, according to Willis. In a study of American high school students, Faunce found that "our conception of self, and, consequently, our degree of concern for achievement in various areas, is anchored primarily in ongoing social relationships in recurring social settings,"[36] a finding similar to that of Willis.

The School Climate and Effective Schools

Many things about schools are familiar: corridors, classrooms behind closed doors, a big clock, signs directing us to the school office. But there is something unique about each school's environment or atmosphere, something intangible. This forms the school *climate.*

School Culture. Each school has a *culture* of its own, like a miniature society. This is part of school climate. It consists of the values, attitudes, beliefs, norms, and customs of those making up the system. Each school's climate includes its rituals and ceremonies.[37] A key purpose or function of this culture is to bring about a group feeling of loyalty. Pep rallies, cheering at athletic events, assemblies, singing, devotions, fire drills, honors and awards ceremonies, opening exercises, commencement, and even passing to classes constitute ceremonies common to most schools, but these are unique in each school. Many ceremonies take place around athletics; athletes are often leading figures among the students and may even be given special privileges and status in the school. Similar ceremonies are found at the college level in fraternities and sororities; they distinguish participants from the more "serious" world of academics and professors, and provide a buffer between the two.

Students are assigned to a public school by chance of residence. The school climate or culture reflects the immediate community in which the school is located and its students' characteristics. The climate affects student self-concept, attitudes and performance, expectations of teachers in schools, and the academic norms of each school.

Norms in both the school setting and the larger culture encourage distance between teachers and students. A new teacher who tries to be too friendly to students may receive sanctions from teachers, ranging from teasing to ostracism. In most school situations, teachers maintain distance as a sign of authority, and perhaps also to discourage close relations, which might lead to indiscretions between students and teachers.

Teachers represent the culture of the adult society and the dominant group; students have a more limited cultural boundary centered on age-peer group, school, and local community. The world view held by the two groups is a separating influence. Teachers are considered "different" by students; mystique surrounds them. Recall your impressions of various teachers, the rumors that circulated about them, and nicknames they were given. Students make their own culture, which is passed on to each new generation entering the school; it involves language, dress, humor, music, games, and hazing.

Effective Schools: What Works?

We can all document problems found in schools, but how do we define effective schools? One of the most quoted definitions of effective schools comes from Edmonds: Effective schools are those where working-class kids score as well as middle-class kids on skills tests.[38] The concept of effective schools addresses both formal structural variables and informal climate variables, recognizing the interrelationship between the two.

Edmonds's[39] findings concerning characteristics of effective schools have been confirmed or slightly modified by a number of studies, including commission reports. Schools with high student achievement and morale show the following characteristics:

1. vigorous instructional leadership,
2. a principal who makes clear, consistent, and fair decisions,
3. an emphasis on discipline and a safe and orderly environment,
4. instructional practices that focus on basic skills and academic achievement,
5. collegiality among teachers in support of student achievement,
6. teachers with high expectations that all their students can and will learn, and
7. frequent review of student progress.[40]

Running through all of these characteristics is the idea of a school climate that emphasizes and rewards academic achievement, the importance of scholastic success, and the maintenance of order and fair discipline. A necessary complement to the above is positive home-school relations: a supportive home environment for students, involvement of parents with the school, and support of students doing homework. In addition, careful manipulation of the structure to group students with the goal of enhancing self-esteem and feelings of accomplishment is recommended by some reports.[41]

Ultimately, it is impossible to have effective schools without *effective students*.[42,43] Efforts to improve schools must take into account the diversity in types of students schools are dealing with and the needs of these students. Students are the ones who must learn and achieve with the help of schools, parents, peers, and other factors that influence the process.

These relationships within the school and classroom context make up the system of education that must be manipulated to improve schools and make them more effective.

Classroom Climate

The class has generally been viewed as a self-contained system, sealed off from society. Psychologists and sociologists have concentrated on the "one teacher—many students" model, rather than viewing the classroom in a broader context. The classroom has also been equated with a crowd situation:[44] many people in close proximity and a central figure trying to maintain control, often through the use of discipline. Whatever the model, the dynamics of classroom behavior cannot be understood unless the importance of the environment is recognized. Did Johnny have breakfast this morning; did Linda have an argument with her best friend; are Stephen's parents separating; does the teacher have personal or professional problems?

Routines are imposed on students in classrooms in order to maintain control and discipline. In fact, the instructional patterns are remarkably similar. Students play passive learning roles and are seldom actively involved in thinking or hands-on activity. Teachers call the shots and determine the activities.

Classrooms, because of their structure and organization, assume certain behaviors and attitudes on the part of students—delayed gratification, for example, and support of group cohesion and purpose over individual desires. These attitudes are not easily taught in school but are necessary components of the teaching situation. Children must begin to acquire the behaviors and attitudes necessary for classroom learning before coming to school. The school experience can be meaningless for "unprepared" children. Problems in families, lack of discipline in some homes, and the influence of television have not aided the adjustment to traditional classrooms. Preparation for school can no longer be assumed by teachers. What can be done to prepare students? Suggestions range from solving societal-economic problems in order to increase family stability, to "deschooling society," as described in Chapter 11.

Students understand their classroom experiences in many different ways, most of which are influenced by relations among students. Especially for early adolescents, social and personal development needs suggest that cooperative learning activities are important and effective.[45]

Classroom climate can produce antischool feelings, especially in competitive, restrictive classrooms, or it can produce students who are motivated toward self-improvement, academic success, and enjoyment of learning. Where student motivation is low, increasing teacher concern and involvement may reduce classroom problems. However, an unfortunate downward trend in positive, encouraging teacher behaviors occurs as students progress through levels of school. By the high school years, "the frequency of teacher praise, encouragement, connection with guidance, and positive interaction with students had dropped by nearly 50 percent from the number of observed occurrences at the early elementary level."[46]

Classroom Codes: Interaction in the Classroom.   A major process in the school system is interaction. Messages concerning expectations, power relations, and attitudes toward others and the learning process are passed through verbal and nonverbal cues. The type and extent of classroom interaction is related to teacher styles, which can be grouped into three types:

- *Authoritarian:* Formal power is vested and used by the teacher.
- *Democratic:* Students are involved in the decision making that affects classroom activities.
- *Laissez-faire:* There is general freedom in the classroom.

Learning takes place in many different settings and classroom structures.

The daily student-teacher interactions and interpersonal relations determine the atmosphere of the classroom. In the average classroom a routine develops, though a day in a classroom is seldom really routine. Consider the fact that between 300 and 600 interactions take place in one hour of class time. Consider also that for every spoken message there are several unspoken messages given through tone, gesture, and facial expressions. The silent language can tell us more about the atmosphere of the classroom than any spoken words.

Basil Bernstein, an English sociologist who has written extensively on processes in schools, is concerned with the processes that take place in classrooms, the rules that govern interaction, power relationships between teachers and students, and how these relate to the social class of students. He argues that these classroom dynamics lead to the social reproduction of class. Classrooms have interaction "codes"—rules, practices, and agencies regulating communication that determine the distribution of power. "Code" refers to a "regulative principle which underlies various message systems, especially curriculum and pedagogy." *Pedagogy* refers to the transmission of knowledge, usually through structured curricula. Among the "codes" are hierarchy—the interaction between the transmitter (teacher) and acquirer (student); the sequencing and pacing, or progression and rate at which information is transmitted; and the criteria, or whether the student accepts as legitimate or illegitimate what is being transmitted in the educational process. All of these factors affect the student's learning. Control, then, relates to the power structures and social division of labor. Those who control *what* knowledge is transmitted in the curriculum also have control over *how* knowledge is transmitted—the materials, organization, pacing, and timing of knowledge transmitted and received.[47]

In a test of Bernstein's concept of "pedagogical codes," Kalekin-Fishman studied the way messages are transmitted between teachers and students in kindergartens in Germany and Israel. The "noise" patterns in classrooms reflected the goals and structure of classrooms. For instance, a teacher's authoritarian directives were more effective in some settings, such as working-class areas, in bringing about desired results, whereas teachers as "facilitators" produced more "white noise" or undifferentiated sound in the classroom. The different pedagogical codes do affect the learning environment. Acoustical environments can enhance or detract from classroom goals.[48]

Student Friendship and Interaction Patterns in the Classroom. Student friendship patterns and interactions vary depending on whether the classroom is structured in an open or a traditional manner. Open, flexible, and democratic classrooms stress the affective or emotional growth of students. According to a study of friendship patterns,[49] affective classrooms include increased interaction and shared activities, more uniform distribution of popularity among students, and an increased opportunity for students to be good at some task. "Open classrooms decrease isolation, increase longevity of friendships, and foster more uniform distribution of popularity." In testing reasons for the differences between traditional and open classes, Hallinan considered the context in which students meet friends. Students in open classes had fewer best friends.[50] In traditional classrooms, children have potential friends from imposed seating assignments. Cross-sex best friends are tolerated, but are not permitted to join friendship cliques. Interestingly, in this later study she found that the larger the class size, the more sociability and the fewer number of isolates. While more children in large classes reported having best friends, fewer were cross-sex friends. Friendliness and popularity were positively correlated with intelligence, physical attractiveness, and social awareness.

For adolescents, having a best friend is important as a source of mutual intimacy, characterized by acceptance, understanding, self-disclosure, and mutual advice. Loyalty and commitment become increasingly important aspects of friendships as adolescents become older.

There are clear differences between female and male popularity and friendship patterns: Females are closely knit and egalitarian, sharing intimacies and problems; males are loosely knit, with clear status hierarchies based on shared activities such as sports.[51]

Eder[52] describes a hierarchy of cliques that are evident among girls in junior high school. Popular girls avoid interactions with lower-status girls, but this engenders dislike toward the popular girls, hence a cycle of popularity. Many girls want to appear friendly and nice and interact with people they dislike to avoid a "snobbish" or "stuck-up" label.

The organizational structure of the school can also affect interactions. For instance, ability grouping constricts the number and variety of students with whom one comes in contact. A recitation mode of instruction results in ranking students by ability to perform orally.[53] These structures, in turn, influence student contacts, such as racial interactions in schools where groupings break down along racial lines. Students are only one-sixth as likely to choose a cross-race than same-race peer as a friend. Personal characteristics of individual students have the strongest effect, but tracking is also important.[54] Interracial friendships influence college aspirations and attendance. The closer the peers, the greater the influence, especially in the same track and gender.[55]

Popularity of boys and girls in elementary school relates to gender socialization. Boys achieve high status because of athletic ability, coolness, toughness, social skills, and success in cross-gender relations. Girls are popular because of their parents' socioeconomic status, their appearance, social skills, and academic success.[56]

Special events or organizational changes can alter the classroom routine and also affect classroom participation: when a substitute teacher comes; when a child moves from one reading group to the next level group; when the principal visits the classroom; when testing days are held; and when the school has a special assembly or holiday program. Teachers often manipulate the classroom situation in order to have better control over interaction patterns of individuals or groups of students. Moving seats, rearranging desks, and regrouping students all influence interaction patterns and climate.

In a review of research literature on the effect of interaction patterns on reading achievement, Bank, *et al.,* concluded that there is some support for the following hypotheses:

1. *Discrimination:* Teachers treat boys and girls differently because of the differential fit between their respective gender roles and the school's expected student role.

2. *Feminization of reading:* American teachers and students look upon reading as a feminine activity, and this affects motivation and expectations.

3. *Differential response:* Teachers do not respond to students' sex per se but do respond to their behavior, and boys and girls behave differently.

4. *Sex-relevant teaching styles:* Different teachers have different views of what and how teachers should teach, and the teaching styles common in the United States may serve girls more effectively than boys.[57]

For the most part different experiences of boys and girls in elementary school classrooms result from gender role expectations; there are subtle differences in teaching boys more self-reliance and independence and girls more conformity and responsibility.[58]

Seating Arrangements and Physical Conditions in Classrooms. Most classrooms are set up so that the teacher is the center of activity; students face the teacher and are placed so that maximum attention can be focused toward the central point.[59] In this way, students' attention can be better controlled by teachers. If a student is inattentive, or a group of students is disruptive, seat reassignment may solve the problem.

The location of a student's seat affects both that student's behavior and the teacher's attitudes toward the student. Studies in elementary and college classrooms show that those students sitting in the front or center of the classroom participate more and achieve better. These students are also regarded more highly by teachers and peers. Teachers tend to be more permissive in their verbal interactions and use fewer formal directives with pupils who are near the front. In college classrooms, students in these positions tend to be brighter and more interested, to get better grades, and to like the instructor better, perhaps because they can see and hear better, are more involved, and can watch and participate more.[60]

A comparison between the effectiveness of row versus table seating in elementary classrooms was made by Kevin Wheldall.[61] In observations of both arrangements, he found that not only did students in his study prefer row seating, but that 15 percent more "on-task behavior" (specific academic task performed without disruption) occurred in rows. In addition, discipline problems were reduced and teachers made more positive commands when students were in rows. This limited study challenges some ideas of the value of more informal groupings; however, it does not argue against the value of table arrangements for the many cooperative tasks in the classroom.

Attention has also been paid to the physical conditions that produce the best working conditions. The ideal temperature for optimum learning in the classroom is in the low 20°C, with variability depending on such factors as activity, clothing, and amount of stress. Little research has been done on lighting, though windowless schools are not considered advisable. The "electrical atmosphere," or ionization of the climate, may affect learning and performance, with negative ionization thought to be beneficial.[62] Other factors, such as wall color, shape of room, and noise level in and outside the classroom, all have some effect on learning, though evidence in this field is scanty. Even music played in the classroom was found to raise the on-task performance of male fifth-grade students.[63] Figure 7-2 shows physical conditions that may affect learning. Note the relationships suggested between psychocultural, biological, and physical factors.

Concerns about classroom and school health hazards abound. Estimates are that one in eight schools is old, delapidated, and in poor condition for learning; 25 percent lack space, maintenance, and safety. These figures will not be alleviated by the decrease in enrollments, estimated to fall in the United States from 41 million in 1992 to 38.7 million in 1996.[64] But funds to repair buildings are lacking. Building contaminants such as carbon dioxide, carbon monoxide, water vapor, nitrogen dioxide, asbestos, formaldehyde, bioaerosols, bio-effluents, lead, and radon exist in almost every school building.[65]

Size of School and Classroom. One assumes that "smaller is better" in the classroom; that smaller classes mean fewer control problems, less work for teachers, and more interaction and communication. However, there is mixed

FIGURE 7-2   Schematic representation of factors to be considered when determining human thermal environment.

Source: Rohles, F. H., "Environmental Ergonomics in Agricultural Systems," *Applied Ergonomics,* Vol. 16, No. 3, 1985, pp. 163–66 (chart p. 163). Reprinted by permission of the publishers Butterworth-Heinemann Ltd.

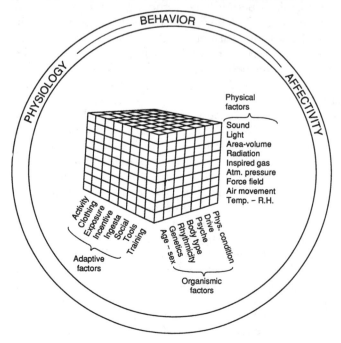

evidence on whether class size itself has a direct effect on the learning process. Certain groups of children—those in lower grades and with lower academic abilities—gain by being in smaller classes, when the teaching methods are adapted to take advantage of the intimate setting. In a study of reading and math skills, primary students in classes of 20 students for two years scored significantly better on standardized tests than did those in classes of 26 or more.[66]

The research findings on optimum numbers for small-group activities within classrooms are somewhat inconclusive.[67] In an analysis of the many research studies related to class size and student gain, researchers conclude that "the classroom practice of teachers working with large groups, rather than small groups, is associated with greater student gain." The researchers found that students learn less when they work in small groups without adult supervision.[68] This may not show the failure of small groups as a teaching technique, but the inexperience of teachers using this technique in keeping all students involved and on task in well-structured, self-motivated, small-group activities. So although most data to date do not support the value of small-group activities over whole-class activities for student gain, there may be ways of structuring small groups for maximum benefit.[69]

Smaller school size was recommended by the Panel on Youth,[70] chaired by James Coleman, because of the impact on social interactions. Students can play a more active role in school life and interact more informally with teachers and administrators in smaller schools. In contrast, the climate in large schools leads students to be more passive with adults, to be followers, to depend on others to manage their affairs, and to have fewer leadership opportunities. Percentage of participation decreases with increased size of the school. Certain types of activities, such as hobby clubs, can increase in size to include any number, but other activities—athletic teams, music, and drama— are inelastic; students attending larger schools are at a disadvantage because a smaller percentage of the school population can participate.[71]

Architecture of Schools.   Architects' designs reflect the purpose that a building is to serve; in turn, the design influences activities within a building, and how these will interact with surrounding activities and buildings.[72] School architectural style and sites make schools stand out among buildings, indicating their distinct function. Whether school buildings are squeezed between other buildings or located on sprawling campuses, their fenced-in area or other physical separation distinguishes them from the community-at-large. Some educators object to this physical isolation from the surrounding community. Separation isolates schools from valuable interactions with the wider community. Yet it serves the function of concentrating students in one place for one specific activity.[73]

The school is composed of many dynamic parts that fit together, from buildings that make possible certain interaction patterns to the atmospheres or climates that influence the learning process. All these are part of the complex informal system of education. We now turn to a third major aspect of the informal system: power relationships.

POWER DYNAMICS AND ROLES IN THE INFORMAL SYSTEM

In the classroom there is a delicate balance between formal expectations and informal processes. Many rules prescribing formal behavior in schools are informally transmitted. Some argue that this informality serves the school and classroom well; the classroom is less bureaucratic than many formal organizations,[74] providing a transition from home to workplace. When students are not hampered by formal rules there is more likely to be unconscious assimilation of rules. Through this informal process students learn to deal with the formal and informal expectations of organizations. Broadly defined, *power* refers to both actual practice that promotes teacher and adult interests, and to a nebulous force that need not always be exercised in order to control or secure desired outcomes.[75]

Theoretical Explanations of Power Dynamics in the Classroom

The theoretical approaches that have been discussed in other chapters are also important in discussions of power dynamics. *Functional theorists* emphasize the consensus resulting from the socialization function of the classroom as it prepares students for societal roles.[76] Another primary function is that of selection and allocation, which begins in elementary classrooms and continues throughout schooling. Not only achievement but also obedience and cooperation are important aspects of schooling. Children learn quickly what is expected of them, and their cooperation makes the school system work. Those most successful in meeting achievement and behavioral expectations do best in the school system. Students are "selected" according to how successfully they have been socialized into the system and how well they cooperate with those in power.

Conflict theorists have other interpretations of classroom dynamics. They see a power struggle between school staff, representing the dominant group and values of the adult world, and students who must be controlled, coerced, and coopted by using a variety of strategies. The theme of conflict in the classroom is dominant in Waller's book,[77] written in 1932. He describes the difference between adult and student cultures, mechanisms to maintain the social distance between the two, and the "battles" in classrooms over requirements.

Capitalism, which demands that schools prepare a loyal, docile, disciplined work force for society, is seen as a societal force behind the "coercion" in classrooms:

> Schools foster types of personal development compatible with the relationships of dominance and subordinancy in the economic sphere . . . through a close correspondence between the social relationships which govern personal interaction in the workplace and the social relationships of the educational system.[78]

From this perspective conflict is seen as built into the dynamic system. Power influences how "cultural capital" is transmitted and reproduced. Teachers control the use of space and time, initiate interactions, and define the rules. Thus the routines and rituals of schools represent the dominant value system that the schools are passing on to young people. Those who are successfully selected, classified, and evaluated in school are likely to be successful in society as adults.[79,80] Schools alone do not determine their own internal power structure or their unequal outcomes. Rather, we must view schools within the larger societal context of social class, ideological, and material forces.[81]

From the *interactionist perspective,* each member of the class has a distinctive perception of the world of the classroom. Each individual's plan of action is dependent on how she or he views the world and responds to it. Many factors affect perceptions. Consider Howard Becker's classic study of Chicago teachers.[82] Their perceptions of students were related to cultural differences and class origins among pupils, which in turn related to the degree of trouble teachers had with students.

Helen Gouldner's study of minority children found that students were labeled early in their school careers and put into rigid, inflexible tracks. For instance, one teacher grouped students into "tigers, cardinals, and clowns"; labels given were internalized by pupils and acted as a self-fulfilling prophecy. Tigers received the most positive interaction, while those in lower groups were given less attention. The groups were correlated by researchers with students' social class, tigers being from higher classes than the other groups.[83] These different expectations based on class influenced the selection and allocation process, with students from lower-class backgrounds at a disadvantage. In addition, student perceptions of their own chances for success influenced their decisions about what role to play in school, as we have discussed.

The "dramaturgical model" is one that takes into consideration the many variables that influence the classroom system.

> [In] . . . the dramaturgical model, the essential elements of a situation are: the 'stage' (the school or classroom, etc.); 'props' (desks, cupboards, books, blackboards, etc.); 'players' (teachers and pupils, each with his or her own intentions, biography, and mix of background cultures); 'scripts' (or roles; i.e., formal expectations of others, and of self); point in time at which all these properties come together; and an important property which is the result of actual expectations of others, and of self. . . .[84]

Much research concerning the formal and informal school organization uses or presupposes this type of model.

Students and the Informal System

Student culture, that complex of "strange customs," constitutes a "participation mystique, complex rituals of personal relationships, a set of folkways, mores, and irrational sanctions, a moral code based upon them."[85]

When we enter a school or observe playground activity, we see this unique culture manifest itself. The norms that control behavior of peer group members are strong. One need only observe the conformity in dress, gestures, language, and slang to discover what is acceptable in a particular school. Fads and crazes are key aspects of student culture, holding the group together.

Playground activities and games help set the students' world apart from the adult culture. Even in playground games, children are learning to relate to their peers by following rules, taking turns, and verbally and nonverbally expressing themselves. These behaviors will carry over into their formal encounters with the adult world and are an important socializing agent in the child's life.

Student Peer-Group Influence.   The student subculture has strong influence in determining what happens in school. Because students are grouped together by age and subjected to a series of age-related requirements, they develop a separate subculture with norms, expectations, and methods or "strategies" for coping with these demands. This subculture evolves as a result of the long period of school training, necessary for industrial societies, that delays the entry of young people into the adult world. In *The Adolescent Society,* Coleman[86] wrote that the strength of this subculture lies in its power over its members. He found that for an adolescent, the disapproval of one's peers is almost as hard to accept as that of one's parents, and that one pays a price for nonconformity. For most adolescents, their peers are a reference group that influences their dress, mannerisms, speech patterns, preferences—their whole way of life. High school subcultures often place high value on athletics for males and leadership activities for females, but little value—for either sex—on being very bright or academically oriented. For girls, good grades are often seen as detracting from popularity. Some students even try not to appear smart for fear of losing peer-group approval. The students with highest status in high schools tend to be from the dominant socioeconomic status group in the school, oriented toward school activites, and not primarily concerned with gaining adult approval. Students who are academically outstanding gain little peer acceptance or reward and are sometimes ridiculed. Coleman suggests that schools could shift the focus "so that the norms of the [adolescent social] communities themselves reinforce educational goals rather than inhibit them."[87] However, in those high schools where students have high educational and occupational expectations, competition for grades can be intense. High achievement in these schools is rewarded, and some students may even resort to cheating rather than do poorly.

Student peer groups are often formed around neighborhood friendships, which may have existed since grade school. Their activities may have little to do with the academic aspects of school, though they can influence academic achievement and other organizational aspects, such as extracurricular activities.[88]

Peer groups serve a number of purposes for their members: Young people of equal age and status in the social and educational system can express themselves freely; experiment with social interactions and friendships, while learning to get along with others; learn sex roles; and serve as a reinforcer for norms, rules, and morality. Age-mates are important in this process because they are thrown together in school activities.

Student actions are constructed within the framework or environment of the school. Philip Cusick outlines key parts of this *sociocultural environment,* which had the *intended effects* of denying freedom of activity and lumping students in an undifferentiated mass, and the *unintended effects* shown in Figure 7-3.[89] As Cusick discovered in the high school he studied: "The tendency of the students . . . to maintain tight, in-school groups was a natural, but unrecognized, consequence of the school's basic organizational structure. As long as the supporting structure exists, the students will probably continue to form groups. . . ."[90]

Within this alienating culture of high school, it is important to have friends with whom to walk, sit at lunch, and attend activities. There is usually a core of elite "jocks" and good-looking female students, and some schools may have high-status music and drama groups. There are, unfortunately, social isolates who have no friends and therefore no "protection" in the system.[91] Generally, their number is small. In his study of high schools, Hargreaves[92] describes two main student groups or subcultures: those with positive and those with negative orientations. Students with positive orientations toward the values of schools end up in the higher groups, which reinforce their orientations; negative students end up in the lower groups. For members of the negative subcultures, peer culture becomes the primary identification, whereas positive students are influenced by school values as well as by peers.

School organization sometimes contributes to the polarization of students through ability grouping, or "streaming," as do social class differences

FIGURE 7-3　Relationship between student behavior and the school organization.

Source: Cusick, Philip A., *Inside High School: The Student's World* (New York: Holt, Rinehart and Winston, 1973).

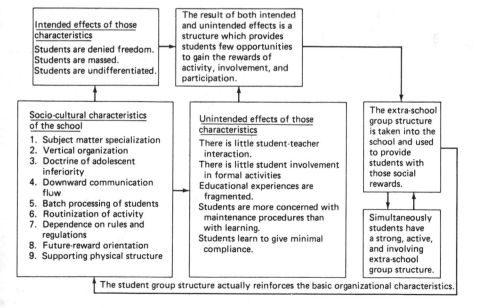

in students. Willis gives evidence that those from working-class or lower-class backgrounds may see little hope for an improved future and concentrate in negative orientation groups:

> . . . [A]nti-school culture provides powerful informal criteria and binding experi-ential processes which lead working-class lads to make the "voluntary" choice to enter the factory, and to help reproduce both the existing class structure of employment, and the "culture of the shop floor" as a segment of the over-arching working-class culture.[93]

There is evidence that the influence of peer groups is growing in many countries as the influence of family on adolescents decreases. Although the family in America used to have the dominant influence on adolescent values and behavior, the home as a socializing agent is now in competition with peer groups for the child's attention.[94]

Student Strategies.   Student "coping" strategies, or ways of adapting to the power structure of school culture, are major aspects of the informal sys-tem. Students develop strategies related to their own needs, based on their own experiences with schooling, self-concept, peer-group relations, ability grouping, and other factors. School requires strategies very different from those learned at home in early socialization, though this early learning is crucial to the student's success in school. The child is gradually eased into the competitive, judgmental, disciplined world of school. The social distance be-tween students and teachers is established early because teachers have author-ity as a result of their position in the educational system. Thus, students begin to learn strategies to cope with the world of the school and classroom from an early age.

Much of the research in this area is recent and is an offshoot of the interactionist theoretical approach, which contends in part that we construct our realities within an environmental context and behave in accordance with those constructions. From this perspective, the development of strategies can be seen as a kind of negotiation requiring students to understand the teachers' roles and needs while attempting to maximize their own interests. Students' attitudes vary from almost complete compliance with the teacher's goals to total lack of commitment. Teachers have power, but getting students to do what is desired takes strategies other than the direct use of power.[95] "Negotia-tions" between individual students, students and teachers, and the class as a group are constantly changing, although some interactions are fairly routine.

Different strategies are appropriate at different times in the matura-tional development of students. Learning how to work and solve problems may be key at one time, while mastering skills in taking examinations is the focus at another stage in the student's career.[96] Turning points in children's careers can change them from "drifters" to "experts," or from excited stu-dents to bored ones.

Martyn Hammersley and Glenn Turner[97] have developed an interac-tional model that takes into account student and teacher strategies. It begins "with the analysis of pupil action, identifying the intentions, motives and perspectives which underlie it." The student considers possible actions, their costs and payoffs, and makes a decision based on the perceived and actual consequences of various behaviors. The teacher sets guidelines, expectations, or "frames" that operate in the classroom situation or that relate to specific segments, lessons, or problems. Students may conform to teacher "frames" or set up alternative options or "frames" that deviate from the teacher's. Whether students conform or deviate depends in part on student peer-group behaviors and on their involvement in the lesson content.

The sociocultural structure of the school is also important in determining student experiences and strategies. Recognizing this, Robert Merton developed a typology of students' reactions to school goals and means (the school's methods of attaining goals). Individual student reactions to school goals and means range from acceptance to rejection, as indicated by Merton's four types:

1. *conformity:* acceptance of goals and means,
2. *retreatism:* rejection of goals and means,
3. *ambivalence:* indifference, and
4. *rejection with replacement:* something else in mind.[98]

Peter Woods,[99] testing the goals-means typology on English public boarding school boys, has revised this model to make it represent more of the variations in individual pupils' responses. He adds to the goals-means typology several categories:

1. *Colonization.* "This mode combines indifference to goals with ambivalence about means." The students accept school as a place where they must spend their time and try to maximize available gratifications, permitted and not, official and unofficial. Parts of the school system are acceptable to them, but illegal means may be used to cope, such as copying work or cheating in tests.
2. *Indulgence.* There is a strongly positive response to goals and means.
3. *Conformity.* This is broken down into several categories:
    a. *Compliance.* Students "feel some affinity for and identification with the goals and means."
    b. *Ingratiation.* Students "aim to maximize their benefits by earning the favor of those with power, and are usually undisturbed by unpopularity among their peers."
    c. *Opportunism.* Students show "less consistent application to work and frequent but momentary leanings toward other modes," trying them out before settling on one. This can result in fluctuations of behavior.
4. *Intransigence.* Students adopting this strategy are indifferent to the school's goals and reject its means to achieve goals through rules, rituals, and regulations. They may disrupt lessons and even physically assault staff or destroy property. Appearance may distinguish this type of student—hair, dress, shoes, or boots. These students are generally difficult for the school to deal with.
5. *Rebellion.* Students reject the school's goals and means, but they substitute others. This is common later in school careers. The replacement of goals makes this group less of a threat than the intransigents.

In this model, developed by Merton and modified by Woods, student strategies in relation to school goals and means of achieving goals are laid out for students in elementary and high school. At the college level, strategies differ because of the different demands and nature of the situation. College students' coping mechanisms are oriented to the work they must complete in each class. Snyder[100] documents many of the gaps between the hidden and formal curricula in higher education; that is, the implicit demands *versus* the visible ones, which can be recognized more easily.

In an early report on student culture and strategies, E. C. Hughes and colleagues[101] studied a medical school subculture. Faced with tremendous pressure because of formal requirements, the students developed coping mechanisms by devising strategies to reduce work pressure and establishing norms for work expectations—agreed upon by the peer group, though not by faculty. They focused on material on which they would be tested and took shortcuts, determined by what they felt to be important to their future, in certain laboratory and clinical work. These strategies effectively altered the medical school faculty expectations.

Some college students quickly discover that those who master the hidden curriculum, who learn to "play the system," have learned important coping strategies. For example, C. M. L. Miller and M. Parlett[102] write about "cue-consciousness," the degree to which students pick up cues from professors on such things as exam topics and favored subject areas. They describe three types of students:

1. *Cue-conscious:* These students rely on hard work and luck to do well. They are less well-prepared for exams because they try to learn more topics. They pick up a limited number of cues.
2. *Cue-seekers:* These students learn selectively. They often actively seek information from faculty and try to make a good impression while seeking cues as to which topics are important.
3. *Cue-deaf:* These students pick up virtually no cues about what is important and try to study all of the material rather than being selective.

The researchers found a correlation between the most cue-conscious students and high exam scores.

In recent years some researchers have studied students' learning styles. Each person has dominant modes of learning; if teachers can be aware of the range of individual variations and class profiles in learning styles, they can plan lessons to match dominant modes or the variety of learning styles. Students who know their style can adapt study patterns. We learn from auditory stimuli, visual stimuli, and tactile stimuli; in cooperative groups, in competitive situations, or in isolation. Several scales to evaluate learning styles have been developed. The following are sample statements from the Grasha-Reichman[103] learning styles inventory. (Students respond on a scale from "agree" to "disagree.")

1. Most of what I know, I learned on my own.
2. I find the ideas of other students relatively useful for helping me to understand the course material.

3. I try to participate as much as I can in all aspects of a course.
4. I study what is important to me and not necessarily what the instructor says is important.
5. I think an important part of classes is to learn to get along with other people.
6. I accept the structure a teacher sets for a course.
7. I do not have trouble paying attention in classes.
8. I think students can learn more by sharing their ideas than by keeping their ideas to themselves.
9. I like to study for tests with other students.
10. I feel that I must compete with the other students to get a grade.

The researchers analyze the responses of each student and of the class; with this information, both students and teacher have a better understanding of which style of learning is most effective.

Student strategies result in a variety of individual roles, and a variety of labels: conformists, drifters, planners, retreatists, intransigents, rebels, teacher's pet, nobodies, troublemakers, jocks, dumb kids, brains, eggheads, popular, "sleepers or hand-wavers."[104] Any label can change. However, once labeled, a child may come to behave more and more in the manner expected, carrying out the self-fulfilling prophecy.

When evaluating student strategies, it is important to consider the entire system within which the student is operating, including the power dynamics, strategies of other students and teachers, and the sociocultural structure or goals and means of the school. Briefly, we now consider the strategies of the holders of the reciprocal role: teachers.

Teacher Strategies and the Informal System

Different teacher strategies are necessary in each new circumstance. The philosophy of the teacher and school, the organization of school and classroom, resources available, number of students and their interest level—all affect the goals and strategies of teachers.

Martyn Hammersley outlines several alternative techniques or strategies that may be used by teachers to deal with classes:

1. Formal organization implies that the teacher is the center of activity; typical strategies are to have students recite material, or do question-and-answer and written work. Informal organization implies groups of students working together and more interaction between class members.
2. The teacher may supervise student action and intervene when deviation occurs. Alternatively, the teacher may act more as participant.
3. The teacher may make use of orders and demands backed by coercion and the authority of the position. Alternatively, the teacher may make personal appeals to the rights and obligations of any person, backed by legitimate resources.
4. Class or school tests may be used for comparison of student performance. Alternatively, there may be no formal assessment. Many commonly used informal strategies of grouping are based on age, ability, or "troublemakers" versus random grouping based on student choice, friendship groups, or no formal grouping.[105]

Techniques employed by teachers influence the climate of the classroom and type of learning taking place, though on many dimensions there is no clear evidence which technique is more effective.

Students often challenge teacher authority, and teachers often end up going further in adjusting to students than students to teachers. Students in lower tracks, according to Mary Haywood Metz, most often use physical and verbal disorder strategies in challenging, while those in higher tracks test the teacher's mastery of the subject. Students challenge teachers on the ground where they feel most competent.[106] New teachers, even when armed with the best training and teaching techniques, must experience the realities of the classroom to develop their own strategies to meet goals for their classes.

Consider the task of getting and keeping student attention. Teachers have plans in mind for the activities and lessons of the day, but they must convince students of the importance of the lesson and motivate them to comply—or even to participate. The teacher must defend the lesson from disintegration and internal defection. The student is being asked to pay attention to the "official environment"—that is, what is going on in the class directed by the teacher—rather than to a friend, comic book, or other distraction. In the typical situation, teachers are at the front of the classroom with students facing them. They watch for inattention and may use strategies such as questioning to get attention. Students may attempt to disguise illicit activities. Teachers can exert power in the form of control over valued things—recess, physical education, games.

In a survey of teachers, many commented that teacher strategies change over time to adapt to changing students. "Quiet, docile, seen but not heard, students have been replaced by more open, expressive, impatient, challenging, questioning, aggressive and assertive youngsters."[107] Most people see deviant students as detrimental to the classroom situation. However, some teachers find that using disruptive students as a "resource" may turn them into an asset. Deviants are *products* of the social organization of the classroom; by considering three factors in their place in the total social context, teachers may discover how to manipulate the classroom structure to their benefit: (1) how ranks of deviants are established; (2) how deviant status is maintained; and (3) how deviants contribute to maintaining order or gain from their disruptions.[108]

Students today have a need to be entertained; they expect instant gratification. Attention spans are shorter. They need more attention, are harder to please, have higher expectations of teachers, are less willing to put forth effort to learn, and are motivated by external rather than internal rewards.

Decision Making in the Classroom.   We have discussed teachers' roles in the educational system in Chapter 6, and the effect of teacher decisions and actions on students' achievement in Chapter 4. Implicit in these discussions is the teacher's role as primary decision maker in the classroom, decisions concerning "lesson content, teaching style, the motivation of the class, the incentives or disincentives to apply, the resources to use, the moments to change pace,"[109] and so forth. However, what really happens in the classroom and what influences the decision-making process is more complex. Most of the research on this topic comes from "interaction" theorists and the "new sociology of education" and focuses on the dynamics of classroom interaction and how individuals perceive the situation. It is not easy to observe these dynamics, but, despite methodological difficulties, the "how and why" of decision making is now a topic of concern.

Most of a teacher's decision-making behavior is almost instinctive, based on experience. But teachers do have decision-making strategies, conscious or unconscious. They may be "situationally specific decisions, or negotiative strategies," used to deal with special circumstances that arise.

Teachers' strategies, especially those of the new teacher, are often based on a "paradigmatic, or ideal, world." However, students deviate from ideals, forcing teachers to deviate from their ideal models to the "pragmatic or realistic component of their perspective."[110]

Using a role conflict model, which focuses on incongruities in the teacher's role, we can see how decision making is influenced not only by the views and expectations of students, parents, other teachers, and administration, but also by teachers' own definitions of the task to be performed. Teachers must consider what they can and cannot, will and will not do. "Thus, interactionists have pointed to the importance of threat, bluff, persuasion, the exploitation of rules and expertise, and bargaining in the exercise of power." Decision making is a complex process influenced by many interacting elements. Teacher dissatisfaction and burnout are increased when teachers are given little control in determining the classroom environment.[111] A supportive "community" can increase teacher satisfaction.[112]

In order to understand the educational system, we must recognize the importance of processes in the informal system. Also crucial to dynamics of schools is the environment, our next topic.

SUMMARY

To understand the processes taking place within the school and classroom, one must be aware of the informal system, an important area of social research. In this brief discussion we have attempted to acknowledge its importance for complete understanding of the system and its integral part in a systems approach.

I. The "Hidden Curriculum"

This part of the informal system includes the curriculum students learn that is not part of the formal curriculum—implicit demands, values, latent functions. Some conflict theorists argue that schools reproduce students' social class, largely through the hidden curriculum. Students experience schools differently depending on their class backgrounds.

II. The Educational "Climate" and School Effectiveness

The climate or atmosphere of schools and classrooms includes the school's architecture, type of classroom, ability and age grouping, and other aspects of the school. Value climate influences motivations, aspirations, and achievement of students. Factors such as home environment, self-concept, and school values influence the effectiveness of schools. The school culture is distinctive in each school.

Interaction patterns in classrooms are also part of the climate. Factors, such as gender, that affect interaction are discussed.

III. Power Dynamics and Roles in the Informal System

Power dynamics are present in any hierarchical system. In schools a look at the teacher-student relationship acquaints us with some of the issues. Both students and teachers develop coping strategies to deal with the dynamics. Students take on roles that vary from elementary school to higher education. Peer groups are an important part of the students' lives, insulating them from the alien adult demands of school.

Power in schools can be actively used or can be seen as latent potential to keep students in line. Functional theorists argue that students learn societal roles by cooperation with adult-enforced rules, whereas conflict theorists feel that there is constant potential for conflict because of power dynamics.

Students develop a culture that serves to insulate them from adult demands. This includes coping strategies for dealing with school. Peers influence behaviors, values, and attitudes, and serve a number of purposes for members of the student group. Teachers also attempt to maintain a delicate balance between overt use of power and gaining student cooperation.

Teachers must make decisions about strategies to use in the classroom; numerous factors affecting these decisions were discussed. The strategies used range from power to subtle cues to changing the physical or social arrangement of the class.

One of the biggest concerns of teachers and parents alike is discipline and control in the classroom. A number of different techniques, based on a broad range of philosophies, can be used.

PUTTING SOCIOLOGY TO WORK

1. Interview a sample of students concerning their outstanding memories of school experiences.
2. Describe the student peer subculture in your high school and college. Were there social isolates, and can you recall their characteristics? Compare your high school with a high school today through observation or interviews.
3. What were some roles students played in your high school? Talk to some students about roles they play today.
4. Discuss "coping strategies" used by you and other students to "get by" in college.
5. What are some strategies used by teachers you observe in high schools to get students to cooperate?

NOTES

[1] Jackson, Philip, *Life in Classrooms* (New York: Holt, Rinehart and Winston, 1968), p. 5.

[2] Holt, John, *How Children Fail* (New York: Pitman, 1968), pp. xiii, xiv.

[3] Meighan, Roland, *A Sociology of Educating*, 2nd ed. (Eastbourne, East Sussex, England: Holt, Rinehart and Winston, 1986), p. 66.

[4] Snyder, Benson R., *The Hidden Curriculum* (New York: Alfred A. Knopf, 1971).

[5] Hargreaves, D., "Power and the Paracurriculum," in C. Richards (ed.), *Power and the Curriculum: Issues in Curriculum Studies* (London: Driffields Nafferton Books, 1977), pp. 126–37.

[6] Bowles, S., and H. Gintis, *Schooling in Capitalist America* (London: Routledge & Kegan Paul, 1976).

[7] Hargreaves, D. H., "The Two Curricula and the Community," *Westminster Studies in Education*, Vol. 1, 1978.

[8] Besag, Frank P., and Jack L. Nelson, *The Foundations of Education: Stasis and Change* (New York: Random House, 1984), pp. 24–25.

[9] McLaren, Peter L., "The Ritual Dimensions of Resistance: Clowning and Symbolic Inversion," *Journal of Education*, Vol. 167, No. 2, 1985, pp. 84–97.

[10] Anyon, Jean, "Social Class and the Hidden Curriculum of Work," *Journal of Education*, Vol. 162, 1980, pp. 67–92.

[11] Lubeck, Sally, "Kinship and Classrooms: An Ethnographic Perspective on Education as Cultural Transmission," *Sociology of Education*, October 1984, p. 230.

[12] Holt, *How Children Fail.*

[13] Coleman, James S., *et al.*, *Equality of Educational Opportunity* (Washington, D.C.: U.S. Department of Education, 1966).

[14] Jencks, Christopher, *et al.*, *Inequality: A Reassessment of the Effects of Family and Schooling in America* (New York: Basic Books, 1972).

[15] Coleman, James S., *et al.*, *Public and Private Schools*, National Center for Educational Statistics (Washington, D.C.: U.S. Government Printing Office, 1981).

[16] Center for Education Statistics, *The Condition of Education* (Washington, D.C.: U.S. Department of Education, 1987), p. 74.

[17] Sewell, William H., and Robert M. Hauser, "The Wisconsin Longitudinal Study of Social and Psychological Factors in Aspirations and Achievements," *Research in Sociology of Education and Socialization*, Vol. 1, 1964, pp. 59–99.

[18] Mickelson, Roslyn Arlin, "The Attitude-Achievement Paradox Among Black Adolescents," *Sociology of Education*, Vol. 63, No. 1, January 1990, pp. 44–61.

[19] Dreeben, R., and Gamoran, A., "Race, Instruction, and Learning," *American Sociological Review*, Vol. 51, No. 5, 1986, pp. 660–69.

[20] Garner, Catherine L., and Stephen W. Raudenbush, "Neighborhood Effects on Educational Attainment: A Multilevel Analysis," *Sociology of Education*, Vol. 64, No. 4, October 1991, pp. 251–60.

[21] Faunce, William A., "School Achievement, Social Status, and Self-Esteem," unpublished manuscript, Michigan State University, 1981, p. 17.

[22] Brookover, Wilbur B., Edsel L. Erickson, and Lee M. Joiner, *Self-Concept of Ability and School Achievement*, III, Cooperative Research Project 2831 (East Lansing: Educational Publication Services, Michigan State University, 1967).

[23] Jackson, *Life in Classrooms.*

[24] Brookover, Wilbur, *et al.*, *Elementary School Social Environments and Achievements* (East Lansing: College of Urban Development, Michigan State University, 1973).

[25] Brookover, Wilbur, and Jeffrey M. Schneider, "Academic Environments and Elementary School Achievement," *Journal of Research and Development in Education*, Vol. 8, 1975, pp. 82–91.

[26] Brookover, Wilbur, *et al.*, *School Social Systems and Student Achievement: Schools Can Make a Difference* (New York: Praeger, 1979); also, *Creating Effective Schools* (Holmes Beach, Fla.: Learning Publications, 1982).

[55] Hallinan, Maureen T., and Richard A. Williams, "Students' Characteristics and the Peer-Influence Process," *Sociology of Education*, Vol. 63, No. 2, April 1990, pp. 122–32.

[56] Adler, Patricia A., Steven J. Kless, and Peter Adler, "Socialization to Gender Roles: Popularity among Elementary School Boys and Girls," *Sociology of Education*, Vol. 65, No. 3, July 1992, pp. 169–87.

[57] Bank, B., B. Biddle, and T. Good, "Sex Roles, Classroom Instruction and Reading Achievement," *Journal of Educational Psychology*, Vol. 72, 1980, pp. 119–32.

[58] Brophy, Jere, "Interactions of Male and Female Students with Male and Female Teachers," in *Gender Influences, Classroom Interactions* (Madison: University of Wisconsin, 1985).

[59] Hammersley, M., "The Mobilization of Pupil Attention," in M. Hammersley and P. Woods (eds.), *The Process of Schooling: A Sociological Reader* (London: Open University Press and Routledge & Kegan Paul, 1976), pp. 105–6.

[60] Stires, Lloyd, "Classroom Seating Location, Student Grades, and Attitudes: Environment or Self-Selection?" *Environment and Behavior*, Vol. 12, 1980, pp. 241–54.

[61] Wheldall, Kevin, "A Before C, or the Use of Behavioral Ecology in Classroom Management," in K. Wheldall (ed.), *The Behaviorist in the Classroom: Aspects of Applied Behavioral Analysis in British Educational Contexts* (Birmingham, England: Educational Review Publications, 1981).

[62] Kevan, Simon M., and John D. Howes, "Climatic Conditions in Classrooms," *Educational Review*, Vol. 32, 1980, pp. 514–25.

[63] Davidson, Charles W., and Lou Anne Powell, "The Effects of Easy-Listening Background Music on the On-Task Performance of Fifth-Grade Children," *Journal of Educational Research*, Vol. 80, No. 1, 1986, pp. 29–33.

[64] Education Writers Association, *Wolves at the Schoolhouse Door: An Investigation of the Condition of Public School Buildings* (Washington, D.C.: Education Writers Association, April 1989).

[65] Greim, Clifton, and William Turner, "Breathing Easy Over Air Quality," *The American School Board Journal*, November 1991, p. 29.

[66] McGiverin, Jennifer, David Gilman, and Chris Tillitski, "A Meta-analysis of the Relation Between Class Size and Achievement," *The Elementary School Journal*, Vol. 90, No. 1, September 1989, p. 52–55.

[67] Boocock, Sarane Spence, *Sociology of Education: An Introduction*, 2nd ed. (Boston: Houghton Mifflin, 1980), pp. 168–70.

[68] Medley, Donald M., *Teacher Competence and Teacher Effectiveness: A Review of Process-Product Research* (Washington, D.C.: American Association of Colleges for Teacher Education, 1977).

[69] *Ibid.*, p. 76.

[70] Coleman, James S., *et al., Youth: Transition to Adulthood* (Chicago: University of Chicago Press, 1974), pp. 154–56.

[71] Morgan, D. L., and D. F. Alwin, "When Less Is More: School Size and Student Social Participation," *Social Psychology Quarterly*, Vol. 43, 1980, pp. 241–52.

[72] "Architecture and Education," editorial introduction, *Harvard Educational Review*, Vol. 39, No. 4, 1969, p. 20.

[73] "An Architectural Revolution Is Going On Inside Schools," *The American School Board Journal*, August 1990, p. 9.

[74] Dreeben, Robert, "The School as a Workplace," in R. Travers (ed.), *Second Handbook of Research and Teaching* (Skokie, Ill.: Rand McNally, 1973), pp. 450–73.

[75] Meighan, *Sociology of Educating*, p. 263.

[76] Parsons, Talcott, "The School Class as a Social System," *Harvard Educational Review*, Vol. 29, pp. 297–318.

[77] Waller, *Sociology of Teaching*.

[78] Bowles, Samuel, and H. Gintis, *Schooling in Capitalist America* (New York: Basic Books, 1976), pp. 11–12.

[79] Bernstein, *The Structuring of Pedagogic Discourse*.

[80] Bourdieu, P., and J. Passeron, *Reproduction in Education, Society and Culture* (London: Sage, 1977); Willis, *Learning to Labour*.

[81] Apple, Michael W., "Analyzing Determinations: Understanding and Evaluating the Production of Social Outcomes in Schools," *Curriculum Inquiry,* Vol. 10, 1980, pp. 55–76.

[82] Becker, Howard S., "The Career of the Chicago Public Schoolteacher," *American Journal of Sociology,* Vol. 57, 1952, pp. 470–77.

[83] Gouldner, Helen P., *Teacher's Pets, Troublemakers and Nobodies: Black Children in Elementary School* (Westport, Conn.: Greenwood Press, 1978).

[84] Woods, Peter (ed.), *Pupil Strategies: Explorations in the Sociology of the School* (London: Croom Helm, 1980).

[85] Waller, *Sociology of Teaching,* p. 103.

[86] Coleman, James S., *The Adolescent Society* (New York: Free Press, 1961).

[87] Coleman, James S., "The Adolescent Subculture and Academic Achievement," *America–Journal of Sociology,* Vol. 65, 1960, pp. 337–47.

[88] Garner, "Neighborhood Effects," p. 251.

[89] Cusick, Philip A., *Inside High School: The Student's World* (New York: Holt, Rinehart and Winston, 1973), pp. 216–217.

[90] *Ibid.,* pp. 208–209.

[91] *Ibid.,* p. 173.

[92] Hargreaves, D., *Social Relations in a Secondary School* (London: Routledge & Kegan Paul, 1967).

[93] Willis, *Learning to Labour,* pp. 53–54.

[94] Goodlad, John I., *A Place Called School* (New York: McGraw-Hill, 1984).

[95] Woods, *Pupil Strategies.*

[96] *Ibid.,* pp. 11–28.

[97] Hammersley, Martyn, and Glenn Turner, "Conformist Pupils?" in Woods, *Pupil Strategies,* pp. 24–49.

[98] Merton, Robert, *Social Theory and Social Structure* (Glencoe, Ill.: Free Press, 1957).

[99] Woods, *Pupil Strategies,* pp. 14–18.

[100] Snyder, *Hidden Curriculum.*

[101] Hughes, E. C., *et al.,* "Student Culture and Academic Effort," in N. Sanford (ed.), *The American College* (New York: Wiley, 1962), pp. 515–30.

[102] Miller, C. M. L., and M. Parlett, "Cue-Consciousness," in Hammersley and Woods (eds.), *The Process of Schooling,* pp. 143–49.

[103] Grasha, Anthony F., "Grasha-Reichmann Student Learning Styles Questionnaire," Faculty Resource Center (Cincinnati, Ohio: University of Cincinnati, 1975).

[104] Jackson, *Life in Classrooms,* p. 86.

[105] Hammersley, Martyn, and Peter Woods, *Teacher Perspectives* (Milton Keynes, England: Open University Press, 1977), p. 37.

[106] Metz, Mary Haywood, *Classrooms and Corridors* (Berkeley: University of California Press, 1978), pp. 91–92.

[107] Hedin, Diane, and Dan Conrad, "Changes in Children and Youth Over Two Decades: The Perceptions of Teachers," *Phi Delta Kappan,* June 1980, pp. 702–5.

[108] Stevenson, David Lee, "Deviant Students as a Collective Resource in Classroom Control," *Sociology of Education,* Vol. 64, No. 2, April 1991, pp. 127–33.

[109] Eggleston, John (ed.), *Teacher Decision-Making in the Classroom* (London: Routledge & Kegan Paul, 1979), p. 1.

[110] Hammersley, Martyn, "Toward a Model of Teacher Activity," in Eggleston, *Teacher Decision-Making,* p. 184.

[111] Lee, Valerie E., Robert F. Dedrick, and Julia B. Smith, "The Effect of the Social Organization of Schools on Teachers' Efficacy and Satisfaction," *Sociology of Education,* Vol. 64, No. 3, July 1991, pp. 190–208.

[112] Rosenholtz, S. J., *Teachers' Workplace: The Social Organization of Schools* (New York: Longman, 1989).

8

THE EDUCATIONAL SYSTEM AND THE ENVIRONMENT
A Symbiotic Relationship

Our environment surrounds us. It encompasses us. No one and nothing exists in a vacuum, for we cannot exist outside our environment. That environment differs for each of us just as it differs for each educational system. What makes our environment unique depends on our background experiences, the family into which we were born, the individuals and institutions with which we come into contact.

As college students, we pay tuition, take classes, study, receive grades, and eventually graduate. The roles we carry out as students are dictated by our educational environment. Also in our environment are other factors: family, church, job, children, friends. Events related to one set of behaviors or roles will affect the other roles we play because they all interrelate. Let us suppose that we have an important exam coming up. We may experience role conflict because of time pressure. Perhaps our family or friends will be neglected; perhaps we will decide not to spend much time studying for the exam. Every element of our environment is affected by demands for other elements.

In this chapter we consider the meaning of environments and examples of institutional environments of schools: family, religion, politics and the legal system, economics, and communities. As part of the larger societal system, school systems are surrounded by pressures from ideological groups, political systems, economic conditions, and other trends in society. Each sphere of society is interrelated; schools cannot ignore the political, economic, and cultural-ideological spheres that make up their environments.[1]

THE ENVIRONMENT AND THE EDUCATION SYSTEM

Educational systems have environments that give them purpose and meaning and define their functions and limitations. Schools are particularly vulnerable to environmental influence where issues relate to the function of socialization of the young. Children are often seen as sponges, waiting to absorb the knowledge presented to them, and many parts of the environment—government, community pressure groups, religious and other special-interest groups—demand input into what children are taught and how it is taught.

Population changes, technological advances, fads, and social movements are some of the environmental factors that influence the functions of education. For example, in the 1960s, there was much experimentation with avant-garde programs in the United States, producing ideas that influenced the public schools. In the 1970s, there was great concern with establishing more discipline in schools; "back-to-basics" became the theme of many. Such movements constitute environmental pressures on the schools.

In our discussion of the internal workings of the system, we saw the connection between the many individual positions people hold in educational systems and the structural units of the school organization. But no organization, unit, or individual can exist without being dependent upon and influenced by the environment. Figure 8-1 again emphasizes the relationship between the organization and its environment.

All individuals and organizations depend on their environments in order to survive and to meet needs; in turn, they affect the environment in which they live by leaving personal or institutional imprints on individuals and institutions.

The interdependence of organization and environment can be seen clearly in many systems. Picture the complexity of a system such as New York City and the chaos that occurs when one part of that system malfunctions.[2] If the power goes out, or the sanitation engineers, subway workers, telephone operators, or school-teachers go on strike, the city's interdependent structure breaks down and all parts of the system are strained to the breaking point. New York City's school system is likewise complex; it employed 61,991 teach-

FIGURE 8-1   Environments of school systems.

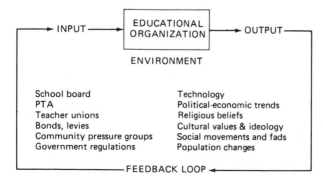

ers in 1986–87, several thousand administrators and technicians, and served 939,142 pupils. It is spread over the five boroughs of the city and services many different populations and communities.[3] The interdependence of parts of this tremendous school system forces it into a delicate balancing act between competing interests.

Types of Environments

Some parts of our environment are more important to our survival than others; these are immediate environments. Less important to survival are secondary environments. Our families are key to our emotional, physical, and financial well-being, whereas a Friday night party is not a matter of survival for most of us. For an organization, the relevant parts of the environment fall into a number of categories: government, including local, state, and national legislatures and agencies; the judicial system; financial support units; the "physical" community surrounding each school, including the demographic composition (age, sex, religion, race, and social class); interest groups in the community; the technological environment, including teaching innovations and new scientific research; consumers of educational system products, such as those who hire graduates or incorporate new knowledge from education systems; and religious institutions.

The distinction between immediate or primary environments and less crucial secondary environments is not always clear. Importance can change over time, but the fact remains that there are differing degrees of importance in environmental factors. Recognizing this allows us to single out those environmental factors that most affect decision making in a school system at any one time. The school is affected less as environmental units become farther removed, just as ripples in a pond become weaker as they move out from the center.

Organizations are not encapsulated, but depend on the environment for resources, materials, people power, and, ultimately, existence. The importance, or salience, of environmental units for educational systems can be pictured on a continuum (Figure 8-2). The salience of environmental units will vary depending on the individual school situation being considered.

Another point needs to be explained. We generally consider the individuals who fill positions in the schools—the administrators, teachers, students, and

FIGURE 8-2 Environmental salience.

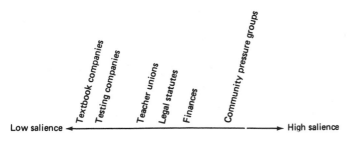

support staff—to be parts of the internal organization. These groups fill the positions in the internal structure of the school and carry out the processes of the school. They provide the bases for the informal relationships in the school. However, there is no question that each of the position-holders in the school brings a unique background and personality into the school, which could be considered an "environmental influence." (Some sociologists consider students as clients of the school system, and in this way a part of its environment.) Further, some school personnel, such as principals, school counselors, and social workers, carry out roles to provide a bridge between the school and home or community environment. These "boundary-spanning" roles facilitate the movement of ideas and products in and out of the school system, and are essential in maintaining relations and contact with the environment.

To summarize, the importance of environmental units must be viewed as varying in degree; some are crucial to the well-being, even survival, of the organization at a particular time. Effects of problems in one sector of the system's environment or in relations with the environment will have ramifications for other sectors, depending on that part's salience to the survival of the system.

In this chapter we focus on the institutional environment of the school. However, there are many elements to any school's environment, from the individuals who make it up to the ancillary organizations that surround it, put pressures on it, and provide services to it.

THE SCHOOL SYSTEMS' ENVIRONMENTS: INTERDEPENDENCE BETWEEN INSTITUTIONS

- Parents and community members disenchanted with schools are demanding that schools and teachers become accountable for the education they are providing. This is resulting in many school districts' and even states' requiring standardized tests to measure achievement levels.
- Are parents in contempt of court if they send their children to nonaccredited religious schools? Should both "scientific creationism" and evolutionary theory be taught in schools?
- Courts in numerous districts are dealing with questions regarding separation of church and state: Can public school districts provide such services as transportation, remedial classes, and counseling to religiously affiliated schools?
- Financing schools leads to controversies when some districts have more property tax money for education than others.
- Hot debate rages in communities between special-interest groups representing differing points of view on minority studies, selection of textbooks, role of the schools in sex education, and numerous other issues.

In this section we look into some of the environmental pressures and resulting issues affecting schools:

1. home influences and pressures,
2. separation of church and state in education,

3. school financing,
4. governmental regulations and court rulings, and
5. influence of the community and special-interest groups on schools.

Home and Family Influences on School

When children walk into the school building they bring with them baggage from home: ambition, motivation, pressures, expectations, physical and mental strengths or weaknesses, and sometimes abuse, insecurities, stress, and other problems. In Chapter 3 we discussed the influence of the family on achievement of students. Here we reemphasize that link between the family institution and education.[4]

Parents affect children's educational aspirations and attainments in several major ways. According to Cohen,[5] boys and girls are strongly influenced by the "defining" behavior of parents through which expectations for appropriate behavior are established. Also important, especially for girls, is "modeling" or emulation of parents. Family influence is strong across social class, but mothers with higher educational status are more involved in school activities, have more contact with teachers, and choose college-preparatory courses for their children. Children of parents who are involved in schools have higher school performance levels.[6,7] On the other hand, children from homes and neighborhoods considered "socially deprived" experience negative effects on their educational attainment.[8]

In ongoing research at the Center for Research on Elementary and Middle Schools, Epstein found that teachers who involve parents in home activities, especially reading, with their children have positive learning results for children.[9,10] Single parents tended to feel pressure to help with home learning; married parents assisted more at school.[11] Her research shows the impact of the home environment and involving parents in the education of their children.[12]

When we combine the influence of parents, peers, and teachers, we have strong effects on students' attitudes toward school, homework, achievement, and other aspects of schooling in the U.S.[13] However, data from the Netherlands and Germany point to the declining effects of family on educational attainment, with differences between siblings becoming greater. Researchers attribute this to the increase in individualism and decline of family influence.[14]

Parents' investment in their children and support for higher education is related to their views of status attainment. Some parents see children as an investment, following the "human capital theory." Others view payment for education as "resource-dilution," often related to how many children are in the family compared to available resources. For instance, parents are more willing to pay for higher education for their children if their parents paid for their education, and they see this as a responsibility; they are also more willing to pay if the number of children in the family does not drain their resources.[15]

The Institution of Religion: Separation of Church and State

In a large number of societies, religion and state are synonymous, and the educational system reflects the beliefs and values of both. Religious minorities may have their own schools, or tolerate the dominant religious themes. In England, for instance, holidays of non-Christian students living in England are often discussed to promote intercultural understanding.

In the United States, a unique experiment was attempted. Since the time of our nation's founding, the principle of separation of church and state has been espoused. It is expressed in the First Amendment, which states: "Congress shall make no law respecting an establishment of religion, or prohibiting the free exercise thereof." The framers of the U.S. Constitution built in guarantees to avoid the religious conflicts that had arisen in many other countries. The government's responsibility was to protect the rights and freedoms of all and favor none. Yet keeping church and state distinct has not always been a matter of conflict. The roots of the problem lie in our pluralistic society, where freedom of worship is an integral part of the value system and political ideology.

We have seen in our open systems model the interdependence of each institution with all others. Where religion has become segmented from the rest of daily life spent in institutions of family, economics, politics, and education, conflict is not likely to arise. But where religion is integrated into all aspects of a person's life, including education, demands for representation of this part of life take the form of pressures on the school from the religious environment.

Two types of cases have dominated the courts. First are those that claim that the school is infringing on individual beliefs; saying prayers in class or at ceremonies or teaching the theory of evolution are examples. Other cases occur when school official or policies prevent individuals from participating in religious activities during school and in school, such as religious use of school facilities.

As early as 1948, religious released-time classes in public school buildings were ruled unconstitutional.[16] In 1962, an extremely controversial ruling was passed by the Supreme Court against required recitation of prayers in public school (*Engle v. Vitale*, 370 US 421). Several states passed laws allowing for voluntary prayers; Illinois, Connecticut, Arkansas, Massachusetts, and others passed laws allowing for a "period of silence," "in silent contemplation of the anticipated activities of the day." This has been ruled constitutional because it does not "advance religion." Reciting the Lord's Prayer and forcing students to recite the Pledge of Allegiance have been ruled unconstitutional.

In 1963, the decision in *Abington Township, Pa. v. Schempp* was passed down, putting a different emphasis on religious education: "One's education is not complete without a study of comparative religion and its relationship to the advancement of civilization. . . ." The argument was that we cannot ignore religions as a field of academic study since they make up a large part of many people's lives. Organizations exist to help provide schools with interpretations of the meaning of the law and materials for classroom use.[17] Therefore, schools can teach *about* religion, comparative religion, history of religion, or the Bible as literature, but *not* a subject that promotes religion.[18]

A related controversy has to do with providing parochial schools with instructional materials and services from public monies. In a 1975 Supreme Court case (*Meek v. Pittenger*), the conflict between strict and loose constitutional constructionists came to a head. The court ruled that "a state government may lend secular textbooks to pupils attending parochial and other religiously oriented schools." Government may also provide nonpublic schools with the following: buses; lunches; fire protection; water; police; sewers; tax exemptions; standardized tests and scoring; in-school diagnosis of speech, hearing, and psychological disorders; therapy, guidance, and remedial services *off* the school premises; payment for field trips; and *loans* to students of instructional materials and equipment. However, it was ruled unconstitutional to make *direct* loans of instructional materials and *direct* provision of auxiliary services such as counseling, testing, therapy, and remedial aid, because such services result in the direct and substantial advancement of religious activities.[19]

In *Aguilar v. Felton,* the public schools were legally required to administer federal aid, but questions about how to do so remain. Some court support has come for not providing aid for equipment such as computers and photocopiers which could be used for religious purposes.[20] Clearly, there is a fine line between the acceptable and nonacceptable, and more test cases are being brought to the courts.

Another issue in the church-state controversy is the clash between state standards and those of private schools. A case in point occurred in Darke County, Ohio, in 1976, when the Tabernacle Christian School, serving the Dunkard religious group, was told that it failed to comply with the state board of education requirements, and that parents would be charged with failure to send children to school. This was seen by supporters and sympathizers of the school as an attempt to crush evangelical Christian schools. Other cases involve conflicts between religious groups such as the Amish and the states in which they live, centering around attendance laws. The church groups would prefer to have control over both the type and the amount of schooling children receive. Accommodations between the state and religious groups have been reached in most areas.

One of the most controversial cases in recent years involving separation of church and state was heard before the Little Rock, Arkansas, state courts in 1981 and 1982. Referred to popularly as Scopes II, *McLean v. Arkansas Board of Education* was similar to the 1925 trial of John Scopes for teaching evolutionary theory in the classroom. The 1981–82 case dealt with requiring equal time in the classroom for "scientific creationist" and "evolutionist" theories.

These cases have centered on the battle between "absolute truth" believed by creationists and "relative truth" of those who have been labeled by Fundamentalist Christians as "secular humanists."[21] Those in favor argued that evolution is not a proven theory and that other theories should receive equal time; those opposed maintained that the creationist view is taken from the Bible and would be bringing religion into the classroom. After lengthy expert testimony the court ruled that allowing the creationist view to be taught would be a violation of church and state separation. The case was particularly important because it set a precedent for cases being considered in 18 other states. One of these was brought before the Supreme Court in June 1987; the argument was that "creation science" had as much right to be taught in the classroom as evolution. Proponents argued that creation is a respectable scientific theory, that life forms did not evolve but appeared suddenly, and that this thesis should be given equal time. But by a 7 to 2 vote the Court again held that this was a subterfuge to bring the Bible back to class and violate First Amendment rights.[22]

Recent court cases return to the issue of prayer in schools and to the complex issue of extracurricular religious clubs. In a 1981 ruling (*Widmar v. Vincent*), the Supreme Court granted public university students the right to form religious clubs on campus; in a June 1990 ruling (*Westside Community Schools v. Mergens*), it extended the ruling to apply to secondary schools under some circumstances. The Equal Access Act states that if a school allows any non-curriculum-related clubs to meet—recreational, political, philosophical—it must also allow religious groups to meet.[23]

A second case (*Weisman v. Lee*) relates to the constitutionality of including prayer at graduation or promotion ceremonies. One side argues that invoking God's name should be upheld as constitutional; others argue that this violates the rights of separation by favoring some religions over others and by making nonadherents feel that they are "outsiders and the public school system does not belong to them."[24]

The Economics of Education: Financing Schools

Most societies view education as an investment in the future. Training youth functions to socialize them into productive roles in society, prepares them to contribute to society, and "selects" them for future roles. In many countries, central governments provide local districts with funds to carry out equitable public education. These policies are based on goals of efficiency, equity, and liberty. However, wealthy members of society may buy their children elite educations, thus ensuring them high positions that reproduce the stratification system.

Schools serve the ever-growing expansion and technological sophistication of the economic sector. This is reflected in the rapid growth of schools to train populations for jobs. Growth of schooling in the United States has been dramatic. From 1890 to the 1960s, secondary education expanded from an enrollment of 7 percent of the high school–aged people to over 90 percent.

The growth of schools is seen by functionalists as meeting the economic needs for an educated labor force. The two go hand in hand to support the economy of nations. The growth and improvement of schools enhances worker skills and character traits, which in turn improves economic growth and social progress.[25] More schooling for individuals opens more economic possibilities for individuals and nations.

A counterargument to the functional, social progress model states that educational improvements alone do not cause social development.[26] Schools serve as sifting and sorting institutions. Conflict theorists see schools as training individuals to meet the economic, occupational demands of society. Training stratifies by credentialing individuals for the labor force, just as testing sorts individuals, but it does not necessarily imply social progress.

The financial environment of schools in the United States is in turmoil. Actual dollars for education keep rising, but school costs are rising faster than inflation. What is the problem? The case of oil-rich states provides one example.

The states of Louisiana, Oklahoma, Montana, New Mexico, North Dakota, Texas, and Wyoming derive 25 to 33 percent of their school support from oil revenues, and Alaska up to 70 percent. When there is a recession and oil prices drop, money for education is lost. Other states have different mechanisms for obtaining revenue, often not as closely tied to industry.

Inner-city schools with higher expenditures are particularly hard hit: teachers' unions in cities are strong and often successfully demand more pay; school buildings need repairs; need for special programs such as compensatory education are greater in inner cities; turnover of students is higher. Unfortunately, as the tax rates go up to support the schools, some residents move to the suburbs, further reducing the city's tax base.

School financing occurs at three levels: local, state, and federal (Figure 8-3). Local has always, on balance, provided the most funds; however, this balance is changing.

FIGURE 8-3   Sources of revenue for public elementary and secondary schools, 1970–89.

Source: U.S. Department of Education, National Center for Educational Statistics, *Statistics of State School Systems; Revenues and Expenditures for Public Elementary and Secondary Education;* and Common Core of Data surveys; reprinted in *Digest of Education Statistics* (Washington, D.C.: U.S. Department of Education, 1990), p. 46.

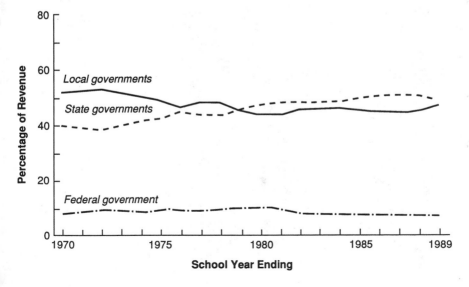

Local Funding.   The idea was to keep financial control local, but gradually the percentage of funding coming from the community has decreased. Property taxes have been the main collection method, but the disparities between districts are great. Inner cities continue to lose their tax base, with wealthy individuals moving to suburbs and industries relocating; therefore, suburbs have greater tax bases to provide better schools. Should property taxes not provide adequate funds, bond levies can be put up for vote, but the record of success does not bode well for schools depending on this source.

Across America, large districts and small towns alike faced shortages of funds. In the early 1960s, local tax levies provided 6 percent of the school budget. By 1974, that figure was 26 percent and growing. Today, 46 percent of total school revenue comes from local funding sources. Taxpayers are rebelling against this heavier burden. In the 1990s, school finance reform is a top priority; state support is providing an increasing proportion of the budget, while local and federal taxes provide less. The local tax base is affected by crises such as the closings of military bases and the bankruptcies of industries and savings and loans. Local districts are resorting to four-day workweeks, selling kids' art, and holding lotteries.

State Funding.   In recent years, state funding of education has increased to almost 50 percent of the total funding; the money comes primarily from sales taxes and personal income taxes. Over 40 states have statewide sales taxes, which make up over 30 percent of state revenues. Personal income tax makes up the remainder—about 25 percent. In 1988, states put $89 billion

Schools depend on levy passage for revenues.

into local education, up 60 percent from 1982 figures. These tax rates vary by state. An increasing number of states are using lotteries to raise funds for education.

The concern in distribution of funds is how to be fair to all groups and areas of a state. State monies come to local districts through four main methods:

1. *Flat grants* provide the same amount to all districts for all students regardless of special needs; some states modify this to provide more for poor districts.
2. *Foundation plans,* the most common approach since the *Serrano* case (see below), provide for a minimum annual expenditure per student.
3. In *power-equalizing plans,* "the state pays a percentage of the local school expenditures in inverse ratio to the wealth of the district."
4. *Weighted-student plans* allow students to be rated according to their special needs: bilingual, disabled, vocational education.[27]

Several of these plans attempt to take into consideration the differential in local ability to support schools and special needs of some districts, thus attempting to provide more equality between schools.

A continuing debate, which has reached the courts in a number of states, concerns the use of property taxes to help finance schools. The argument of those opposed to this is that wealthier districts have more money to pour into schools and can afford a better-quality education for their children. Thus, states are seeking ways to reduce the disparities in funding between local districts. In New Jersey, the "Robin Hood plan" would redistribute state funds to less affluent districts; in Louisiana, formerly tax-exempt sources are being asked to pay school property taxes. Some districts are requiring students to pay school fees to offset costs.

Two well-known court cases addressed the issue of local school funding through property taxes. In 1971, in the case of *Serrano v. Priest,* the California Supreme Court ruled that "this funding scheme invidiously discriminates against the poor because it makes the quality of a child's education a function of the wealth of his parents and neighbors."[28] This landmark ruling affected school funding in many other states. In a 1973 Texas case, *San Antonio v. Rodriquez,* it was argued that education is a fundamental right and all schools should have the same financial base. This case reached the U.S. Supreme Court, which held that "education is not a fundamental interest or right," and rejected the case against property tax support. The use of property taxes for schools was left undisturbed, though states were urged to devise new taxing and spending plans. "Poor schools remain poor, rich schools remain rich, and equalization is still a long way off."[29] Many other cases have been going through court systems, resulting in a redistribution of funding for education between local, state, and federal, with the percentage of local funding down.

Federal Funding.   Federal funding for education is influenced by the economic state of the nation. When recession plagued the United States in the early 1980s, available monies from government revenues dropped. A nation's priorities also influence where money is channeled.

During the Reagan and Bush administrations, the philosophy was to leave education and decision making to state and local governments. Thus, federal programs for disadvantaged students, except for Head Start, were reduced. Twenty-seven federal programs were put together into single grants to states, resulting in some programs being lost at the state level, especially if they were unpopular among more powerful groups in the state; this caused many to argue that the federal government should support programs to enhance equal opportunity.[30] Urban schools are likely to suffer most from loss of programs and money.[31] The budget for fiscal 1991 is summarized in Table 8-1. The end result is that the United States spends less money per student on education than other industrial nations (Figure 8-4).

Several ideas have been proposed to improve funding of education: Tuition tax credits, vouchers, private-sector support, and lotteries are among the most common. Vouchers, for instance, have generated controversy in various circles. The basic idea is that children and their families would receive a voucher to pay for a school of their choice, or schools that would meet special needs of students. Some critics of this idea argue that it could lead to segregated schools, challenge teacher unions, allow special-interest groups to dominate education, and destroy the concept of mass education.

The political climate and philosophy directly affects funding for education. Our next environmental institution is the political sector.

Because of financial pressures, schools are put in the situation of having to market themselves to the environment, sell their program advantages, justify their staffing, prove their results. The programs that are considered by the community to be "frills" are scrutinized most carefully. Thus, extracurricular activities, sports, music and art programs, counseling services, yearbooks,

TABLE 8-1   Budget for Fiscal 1991 (in thousands)

Sample Program	FY91
Chapter 1 aid to the disadvantaged	$6,214,757
Impact aid	780,720
Chapter 2 block grants	484,444
Emergency immigrant education	198,014
Education for the disabled	2,467,446
Vocational and adult education	1,245,536
Student financial assistance	6,709,584
Guaranteed student loans	4,539,780
Higher education programs	762,638
Educational research and statistics	135,070
Libraries	142,898
Departmental management	392,386
Total Education Department budget	$27,426,292

Source: "Databank: Final Education Department Budget for Fiscal 1991," *The Chronicle of Higher Education,* November 7, 1990, p. 10.

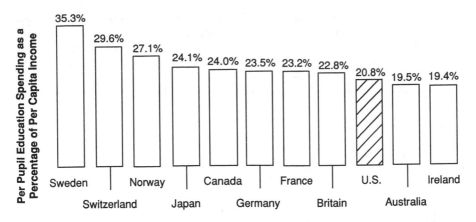

FIGURE 8-4   "Back of the class": The U.S. is among the stingiest industrialized nations in per student education spending.

Source: "Shortchanging Education: How U.S. Spending on Grades K–12 Lags Behind Other Industrialized Nations," Economic Policy Institute; reprinted in "The President's Worst Subject," *U.S. News & World Report,* August 6, 1990, p. 46.

newspapers, debate teams, plays, and concerts are often first to go in a budget crunch. The financial environment of the school has a great impact on the type of school programming and planning that takes place.

School Partnerships. Corporate America, realizing that its future work force is at stake, is paying more attention to schools. This attention takes several forms, from outright cash donations to operating schools on corporate premises. More than 50 percent of the nation's 15,889 school districts, representing 65 percent of students, have some partnership program with parents or business or civic groups. Thirty-one percent of these partnerships involve direct support such as tutoring, mentoring, job training, career awareness, and student recognition awards; 33 percent focus on curriculum and instruction programs; 14 percent focus on professional development efforts with staff; and 22 percent focus on districtwide policy and program initiatives such as dropout and substance-abuse prevention.[32]

Foundations are particularly active in awarding grants to school districts for projects; some are diverting funds that formerly went to universities in attempts to shore up elementary and secondary schools. Local small businesses donate for special programs, libraries, and sports programs.

The link between corporations and students from inner-city schools who go on to attend college is encouraging some students to continue with their high school educations. Corporations have offered to pay all expenses for students who complete high school and attend college. However, corporations also express frustration over not always knowing the outcomes of their cash and in-kind contributions to schools. Measuring effectiveness is difficult, and many corporate leaders are questioning whether their efforts are having any impact.

Some school personnel question the role of business in public education, fearing undue influence from the corporate sector—which has money to direct curriculum and policies; others feel that corporate partnerships are a hope for infusing more funds into poor school districts and for trying out creative ideas to improve achievement levels.

The impact of school funding problems will fall in several areas:

1. classroom size has leveled off, but may start increasing with rising student numbers,
2. most school districts need to update old buildings,
3. smaller schools become more appealing because of lower costs,
4. schools can save energy through lowering thermostats and other practices,
5. teacher layoffs are still occurring in some areas, but are leveling off in others,
6. administrative layoffs are occurring, especially in nonteaching areas such as coordinators, directors, and assistant superintendents
7. states are experiencing lower incomes and are cutting state budgets, including school budgets.[33,34]

The Political and Legal Institution

Governments have direct involvement in education, whether through ideological beliefs, funding, or setting policy. Many systems are controlled by the central government, usually through a ministry of education. Others are influenced by the federal government, which has legal and financial control and influence over schools.

Some of the political issues facing schools are worldwide, others unique to particular systems. For instance:

1. Should children be provided with broad, comprehensive education or tracked, with some taking vocational education and others academic courses?
2. Should schools be administered from a central "ministry of education" or a local authority?
3. Should parents be allowed to educate their children in schools of their choice (even if unaccredited, such as some church schools), or should children be required to go to accredited schools?
4. Should vouchers be given to parents to choose their children's school?
5. Should groups of parents with particular ideological concerns be allowed to ban textbooks from schools because they are offensive to the group?
6. Should controversial community or societal issues such as AIDS and sex education be brought into the classroom?

In four specific categories, education and politics cannot be separated:

- *Structural politics,* centered upon the nature and strength of the alignment of the school with the economy (for example, conflicts over differentiated and vocational education) and conflicts over the structure of authority relations within schools (for example, conflicts over the centralization of administrative authority, unionization, and professionalism);

- *Human capital politics,* generated by the efforts of parents or communities to enhance the rates of return to their children or school population relative to other children or school populations;
- *Cultural capital politics,* created by conflicts over competing definitions of legitimate knowledge; that is, conflicts over the distribution of symbolic authority in the society (for example, conflicts over curricula content or textbooks);
- *Displacement politics,* in which educational issues (often, though not always, conflicts of a cultural capital kind) become proxies for other noneducational conflicts in the community.[35]

Schools have always been the testing ground for societal changes and conflicts. In the United States, this means responsibility for public education and "promoting the general welfare."

Early in U.S. history, the federal government was involved in setting aside land for education and raising funds as ordained in the Northwest Ordinance of 1785 and the Morrill Act of 1862, and passing laws to ensure education for specific groups of students. Recently, this has involved laws guaranteeing education for disabled students.

Courts at each level of the system hear education cases on interpretations of the law, ranging from desegregation to education for the disabled to voucher systems. Community residents or interest groups initiate cases that are brought before the courts; we have seen several examples throughout the book: textbooks, creationism, busing and integration, special education, and many other issues.[36]

One example of the enormous impact legislation can have on schools is seen in a federal government ruling that some predicted would have as profound an effect on education as the 1954 *Brown v. Board of Education* case, or the 1964 Civil Rights Act. Public Law 94-142, the Education for All Handicapped Children Act, enacted in 1975, requires schools to "mainstream" disabled children from ages 3 to 21.

Before the passage of PL94-142, 1 million disabled children would have been excluded from the public school system. Arguments for integrating these children include the following:

1. The disabled can achieve higher levels academically and socially if not isolated.
2. Regular school settings help them cope with the world in which they must live as adults.
3. Exposure to the disabled helps other children understand differences between children.

Opponents of the law argue that many disabled children will suffer from the taunting of classmates and from untrained teachers trying to make the program work. They recommend caution in placements, special training for teachers, and limited numbers of disabled children in classrooms.

Although President Bush claimed to be "the education president," critics argue that his plans have not been carried through or backed up by money. The idea of having the United States be No. 1 in math and science by the year 2000 is rhetoric at the current rate of funding, claim many educators.

Governmental bodies and agencies at various levels in the school's environment have responsibility for passing and enforcing legislation related to the functioning of schools, and therefore have an impact on the school's internal operation. The whole educational system is affected. The structure must be altered to include appropriate materials, physical facilities, and support personnel; roles must be redefined to include new expectations; school goals must be restated to avoid conflicting statements. Laws requiring change in schools, classrooms, curricula, and individual role responsibilities mean a restructuring of the system and have repercussions for structure and positions at each level.

States have become increasingly involved in educational reform; hardly any areas have remained untouched, as is illustrated in the following list of legislative activities:[37]

I.   Administration/Leadership
   A.   Training for school board members
   B.   Changes in certification for administrators
   C.   Competency testing for all administrators or for initial certification
   D.   Evaluation programs for administrators
   E.   Establishment of principals' academies and administrative staff development programs

II. School District
   A.   Academic bankruptcy or curricular accountability
   B.   Long-range planning (accountability)
   C.   Programs to lower class size and target instructional resources
   D.   District consolidation or reorganization

III. Early Childhood
   A.   Prekindergarten programs
   B.   Mandatory kindergarten and/or full-day kindergarten
   C.   Early intervention and programs for at-risk or disabled students
   D.   Prime-time programs and smaller classes for early elementary years

IV. Finance
   A.   Tax increases for reforms
   B.   Funding innovations, especially incentive programs
   C.   Teacher salary increases, career ladders, or merit-pay programs

V.   General
   A.   Adult literacy
   B.   Computers/technology
   C.   Incentive programs for schools and districts
   D.   Governance changes
   E.   Changes in length of school day and year
   F.   Parental involvement
   G.   Programs for special populations (gifted, disabled, etc.)
   H.   Mandated discipline plans
   I.   Guidance/counseling

VI. Postsecondary
   A.   Changes in admissions requirements
   B.   Efforts to improve quality of undergraduate students
   C.   Program consolidation

VII. Students
   A.   Programs for at-risk youth
   B.   Changes in the curriculum

C. Increased requirements for high school graduation
D. Competency testing
E. Academic recognition
F. Changes in policies regarding placement, promotion/retention, and remediation
G. Home instruction
H. Choice programs

VIII. Teachers
A. Instructional time
B. Teacher shortages
C. Certification changes
D. Preservice training
E. Alternate certification
F. Competency testing/evaluation
G. Career ladder plans and merit-pay plans
H. Staff development
I. Forgivable loans to attract new teachers

Communites and Their Schools

Parents complain that the school should not be teaching about sex. Businesses put pressure on the school to train students in industry-oriented computers and technology. Immigrant groups want the school to teach students in their native languages. Peer groups compete with schools for the attention of students. All of these examples show the vulnerability of the school system to environmental pressures from a variety of community sources. The composition of the community in which schools are located determines the "raw material" entering the local school.

Businesses have become increasingly involved in schools, especially in some large cities where high school students are given internships, graduates are promised jobs, and those going to college are given tuition. Business leaders consider this support to be in their interests to provide more employment, a trained labor force, and more livable cities.

Peer groups become increasingly important for children as they progress through the teen years; each child is likely to be influenced by several different groups—some formally organized by the school, as in team sports; some community activities through religious groups or scouts; and some informal and neighborhood and peer groups.

Special-interest groups make constant demands on the school:

- More money should be funneled into athletic programs.
- Sex education is not the role of the schools, but should be taught at home.
- Teaching our cultural heritage should be a high priority for schools.
- Students should learn discipline and respect in the school in order to become solid citizens.
- Minority students should have special cultural programs.

At some time, most of us will take sides on an issue that is confronting the school system. It may involve the proper role of schools, the educational content of curricula, or the hiring or firing of personnel. Because of the school's vulnerability to environmental demands, administrators must consider the varying demands made upon them. The school administration is in a double bind. It is under pressure to consider all opinions on an issue, yet not all views can be accepted. Teachers may demand academic freedom in covering their disciplines, and this may conflict with community concerns.

Over the years, minority groups have requested that a number of programs be added to the school curriculum; black studies, Hispanic studies, women's studies, and others were initiated. More recently, grant money from such philanthropic organizations as the Ford and Rockefeller foundations has been funding projects in ethnic studies, based on arguments put forth by Michael Novak and others.[38] Many educators agree that the standard curriculum—originally designed to socialize children to be like the dominant group in society, and to assimilate groups to be "Americans"—is in need of revision. Trends today are in the direction of inter-cultural programs supporting the diversity of groups dealt with in the system. This could eventually put each group into perspective in the national picture, and stress respect for cultural diversity and pluralism.

Minority programming is one example of an issue put forth by special-interest groups. The stronger the power base of the interest group pushing an issue in a community, the more consideration the issue is likely to receive. Some small groups have had disproportionate influence because they were willing to speak out. The school's institutional environment shapes the internal processes of schools around the world, making each a unique organization within the educational setting.

SUMMARY

I. The Environment and the Education System

Schools respond to the many and varied demands of their environments in order to survive. Because they depend on the environment for resources, demands from the environment cannot be ignored. In this chapter we have focused on the institutional environment of schools: family and home, religious groups, financing and the economy, political and legal systems, and the community.

Conflicts of interest are an inherent part of the schools' environment, with opposing groups demanding that their views dominate. In order to receive the resources necessary for survival, schools must expend more energy dealing with the demands of the more salient parts of the environment.

II. The School Systems' Environments: Interdependence Between Institutions

Key institutions that make up the environment include the home, religious organizations, financial environment, government and legal systems, and the community and special-interest groups.

1. Children bring their attitudes toward school, among other attributes, from home. Parents have varying degrees of involvement in schools; the more active the parents, the more positive the results for their children's school experience.
2. In some societies, religion and the state, including education, are one and the same. In the United States, the separation of church and state has caused conflict on several issues, most notably what constitutes teaching religion in schools and what to teach in the classroom. The "creation story" issue is a prime example.
3. Funding of education comes from three primary sources: federal, state, and local levels. The percentage supplied by each of these has shifted over the years. Court cases have challenged some local plans for financing schools as being unfair to poor districts, and in recent years there has been an increase in state funding. Funding comes from several sources: personal income tax, sales tax, property tax, levies, and—in some states—lotteries. Methods of distribution of funds also vary by state, with "foundation plans" being most common. Federal funding supports special programs for minorities, the disabled, and other targeted projects. Proposals for change, including tax credits and vouchers, continue to be discussed.
4. Government involvement in education involves passing laws and setting policies. While local control is paramount, the federal government has great leverage by restricting funding of education to those who fail to adhere to federal educational guidelines. Where there are questions related to laws and policies, the courts are asked to make judgments; for instance, laws setting policy for education for the disabled have dramatically affected this group, and cases brought before the courts continue to test the law.
5. Communities provide the "raw material" entering the schools, as well as influencing the type of education offered in a particular community. Composition of the community determines the need for special programs such as bilingual education. Special interests in the community also put pressure on schools to accommodate their interests.
6. The school environment has a dramatic effect on the internal functioning of schools. We cannot completely understand schools without considering this crucial element in the educational system.

PUTTING SOCIOLOGY TO WORK

1. Describe the parts of your environment that affect your role as a student. Do any of these cause role conflict?
2. What are some movements or population trends affecting your school district? Ask teachers and principals what they perceive to be pressures on the schools related to current trends. Compare current influences with those of the 1960s (see also Chapter 10).
3. What are your local schools' immediate and secondary environments? Diagram them.
4. Discuss several examples of school system change brought about by environmental feedback.

NOTES _____

[1] Apple, Michael W., and Lois Weis, "Seeing Education Relationally: The Stratification of Culture and People in the Sociology of School Knowledge," *Journal of Education*, Vol. 168, No. 1, 1986.

[2] Rogers, David, *110 Livingston Street* (New York: Vintage Books, 1969), p. 211.

[3] Data from New York City Board of Education.

[4] "Children Under Stress," *U.S. News & World Report,* October 27, 1986, pp. 58–64.

[5] Cohen, Jere, "Parents as Educational Models and Definers," *Journal of Marriage and the Family,* Vol. 49, May 1987, pp. 339–51.

[6] Stevenson, David L., and David P. Baker, "The Family-School Relation and the Child's School Performance," *Child Development,* Vol. 58, 1987, pp. 1348–57.

[7] Baker, David P., and David L. Stevenson, "Mothers' Strategies for Children's School Achievement: Managing the Transition to High School," *Sociology of Education,* Vol. 59, July 1986, pp. 156–66.

[8] Garner, Catherine L., and Stephen W. Raudenbush, "Neighborhood Effects on Educational Attainment: A Multilevel Analysis," *Sociology of Education,* Vol. 64, No. 4, October 1991, pp. 251–62.

[9] Epstein, Joyce, "Toward a Theory of Family-School Connections: Teacher Practices and Parent Involvement Across the School Years," in Klaus Hurrelmann and Franz-Xavier Kaufman (eds.), *The Limits and Potential of Social Intervention* (Berlin/New York: DeGruyter/Aldine, 1987).

[10] Epstein, Joyce, "Effects on Student Achievement of Teachers' Practices of Parent Involvement," in S. Silvem (ed.), *Literacy Through Family, Community, and School Interaction* (Greenwich, Conn.: JAI Press, 1988).

[11] Epstein, Joyce, "Single Parents and the Schools: The Effect of Marital Status on Parent and Teacher Evaluations," Report 353 (Baltimore: Johns Hopkins University, Center for Social Organization of Schools, March 1984).

[12] Epstein, Joyce, "Target: An Examination of Parallel School and Family Structures That Promote Student Motivation and Achievement," Report 6 (Baltimore: Johns Hopkins University, Center for Research on Elementary and Middle Schools, January 1987).

[13] Natriello, Gary, and Edward L. McDill, "Performance Standards, Student Effort on Homework, and Academic Achievement," *Sociology of Education,* Vol. 59, January 1986, pp. 18–31.

[14] Dronkers, Jaap, "Is the Importance of Family Decreasing?" presented Summer 1991, Social Stratification, International Sociological Association, Columbus, Ohio.

[15] Steelman, Lala Carr, and Brian Powell, "Sponsoring the Next Generation: Parental Willingness to Pay for Higher Education," *American Journal of Sociology,* Vol. 96, No. 6, May 1991, pp. 1505–29.

[16] "Elected Silence," *American,* February 4, 1978, pp. 72–73.

[17] Uphoff, James K., Nicholas Piediscalzi, and James V. Panoch, "Public School Religion Studies: A New Freedom Through a Slow Revolution," *Intellect,* September 1976, pp. 97–98.

[18] "Teach About Religions, but Not Religion," *The Christian Science Monitor,* September 5, 1985, p. 25.

[19] Brickman, William W., "Textbooks, Auxiliary Services, and Parochial Pupils," *Intellect,* September 1975, p. 113.

[20] Crawford, James, "Chapter 2 Limits Set in Suit Settlement," *Education Week,* September 17, 1986, p. 15.

[21] "Keeping God Out of the Classroom," *Newsweek,* June 29, 1987, p. 23.

[22] "Louisiana Creationism Law: A 'Religious Purpose'," *Education Week,* August 4, 1987, p. 23.

[23] Sendor, Benjamin, "Religious Clubs Gain 'Equal Access' to Schools," *The American School Board Journal,* September 1990, p. 15.

[24] Walsh, Mark, "Justices Weigh Allowing Prayers at Graduation," *Education Week,* November 13, 1991, p. 1.

[25] DeYoung, Alan J., "Economic Underdevelopment and Its Effects on Formal Schooling in Southern Appalachia," *American Educational Research Journal,* Vol. 28, No. 2, Summer 1991, pp. 297–315.

[26] *Ibid.*

[27] Ornstein, Allan, and Daniel Levine, *Foundations of Education*, 3rd ed. (Boston: Houghton Mifflin, 1985), pp. 258–59.

[28] Hutchins, Robert M, "Two Fateful Decisions," *Education Digest*, Vol. 40, April 1975, pp. 17–20.

[29] Brodinsky, Ben, "Something Happened: Education in the Seventies," *Phi Delta Kappan*, Vol. 6, December, 1979, p. 241.

[30] Van Scotter, Richard D., *et al.*, *Social Foundations of Education*, 2nd ed. (Englewood Cliffs, N.J.: Prentice Hall, 1985), p. 163.

[31] Spring, Joel, *Education and the Rise of the Corporate State* (Boston: Beacon Press, 1972).

[32] *The Chronicle of Higher Education*, Vol. 11, No. 12, November 20, 1991, p. 15.

[33] Ornstein, Allan C., "School Budgets in the 1990s," *The School Administrator*, October 1989, pp. 20–21.

[34] Natale, Jo Anna, "Just Deserts," *The American School Board Journal*, March 1990, p. 21.

[35] Apple and Weiss, "Seeing Education Relationally," p. 8.

[36] *Education Week*, November 5, 1986, pp. 16–17.

[37] Pipho, Chris, "States Move Reform Closer to Reality," *Phi Delta Kappan*, December 1986, pp. K4–K5.

[38] Novak, Michael, *The Rise of the Unmeltable Ethnics: Politics and Culture in the Seventies* (New York: Macmillan, 1972).

9

THE SYSTEM OF HIGHER EDUCATION

"The path from school to college is poorly marked."[1] Some of us have models—older siblings, parents, or help from a counselor—to point the way through college-preparatory curricula, college testing, the application and selection process, and admission. Others have little guidance, and often these are the very students who have less chance of going to college and succeeding in higher education. Elementary and secondary schooling are compulsory, but we choose whether to attend an institution of higher education. The atmosphere, the professional manner of the faculty, the organization of the system—all have unique features as compared to primary and secondary school.

In this chapter we deal with the system of higher education—its development and meaning; access to the system; the structure, process, and role relationships within the system; environmental pressures toward change; and outcomes and reforms in higher education. The open systems model helps us draw together the many aspects of higher education and see them in relation to the total system (Figure 9-1). This model shows the parts of some systems of higher education today. However, it would look unfamiliar to many institutions that have existed throughout history.

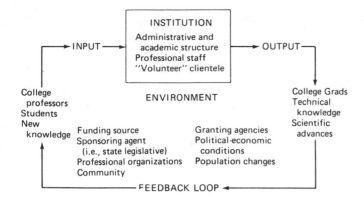

FIGURE 9-1   Systems model of higher education.

HISTORY AND DEVELOPMENT OF HIGHER EDUCATION

Walking through the colleges at Oxford and Cambridge universities in England, one is reminded that many traditions in higher education were established in the twelfth and thirteenth centuries in those very settings, with their courtyards, spires, formal gardens, long halls with stained-glass windows, and statues of notable early scholars. In the ancient library at Oxford University, medieval scholars sat and studied just as students in jeans with backpacks do today. The tradition of transmitting knowledge began with the early universities: Paris in France, Bologna and Venice in Italy, Salamanca in Spain, and Oxford and Cambridge in England.[2] These universities established a delicate balance between independence and autonomy over their decision making and interaction with the church and state, a balance that set precedents for church-state-institution relations through the centuries and up to the present time.

Historical Functions of Higher Education

In the nineteenth century, a new mission or function was added to the traditional one of transmitting knowledge. Research became an end in itself.[3] This new mission created tension between teaching and research, causing strains on the teacher-student relationship and between faculty members with different orientations and interests. This tension is familiar to us today as professors divide their time between students and research. In many countries, research wins out because more monetary and prestige rewards are attached to these activities than to teaching.[4]

Two further missions or purposes have developed during the present century: providing services to the community, and creating an ideal democratic community within the institution.[5] Both have created dilemmas for the university, as we shall see.

Over time changes have occurred in the governance, the administrative structures, the curriculum, and the composition of the student body in higher education. In the twentieth century, new disciplines developed rapidly, requiring adaptation of existing structures. Pressure for more representative multicultural curriculum and higher educational opportunities for more segments of populations around the world became key issues.

Trends in Development of Higher Education

Higher education developed somewhat differently in the United States compared with European countries such as England and Spain. In the colonial period, several small colleges were established in the United States, most sponsored by religious groups but run by lay persons, a pattern that was also typical in Scandinavian countries. In the period that followed, many other colleges sprang up—and many died. The colleges were meant to serve men from "respectable families" and a few lucky young men selected from poor families. Generally, they were established by upper-middle-class men, and perpetuated the existing distinctions between social classes in the United States. In 1776, only about one man in 200 had a college education, but many other young men learned from tutors or were self-taught.[6] Women were excluded from higher education at this period; however, a few women met in small private groups to receive training from broad-minded male professors at nearby universities.

It was not until after the Civil War, with the passage of the Morrill Act, that many states established public land-grant colleges and universities with the purpose of providing liberal and practical education for a wide range of students. Public teacher-training colleges, or "normal schools," also sprang up to meet the growing need for teachers. The first American colleges to provide graduate education and thus become universities were Harvard University, chartered in 1869, and Johns Hopkins, in 1876.

By 1900, there were several hundred small, private, undergraduate colleges, most with a "classical" curriculum of Greek, Latin, mathematics, morals, and religion. In addition, more specialized colleges, forerunners of today's professional schools, were emerging—for example, the Massachusetts Institute of Technology (MIT) and the California Institute of Technology, both specializing in engineering.

England today has a relatively small number of higher-education institutions, which fall into the categories of universities, polytechnics, and colleges; they enroll only about 15 percent of individuals in the college-age range. In contrast, the United States has over 3,500 higher education institutions, including two-year-colleges,[7] and enrolls over 50 percent[8] of the age range from 18 to 22—the highest percentage in the world. Canada, New Zealand, and Australia come next in percentage attending institutions of higher education. Various historical factors have led to the more restrictive model in England and the mass education model in the United States, among them the great diversity of student population in the United States. However, England is expanding its model to provide education equivalent to the two-year college, as we shall see.

The advent of two-year colleges, sometimes called community or junior colleges, is a twentieth-century phenomenon. They provide terminal degrees or act as feeders for four-year colleges and universities, or both. This unique American institution serves multiple purposes: a focus on students, remedial education where needed, vocational courses, community service, and nontraditional and minority student accessibility.[9,10] In 1988, almost half of the 1.1 million minority students in higher education were enrolled in community colleges.[11] In the fall of 1992, 50 percent of the 14 million U.S. students going to college enrolled in community colleges.[12] Of the 50 percent in higher education who attend community colleges, only 12 percent graduate from four-year colleges.[13] Therefore, some argue that these colleges serve as a sieve to eliminate poor and minority students or prevent them from moving up the educational ladder. Another potential problem lies in the shift in the purpose of many community colleges toward service to the corporate culture, with custom-contracted training programs. Because this is more of a community and vocational purpose, the traditional liberal arts and transfer functions of community colleges are weakened.[14]

The student population in two-year institutions has expanded more rapidly than that of four-year colleges, and the number of two-year institutions is increasing. However, relatively few two-year students transfer to four-year colleges, and probably less than 5 percent ever get a B.A. degree.[15,16]

Burton Clark observes that junior colleges in California in the 1950s served two functions: to provide terminal two-year degrees and to give a *small* group of students the preparation to transfer to four-year institutions. When it became clear that *many* students wished to transfer, they were dissuaded by the junior college and told of their academic weaknesses and the virtues of the career-oriented two-year terminal programs. Clark calls this the "cooling-out function."[17]

Until 1970, two-thirds of community college students transferred to four-year schools; by 1980, 70 percent of community college students were in two-year vocational programs. In a recent review of the situation, several reasons for this dramatic shift in purpose were suggested, from changes in students' choices of programs to community business leaders' exerting influence over what happens in community colleges. In fact, research shows that the community colleges themselves may have pursued the more vocational and semiprofessional course because it was an available niche in the higher education marketplace.[18] Conflict theorists might argue that junior colleges effectively filter out marginal students, who are often minority students, from the higher education system.[19] Students with modest or poor academic skills are directed into occupational programs preparing them for "middle-level" jobs.[20] Hispanic students are disproportionately tracked into two-year colleges, for instance.[21]

Many educators are concerned about the drop in the numbers of transfers, though articulation programs with universities have increased.[22] Some argue for the importance of the transfer function because it confirms the academic purposes of community colleges; many students *do* aspire to a four-year degree but are discouraged in the process; and claims to be egalitarian *depend* on the transfer function, which purports to give all students an opportunity for a four-year higher education.[23]

Who transfers? A student's academic performance in community college is the strongest predictor of transfer. Family background and high school factors are also important, though socially and academically disadvantaged students have access to community colleges. Chances of transferring are increased if students live on campus and have work-study jobs. Black and Hispanic students are more likely than white students to be motivated to transfer because selection has taken place to a greater extent at the high school level, where uncommitted students dropped out.[24] Yet, these are not the students who are most likely to transfer.[25]

What effect do community college degrees have on occupational placement and success? The type of college we enter shapes our occupational status. Community college male entrants achieve lower occupational status than those who begin at four-year colleges. For women, occupational return for each additional year of education is lower for community college entrants than for four-year entrants.

> On average, community college entrants achieve a lower occupational status than four-year college entrants, net of other variables. Community colleges do not provide two years of a college education; they provide a different kind of education. Community college entrants may take courses that are not readily transferable to four-year institutions. Tracking within community colleges may influence the deleterious impact of community college entrance on adult occupational attainment.[26]

According to recent studies, students who enter community colleges have limited occupational and economic status advantages over students who take a job after high school. Considering the loss of work experience, the economic payoff is modest.[27] Completing the associate of arts degree may actually hinder a student's chances of getting additional years of education.[28] Community college, then, can perpetuate stratification in higher education.[29]

Vocational education offered at community colleges leads to certain types and levels of jobs such as building trades or electronic or business skills; it benefits employers who need skilled workers, and may give workers an opportunity to rise above low-paid, dead-end jobs,[30] but may also lock them into lower-level positions, as feared by conflict theorists.

Many community colleges are contracting with businesses to provide training, courses, and workshops for employees. However, some theorists point to the conflicting interests of those involved and fear that community colleges may find the financial benefits more appealing than their educational autonomy and serving the educational needs of their unique student constituencies. Two-year colleges serve a distinct role and, despite some controversy, are expanding their presence around the world.

Today the two-year college idea is spreading to other countries. For example, Britain is adding "sixth-form" colleges to many comprehensive schools; these are similar in structure and function to two-year colleges. Japan also offers selected courses of study at two-year colleges.

THEORETICAL APPROACHES TO HIGHER EDUCATION

Higher education has expanded rapidly around the world in the past half-century. Major theoretical questions are *why* and *what are the results?* Another major theoretical debate has centered on *access to higher education;* whether some groups have greater opportunity than others. Let us look briefly at these two debates through the eyes of functional and conflict theorists.

The Expansion of Higher Education

Functionalist or consensus theorists think that universities can go a long way toward solving societal problems through development and use of new knowledge; conflict theorists argue that universities often perpetuate the status quo and that more basic societal change is needed if we are to alter the current state of inequality.

Functional Approach. According to a functionalist perspective, higher education has developed rapidly in the United States and other countries, for several reasons. First, higher education is desirable to help improve individual opportunities. Second, higher education increases the possibility of equal opportunities by teaching the skills required in a complex technological world, and thereby improving an individual's ability to compete and fit into the system in a productive way. Third, society needs higher education to help prepare individuals to fill essential roles; this argument has been put forward to expand higher education in developing regions.

Conflict Approach. Conflict theorists view the growth in higher education as directly related to changes in the needs of the capitalistic system. They believe that higher education, like primary and secondary education, is structured to serve the needs and perpetuate the advantaged position of the elite. Just as the secondary schools channel students into vocational or academic tracks, so too the higher education system can be viewed as a series of tracks. The illusion of upward mobility is present, but its reality has been questioned. There is a major difference in the occupational status of the student graduating from two-year college or technical school compared with that of the elite university-trained student. Samuel Bowles and Herbert Gintis interpret most of the system of higher education as " . . . channeling students to lower-level white-collar occupations that permit little autonomy or discretion. Only in universities preparing students for elite status do we find a great deal of choice and discretion and long-range work without supervision.[31] These authors are doubtful that even an elite education encourages students to raise questions about the system and its legitimacy. Research funding is also guided by the interests of the elite and perpetuates the status quo.

To understand the politics of "gatekeeping,"[32] or who has access to elite colleges, one must study all parts of the educational system: those who make decisions about access, the criteria they use, and what type of university they are trying to create. The admissions process probably reflects the university's position in the larger society and how selective it can be. Therefore, the struggles for access in the society are reflected in the admissions process.[33]

Access to Higher Education

The issue around the globe is who gets into what university, and why. True or not, the belief in most countries is that education is the road to advancement and success. In many societies, the elite do dominate the halls of ivy, and as the opportunity structures change with modernization, others in society are demanding a share of the system.

Old universities around the world are pressured to reconsider their restrictive entrance requirements, and new universities are opening their doors to new groups of students. For example, in Malaysia, the national university now serves primarily Malays, the indigenous group that until recent years was underrepresented in higher education compared with Indian and Chinese groups in the population.

In the United States, the picture differs. Entrance to elite universities is similar to that in England and Japan, although there is no university exam here. However, 90 percent of the public institutions in the United States have "open-door policies," meaning that any high school graduate will be admitted. Private schools are divided between open-door (47 percent) and selective (48 percent) admissions. Since 1980, public four-year institutions have become more selective, meaning that expectations for high school coursework and achievement test scores have increased. With this gradual closing of the doors has come protest over access to systems and elitism in higher education.

Stratification and Equal Opportunity in Higher Education

In the United States, several factors are considered by college admissions officers—high school grades, activities, recommendations, and test scores. Yet controversy centers on test scores. Those in favor of using test scores in the admissions process argue that scores help screen out students who "can't make it." The scores of minority students, who make up 20 percent of the test takers, have improved somewhat; on the ACT, scores of minorities rose slightly while white scores dropped one-tenth of a point, as shown in Table 9-1.[34] Critics of the achievement tests argue that the tests do not give an accurate representation of what students have learned, that students who can afford it can be coached to raise their scores, that the tests do not measure what they say they do, and that they are unfair to minority students.[35]

In many countries, one exam for university entrance determines one's future. Pass or fail—simple as that! This has created a category of young people in Japan called "ronin," students who failed the exam for the university of their choice and spend an extra year or more studying to retake the entrance exam. However, some students in Japan simply give up the competitive

TABLE 9-1   Average Test Scores by Sex and Racial and Ethnic Group

	SCHOLASTIC APTITUDE TEST (SAT) SCORES, 1991			
	Verbal Section		*Mathematical Section*	
	1991	*1-Year Change*	*1991*	*1-Year Change*
Men	426	− 3	497	− 2
Women	418	− 1	453	− 2
American Indian	393	+ 5	437	0
Asian	411	+ 1	530	+ 2
Black	351	− 1	385	0
Mexican-American	377	− 3	427	− 2
Puerto Rican	361	+ 2	406	+ 1
Other Hispanic	382	− 1	431	− 3
White	441	− 1	489	− 2
Other	411	+ 1	466	− 1
All	422	− 2	474	− 2

Note: Each section of the Scholastic Aptitude Test is scored on a scale from 200 to 800.

	AMERICAN COLLEGE TESTING (ACT) SCORES, 1991	
	Score	*1-Year Change*
Men	20.9	−0.1
Women	20.4	+0.1
American Indian	18.2	+0.2
Asian	21.6	−0.1
Black	17.0	0.0
Mexican-American	18.4	+0.1
Other Hispanic	19.3	0.0
White	21.3	+0.1
All	20.6	0.0

Note: The American College Testing Program's ACT Assessment is scored on a scale from 1 to 36.

Source: The College Board, American College Testing Program; reprinted in *The Chronicle of Higher Education Almanac,* August 26, 1992, p. 9.

battle for top university placement; more often these are children of blue-collar workers, thus perpetuating the existing class system.

Gaining admission to Oxford University in England typifies the process of entrance to elite universities of the world; the university's entrance exam is most important. Next come the British A-, O-, and S-level exams, which each graduate takes. Socioeconomic variables (especially the type of school from which the student graduated) are highly significant in determining university admission.

Partly as a result of the controversy over access, many institutions have open admissions policies, our next topic.

Elite versus Public Colleges

Students from lower socioeconomic backgrounds are most likely to go to colleges with lower selectivity, such as open-enrollment institutions, regardless of their ability, achievement, and expectations. Though high school students in the United States know that *some* school will accept them, fewer middle-class students are enrolling, especially in selective schools. Elite boarding school students have the highest probability of attending highly selective colleges and universities (61 percent from elite schools versus 39 percent for a general sample of college-bound students).[36] Admissions officers are working toward diversifying the student populations at their campuses, usually voluntarily, but these efforts have caused controversy and raised affirmative action questions.

Admissions and the Courts

Admission of minority students has not always been a voluntary decision by the institution. The government has put pressure on institutions by offering funding for special programs, passing affirmative action legislation, and denying research funds to universities that do not comply with government-set standards in minority admissions and staff hiring.

Increasingly the courts have become involved in major decisions affecting the direction of education at all levels—this sector of the educational systems' environment has taken on increased importance. In higher education, court decisions and their implications have ranged from admissions and affirmative action to financing school sports and questions of students' rights. Two cases related to equal opportunity demonstrate the role of the courts in the environment of higher education.

What is considered preferential treatment of minorities by some has not gone unchallenged. In 1970–71, DeFunis, denied admission to the University of Washington law school, claimed that minority students with lower scores were given preference. The case reached the Supreme Court, which ruled in his favor but left unclear the issue of minority admissions and quota systems.

Admissions officers hoped that the 1978 *Bakke* case would resolve the unanswered questions about minority preferential treatment in minority quotas resulting from *DeFunis*. In this case, the medical school at the University of California at Davis set up quotas. Bakke came close to admission, but special applicants with lower scores were admitted. Bakke filed suit, arguing reverse discrimination. The Court supported the idea that institutions may attempt to achieve racial balance through admissions and affirmative action programs. But the idea of *protecting individual rights* was not to be ignored in admissions; thus, types of race-conscious plans other than quota systems should be adopted. This eagerly awaited decision left almost as many questions unanswered as answered. Postmortems ranged from disappointment that the Court was stepping backwards in the push for minority progress, to realization that more cases must be heard to test the ramifications. We have not heard the end of this difficult issue.

CHARACTERISTICS OF HIGHER EDUCATION IN THE UNITED STATES

Higher education is a catch-all term for programs offering some academic degree after high school. In general, however, we will not be referring to vocational or occupational training programs in this section.

In selecting our college, we can pick from two-year, four-year, or university systems, public or private. Once we have made our selection, we move into the system where we will remain until either (1) we are graduated after two or four years, (2) we drop out, or (3) we transfer.

There are more than 3,500 institutions of higher education in the United States.[37] John D. Millett has suggested several categories to use in classifying them (see Table 9-2). First, *sponsorship* is an important division, with two main

TABLE 9-2   Classifying Institutions of Higher Education

SPONSORSHIP	
Public	*Private*
Federal	Nonsectarian
State	Religious
Local	Protestant
	Roman Catholic
	Other

STUDENT COMPOSITION	
Coeducational	Student age
Men only	Race and ethnic composition
Women only	Foreign student

TYPES OF PROGRAMS	
Two-year: technical, institutions	A.A. or A.B. degree, feeder for four-year
Four-year	
M.A. or other graduate level	
Ph.D.-granting	
Professional schools	

Source: Millett, John D., "Similarities and Differences Among Universities of the United States," in Perkins, James A. (ed.), *The University as an Organization: A Report for The Carnegie Commission on Higher Education* (New York: McGraw Hill, 1973), p. 39. Reprinted by permission.

categories—public and private. Within the public category, institutions of higher education exist at the local, state, and even federal level. Most often public institutions are state-sponsored. Locally sponsored institutions tend to be two-year colleges and technical training institutions. More than half of the private institutions are religiously affiliated, usually with Protestant and Roman Catholic parent organizations.

Second, *student composition* tells us something about the institutions: percentage of males, females, minorities, foreign-speaking students; age and background of students (Table 9-3).

Third, *types of programs* distinguish one institution from another: two-year, four-year, master's or graduate level, Ph.D.-granting, professional schools such as law or medicine. Many of the institutions develop certain specialty areas or professional schools for which they become well known. Some institutions, especially public, state-sponsored systems, have moved toward multi-campus facilities. The University of California is a case in point, with its nine university campuses, 19 four-year state universities, and more than 100 two-year programs, which can either be terminal or feed into the other parts of the system.

TABLE 9-3   Characteristics of Freshmen, Fall 1991

	Total	Men	Women
Racial and ethnic background:			
American Indian	1.5%	1.5%	1.6%
Asian-American	3.1	3.3	2.8
Black	9.2	8.0	10.3
White	83.4	84.5	82.4
Mexican-American	2.7	2.4	3.0
Puerto Rican-American	0.6	0.6	0.6
Other	1.9	1.9	1.8
Estimated parental income:			
Less than $6,000	3.3%	2.6%	3.8%
$6,000–$9,999	3.3	2.7	3.8
$10,000–$14,999	5.3	4.3	6.3
$15,000–$19,999	5.3	4.5	6.0
$20,000–$24,999	6.7	6.2	7.1
$25,000–$29,999	7.2	6.7	7.7
$30,000–$39,999	14.0	14.2	13.9
$40,000–$49,999	13.7	13.9	13.4
$50,000–$59,999	11.9	12.4	11.4
$60,000–$74,999	11.4	12.1	10.8
$75,000–$99,999	8.0	9.2	6.9
$100,000–$149,999	5.0	5.9	4.2
$150,000–$199,999	2.1	2.3	1.9
$200,000 or more	2.8	3.0	2.6

Source: "Attitudes and Characteristics of Freshmen," *The Chronicle of Higher Education Almanac,* August 26, 1992, p. 11.

Within each classification, there may be further variations. For instance, Peter Blau[38] has identified 18 types of professional schools:

Architecture	Journalism	Optometry
Business	Law	Pharmacy
Dentistry	Library science	Public health
Education	Medicine	Social work
Engineering	Music	Theology
Forestry	Nursing	Veterinary medicine

These schools vary as to size, financial resources, graduate or undergraduate training, affirmative action and sex distribution, and according to specific attributes of the universities with which they are affiliated. The variations between systems of higher education are great. What they have in common is their service to students who have completed 12 years of schooling and who are voluntarily furthering their education.

Higher education experienced a period of phenomenal growth and has now leveled off. We look at these trends and their implications next.

Growth of Higher Education

According to Joseph Ben-David, the growth of American higher education since the late nineteenth century (and especially in the 1960s) has been phenomenal as compared with any previous time. Despite the rapid increase in the size of institutions of higher education, he argues, the teaching quality has not diminished and the dropout rate has remained the same throughout the period he discusses.[39] Recent data show enrollment increases up 3.2 percent in the fall of 1991, to over 14 million students. Much of this growth was at the two-year colleges.[40] This number is expected to rise to 16 million in 2002.[41] The minority population in these figures is also rising, while the white population is dropping slightly.

The "Body-Count Game" and the Credential Crisis

Does everyone have the right to go to university? To receive some form of higher education? If not, who should decide who has the right? And, ultimately, must some people entering higher education fail?

Following the period of rapid expansion of numbers of both students and faculty in the 1960s, institutions are now faced with lower enrollments and may be forced into playing "the body-count game": "One way to obtain a higher body count in a college or university is to lower admission standards. By making it easier for students to enter, institutions of higher education can reach out to a new clientele not previously eligible for admission."[42] One effect of this game is that students formerly eligible only for junior or two-year colleges may now gain admission to four-year colleges or universities. Yet some charge that opening college doors unselectively and expanding college faculty rapidly to meet the influx lowers the quality of higher education.

Another recent issue is a "credential crisis," which has arisen because graduates can no longer be guaranteed a job after college. Large numbers of college graduates remain unemployed or are returning to graduate school to improve their chances of employment.[43] Various new types of credentials are being proposed and requirements for jobs are being raised, not as a result of new educational knowledge, but because of the increased number of people seeking higher-level jobs in the system. The inflation of credentials is closely related to the economic and stratification system; students want higher credentials to get better jobs to have higher status. However, the image of college and university as "a sure route to the better life" is losing ground. This narrowing gap between high school and college credentials is directly related to the failure of the economy to provide more and higher-paying jobs for the larger number of college graduates. In fact, many college graduates accept positions unrelated to their college majors. The functionalist interpretation of expanding educational opportunities to meet societal needs is challenged by the current economic picture. Tensions produced by the presence of large numbers of dissatisfied graduates could, according to conflict theorists, force a restructuring of the economic system, and in turn of the educational system.

FUNCTIONS OF THE HIGHER EDUCATION SYSTEM

Higher education serves certain functions or purposes in society. What these purposes are or should be is a matter of debate and may cause conflict between parents, educators, students, government officials, and other groups in society. In the following discussion we consider the university as a community, the functions of the university, and conflicts over functions.

The University as a Community

One way to consider the functions of the university is through the concept of *community:* what members have in common, the division of labor, and the interdependence between members.[44] Universities are communities with an overall academic program, centralized physical settings, a form of governance, and a range of services. One can eat, sleep, and work there. Perhaps the best way to describe the modern university is one institution fulfilling numerous functions, or, to use Clark Kerr's term, a "multiversity."[45]

The full university, with its expanse of programs, research facilities, graduate and professional schools, and support services, has set the standards for all academic systems of higher education. Yet it is caught between contradictory goals, especially in the area of organizational structure and autonomy. Bonds such as shared beliefs, attitudes, and values, which traditionally held the university together, have been distintegrating as more formal structures, rules, and procedures replaced them.[46] Questions have been raised about some basic values of the university community—the nature of the academic program; whether to teach factual knowledge, or also values and feelings, and even practical skills; the meaning of freedom of inquiry for scholars; and what should be included in the activities of a university.

The Function of Research

The expansion of knowledge is a generally accepted purpose of higher education, especially in universities with strong research components. The direction and extent of research programs has been determined largely by the financial support provided by business, industry, and government. This influence on the direction of research efforts has led some researchers to ask, "knowledge for whom?" Some research, especially in pure rather than applied science, is being eliminated because it is not a priority in this time of financial cutbacks. This could lead to future gaps in our knowledge, some argue.

The Function of Teaching

Concerns such as that regarding the balance of teaching and research roles of professors dominate institutions of higher education, especially those with graduate programs. Standford University took the lead recently when it announced that evaluation of teaching would be a significant part of the promotion process. A number of disciplines are producing teaching materials and promoting professional development in teaching. Professional schools are also putting more emphasis on the art of teaching.

Concern has been expressed that medical schools are maintaining the status quo, not moving with the times in what they teach, and involved in too much research and clinical work at the expense of teaching. Planning for the future in such areas as ambulatory care is not receiving adequate attention, according to some critics.[47]

The Function of Service

Another function or purpose of the university is that of public service in the wider community. The faculty are expected to disseminate knowledge developed in research programs through such channels as publications, the media, and teaching and lecturing. This diffusion of ideas has wide repercussions, even to the point of stimulating social change in countries around the world. The degree to which scholars should become involved in attempts to sway opinions through social awareness or act to bring about changes is a matter of debate. Students in many colleges are involved in community service work, sometimes as a required part of their education.

The Function of the "National Security State"

Higher education, sometimes assumed to operate autonomously, is in fact central to the training of individuals for high-level technical human resource requirements; this is seen by some as necessary to national security and for a developing economy. Some argue that the university power structure is headed by boards of trustees who serve corporate interests, and that their interests are felt in the organization of universities.[48] Liaisons between universities and the corporate world, created by students employed in these organizations and research funded by private interests, provide evidence for the links.

University professors create ideas in laboratories; some of these ideas become commercial products. Structures for transferring the technology from labs to commercial use are most often controlled by university administrations, who use the idea of "the public good" to control the transfer; university faculty, however, hold that scientific norms should guide the transfer of technology. How the information is transferred affects who receives credit, patents, and financial benefits.[49]

Conflicts Over the University's Function

It is a crisp autumn Saturday afternoon. The stands are packed for the big game, the traditional rivalry that will determine who goes to the bowl. College athletics is big business worth millions of dollars, and the issues surrounding athletics have become major targets in the conflicts over the functions of a university. "Division I football programs will raise and spend nearly one billion dollars while entertaining 25 million spectators. . . ."[50] This is a big money-maker and attracts new students. Critics argue that athletics is not part of the major function of universities—the acquisition and transmission of knowledge, service, or other traditional functions. This case illustrates the conflict over the academic function of universities versus a big-business orientation.

The Academic Function of Universities versus Big Business

Issues that have been raised in recent years illustrate the conflicts. We will refer to the "athlete as a hunk o' meat" issue. Scouts and recruiters see star high school players and sign them up. It is illegal to offer rewards or bribes such as cars or fancy living, but it has been known to happen.[51] What is more common is that pressure to succeed in athletics is so great that there is temptation to skirt the rules. Reports of grade fixing at several institutions have caused scandals and led to sanctions against individuals and institutions. Young women and men with weak academic backgrounds are recruited to compete, but they often fail to make progress toward a degree. This hits minority students particularly hard. Findings from a study by the National Collegiate Athletic Association (NCAA) show that African-American athletes attending Division I colleges are five times more likely to enter college with weaker credentials than other students, and are half as likely to graduate. Only 26.6 percent of African-American students earn degrees in five years, compared with 52.2 percent of white students, and blacks are twice as likely to leave college with bad academic standing. However, African-American athletes' academic performance was comparable to that of other African-American college students.[52]

Using participant observation, two sociologists spent several years studying athletes at a Division I college, observing the conflicting roles of players. Most players come to college expecting to play ball, have a social life, and earn a degree, and perhaps go on to the NBA or other professional leagues. However, many quickly become disillusioned, and some feel exploited by the fans and even the coaches, who are interested in them only as long as they can perform well. The problem is that the athletes come poorly prepared for academics, and training is all-consuming. They are often housed separately, isolated from campus, and made to feel like outcasts. Some of the middle-class athletes graduate, but few recruited from the ghetto do so.[53]

The second problem is the lack of support athletes get once they enter college. In other words, they are used as long as they can play for the team; then they are dropped, leaving them little future. Several proposals have been made to curb the "meat market" phenomenon. In order to play during the freshman year, athletes must have a 2.0 high school average in core courses and an SAT combined score of 700 or ACT of 15. Foes of this requirement argue that it places a heavier emphasis on racially biased tests.[54] Another proposal is to let athletes play five years, giving them more time to complete their college work. Programs for special tutorials, restrictions on "the season" and practice time, and counseling services are being put in place in many schools and could help weak students. Tutoring and mentoring programs at many universities are meant to supplement the athletes' programs; some help, some don't. Some of those athletes who flunk out or drop out end up sweeping floors or doing other menial labor. The academic "teaching" function is brought into question when emphasis is on "big business," but recent attention is focusing efforts, such as those listed above, on bringing this function into balance. There is one bright spot—students who have participated in varsity sports are more likely to do better in the job market than those who did not, according to some findings.[55]

What Type of Curriculum?

Conflicts persist over curricular issues. On the one hand are those who would have the university retain its traditional focus on a liberal education in the arts and sciences, which transmits to students knowledge for its own sake and produces a well-rounded person. On the other hand are those who advocate a practical, career-focused training that stresses the social utility of the knowledge transmitted.[56] These conflicts are particularly relevant today, when universities and colleges have faced periods of dropping enrollments, and when economic conditions put pressures on students to get a degree they can "use"—one that will be functional and lead directly to employment. Only a few elite schools may be able to resist the pressures to diversify the curriculum and introduce more applied or practical programs as opposed to "pure" arts and sciences. For most institutions, ability to adapt to changing or conflicting environmental demands may determine survival.[57]

Societal conflicts are reflected in debates over curriculum content and pressure to be "politically correct." Racism, discrimination, prejudice, intolerance, differential treatment, sexual harassment, homophobia—all are hot topics on university campuses. After the 1960s, there was a transformation from activism to "MEism," but we are seeing a recurrence of activism in the 1990s.[58]

Extremes range from those who would throw out the "old" curriculum and replace it with entirely new materials sensitive to abuses of the past, to "hate speech" and racial/sexual incidents on campuses. The debate is between competing responsibilities to protect freedom of speech *and* to protect students, faculty, and staff who are victims of hate crimes.[59] The Supreme Court is even reviewing cases of bans on "hate speech,"[60] and has ruled in one decision that "hate speech" is free speech.

In universities across the country, from Duke to Stanford, traditional "Western" curricula are being challenged by concerned students and professors, many of whom attended college themselves in the "radical" 1960s. Stanford now requires students to take courses in world cultures, diversity, and gender issues.[61] Most colleges are "internationalizing" their curricula, to include Third World and environmental concerns; the numbers of students majoring in these fields are also increasing.[62] Requirements to engage in community service show a curricular trend toward citizenship development.[63]

Conflicts over purposes can also be seen in the changing roles of various members of the university community. For instance, in the 1950s administrators were expected to watch over their students like parents; hence the term *in loco parentis*. Dormitory hours were rigid, lights-out regulations were enforced, separation of the sexes in living quarters was expected, and the atmosphere was one that not only perpetuated an adolescent dependence, but carried the home structure to the school. Following student discontent and attacks on the university administration in the 1960s, most administrators have gradually reduced or eliminated this role.

HIGHER EDUCATION AS AN ORGANIZATION

Higher Education Structure and the Bureaucratic Model: Does It Work?

According to John Corson, the answer to this question is "No." "For too long, colleges and universities have borrowed their governance models from business and public administration. Neither is appropriate for most functions of academic institutions."[64]

Universities face particular contradictions when trying to run on a bureaucratic or business model, yet that is what most are doing. The hierarchical charts of universities may resemble business organizations, but most of the similarities stop there.

1. There are two distinct structures in the university: the flat academic structure and the hierarchical administrative structure.
2. Many of the employees are knowledge specialists, professionals who by tradition expect autonomy and academic freedom; they may have only temporary loyalty to the institution but permanent allegiance to their disciplines.
3. Colleges are to a large extent detached from the community and larger society in pursuing their primary activities—transmitting knowledge and conducting research.

4. Teaching and research require individual faculty autonomy over the end product.

5. Policy decision making is spread throughout the organization, and students sometimes have a substantial voice in issues.

Let us consider the problems of hierarchy and decision making in greater detail.

The Dual Hierarchy.   Academic institutions have two hierarchies. The *academic structure* of the university, with its many departments and programs, has one form of hierarchy, usually based on rank and tenure. Although faculty members hold differing ranks, their formal status within the university is the same. However, informal influence, power, responsibilites, and salary may differ. The *administrative structure* approximates more closely the business model and Weber's bureaucratic division of labor. At the top of the hierarchy are the president and other top administrators, including deans. Other administrative personnel carry out diverse functions, providing health services, bookstores, food services, building and grounds maintenance, financial services, and counseling.

The university fails to be really effective using the business model, according to Ann and Robert Parelius,[65] because it is primitive compared with business and industry. For instance, there is a general lack of solid statistical analysis on which to base decisions. The structural looseness of the university, with its focus on academic freedom, allows for little centralized decision making. The professional faculty expect to make decisions in their areas of expertise, and resent others' usurping this power or making rules that infringe on this "right"; this is especially true in the area of hiring, promotion, retention of faculty, and curriculum matters. Once faculty members are granted tenure by their peers, their independence from administrative decisions is increased. Finally, there is inherent conflict between providing a good education and running an administratively economical and efficient operation—as is called for in business or a bureaucratic model.

These problems and inconsistencies have been accentuated by the rapid increase in size and corresponding administrative complexity of the "multiversity." With added departments, programs, and research components, the administrative structures increase in complexity along with the academic structure.

The University Hierarchical Structure and Decision Making.   Despite the incongruities, it is useful to use characteristics of the bureaucratic model after describing the university, since this model is closer than any other to the realities of the situation. There are seven levels within the higher education hierarchical structure.

1. *Department.* This is an administrative unit with a head or chair who may be appointed or elected, or the position may rotate among department members. The chair is accountable to both department members and higher-level adminis-

trators. The position has inherent role conflict, since a chair must both support faculty and sit in judgment on them for salary increases and, sometimes, promotions. Departments are hierarchically structured, the usual ranks being instructor, assistant professor, associate professor, professor. Power and decision making for the unit is usually distributed among members, who use democratic procedures to make major unit decisions.

2. *College.* Several related disciplines are grouped as a college with a dean as administrative head. Professional schools in universities have similar status. At this level of the administrative hierarchy, decisions are made about finances, salaries, scheduling, new programs, and so forth, which affect all unit parts.

3. *Administration.* The president or chancellor, vice-president, and deans and assistants may or may not be faculty members. They have responsibility for various aspects of the university, including academic matters, student services, and financial matters.

4. *Faculty representative bodies.* Faculty councils or senates composed of representatives from the various colleges and schools have decision-making power over academic issues.

5. *Board of trustees.* These lay persons from the community have ultimate legal responsibility. Members are usually selected through election, by other board members, or through appointment by state governors. Most boards will give their formal approval to recommendations of the institution's president and faculty senate. In recent years, central committees have been formed as coordinating structures for some multicampus universities. These "superboards" have ultimate control just as boards of trustees, but remove decision making even further from the faculty and individual campus.[66] "Of approximately 48,000 people who held voting positions on governing boards last spring, 90 percent were white, 80 percent were men, 42 percent held positions in business or had retired from such positions in business—making business more heavily represented than any other field—and 70 percent were at least 50 years old, including 32 percent who were at least 60."[67] Since 1976, this represents a rise from 15 percent to 20 percent women and from 5.9 percent to 11.4 percent blacks.

6. *Regional accrediting associations.* There are six voluntary associations around the country that evaluate institutions' achievements in comparison with their goals, using professionals from within the region. The attempt is not supposed to equalize or standardize institutions, but to help institutions achieve the standards they set for themselves.

7. *National organization.* While there is no formal national control of decision making in the United States, as is the case in many countries, the federal government does wield its influence in many ways. To some extent a national education policy has been developed in response to international pressures and competition and national needs in areas of economics, politics, and the military. The manifest function of government in higher education can be seen in the reaction to the Soviet Union's launching of *Sputnik* in 1957, when the U.S. government funded many scientific programs and curriculum changes.[68] Federal funding has had a major influence on what research an institution pursues, and may constitute the financial support of entire programs in the university. If an institution is judged to be negligent in its affirmative action policies, funding will be withdrawn. Many institutions would suffer severe crises if they lost federal support.

Burton Clark summarized the nature of academic control in the United States: The national center possesses relatively little formal authority; the middle levels (state, multicampus, and universitywide) are strongly organized, with trustee and administrative authority predominating over faculty prerogatives; the lower levels (college and department) retain impressive decision-making powers over personnel and curriculum—areas in which professors care most about exercising collegial rule. The various levels and the several major forms of authority constitute a set of countervailing forces. In organization and authority, the "system" is not only inordinately large and complex but also fundamentally disorderly.[69]

Control and Decision Making.   Major decisions are made or approved by the institution's president and board of trustees. The multiplicity of diverse programs is coordinated through the administrative hierarchy. While the number of coordinating structures has been increasing, demands are also increasing for decentralized decision making, with power held by individual units.

Lower-level participants in the university wield power that is not always recognized officially, but is influential in decision making. For instance, office workers have access to and control over people, information, and technology. Many office workers are irreplaceable because of the knowledge they hold. However, their compensation is seldom commensurate with their subtle power.[70]

Students have varying degrees of power in the decision-making structure. They are with the organization for a short time; they bring new perspectives; they pass through and leave their mark. Because of their short stay in the institution, students are not usually primary decision makers, but they may provide much-needed impetus for evaluation and change of the status quo.

ROLES IN HIGHER EDUCATION

Each of us has a role in the system of higher education. This is only one of our many roles, and herein lies one of the problems for higher education, as for any organization—it must compete for the loyalty of members who have multiple role obligations. A student may have family, work, and other role obligations. Faculty members have multiple loyalties, which lead to problems for the organization. Keep in mind the dilemma of conflicting role obligations as we discuss major roles in the system of higher education.

Roles in Higher Education: The Clients

Without students there would be no institutions of higher education, and most professors would be out of work. Students are clients of the system, buying a service, and members of the system, playing an integral part in its functioning. At different times students have held different degrees of power in the system, from an ineffectual group that comes and goes and has little real power, to a group that, by their choices, determines which faculty members, programs, and even universities will survive.

The students of the 1950s were a cautious "silent generation." By the 1960s, students began to demand a major role in the governance of universities and other institutions and to create pressures for change. This politically active student population flexed its muscles with the Free Speech Movement at Berkeley; it went on, in greater strength, to the Vietnam War protests in the late 1960s and 1970s. What was remarkable about the revolt of the 1960s was that the "values and habits of the youth culture had a profound impact on adults, and many of the ideas and practices of the youth culture were adopted by adults."[71] Changes initiated by students affected all members of higher education because of their reciprocal role involvements.

Through the baby-boom years, college enrollments expanded dramatically; then came the bust and retrenchments. Between 1979 and 1985, the number of 18-year-old high school graduates decreased by a half-million. Colleges feared that there would not be enough students to keep them alive, but increasing recruitment among nontraditional students, a recession that kept students nearer their home institutions, and increases in the number of high school graduates attending college forestalled disaster for many small institutions. College marketing budgets have increased dramatically—direct mail, telephone contacts, invitations to visit, and scholarships to academically talented students.[72] Ironically, at a time when it seems that underrepresented groups might have an advantage, many colleges have not lowered but have increased their admissions requirements and expectations, recruiting students with high SATs and those from wealthier areas rather than poor, disenfranchised minority students.

The profile of the typical college student is becoming more diversified, with older nontraditional students, minority students, and married students attending college in greater numbers. African-Americans have been the only group experiencing declining numbers in higher education since 1980, a problem of great concern to many educators.

Over 14 million students enrolled in higher education for the 1991–92 academic year, up 1.1 percent from the previous year. This was welcome relief to colleges that had seen a drop in numbers of freshmen in 1990. Private college enrollments were up 2.7 percent, and public institution enrollments were up 0.6 percent. Part of the increase may be because of poor job prospects.

Between 1976 and 1989, students aged 22 and older increased from 37.9 percent to 45.8 percent of the college population.[73] Minority enrollments increased from 18 percent in 1976 to 21 percent in 1988, but with a drop for African-American students.[74] Native American enrollments rose, and today there are 24 tribally controlled colleges in the United States.[75]

Some charge that higher standards for high school graduation and college admission have caused the difference between the 70 percent acceptance rate of African-American applicants compared to the overall acceptance rate of 76 percent. Table 9-4 shows the percentage of students from different backgrounds enrolled in college.

One "new" student group is first-generation college students. They face unique "academic and social challenges over and above those encountered by others." They are more often from lower- or working-class homes with more authoritarian family structures, are expected to contribute as workers to the family, and feel more control over their gender roles and values. They often

TABLE 9-4   1988 Enrollment, by Type of Institution

	Total	American Indian	Asian	Black	Hispanic	White	Foreign
Public							
Four-Year . . .	42.5%	36.0%	42.3%	39.7%	31.7%	43.3%	50.2%
Two-year . . .	35.4	51.6	39.4	38.3	54.6	34.1	15.6
Private							
Four-year . . .	20.2	9.5	17.6	18.4	11.8	20.7	33.3
Two-year . . .	2.0	2.9	0.8	3.6	1.9	1.9	0.9
Total	100.0%	100.0%	100.0%	100.0%	100.0%	100.0%	100.0%

Note: This table shows, for example, that while 42.5 percent of all students were enrolled at 4-year public institutions in 1988, only 36.0 percent of American Indian students attended such institutions.

Source: National Center for Education Statistics, "Fall Enrollment in Colleges and Universities" (U.S. Department of Education, February 1990).

live at home rather than on campus, increasing the dependency relationship to family. This instills obedience to parents, respect for authority, and conformity to subcultural identity.[76]

Gender and Race in Higher Education

The number of women attending college in the United States has doubled since the 1970s. In fact, college women outnumber men by 6.8 million to 5.9 million. Part of the increase results from "nontraditional"-age women returning to college. However, there is evidence that women's participation in higher education in non–core developing nations is being hindered by multinational corporations, which hire men in high-status occupations, thus creating less demand for educated women.[77]

Women's achievement in math and science courses at all levels of education continues to occupy the efforts of researchers. In college, women's and men's grades are similar in math courses through calculus.[78] However, men have increased their domination of mathematic-intensive fields, fields that generally command higher income potential (Figure 9-2).[79]

The median annual income of full-time male workers 25 years and over in 1989 was $30,465, with college graduates averaging $38,565 and those with five years or more of college $46,842. Women averaged $20,570, with college graduates receiving $26,709 and those with five years or more of college, $32,050[80]

A hope for some institutions of higher education with dropping enrollments lies in attracting women from nontraditional age categories. In recent years, this group has been a target for admissions officers. These women are already entering, or returning to, college in large numbers. There are over 1 million "reentry women" in higher education. They are a diverse group of students: "31 percent are entering college for the first time, 56 percent for the second time, 13 percent for the third time." Their motivations are often

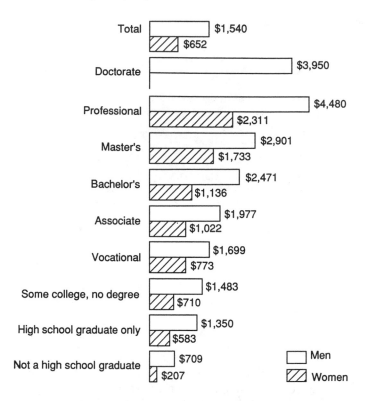

FIGURE 9-2   Men earn more than women at all degree levels. Mean monthly earnings for adults 18 and over, by degree level, spring 1987.

Note: There were not enough women with doctorate degrees in the survey to list their mean monthly earnings.

Source: U.S. Bureau of the Census, February 1991.

economic: to prepare for entry or a return to the work force. Institutions are developing recruitment programs to focus on this group, but the cost of support programs such as refresher courses, child-care facilities, increased admissions staff, and development of new courses may not be offset by the additional tuition.[81]

Many reentry women are attempting to fulfill two sets of expectations: family roles and educational roles. "They grow up expecting that home and family would be a satisfying lifetime goal, only to find that somewhere along the way the rules were changed."[82] That "rule change" has caused many women to take on the educational role. Survey data indicate that most reentry women are committed to their studies and have confidence and energy, although it is early to evaluate their success rates at coping with the two sets of expectations. Sophie Freud Loewenstein describes the challenge and conflict:

My identity is an integration of my most meaningful roles: enthusiastic student, painfully maturing mother, struggling wife, and empathetic social-work coun-

selor. . . . Self-definition came first through motherhood and later, more autonomously, through work and competence. I had to proceed simultaneously on all
fronts to master the complexities of many roles.[83]

More younger women are completing college and entering graduate
school, and holding multiple roles, according to Giele, et al., because of the
increasing industrialization and specialization required in modern society.[84] In
time, older women students may be reduced in numbers as more young
women take on multiple roles at younger ages.

Many colleges are offering more nondegree courses for adults through
continuing education of lifelong learning programs. Not only do these enable
interested adults to learn for pleasure, but they also help offset budget deficits
in programs being run at a financial loss. Courses are taken by a wide range of
adults—"do-it-yourselfers"; senior citizens; those who have a specific motivation, such as learning a language for a holiday trip abroad; those who wish to
prepare for college reentry, to have contact with others, to increase mental
stimulation, or just to have fun.[85]

Most women students seem reasonably satisfied with their college experience, including professors, other students, and classroom and study conditions.[86] However, controversies over the value of single-sex colleges have
erupted—most notably in the case of Mills College in California. Students at
women's colleges tend to be very satisfied with their experiences. They perceive the acquisition of skills and abilities to be high, and educational aspirations, including the likelihood of attending graduate school, are also high.[87]
Women at formerly all-male campuses still express frustration with age-old
traditions and old-boy networks that disadvantage women.[88]

Graduation ceremonies mark transitions to new beginnings.

Several studies have suggested that faculty and male graduate students may be openly antagonistic to female students, refusing to take them seriously or to provide necessary intellectual support. Charges of the sexual exploitation of female graduate students by male faculty have also been voiced frequently, and there is evidence that women have been discriminated against in admissions and financial aid.[89]

By and large, women are gaining ground; however, the story for other minorities is mixed. One-third of the nation will be African-American or Hispanic by the early part of the next century. Yet the numbers of those groups in higher education do not reflect this diversity (Box 9-1). There are many plans to increase the numbers,[90] but only time will determine their success.

Factors Related to Student Success or Failure.   Student success in higher education is based not only on individual goals, motivations, and abilities, but also on social class, race, sex, and early labeling. "Success" or "failure" begins early in life with the labeling of children. By the high school years, teachers, counselors, students, and parents have a fair idea of the student's academic ability. Tracking into college-preparatory or vocational courses is often an easy decision. Conflicts arise for those who have high aspirations but little support in the form of teacher recommendations, test results, counselor evaluations, and parental encouragement.

The system provides for open competition and rewards high achievers with acceptance to the better academic institutions. This has been referred to as "contest mobility." However, "sponsored mobility" removes some of those slots from open competition, since it singles out some favored or elite students and trains them for particular positions in society.[91]

Other students are not prepared for the college experience. Basic skills in reading, writing, and math, plus lack of college-preparatory curricula, put students "at risk" in college. In the report *Access to Quality Education,* the authors recommend early diagnosis and remedial action to build basic skills of students while they are still in high school. Nonetheless, many colleges are offering special services in remedial and developmental education (Table 9-5).

Although minorities make up over 21 percent of the U.S. population, only 15 percent are enrolled in higher education. The problem often begins in earlier years of schooling, and many universities find themselves offering remedial courses for low-achieving students with weak skills. Urban universities in particular are being hit by underfunding and cutbacks in services, making them unable to respond effectively to many minority students' needs.

One-half of the African-American students who enter college fail to complete their degree work, not because of ability level, but because of poor academic preparation and campus climates. Those who do graduate have lower grades and less chance of going on to graduate school. The number of Ph.D.'s granted to African-Americans dropped between 1977 and 1990, from 1,116 to 828.[92] However, the number showed an increase in 1991 (Table 9-6).

Even with adequate preparation, many minority students feel undervalued, stigmatized, and vulnerable. It is as though others look for reasons to "confirm" racial inferiority.[93] College is an impersonal, unfamiliar,[94] even hostile world for many. It challenges self-respect and self-esteem,[95] especially if one is insecure about one's ability to cope with college work and believes that others are questioning that ability, too.[96] The exclusion of African-American students becomes a "silent killer" on predominantly white campuses.[97]

Recent racial incidents on campuses do not help efforts to integrate African-Americans and improve their self-esteem. One explanation is that these incidents are sparked by the competition for scarce resources[98]—grades, acceptance to competitive programs, graduation, and ultimately jobs and income. Disparities still exist between African-American and white students by educational attainment.[99] Methods of assessment need to take into account self-esteem and insecurity, and give support for improvement.[100]

Student Subcultures or Peer Groups. Students belong to peer groups, which have great influence over their activities, interests, and academic success. Some years ago, a typology of student subcultures or peer groups was developed by Burton Clark and Martin Trow.[101] Students were categorized into one of four types: *collegiate*—sports, dates, fun, fraternities and sororities, "Joe College," some money; *vocational*—job preparation, no-nonsense attitude, financially less well-off, often working, married; *academic*—intellectual, identification with faculty, time spent in library and lab, planning graduate and professional training; *nonconformist*—several types: the aggressive intellectual, the student seeking personal identity, and the rebellious student. With the radical student movements of the 1960s, new student types emerged that did not fit clearly into these categories. However, while these types may have altered, the concept of a "reference group" that provides both a sense of belonging and a model for behavior has not changed.

Fraternities and sororities function to provide group identity for some students in higher education. These "formalized" peer-group relationships generally fall into the collegiate subculture. They provide an alternative to the academic side of college life. Although Greek organizations declined in number during the 1960s, since the mid-1970s they have increased in strength and number on many campuses. This peer-group pressure has led to some serious charges, from hazing of pledges in sororities and fraternities[102] to date rape and even gang rape,[103] sometimes linked with alcohol usage. The good news is that drug and alcohol use is down somewhat on campuses.

The vocational subculture has increased in recent years with economic pressures, competition for jobs, and many first-generation college students trying to improve their chances for upward mobility.

The Graying of College Graduates

During the 1980s, the traditional college-age population of 18- to 22-year-olds dropped by 2.7 million students. However, the overall number of college students rose by 1.8 million. Why? The increase in the number of students over age 25 rose significantly; the average college student is now over 25 years old.[104] The Census Bureau reports that 320,000 students aged 50 and

BOX 9-1   *FOCUS ON MINORITIES: HIGHLIGHTS OF THE REPORT*

This report reviews the progress toward the full participation of minorities in higher education during the past three decades.

The Potential Supply

- Minorities are a growing proportion of the traditional college-age population. By the year 2025, they are expected to make up nearly 40 percent of all 18- to 24-year-olds.
- Minority high school graduation rates have increased significantly in the past 20 years but still lag behind white rates. *Hispanics have the lowest rates— only 62 percent* of 18- to 24-year-old Hispanics have high school diplomas, compared with 83 percent of whites.
- The academic preparation of black and Hispanic high school students continues to lag despite progress in recent years. Data from the National Assessment of Educational Progress (NAEP) reveal that 17-year-old black and Hispanic students, on average, read only about as well as 13-year-old white students.

College Participation and Enrollment

- College participation rates among black and Hispanic college-age youth peaked in the mid-1970s and have declined since then.
- Total minority enrollment increased 21 percent from 1976 to 1984, nearly three times the rate of whites. However, much of this increase occurred before 1980. From 1980 to 1984, black enrollment declined, as did that of Native Americans.
- Far outpacing other groups, Asian-Americans nearly doubled their 1976 enrollment level by 1984. This fast-growing minority group now makes up more than 3 percent of total enrollments, compared with their 2 percent representation in the population generally.
- Except for Asian-Americans, the representation of minorities drops dramatically at the graduate and professional levels. Blacks, who make up about 13 percent of college-age youth, are 9.5 percent of all undergraduates and only 4.8 percent of graduate students.

Retention and Success

- Only about half of all high school seniors go on to college full-time immediately after graduation. Only half of those enrolling in four-year institutions achieve senior status four years later.
- Students on the "fast track" are those who achieve senior status four years after high school graduation. One in three Asians in the class of 1980 was on the "fast track," but only one in seven blacks and one in 10 Hispanics.
- The factors most closely associated with both initial enrollment and later persistence in college are high school grades, family income, and parents' education. Students who earn As in high school are 25 times more likely to be on the "fast track" in college than students who earn Cs. Students who come from high-income families are four times more likely to persist than those from low-income families.

- Many minorities begin their education in two-year institutions, and success to the bacalaureate depends on transfer to a four-year institution. National and state studies, however, point to a deteriorating number of transfers from community colleges. This can be caused by high dropout rates, the lack of effective articulation agreements among colleges, and roadblocks to accepting credit placed by four-year institutions and accrediting bodies.

- In the 1960s and 1970s, institutions responded to increased numbers of minorities by forming separate counseling and support programs. More recently the trend has been to integrate these services into broader efforts to improve the academic preparation of all students in need of help.

- Anecdotal reports from the campuses indicate that little progress has been made in race relations. Racial and ethnic groups often go their separate ways, creating a climate that may isolate students and reinforce stereotypes. Minority students may become disconnected from the life of the campus, a situation that lessens their retention and success.

- Effective remedial and counseling programs are critical to retention. Yet many programs are poorly funded and receive low priority from institutional leaders.

- The aspirations of students themselves can affect retention and success. States are considering a variety of "mentoring" efforts to raise the sights of minority students.

Minority Representation in the Professions

- While the black middle class has grown substantially since World War II, black representation among such professional groups as accountants, physicians, college professors, engineers, lawyers, and judges is far below their numbers in the population. For example, only about 2.6 percent of the employed engineers in the nation are black.

- The Hispanic population is a diverse group consisting largely of Puerto Rican–Americans, Mexican-Americans, and Cuban-Americans. Even with the relative success of Cuban-Americans, Hispanics remain underrepresented in the professions and overrepresented in low-skill, low-wage jobs. For example, Hispanics make up more than 11 percent of the teachers' aides but only about 3 percent of the elementary and secondary school teachers in America.

- The number of minority doctoral recipients has grown substantially in recent years, but the progress of various groups differs significantly. About the same number of Hispanic doctorates are awarded annually as Asian-American, yet the Asian-American population is half the size of the Hispanic population.

- Only about 900 doctorates are awarded to blacks annually, a number that has declined since the 1970s. While blacks have diversified their interests in recent years, a majority of doctorates are still awarded in education. Blacks and Hispanics remain severely underrepresented among science and engineering doctorates, greatly limiting the available faculty pool.

Source: Mingle, James R., *Trends in Higher Education Participation and Success* (Denver: Education Commission of the States and State Higher Education Executive Officers, July 1987).

TABLE 9-5   Remedial and Developmental Services

TYPE OF SERVICE	NUMBER AND PERCENTAGE OF INSTITUTIONS OFFERING SERVICE				
	Two-year Public	Two-year Private	Four-year Public	Four-year Private	All Institutions
Preadmission summer program	227 25%	56 19%	210 42%	321 29%	814 29%
Reduced course load	491 56%	136 47%	319 63%	760 68%	1,706 61%
Remedial instruction	827 93%	161 56%	381 76%	600 53%	1,969 70%
Tutoring	758 85%	179 62%	464 92%	867 77%	2,268 81%
Special counselor	499 56%	101 35%	368 73%	599 54%	1,567 56%
Learning center	725 82%	83 29%	348 69%	507 46%	1,663 59%

Source: "Demographics," p. 25. Data from *College Entrance Examination Board Annual Survey of Colleges, 1986–87: Summary Statistics* (New York: College Entrance Examination Board, 1986).

TABLE 9-6   Americans Who Received Ph.D.'s in 1991

	Number	One-year Change	Ten-year Change
American Indian	128	+33.3%	+50.6%
Asian	762	+19.0	+63.9%
Black	933	+4.0	−7.9
Hispanic	708	−1.4	+52.6
White	21,859	−1.3	−0.6
Race unknown	331	—	—
Total	24,721	−0.7%	−1.4%

Source: National Science Foundation; reprinted in "Recipients of Doctorates from U.S. Universities," *The Chronicle of Higher Education,* Vol. 38, October 16, 1991, p. A20.

older attended college in the United States in 1991.[105] The older, nontraditional students are upgrading their job skills, changing careers, and seeking personal improvement by taking classes for credit or audit. Education becomes important in retooling for the paid labor force that many older people enter. Financial aid, including federal and state assistance, is available to help older citizens pay for schooling.

This demographic shift is having an impact on curricula and on campus life. Evening and weekend classes have increased; more convenient off-campus sites have been established, especially in metropolitan areas; much of the course work can be done at home; and some universities provide transitional programs for older students.

However, many older students accept the stereotypes imposed upon them, fearing to go back to school after so many years. They fear that they might prove to themselves or others that they are unable to cope with the college crowd, the work, the new and demanding environment, or the stress. Although there may be some performance decline with age, many older people remain at top productivity[106] and enjoy college life. Older people make good students, and are highly motivated and dependable.[107]

The postwar baby boom increased the number of births from 2.75 million in the 1940s to 4.35 million in the 1960s. By 2020, the population over age 65 will be 42.8 percent of the total U.S. population. This group will also be living longer because of continuing medical advances.[108] As this group ages, it will be more active than its predecessors. Though ageism has historically plagued older cohorts, the baby-boom generation will probably defy most of the age-related stereotypes because of its proportion of the population. Older workers retiring later in life, changing careers, and training to remain current in their fields will be common. Performance studies do not show marked decline in ability; the literature shows that adult cognitive abilities, for most people, improve with longevity, barring health problems.[109]

Federal and state legislation addressing the needs of older people has also been passed in some countries. For instance, in 1976 the U.S. Lifelong Learning Act was passed to ensure educational opportunity for all citizens "without regard to restrictions of previous education or training, sex, age, handicapping condition, social or ethnic background, or economic circumstances." The bill states that "lifelong learning is important in meeting the needs of the growing number of older and retired persons.[110]

This federal legislation, although never funded, did provide opportunity for access to higher education through state-sponsored programs. For example, all state-funded colleges and universities in Ohio must provide free enrollment, on a space-available basis, to those 60 years and older.[111] Many older students do not wish preferential treatment, preferring to have their course work judged on the same basis as that of the more traditional students. Countries that make use of their older citizens can enhance their economic and social systems.[112]

Roles in Higher Education: The Faculty

Universities expect professors to teach well, be knowledgeable and current in their disciplines, and produce work that will be influential and prestigious. The institution thus gains prestige, which in turn produces resources. Students, parents, and others in the institution's environment also hold certain expectations of faculty. The following section deals with some specific aspects of this role.

Characteristics of Faculty.   Sociologists identify groups of people in part by the characteristics they have in common. Faculty are no exception. They can be characterized by their race, sex, and religious affiliation (just as students were in the preceding section; see Table 9-7). In 1940, 15,000 people were employed on the faculties of U.S. colleges and universities. The 1960s

TABLE 9-7   Faculty Attitudes and Characteristics: Results of a 1989–90 Survey.

Age on December 31, 1989

Less than 30	2.2%
30–34	8.0
35–39	13.4
40–44	17.3
45–49	18.9
50–54	15.7
55–59	12.8
60–64	8.3
65–69	2.9
70 or more	0.5

Sex

Male	71.2%
Female	28.8

Highest Degree Earned

Bachelor's	3.2%
Master's	28.1
L.L.B. or J.D.	0.7
M.D. or D.D.S.	0.4
Ed.D.	4.7
Ph.D.	56.3
Other first-professional	0.6
Other degree	4.0
None	2.0

Racial and Ethnic Background

American Indian	0.9%
Asian-American	3.2
Black	4.0
Mexican-American	0.8
Puerto Rican–American	0.4
White	90.4
Other	2.1

Marital Status

Married	75.9%
Separated	1.3
Single, never married	10.9
Single, with partner	2.4
Single, divorced	8.3
Single, widowed	1.2

Year Highest Degree Earned

1951 or earlier	2.6%
1952–1956	3.2
1957–1961	5.7
1962–1966	11.3
1967–1971	17.8
1972–1976	18.0
1977–1981	15.6
1982–1986	16.5
1987–1989	9.2

HOW PROFESSORS SPEND THEIR TIME

Proportion Reporting Number of Hours per Week

	0	1–4	5–8	9–12	13–16	17–20	21–34	35–44
Teaching	0.3%	7.2%	26.2%	32.0%	17.6%	10.1%	5.9%	0.5%
Preparing for teaching	0.3	8.4	22.9	25.2	17.3	13.8	9.4	2.0
Research and scholarly writing	20.2	27.9	16.4	12.4	7.3	6.7	6.3	1.8
Advising or counseling students	2.6	56.6	29.5	8.0	2.0	0.9	0.4	0.1
Committee work/meetings	4.6	68.8	20.6	4.3	1.1	0.3	0.1	0.0
Other administration	36.5	38.6	11.5	5.8	3.0	2.3	1.7	·0.4
Consultation with clients or patients	68.8	20.7	6.3	2.2	0.8	0.6	0.4	0.1

Source: Astin, Alexander, William Korn, and Eric Dey, *The American College Teacher; National Norms for the 1989–* *Faculty Survey* (Los Angeles: Higher Education Research Institute, UCLA, March 1991).

brought a tremendous increase in numbers of faculty along with increases in the student body, and by the 1970s faculty numbered over 600,000. (By 1990, the number of faculty had dropped to 515,000.) With the growth came changes in the composition of faculties.

The proportion of females and males on the faculty varies depending on the program. In nursing and home economics, women make up nearly 100 percent of the faculty, but in engineering and agriculture they constitute less than 1 percent of faculty ranks. Women were found most frequently in teaching rather than research institutions and in departments with low prestige.

There has been little change in the percentage of African-American faculty in institutions of higher learning in the past four decades, and there may have been a relative decrease. The numbers within each age group have remained fairly constant. The percentage of faculty from various socioeconomic backgrounds has also changed little in recent years, with an average of 24 percent coming from manual or blue-collar backgrounds and the rest from higher socioeconomic backgrounds.

To have increases in the number of faculty, more students must be coming through the pipelines. We have already seen that there has been a drop in the number of African-Americans going to graduate school and receiving Ph.D.'s. The same is true for students coming from manual or blue-collar backgrounds, but they receive no special consideration because they are not considered an "official" category.[113] Faculty representation from Catholic and Jewish backgrounds about doubled in the first half of the twentieth century, but has leveled off or dropped in recent years. In addressing the question of whether religious minorities are represented in academia to the same extent they are in the population, Robert Wuthnow finds the gap closely very slowly, though Jewish representation on faculties compared to Jewish percentage in the total population is increasing. This increased representation of Jews is even more pronounced among students than it is among faculty.[114]

Faculty Issues in Higher Education

Three issues related to the role of faculty in higher education have been particularly important in recent years: professionalism, collective bargaining, and status of women faculty and staff in higher educational institutions.

Professionalism and Orientation: The Faculty Role.   Faculty members go through several years of intense training in order to become professionals. The primary mark of acceptance into professional status is the highest degree in the field: the Ph.D. (Doctor of Philosophy), L.L.D. (Doctor of Laws), M.D. (Doctor of Medicine), and so on. During the education period, intensive training and professional socialization take place as the graduate students learn not only their subject areas but also the appropriate attitudes, behaviors, and ethics of their discipline. Typically, graduate school training for a Ph.D. involves three or four years of course work, followed by comprehensive examinations and a major work of original research—the dissertation. Having been through an intense common experience, graduates become part of a "fraternity," protecting the entrance gates of the discipline by maintaining the traditions. These traditions are most highly protected in the most prestigious professions, such as medicine.

This socialization process has had its critics. Some graduate students complain that their training lacks relevance to the professional tasks they will be performing. Some have limited practical experience. Others claim that they receive little or no training in teaching techniques, and that their research focus is usually very narrow. Some universities do offer graduate students training in teaching techniques; seminars for teaching assistants (TAs) have been offered at several universities.[115] Training, according to one such program, attempts to accomplish three goals:

1. to come closer to ensuring that undergraduate students are competently and conscientiously taught,
2. to add something to the meaning of an advanced degree conferred by the department, and
3. to strengthen the student's bargaining position when he or she seeks full-time employment.[116]

More institutions are emphasizing the importance of quality teaching as student populations have become less stable.

Once on the job, faculty members face differing role expectations. Teaching is the primary task at the two-year institutions and at the four-year liberal arts colleges,[117] whereas research takes a large percentage of faculty time at most universities. The orientation of faculty is also related to the type of institution. "Cosmopolitan" faculty—those who have attachments and professional interests outside their institution—develop their research and writing in relation to a wider audience; they attract more grant money and prestige. "Local" faculty focus their attention within the institution, are active and concerned about institutional matters, and tend to be more loyal to the institution. Though both types are found at all institutions, higher percentages of "local" faculty are likely to be found at two- and four-year colleges.

The most prestigious institutions, which attract the most prominent faculty members, also have problems retaining them. These faculty teach less, and spend a great deal of time consulting, lecturing, attending conferences, or working at other institutions as visiting scholars or lecturers. Committee assignments and teaching often fall to younger faculty members. Universities tolerate this because having respected, well-known faculty enhances the prestige of the university and may attract other top scholars and students as well as more funds.

A difficult problem for many faculty is the incongruity between the demands of teaching and research. This dilemma often hits young scholars hardest; they must "prove themselves" in order to be retained and given tenure. This means performing well not only in teaching and university service, but also in research and publishing, which are seldom listed as part of the "job requirement." Young faculty members with family responsibilities may be forced to make hard decisions between family and career. Some argue that faculty have been pushed to "get it written rather than get it right." College faculty are hired to teach students, but are expected to publish—or perish.

Professionals, Unions, and Collective Bargaining. Academic professionals are characterized by belief in academic freedom, autonomy over decisions related to their discipline and educational process, and service to the community. Many faculty members are reluctant to address their grievances to the administration through a mediating union, preferring instead to retain control over problem solving. The American Association of University Professors (AAUP) has traditionally represented faculty interests, setting down guidelines for salaries, promotion, and policies. The Association's only "clout" with institutions has been the backing of the membership and the threat to blacklist an institution so that faculty would resist taking employment there.

Since faculty members belong to representative organizations in the form of professional associations and the AAUP, the idea of organizational membership is an established one. (In fact, on unionized campuses today AAUP represents faculty interests in such areas as due process and faculty salaries.) However, support for union representation among faculty varies considerably. At two-year institutions, faculty are more likely to consider themselves "employees," to follow more closely the secondary school model, and to expect to gain by union representation. Faculty at prestigious universities are less likely to "stoop" to use of union bargaining agents since they have less to gain by being represented. Many already have high salaries relative to others, and they have the flexibility to relocate if they are dissatisfied. The American Federation of Teachers (AFT) and the National Education Association (NEA) are unions that have been trying to attract college faculty.

In recent years, many factors have made faculty unions and collective bargaining look more attractive to large segments of the academic community. Higher education has expanded rapidly, especially at the two-year college level, which has fewer faculty members with terminal Ph.D. degrees. Economic problems have caused an uncertain job market in academia. Administrative decision making has become further removed. Young faculty members come from more varied backgrounds, providing a large core of faculty open to collective bargaining as a tactic.

The primary accomplishment of unions and collective bargaining, according to an ongoing study of academic governance and collective bargaining in higher education, is "the regularization of personnel procedures through a grievance system,"[118] not necessarily improvement in faculty salaries. This includes policies for retrenchment in case of economic necessity.

Gender Issues in Higher Education. Women are more heavily concentrated in the two-year institutions than in universities, and in all institutions the percentage of women with tenure is lower than their percentage of the total faculty, meaning that women are concentrated in the lower ranks. One reason for this pattern, according to women's studies scholars, is the long tradition of male-dominated academic institutions. Traditional approaches to research are based on the male life cycle, following an established series of steps to success.[119] Women, however, may pursue research with different career assumptions, such as entry into professions after childbearing years or shared academic positions. There is little recognition that other patterns also can lead to success, an attitude that has penalized women who are competent and effective—with consequent loss to the academic community.

"Women working on campuses face hostile environments," concludes a recent study of conditions facing women in academia. Not only is sexual harassment a continuing problem, but discrimination in the form of less pay for the same job, lower positions, and fewer promotions is common.[120,121] The proportion of female faculty has remained the same in recent years, with women making up 13.6 percent of full professors (one in three Ph.D.'s is female[122]). There are fears, however, that with economic hard times even fewer women will be tenured and promoted. Women are dismissed in disproportionate numbers when faculty and staff are laid off.[123] Women and minorities are less frequently hired in positions from which they have been excluded in the past, such as administrative positions. Also, women faculty are found disproportionately in female-dominated fields and lower-paying, lower-prestige institutions.[124]

Roles in Higher Education: Administrators

Administrators must be jugglers, maintaining a delicate balance of good will between the environmental factors crucial to the institution and the academic interests of faculty and student body.

In public institutions, primary authority over fiscal matters and programs falls to a state (or local) board of trustees or regents, and may depend on the attitudes and prejudices of state legislators and governors, who presumably reflect the mood of the public.

At private institutions, administrators depend in part on support and private funds, often from alumni. But again, this funding is tenuous and depends on retaining the good will of donors. In the case of one prestigious institution, pressure from alumni influenced decision making. The alumni newsletter reported various impending changes in the traditional structure of the university: admitting women to the formerly all-male school; opening the doors to more minority students; and reconsidering the practice of giving preference in admission to relatives of alumni. Cries of outrage were heard from alumni who threatened to or actually did cease to contribute. The issues became policy, but in modified forms more acceptable to alumni.

The system of higher education cannot be understood without referring to the environment. The next section in our chapter considers some examples of the higher education environment.

ENVIRONMENTAL PRESSURES ON HIGHER EDUCATION

Environmental pressures affecting the higher education system come from government, the courts, teacher organizations, publishing companies, churches, community, parents, and other interest groups (Figure 9-3). Institutions of

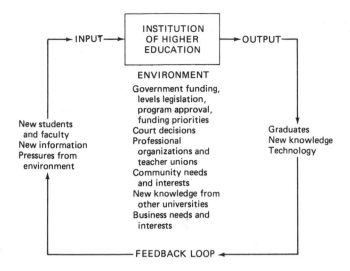

FIGURE 9-3   Open system model of higher education.

higher education are playing a game of survival; whatever parts of the environment are most crucial to that survival will have the greatest impact on decision making and changes that take place. Let us consider several key sources of environmental influence on higher education.

Government Influence on Funding of Higher Education

Government has a degree of power over institutions of higher education through the control of money. The combined federal, state, and local government funding for higher education institutions decreased from 49.3 percent to 43.8 percent of the institutions' budgets between 1980 and 1988 (see Box 9-2).[125] Government influence over public institutions is greater, though private institutions often depend on governmental support for research and special programs. State and local governments provide almost half of the revenues for public institutions; tuition and fees play the largest role in most private institutions. Religiously affiliated institutions are generally least dependent on and influenced by government. The largest expenditures in higher education are for institutions.

If priorities for funding programs and research are established by the government in AIDS and cancer research or mental retardation, for example, then researchers are drawn to these areas to seek support funding. Some fields have higher funding priorities than others, and in fact may be kept alive by funding. Change in the funding priorities can bring about change in the number of faculty and staff in an academic department. Those staff on "soft money," or funded projects, may be cut back or not renewed. Laboratory or other facilities, faculty teaching loads, number of students attracted to a de-

BOX 9-2   *COLLEGE REVENUES*

During the 1980s, colleges and universities came to rely more heavily on tuition and fees and less on help from the state and federal governments, according to data compiled by the National Center for Education Statistics.

In fiscal year 1980, tuition and fees accounted for 20.4 percent of revenues at colleges and universities, the center says; by fiscal year 1988, the figure was 23.7 percent. For public institutions, the figures were 12.5 percent and 15 percent, respectively; for private institutions, the figures were 35.9 percent and 39.1 percent, respectively.

Over the same period, federal funds declined from 15.2 percent to 12.6 percent of overall revenue. The decline held true for both public and private institutions. Public institutions saw their percentage of revenue from federal sources decrease from 13.1 percent to 10.3 percent, while private institutions experienced a drop from 19.4 percent to 16.6 percent.

While state governments remained the largest source of revenue for public institutions, their share declined from 46.3 percent to 43.4 percent over the period.

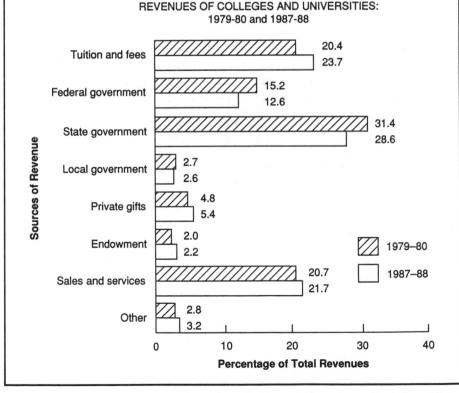

REVENUES OF COLLEGES AND UNIVERSITIES:
1979-80 and 1987-88

Note: The data are available in the report "Current Funds Revenues and Expenditures of Institutions of Higher Education Fiscal Years 1980–88."

Source: National Center for Education Statistics; reprinted in "College Revenues," *Education Week,* November 13, 1991, p. 3.

partment as majors, and even a department's or institution's chances for survival can rest on levels of government support.

Recent scandals about misuse of research funds and excessive overhead or "indirect costs" are causing funding agencies to scrutinize college budgets more carefully.[126,127]

Colleges also receive funding from alumni, corporations, foundations, and religious organizations. Monies are often earmarked for special projects. These contributions rose 10 percent in 1990, but the recession is having an impact on funding from all sources. In the early 1990s, most institutions are experiencing lean times, trimming their expenditures, and raising tuition and fees to cover costs (Tables 9-8, 9-9).

The cost of financing a student's education is resting more heavily on families as tuition costs increase. A recent study looked at the effect of female and male siblings in a family on the financing of college. Having a number of sons in a family is more of a liability for parents than having daughters, partly because parents are more likely to encourage sons to enroll in college; if a daughter attends, they support her as well, but more effort goes into finding money for males.[128]

The federal government provides grants and loans for students with financial need to help them meet the costs of college. Controversy erupted in late 1990 when the U.S. education secretary announced a ban on scholarships based exclusively on race; race could be used as only one factor in awarding scholarships in order to increase diversity on campuses, or used to remedy proven discrimination. How to achieve equality of educational opportunity is an issue at every level of education.[129]

Higher education has socioeconomic implications beyond the individuals who attain an education. The private economy in capitalist states is stimulated

TABLE 9-8   Year-by-Year Changes in Tuition and Fees at Four-Year Institutions

	Public	*Private*
1981–82	+16%	+13%
1982–83	+20	+13
1983–84	+12	+11
1984–85	+ 8	+ 9
1985–86	+ 9	+ 8
1986–87	+ 6	+ 8
1987–88	+ 6	+ 8
1988–89	+ 5	+ 9
1989–90	+ 7	+ 9
1990–91	+ 7	+ 8
1991–92	+12	+ 7

Note: Beginning in 1987–88, data are weighted by enrollment.

Source: The College Board; reprinted in *The Chronicle of Higher Education*, October 23, 1991, p. A30.

TABLE 9-9   Average College Costs, 1991

	PUBLIC COLLEGES		PRIVATE COLLEGES	
	Resident	Commuter	Resident	Commuter
Four-year colleges				
Tuition and fees	$2,137	$2,137	$10,017	$10,017
Books and supplies	485	485	508	508
Room and board*	3,351	1,468	4,386	1,634
Transportation	464	793	470	795
Other	1,147	1,153	911	1,029
Total	$7,584	$6,036	$16,292	$13,983
Two-year colleges				
Tuition and fees	$1,022	$1,022	$5,290	$5,290
Books and supplies	480	480	476	476
Room and board*	—	1,543	3,734	1,529
Transportation	—	902	519	786
Other	—	966	895	925
Total	—	$4,913	$10,914	$9,006

Note: The figures are weighted by enrollment to reflect the charges incurred by the average undergraduate enrolled at each type of institution.

*Room not included for commuter students

—Insufficient data

Source: The College Board, reprinted in *The Chronicle of Higher Education*, October 23, 1991, p. A30.

by government spending on higher education—especially on research—more than spending in general. Spending on research activities has long-lasting effects on private production. This is especially true since the university is a primary location for pure research, whereas industry in the United States spends money on applications.[130]

With government and family working together to help finance higher education, we have another example of the impact of environment and the interdependence of institutions. Government has also worked with schools in developing and funding curricula to meet national priorities.

The Courts and Affirmative Action

Affirmative action legislation prohibits instituions from discriminating on the basis of race, sex, or creed, and may allow or even require preferential treatment of minorities. Governmental control is wielded largely through government funds, on which most institutions are dependent. If an institution is found to be out of compliance, funds may be withheld.

Prior to this legislation, faculty at universities have often hired through the "old-boy network." Professor X called Professor Y and praised his student, pushing him for an opening about which he had heard through the academic grapevine. The job was not advertised, but was filled through word of mouth and friendship networks. While this informal system still functions to some extent, through personal recommendations, affirmative action now requires jobs to be well advertised, and all qualified applicants to be considered.

Affirmative action also affects educational programs or activities receiving federal funds. Title IX forbids any discrimination on the basis of sex at any educational level. It has been especially influential in school sports programs. Although there has been controversy over the meaning and intent—should girls be allowed to play on the high school football team?—the clear impact seems to be on funding for equal facilities, equipment, and programs for men and women.

Have efforts to improve racial and sex balance and opportunity proven successful? Educational gains have been made by racial and ethnic minorities; however, the dropout rate is still high for minorities.

Environmental Feedback and Organizational Change

"On September 30, 1964, five students concerned with civil rights were cited by the dean of men at the University of California, Berkeley, for violating rules which prohibited political propagandizing on campus."[131] According to Neil Smelzer's theory of collective behavior,[132] this was the "precipitating factor" that stimulated the confrontations between students and university administrators that lasted for four months and set an example for student protests at other campuses around the world. Such events as the following occurred:

> On December 2, 1964, 1,000 students, their morale bolstered by folk singer Joan Baez, occupied the administration building [at Berkeley]. What ensued was the sensational spectacle of some 700 police and sheriff's deputies bodily removing the unrelenting demonstrators. Instantaneously and spontaneously the number of sympathizers and collaborators multiplied.[133]

A university is concerned with its public image because of the effect image has on the public and private monies it receives and on the students it attracts. The Berkeley Free Speech Movement changed both the environmental image and the decision-making structure of the University of California. Many attempted to analyze the events. Some argued that the movement was the result of students trying to seize power in the educational system; others argued that they were responding to such concrete deprivations as lack of freedom of speech.[134] In the years following the uprisings, there were intense debates over the purpose of the university, and pressures for change were felt by most institutions of higher education. In some cases, the institutions incorporated more students into the decision-making structure or were more tolerant on the issue of free speech. Other institutions reacted in the opposite way, tightening control over decision making in response to community pressures.

This example indicates that feedback from the primary environment— the students viewed as clients—and from the secondary environment—the community—bring about alterations and change. The dramatic and intense reaction at Berkeley was a form of feedback demanding attention and action, which led to change and long-term searching for alterations and improvements in the system.

The variables affecting change in each situation will differ, but the process of constant change can be traced and studied through the open systems model. Using this approach, the organization does not appear static—a criticism frequently made of functional analysis of organizations; nor will change necessarily be seen as resulting from continuous power struggles between factions or interest groups—as in conflict theory. Rather, change can be seen as a natural part of organizational process and function. Change is an ongoing, dynamic process in any system; organizations must rely on feedback from the environment and must constantly adapt and alter to meet changes in environmental demands if they are to survive.

OUTCOMES OF HIGHER EDUCATION

Higher Education: Attitudes, Values, and Behaviors

Many researchers are interested in the effect of higher education on student values. In a study that laid the groundwork for many others, Theodore Newcomb[135] found that liberal faculty attitudes on public issues influenced the attitudes of entering students at Bennington College. Yet these newly acquired liberal attitudes did not persist after graduation, if students had come from more conservative family and community backgrounds. Recent follow-up studies of Bennington students reached similar conclusions. In another study conducted shortly after the first one at Bennington, Philip Jacob[136] reached a different conclusion: that college experience itself does little to change student value systems, but that peer influence has a great effect. Values are shaped by multiple factors: the institution attended; the family, social, and political backgrounds of the students; peer association; influential faculty; residential versus commuter institutions; and other influences.[137]

Changes in student religious and moral attitudes and values from 1948 to 1984 have been traced by Hoge and others.[138] Certain trends, established in the first part of this period, continued in the second:

1. Church attendance and felt need for religion continued to drop.
2. Interest in careers in corporate business continued to drop.
3. Fear of communism continued to drop.
4. Emphasis on collegiate extracurricular activities and on fraternities continued to drop.
5. Alienation from the military service and from national ideology continued to rise.
6. Support for equal opportunity employment and for a minimum wage continued to rise.

Between 1974 and 1984 several moral trends and religious attitudes changed greatly, from the liberalism and individualism that grew between 1948 and 1967, toward increased traditionalism. The authors conclude that "a return of the fifties is occurring in two respects. First, there is a growing conservatism, religiously and morally. Second, there is a growing privatism, in the sense that students have more concern about personal and family life issues, less about broader social and political issues. This is seen in the increased rejection of the view that Americans have a moral obligation to reduce their consumption and limit their families. . . ."[139]

Regardless of the type of institution, student major, and grades, achieving a college or advanced degree enhances participation in political and community activities.[140]

The Value of a College Education

Do higher education credentials lead to higher occupational status and higher future earnings? The college attended has proven more significant than college grades or job performance in predicting future status and earnings.[141] Students who have gone to a prestigious school have greater chances for higher earnings, although individual initiative is also important. Training in graduate school at a prestigious university by a productive faculty member involved in research and publishing instills a professional orientation, and has a positive effect on the graduate's productivity during the first ten years of professional work and probably for a lifetime.[142]

Many students are accepting jobs in areas unrelated to their majors. This and the reduced economic advantages of college are causing young people to ask if college is worth the time and money. Consider Figure 9-4. The comparison shows that college graduates earn more than high school or elementary graduates, but that these figures for African-American males declined since the mid-1980s. Beginning salaries of bachelor's degree graduates are compared in Figure 9-5. Note that the gap between disciplines is narrowing.[143] College type and quality are important determinants of returns from education in terms of salary and prestige. When students' ability and socioeconomic status are held constant, the findings are less conclusive, but still important.[144] Demographic variables such as sex are also influential. In a comparison of occupational achievement for men and women, women had a narrower range of occupations and lower returns. Also, they were less likely to realize their occupational expectations; they may have been socialized to expect less than men, but the opportunity structure is a major factor in determining women's roles.

The less tangible results of college have been summed up by Alexander Astin in his *Four Critical Years.*[145] College helps students develop a more positive self-image and greater interpersonal and intellectual competence. They adopt more liberal political views and attitudes (which may or may not last) toward social issues. And their religious orientation decreases.

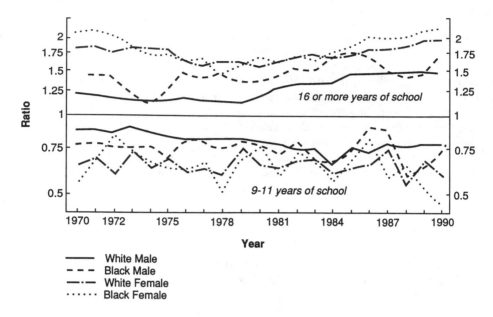

FIGURE 9-4   Ratio of median annual earnings of wage and salary workers 25 to 34 years old with 9–11 and 16 or more years of school to those with 12 years of school, by sex and race/ethnicity, 1970–90.

Note: 1 on the scale represents earnings equal to those with 12 years of school, 2 represents double their earnings, .5 represents half their earnings. The scale on the graph makes the distance between 1 and 2, or doubling, the same as between 1 and .5, or halving.

Source: U.S. Department of Commerce, Bureau of the Census, March Current Population Survey; reprinted in National Center for Education Statistics, *The Condition of Education, 1992,* Vol. 2, Postsecondary Education, (Washington, D.C.: U.S. Department of Education, 1992), p. 85.

PROBLEMS AND REFORM IN HIGHER EDUCATION

With the increasing pressure on the educational system for accountability, higher education is in the critical eye of the public and policymakers. The ivory tower is coming under more challenges, and many institutions are responding to problems: Improve quality of teaching, evaluate the educational program, increase access for minority students, and prepare students with knowledge and skills for a good future.

Colleges are also criticized for certain "unethical" practices, and many are addressing these problems. Grade inflation between the 1960s and 1970s was rapid, but has leveled off; cheating by students is being firmly addressed in many institutions, with misconduct policies and procedures in place; curriculum and credit given for courses is undergoing both internal and external review. Reports of misuse of funds are being investigated and curriculum reform is a constant process.

All organizations have their critics; higher education is no exception.

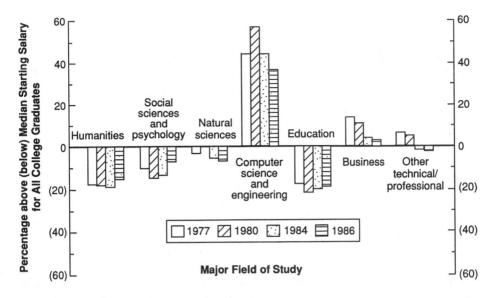

FIGURE 9-5   Differences in median starting salaries of college graduates, by major field of study: years of graduation 1977, 1980, 1984, and 1986.

Source: U.S. Department of Education, National Center for Education Statistics, Recent College Graduates surveys; reprinted in National Center for Education Statistics, *The Condition of Education, 1991,* Vol. 2, Postsecondary Education (Washington, D.C.: U.S. Department of Education, 1991), p. 59.

Some critics have an ideology to back their reformist critiques. In recent years several authors have made sweeping criticisms of higher education, especially of humanities and social sciences. The conflict centers around views about the correct way to learn and the correct knowledge to learn. Issues of "political correctness" on campuses, stimulated in part by these critics, are bringing about changes in curriculum and dominant issues on campuses. The conflicts represent an underlying tension between privilege and patriarchy on the one hand, and affirmative action and cultural diversity issues on the other.[146]

Some critics argue that with the tenuring of radical professors who were influenced during the 1960s has come a shift in the educational agenda; academic missions; administrative policies; hiring; control of academic journals; and ultimately the philosophy, substance, and direction of institutions of higher education.[147] These radical professors, the critics argue, set the code of conduct and instructional norms.[148] For instance, Stanford University voted to change its traditional curriculum to include "works by women, minorities, and persons of color."[149] *Profscam* received attention for its sharp rebuke of professors who are outdated and are trying to escape teaching. With job security and freedom to do what they like, some do nothing at all, it claims.[150]

Other critics attempt to be unbiased, study trends and conditions, and recommend changes. One such set of proposals comes from *The University as an Organization.* According to Corson, five proposals seem to be gaining approval among experts in the field:

1. The university must be recognized as being made up of groups, each of which is relatively independent of the institution and of each other. This implies that a restructuring is necessary; the business model will not work well where many autonomous units exist with competing loyalties such as professional associations outside of the institution.
2. The governance of such a community requires structure and processes that will facilitate the engineering of consensus; such a community cannot be governed with the structure and processes that rely on authoritative command.
3. A community agency . . . that includes representatives of all seven elements of the membership of the university is needed as a mechanism through which the president and the board can build essential consensus.
4. The authority of the president to lead what is a large and complex enterprise needs to be strengthened and reaffirmed.
5. A system of accountability must be (and gradually is being) established.[151]

Not all views are negative. Positive aspects of ethical conduct in higher education include the following: There is expanded equality of opportunity; the university is serving as a forum for discussion of national issues; many students are serious about school, are satisfied with their instruction and academic programs, trust their teachers and feel they are available, and are learning as much as ever.

Several areas have been specific targets for reform movements in recent years: athletic programs and colleges of education. The package put forth by the commissioners of eight major sports conferences include the following reforms, among others:

1. to upgrade academic expectations for freshman athletes,
2. to show academic progress toward a degree,
3. to limit the competitive season length and number of hours of practice a day, and
4. to limit the number of contests played in a season.

The commissioners expect that these reforms will eliminate some of the criticism about the misuse and abuse of athletes.[152]

Colleges of education are particular targets because their products are visible and measurable. Some commission reports push for increasing the status of education as a major, while others argue that students should major in a subject area and take education during a fifth year.[153] See Box 9-3 for a list of objectives for higher education recommended by then–Secretary of Education Cavazos.

The conventional wisdom is that universities are for the conservation, advancement, transmission, and interpretation of knowledge. The permanence of purpose implied by the almost universal acceptance of the definition throughout most of the twentieth century does not necessarily require permanence of method or curriculum content. Far from being detached from society, universities are very much a part of their environment, and their staff and students experience the societal tensions and strains caused by rapid economic and technological changes.

BOX 9-3   *SIX GOVERNMENT OBJECTIVES FOR HIGHER EDUCATION IN THE UNITED STATES*

By 2000, [Secretary of Education] Cavazos said, institutions should:

- Decrease by half the difference in degree-completion rates between minority students and all students. Cavazos said that 33 percent of all students do not earn a degree within 12 years of entering higher education, compared with 55 percent of black students and 51 percent of Hispanic students.
- Increase from 10 percent to 50 percent the population of bachelor's-degree recipients who are proficient in a second language.
- Ensure that all associate- and bachelor's-degree recipients are proficient in college-level mathematics and science.
- Ensure that all graduating students are able to write coherent, grammatically correct papers, and display a basic knowledge of world history, geography, and culture.
- Increase by 25 percent the number of American citizens completing doctoral programs in the basic arts, mathematics, sciences, engineering, and technological disciplines. The changes should include 50-percent increases in the numbers of women, blacks, American Indians, and Hispanics.
- Ensure that all students leaving post-secondary institutions have critical-thinking and problem-solving skills needed to contribute to the economic and political life of the nation.

Source: DeLoughry, Thomas J., "Secretary Cavazos Offers Colleges Six Objectives to Improve Students' Education in the 90's," *The Chronicle of Higher Education*, January 31, 1990, p. A21.

SUMMARY

There is no one system of higher education. To the extent that generalizations can be made across systems, we have discussed some common characteristics and problems: the development and meaning of higher education; access to the system; the structure, process, and role relationships within the system; the environmental pressures toward change; and some outcomes and reforms in higher education.

I. History and Development of Higher Education

Organized higher education dates back to the twelfth and thirteenth centuries. Over time, its structure and functions have changed dramatically. It now has a two-part structure—administration and faculty—and has taken on several additional functions such as research and service. The twentieth century has brought the two-year college, and with it new structures and functions.

II. Theoretical Approaches to Higher Education

We can gain a better understanding of how sociologists view higher education through functional and conflict theories. The systems model helps integrate aspects of higher education for a more comprehensive view. The issue of access to higher education, who gets in and why, is of major concern to educational theorists. They focus particularly on the admissions process and testing, and public versus private institutions. There have been legal challenges to admissions decisions to professional schools, with unclear outcomes.

III. Characteristics of Higher Education in the United States

Institutions vary depending on sponsorship, student composition, types of programs, and degrees offered. The rapid growth of higher education threatened to weaken the value of college. Changing enrollments and economic patterns also force cuts in programs and staff.

IV. Functions of the Higher Education System

The university can be viewed as a community, and in some cases as a "multiversity." With growth has come controversy over functions of the university: what form of curriculum to adopt; the relationship between research and teaching; and what role service to community should play. Controversy over the academic function of the university is illustrated by the role of "big business" sports on some campuses and the type of curriculum the university should have.

V. Higher Education as an Organization

Higher education has been administered using a bureaucratic model, which many argue is not appropriate for the unique composition of the university. Decision making varies by constituency in the university, as do areas of decision-making responsibility. For instance, faculty generally retain control of curriculum matters.

VI. Roles in Higher Education

Students are becoming a more diversified group, with older students, minorities, and married students attending college in greater numbers. Of concern is the drop in black student enrollment. More women students are moving through the system and into graduate school today, assuming multiple roles, than in the past. Colleges wrestle with the problem of underprepared students who lack necessary skills to complete college.

Three issues facing faculty were discussed: professionalism, collective bargaining, and gender issues.

VII. Environmental Pressures on Higher Education

Several issues related to the environment of higher education were used to illustrate its importance: funding of higher education, court actions, and community pressure on programs.

VIII. Outcomes of Higher Education

Outcomes of higher education include the value, attitude, and behavioral changes that take place and the financial outcomes of having a college education.

IX. Problems and Reform in Higher Education

Finally, some problems and reforms in the areas of challenges to the higher education system and ethics were briefly discussed, including several critiques of faculty and curriculum. Proposals for reform were listed.

PUTTING SOCIOLOGY TO WORK

1. List the institutions of higher education in your geographical area.
    a. What is the purpose served by each? (What courses and degrees are offered, who is served?)
    b. What sorts of students go to each?
    c. What did your high school classmates do after graduation? college? work? other?
    d. Are there indivduals who have not been accommodated by higher education in your area after high school?
    e. Do you see any gaps in the system of higher education in your area?
2. Think of a recent controversy in your institution. Put yourself in the place of other students who represent differing viewpoints on the controversy; of a faculty member (or members); of an administrator involved with the controversy. How do they differ in their perpsectives on the controversy? It may be useful to interview those involved.
3. Consider several issues in higher education that were raised in the text or others that are of concern to you. Explain how a functionalist and conflict theorist would interpret these issues differently.
4. What problems do you see in the program or curriculum of your institution or in your major area? Designate alternatives to the present system at your institution that could help solve the problems.
5. Who holds formal power and decision-making rights in your institution in various areas? Who holds informal power? Give some examples. It may be useful to interview others on this question.
6. With what areas of the environment must your institution interact? Talking with an administrator about pressures on the university would be informative here.

NOTES

[1] Boyer, Ernest L., *College: the Undergraduate Experience in America* (New York: Harper and Row, 1987).

[2] Perkins, James A. (ed.), *The University as an Organization: A Report for The Carnegie Commission on Higher Education* (New York: McGraw-Hill, 1973), p. 3.

[3] *Ibid.*, pp. 6–7.

[4] Ballantine, Jeanne, "The Role of Teaching Around the World," *Teaching Sociology*, Vol. 17, No. 3, July 1989, pp. 291–96.

[5] Perkins, *The University as an Organization*, pp. 10–13.

[6] Jencks, Christopher, and David Riesman, *The Academic Revolution* (Garden City, N.Y.: Doubleday, 1968), pp. 90–91.

[7] "Percent Enrolled in College in October Following High School Graduation, by Sex, Type of College, and Race/Ethnicity: 1968–1988," *The Condition of Education*, Postsecondary Education, National Center for Education Statistics, Vol. 2, 1991, p. 102.

[8] Trow, Martin, "Comparative Perspectives on British and American Higher Education," paper presented at American Sociological Association meetings, Chicago, August 1987.

[9] Vaughan, George B., "Institutions on the Edge: America's Community Colleges," *Educational Record*, Vol. 72, No. 2, Spring 1991, pp. 30–33.

[10] Grubb, W. Norton, "The Decline of Community College Transfer Rates: Evidence from National Longitudinal Surveys," *Journal of Higher Education*, Vol. 62, No. 2, March/April 1991, pp. 194–217.

[11] Eaton, Judith S., "Encouraging Transfer: The Impact on Community Colleges," *Educational Record*, Vol. 72, No. 2, Spring 1991, pp. 34–39.

[12] "All Things Considered," National Public Radio, August 25, 1992.

[13] Lieberman, Janet E., "A Plan for High School/Community College Collaboration," *The College Board Review*, CLIII, Fall 1989, pp. 14–19.

[14] Pincus, Fred L., "Contradictory Effects of Customized Contract Training in Community Colleges," *Critical Sociology*, Vol. 16, No. 1, Spring 1989, pp. 77–91.

[15] Pincus, Fred L., and Suzanne DeCamp, "Minority Community College Students Who Transfer to Four-Year Colleges," paper presented at American Sociological Association meetings, Atlanta, August 1988.

[16] Olivas, Michael, *The Dilemma of Access: Minorities in Two-Year Colleges* (Washington, D.C.: Howard University Press, 1979).

[17] Clark, Burton R., "The Cooling-Out Function in Higher Education," *The American Journal of Sociology*, Vol. 65, 1960, pp. 569–76.

[18] Brint, Steven, and Jerome Karabel, *The Diverted Dream: Community Colleges and the Promise of Educational Opportunity in America, 1900–1985* (New York: Oxford University Press, 1989).

[19] Velez, William, "Finishing College: The Effects of College Type," *Sociology of Education*, Vol. 58, No. 3, 1985, pp. 191–200.

[20] Clark, Burton, "Cooling Out Function Revisited," *New Directions for Community Colleges*, Vol. 32, 1980, pp. 15–31.

[21] Velez, William, and Rajshekhar G. Javalgi, "Factors Affecting the Probabilities of Transferring from a Two-Year College to a Four-Year College," unpublished paper.

[22] Eaton, Judith S., "Minorities, Transfer, and Higher Education," *Peabody Journal of Education*, Vol. 66, No. 1, Fall 1990, p. 58.

[23] Grubb, "The Decline of Community College Transfer Rates," p. 194.

[24] Velez, "Finishing College," p. 13.

[25] Lee, Valerie E., and Kenneth A. Frank, "Students' Characteristics That Facilitate the Transfer from Two-Year to Four-Year Colleges," *Sociology of Education*, Vol. 63, No. 3, July 1990, pp. 178–93.

[26] Monk-Turner, Elizabeth, "The Occupational Achievements of Community and Four-Year College Entrants," *American Sociological Review*, Vol. 55, No. 5, October 1990, p. 725.

[27] Monk-Turner, Elizabeth, "Is Going to a Community College Better Than Not Going to College at All?" unpublished manuscript, 1992.

[28] Monk-Turner, Elizabeth, "Factors Shaping the Probability of Community vs. Four-Year College Entrance and Acquisition of the B.A. Degree," unpublished manuscript, 1992.

[29] Lee, "Student's Characteristics," p. 191.

[30] Pincus, Fred L., "Customized Contract Training in Community Colleges: Who Really Benefits?," paper presented at American Sociological Association meetings, Washington, D.C., August 1985.

[31] Bowles, Samuel, and Herbert Gintis, *Schooling in Capitalist America: Educational Reform and the Contradictions of Economic Life* (New York: Basic Books, 1976).

[32] Karen, David, "Toward a Political-Organizational Model of Gatekeeping: The Case of Elite Colleges," *Sociology of Education*, Vol. 63, No. 4, October 1990, pp. 227–40.

[33] Collier, Paul, and Colin Mayer, "An Investigation of University Selection Procedures," *Supplement to the Economic Journal*, Vol. 96, 1986.

[34] *The Chronicle of Higher Education*, September 25, 1991.

[35] Crouse, James, "The Time Has Come to Replace the SAT," *The Chronicle of Higher Education*, February 26, 1986, p. 40.

[36] Karen, "Toward a Political-Organizational Model," p. 238.

[37] "Number of Colleges by Enrollment, Fall 1988," U.S. Department of Education; from *The Chronical of Higher Education Almanac*, September 5, 1990, p. 13.

[38] Blau, Peter M. *et al.*, "Dissecting Types of Professional Schools," *Sociology of Education*, Vol. 52, 1979, pp. 7–19.

[39] Ben-David, Joseph, *American Higher Education* (New York: McGraw-Hill, 1972), pp. 5–7.

[40] U.S. Says Fall Enrollments Rose 3.2%, Topping 14 Million for First Time," *The Chronicle of Higher Education*, January 8, 1992, p. A41.

[41] Evangelauf, Jean, "Enrollment Projections Revised Upward in New Government Analysis," *The Chronicle of Higher Education*, January 22, 1992, p. A1.

[42] Ashworth, Kenneth H., *American Higher Education in Decline* (College Station: Texas A&M University Press, 1979), p. 53.

[43] Wilson, Robin, "Job Prospects for 1991 College Graduates Are the Bleakest in at Least 20 Years, Study Finds," *The Chronicle of Higher Education*, December 19, 1990, p. A26.

[44] Sanders, Irwin T., "The University as a Community," in Perkins, *The University as an Organization*, p. 57.

[45] Kerr, Clark, *The Uses of the University* (Cambridge, Mass.: Harvard University Press, 1963).

[46] Perkins, James A., "Missions and Organizations: A Redefinition," in Perkins, *The University as an Organization*, p. 258.

[47] Evangelauf, Jean, "Leaders Accuse Medical Schools of Failing Society by Maintaining Status Quo," *The Chronicle of Higher Education*, November 12, 1986, pp. 1, 22.

[48] Rhoades, Gary, and Sheila Slaughter, "Professors, Administrators, and Patents: The Negotiation of Technology Transfer," *Sociology of Education*, Vol. 64, April 1991, pp. 65–77.

[49] *Ibid.*, p. 75.

[50] "Our Schools for Scandal," *Newsweek*, September 15, 1986, p. 84; "College Sports' Real Scandal," *U.S. News & World Report*, September 15, 1986, p. 62.

[51] "College Sports' Real Scandal," p. 62.

[52] Lederman, Douglas, "Black Athletes Who Entered College in Mid-'80s Had Much Weaker Records Than Whites, Study Finds," *The Chronicle of Higher Education*, July 10, 1991, p. A30.

[53] Adler, Patricia A., and Peter Adler, *Backboards and Blackboards: College Athletes and Role Engulfment* (New York: Columbia University Press, 1991).

[54] Lederman, Douglas, "Proposal to Let Athletes Play for 5 Years Touted as Cure for Many of Sports' Ills," *The Chronicle of Higher Education*, November 12, 1986, p. 41.

[55] Lederman, Douglas, "Students Who Competed in College Sports Fare Better in Job Market Than Those Who Didn't, Report Says," *The Chronicle of Higher Education*, September 26, 1990, p. A47.

[56] Millett, "Similarities and Differences," p. 44.

[57] Coser, Lewis A., *The Functions of Social Conflict* (Glencoe, Ill.: Free Press, 1956).

[58] Altbach, Philip G., and Robert Cohen, "American Student Activism: The Post-Sixties Transformation," *Journal of Higher Education*, Vol. 61, No. 1 January/February 1990, pp. 33–48.

[59] Munitz, Barry, "California State University System and First Amendment Rights to Free Speech, *Education*, Vol. 112, No. 1, Fall 1991, p. 4.

[60] Jaschik Scott, "High Court to Weigh the Constitutionality of 'Hate Speech' Ban," *The Chronicle of Higher Education*, June 19, 1991, p. A15.

[61] "Minority Update," *The Chronicle of Higher Education*, December 19, 1990, p. A16.

[62] Dodge, Susan, "More College Students Choose Academic Majors That Meet Social and Environmental Concerns," *The Chronicle of Higher Education*, December 5, 1990, p. A31.

[63] Morse, Suzanne W., "Renewing Civic Capacity: Preparing College Students for Service and Citizenship," *ERIC Digest*, Report EDO-HE 89-8.

[64] Corson, John J., "Perspectives on the University Compared with Other Institutions," in Perkins, *The University as an Organization*, pp. 155–69.

322   *The System of Higher Education*

65 Parelius, Ann, and Robert J. Parelius, *The Sociology of Education*, (Englewood Cliffs, N.J.: Prentice Hall, 1978), pp. 139–40.

66 Clark, Burton R., *Structure of Academic Governance in the United States*, working paper, Institute for Social and Policy Studies (New Haven, Conn.: Yale University, 1976).

67 Jacobson, Robert L., "Typical College Trustee, Survey Finds, Is a Middle-Aged, White Businessman," *The Chronicle of Higher Education*, February 12, 1986, p. 23.

68 Spring, Joel, *The Sorting Machine* (New York: David McKay, 1976), pp. 96–97.

69 Clark, "Structure of Academic Governance," p. 36.

70 Reyes, Pedro, and Donald J. McCarty, "Factors Related to the Power of Lower Participants in Educational Organizations: Multiple Perspectives," *Sociological Focus*, Vol. 23, No. 1, February 1990, pp. 17–30.

71 Ross, Murray G., *The University: The Anatomy of Academe* (New York: McGraw-Hill, 1976), p. 122.

72 Rothman, Robert, "Enrollment Gains Linked to Marketing," *Education Week*, October 15, 1986, p. 8.

73 DeLoughry, Thomas J., "14.1 Million Students Expected to Enroll in Colleges This Fall," *The Chronicle of Higher Education*, September 4, 1991, p. A47.

74 Wilson, Robin, "Many Institutions Report Sharp Drops in Freshman Rolls," *The Chronicle of Higher Education*, October 3, 1990, p. A35.

75 *Tribal Colleges: Shaping the Future of Native America* (Princeton, N.J.: The Carnegie Foundation for the Advancement of Teaching, November 1989).

76 Billson, Janet Mancini, and Margaret Brooks Terry, "In Search of the Silken Purse: Factors in Attrition Among First-Generation Students," *College and University*, Fall 1982, pp. 57–76.

77 Clark, Roger, "Multinational Corporate Investment, and Women's Participation in Higher Education in Noncore Nations," *Sociology of Education*, Vol. 65, No. 1, January 1992, pp. 37–47.

78 Bridgeman, Brent, and Cathy Wendler, "Gender Differences in Predictors of College Mathematics Performance and in College Mathematics Course Grades," *Journal of Educational Psychology*, Vol. 83, No. 2, June 1991, p. 283.

79 Wilson, Kenneth L., and Janet P. Boldizar, "Gender Segregation in Higher Education: Effects of Aspirations, Mathematics Achievement, and Income," *Sociology of Education*, Vol. 63, No. 1, January 1990, pp. 62–74.

80 National Center for Education Statistics, *Digest of Education Statistics 1991*, Washington, D.C.: U.S. Department of Education, November 1991, pp. 378–79.

81 Bennett, Stephanie M., "The Re-entry Woman: Prospects and Challenges," *Vital Speeches*, Vol. 46, 1980, pp. 502–5.

82 Folland, Laura Enice Pickett, and Ruth Hoeflin, "Adult Women in College: How Do They Fare," *Journal of Home Economics*, Vol. 69, 1977, p. 28.

83 Loewenstein, Sophie Freud, "The Passion and Challenge of Teaching," *Harvard Educational Review*, Vol. 50, 1980, pp. 10–11.

84 Giele, Janet Zollinger, *et al.*, "Changing Educational and Occupational Histories of Women College Graduates, 1934–1982," paper presented at American Sociological Association meetings, New York, August 1986.

85 Survey by author of students in continuing education classes, unpublished.

86 Babbitt, Charles E., and Harold J. Burbach, "Women and the College Environment: A Study of Organizational Satisfaction, Compliance and Academic Achievement," *Sociological Focus*, Vol. 18, No. 1, 1985, pp. 37–47.

87 Smith, Daryl G., "Women's Colleges and Coed Colleges: Is There a Difference for Women?" *Journal of Higher Education*, Vol. 61, No. 2, March/April 1990, p. 181.

88 Collison, Michele N-K, "20 Years Later, Women on Formerly All-Male Campuses Fight to Change Their Institutions' 'Old Boy' Images," *The Chronicle of Higher Education*, Vol. 37, No. 15, December 12, 1990, p. A23.

89 Parelius and Parelius, *Sociology of Education*, pp. 217–18.

[90] "Achieving Campus Diversity: Policies for Change" (Denver: Education Commission of the States, 1990).

[91] Turner, Ralph H., "Sponsored and Context Mobility," *American Sociological Review*, Vol. 25, 1960, pp. 855–67.

[92] Steele, Claude M., "Race and the Schooling of Black Americans," *The Atlantic Monthly*, April 1992, pp. 68–78.

[93] *Ibid.*

[94] Thompson, Chalmer E., and Bruce R. Fretz, "Predicting the Adjustment of Black Students at Predominantly White Institutions," *Journal of Higher Education*, Vol. 62, No. 4, July/August 1991, pp. 437–49.

[95] Lieberman, Janet E., "The LaGuardia-Vassar Connection," *Educational Record*, Vol. 72, No. 2, Spring 1991, p. 43.

[96] Kraft, Christine L., "What Makes a Successful Black Student on a Predominantly White Campus?" *American Educational Research Journal*, Vol. 28, No. 2, Summer 1991, pp. 423–43.

[97] McClelland, Katherine E., and Carol J. Auster, "Public Platitudes and Hidden Tensions: Racial Climates at Predominantly White Liberal Arts Colleges," *Journal of Higher Education*, Vol. 61, No. 6, November/December 1990, pp. 607–39.

[98] Magner, Denise K., "Racial Tensions Continue to Erupt on Campuses Despite Efforts to Promote Cultural Diversity," *The Chronicle of Higher Education*, June 6, 1990, p. A30.

[99] Kameen, Marilyn C., and Manuel J. Justiz, "Using Assessment in Higher Education to Improve Success for Minority Students," *Peabody Journal of Education*, Vol. 66, No. 1, Fall 1990, p. 46.

[100] *Ibid.*

[101] Clark, Burton, and Martin Trow, "The Organization Context," in Theodore Newcomb and Everett Wilson (eds.), *College Peer Groups: Problems and Prospects for Research* (Chicago: Aldine, 1966), pp 17–70.

[102] Nuwer, Hand, *Broken Pledges: The Deadly Rite of Hazing* (Marietta, Ga.: Longstreet Press, 1990).

[103] Sanday, Peggy Reeves, *Fraternity Gang Rape: Sex, Brotherhood, and Privilege on Campus* (New York: New York University Press, 1990).

[104] U.S. Bureau of the Census, "Projections of the Population of the United States: 1975–2050," *Current Population Reports*, Series P-25, No. 601 (Washington, D.C.: U.S. Government Printing Office, 1991).

[105] Rix, S., *Older Workers, Choices and Challenges* (Santa Barbara, Calif.: ABC Clio, 1990).

[106] Burtles, G. (ed.), *Work, Health and Income Among the Elderly* (Washington, D.C.: Brookings Institute, 1987).

[107] Cox, Harold, *Later Life: The Realities of Aging*, 2nd ed. (Englewood Cliffs, N.J.: Prentice Hall, 1988).

[108] Hale, Noreen, *The Older Worker* (Oxford: Jossey-Bass, 1990).

[109] Lowy, Louis, and Darlene O'Connor, *Why Education in the Later Years?* (Lexington, Mass.: D.C. Heath, 1986).

[110] U.S. Code Congressional and Administrative News, Laws of the 94th Congress, 2nd Session 1976, 90 stat. 2086-2089.

[111] Ohio Revised Code 3345.27, Amended Senate Bill 497.

[112] This section was written by Mary French, graduate student, Wright State University, with information from *Education Week*, Vol. 11, No. 13, p. 3.

[113] *The Chronicle of Higher Education Almanac*, August 28, 1991, p. 29.

[114] Wuthnow, Robert, "Is There an Academic Melting Pot?" *Sociology of Education*, Vol. 15, 1977, pp. 7–15.

[115] In sociology, training was given by Emory S. Bogardus in the 1920s; more recently, Everett Wilson and William D'Antonio pioneered such courses. See Goldsmid, Charles A., and Everett K. Wilson, *Passing On Sociology* (Belmont, Calif.: Wadsworth, 1980), pp. 42–44.

[116] From "Seminar Practicum on Teaching Sociology," Reece McGee, Purdue University, 1992.

[117] McGee, Reece J., *Academic Janus* (San Francisco: Jossey-Bass, 1971), pp. 191–94.

[118] Kemerer, Frank R., and J. Victor Baldridge, "Unions in Higher Education: The Going Gets Tougher," *Phi Delta Kappan,* June 1980, pp. 714–15.

[119] Gilligan, Carol, "Women's Place in Man's Life Cycle," *Harvard Educational Review,* Vol. 49, 1979, pp. 431–46.

[120] Blum, Debra E., "Environment Still Hostile to Women in Academe, New Evidence Indicates," *The Chronicle of Higher Education,* October 9, 1991, p. A1.

[121] Lomperis, Ana Maria Turner, "Are Women Changing the Nature of the Academic Profession?" *Journal of Higher Education,* Vol. 61, No. 6, November/December 1990, p. 643.

[122] McMillen, Liz, "Women in Academe Say They Bear Brunt of Staffing Cutbacks," *The Chronicle of Higher Education,* Vol. 38, No. 12, p. A1.

[123] Konrad, Alison M., and Jeffrey Pfeffer, "Understanding the Hiring of Women and Minorities in Educational Institutions," *Sociology of Education,* Vol. 64, July 1991, pp. 141–57.

[124] Tolbert, Pamela S., and Alice A. Oberfield, "Sources of Organizational Demography: Faculty Sex Ratios in Colleges and Universities," *Sociology of Education,* Vol. 64, October 1991, pp. 305–15.

[125] "College Revenues," *Education Week,* November 13, 1991, p. 3.

[126] Cordes, Colleen, "National Science Foundation Does Little to Monitor University Spending on Research, Congress Told," *The Chronicle of Higher Education,* October 2, 1991, p. A29.

[127] "White House Imposes New Limits on Overhead Rate for Federally Financed Research at Universities," *The Chronicle of Higher Education,* October 9, 1991, p. A31.

[128] Powell, Brian, and Laia Carr Steelman, "The Liability of Having Brothers: Paying for College and the Sex Composition of the Family," *Sociology of Education,* Vol. 62, No. 2, April 1989, pp. 134–47.

[129] Jaschik, Scott, "Scholarships Set Up for Minority Students Are Called Illegal," *The Chronicle of Higher Education,* December 12, 1990, pp. A1, 21.

[130] Sanders, Jimmy M., "Short- and Long-Term Macroeconomic Returns to Higher Education, *Sociology of Education,* Vol. 65, No. 1, January 1992, pp. 21–36.

[131] "Ten Years Later: Berkeley After the FSM," *Christian Century,* December 4, 1974, p. 1149.

[132] Smelzer, Neil J., *Theory of Collective Behavior* (New York: Free Press, 1962).

[133] "Berkeley Revisited," *Newsweek,* September 6, 1965, p. 51.

[134] *Ibid.*

[135] Newcomb, Theodore M., *et al., Persistence and Change: Bennington College and Its Students After Twenty-five Years* (New York: Wiley, 1967).

[136] Jacob, Philip E., *Changing Values in College: An Exploratory Study of the Impact of College Teaching* (New York: Harper & Brothers, 1957).

[137] Rose, Peter I., "The Myth of Unanimity: Students' Opinions on Critical Issues," *Sociology of Education,* Vol. 37, 1963, pp. 129–49.

[138] Hoge, Dean R., "Changes in College Students' Value Patterns in the 1950's, 60's, and 70'," *Sociology of Education,* Vol. 49, 1976, pp. 155–63.

[139] Hastings, Philip K., and Dean R. Hoge, "Religious and Moral Attitude Trends Among College Students, 1948–1984," *Social Forces,* Vol. 65, No. 2, 1986, pp. 370ff.

[140] Lindsay, Paul, William E. Knox, and Mary N. Kolb, "Lasting Effects of Higher Education on Civic Commitment: A Longitudinal Study," paper presented at American Sociological Association meetings, Cincinnati, Ohio, August 1991.

[141] Hurn, Christopher J., *The Limits and Possibilities of Schooling* (Boston: Allyn and Bacon, 1978), pp. 38–39.

[142] Reskin, Barbara, "Academic Sponsorship and Scientists' Careers," *Sociology of Education,* Vol. 52, 1979, pp. 129–46.

[143] Wilson, Robin, "Job Prospects for 1991 College Graduates Are the Bleakest in at Least 20 Years, Study Finds," *The Chronicle of Higher Education*, December 19, 1990, p. A26.

[144] Solmon, Lewis C., and Paul Wachtel, "The Effects on Income of Type of College Attended," *Sociology of Education*, Vol., 48, 1975, pp. 75–90.

[145] Astin, Alexander W., *Four Critical Years* (San Francisco: Jossey-Bass, 1977), p. 211.

[146] Wilkinson, Doris Y., "The American University and the Rhetoric of Neoconservatism," *Contemporary Sociology*, Vol. 20, No. 4, 1991, pp. 550–51.

[147] Kimball, Roger, *Tenured Radicals: How Politics Has Corrupted Our Higher Education* (New York: Harper & Row, 1990).

[148] *Ibid.*, p. 28.

[149] Sykes, Charles J., *Profscam: Professors and the Demise of Higher Education* (New York: St. Martin's Press, 1988).

[150] Bloom, Allan, *The Closing of the American Mind* (New York: Simon & Schuster, 1988).

[151] Corson, John J., "Perspectives on the University Compared with Other Institutions," in Perkins, *The University as an Organization*, pp. 168–69.

[152] Lederman, Douglas, "Early Reports Show Widespread Backing for New Reform Plan," *The Chronicle of Higher Education*, April 18, 1990, p. A37.

[153] Astin, Alexander W., *The American Freshman: 20-Year Trends, 1966–1985* (Washington, D.C.: American Council on Education, 1986), p. 261.

10

EDUCATION SYSTEMS AROUND THE WORLD
A Comparative View

Aminu is 8. He falls somewhere in the middle of nine brothers and sisters. He and his family live in a small, rural village in West Africa, in the northern part of his country. Farming is the primary occupation of the villagers, with each family tilling its own plot. Aminu's family uses a hand plow in the fields; it's not an easy life, but the family generally has enough to eat—mostly a starchy diet of millet, cassava roots, bananas, and some bits of meat. Aminu has other relatives living in the village too—cousins, aunts and uncles, and grandparents.

From an early age Aminu helped the family in the fields; his father taught him about farming and his grandfather about his family and religion. Though he was one of many children, there was always some relative to whom he could turn for help. His life was secure and happy.

At age 6, he began attending the village school. All the children went there from ages 6 to 9, as mandated by the central government. Aminu didn't much mind; he saw his friends there and could play during free time. The teacher was a young local man who had been away to secondary school and came back to take charge of the one-room schoolhouse located in the village meeting hall. Molam Hassan seemed a nice man but was very strict and frequently resorted to striking pupils or punishing them by making them stand in a corner. With older and younger children in one class, it was difficult to teach materials pertinent to all. Aminu learned basic mathematic functions, which he rather enjoyed doing, though he saw no use for them. He could read simple books. They were about English boys and girls going on picnics with their dog. Aminu studied the Koran and learned to recite passages. He disliked being called on to stand in front of the class and recite, for if he forgot, he would be punished. He had no time, peace, or quiet to sit down at home and learn the recitations. But writing was worse. The children were required to write down dictations, and Aminu could never get it right.

When planting and harvest time came, Aminu and his brothers stayed away from school to help with the farming. When anyone was sick, the children took turns staying home and helping. One time Aminu missed a month of school to help his father and travel with him to the big town 20 miles away.

At the end of this school year, Aminu will leave school along with most of his friends. Only two boys are considering going on to the secondary school in the big town, the two top boys in the school. One has relatives in town with whom he can live. But the other is doubtful about going; his father needs his help and cannot afford the additional money his son would need to live away from home, though the education is free. Besides, many of the villagers are critical of boys who have left to study; they seldom return, and when they visit, they seem to have a superior air.

Joan is 10. She lives in an urban area in Britain. Her parents have a nice home in a residential section of town from which her father commutes to his business each day. Joan began school at age 3 in a private nursery, where she learned her letters, numbers, and nursery rhymes, and to follow rules, routines, and schedules. Then she went to infant school and primary school near her home, and she is to enter a girls' public school next fall. ("Public school" in Britain is equivalent to private school in the United States. Tuition must be paid. Attending public school is generally considered to be preparatory to getting into a good university.) Here she will study the regular academic subjects, including Latin and French, plus horseback riding and a musical instrument. She particularly likes drawing and will have private lessons. Joan's parents stress education; she studies or reads for at least one hour each evening and is rewarded when her reports are good. Her parents both read a great deal and have many books, magazines, and newspapers in the home. Her mother was trained as a teacher; her father studied mathematics at Oxford and is a successful businessman. She has one brother, who is at a public school for boys.

Joan is a good student and applies herself. When she completes public school she thinks she would like to go on to the university, and she probably will.

These two scenarios provide a glance at two educational systems representing two worlds through which children are passing. The division is not only between two children, but between two countries and two worlds: one rich and developed, the other poor and developing. This distinction must be kept in mind as we consider the world system of education. For as different as they are, there are also commonalities in these two education systems. In this chapter we explore some of these commonalities and differences.

CROSS-CULTURAL EDUCATIONAL STUDIES

Many sociologists have an interest in cross-cultural research, for it provides new insights, ideas, and perspectives on their own societies. It provides information on what is unique in educational systems, for example, and what is universal. Cross-cultural research is not always easy to do because systems of education are difficult to compare and have different underlying ideologies and goals. Sociologists have been major contributors to the field of comparative education: developing useful methodologies, identifying key variables, constructing analytical models, and carrying out research projects.

Comparative Education as a Field of Study

The field of comparative education has moved from primarily descriptive data and case studies of specific problems in selected countries to a "multi-disciplinary field that looks at education in cross-cultural context" using a variety of methodologies.[1,2] Edmund King sees the field as having progressed through four historical phases of development:

1. the nineteenth-century use of comparative study for the establishment of particular institutions, such as universities, technical institutions, teachers' education, progressive schools, and so forth,
2. the twentieth-century attempt to guide the universalization of particular institutions, such as elementary schools, secondary schools, and various ancillary services,
3. post-1945 attempts to guide overall national appraisal of formal education and its interrelated development, but with growing international and comparative awareness of major educational trends and problems, and
4. post-1960 attempts to guide what are essentially political-economic and social decisions in an international perspective by using insights, evidence, and techniques from comparative researches in education.[3]

In the last decade several themes, influenced by worldwide trends and issues, have dominated cross-cultural studies in education. Three of these themes are discussed shortly: curriculum issues, international tests, and legitimacy of knowledge. New theoretical approaches—Marxist, neo-Marxist, and feminist—have been added to existing theories to enrich the field.[4] Though the United States has played a major role in the development of the field of comparative education, countries such as the People's Republic of China, with its supportive governmental policies, are making valuable contributions to the field.[5]

Many dimensions of education have been compared cross-culturally: quality, quantity, internal structure, differentiation, goals, materials, resources, teaching techniques, effectiveness, curricula, social control, and so forth. Methodological problems such as differences in school starting ages, curricula, types of schools, testing and record-keeping techniques, and the expense of cross-cultural research all complicate efforts to find standard comparative techniques and data. An example is seen in an extensive study of 20 countries

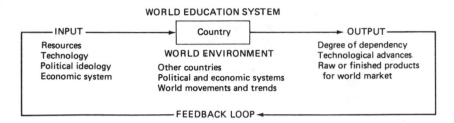

FIGURE 10-1   The world education system shows interdependence among countries.

that had to be constructed in many different languages.[6] The United Nations has established some common measurements to be used by member countries, and as these techniques are adopted, areas for comparative analysis are expanding. Though some researchers are doing international comparative studies, to date, sociologists of education in different countries tend to focus on questions most relevant to their particular settings. This leads to a variety of research questions, theoretical approaches, and methodologies.[7]

Comparative Education and the Systems Approach

We cannot ignore the interaction between education and other institutions in societal systems. The systems approach is again useful for piecing together these dynamics.

Using the open systems approach helps us conceptualize the world context within which each country exists (Figure 10-1). From this perspective the world system is the environment for individual countries. How they interact economically and politically and their level of development with the world system influence the type of education system they develop. Complex as the world scene may be, attempts must be made to develop and test propositions so that educational policy may be used in scientific research.

APPROACHES TO CROSS-CULTURAL STUDIES OF EDUCATIONAL SYSTEMS

What do we wish to compare, and how should we do it? Recent comparative studies show the diversity in research: gender issues, in-school variables, dysfunctional aspects of schooling, the role of the state, curriculum and textbook issues, comparative test results, and a variety of other themes.[8] These underlying questions lead to the following five approaches, which are by no means inclusive of the approaches that exist:

1. models comparing countries on specific aspects of education such as subject area achievement,

2. approaches identifying key elements in the internal structure of educational systems that can be compared cross-culturally,

3. societal system "strategies" or approaches to the development of educational systems to meet the needs of society,

4. models showing the link between mass education curricula and expansion of nation-state and standard curricula and structures,[9] and

5. models showing the interrelationships between societal institutions and the environment.

Many approaches to cross-cultural studies present models or typologies. A model is like the frame of a house: It provides the foundation and supports for each unique unit. We vary the rooms, the decor, the outside covering. Yet each house has a foundation based on common principles of construction. Likewise, a model provides a framework for developing or studying the same types of systems; in this case, education systems. A model is useful insofar as it reflects reality when matched against actual cases. Models commonly relate to either specific aspects of education or comparisons of systems. An example of a "specific aspect" study on achievement may help clarify.

Comparative International Studies of Achievement

The International Association of the Evaluation of Educational Achievement (IEA) carried out the most extensive cross-cultural research endeavor ever. The original study is destined to become a classic in the field, not only because of its extent and its advanced cross-cultural methodological techniques, but because such a multimillion-dollar project may never again be possible.[10] A number of volumes have resulted from the study, with topics ranging from the significance of study to methodology to comparative findings, and follow-up studies have provided additional data for comparisons.

A primary purpose of the study was to identify key characteristics affecting national systems of education and relate them to outcomes of learning.[11] The study analyzed school subjects—math, science, reading comprehension, literature, civil education, and French and English as foreign languages. Test results were compared for 10-year-olds and 14-year-olds, and for the year before students left school. Key variables included age of school entry and leaving, size of school and classroom, proportion of total age cohort in school at termination time, specialized versus comprehensive curricula, student socioeconomic status, and sex differences.

The IEA studies show only modest differences in achievement among advanced, primarily European, countries, though the range between subject areas such as math, science, and reading comprehension varies greatly. Differences that do exist can be explained by differences in school structure or curriculum.

If one compares less developed countries with advanced ones, the differences are great. One suggested reason for the discrepancy is that children in

Children around the world attend primary schools, though the settings vary greatly.

less developed countries "arrive at school with substantially less development of the skills most relevant to school performance.[12] The schools are unable to compensate for the deficits. However, controlling for the differences in facilities, teachers, and students, the schools' achievement level is about the same as in advanced countries.

Such a vast amount of data was collected and processed and so many hypotheses were tested that it is impossible to summarize the findings accurately and completely. However, this much can be concluded: after a country reaches a "critical threshold," educational efficiency between nations is similar. Differences between developed countries are probably best explained by how many resources are put into what aspects of education.

A recent study by the Educational Testing Service found that U.S. test-takers aged 9 and 13 lag far behind their peers in international rankings. Of the 15 mostly industrialized recorded, math and science scores of 13-year-olds were highest in Korea and Taiwan, and lowest in Jordan, the United States, and Spain. No clear correlation was found between length of the school day or year, money spent, or use of innovative instructional techniques. Findings did indicate that "high expectations produced high achievement."[13]

THEORETICAL PERSPECTIVES AND TYPOLOGIES IN COMPARATIVE EDUCATION

Education is viewed by much of the world's population as a gateway to opportunity. Many bright, eager African children beg foreign visitors to help them get more education, while children in many countries think they would like nothing more than to be free of the compulsory burden. But what can education actually do for the people of a nation? There is not a clear cut answer to this question; it is riveted with ideological differences of opinion that permeate the field of comparative education. What is needed is to recognize ideological differences and work with them to gain a deeper understanding of education's role in world development.

If we believe that systems of education reflect the desires of capitalists and the elite in society, and is organized to perpetuate their status, our discussion of comparative education will have a conflict perspective. If, on the other hand, our view holds that education systems are the great "levelers" of society, providing individuals with an opportunity to get ahead, and providing society with the skilled human power needed for economic development, our perspective will be functional. Either perspective might be used, depending on the view of the researcher and the nature of the research questions being asked.

Modernization and Human Capital Perspectives

Many researchers are looking at the relationship between education and economic growth and development. Modernization and human capital perspectives, which dominated theory in the comparative field in the 1960s and early 1970s, pointed to the importance of education in transforming individuals' beliefs, values, and behaviors into those necessary for economic modernization—diligence, rational calculation, orderliness, frugality, punctuality, and achievement orientation[14]—and new social values such as meritocracy—getting ahead on one's own ability.

While it is clear that there is a relationship between the global economy and the role of education,[15] this approach has been criticized for several reasons:

1. Meritocracy is an ideal reached in few countries. Review of data from 20 countries representing different types of political-economic systems shows that "Eastern European nonmarket economies" (Poland, Czechoslovakia, Hungary, the former USSR) were closer to ideal meritocracy than the industrial market economies of Western Europe (France, Great Britain, Switzerland, Netherlands, Germany, Finland, Sweden). Contrary to widespread beliefs, Japan and the United States are very far from ideal meritocracy—much farther than some less developed countries.[16]

2. There is a built-in "ethnocentric" assumption that all nations will emulate the Western model of development. In fact, countries may not lose their indigenous educational systems as they adopt Western ones; in one case study traditional Islamic schooling was maintained along with the increase in Western schooling.[17]

3. Making individuals "modern" through education may not result in a modern society.[18] Lack of jobs and low wages for the educated may cause discontent and some "brain drain."

Two alternative views, world systems perspective and dependency theory, challenge the claim that education is a positive force in economic development.

> Dependency and world system scholars argue that: (1) the global capitalist economy is a holistic system characterized by structural inequalities both between and within nation-states; (2) the economies of Third World nations were systematically plundered and *underdeveloped* in earlier historical epochs and now constitute a peripheral component of the global system which continues to supply raw materials and cheap labor to the industrial centers; (3) the expropriation of profit and surplus value by core nations and multinational corporations depended upon the complicity and power of national elites who were usually educated in Western school systems; and (4) by seeking to maximize returns to foreign investments and by setting national priorities according to foreign standards, the actions of the national bourgeoisie have intensified internal inequalities, reinforced the dependency of Third World nations, and retarded long-term economic development.[19]

These theorists look instead to "a nation's structural position in the world economy, trade flow, dependence on primary product exports, state strength, degree of foreign investment, and the presence of multinational corporations."[20] Education plays a minor role in determining or influencing economic development, according to these views.

More recently, some reproduction theorists have argued that education *does* affect development: Western-educated Third World leaders have perpetuated former colonial patterns that keep their countries in dependent positions. "Education reproduced and reinforced the class structure of peripheral nations," strengthening the position of national elites.[21] Although some economic growth has taken place, the profits go outside the country and the masses see little change.

"Legitimation of Knowledge" Perspective

The study of comparative educational knowledge has gone through two broad phases of development, according to Welch.[22] The first was to study the process whereby educational knowledge becomes "legitimate" (that is, accepted by the citizens), and how that knowledge base changes over time. The second was to consider the relationship between the legitimation of educational knowledge and power relations in the modern state. Conflict or "critical" theorists have taken the lead in these discussions. They use as a foundation writings by Max Weber, Karl Marx, Jurgen Habermas, and others.

In the 1970s, with the advent of the "new" sociology of education, Michael Young[23] and others no longer assumed that education represented the social consensus or agreement of citizens of a country; in fact, "critical" sociologists questioned every assumption and structure. Some viewed education as a form of "ideological domination" by those in power to control the knowledge taught and to stay in power.

Three central questions are related to the issue of legitimate knowledge: How does certain knowledge become legitimate? Under what circumstances does it become changed? And what does a cross-national comparison of such processes tell us?[24] The hypothesis underlying these questions was that in the process of knowledge transfer (education of children), some groups in society may be left out of decision making about curricula.[25]

The underlying theme in much of the recent writing is that curriculum and acceptable knowledge transmission are *not* neutral, but rather are driven by social elements such as who is in power and who has economic control.[26,27] Some argue that the form schooling takes, such as "comprehensive school structure" in Europe, is influenced by the needs of capitalist labor markets.[28]

Even the day-to-day routines that take place in schools around the world have been the subject of study for their hidden messages. This "hidden curriculum" is exemplified in the African thought process.[29] Science education is more closely associated with a Western cause-effect view of the world than with a world view from traditionally agricultural, religious countries. As science becomes an integral part of most countries' basic curriculum, these new Western world views are transmitted. Some argue that these "hidden messages" lead to a more rapid increase in a country's standard of living.[30] But such a world view may also perpetuate stratification systems by giving some members of society more access to elite education.

Despite the conflicting views over the role of education in societies, all nations have some form of formal education. In the next section we consider cross-national studies in comparative education: rich versus poor countries, studies of internal structure of educational systems, and societal strategies for education.

Rich Versus Poor: An Educational Typology

Nepal is one of the poorest countries of the world, with a per capita income of $180; it is better off than Mozambique, and only slightly ahead of Chad, Bangladesh, and Ethiopia. Ninety percent of its 15 million citizens engage in agriculture, most subsistence-level. Fifty-two percent of the children are undernourished, and 11 percent suffer from severe malnutrition. Life expectancy is 51 years. Population growth does not help the situation. Eighty-eight percent of the women and 74 percent of the men are illiterate. However, attendance in primary school rose from 20 percent in 1965 to 82 percent in 1987, and secondary school attendance is now about 25 percent[31]; the poorest have the lowest literacy. Despite various government programs to improve the basic health, welfare, and educational level, many barriers must be overcome. Subsistence agriculture demands all hands; girls are involved in household chores and child care; and long distances from school and teacher quality affect attendance rates. The government has implemented a vast system of adult education that is reaching thousands; they hope to break the cycle of illiteracy in this way. This is but one example of barriers to formal education in developing countries.[32]

Learning takes place in many ways and settings: For the rich, much learning is formal, in classrooms and specially designed buildings. For the poor, there may or may not be a classroom. Often formal learning is a small part of the poor child's education; mostly he or she learns informally through imitating elders and learning the family trade. An anthropology professor once warned that before we scoff at informal learning we should consider its impact. He asked us to imagine ourselves transferred to the Kalahari Desert. How would we survive? Where would we find food and water? Without help we would be likely to perish. Yet the Hottentots and Bushmen survive and flourish there; they have been learning survival techniques, passed on through the generations, from early childhood. The film "The Gods Must Be Crazy" showed the contrasts between the lives of Europeans and Bushmen.

There are over 500 million primary and secondary school students in the world, and 15 million professional teachers. Yet this is not the whole picture, for the proportion of children at primary school in Somalia is 15 percent,[33] whereas in rich Western countries it is 100 percent. The number of children in school in any country is closely related to that country's wealth and level of economic development. Illiteracy and economic development are related; Third World countries that are struggling economically also have the highest illiteracy rates. Illiteracy is so severe in India that educational leaders are considering closing all high schools, colleges, and universities for up to a year to mobilize a campaign to teach people to read. (Illiteracy rates for men and women in selected regions were listed earlier in Figure 4-1.)

Unfortunately, the quality of schools in many of the poorest Third World countries is eroding and public spending per pupil is dropping. Although middle-income countries show a rise in school quality, the overall comparison of Third World countries with industrial nations is great and the gap is widening. Why the differences? The reasons are many, but they center around the position of Third World countries in the world system. Influencing the educational situation are the level of wealth in a country; the rapid growth in enrollments, which forces limited resources to be spread even thinner; and other factors related to dependent and debtor nations.[34]

Within many countries there are unofficially two education systems: one in rural areas and the other in urban areas. Village schools, as seen in the opening scenario in this chapter, have fewer resources, often less qualified teachers, and less parental support. They may be state-run or attached to a local temple or mosque; religious education may be the main emphasis.[35] Urban schools in developing nations are usually organized and run on a Western or colonial model, often patterned after the English or French forms of education; many serve the nation's elite population. In former French colonies in Africa, for instance, farmers receive a much smaller share of educational support than do white-collar citizens.[36] Within the poor nations are families who cannot afford to take advantage of available preschool and elementary education because their children's hands are needed to help with the farm work. Survival has priority over schooling; early-childhood intervention programs may provide useful information and support to the family and child.[37] Cross-cultural analysis of elementary school curricula show worldwide standardization in major subject areas, reflecting ideologies, rules, and customs that are transnational in character.[38] Secondary education is even more elusive for rural children of developing nations, for they may be required to pay for transportation or boarding, books, and clothes. The education system, then, often serves to perpetuate inequality by being available only to elites, usually those from urban areas.

Inequality is found in wealthy, developed, industrial societies as well as poor, emerging, developing, modernizing ones. The inequalities between people may be related to class, race, sex, and religion as well as to rural versus urban residence. Even the age at which children start school and the pre-primary enrollment rates vary by country. For instance, in Finland and Norway, many children do not start school until age 7, whereas in Spain, Belgium, France, and the Netherlands, more than 90 percent of 4-year-olds are in school.[39]

Each societal system of education is also influenced by the larger world system. Few societies in today's interdependent world can be studied without careful consideration of the world community. Yet this is not an easy task, because comparing complex and different systems presents methodological difficulties.

National Structures of Educational Systems and Curricula: Comparative Variables

Internal variables can be compared across different systems. One example, is the recent comparative work on national classroom curricula, per pupil expenditures, texts, and teacher training.[40] With the rapid expansion of formal schooling,[41] there are both variations and similarities. Math and science curricula are common throughout, and there is increased interest in modern foreign languages, depending on what the international powers are at the time.[42] Teacher training has also been compared across countries.[43] Evidence indicates that the national expenditures devoted by developing countries to educational systems have a major impact on student achievement.[44] Another example is seen in the general model developed by D. W. Livingston,[45] who set forth a group of activities that are key elements in any educational system: legal procedures, financing, staff development and maintenance, educational research, program control, centralization, provision of educational facilities, provision of auxiliary services, instruction, and administration. Livingston goes on to suggest interrelationships between these key elements. Variables unifying these elements—those on which data can be collected to fill in the frame—include enrollment, centralization, degree of control and from what sources, number and types of programs offered, auxiliary services offered, and so forth. Thus, in a cross-cultural study these elements provide the framework by which to compare countries.

Whatever theoretical perspective one holds, it can be agreed that education does not stand alone in society. Education must be considered in relation to other institutions in the society, and in relationship to that society's international environment. This is particularly important in the case of developing nations, many of which are in a postcolonial period and have inherited the former colonial power's system of education. In the following section, examples of institutional interdependency models are discussed.

CROSS-CULTURAL APPROACHES TO EDUCATIONAL SYSTEMS: WORLD AND INSTITUTIONAL INTERDEPENDENCE

Approaches to institutional interdependence can be global, as in the case of the "world system" perspective;[46] cross-national, as in the case of Williamson's[47] economic-political typology of societies or studies of curricula, knowledge, or tests; or national, with applicability to comparative studies. In the first, the world is conceptualized as a system with interdependent units. Internal and external change is linked to relationships between countries. Much research related to this theory has dealt with economic and political institutional characteristics, though cultural and ideological elements have been examined as well. More recently, this approach has been expanded to take an international view of forces that produce similar patterns of social change.

World System Analysis

A global perspective views education within the transnational social structure and system, and observes the effects of this system on subunits, or nation-states. Both ideological systems and organization affect the directions of educational development. For instance, most countries are caught up in the "myth of progress."[48] Since all states respond to this common global ideology, rates of educational development have been similar, with the underlying assumption that growth is good for society and the individual. Individual governments have expanded their role in financing and controlling education.

An example of world system analysis is seen in the theoretical model developed by Robert Arnove,[49] who uses "dependency theory" to explain the relationships of societies and education. A chain of exploitation exists at several levels: metropolitan (developed) countries over peripheral (developing) countries; centers of power in Third World countries over peripheral rural areas; and so on down to the village level. In this system, the peripheral areas may gain by getting needed resources, but the price is domination (by the metropolitan or center areas) over local affairs—curricula, texts, and reforms, for example.

To illustrate the world system of education, Arnove points to the many international organizations coordinating education worldwide: the Ford and Rockefeller foundations, the World Bank, UNESCO, UNICEF, and so on. These organizations have the power and money to promote new ideas or programs, some of which may be highly successful, others disappointing—as in the case of rural India, where emphasis on "nonformal education" gave the government an excuse not to provide classrooms for students.

Another example of international influence is seen in the fact that "66 percent of all East African higher education faculty have been Rockefeller Foundation scholars." To conflict theorists, this exemplifies American philanthropy shaping African universities to become pro-American and favorable toward American corporate needs.[50] Arnove also points to the "production of knowledge as big business." Thirty-four industrialized countries with 30 percent of the world's population, produce 81 percent of the world's book titles, for example.[51]

Education and Economic Institutions

Most countries believe that there is a relationship between education, economic development, and modernization. Governments act on this premise even though the facts do not always uphold it. They invest in education, and thus education reflects the political philosophy of a country, and the goals of the group in power. Many governments have the power to adopt or reject educational programs, or even to totally revamp the education system, as in China and Cuba during the communist revolutions. If the government establishes certain priorities for the society, the education system is likely to reflect these in curriculum, texts, and other aspects of the program.

In order to meet a country's goals, trained personnel are needed. Human capital theorists such as Gary Becker argue that individuals are like pieces of machinery—a capital good—and can increase their value in the labor market by increasing their education, especially training in occupational skills.[52] (This argument is challenged by Samuel Bowles and Herbert Gintis, among others, who contend that individuals are labor, not capital.) However, the system of supply and demand of educated persons does not always work perfectly, for several reasons. For instance, those from developing countries who receive a higher education will be among the elite. But the prestigious fields for which their training prepares them are not necessarily those where the country's needs lie. India, for instance, has many trained lawyers and engineers who cannot be absorbed into the system. This has caused a number of highly-skilled individuals to leave India. The assumption that high-level training will lead to economic development is not upheld when the training does not correspond with the country's needs.

Unfortunately, much of the supply-demand problem has arisen because of unsuitable models of education adopted from or left by colonial powers. Structures left from the colonial period still influence power relationships, as seen in the case of the lower status of women in former colonial societies (referred to as "gender colonization"). Until these relationships are altered, countries cannot use their human resources, especially women, to the fullest.[53] Multinational corporations hire large numbers of workers in Third World countries.[54] When both the host countries and the multinational corporations see the value of economic development in education, women's progress may be enhanced.

Illiteracy and low levels of schooling are the major social problems confronting the Third World. These problems can inhibit economic growth and political stability. Some emanate from Western colonial educational models, which favor elites. Various countries are breaking this unproductive mold and developing different definitions and forms of education, recognizing the diversity between national needs. Educational reforms relate to religious, social, economic, and political ideologies. Countries as varied as Iran, Nicaragua, and Tanzania have begun to move away from Western models.[55]

Many comparative educationists advocate new programs of education based on the countries' needs. Tanzania has received attention in this respect for its program called "education for self-reliance," advocated by Julius Nyerere to train people in needed skills. The assumption that if a country invests in education there will be corresponding economic growth may not hold up under scrutiny.

Some European countries import "foreigners" to work in their countries and educate them in their host and home languages with the idea that they can be sent home should the market economy have less demand. Other European countries, such as Sweden, France, Netherlands, and the United Kingdom, are making attempts at multicultural education.[56]

Stages of Economic Development and Educational Change

The development of educational systems can be related to three technological stages, according to King. In the first stage only a limited number of people, a privileged few, are involved in education—cloistered monks, for example. The second stage involves education that reaches farther, training a core of the population for factory work and the civil service and to be leaders of business, industry, and government. Third is the training required for the technological age, for the "communication society," where the relationship between education, work, and society is stressed.[57] Daniel Bell calls this the "post-industrial society"; an example is the United States, where one-half of the work force is involved in "information functions."[58]

Modernization Theory and "Modern Man." As a society moves through these stages, changes besides those in skill education and literacy take place. The values of the population and attitudes toward education and development also change, according to Alex Inkeles and David Smith's functional perspective of the modernization process. A society that puts emphasis on economic development needs what they call "modern man." Modern man has "those personal qualities which are likely to be inculcated by participation in large-scale modern productive enterprises such as the factory . . . if the factory is to operate efficiently and effectively.[59] These personal qualities are:

1. openness to new experience,
2. readiness for social change,
3. growth of opinion, disposition to hold or form opinions, awareness of diversity of opinions, and the placing of positive value on variations in opinion,

4.   interest in acquiring facts and information,
5.   acceptance of fixed schedules, punctuality, present-time orientation,
6.   belief that man can exert control over his environment, advance his goals,
7.   long-term planning in public affairs and private life,
8.   calculability or trust in world and others,
9.   valuing technical skill,
10. educational and occupational aspirations,
11. awareness of and respect for the dignity of others, and
12. understanding of production and decision-making process.

These 12 personal qualities were closely related to other factors in the individual's background experience and society: kinship and family, women's rights, religion, the role of the aged, politics, communications, consumerism, social stratification, and work commitment. This "modern man" places a high value on formal education and schooling in skills such as reading, writing, and mathematics, and has the skills and attitudes needed for economic development.

The Challenge of Becoming Modern.   The industrial revolution was a simple, gradual transition in its early stages. One development led naturally to another and to the increased investment of capital. Today, developing countries face pressures to make that transition rapidly. The technology is available, but economic development requires a change in the whole structure and value system of society. Subsistence agricultural societies must make enormous transitions to become "modern." Imagine for a moment a traditional, largely rural, agriculturally based country, its internal structure reliant as much on extended family (kin) relationships as on any central or even regional government. In order to modernize, leaders must gain support for massive and rather rapid changes involving all institutions in the society. Transportation and communication, health systems, economic planning, capital to build, an education system for many levels and types of knowledge and skills—all these will be needed. Developing the human capital necessary to carry out the economic development requires willingness to modernize and be mobile, motivation to pursue the education or training needed, and cooperation with the goals set by those in power. In other words, economic development depends on the attitudes and values of the population quite as much as on the technological machinery and necessary capital.

Dependency on rich nations may occur in the development process, for it takes massive input of capital and expertise for such a mobilization. Countries often bargain for aid from the developed world—socialist or capitalist—with the implicit understanding that they own some degree of allegiance to the provider.

Education and Political-Economic Institutional Systems

Major political-economic divisions between societies and broad generalizations about the implications of those divisions for education systems have been laid out by sociologists. Socialism ranges from Marxism to social democracy, capitalism from free market economies to state-regulated capitalism and the welfare state. Socialist models put special emphasis on "egalitarian and relevant" education, as we shall see in the Chinese example; capitalist models, predominant in Western Europe and the United States, tolerate inequality and often stress "classical" rather than relevant subjects, as we shall see in the case of Britain. In most cases, education systems reflect the position of the dominant group in society.

In a systems model that illustrates the interdependence of institutions, Williamson combines elements from the political and economic institutions. He contends that the education system reflects the political structure and distribution of power in society. It is also important to understand the historical comparative context of a country in order to encompass its past, present, and future environments. This is especially important in cases of postcolonial education systems. Williamson divides the world into four predominant types of societies.[60]

Developed Socialist Societies.   The former U.S.S.R. and other Eastern European societies must be understood as socialist societies whose special features flow historically from the program of industrial development followed by Lenin and Stalin. The Soviet system provided the model for the development of a number of agricultural countries.

Underdeveloped Socialist Societies.   These are peasant societies that are building socialist societies, with the former Soviet Union as the dominant model. Since most are predominantly agricultural, accumulating capital for industrialization is difficult. This has forced them into a dependency role in relation to the former U.S.S.R. Underdeveloped socialist societies face the structural problem of involving peasants and rural workers in revolutionary change; they must satisfy both immediate demands for a better life and longer-term demands for capital accumulation, which involves sacrifice and deferred consumption.

Advanced Capitalistic Societies.   Capitalism has been described in many ways and has undergone many changes over the years. The main features of capitalism as described in classical theory include the following:

1. private ownership of the means of production,
2. a free market in labor,
3. the concentration of production into factories and the incorporation of agriculture into the capitalist market,
4. production geared to a market and aimed at realizing profit,
5. the rationalization of economic life to principles of clear capital accounting, and
6. production geared to a world market.

A social scientist's views of changes in the capitalistic system, according to Williamson, include the following:

1. Capitalist industry has given way to corporate industry through the spreading of shared ownership and technical change.
2. The basis of social conflict is no longer the division of society into classes; rather it is the outcome of different social groups carrying different amounts of authority.
3. The anarchy [lack of control or planning] of the market mechanisms of capital formation have given way to planning in which the state plays a crucial role.[61]

These latter characteristics more closely represent "capitalist" societies in today's world.

Dependent Societies. These societies are characterized by an "interdependence of poverty, low income, low productivity, high mortality rates, urban squalor, economic dependence, political corruption and illiteracy," and account for about two-thirds of the world's population. In Williamson's view, economic backwardness is the result of poor societies having had their economic and social systems distorted by the overseas expansion of capitalist enterprise. Thus, poverty is not intrinsic to these societies, but results from historical factors such as colonialism. These societies often must become dependent on Western aid and expertise in their efforts to modernize, thus perpetuating their dependent status in the world economy.

From this economic-political typology comes the model shown in Figure 10-2, combining the level of economic development and the political orientation of sample countries. Williamson argues that "education is not a commodity, but a programme of action"[62] in that it has political and ideological dimensions. These help explain variations in form and content between countries. Models of change or development in education reflect these political-ideological underpinnings and define what a society is about and what actions it takes. Of course, there are varying degrees of support for the ideology of political groups in control, and this may in turn influence the support for education systems reflecting the dominant ideology. If a group in society feels that it is not receiving its share of resources, it may oppose the existing system.

This and similar typologies based on institutional interdependence are

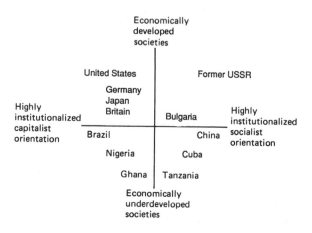

FIGURE 10-2
Models of development and type of economy.

Source: Williamson, Bill, *Education, Social Structure, and Development* (London: Macmillan, 1979), p. 36. Used with permission.

closely related to the open systems approach; they make paramount the relationship between the institution of education and other institutions in the national system and international environment. As socialist societies change, these models will need to be redesigned.

Education and the Institution of Religion

Within one country—even within one village—the relationship between education and religion is complex and sometimes contradictory. A few examples may clarify:

- *Northern Nigeria.* A Koranic school for boys stresses traditional religious beliefs, attitudes, and behavior patterns, and is not supportive of change. It exists next to a state-run village school, formerly run by Christian missionaries, which stresses "modern" attitudes and the importance of education in "getting ahead."
- *Northern Ireland.* The Catholic parochial schools and the state schools attended primarily by Protestants protect and perpetuate a distinction between segments of the society, and the hostilities between the two religious groups.
- *Iran.* Fundamentalist Muslim schools support the status quo and reflect the leadership and views of Muslim imams, or religious leaders.
- *United States.* Fundamentalist Christian schools stress some values opposed to the constitutional separation of church and state; they express the group's alienation from the technological society. Examples of the latter are controversies about textbooks and the questioning of certain scientific teachings on evolution.
- *Israel.* Religion and education work hand in hand to accomplish the goals of the state. Hebrew language and religious training provide unifying themes in an otherwise heterogeneous society.

Religion is often closely linked to a group's ethnic, racial, or national origins; therefore, it may provide for the group a point of stability in a time of rapid and confusing change in which norms break down—a situation sociologists refer to as "anomie." Attitudes toward change are reflected in religious schools, or in state schools where the religion is represented. If a change is consistent with the principles of the religion, the church may in fact be a leader in that change. However, religion may also serve to retard change, especially if the change threatens the principles of the belief system.

Family, Social Class, and Education

Much evidence exists documenting the importance of one's family background for educational achievement. The family is the primary social bond and purveyor of values. Here we develop an attitude toward ourselves and what we can become; we develop expectations concerning our education. It is in the environment created by the family that we receive informal education, and also encouragement, support, and models of behavior for formal educational pursuit. Deviation from this early influence probably means that some alternative model is available to us and is seen as realistic: The child may be influenced by a teacher, minister, or older child; the community may require children to attend school and encourage the brightest to continue, perhaps even providing support.

Recent findings of the IEA indicate that families may not have as strong an influence in societies with lower standards of living than the United States. In these countries the school offers more help to individuals, and school resources may be more beneficial in developing countries to offset the poverty of the home.[63] However, in developing "peripheral" communities, some families may be too poor to take advantage of educational opportunities; formal education may not be a realistic part of their lives. Thus, the cycle of poverty for some and great opportunity for others—both in individual countries and in the world—is perpetuated. Paulo Freire, a Brazilian who has worked with developing education for the poor, has written about what he sees as the hopelessness of the poor classes, caused in part by their inability to see beyond immediate problems and to look at the world critically. This inability—"semi-intransitive consciousness"[64]—allows a system of educationally elite landowners to dominate rural, uneducated peasants. The peasants adopt a fatalistic attitude about life, supported by supernatural religious beliefs, which serves to hold them in their inferior places.

As a society becomes more literate, certain attendant changes occur: urbanization, mobility, and modernization. These have a direct bearing on the family. Extended families begin to break down; the birth rate decreases and urbanization increases; it is difficult to house and feed a large family in an urban, mobile society. Women's status often changes with entry into urban life as many women enter the industrial work force and have fewer children. Again, changes in one part of society inevitably affect other parts.

In some societies, the position of one's family in the social structure affects both one's chances for education and one's place in an educational system developed to meet the needs of the various social classes—as perceived by a powerful elite. Turner has suggested that the "accepted mode of upward mobility shapes the school system."[65] He has compared English and American schools, concluding that the values in England support what he calls the "sponsored" form of mobility, where elites select elites and perpetuate themselves. This compares with "contest" mobility in America, where an individual's abilities are taken into account. These values underlie the institution of education in each country.

Parents in developed countries generally want to have a say in their children's education, to "manage" their school careers. For instance, in American schools, parents who manage the daily activities of their children raise the academic standing of their children. In Germany, parental management differs by the type of secondary school the child attends. In Japan, parents support schooling activities outside of the formal setting, which enhances examination preparation and future opportunities.[66] Parents want to choose the school their children will attend, including the religious affiliation, pedagogy, and curriculum. Minority and immigrant parents may make special efforts to influence their children's education.[67,68]

The interdependence between education and other institutions in society can help us focus on important variables as we attempt to understand very different educational systems.

Higher Education Around the World

In 1989, students in China occupied Tienanmen Square in a fight for democracy in that communist stronghold. The government routed out the dissidents; some leaders were imprisoned, others went underground. Students at the universities are now closely watched, and new students must go through intensive political indoctrination. Yet underneath the surface, the democratic movement still festers.[69] Institutions around the world, from China to South Africa, experience student activism over issues of concern. They also share common trends: rapid growth in demand, rising expectations, increased financial support, growing involvement in society through research and continuing education, diversification of the types of education offered, and student activism and disorder.

Around the world, higher education systems are changing, generally providing more access to a wider range of students and drawing financial support from more sources, including business and private contracts. The new European Community will result in more collaboration and internationalizing of higher education in European countries.[70,71] Student exchanges are increasing around the world. Study results of exchange students from the United States indicate that they are more interested in current events and international affairs, and have increased appreciation for foreign cultures.[72]

Some countries are losing their best and brightest when they cannot provide job opportunities after education. This "brain drain" means that record numbers are going abroad for education and job opportunities. In the United States, 23 percent of doctorates in 1990 were awarded to temporary residents.[73] Note the drop in the number of doctorates awarded to Americans compared with doctorates being granted by U.S. universities to foreign students.[74]

For many countries struggling to advance, some forms of higher education may be inappropriate. Until developing countries can absorb their graduates, the brain drain will remove some of the young talent. Many students, especially in developed countries, are demanding a more vocationally oriented, practical education to help them get jobs. These societal needs and institutional demands may change the structure of higher education.

CASE STUDIES OF EDUCATIONAL SYSTEMS

Educational systems in newly developed nation-states have developed along the same lines as the first European systems. Education was seen as a way to unify and give identity to the nation-states, needed for individual and national progress.[75]

Ramirez and Boli argue that economic competition between states has caused the pressure for all nations to organize education systems in similar ways, leading to the universality of state schooling and similarities between systems. Pressures from the economically integrated and dependent developed world have caused newer nations to commit themselves to state-funded mass education models as part of nation building.[76] This trend is seen in the spread of common national curricula.

The worldwide growth of similar education systems is seen in increased enrollments; establishment of educational ministries; compulsory education laws; increasing state funds; educational opportunity for all, including women and minorities; and schools serving the purpose of a socializing agent.

Despite this world interrelationship, social scientists must be cautious not to assume that all systems are similar because of cross-national pressures and dominant powers. Each system brings its own country's unique culture into the system, even though education may be influenced by colonial models and world trends.[77]

In the following case examples we see both the similarities and the differences in three educational systems. These case studies represent systems that fall into different sectors (see Figure 10-3) of Williamson's political-economic typology.[78] Britain is located in the economically developed countries' sector, with a political system more clearly capitalistic than socialistic in orientation. China represents a system in the socialist tradition. Finally, Ghana, a former colony of Britain, is economically dependent and developing along capitalistic political lines.

Discussions of each country will include the following: the historical background leading up to the present system; the national goals for the education system; structural aspects of education, such as the number of years of schooling and type of curriculum; equality or inequality in the education system; and higher education.

Education in Britain

Development of Education in Britain. Britain is the land of monarchy, peerages and nobility, pomp and circumstance, a land that once ruled one-third of the world. It is also a land that was devastated by two world wars, that experienced extreme poverty in the wake of industrial prosperity, and that has a legacy of immigrants from former colonies who have moved to Britain and must be educated and integrated into the society.

Britain was one of the early industrialized and urbanized countries. The process took place gradually, aided by a mobile peasantry able to provide the needed labor, and by an international trade market anxious to buy goods. During this evolution, the class structure in Britain was strengthened and was reflected in the education system.

Marxist interpreters have described the development of education in Britain as serving the needs of the elite. An educated mass was needed for the expansion of capitalism, with a trained labor force for various levels of industry. Morality, obedience, and frugality could be taught through the schools and these goals were reflected in curricula. The subordination of the lower orders had several aims—political control, the suppression of crime and

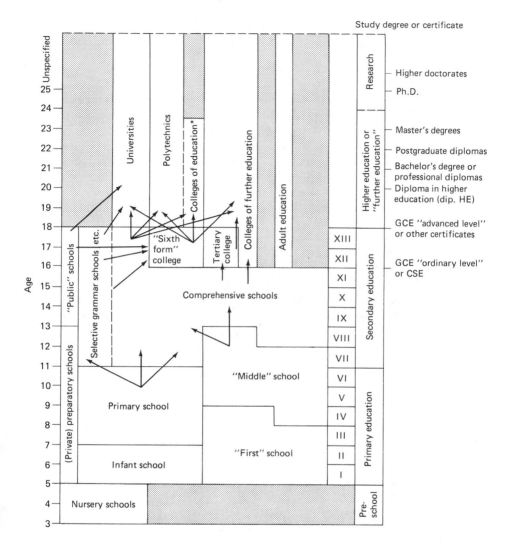

FIGURE 10-3   School system in England and Wales: in transition during the 1970s and 1980s. The number of colleges of education was rapidly reduced as many merged with polytechnics or, alternatively, took on a new role as institutes of higher education.

Source: King, Edmund J., *Other Schools and Ours: Comparative Studies for Today,* 5th ed. (London: Holt, Rinehart, and Winston, 1979), p. 177.

drunkenness, the propagation of Christian morality, and preparing the lower orders for a life of industry and toil.[79]

As the working classes grew and became more organized, they demanded greater access to education, among other rights. This was to the advantage of the elite, who needed an ever more sophisticated and skilled labor force. First, secondary education opened to the working class, and compulsory attendance was eventually extended to 11 years, beginning at age 5. Parents were and are required to see that their children receive an education for this period. During the period after World War II, education was free for all—even university, if one qualified. But the school divisions still perpetuated class distinctions: grammar schools; secondary comprehensive schools with academic programs; and secondary technical schools representing trade-training programs. Increased access to higher education took place in the 1960s with the establishment of additional universities, polytechnics, colleges, and the Open University.

Educational goals for the elite and middle class were a different matter. English "public schools," similar to private schools in many countries and too expensive for the commoner, served those who wished to retain a social distinction, and they still do. These schools provide both excellent academic foundations and also training in the art of being "ladies and gentlemen," fostering the mannerisms and speech patterns typical of the elite. They give the well-rounded education necessary to pass entrance exams for elite universities such as Oxford and Cambridge. A disproportionate number of senior civil servants and business and professional leaders were and are drawn from these schools, although highly qualified students from lower classes have some chance to attend elite schools as scholarship students.

Because of high unemployment, especially among the young who leave school at age 16, "post-compulsory" sixth-form education has been instituted to prepare young adults for a vocation or to continue college training. Work-study plans have also been proposed. There are government-sponsored training programs, but only a small proportion of those in need can be accommodated. Thus, large numbers of youth are leaving school disillusioned and with little hope of employment.

Control and Decision Making in Education.   Historically, local control has been valued in Britain, and it still is. The national government Department of Education and Science carries out national research and planning, and recommends major revisions in the structure of education, but the day-to-day decisions and running of the school are retained by local communities. "Local Education Authorities (LEA) have wide-ranging power and duties covering the whole of education (except universities), and extending from pre-school to higher education. . . ."[80] Each school has a governing body ideally consisting of equal numbers of local authority representatives, school staff including the head teacher, elected parents, students in older classes, and community representatives; LEAs have responsibility for the management of schools and the proper conduct of administrators. Both county (state-supported) and voluntary (usually church) schools are under the jurisdiction of LEAs.

Structure of the Education System.   State-supported British infant and primary schools have received a great deal of attention, and have provided models for many elementary schools in the United States and around the world. The widely read Plowden Report[81] (1967) detailed the system of British primary education and evaluated its problems. These schools are noted for their informal and open approaches to education. The visitor to a British primary school has the feeling of entering a child's world. From the ceiling hang mobiles; the walls are covered with artwork; books and educational toys line the walls. Classroom activities are minimally structured, with emphasis on individualized work. Curricula include plenty of active time, music, art, time for special projects, and a range of opportunities for TV education, theater trips, and museum visits.

Figure 10-3 diagrams the structural levels of British education. Although several aspects of the system are in transition, this chart gives a general idea of the stages or levels through which a student passes.

Some 80 percent of the secondary school students attend comprehensive schools, which were formed in the 1970s to counter the streaming of children into elite and working-class schools. They combine what were formerly grammar (more academic) and secondary-modern schools. The remaining 20 percent go to the few remaining state grammar schools or to "public" schools. Within comprehensive schools there is some differentiation between students on the basis of academic versus vocational tracks, but the stated goal is to identify talent and allow children to develop their capabilities.

"Public" schools—such as Eton, Harrow, Rugby, Winchester, and other elite secondary schools—serve a unique role. Eton, for instance, is set in a small town a short distance from Windsor Castle. The young men can be seen walking purposefully, surrounded by stately old buildings alive with English tradition. "You are destined to be a statesman and gentleman," Eton seems to say to its inhabitants. Following rigid rituals and ceremonies and dressed in their uniform of black-and-white pin-striped trousers, white bow ties, black vests and waistcoats, and braided tailcoat, an Eton lad would never be mistaken for a comprehensive school student.[82]

Composition of British Schools. In 1991, there were 55.5 million people in the United Kingdom (including Northern Ireland), an area the size of the state of Oregon. Of this population, 9.2 million are schoolchildren attending 30,500 state secondary schools and 2,500 independent schools. About 1.5 million students aged 16 and older are full-time students or "sandwich" students, both working and going to school. (For Europe, this is a relatively low number of students.) Nine-tenths of students go to comprehensive schools, and the remainder go to grammar or secondary modern schools.[83]

The Education Reform Act of 1988 reflects international pressures for change. The primary impact is that all schools will follow a common curriculum, prescribed by law, in ten subjects: English, mathematics, science, technology, a modern foreign language, history, geography, art, music, and physical education.[84] Implementation is currently taking place.

Effective schools in Britain share many characteristics with effective schools in other countries. A study conducted in London singled out characteristics of effective primary schools: small school and class size, teacher planning periods and involvement in curriculum planning, lesson plans, progress reports on each child, low turnover of all school personnel and students, and an orderly work environment.[85]

Exams and Credentials.   Britain is a highly "credentialed" society, placing great emphasis on exams and certificates. Exams are given in subject areas. At about age 16, students take the General Certificate of Secondary Education in major subjects such as mathematics and literature: following two more years of study, students take Advanced or A-level exams; between these two are the AS exams, equivalent to two General Certificate exams or one A-level exam. Universities generally require three A-level exams for entrance.

There is yet another very prestigious exam—the International Baccalaureate—taken by sixth-form (16- to 18-year-old) students, and requiring competence in six subject areas: one's native tongue, a foreign language, the study of man (history, geography, social science, or philosophy), experimental science, mathematics, and an art or advanced work in one area.

Critics argue that those who can afford the "elite" education are best prepared for A-levels and elite-university entrance exams, and that the exam system helps perpetuate the class system.

Inequality in Education and Occupational Mobility.   Great strides have been made toward providing opportunity for students of all social backgrounds to move as far as possible in the education system. However, there are at least two kinds of problems encountered in this endeavor. The Plowden Report and more recent studies point up the special problems of deprived neighborhoods such as inner-city areas where health and housing standards are low, and child mortality high; the Plowden Report recommended that schools in these blighted areas be given extra funds from the 7 percent national educational budget. Living in these areas are many from immigrant groups and those who fall into the poorest classes of society. The report also said that educational disadvantage cannot be solved in schools alone.[86]

Another problem inhibiting mobility is the distinction between "public" schools and state-supported schools. With the tradition behind the elite schools and the excellent education they provide, plus the tendency for elite universities and government and industry to fill their top ranks with graduates of these schools, mobility at the top remains the prerogative of a limited, select group. Education reflects the history and traditions built up over long periods in Britain. Complete equality seems impossible without altering the basic structure of the education system.

What does educational inequality mean for occupational attainment? Depending on the measures used, we can generally say that one's class origins are more important in Britain than in the United States in occupational attainment. In the United States, educational attainment is more important, especially for one's first job placement.[87] However, the degree of openness or mobility is about the same when we look at occupational status ten to 20 years after labor force entry; but the process of career mobility in the two countries differs.[88]

Higher Education in Great Britain: Elite Versus Mass Education.   Oxford and Cambridge universities—prestigious institutions with spires, courtyards, and long traditions—have been the models for educational systems around the world. Classical, traditional education can be obtained from robed dons behind the cloistered walls. Students are affiliated with a college in the university.

For centuries these universities provided access to high positions and perpetuated the intellectual elite. With the worldwide trend toward more access to all levels of education by all groups in society, and the need for a more educated populace to fill the technical positions in an industrialized society, several changes have occurred: The great universities opened their doors a crack to let in larger numbers of qualified students from state-supported schools, and other institutes and colleges were developed to meet growing needs for trained personnel. University access is still limited, and children of professionals stand a much better chance of acceptance than do those from lower socioeconomic levels. Universities are reserved for the best students, while the other institutions of higher education give access to those who fail university entrance or who wish to pursue specialized studies. There are also differences in treatment of female and male faculty at universities. Women are paid an average of $3,520 less than men, regardless of age and discipline.[89]

A number of polytechnics were developed, beginning in 1966, to meet the need for trained engineers, technical experts, and technicians. They are closely associated with business and industry. In addition, there are a number of specialized, prestigious institutions.

Another development in British higher education is the Open University. Begun in 1971 to give opportunity to people who might not otherwise be able to attend university—teachers, those working, those at home—the idea caught on to the extent that, by 1976, the Open University received about 53,000 applications and was enrolling up to 20,000 students a year. The Open University currently enrolls about 24,500 new students a year, including 5,900 master's and 625 doctoral students.[90] Open University students pay tuition and sign up for courses. They tune in to lectures on British Broadcasting Corporation (BBC) radio or TV. Texts are developed for the courses, and assignments are sent to tutors who correct and return them. At the end of the year students take examinations. A wide range of courses is offered through the Open University, with most degrees being given in general arts and science. The average student takes six years to complete a degree, compared with three or four years for students in residence on a campus, and the dropout rate is higher than at campuses.

The number of Open University students is growing rapidly as the program enters its third decade, and is expected to increase from the current 45,000 to 95,000 by the year 2000. Open University has graduated 100,000 students, mostly adult homemakers and full-time employees wishing to upgrading credentials.[91]

Recently, British campuses have faced a significant increase in enrollments—a projected 20 percent between 1991 and 1994—in part owing to reduced job opportunities. Changes being initiated to help cope with the increased demand are familiar: larger classes, use of teaching assistants, and availability of intensive "24-month degrees" in some fields of study that normally take three years to complete.[92] In the future Britain will face pressures to open its educational system further and provide opportunities for the many unemployed working-class and immigrant members of the society.

Education in the People's Republic of China

China's closed door policy kept the West out for many years. However, recently China opened its doors again to the West. This huge country whose population is projected to reach 1.275 billion in 2000, and which covers almost a quarter of the world's land surface, is selectively allowing its officials and scholars to make forays into the world outside, and now admits both curious tourists and foreign scholars into the vast reaches of China.

Recent Historical Events Affecting Education.   Several key dates mark major transitions in China: In 1949, the Chinese Communist Party won national power and declared the founding of the People's Republic of China. At this time the borders closed to the outside world. In 1976, Chairman Mao (Mao Tse-tung) died; this event ushered in a new era of changing policies and programs, and further opened China's borders to the outside world.

In 1989, protests led by university students were forcefully repressed, and contacts with Western countries were curtailed. The situation has eased somewhat recently. Though the Chinese have some suspicions about the motivations of Westerners, most exchanges are returning to prerevolution levels. Social sciences research, however, is restricted because of China's suspicions that the West is spying on China's social situation.[93]

No period can be ignored in reviewing Chinese education; each has been a reaction to the previous era, yet each reflects the changing political-economic scene. Today, tensions can be seen between four competing purposes of education in China: "to modernize the economy, to provide sources for education as a universal citizen right, to establish paths for the recruitment and circulation of elites, and to share a political ideology that reformulates varying political interests. . . ."[94]

Status and Structure of Education in China.   A typical day in a Chinese elementary school includes courses in Chinese, math, physical education, music, drawing, painting, and moral (political) education. Language study takes up to one-third of the day. The day starts with an exercise period, followed by four periods in the morning. There is a two-hour break for lunch and rest, followed by three more periods. After school, which ends about 4:00 P.M., some students stay for special help. After school on Saturday morning there are organized activities such as sports.[95] Foreign language study begins in third grade; history, geography, and science begin in fourth through sixth grade. Classes range in size from 40 to 55 students.

According to Chinese statistics, 98 percent of primary-aged children attend school. Forty percent of secondary-aged children attend school, with boys outnumbering girls by a small percentage.[96] About 5 percent of the 7 million high school graduates in China enter university, and these students compete for scholarships to pay for their education. Table 10-1 shows the status of educational institutions in China.

China's goal to have 75 percent of the population receiving nine years of compulsory education by 1995 is realistic, especially in urban areas. Children will attend primary school from 7 to 12 years (some will begin younger) and secondary school from 12 to 17 years.[97,98] China is also concerned about improving adult literacy, seeing this as essential for economic growth.[99] As far back as 1949, Chairman Mao said: "Sweeping away illiteracy from 80 percent of the population is an important mission for New China. We must work energetically to realize this goal, so that workers and peasants can easily grasp scientific learning [and] become weapons for [class] struggle and [socialist] construction—complete and developed weapons for the people's democratic dictatorship."[100] Schools in China have been the site for political indoctrination,[101] and at times the secondary curriculum focused on industrial and agricultural courses.

Authority structures in Chinese schools are based on personal ties and networks, and loyalty to the political system. Because the party leadership perceived weaknesses in education, structural changes are taking place in the educational system. These include the growing importance of local districts obtaining their own financial resources for schools, expansion of vocational and technical learning, and demands for new teaching techniques to improve creativity and independence.[102] "The political climate of the early 1990s formally reasserts the authority of the Party, including its role in running the schools. Yet the economic and demographic pressures that prompted changes in authority relations have not subsided."[103]

Recent changes in government policy concerning education make the picture muddled. For instance, with the move toward individual rather than

TABLE 10-1   Education in China

	Institutions	Full-Time Teachers (Thousands)	Students (Thousands)
Kindergartens	166,526	491	12,571
Primary schools	853,740	5,369	135,571
Lower secondary schools	75,867	2,097	38,643
Upper secondary schools	17,847	459	6,898
Secondary technical schools	2,293	118	811
Teacher-training schools	1,008	42	511
Agricultural schools	4,622	55	907
Vocational schools	2,380	48	837
Special schools	330	6	39
Higher education	902	315	1,443

Source: U.S. Area Handbook, *People's Republic of China* (Washington, D.C.: U.S. State Department, 1983).

collective responsibility has come an emphasis on rural self-sufficiency, including local funding of rural schools. But many children have left school to participate in individual family money-making ventures.

Higher Education in PRC.   China has long held the belief that education and the economy are integrally linked. Hence, most changes have reflected current thinking along these lines. Higher education is undergoing radical change, with increased emphasis on science, applied research, foreign languages, the emergence of business schools, and restructuring of the management of education in the form of a Western model of scientific management. How long these measures will last is uncertain in the rapidly changing environment of Chinese education.

During the Cultural Revolution the Ministry of Education in China was dismantled; it was reestablished in 1975. Major changes began in 1976, with the separation of politics and higher education decision making—putting education in the hands of academics, the Ministry, and local committees. The Ministry controlled programs, curricula, and admissions. In May 1985, a State Council Education Commission replaced the Ministry to allow for closer regional control and to reflect the needs of regions.[104]

Emphasis on applied research has led to a professorate concerned with contract research more than pure research or teaching. Some have pointed out the danger of this shortcoming. Joint university projects with other countries—the United States, Canada, Japan, and Western Europe—are often initiated by the Chinese and generally involve mutual sharing and respect rather than control by the industrialized; yet there is concern that the "foreigners" do not understand the culture with which they are interacting.[105]

Universities have been under the strictest controls and intense political indoctrination since restrictions after the fall of the Maoist Gang of Four in 1976.[106] After the rebellious "counterrevolutionaries" protested at Tienanmen Square, students have been required to study ideology and be repoliticized.[107] Freshmen at Beijing University are required to serve in the military for one year.[108] Unhappy students have been sent to remote factories to gain "socialist experience."[109]

Efforts to contain Western influence take the form of curtailed exchanges, often available only after five years of work; repoliticalization programs; and limits on the type of research allowed. The government is trying to seek a balance between the need for scholars and Western knowledge, and the need for loyalty and indoctrination; one still sees patterns of patron-client relations, where political rulers offer prestige, privilege, and protection in return for support from scholars.[110] It remains to be seen whether allowing intellectuals freedom to pursue their research is compatible with repressing independence and democracy.

China has had a period of independence from the influence of other nations; however, much of Africa labors under a colonial legacy that has major implications for education.

History of Education in Colonial Africa

In the nineteenth and early twentieth centuries, Europeans conquered most of Africa. Ostensibly the purposes were ending the slave trade, spreading Christianity and civilization, and opening the area for trade. Hardly mentioned were the expansion to new lands and the wealth of raw products that the colonial powers enjoyed.

Early in the colonial period, missionaries set up schools to teach Christianity and Bible studies. Colonial governments also organized schools according to the mother country's system of education. Their purpose was to teach the language of the colonizing power and develop a cadre of Africans to help fill lower posts in colonial administration, as well as to develop understanding and acceptance of European-style law and order. Many Europeans wanted to limit African education to technical, vocational, and agricultural skills, which would be helpful to them in exploiting the resources of the countries. However, Africans saw this type of training as an attempt to keep them in their places, and sought the academic education of the Western elite. Some went abroad to receive this training, with European encouragement.

Those few Africans who moved up the colonial education ladder adopted European views and worked for colonial administration. They were often alienated from their own people and traditions, strangers in their own lands. With independence, some of these same European-educated Africans became postcolonial leaders; their proposals were often greeted with skepticism by the people.

History of Ghanaian Education.   The Portuguese, the Dutch, the Danes, and then the British ruled the "Gold Coast," as Ghana was called. It was a prize colony, rich in mineral resources and later valued for its cocoa plantations. During their rule from 1844 to 1957, the British developed trade relations with other countries; when it achieved independence in 1957 Ghana was economically stable and its institutions were based on British models. However, since independence three different governments have ruled and been overthrown. This political instability has in turn affected the institutions in society, including education; 1961–66 was period of rapid expansion of education at all levels in Ghana. After 1966, however, enrollment in public primary schools in many parts of the country declined steadily.[111]

The early rapid growth was curtailed when a military government took over in 1966. The government ordered a study of the system, which resulted in the following recommendations: "reorganizing and adopting new approaches to teacher training; creating new places at secondary Form I level and strengthening the secondary base in advance of university expansion; and considering the country's needs in the development of technical education."[112] However, there has been little change in the education system structure since 1966. This could be related to mistrust of the government by the people, the rich-poor division in the population, lack of opportunity, or the government's lack of planning and movement in the area of education. Enrollments showed a peak of 66.8 percent in 1965 for children from 6 to 11 years, and a drop of almost 14 percent for this age group in a seven-year period to 1972.

In 1974 the government again designed an experimental structure for education. However, 90 percent of students will follow the old system. By 1983 the primary school enrollment during the first six years of school was 79 percent (89 percent of boys, 70 percent of girls); middle schools enrolled 38 percent of the school-aged children (48 percent of boys, 28 percent of girls). Today, approximately 71 percent of boys and 63 percent of girls are enrolled in primary school, 40 percent and 32 percent, respectively, in secondary school. Only 2 percent go on to higher levels of education, and these figures are better than those for many other African countries.[113]

The illiteracy rate in Africa is 52.7 percent, but with overwhelming problems of poverty and hunger, literacy takes a back seat. However, Third World countries cannot compete with developed countries if their populations are illiterate. Some countries have had elimination of illiteracy in their goals. For instance, in both Tanzania and China, motivation to reduce illiteracy has had both political and economic objectives.[114]

Forms of Education.   Education existed in Ghana and other African nations long before modern boundaries and European systems were introduced. It is important to distinguish, therefore, between traditional and formal education in many African countries.

> There were systems of education in Africa before the colonial period; for every community must have a way of passing on to the young its accumulated knowledge to enable them to play adult roles and so ensure the survival of their offspring, and the continuity of the community.
>
> In African communities, the older generation passed on to the young the knowledge, the skills, the mode of behaviour and the beliefs they should have for playing their social roles in adult life.
>
> The young were taught how to cope with their environments; how to farm, or hunt, or fish, or prepare food, or build a house, or run a home. They were taught the language and manners, and generally the culture of the community. The methods were informal, the young learnt by participating in activities alongside their elders. They learnt by listening, by watching, by doing. In many practical ways they learnt how to live as members of their community.[115]

Many educators are asking how traditional systems can be used as a base for meeting the educational needs of modernizing countries. Options range from continuing French, English, or other colonial models, to developing completely new indigenous types of education. Formal schooling is still primarily for the urban elite. The question becomes this: What kind of education to offer in rural peasant communities?

"Nonformal" education and "basic" education have received the attention of many African educators. They are distinguished from "formal school" by the following facts:

1. (Formal) schooling is just a part of education.
2. Education cannot be conceived of as taking place at certain ages, stages, times and places. It is always unfinished business.
3. Educational opportunities, formal and non-formal, must relate to each other both horizontally (e.g., school, home, mosque, media, work experience) and vertically throughout the different stages of a learner's life.
4. There are many paths to learning, no one path being better or worse than another, only more efficient or more appropriate.
5. Methods, materials, and delivery systems must also vary to suit purposes and means available.[116]

"Nonformal" and "basic" education seem to work together. Neither puts age or time strictures on education; both provide many varied paths to education, individual attainment of goals, and lifelong learning; and both involve various agencies—family, school, community. Subjects range from functional literacy to knowledge of processes such as health and sanitation; crops and animals; and household skills, including caring for the sick, making clothes, and civic knowledge. An attempt at nonformal, grass-roots education is seen in the Community Development experiment, which has been tried in several communities. Informal courses or training in preventive medicine, health, nutrition, cooking, sewing, and other skills are made available to any person in the villages. Another example of nonformal education is the Mancell Girls' Vocational Institute in Kumasi for women aged 13 to 28. Over 1,000 students have been enrolled in one-year courses in "skills required for self-development and for jobs in laundry, baking, sewing, dressmaking, designing, and catering."[117] Other programs have been developed to preserve African ways but teach Western thought.

A related curriculum issue has to do with the language used for teaching. If the former colonial power's language is used, some feel that it imposes "linguistic imperialism on the country"; but if a native tongue is used, one group might gain dominance over another. Therefore, several countries are promoting learning for each group in its mother tongue to preserve cultural diversity and avoid conflicts.[118]

This question remains: Will "basic" or "nonformal" education and mother-tongue teaching meet the needs of individuals and countries, or will their implementation perpetuate the rich-poor dichotomy without significantly raising the developing countries from the poverty level? For many countries, the question is how to maximize development and still preserve national cultures and traditions.

Structure of the Ghanaian Education System. Children in Ghana enter school at age 6. Some go on to secondary school at age 12, which lasts five years (Figure 10-4). The stated goal is compulsory education for ten years, but Ghana has a long way to go to achieve literacy.

The subjects taught in secondary schools generally follow the British model: language, mathematics, general science, social studies, religious educa-

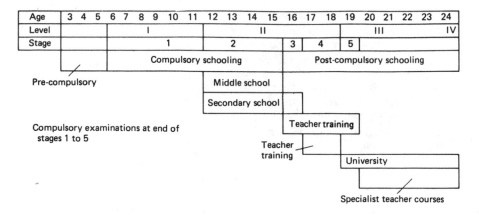

FIGURE 10-4   Structure of the education system in Ghana.

Source: Country Education Profiles (Paris: UNESCO, Internal Bureau of Education), p. 34.

tion, and physical education. The exception is "cultural and practical activities," which focus on African heritage and necessary skills for daily life. Examinations also follow the British model. Institutions for higher education include universities, technical and craft institutes, polytechnics, and vocational schools. Vocational training is also provided in some communities outside the formal school setting.

Equality of Opportunity in Ghanaian Education.   Sons and daughters of the urban elite have a disproportionate share of places in education as one progresses upward through the system; this includes places as teachers. However, there is now an economic motivation for basic education for all—to be competitive in the world and achieve social equality.[119]

The differences between the elite and the masses are to some extent regional. For instance, in northern Ghana, 80 percent of the people have never been to school. Here is an example of problems faced by one tribal group in northern Ghana, the Sisala:

> . . . [T]he conditions to which the younger generation of educated Sisala must adjust are more severe and frustrating, particularly in respect to educational mobility. Most of the middle school graduates apply for entrance into the teacher training colleges and secondary schools, but few are able to qualify. This is due not only to the nationwide competition but also to political patronage and corruption. Gifts or "dashes" to such politicians in return for favors rendered is an all-too-common occurrence which has created an attitude of cynicism among members of the younger generation. Even in those cases in which students do qualify, financial assistance is frequently a problem, for many parents either are unable to furnish the necessary funds, or because of their lack of understanding, feel that their children have had enough education and should return to help their families. All these factors serve to limit the possibilities for educational advancement.[120]

One final point on the topic of equality: Ability to speak the English language has become a potent force of "academic colonialism," separating the educated elite from the rural illiterate.[121]

While each African system is unique, some general observations apply to many postcolonial countries. Education was seen as a high priority following independence from colonial control, for it was thought that through education countries could become truly independent of foreign domination and provide the indigenous leadership needed for technological development, industrialization, business, and politics in the long push toward modernization. The educated elite of these countries could afford to send their children abroad, where they often pursued prestigious fields such as engineering or law (but also Greek and Latin, less directly useful in modernizing a country). Returning students brought with them not only their expertise but also foreign ideologies and models for curricula. However, the development of technical and agricultural skills, emphasis on preventive medicine within the context of traditional tribal medicine, and integration of new knowledge with existing values and traditions may be more relevant to the needs of the nations than European models of education.

Some members of the African elite rejected their own countries' traditional values, cultural uniqueness, and tribal ties in favor of Western models. Others became dissatisfied and alienated because they were overeducated for the available jobs. There is high prestige in being a lawyer or an engineer, but a developing country can absorb only a limited number of them. It might better use schoolteachers and agricultural technicians.

In many Third World countries such as those in West Africa, international funding agencies have attempted to direct the development of education. However well-intended the efforts, these, too, may cause problems: "educational development agency policies that tend to emphasize agency goals rather than country needs; development projects; multiple development agency competition for control of the education sector; and the competition within and among development sectors for access to agency funding." These factors result in "loose coupling" or fractionalization of education.[122]

Higher Education.   Africa has many fine universities, some of which have difficulty integrating their programs into life on the continent.[123] Others, offer a combination of indigenous and Western education. For instance, the University of Ghana at Accra offers some excellent programs in traditional African arts, music, dance, and oral traditions in literature, as well as courses of study patterned after European models. In Nigeria, the plan is to improve the technological base by providing an appropriate mix of students, with 60 percent in sciences and 40 percent in arts, but reality is far from these figures. Some universities are centers of political activity, spearheading pro-democracy drives that sometimes result in violence.[124] Meanwhile, a high percentage of university graduates are disillusioned because they cannot find jobs.[125]

In the future, African leaders searching for ways to improve standards of living will be looking at new models of education. While political factors may prevent rapid changes in educational systems, there is greater awareness of the problems, and alternative educational models are becoming more prevalent.

Children around the world receive some formal education, but the amount and circumstances vary greatly depending on the country's culture and place in the world political-economic system.

SUMMARY

This chapter is about education around the world. It covers theoretical approaches, typologies, and examples of three educational systems in very different societies.

I. Cross-Cultural Educational Studies

The field of cross-cultural educational studies has been largely descriptive in the past, using case studies of selected countries. Theories and typologies are advancing our knowledge of the area. The systems approach helps us conceptualize the links between countries. One approach to comparative studies has been assessment of achievement in different subject areas across societies.

II. Theoretical Perspectives and Typologies in Comparative Education

Recent theoretical approaches contrast functional and conflict theoretical approaches; several of these focus on the relationship between educational and economic growth and development. Earlier theories focused on changing individuals to fit modern society. However, this approach has been criticized for a number of reasons.

Cross-cultural studies all into several types: contrasting rich and poor nations, studying the internal structures of educational systems, and studies of institutional interdependence.

III. Cross-Cultural Approaches to Educational Systems: Institutional Interdependence

Institutional interdependence means that each institution is affected by each other institution. A change in one means that adaptations will be necessary in others. World system analysis stresses the interdependence of nations of the world, with "metropolitan" centers and nations dominating over "peripheral" areas.

In comparing nations, most emphasis has been put on political-economic systems as they influence educational systems. Williamson's typology illustrates this point. Relationships of education to religion and family were discussed. Examples of "world environment" were given.

Higher education structures have ranged from Western forms to indigenous models. A problem faced by some countries is that elite students are educated in foreign countries and bring back Western political and legal models; these models are not necessarily best for countries struggling with development and literacy. Also, some of the educated elite may not find need for their skills in their developing countries and may become alienated.

IV. Case Studies of Educational Systems

Three countries' systems of education were discussed—those of Britain, the People's Republic of China, and Ghana. Each exemplified some unique features and problems.

PUTTING SOCIOLOGY TO WORK

1. Talk to several international students about educational systems in their countries. Ask about the structure, access for various groups and classes of students, and how their systems differ from that of the United States.
2. Find out how you would be educated in your major field if you were studying in another country of your choice.
3. Select two developing countries, one capitalist, the other socialist. How do their educational systems differ? Can this be attributed to their political ideologies?
4. Put yourself in the position of a minister of education in a developing country. What would be your primary concerns in planning the educational program?
5. Pose a question about cross-cultural educational systems. Which of the theoretical approaches would be useful in dealing with your question?

NOTES

[1] Epstein, Erwin H., "The Problematic Meaning of 'Comparison' in Comparative Education," in Jurgen Schriewer and Brian Holmes (eds.), *Theories and Methods in Comparative Education* (Frankfurt am Main: Peter Lang, 1988), pp. 3–23.

[2] Altbach, Philip G., and Gail P. Kelly (eds.), *New Approaches to Comparative Education* (Chicago: University of Chicago Press, 1986).

[3] King, Edmund J., *Other Schools and Ours: Comparative Studies for Today,* 5th ed. (London: Holt, Rinehart & Winston, 1979), p. 32.

[4] Hall, W.D. (ed.), *Comparative Education: Contemporary Issues and Trends* (London: Jessica Kingsley, 1990).

[5] Altbach, Philip G., "Trends in Comparative Education," *Comparative Education Review,* Vol. 35, No. 3, August 1991, pp. 491–507.

[6] *Second International Mathematics Study: Summary Report for the United States,* National Center for Educational Statistics (Washington, D.C.: U.S. Department of Education, May 1985).

[7] Cowen, Robert, "Comparative Education in Europe: A Note," *Comparative Education Review,* Vol. 24, 1980, pp. 98–108.

[8] Altbach, "Trends in Comparative Education," p. 506.

[9] Benavot, Aaron, *et al.,* "Knowledge for the Masses: World Models and National Curricula: 1920–1986," *American Sociological Review,* Vol. 56, No. 1, February 1991, pp. 85–100.

[10] Passow, A. Harry. *et al., The National Case Study: An Empirical Comparative Study of Twenty-One Educational Systems* (New York: Wiley, 1976), pp. 12–13.

[11] *Ibid.,* p. 12.

[12] Inkeles, Alex, "National Differences in Scholastic Performance," in Altbach, Philip G., Robert F. Arnove, and Gail P. Kelly, *Comparative Education* (New York: Macmillan, 1982) pp. 210–31 (esp. p. 228).

[13] Educational Testing Service, "Learning Mathematics" and "Learning Science" (Princeton, N.J.: Center for the Assessment of Educational Progress, 1992).

[14] Slomczynski, Kazimierz M., and Tadeusz K. Krauze, "The Meritocratic Relationship Between Formal Education and Occupational Status: A Cross-National Analysis," paper presented for XIth World Congress of Sociology, New Delhi, August 1986.

[15] Welch, Anthony, "Knowledge and Legitimation in Comparative Education," *Comparative Education Review*, Vol. 35, No. 3, pp. 508–31.

[16] Krauze, Tadeusz, and K. M. Slomczynski, "How Far to Meritocracy? Empirical Tests of a Controversial Thesis," *Social Forces*, Vol. 63, No. 3, 1985, pp. 623–42.

[17] Morgan, William R., and J. Michael Armer, "Islamic and Western Educational Expansion in a West African Society: A Cohort Comparison Analysis," paper presented at American Sociological Association meetings, Chicago, August 1987.

[18] Benavot, Aaron, "Education and Economic Growth in the Modern World System, 1913–1985," paper presented at American Sociological Association meetings, Chicago, 1987.

[19] *Ibid.*, p. 8.

[20] *Ibid.*, p. 8.

[21] Carnoy, Martin, "Education for Alternative Development," *Comparative Education Review*, Vol. 26, 1982, pp. 160–77.

[22] Welch, "Knowledge and Legitimation."

[23] Young, Michael (ed.), *Knowledge and Control: New Directions in the Sociology of Knowledge* (London: Collier Macmillan, 1971).

[24] Welch, "Knowledge and Legitimation," p. 515.

[25] Cowen, Robert, "The Legitimation of Educational Knowledge: A Neglected Theme in Comparative Education," *Annals of the New York Academy of Sciences*, 1975, p. 283.

[26] Archer, Margaret, *The Social Origins of Educational Systems* (London: Sage, 1979).

[27] Habermas, Jurgen, *Knowledge and Human Interests*, 2nd rev. ed. (London: Heinemann, 1978).

[28] Levin, Henry, "The Dilemma of Secondary School Comprehensive Reforms in Western Europe," *Comparative Education Review*, Vol. 22, No. 3, 1978, pp. 434–51.

[29] Horton, Robin, "African Myths and Western Science," in Young (ed.), *Knowledge and Control*, 1971.

[30] Benavot, *et al.*, "Knowledge for the Masses," 1991.

[31] UNICEF, *The State of the World's Children, 1991* (Oxford: Oxford University Press, 1991).

[32] Shrestha, Gajendra Man, *et al.*, "Determinants of Educational Participation in Rural Nepal," *Comparative Education Review*, Vol. 30, No. 4, 1986, pp. 508–22.

[33] *Poverty: World Development Report, 1990* (New York: Oxford University Press for The World Bank, 1990).

[34] Fuller, Bruce, "Is Primary School Quality Eroding in the Third World?" *Comparative Education Review*, Vol. 30, No. 4, 1986, pp. 491–508.

[35] *Ibid.*

[36] Mingat, Alain, and Jee-Peng Tan, "Who Profits from the Public Funding of Education: A Comparison of World Regions," *Comparative Education Review*, Vol. 30, No. 2, 1986, pp. 260–70.

[37] Halpern, Robert, "Effects of Early Childhood Intervention on Primary School Progress in Latin America," *Comparative Education Review*, Vol. 30, No. 2, 1986, pp. 195–215.

[38] Benavot, Aaron, David Kamens, Suk-Ying Wong, Yun-Kyung'Cha, and John Meyer, "World Culture and the Curricular Content of National Educational Systems, 1920–1985," paper presented at American Sociological Association meetings, Atlanta, August 1988.

[39] "Preprimary Enrollment Rates in Western Countries," *Education Week*, January 29, 1992, p. 7.

[40] Benavot, Aaron, "Curricular Content, Educational Expansion, and Economic Growth," *Comparative Education Review*, forthcoming 1992.

[41] Najafizadeh, Mehrangiz, and Lewis A. Mennerick, "Worldwide Educational Expansion from 1950 to 1980: The Failure of the Expansion of Schooling in Developing Countries," *The Journal of Developing Areas*, Vol. 22, April 1988, pp. 333–58; and "Third World Educational Development from the 1950s to the Present and Beyond," paper presented at American Sociological Association meetings, Washington, D.C., August 1990.

[42] Cha, Yun-Kyung, "Effect of the Global System on Language Instruction, 1850–1986," *Sociology of Education*, Vol. 64, January 1991, pp. 19–32.

[43] Gumbert, Edgar B., *Fit to Teach: Teacher Education in International Perspective* (Atlanta: Center for Cross-cultural Education, 1990).

[44] Heyneman, Stephen P., "Education of the World Market," *The American School Board Journal*, March 1990, p. 28.

[45] Livingston, D.W., *A General Model of the Internal Structure of National Education Systems* (Baltimore: Johns Hopkins University Press, 1968).

[46] Wallerstein, Immanual, *The Modern World System* (New York: Academic Press, 1974).

[47] Williamson, Bill, *Education, Social Structure and Development* (London: Macmillan, 1979), pp. 36–46.

[48] Ramirez, Francisco O., and John Boli-Bennett, "Global Patterns of Educational Institutionalization," in Altbach, Arnove, and Kelly, *Comparative Education*, pp. 15–36 (esp. p. 18).

[49] Arnove, Robert F., "Comparative Education and World-Systems Analysis," *Comparative Education Review*, Vol. 24, 1980, p. 49.

[50] Berman, Edward H., "The Foundation's Role in American Foreign Policy," in Robert Arnove (ed.), *Philanthropy and Cultural Imperialism: The Foundations at Home and Abroad* (Boston: G. K. Hall, 1980).

[51] Arnove, "Comparative Education," p. 57.

[52] Becker, Gary S., *Human Capital: A Theoretical and Empirical Analysis with Special Reference to Education*, rev. ed. (Chicago: University of Chicago Press, 1980), and Bowles, Samuel, and Herbert Gintis, "The Problem with Human Capital Theory," *American Economic Review*, Vol. 65, 1975.

[53] Acosta-Belen, Edna, "From Structural Subordination to Empowerment: Women and Development in Third World Contexts," *Gender and Society*, Vol. 4, No. 3, September 1990, pp. 199–320.

[54] Fisher, George M.C., "World-Class Corporate Expectations of Higher Education," *Educational Record*, Fall 1990, pp. 19–21.

[55] Najafizadeh, Meharangiz, and Lewis A. Mennerick, "Defining Third World Education as a Social Problem: Education, Ideologies and Education Entrepreneurship in Nicaragua and Iran," *Perspectives on Social Problems*, Vol. 1, 1989, pp. 283–315.

[56] Lynch, James, "Multicultural Education in Western Europe," *Phi Delta Kappan*, April 1983.

[57] King, *Other Schools and Ours*, pp. 36–44.

[58] Bell, Daniel, *The Coming of the Post-Industrial Society: A Venture in Social Forecasting* (New York: Basic Books, 1973).

[59] Inkeles, Alex, and David H. Smith, *Becoming Modern: Individual Change in Six Developing Countries* (Cambridge Mass.: Harvard University Press, 1974), pp. 19–32.

[60] Williamson, *Education*, pp. 37–46.

[61] *Ibid.*, p. 37–38.

[62] *Ibid.*, p. 4.

[63] Passow, *et al.*, *National Case Study*.

[64] Freire, Paulo, *Education for Critical Consciousness* (New York: Herder & Herder, 1973); and *Pedagogy of the Oppressed* (New York: Herder & Herder, 1970).

[65] Turner, Ralph, "Sponsored and Contest Mobility," *American Sociological Review*, Vol. 25, 1960, pp. 855–67.

[66] Baker, David P., and David L. Stevenson, "Parents' Management of Adolescents' Schooling: An International Comparison," Chapter 20 in Klaus Hurrelmann and Uwe Engel (eds.), *The Social World of Adolescents* (New York: Walter de Gruyter, 1989), p. 348.

[67] Baker, David P., and David Lee Stevenson, "Institutional Context of an Adolescent Transition: Going from High School to College in the United States and Japan," *Journal of Adolescent Research*, Vol. 5, No. 2, April 1990, pp. 242–53.

[68] Glenn, Charles L., "Personal Reflections," from *Choice of Schools in Six Nations* (Washington, D.C.: U.S. Department of Education, December 1989).

[69] China: What Price Peace?" *U.S. News & World Report*, June 19, 1989, p. 20; and "In Beijing, Big Brother Is the Anchorman," *U.S. News & World Report*, June 26, 1989, p. 37.

[70] Cerych, Ladislav, "EC '92: What Will It Mean for Higher Education?" *Educational Record*, Spring 1990, pp. 38–41.

[71] Woodhall, Maureen, "Sharing the Costs of Higher Education: An International Analysis," *Educational Record*, Fall 1991, p. 30.

[72] Carlson, Jerry S., Barbara B. Burn, John Useem, and David Yachimowicz, *Study Abroad: The Experience of American Undergraduates* (New York: Greenwood Press, 1990).

[73] *Source:* National Science Foundation, 1991.

[74] DeMartini, Joseph R., review of *Study Abroad*, in *Contemporary Sociology*, Vol. 21, No. 1, January 1992, p. 76.

[75] Benavot, "Curricular Content."

[76] Ramirez, Francisco O., and John Boli, "The Political Construction of Mass Schooling: European Origins and Worldwide Institutionalization," paper presented at American Sociological Association meetings, Chicago, August 1987.

[77] Archer, Margaret S., "Cross-national Research and the Analysis of Educational Systems," paper presented at American Sociological Association meetings, Chicago, August, 1987.

[78] Williamson, *Education.*

[79] *Ibid.*, p. 55.

[80] King, *Other Schools and Ours*, p. 211.

[81] Central Advisory Council for Education, *Children and Their Primary Schools* (London: H.M. Stationery Office, 1967).

[82] *London Sunday Times Magazine*, December 14, 1980, p. 94.

[83] British Department of Education, *Annual Abstracts of Statistics: 1992* (London: Central Statistical Office, 1992).

[84] Davies, Martin R., "The English National Curriculum: A Landmark in Educational Reform," *Educational Leadership*, Vol. 48, No. 5, February 1991, p. 28.

[85] Mortimore Peter, *et al., School Matters* (Berkeley: University of California Press, 1988).

[86] Garner, Catherine L., and Stephen W. Raudenbush, "Neighborhood Effects on Educational Attainment," *Sociology of Education*, Vol. 64, No. 4, October 1991, p. 251.

[87] Kerckhoff, Alan C., Richard T. Campbell, Jerry M. Trott, and Vered Kraus, "The Transmission of Socioeconomic Status and Prestige in Great Britain and the United States," *Sociological Forum*, Vol. 4, No. 2, 1989, pp. 155–77.

[88] Winfield, Idee, *et al.*, "Career Processes in Great Britain and the United States," *Social Forces*, Vol. 68, No. 1, September 1989, pp. 284–308.

[89] "Female Professors in Britain Paid Less Than Males, Study Finds," *The Chronicle of Higher Education*, Vol. 38, No. 5, September 25, 1991, p. A46.

[90] Walker, David, "Britain's Pioneering Open University Begins Its Third Decade with a New Vice-Chancellor and Big Expansion Plans," *The Chronicle of Higher Education*, June 19, 1991, p. A25.

[91] *Ibid.*

[92] Walker, David, "Britain's Campuses Expect to Face a Rush of Students," *The Chronicle of Higher Education*, Vol. 38, No. 8, October 16, 1991, p. A51.

[93] "Chinese Academy Considering New Restrictions on Joint Research," *The Chronicle of Higher Education*, Vol. 37, No. 42, July 3, 1991, p. A27.

[94] Robinson, Jean C., "Stumbling on Two Legs: Education and Reform in China," *Comparative Education Review*, Vol. 35, No. 1, pp. 177–89.

[95] Hauser, Mary, Curtis Fawson, and Glenn Latham, "Chinese Education: A System in Transition," *Principal*, January 1990, pp. 44–45.

[96] The World Bank, *World Development Report 1990: Poverty* (Oxford: Oxford University Press, 1990), pp. 234–35.

[97] *United Nations World Fact Book* (Paris: UNESCO, 1986).

[98] Pepper, Suzanne, *Post-Mao Reforms in Chinese Education: Can the Ghosts of the Past Be Laid to Rest?* No. 10 (Indianapolis, Ind.: Universities Field Staff International, Inc., 1986).

[99] Stites, Regie, and Ladislaus Semali, "Adult Literacy for Social Equality or Economic Growth? Changing Agendas for Mass Literacy in China and Tanzania," *Comparative Education Review,* Vol. 35, No. 1, February 1991, pp. 44–75.

[100] *Ibid.,* p. 73.

[101] Kwong, Julia, *Cultural Revolution in China's Schools: May 1966–April 1969* (Stanford, Calif.: Hoover Institution Press, 1988).

[102] Delany, Brian, and Lynn W. Paine, "Shifting Patterns of Authority in Chinese Schools," *Comparative Education Review,* Vol. 35, No. 1, pp. 23–44.

[103] *Ibid.,* p. 43.

[104] Kwong, Julia, "In Pursuit of Efficiency: Scientific Management in Chinese Higher Education," *Modern China,* April 1987.

[105] Hayhoe, Ruth, "Penetration or Mutuality? China's Educational Cooperation with Europe, Japan and North America," *Comparative Education Review,* Vol. 30, No. 4, 1986, pp. 532–59.

[106] Sautman, Barry, "Politicalization, Hyperpoliticization, and Depoliticization of Chinese Education," *Comparative Education Review,* Vol. 35, No. 4, November 1991, pp. 669–89.

[107] Robinson, "Stumbling on Two Legs."

[108] "Forcing Beijing University Students to Serve a Year in the Military," *The Chronicle of Higher Education,* Vol. 38, No. 8, October 16, 1991, p. A51.

[109] Lubman, Sarah, "Facing Widespread Discontent, China May Relax Rules Limiting Graduate Education and Overseas Study," *The Chronicle of Higher Education,* Vol. 37, No. 2, September 12, 1990, p. A37.

[110] "Forcing Beijing University Students."

[111] McWilliam, H. O. A., and M. A. Kwamena-Poh, *The Development of Education in Ghana* (Harlow, Essex, England: Longman, 1975), p. 116.

[112] McWilliam, *Development of Education,* p. 117.

[113] The World Bank, *World Development Report,* p. 234.

[114] Stites and Semali, "Adult Literacy for Social Equality or Economic Growth?"

[115] Busia, K. A., *Purposeful Education for Africa* (London: Moutin, 1964), p. 5.

[116] Hawes, Hugh, *Curriculum and Reality in African Primary Schools* (Harlow, Essex, England: Longman, 1979), p. 163.

[117] Sine, Barbacar, "Non-Formal Education and Education Policy in Ghana and Senegal" (Paris: UNESCO, 1979).

[118] Akinnaso, F. Niyi, "On the Mother Tongue Education Policy in Nigeria," *Educational Review,* Vol. 43, No. 1, 1991, p. 89.

[119] Stites and Semali, "Adult Literacy for Social Equality or Economic Growth?" p. 74.

[120] Grindal, Bruce, *Growing Up in Two Worlds: Education and Transition among the Sisala of Northern Ghana* (New York: Holt, Rinehart and Winston, 1972), p. 92.

[121] Williamson, *Education,* pp. 150–51.

[122] Nagel, Joane, and Conrad W. Snyder, "International Funding of Educational Development—External Agenda and Internal Adaptations: The Case of Liberia," paper presented at American Sociological Association meetings, Chicago, August, 1987.

[123] Sherman, Mary Antoinette Brown, "The University in Modern Africa," *Journal of Higher Education,* Vol. 61, No. 4, July/August 1990, p. 363.

[124] Morna, Colleen Lowe, "Africa's Campuses Lead Pro-Democracy Drives," *The Chronicle of Higher Education,* Vol. 37, No. 13, November 28, 1990, pp. A1 and 40.

[125] Chuta, E. J., "Free Education in Nigeria: Socioeconomic Implications and Emerging Issues," *Comparative Education Review,* Vol. 30, No. 4, 1986, pp. 523–31.

11

EDUCATION MOVEMENTS AND REFORM

Which school is more effective: a traditional school, with stress on basic skills and discipline, or an alternative "open" school, with freedom of movement, less structural rigidity, and greater student participation in decision making? In which school would you learn the most: one with group instruction and students progressing through the same material at the same rate, or one with individual instruction and students progressing at their individual rates? These kinds of questions underlie this chapter on educational movements and reform.

Since the early 1980s, numerous commissions, task forces, and individuals have produced documents lamenting the condition of education in the United States and arguing the need for reform. States have followed suit with hundreds of reports and proposals for reform, many of which are in operation. One notable area is that of accountability; over 35 states now require prospective teachers to pass a test before entering the classroom, and many others require students to pass achievement tests at various levels before they can move to the next or be graduated.

As you read, consider how the major educational movements discussed have affected your own educational experience. Such movements are common in the United States, facilitated by the lack of centralization in the country's educational system. In addition, each school district has ultimate jurisdiction over its own educational decision making, a factor that encourages many points of view on education. The United States takes pride in local control of schools, a plan originated to take into account the diverse local population needs. Countries with more centralized educational decision making and more homogeneous populations have less diversity in educational programs and fewer popular movements for change.

In recent years, demands for accountability and court cases on desegregation and financing have led U.S. state legislatures and boards of education to play a greater role in educational decisions that affect the local level.[1] The following outline indicates some of the many areas of state concern and shows the interdependence of government and education.

I. Administration/Leadership
   A. Training for school board members
   B. Changes in certification for administrators
   C. Competency testing for all administrators or for initial certification
   D. Evaluation programs for administrators
   E. Establishment of principals' academies and administrative staff development programs
II. School District
   A. Academic bankruptcy or curricular accountability
   B. Long-range planning (accountability)
   C. Programs to lower class size and target instructional resources
   D. District consolidation or reorganization
III. Early Childhood
   A. Prekindergarten programs
   B. Mandatory kindergarten and/or full-day kindergarten
   C. Early intervention and programs for at-risk or handicapped students
   D. Prime-time programs and smaller classes for early elementary years
IV. Finance
   A. Tax increases for reforms
   B. Funding innovations, especially incentive programs
   C. Teacher salary increases, career ladders, or merit-pay programs
V. General
   A. Adult literacy
   B. Computers/technology
   C. Incentive programs for schools and districts
   D. Governance changes
   E. Changes in length of school day and year
   F. Parental involvement
   G. Programs for special populations (gifted, disabled, etc.)
   H. Mandated discipline plans
   I. Guidance/counseling
VI. Postsecondary
   A. Changes in admissions requirements
   B. Efforts to improve quality of undergraduate education
   C. Program consolidation
VII. Students
   A. Programs for at-risk youth
   B. Changes in the curriculum
   C. Increased requirements for high school graduation
   D. Competency testing
   E. Academic recognition
   F. Changes in policies regarding placement, promotion/retention, and remediation

        G.   Home instruction
        H.   Choice programs
VIII.   Teachers
        A.   Instructional time
        B.   Teacher shortages
        C.   Certification changes
        D.   Preservice training
        E.   Alternate certification
        F.   Competency testing/evaluation
        G.   Career ladder plans and merit pay plans
        H.   Staff development
         I.   Forgivable loans to attract new teachers[2]

Some of the reforms seem most easily mandated at the state level rather than leaving them to local districts to carry out in order to obtain similarities between district policies. Recommendations for reforms focus on accountability in standards for teachers and students, longer days and more school days in the year, more stress on academic requirements for all students, higher graduation requirements, and higher standards and more recognition and pay for teachers.[3]

Societal attitudes swing like a pendulum, from right to left and back again (Figure 11-1). Education is but one area of society, and the educational pendulum reflects broader societal trends, movements, and attitudes,[4] as we shall see in our discussion of movements.

Theoretical approaches also enter into an understanding of movements. Some conflict theorists argue that attempts by conservatives and minority groups to stress basics will only widen the gap in the opportunity structure. The argument is this: The more fundamentals, rigidity, and discipline the schools stress, the more compliant will be the laborers created. This in turn perpetuates the unequal class structure by creating a well-trained work force—exactly what those in power need to perpetuate the class differences. Conflict theorists argue that only a restructuring of the obsolete educational and economic systems can lead to expansion of the opportunity ladder. If one accepts this theory, it seems ironic that many persons in those very groups that would be most hurt by stress on basics and discipline—minorities—are among those pushing for conservative change.

FIGURE 11-1   The pendulum of attitudes swings from right to left and back.

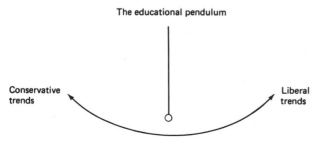

The role of schools in preparing young people for the workplace has been in the forefront of educational reform movements, and there is a correspondence between schools and workplaces. However, conflict theorists are concerned that schools are controlled by the state; schools also produce the workers for the capitalistic system. Strong democratic social movements for equal opportunity in schools and society can help counter what conflict theorists see as reproduction of the social class system.[5]

The view of functionalist theorists is very different. They believe that more stress on basics, discipline, and accountability will help people achieve a niche in the competitive society. Education in the basics would provide opportunity, even though it is unlikely to create a fundamental change in the stratification system of society.

THE NATURE OF EDUCATIONAL MOVEMENTS

Systems change because of constant internal and external pressures from many sources. Figure 11-2 notes some sources of change in educational systems. You can undoubtedly think of more.

When change is brought about in one system or subsystem of society, such as education or politics, it will affect other systems. Social movements are one major indication of the direction in which a society is moving and of the constant pressure for change on parts of the system.

The concept of social movement has been used to refer to numerous collective efforts for change—women's rights movement, civil rights movements, prohibition movement, antiwar movement, right-to-life movement.

FIGURE 11-2   Sources of change in the school system.

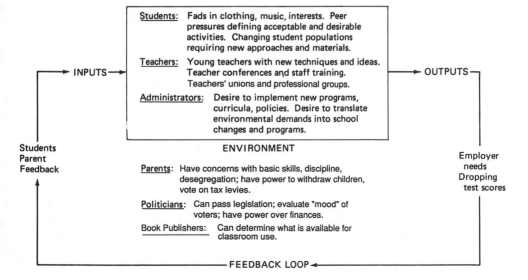

Movements arise because large groups of people are dissatisfied with existing conditions. They focus around a general guiding ideology or philosophy, a strong idealism and dedication to this ideology on the part of adherents, and some form of action.

There has never been a time when all members of a society were content with the society or its education system. The supporters of a movement are generally attempting to bring about or resist some change in society; their motives for involvement in a movement vary from idealism to the personal satisfaction of belonging to a group of believers and having a "cause." Problems in society may first come to light because of a growing social movement. If a movement "catches on" and attracts large numbers of adherents it is likely to have a direct impact on the existing system. It often starts out as a small fringe group bucking in the general trends; with the development of leadership and a communication network such as a newsletter, and with the attention of the media, more people are attracted to the movement. Eventually ideas from the movement may be adopted by schools or other institutions and become "institutionalized"; that is, accepted as integral parts of society. Some social movements attract few followers and eventually die.[6] These are often groups pushing for ideas that are not easily integrated into the existing system—as, for example, educational technology and TV. Any large social movement is likely to include splinter groups or smaller groups of reformers or radicals supporting specific, related ideologies and causing internal dissent as supporters quarrel over means and ends.

Movements may be organized, or they may be unstructured and without clear leadership, as in the case of the counterculture movement from which free schools were spawned. However, common threads or ideologies, such as the desire for individuality and freedom, hold movements together. Leaders who have written influential books that generate and espouse the movements' philosophy and ideological bases provide common focal points.

Several typologies of movements have been constructed. Following is a summary of those types of social movements most relevant to our discussion:

1. *Reform movements* believe that certain reforms are necessary, usually in specific areas of society.
2. *Regressive movements* aim to "put the clock back," reverse current trends, and return to a former state of affairs.
3. *Revolutionary movements* are deeply dissatisfied with the existing order and seek to reorganize society.
4. *Utopian movements* include "loosely constructed collectivities that envision a radically changed and blissful state," such as the 1960s counterculture movement.[7]

From the counterculture movement of the 1960s emerged the free school movement. This movement came in reaction to structured, authoritarian schools and led to the development of schools with freedom of choice and little structure. Initially, this was a fairly isolated, utopian movement. As more people learned about it and its ideology, several things happened (Figure 11-3). (A) Some were attracted and joined. (B) Others were intrigued, but rather

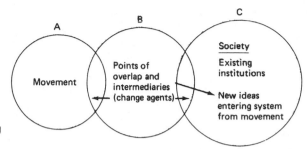

FIGURE 11-3
Educational movements can bring
about change in systems.

than join the movement and give up their positions in the society or educational system, they adopted a middle-ground or compromise position and accepted some ideas that could be adapted to fit within the existing system without major structural change. These people acted as change agents in what now took on reform movement elements. (C) The educational system faced pressures from the educational movements without, and from persons within who wished to adopt the movements' ideas.

Demands for change range from "throw the whole system out and start over," to "there is always room for reform within the existing framework." Most educational policymakers take a cautious middle ground when it comes to changes because gradual change makes planning and adaptation possible without much disruption to the existing system. However, this approach appears unresponsive to some who want major structural and ideological change.

Caution must be exercised in using the label "movement" when referring to very specific or short-term changes. For example, many technological "fads" such as reading machines, talking typewriters, and programmed texts brought about significant structural change in many schools, but would probably not be considered movements. They might be subsumed under a larger "movement" such as "classroom technologies."

The purposes of the remainder of this chapter are twofold: to stress the impact of educational movements on school systems, and to discuss some major educational movements in the United States. Because the ideology behind education helps determine its structure, functioning, and change in the system, an understanding of these major movements is important.

EDUCATIONAL MOVEMENTS THROUGHOUT HISTORY

Early European Education: Purpose and Function for Society

Education has always been a part of a society's way of acculturating its young, of teaching a child to become a member of a society. Education is both informal and formal: informal, in that a child learns the ways of his or her culture by being a member immersed and participating in that society; formal, in that a child is taught by a teacher about certain aspects of his or her culture in a specific place, such as a school.

In ancient Greece and Rome, boys—seldom girls—were educated by wandering teachers called Sophists who taught youngsters the skills needed to develop their reasoning power and rhetoric; that is, the art of persuasion. This form of "formal" education met the needs of the society and times. Philosophers and great teachers such as Socrates, his student Plato, and Aristotle are still studied for their concepts of the educated person, freedom of thought, and rational inquiry.

After the fall of the Roman Empire and the decline of the ancient classical civilization, formal education was found in only a few places, such as religious institutions. Many towns in Europe had monastic schools that conducted elementary education, but at the secondary level only monasteries offered any kind of opportunities. Societies at this time did not rely on a formally educated class to carry out necessary functions. However, education of a formal type could be found at the castle of a great lord where young knights were trained in the skills of military tactics and the code of chivalry. Also, merchant and craft guilds maintained means of instructing apprentices for trade. Universities evolved during the Middle Ages.

An influence from the education of the Middle Ages on today's educational movements is the concept of human depravity. Since lust was considered a sin, all children were conceived in sin and thus were born depraved. Early religious leaders like St. Augustine, and later John Calvin and Martin Luther, stressed that corruptive weakness could be corrected by a strong teacher who used authoritarian methods. Similarly, in the early colonies of New England "Old Deluder Satan Acts" were legislated to save children from the temptation of straying from the faith. Many today still advocate the use of authoritarian methods in the classroom.

During the Renaissance in Europe the concept of the well-rounded and liberally educated person was developed. Great interest was shown in the humanistic aspects of Greek and Latin classics. In contrast to the sectarian education of the Reformation, with its God-centered world view, the secular education of the Renaissance focused on the earthly experience of human beings. These views continue to influence curriculum movements, especially in higher education, which focus on developing well-rounded students.

Another period of European history that had an effect on American education was the "Enlightenment" of the eighteenth century. It was believed that people could improve their lives by reason, by using their minds to solve problems; education would enable society to progress toward a new and better world, and schools were seen as instruments for cultivating the reasoning powers of youth.

Educational Movements in the United States

The Public School Movement.   Until the early nineteenth century, many children in the United States attended only primary schools. Schools at the secondary level were for the elite children. They were sent there to prepare for university, which would lead to occupations in the church or commerce. This pattern perpetuated an elite and commercial class.

Several concerns led to movements for increased opportunity for schooling:

1. With the industrialization of the northeastern part of the United States, many people were concerned about the well-being of children; school provided one alternative to working long hours in the factories.
2. Industrialists were seeking ways to educate and urbanize those coming to towns from rural areas to make them reliable, compliant workers.
3. Many wanted to Americanize and assimilate immigrants.

The school appeared to be the institution that could solve these problems.

Horace Mann, a member of the Massachusetts legislature during the late 1820s and 1830s, was the most forceful advocate and leader of the public school movement. It was Mann who pushed for the establishment of schools for all children free of charge, without religious teaching, and financed through public taxation. He said, "Let the home and the church teach faith and values, and the school teach facts."[8] He also advocated locally elected boards of education to remove control of the schools from conservative churchmen and school masters. Local districts were supervised by and under the influence of a centralized bureaucracy—the state board of education. Mann himself was appointed head of this agency in Massachusetts. Another innovation of Horace Mann's was the professionalization of teachers: Teacher training colleges, or "normal schools," were established; higher salaries were paid to attract better-qualified teachers; and scientific methods were used for the evaluation of teachers. This reform movement came at a time when societal needs favored development of mass education. Following Massachusetts's lead, people in other states pressed for laws establishing universal, free, primary education. This movement also extended to secondary education, but it was not until after the Civil War, with the need for a highly educated labor force, that the cry of "more education for more people" really made an impact.

The Progressive Education Movement. Just as the movement for public education during the first half of the nineteenth century paralleled the wider social trend to integrate newcomers into an industrial society, the progressive education movement extending into the 1920s and 1930s paralleled the political progressive movement of the 1890s.

Controversy exists today over an offshoot of progressive education philosophy: "life skills." Courses in sex and drug education, marriage, parenting, death and dying, values clarification, money management, consumer knowledge, house buying, insurance, and other practical skills are seen by some as essential skills for students to have before leaving high school. Others feel that schools should concentrate on basic skills and that the home should teach life skills.

The Essentials.   Theodore Brameld,[9] who has written extensively on the various movements in American education, has used the term "essentialist" to describe those involved in a 1950s movement opposing progressive education. Essentialists were particularly vexed about an offshoot of progressive education called the life adjustment movement, which they believed reduced education to teaching survival skills such as home economics, driver education, and hygiene—ignoring the intellectual mission of schooling to teach disciplines.

Essentialist critics, such as Arthur Bestor and Robert Maynard Hutchins, decried the "intellectual flabbiness and soft-headedness" of the schools. Navy Admiral Hyman Rickover complained that he could not find enough scientists and technicians to build and run the Navy's nuclear submarines; and many church leaders and their followers deplored the teaching of cultural relativism and the ignoring of the eternal truths. Politically, the decade of the 1950s was a time of fear; Joseph McCarthy stressed the communist threat, with communists lurking in the teachers' lounges and superintendents' offices of the nation's schools. Some saw progressive education as a movement to weaken educational institutions.

Humanistic Education.   American education in the twentieth century follows the pendulum-swing theory. Progressivism was in many ways a reaction to the crimping, stultifying schools of Victorian authoritarianism; essentialism was a reaction against progressivism; and the humanistic education movement of the 1960s and 1970s was in reaction to the authoritarianism that had never been given up by the schools. It was a rediscovery of the teachings of the child-centered progressives.

Leaders of the humanistic movement said that schools should eliminate coercive rules and regulations. More opportunities should be created for students to participate in shaping educational goals, especially at the secondary level. This movement was greatly influenced by the client-centered therapies of such psychologists as Carl Rogers and Abraham Maslow. In practice, educators such as Sidney Simon (Values Clarification) and Lawrence Kohlberg (Stages of Moral Development) presented teachers with a variety of techniques to clarify the values and develop the moral base of their students. Charles Silberman's *Crisis in the Classroom*[10] was a keynote book on humanistic education. His analysis of American education described the schools as overly formal, devitalized, and often inhumane. He looked at the informal classroom of the English primary school as a model for reform. A number of teacher training colleges, most notably the University of North Dakota, adopted the practices of English primary schools and provided learning experiences whereby prospective teachers were trained to sense their pupils' needs and interests and to follow these in the classroom. Humanistic educators insisted that greater attention should be placed on developing the "affective domain," or emotions and feelings, of a child, not just the "cognitive domain," or intellect. Emotions, intellect, *and* the psycho-motor all need attention.

From the humanistic education movement came interest in an area of "preparation for life" called moral education, also known by such terms as moral development, civic education, citizen/moral education, moral sensibility, moral reasoning, and values clarification. Moral education does not "teach" morals; rather, through the use of classroom exercises, it helps children deal with ethical issues that affect them and the world in which they live, and that will be involved in their decision-making processes.[11]

> The whole idea of values clarification is not to instill or introduce any particular values, new or old, but to help students discover those they already have. . . . Moreover, the theory stresses that "exercising" one's values via such paper-and-pencil exercises will help students hold on more firmly to their values.[12]

Critics of humanistic education argue that we should be more directive and absolute, not morally neutral, in teaching values. They also question whether teachers can remain neutral or hide their values in the teaching process.[13]

ALTERNATIVE EDUCATION AND RELATED MOVEMENTS

The alternative education movement does not lend itself to easy definition because it is by definition decentralized. Each subgroup is unique, meeting the needs of those involved. We will divide our discussion into several parts: philosophical basis and definition of alternative education; the English model; and free schools.[14]

From the humanistic philosophical perspective came the origins of the alternative education movement, with its emphasis on the whole child. It is impossible to speak of one philosophy that all in the movement share, but through networks such as *Educational Switchboard, Changing Schools Newsletter, New Schools Exchange, This Magazine Is About Schools,* and various state-centered organizations such as OCEAN (Ohio Coalition for Educational Alternatives Now), a general picture emerges.

The Ohio Coalition for Educational Alternatives Now drafted a working definition of alternative schools, which is shown in Box 11-1.

BOX 11-1 *WORKING DEFINITION OF ALTERNATIVE SCHOOLS*

Alternative schools:

- generally are schools that give people freedom and choice in location, methodology, philosophy, materials, relationships, and expectations;
- generally reflect human qualities of love, openness, informality, flexibility, parental and community involvement, and integration in contrast to segregation;
- generally demonstrate humane schooling that will further intellectual, social, and emotional development; self-knowledge, independence and interdependence; and creativity in an environment of shared responsibility;
- generally minimize failure, competitiveness, authoritarianism, top-down administration, expensive facilities, and labels.

Terms used to describe the schools loosely adhering to these philosophical tenets include "free," "open," "innovative," "experimental," "new," and "radical."[15] Many of these philosophical underpinnings have been spelled out in books that have become the "bibles" of alternative schools advocates.[16]

The Development of Free Schools

Summerhill is a small residential school set in a village in England; it advocates a totally free learning environment and unrestrained spontaneity. The late A. S. Neill,[17] who founded Summerhill in 1921, believed that to become fulfilled adults, children must be allowed to have a "free" experience, unfettered by rules. The few rules of the school are established by the whole community in a democratic way. While regular classes from primary through secondary levels are offered, attendance is voluntary.[18]

Some free schools in the United States have been patterned specifically on the Summerhill model; some have adopted aspects of the model. Several hundred free schools were established in the late 1960s and early 1970s, and many young adults, disenchanted with their own schooling, with what schools do to children through rigidities and corporal punishment, and with the whole power structure of society as reflected by Vietnam and Watergate, decided to establish alternatives for their children.

The free school movement was not, however, just a reaction against repressive school structures, outdated curricula, or ineffective teaching methods, but one against the school as an instrument of the mainstream culture. Many free school advocates were motivated by the philosophy that education should be regarded as a means to a political end. A number of teachers such as John Holt and Jonathan Kozol criticized public schools as inherently corrupt and not possible to reform. In *Free Schools,* Jonathan Kozol[19] emphasized the need for schools independent of the mainstream traditional school system, schools that would stress political awareness and would give students the tools to become agents of change. More recently, he has written on the gulf between rich and poor schools in urban areas.[20] During the 1960s and 1970s a number of street academies and storefront schools were set up in city ghettos for black and other minority children. Although many people shared Kozol's ideas and worked in free schools for the "liberation" of their children, some free schools remained quite apolitical.

Changing the educational power structure was also the goal of some Third World educators. In *Pedagogy of the Oppressed,*[21] Brazilian educator Paulo Freire asserted that literacy among oppressed peasants could be increased by leading these people to an awareness of their cultural reality (the powers that oppress them) and thus giving them the knowledge and its attendant power to fight back against the oppressor. Freire devised a new method of teaching reading that achieved considerable success among the people of poverty-striken northeastern Brazil. The result was an increased politicalization of the peasantry, which was perceived as a threat by the government. Freire was jailed and eventually forced into exile.

This idea of facilitating learning among the illiterate poor as a means toward their liberation parallels the ideas of Ivan Illich,[22] a former priest who operated a "think tank" and training center in Mexico frequented by American educators and reformers. He viewed schools as among several institutions that are coercive, discriminatory, and destructive to the individual. He claimed that by disengaging education from "schooling," deinstitutionalization of the social order would occur, allowing for change. Illich also argued that one does not have to go to school to get an education, and that schools can actually inhibit education.

The largest group of students in free schools are bright children seeking escape from the anxiety and boredom of their schools. There are also students who have experienced academic failure and are potential dropouts. For both of these types of students, free schools meet a need. The student is accepted as a person. Some students appear to thrive in this type of environment, while others who have been turned off to school may gain little in the area of knowledge and may use the experience as an escape.

Factions and feuds arise easily in free schools.[23] In a discussion of parent-run free schools, William Firestone[24] comments that conflicts over goals, governance, and patterns of interpersonal relations can jeopardize the survival of these schools. Some free schools still exist; others dissolved after only a year in operation because of financial problems, conflicts, or the emotional fatigue of the participants.

English Primary Schools

In 1966, the Plowden Report[25] was published in Britain. This important report altered British primary school education, and its findings have influenced education in the United States. In 1978, a follow-up report evaluating primary education in Britain was released, giving a positive account of results of the open primary school model. The report shows a commitment to individualized education and to stress on the basics—reading, writing, and mathematics. In this system, described in Chapter 10, children work at their own level in basic skills, which are taught in conjunction with other subjects such as history, science, music, and art. Advocates of basic skills in both Britain and the United States have questioned whether children learn as well in this individualized broad curricular approach; in response to these critics the 1978 report states the following:

- There is no evidence in the survey to suggest that a narrower curriculum enabled children to do better in the basic skills or led to the work being more aptly chosen to suit the capabilities of the children.
- The general educational progress of children and their competence in the basic skills appears to have benefited where they were involved in a programme of work that included arts and crafts, history, geography, music and physical education, and science, as well as language, mathematics, and religious and moral education.[26]

The report also showed that teachers were most successful in teaching average and slower students, and less successful in challenging brighter stu-

dents. Two particular findings of significance for the open education movement in the United States are that children learn basic skills best when they are
combined and integrated with a rich curriculum program, and that Britain
has been very successful in educating primary children with emphasis on the
whole child, individualized education, informal classroom atmosphere, and an
integrated curriculum. In summary:

> The back-to-basics movement in America and in Britain seems to assume that if
> children will spend longer periods of time working in a narrower way at basic
> skills they will achieve more. Our major national survey suggests that the oppo-
> site is true. If the basic skills are embedded in a web of direct experience on the
> part of the child that engages the many facets of his personality and being, then
> basic skills grow most strongly.[27]

Impact of the Alternative Education Movement

The ending of the Vietnam War and the aging of the counterculture
took the wind out of the sails of protest. During the mid-1970s, many people
had fallen back into an acceptance of the status quo. However, the impact of
the alternative education movement can be seen in many school systems and
classrooms where students are taught in less traditional ways, and in school
districts where alternative types of schools or classrooms are available.

In the early 1970s, many public school systems established "alternative
public schools" for those students who were potential dropouts and could not
function effectively within the traditional high school system. These "fringe"
public high schools included many of the features of private alternative or
free schools. They were informal and small, with personalized learning, student involvement in decision making, innovative learning techniques, and
community involvement. Some major cities have retained alternative high
schools for limited numbers of students.

Open Classrooms

The terms open classrooms, open education, open schools, and open
space all refer to a movement that has its roots in the progressive education
movement. Open classrooms are characterized by the following:

1. concern over quality of teacher-child interaction; warmth, acceptance; children's
   thoughts taken seriously,
2. emphasis on cooperation, not competition; few behavior problems,
3. freedom of movement and use of materials, within certain boundaries; communication between children, and
4. other factors related to positive self-image and willingness to take risks and
   persist.

The teacher is there to facilitate learning and to help students in their
activities. The teacher's role is supportive and guiding and child-centered.
"[C]omparison may be made with a well-stocked specialty shop where the

owner is sensitive to the nature of his customers and tries to meet a range of their needs by making high-quality provisions available and giving guidance whenever necessary."[28] The physical environment gives an atmosphere of informality. Desks are grouped, and areas of the room have different activities available. Open classrooms are most commonly found in elementary schools (see Figure 11-4).

Parents tend to be involved in open classrooms, volunteering help or bringing in projects for the children. Open education results in different interaction patterns in the classrooms; there is generally more interaction among students, and less formal teacher-student interaction. Findings on student academic achievement in open education vary. In an extensive study comparing open schools and traditional ones, James McPartland and Joyce Epstein[29] considered the "duration of exposure to school differences (open or traditional), within-school variations across differences, and consistency of relationship across grades or student subgroups." The openness of the classroom situation was measured by such variables as whether students might sit in any seat, talk with other students, move freely about the room, work individually, and choose what to work on, within limits. Their findings indicate that "students neither lose nor gain significantly in their performance on standardized achievement tests as a consequence of attending open schools.... [Data strongly suggest that] openness of instructional approach is of no important consequence for student academic achievement."[30]

Open education may have particular value for some groups. William Cockerham and Audie Blevins[31] considered the value of open versus traditional education for Native Americans and white rural students. Their contention was that open education would be particularly beneficial for Native American children who come from a culture that holds values similar to those of open education—"cooperation, sharing, and individual responsibility for decision making"—and in fact this was found to be true. The study findings suggest that ". . . open school Indian students have a more positive level of self-identification than students attending traditional schools, either Indian or white. Characteristics of open school education seem to clash less with Indian customs and practices than those of traditional schools."[32]

In times of back-to-basics movements, open education classrooms have come under attacks as "schools without failure," automatically promoting chil-

FIGURE 11-4   Open classroom.

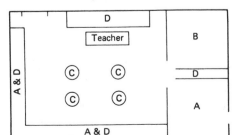

A. Activity centers
B. Quiet space
C. Work tables
D. Resources

dren without identifying lack of achievement.[33] Open education also faces problems of staff training and adapting traditional materials to self-learning. Some open education structures have been replaced by more traditional classrooms with desks and chairs in rows. But many teachers have retained some semblance of the open education atmosphere in their classrooms.

BACK TO BASICS AND ACCOUNTABILITY

Seldom has there been a clearer backlash. From the alternative education movement, the swing of the pendulum is now to the conservative side. The movement referred to as "back to basics" features good, old-fashioned readin', writin', and 'rithmatic with a good dose of discipline thrown in and none of the "frills" such as humanistic education and the arts. Here is a description of one such traditional school:

> The John Marshall Fundamental School (Pasadena, California) is a bastion of tradition-oriented education. Letter grades, regular examination, strict dress codes and detention for delinquents are integral parts of the school's conservative program. Both the faculty and student body are expected to present "an outstanding image" in dress and deportment. The curriculum is strict and basic; it features computational arithmetic (i.e., the old math), reading drill in standard phonics and rigorous homework requirements from kindergarten on. At lunchtime, teachers and volunteer parents move about the cafeteria correcting table manners. There are no graffiti on the Marshall walls; in their place hang framed patriotic sentiments and didactic homilies ("Happiness Is Manners"). A 35-page school handbook spells out the Marshall goals in jargon-free clarity: "Traditional education, order, quiet and control."[34]

Initially the pressure for more emphasis on basic skills came from parents concerned about their children's skill levels. Groups of parents have protested to school boards and superintendents, or have withdrawn their children from "liberal" or experimental schools in reaction to the innovations of the alternative school movement. Today pressure comes from commission reports, state legislators, and concerns of the public over the drop in achievement test scores.

Our historical summary shows that "back to basics" is not new. In Puritan times most schools were set up to teach basic skills and religion so that children could be brought up to have a better understanding of morals, religion, and law. Young boys from elite homes attended grammar schools where Greek and Latin literature were taught; always the emphasis was on basic skills. As the colonies expanded, different types of schools were founded to meet the differing needs of students and society, but always stressing basic skills. McGuffey Readers reigned as the primary texts used in classrooms for almost a century, from 1836 to the 1930s. In addition to basic skills, the text stressed morals and manners (Box 11-2). This is a clear example of cultural transmission of dominant values.

The Council for Basic Education, founded in 1956, acted as a liaison

BOX 11-2 *EXCERPT FROM A MCGUFFEY READER: THINGS TO REMEMBER*

1. When you rise in the morning, remember who kept you from danger during the night. Remember who watched over you while you slept, and whose sun shines around you, and gives you the sweet light of day.

2. Let God have the thanks of your heart, for His kindness and His care. And pray for His protection during the wakeful hours of day.

3. When you are at the table, do no eat in a greedy manner, like a pig. Eat quietly, and without noise. Do not reach forth your hand for the food, but ask someone to help you.

4. Avoid a pouting face, angry looks, and angry words. Do not slam doors. Go quietly up and down stairs; and never make a loud noise about the house.

5. Be kind and gentle in your manners; not like the howling winter storm, but like the bright summer's morning.

6. Do always as your parents bid you. Obey them with a ready mind, and with a pleasant face.

7. Never do anything that you would be afraid or ashamed that your parents should know. Remember, if no one else sees you, God does; from whom you can not hide even your most secret thought.

8. We must do all the good we can to all men, for this is well pleasing in the sight of God. He delights to see his children walk in love, and do good, one to another.

Exercises—What should you remember in the morning? Whom should you thank, and for what should you pray? How should you behave at the table? What should you avoid? How should you behave to your parents? What should you do at night? Whom should you always trust?

Source: McGuffey, William H., *Third Eclectic Reader* (Cincinnati: Wilson, Hinkle, 1857; 2nd ed., 1965), pp. 55–57

group for those interested in basic education, or basic skills. This has not always been easy, since proponents of basic education today have a variety of interests and motives. Some advocate use of the paddle, and stress truth, virtue, justice, religious principles, and dress codes as the primary focus of schools. Others mainly want to be assured that the three R's are being mastered. One council leader comments that some "seem to want to bring back everything from the schools of 1915 except the pot-bellied stove."[35] What holds this diverse group together may only be a common bond of dissatisfaction with schools and a feeling that more stress should be placed on "essentials."

Members of the Council for Basic Education, parents, ministers, business leaders, politicians, and other supporters of "basic skills" argued that schools should be guided by essentialist principles, including the following:

1. The elementary school curriculum should aim to cultivate basic tool skills that contribute to literacy and mastery of arithmetical computation.
2. The secondary curriculum should cultivate competencies in history, mathematics, science, literature, English, and foreign languages
3. Schooling requires discipline and a respect for legitimate authority.
4. Learning requires hard work and disciplined attention.[36]

Having completed such a school curriculum, the students should be able to apply their knowledge to solve many problems. However, some argue that they will also have learned their place in the class structure.

Why has this movement gained strength now? Ben Brodinsky gives the following explanation:

> . . . [N]ostalgia in the 1970s; the public's whetted appetite for accountability; the nation's periodic swing to conservatism; the high divorce rate and the disintegration of the family, leading to demands that the schools provide the discipline which the home no longer can; the excesses of permissiveness; and a bundle of causes in which Dr. Spock, TV, and creeping socialism are crammed into the same bag.[37]

Supporters of "back to basics" argued that there is no proof of improvements from the many innovations, which were "too much and came to quick."[38] Clifton Fadiman, a leading spokesman for back to basics, argued that the "young people who are coming out of high schools which do not stress basic skills are lost, do not know who they are and do not have meaning in their lives."[39] Pointing to the number of promises for educational breakthroughs in the past two decades, John Egerton notes that they have not lived up to their advance billing:

> . . . [W]e have been promised a dozen or more revolutionary breakthroughs, only to discover that most of them had little effect at all—or worse, had a negative impact on learning. Educational television, the "new math," computer-assisted instruction, compensatory education, career education, open education, mainstreaming, tracking and ability grouping, modular scheduling, individualized instruction—one after another the innovations have been trotted out and tried. Almost without exception, they have turned out to be less effective than their advance billing indicated.[40]

Reaction to the failures of promised miracles, to desegregation, and to the ban on Bible-reading and prayers in classrooms; a "break-down in the moral fiber of society"; and a need for "patriotism, morality, manners, adult authority, discipline, order, and quality education"—these have provided the main uniting ideologies for back-to-basics proponents.[41]

What did this mean in terms of changes in the schools? Many open classrooms were eliminated. Courses other than basics—art and music appreciation, sex and drug education, physical education, drivers' education—were questioned or eliminated, as were emphases on the well-being of the whole child and use of counselors and other social service programs. Discipline and basic skills took their place. Only in recent years have we seen the slow return of some social programs and additional courses.

Private Schools

The booming private school business owes a great deal to back-to-basics proponents. Private schools thrive on the discontent of frustrated parents who want reprieve from the conflicts over desegregation, the perceived lack of discipline, and apparent lowering of standards.

There are several categories of private schools: elite preparatory schools such as Choate, Phillips-Andover, Groton, and Lawrenceville, which cater to the wealthy who plan to go to elite colleges; special schools for the disabled, gifted, or retarded; military academies; and religious, sectarian day schools sponsored by Catholic, Jewish, Baptist, Lutheran, Quaker, fundamentalist Christian, and other religious groups. These private schools meet the preferences of many different people holding various beliefs about the role of education.

One type of private school that has experienced tremendous growth in the past decade is the fundamentalist Christian school. Some of these schools were established in reaction to negative feelings about the public schools, others in response to integration of schools. At the core of this movement is a distrust of the educational system, which seems to some to be superimposing an alien value system on their own.

Fundamentalist Christians believe that education and Christian teachings cannot be separated. They object to public school teachings that include such ideas as "man evolved from lower forms of life," denying the literal Biblical interpretation of the Creation; the idea that man is an animal, implying that man does not have a soul; and other specific teachings. Reaction to such teachings in public schools has led to an upsurge of interest in Christian schools. In this, as in other movements, one senses an in-group—out-group or we-they tone. "They" are destroying our children's faith in God, implanting alien ideas in their minds.

In 1991, private school education received a boost from the government with the push for a "choice" system. This would allow parents to select from various schools, which in turn would receive funds from each student enrolled.[42] Thus, more students might be able to attend private schools.

Accountability Movements

The Meaning of Accountability.   Accountability is a close relative of the "back-to-basics" movement and of current calls for assessment. It is a catchword for many recent trends in education rooted in the 1970s, ranging from "educational engineering" to community control of schools. Accountability is both very hard to define and very appealing to a wide variety of people because of its broad general goal to "change education." Some groups see it as a means of controlling education. Accountability means that teachers will have standards of competency and schools will measure outcomes with expenditures.[43,44]

Who Is to Be Held Accountable?   The accountability movement arose in reaction to the humanistic emphasis in education. Of paramount concern was the attempt to account for dollars spent and to hold someone responsible for the output of schools, which is measured by student achievement. Discontent on the part of community members was manifest; bond issues were failing, schools were closing, and a Gallup survey in the early 1970s showed finances to be the number one school problem. With reports of graduating students who could not spell or write a sentence, and who did not know some basic information in science and history, parents turned to the schools and blamed the humanistic emphasis of the 1960s. Demands for helping each child to learn to his or her maximum potential became prevalent. Some educational writers arguing for reforms in the schools supported the idea of accountability. Nat Hentoff, for one, urged parents to speak up against the "great consumer fraud" and demand competent teachers, though he indicated that teachers are almost never fired for incompetence.[45]

Many proposals have been set forth for measuring teachers' performance:

1. performance of students on standardized tests,
2. the increase in students' achievement over a year in the classroom,
3. observation and rating of teachers in the classroom,
4. student ratings of teachers,
5. results of a National Teacher Exam or other teacher exams,
6. evaluation of teachers' instructional objectives, and
7. mutual goals and evaluation of success by teachers and supervisor or principal.[46]

Some incompetent teachers "weed themselves out," but there is a problem in eliminating those who do not remove themselves from the system. Some critics suggest putting more pressure on teacher training institutions to evaluate prospective teachers' ability to relate to children throughout the training period rather than at the end, when they do student teacher training. This would lead some to decide for themselves that they are not suited for the role of teacher, while others could be advised early as to their future in teaching, instead of waiting until they have completed four years of training. Other critics of teacher training institutions indicate that more careful selection of entering students would help solve the problem.[47]

Once a teacher is in the school, in-service training and observation can help to improve skills. According to James Herndon, if we make expectations clear when the teacher is first hired, and then make systematic evaluations, we have better control of the quality of teaching.[48] Competency-based education (CBE) in teacher training institutions requires students to master certain skills before graduation.[49]

Accountability and the Systems Approach.   According to systems analysis, problems in education cannot be attributed to only one source. Teachers are not the only villains, nor are the students. Perhaps the schools are scapegoats, blamed because of expectations that they can solve all of society's problems. Government at all levels is involved, as are all those who serve the school.

Some critics of the accountability movement argue that there are numerous causes for educational problems *besides* the teacher or school administrators: parents, community residents, school board members, taxpayers, and most important, the students themselves. Recently, families and teacher education programs have come in for their share of criticism for school failures.

Bad news in terms of low student test scores, violence in schools, and high dropout rates is among the causes of recent calls for accountability. Many states are requiring students to pass exams at one or more points in their school careers. Some states and local school districts are proposing that teacher pay be tied to student test results. This practice is likely to reduce creativity in classrooms, as teachers teach to the tests.

Humanists point out that accountability may turn the schools from humane, spontaneous, creative places that encourage positive self-concepts and success, to cold formal places with measurement procedures and clearly delineated objectives allowing for little spontaneity and creativity. Numerous people play a role in educating the child. Concentrating on only one aspect of the system and the environment will produce a "bandage effect," but probably will not result in solutions to problems.

The Testing Controversy and Back to Basics

Movements for accountability have increased the power and influence of testing agencies in the school environment. School districts desiring to evaluate their student populations compared with state or national norms rely on standardized tests.

The decline in standardized test scores on the College Boards or Scholastic Aptitude Test (SAT), put out by the Educational Testing Service (ETS) and the American College Testing Program (ACT), has been cited as a major reason for the back-to-basics drive.

The testing controversy is complex; many factors have entered into the decline of scores, and some feel that tests should not be used at all for placement and college entrance. "Standardized tests are the greatest single barrier to equal opportunity, at least in the sphere of education," according to one sociologist. A number of explanations for the dropping test scores have been presented:

1. There may be a change in the types of students taking the test, with some bright students opting out because they can't afford to go to Harvard, and many more students taking the test who formerly wouldn't have considered it.
2. There has been a decline in the number of students taking the test as juniors for practice. While this is not credited with making a big difference in scores, it has affected them.[50] Practice and coaching for the test can also affect scores.
3. Because of changed admissions policies (higher education admissions officers, some from elite colleges, becoming more lenient or not requiring standardized tests for admissions in order to attract more students) and students knowing that the necessity to score high is not as great, scores may be affected. In other words, student motivation to score well may not be as high.[51]
4. Evidence indicates that reading scores, measured by other tests such as NAEP, may actually be improving and that trends in society, such as emphasis on science during the *Sputnik* era, have influenced the academic emphasis at different points in time.[52]

Humanistic arguments include critiques of the whole testing process on several grounds; a person's worth is not a test score, which may be flawed.

More than the test score of individual students must be considered to evaluate students.

Effective Schools and Educational Reform

The buzzword in the halls of education is "effective schools," the newest "social movement." Exactly what is meant by this term varies, but common themes include schools in which students are achieving at a high level or in which achievement has risen significantly. Drawing from multiple studies of effective schools, limited somewhat because they were mostly done in urban schools, we can summarize the characteristics that enable students to achieve at a high level: (1) strong leadership in the schools, (2) frequent evaluation of student progress, (3) an atmosphere of high academic and behavioral expectations and requirements, (4) a school climate conducive to high expectations and serious academic work, and (5) teaching of skills to all students.[53]

How to achieve effective schools is the subject of even more studies and reports. The highest rates of improvement in school achievement have been reported when there is clear articulation of grade-level expectations and standards in each area, clear homework policies throughout the school, and all students are taught the curriculum for their grade level.[54] Other findings focus on instructional techniques, classroom expectations and rules, how students are grouped for subjects, and other specific recommendations, some of which were discussed in earlier chapters. Successful elementary schools have three characteristics in common, according to a comparative study: a sense of purpose, teamwork and sharing between all involved, and staff development.[55]

There is a danger in reform movements such as effective schools that schools, districts, or states will simply attempt to institute a "list" of reforms rather than consider carefully what is best for the school.[56] Some influential reformers argue that the individual school must be the center for efforts to improve schools. In a large research project based on extensive descriptive data from 38 schools in 13 diverse communities, Goodlad[57] investigated the following aspects of schools: school functions, the relevance of schools to students, how teachers teach, circumstances surrounding teaching, curriculum, distribution of resources for learning, equity, hidden curriculum, satisfaction with school quality, and need for school data collection. He argues that school reform must take place at the individual school and classroom level, not at some distant central location. Uniformity imposed from a central office hinders real change, and decentralization of decision making is essential. The strong leadership of a principal who gives teachers power and works with them will have the greatest impact on achievement in the school.

The risk with back to basics, accountability, and effective schools is that some of the ever-growing number of disadvantaged students who fall in the bottom half will be left farther behind and eventually drop out.

Structural and Curricular Changes in the Schools

Changes introduced in educational systems affect structure and role relationships. When movements produce new ideas, concerns, and programs there are often efforts to incorporate them into the existing system. This requires adaptation of the physical and role structure of schools. Structural changes can take place at the system level (for example, magnet schools and vouchers); the school level (for example, tracking students, integrating the disabled, programming for gifted children, installing architectural alternatives); and the classroom level (for example, alternative curriculum models, team teaching, open classrooms).

The "Choice" Movement

Systemwide change has resulted from attempts to integrate schools, as shown by the case of *magnet schools*. These were established in some cities to distribute students and desegregate schools on the basis of special interests or talents: science, mathematics, art and music, and vocational education. The plan is in place in some cities, sometimes as part of a busing-desegration plan. By the fall of 1992, there were 5,000 magnet schools nationwide.

Voucher systems also produce systemwide changes. School districts establish schools with a variety of philosophies, educational programs, kinds of discipline, and services. Communities and parents become involved in both the selection and the operation of schools. Each family receives money vouchers for school-aged children good for a year of education at the school of their choice.

Choice movement leaders have advocated parental and student free choice of schools so that parents can select between educational philosophies and curricula. One goal is to involve parents in the educational decisions regarding their children. Corporations are sponsoring some "model" schools, providing money for programs, equipment, and teacher training.[58,59]

Opponents of choice have several key concerns, among them that urban public schools would become the dumping ground for students not enrolled in other schools, and private schools supported in part by public funds would create further divisions in society by becoming more selective about their student bodies. Some have predicted the demise of public school education and heterogeneous grouping in schools. One critique puts it this way: " 'Choice' plans of the kind the White House has proposed threaten to compound the present fact of racial segregation with the added injury of caste discrimination, further isolating those who . . . have been consigned to places *nobody* would choose if he had any choice at all."[60] However, an early evaluation of Milwaukee's voucher plan indicates that the parental choice program is attracting some students who are more likely to have behavioral problems, and that these parents are more involved in and satisfied with their children's education than those not involved in the plan.[61]

Research does not indicate that a choice system would improve schooling for low-income youth. In fact, it could perpetuate the gap between wealthy and poor youth because high-income youth would continue to receive better education than poor youth.[62]

"Multiculturalism" and "Political Correctness"

"Hey, hey, ho, ho, Western culture's got to go," was the cry at Stanford University in 1987. The next year saw changes in the required course in

Western culture at Stanford, and also saw the debate over what is taught in schools and universities intensify.

"Multicultural curriculum" refers to teaching history and literature, among other subjects, in ways that accurately reflect the different cultural strands in our society and world.[63] Integration of multicultural materials into existing curricula involves inclusion of reading materials by and about minority groups, history that integrates all groups, and other broadened themes that promote understanding of all segments of multicultural society in the United States and around the World.

"Political correctness" refers to fair and accurate inclusion of minorities and women in discussions of history, literature, and other subjects. The movement has served to sensitize the many segments on campus to issues of racism, sexism, and other sensitive areas. The widespread and often acrimonious debate about "PC" centers around what is fair and accurate, and whether traditional values of academic freedom are being threatened by pressure to revise "traditional" curricula.

With the movement toward broadened curricula has come criticism of some educators for teaching traditional curricula or using "outdated" terms or explanations. A backlash began, based in Princeton, New Jersey, and known as the National Association of Scholars. Originally made up of conservative scholars, the organization has become more diverse over the years as more scholars have become concerned about issues of academic freedom.[64]

Dinesh D'Souza, one of the most controversial figures in the debate over the "politically correct" movement, argues that the "issue is not the inclusion of more works by women, or more works by blacks, or more works from outside the Western tradition; that broader representation is proper and justified has been conceded. The real issues—the ones underlying a wide range of campus debates—include the assumption by many that Western values are inherently oppressive, that the chief purpose of education is political transformation, and that all standards are arbitrary."[65,66]

When the controversy dies down, we should see some new and innovative approaches combining traditional and newer approaches to core curriculum in both public schools and higher education.

Technology and the Classroom

Concern over dropping achievement scores brought a flood of cure-alls beginning in the late 1950s. Teaching machines, reading programs, talking typewriters, educational television, tape-cassette machines, and other technological innovations were introduced into classrooms across the nation. Proponents of the new technology argued that schools should take advantage of the technological revolution, just as business and other institutional sectors were doing. "Traditional" classrooms could be changed into individualized instructional centers to meet a wide variety of learning styles and interests. Potential for linking home and school learning excited educators. Computers in the classroom and computer-assisted instruction (CAI) began in the late 1960s.

This is one example of a "fad" that is likely to have a lasting impact because of its importance to future jobs in society.

Other Movements, Reforms, and Fads

"The American educational system is in crisis. In the last decade hundreds of expensive reports and thousands of articles by social scientists and journalists have documented the shortcomings of America's schools. There has been general agreement over the need for change; there has been bitter disagreement over the content and philosophy of that change."[67]

Educational reforms have been proposed to solve everything from major educational concerns to small problems. Some ideas have been tried, succeeded, and been integrated into the system as permanent features; others have failed or died for lack of interest and support. New ideas vary in their rate of acceptance based on a number of factors: political climate, economic conditions, sources and pressures for change, change in routine required at the school and classroom level, and support of classroom teachers.

Some parents choose home schooling for their children.

The language of school reform has changed dramatically over the last 30 years, from concepts like "innovation" to systematic ideas of "restructuring and transformation."[68] The problems leading to this change are the growing numbers of low-income and minority children, dropouts, and failures.

Observers worry that current efforts to reform education are not based on research findings or an overall plan, and are likely to intensify problems rather than begin to solve them.[69] Little dialogue occurs between educational researchers and policy experts and opinion leaders who have influence over action taken.[70] Educators agree on many causes of school difficulties, but without influence, their advice often goes unheeded.

Though some would have us return to "the good ol' days" of education, no period in history has been free of educational critics and problems in schools: high dropout rates, nonreaders, boredom, violence, and undisciplined students. We can predict that the pendulum will continue to swing.[71]

Using the open systems approach helps make clear that one integrated approach to educational policymaking is difficult to accomplish in a system with such diverse environmental pressures and movements. It must take into account the many interdependent parts of the system. Schools are vulnerable to environmental pressures and to the moods of the time; a balanced program is difficult to achieve when each new fad creates upheaval in the system, altering its structure and roles relationships.

SUMMARY

Social and educational movements reflect the diversity of opinion present in a society. They reflect the range of perceived options. Systems experience pressure to change from movements in society; change may involve minor modifications in existing programs or major structural and curricular changes. Movements are only as effective in changing societal institutions as the attention they attract and the feasibility of the programs they propose and stimulate. Some movements seek separation from the existing structure. In this chapter we have reviewed theory of movements; the educational periods that have influenced today's education; movements in the United States, with specific examples; and trends in movements.

I. The Nature of Educational Movements

Educational movements come and go like the swing of a pendulum, reflecting the mood of the times. They influence educational systems as pressure groups from the environment. Some movements stimulate schools outside the traditional or public school system; others press for reform within the system.

II. Educational Movements Throughout History

Three influences from early European education on educational movements and systems today were discussed:

1. influential methods of teaching such as "reasoning power, rhetoric, and the art of persuasion" and rational inquiry;
2. human depravity of children, which encouraged authoritarian methods; and
3. the Renaissance concept of well-rounded, liberally educated persons.

Several movements have dominated educational history in the United States: the public school movement, progressive education, essentialism, and humanistic education.

III. Alternative Education

The alternative education movement came at a time when all institutions in our country were being challenged. It focused on what adherents felt was the oppressive nature of schools. Influential in movement philosophy were Summerhill and the English primary schools. From the movement came free schools outside the existing system, and alternative schools and open classrooms within.

IV. Back to Basics and Accountability

The back-to-basics movement is a backlash against the "permissiveness of alternative education." It stresses basic skills and places less emphasis on "nonessentials." It has given rise to private schools, competency-based education, and other submovements, such as accountability.

Accountability has meant many things, but usually includes teachers' concerns for competency and schools' assessment of outcomes of the educational process while considering expenses.

Effective schools literature is concerned with how to help students achieve; studies point out variables that schools should consider to raise levels of achievement.

Some movements have lasting effect; others, thought to be cure-alls, fizzle. Educational technology, performance contracting, and "new math" did not live up to expectations. Vocational education and some structural changes—magnet schools and voucher systems—have had mixed success. Open education has left a permanent, if limited, mark.

Societal movements are reflected in higher education systems through curriculum and structural changes. Some institutions have produced alternative educational models.

Change related to educational movements has been reflected in proposed innovations, radical reforms, and other alternatives. Many concerns of individual groups are reflected in these changes. Predictions are that concerns for equal education will continue and that practical education will be a focus because of economic conditions.

PUTTING SOCIOLOGY TO WORK

1. Find out what alternatives in primary and secondary education exist in your community.
2. Have any of the "fads" mentioned in this chapter been tried in schools in your community? Are they still in use? What has been their success or failure record?

3. Design a hypothetical school, at any level of the system, of the type you would like to attend. Include features of systems discussed in this chapter, and others you would like to add.

4. Do an informal survey of parents in your neighborhood about their attitudes toward education for their children and toward alternative versus basic education.

5. Spend some time observing in two local schools or classrooms that represent different philosophies.

NOTES

[1] Pipho, Chris, "States Move Reform Closer to Reality," *Phi Delta Kappan*, December 1986, pp. K1–K8.

[2] *Ibid.*

[3] Bickel, Robert, "Student Acceleration: Redefining an Educational Reform," *ERS Spectrum*, Spring 1986, pp. 14–21.

[4] Kellams, Samuel E., "Current General and Liberal Education Reform Efforts: The Cycle Continues," *Educational Studies*, Vol. 26, No. 2, 1985, pp. 117–26.

[5] Carnoy, Martin, and Henry M. Levin, "Educational Reform and Class Conflict," *Journal of Education*, Vol. 168, No. 1, 1986, pp. 35–46.

[6] Heberle, Rudolf, *Social Movements: An Introduction to Political Sociology* (New York: Irvington, 1951).

[7] Robertson, Ian, *Sociology: A Brief Introduction* (New York: Worth, 1989), pp. 383–84.

[8] Blanchard, John F., Jr., "Can We Live with Public Education," *Moody Monthly*, October 1971, p. 88.

[9] Brameld, Theodore, "Social Frontiers: Retrospective and Prospective," *Phi Delta Kappan*, October 1977, pp. 118–20.

[10] Silberman, Charles, *Crisis in the Classroom* (New York: Random House, 1970).

[11] Simon, Sidney B., *Values Clarification: A Handbook of Practical Strategies for Teachers and Students* (New York: Hart, 1972).

[12] Etzioni, Amitai, "Can Schools Teach Kids Values?" *Today's Education*, September/October 1977.

[13] *Ibid.*, pp. 36–43.

[14] This section was written with the assistance of Harden Ballentine.

[15] Capron, Barbara, Stanley Kleiman, and Tedd Levy, "Alternative Schools: Agents for Change?" Social Science Education Consortium *Newsletter*, May 1972, pp. 1–2.

[16] Graubard, Allen, *Free the Children: Radical Reform and the Free School Movement* (New York: Pantheon Books, 1972), pp. 9–10. (1) Critical analyses of the structure and function of the public school system include Paul Goodman, *Compulsory Mis-education;* Jules Henry, *Culture against Man;* John Holt, *How Children Fail* and *The Underachieving School;* Edgar Friedenberg, *Coming of Age in America;* Miriam Wasserman, *The School Fix—NYC, USA;* Paul Lauter and Florence Howe, *The Conspiracy of the Young;* Ivan Illich, *Deschooling Society;* The Schoolboys of Barbiana, *Letter to a Teacher.* (2) Personal accounts of experiences of teaching in public schools and of sometimes attempting free education ideas include Jonathan Kozol, *Death at an Early Age;* Herbert Kohl, *36 Children;* James Herndon, *The Way It Spozed to Be* and *How to Survive in Your Native Land;* Nat Hentoff, *Our Children Are Dying.* (3) Personal accounts of new schools include A. S. Neill, *Summerhill;* George Dennison, *The Lives of Children;* Sylvia Ashton-Warner, *Teacher;* Elwyn Richardson, *In the Early World;* Peter Marin, "The Open Truth and Fiery Vehemence of Youth" (much anthologized). (4) What could very loosely be called theory of free education and advice on how to translate theory into practice, either in new schools or in public school classrooms, include George Leonard, *Education and Ecstasy;* Neil Postman and Charles Weingartner, *Teaching as a Subversive Activity;* Herbert Kohl, *The Open Classroom;* John Holt, *How Children Learn* and *What Do I Do Monday?;* Carl Rogers, *Freedom to Learn;* Robert Greenway and Salli Rasberry, *Rasberry Exercises;*

Joseph Featherstone, articles on British infant schools in *Schools Where Children Learn;* Jonathan Kozol, *Free Schools.*

¹⁷ Neill, A. S., *Summerhill: A Radical Approach to Child Rearing* (New York: Hart, 1960).

¹⁸ Hart, Harold H., *Summerhill: For and Against* (New York: Hart, 1970).

¹⁹ Kozol, Jonathan, *Free Schools* (Boston, Houghton Mifflin, 1972).

²⁰ Kozol, Jonathan, *Savage Inequalities: Children in America's Schools* (New York: Crown, 1991).

²¹ Freire, Paulo, *Pedagogy of the Oppressed* (New York: Herder & Herder, 1970).

²² Illich, Ivan, *Deschooling Society* (New York: Harper & Row, 1971).

²³ Glatthorn, Allan A., "Alternative Schools," *The Review of Education,* Vol. 6, 1980, pp. 63–64.

²⁴ Firestone, William A., "Ideology and Conflict in Parent-Run Free Schools," *Sociology of Education,* Vol. 49, 1976, p. 174.

²⁵ Central Advisory Council for Education, *Children and Their Primary Schools* (London: H.M. Stationery Office, 1967).

²⁶ *Primary Education in England,* A Survey by H.M. Inspectors of Schools, Department of Education and Science (London: H.M. Stationery Office, 1978), paragraphs 8.28 and 8.29.

²⁷ A British Administrator Looks at British Schools" (interview of John Coe by Vincent Rogers), *Phi Delta Kappan,* September 1979, p. 61.

²⁸ Sealey, Leonard, "Open Education: Fact or Fiction?" *Teacher's College Record,* May 1976, p. 620.

²⁹ McPartland, James M., and Joyce L. Epstein, "Open Schools and Achievement: Extended Tests of a Finding of No Relationship," *Sociology of Education,* Vol. 50, 1977, pp. 133–44.

³⁰ *Ibid.,* p. 142.

³¹ Cockerham, William C., and Audie L. Blevins, "Open School vs. Traditional School: Self-Identification Among Native American and White Adolescents," *Sociology of Education,* Vol. 49, 1976, pp. 164–69.

³² *Ibid.,* p. 168.

³³ Ebel, Robert L., "The Failure of Schools Without Failure," *Phi Delta Kappan,* February 1980, p. 386.

³⁴ "Back to Basics in the Schools," *Newsweek,* October 21, 1974.

³⁵ Egerton, John, "Back to Basics," *The Progressive,* September 1976, p. 24.

³⁶ Donohue, John W., "What Happened to Progressive Education?" *America,* Vol. 134, January 1976, pp. 46–50.

³⁷ Brodinsky, Ben, "Back to Basics: The Movement and Its Meaning," *Phi Delta Kappan,* March 1977, p. 523.

³⁸ Nygren, Burton M., "Those 'Innovations' That Nearly Ruined the Schools in the 1960's," *The American School Board Journal,* Vol. 163, 1976, pp. 28–30.

³⁹ Fadiman, Clifton, "The Case for Basic Education," in James D. Koerner (ed.), *The Case for Basic Education* (Washington, D.C.: Council for Basic Education, 1959).

⁴⁰ Egerton, "Back to Basics," p. 21.

⁴¹ *Ibid.*

⁴² *America 2000: An Education Strategy* (Washington, D.C: U.S. Department of Education, 1991).

⁴³ Ornstein, Allan C., *et al., Introduction to the Foundations of Education* (Boston: Houghton Mifflin, 1988).

⁴⁴ Ornstein, Allan C., "Accountability: Prospects for the 1980s," *School and Community,* May 1981, pp. 24–25.

⁴⁵ Hentoff, Nat, "The Great Consumer Fraud," *Current,* March 1978, pp. 3–8.

⁴⁶ Jaffe, Donald L., "How to Evaluate Thee, Teacher—Let Me Count the Ways," *Phi Delta Kappan,* January 1980, pp. 349–352.

⁴⁷ Lyons, Gene, "Why Teachers Can't Teach," *Phi Delta Kappan,* October 1980, pp. 108–111.

[48] National Public Radio, Transcript of Program 134, "How Good Is Your Teacher," interview with James Herndon, NPR and Institute for Educational Leadership, pp. 7–8.

[49] Rosner, Benjamin, and Patricia Kay, "Will the Promise of C/PBTE Be Fulfilled?" *Phi Delta Kappan,* January 1974, pp. 290–95.

[50] Ebel, Robert L., Vincent R. Rogers, and Joan Baron, "Declining Scores: Two Explanations," *Phi Delta Kappan,* December 1976, pp. 306–13.

[51] *Ibid.*

[52] Wilhelms, Fred T., "What Basic Standards? " *Today's Education,* February 1976, p. 15.

[53] Edmonds, Ronald R., "Programs of School Improvement: An Overview," *Educational Leadership,* December 1982, pp. 4–11.

[54] Larkin, Maureen McCormack, "Insights into the School Effectiveness Process," *The Effective School Report from Research and Practice,* March 1984, p. 4.

[55] Mitchell, Anne W., "Schools That Work for Young Children," *The American School Board Journal,* November 1990, pp. 25–28.

[56] Barth, Roland S., "On Sheep and Goats and School Reform," *Phi Delta Kappan,* December 1986, pp. 293–96.

[57] Goodlad, John I., *A Place Called School* (New York: McGraw-Hill, 1984).

[58] Weisman, Jonathan, "Corporations Back Up Calls for Reform by Lending Their Expertise to Schools," *Education Week,* Vol. 10, No. 11, November 14, 1990, p. 10.

[59] Rist, Marilee C., "Angling for Influence," *The American School Board Journal,* April 1990, pp. 20–25.

[60] Kozol, *Savage Inequalities,* p. 63.

[61] Olson, Lynn, "Milwaukee Voucher Plan Found Not to 'Skim' Cream," *Education Week,* Vol. 11, No. 14, December 4, 1991, p. 12.

[62] Manski, Charles F., "Educational Choice (Vouchers) and Social Mobility," Institute for Research on Poverty (Madison: University of Wisconsin, June 1992), p. 1.

[63] Ravitch, Diane, "Multiculturalism Yes, Particularism No," *The Chronicle of Higher Education,* October 24, 1990, p. A44.

[64] Mooney, Carolyn J., "Academic Group Fighting the 'Politically Correct Left' Gains Momentum," *The Chronicle of Higher Education,* December 12, 1990, p. A13.

[65] D'Souza, Dinesh, "Illiberal Education," *The Atlantic Monthly,* March 1991, p. 51.

[66] D'Souza, Dinesh, *Illiberal Education: The Politics of Race and Sex on Campus* (New York: Free Press, 1991).

[67] Ewen, Lynda Ann, "Turning Around the American Dream: The Social Implications of the Changes in Education," paper presented at American Sociological Association meetings, Washington, D.C., August 1990.

[68] Hartoonian, Michael, "Good Education Is Bad Politics: Practices and Principles of School Reform," *Social Education,* Vol. 55, No. 1, January 1991, pp. 22 and 65.

[69] "Research and the Renewal of Education: Executive Summary and Recommendations," *Educational Researcher,* Vol. 20, No. 6, August/September 1991, pp. 19–22.

[70] Gardner, Howard, "The Two Rhetorics of School Reform: Complex Theories vs. the Quick Fix," May 6, 1992, Section 2, p. 1.

[71] Wolfthal, Maurice, "We Won't Reform Schools by Turning Back," *Educational Leadership,* September 1986, pp. 50–52.

12

CHANGE AND PLANNING IN EDUCATIONAL SYSTEMS

This book presents the story of a dynamic system. It is a system that does not and cannot remain stagnant, for there are constant pressures for change. Recall our systems model of the school (Figure 12-1). Everyone in our society is affected by that system. A large segment of our population has a primary involvement with the school system—those who are educated by it or employed by it. It touches the lives of all of us taxpayers, parents, and students.

Schools face constant challenges from within the system and from the environment. Flexibility and adaptation are necessary if an open system such as a school is to survive; it is dependent on the support of both internal and external individuals and groups in order to maintain a viable program and meet needs.

Change affects all aspects of educational systems. Recent pressures for change have focused on "loosening" the social structure and allowing students more flexibility and freedom of choice. Experiments with physical space and learning have been seen in "open space" schools and alternative classrooms. In this final chapter we explore the process of change in educational systems, and some methods that have been proposed to bring about change.

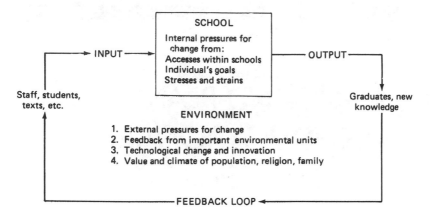

FIGURE 12-1   Systems model of school change.

THE DYNAMICS OF CHANGE

Change is ever present. It takes place in societies, organizations, groups, and individuals. The difficulty lies in coming up with one definition that fits all levels and types of change, planned and unplanned. Here is one definition of change: It is "the process of planned or unplanned qualitative or quantitative alterations in social phenomena."[1] Also, "planned social change refers to deliberate, conscious, and collaborative efforts by change agents to improve the operations of social systems."[2] Let us consider several components of the change process:

- *Identity* of change refers to a specific social phenomenon undergoing transformation.
- *Level* of change delineates the location in a social system where a particular change takes place.
- *Duration* refers to the question of how long a particular change form endures after it has been accepted.
- *Direction* of change may indicate development or decay, progress, or decline.
- *Magnitude* may be based on a three-part scheme of incremental or marginal, comprehensive, and revolutionary change.
- *Rate* of change may be based on any arbitrary scale such as fast or slow. . . .[3]

The process can take place in rapid spurts or it can be gradual and almost evolutionary. It can be planned or unplanned. Planned change often takes place as a result of the "manifest functions" or stated purposes of a system. Unplanned change, in some cases referred to as "latent functions," may result from unanticipated consequences of planned change.

The impetus for change comes from the internal functioning of schools or from the environmental influences on schools. For examples we must use snapshots capturing one moment. Tomorrow's snapshot will be different from today's, for this is the nature of the unending process of change, a process that has been an underlying theme throughout this book.[4]

Change is often seen as a positive, productive process improving our lives. Yet it can also be a threatening, frightening, and conflict-producing force pushing and pulling people with its constant motion. Change often upsets the routines we have established, and as creatures who need some stability, we find this unsettling. The term "future shock," coined by Alvin Toffler, refers to extreme cases of inability to adjust or adapt to rapid social-cultural change.[5] Routines are important. They give us familiar benchmarks; take them away and there is no structure within which to move from one activity to another. It is within this process framework that we look at change in educational institutions.

Change and Levels of Analysis

When we picture change, we must visualize a complex and ubiquitous process. It is useful to be aware of the level at which change is occurring when we are proposing and implementing change and studying its impact. Social scientists generally conceptualize four "levels of analysis" when referring to change in systems such as schools:

1. The *individual level* refers to change that is initiated by or directed toward persons holding roles within the system—teachers, students, or others. For instance, there might be attempts to change teacher attitudes toward a new program.

Children learn in many ways.

2. The *organizational level* refers to change within a school. Perhaps a new curriculum model is introduced that will require changes in the physical and role structures of the school.
3. The *institutional or societal level* refers to large system change. This is usually related to changes in other parts of society. For instance, change in the political institution and structure of a nation will often result in changes in educational policy.
4. The *cultural level* refers to change in societal attitudes and values. These are often the slowest to change, lagging behind technological innovations.

Change occurs at each level of analysis, and major change may affect all. When considering levels of analysis, we can use several types of strategies, depending on whether the change is short- or long-term (see Table 12-1).[6,7]

At the micro or individual level, there may be short-term changes in attitudes and behavior (Type 1). An illustration of this change would be the use of sensitivity training to alter a person's attitudes. An illustration of a more long-term change at the micro level (Type 2) is the training and socialization process of new recruits in an institution. Priests, for example, when they start their training program, learn a new set of attitudes and behavior that affects their entire life. At the group or intermediate level of short term change, normative or administrative change may be brought about. Normative changes take place when a group alters its norms temporarily to experiment with an innovation (Type 3). For example, in a corporation a team sets up a novel computerized information bank. Team members are given freedom to experiment, and they can bend established organizational rules. The change agent (in this case, the manager responsible for the innovation) encourages the team. Once the innovation has been tried and found useful, it is institutionalized.[8,9] At this point, it will become a more long-term change (Type 4) at the organizational level. The original participants in the change effort will be rewarded, this process then providing incentives for others to experiment.

At the societal level of change, short-term (Type 5) change is often the result of innovations or inventions. For example, the introduction of birth-control technology in a receptive society can alter birthrates and population size in a relatively short time period. In the long run, these changes could

TABLE 12-1   Time Dimensions and Target Levels

Time Dimension	Micro (Individual)	Intermediate (Group)	Macro (Society)
	LEVEL OF SOCIETY		
Short-term	Type 1 (1) Attitude change (2) Behavior change	Type 3 (1) Normative change (2) Administrative change	Type 5 Invention-innovation
Long-term	Type 2 Life-cycle change	Type 4 Organizational change	Type 6 Sociocultural evolution

Source: Zaltman, Gerald, and Robert Duncan, *Strategies for Planned Change* (New York: Wiley, 1977), p. 11.

result in major changes in the social structure of the society. The long-term consequences are (Type 6) sociocultural change—that is, the facilitation of the modernization process in an underdeveloped nation.

By recognizing where the change is taking place, we can better understand the process and deal with its consequences.

Sources of Change

Stresses and strains in school systems are major sources of change. *Stresses,* which Olsen[10] describes as "sources external to an organization" and which are part of the system's environment, fall into four main categories:

1. *Population size and composition.* In the early 1960s, there was a need for more teachers to meet the demand of increased student populations from the baby boom; yet now many schools have been forced to close and there is a teacher glut because of the drop in student population. While these trends can hardly be controlled, they can be predicted with some degree of accuracy for future planning.

2. *The human factor.* Individuals in positions of power can bring about change in the climate or structure of the classroom or school system through their personality. For instance, the classroom teacher often initiates change at this level. Individuals holding positions in the system must be considered whether change is being planned, implemented, or analyzed.

3. *Material technology.* There are always new ideas and new materials that could be integrated into the educational system. Whether an invention be major or minor, involving materials or techniques, educators are challenged to integrate the new technology into the system and pass it on through the process of learning.

4. *Natural environment* (including such factors as "climatic adaptation," depletion of vital natural resources, natural disasters, epidemics, and weather conditions). Some schools were required to close their doors owing to fuel shortages during the coldest days of the extreme winters of 1977 and 1978. Blizzards and ice also affect school days and alter schedules. These are examples of natural environment influences.

In addition to the four sources mentioned by Olsen, there are major trends in societies that stimulate change in all institutions: movement toward urbanization, industrialization, modernization, and postindustrial, technocratic society. Yet another source of changes comes from attitudes of the public and educators at any particular time stimulated by social movements reflecting societal concerns.

Strains are sources of conflict and pressure that develop within the internal organization. Many examples of change in the literature focus on strains, though it is important to keep in mind that change in the internal organization is also affected by what is happening in its environment. Let us consider several examples of internal strain in educational systems:

1. *Individuals or subgroups within the organization.* Goals of individuals or subgroups within the organization may be supportive of system goals, or may contradict

them. Conflict can occur when goals differ. If the individual or subgroup is influential or holds a position of power and favors change, then change is likely to result from the conflict. However, as in the case of minorities in the system, success defined as individual gain and upward mobility assumes that these are equally available to all and that all share these goals. This assumption may also lead to conflict.[11]

2. *"Deviant" individuals or groups within the organization.* Students who are rebellious, behavior problems, or potential dropouts create strain in the system because they are not working toward system goals. Therefore, the educational system will frequently devote human and financial resources to reducing or eliminating the strain. "Deviant" teachers who propose alternative methods or structures that would force the system to change can also create strain.

3. *Ideology, goals, structure, and resources.* Strain can develop as a result of incongruencies between a system's ideology and goals, the structure within the system must function, and the resources available to the system. "Open space" schools or schools without walls, built in the late 1960s and early 1970s, are sometimes seen as a hindrance to more rigid programs.

PERSPECTIVES ON CHANGE

Imagine that we have an assignment to outline a process for bringing about change in a school. One important aspect of this process is to identify our perspective on change. When sociologists consider the process of change, two theoretical perspectives dominate the literature. *Structural-functional theory* sees change as a gradual adjustment of a system to stresses and strains. *Conflict theory* sees change as occurring through conflict or more dramatic revolution (see table 12-2).

Structural-Functional Approach to Change

The educational system attempts to maintain order and integration among its principal parts. The system is basically in a state of equilibrium; social control mechanisms help maintain stability and adjustment. Threats to this equilibrium in the form of pressures for change are likely to be seen as dysfunctional or negative for the system, but balancing is a continual process. Pierre Van den Berghe has outlined several aspects of change as perceived from the functionalist point of view:

> Although integration is never perfect, social systems are fundamentally in a state of dynamic equilibrium; i.e., adjustive responses to outside changes tend to minimize the final amount of change within the system. The dominate tendency is thus toward stability and inertia, as maintained through built-in mechanisms of adjustment and social control.[12]

Van den Berghe points out that "dysfunctions," tensions, and deviance exist and persist in systems, but tend to become part of the ongoing system, to be "institutionalized." The system tries to achieve and maintain equilibrium and integration. Change is seen as occurring in a gradual, adaptive fashion; sudden changes leave the core structure unchanged. From this point of view, change stems from three sources: adjustment of the system to environmental demands; growth of the system; and inventions or innovations of group members.

Critics of structural-functional theory point out that the theory does not give a complete view of change. For instance, it cannot account for sudden or revolutionary change, and for systems that are *not* integrated. What may be functional change for one group may be harmful to another.[13] Later in this chapter we discuss several of the strategies for bringing about change through a functionalist approach that maintains order and attempts to achieve change with the least disruption to the system.

Conflict Approach to Change

Change is seen by conflict theorists as inevitable, ever-present, and part of the nature of events. Change is the essential element of social life.

> Change is not only ubiquitous, but an important share of it is generated within the system; i.e., the social structure must be looked at, not only as the static framework of society, but also as the source of a crucial type of change.
>
> Change is intra-systematic or endogenous from inside the system. The origin [of change] often arises from contradiction and conflict between two or more opposing factors. These "factors" can be values, ideologies, roles, institutions or groups.[14]

Conflict between competing interest groups in modern society accentuates the pressure for change in schools and the community. Dominant groups or power holders attempt to protect the system from change that will alter their status or threaten vested interests, such as an education system that favors certain groups. When change does occur it may be the result of a crisis, a conflict over power and decision making. The current conflict over curriculum content provides a case in point. Significant change in schools is unlikely to come about as a result of additional resources, but rather will require change in the structure, roles, and power relationships within schools, according to conflict theorists. Fewer stated strategies for change in educational systems have been developed from the conflict perspective, but change does occur through disruptions, and there is ever-present potential for conflict in the system.

Table 12-2, taken from an article by Lawrence Saha[15] summarizes conceptual and theoretical frameworks of change and their relationship to educational change. Note that the strategies for planning, as well as the outcomes, depend upon the theory employed. The items under each column of the table represent a cluster and are not intended to be linked with particular items in adjacent cells.

When social scientists are studying change, their theoretical perspectives influence their interpretations. For instance, note the difference between the "rationales for educational change" of the structural-functionalists focusing on "system needs" as against the neo-Marxian focus on "social justice and equality."

TABLE 12-2 Summary of Sociological Theories of Education and Implications for Planning

Theoretical Approaches	Theory of Society	Theory of Education	Policy Priorities	Planning Strategies
Functionalist-Consensus	Integrated social institutions Social order based on consensus Homeostasis, i.e. balance-seeking among institutions	Education integrated with other institutions Socialization function Selection and allocation functions Creation of new knowledge "Babysitting" functions, i.e., keep youth off streets and postpone entry to job market	Equal opportunity/meritocracy; each can rise to their level of competence Maximize use of talent Closer links with other sectors of society	Selective educational systems/late selection Human capital, "rates of return" planning Educational expansion as investment Compensatory education programs Remove barriers to social mobility
Conflict (Marxist and non-Marxist)	Conflict and exploitation Power and force to maintain order Constant struggle between dominant and subordinate groups	Education an extension of dominant group power/doubtful autonomy Education reproduces social order	Break correspondence between school organization/structure and the needs of the economy Consciousness-raising and resistance taught in schools	Change structure of schools/work/society Replace dominant ideology in curriculum Education expansion as liberation

Interactionist	Social reality as negotiated and defined by actors Social order result of shared symbols and values	Education a process of definition of reality Classroom interaction the center of education process Classroom is self-fulfilling prophecy	Remove bias from class-room interaction Equality of opportunity and treatment in the classroom	Teacher training—expose teacher bias Focus on positive student self-identity and self-confidence Restructure classroom setting to eradicate "labeling" Reduce emphasis on ex-aminations and class competition
Critical Theory	Oppression by dominant class and dominant ideol-ogy, maintained by hid-den agenda and hidden curriculum	Education serves to main-tain oppression	Remove oppression thru empowerment skills	Curriculum reform Critical enquiry

Source: Saha, Lawrence J., "Bringing People Back In: Sociological Theories of Education and Implications for Planning Strategies," presented at Sociology of Education, International Sociological Association, Amsterdam, July 1992.

Open Systems Approach to Change

The open systems approach is based on the assumption that change, whether evolutionary or revolutionary, is inevitable and ever-present in systems. Systems are constantly in the process of change because of their adaptation to feedback from the environment. This approach provides us with a framework for viewing the total system, locating the impetus for change, and tracing the repercussions of change throughout the system. The theoretical perspectives on change discussed above both have limitations. The open systems approach to change takes the emphasis off stability and equilibrium and looks at the system from a different perspective.[16] It is not locked into a specific theoretical perspective and can therefore help us analyze the type, speed, location, and effects of change on the total system. It does not assume equilibrium or disruption related to change. Systems are not viewed as intransigent or in crisis; rather, change is seen as a normal part of the system, whether it be planned or unplanned. Theories of change can be used in combination with the systems approach to better understand the total impact of the process of change.

Viewed from an open systems approach, change may emanate from inside a school system or a subsystem or may come from environmental sources outside. The environment has a constant impact on the school. Inputs into the school system, such as legal requirements, financial resources, and community attitudes, change constantly, requiring the system to adapt. The change may be rapid, such as that caused by a student movement or fad, or may be slower, as in rising or dwindling student or teacher population.

The school system relies on feedback from the environment in adapting its programs. If, for instance, a goals is to produce students who can find jobs, the school system must be aware of the changing demands for skills. It may even attempt to influence the job market by interacting with business and the community. The school system may attempt to control aspects of its environment. For instance, funding and finances are essential to continue programs. In order to increase security and stability, school systems may become involved in public relations efforts to "sell" themselves to the public. This is especially true with efforts to justify expenditures and get levies passed. There is give and take between the school and its environment, but schools must adapt to environmental demands, which often necessitate change.

The systems approach most often focuses on the organizational level of structure and roles, and gives an overview of the system and its parts. Potential exists for bringing the numerous studies of system change under one umbrella, thus obtaining a view of the whole that is closer to reality than an individual study can provide.

For an outsider looking in or an insider trying to get some perspective on the organization, the open systems approach can help locate elements of particular interest for change in the organization or its environment. This ability to see the relationship of parts to the whole can be crucial in assessing accurately the potential problems in the process and need for change. The open systems approach also aids in the planning of change and thus is more effective than haphazard response to transitory social movements.

BRINGING ABOUT CHANGE

One gets the feeling of a force, a perpetual-motion machine, when viewing change in the educational system. However, resistance from participants and caution on the part of decision makers keep the change process from rushing headlong. These brakes cannot stop the system, but they can slow it. Every part of the educational system is caught up in change, for no part is totally autonomous. What are some of the factors involved in the push toward change? Most of the factors have their roots in organizational or structural rather than individual attributes.

Any time we introduce a major change, we must consider the impact on the whole system, for every part of the system experiences stresses and strains. The impetus for change comes from environmental pressures and educational hierarchies, and is often mandated by a central office. Superintendents have the power and resources unavailable at the local district level to bring about change. But it is the individual school and teachers who must carry out the change. Without their support change is likely to fail.

Individuals in the System

The individuals who hold positions in educational systems influence the rate of change by their initiation, acceptance, or resistance to it. Let us consider examples of administrators and teachers. Impetus for change from administrators has come in such areas as court-ordered busing or integration of teaching staff, mainstreaming of disabled students, measures to cut the budget, new programs such as computer technology and Computer-Assisted Instruction (CAI), restructuring of classrooms for homogeneity or heterogeneity, and reading or testing programs. Generally, initiation for change comes from the more powerful units because they control the resources. Those with less power either will be persuaded to agree, or will feel neutral about the change, or will be unable to mount substantial resistance if they oppose the change. Although it is recognized that school administrators, especially superintendents, play a significant role in innovation and change, study results differ as to the degree of their influence; some administrators are seen as preservers of the status quo and others as forces for change.

Impetus for change may also come from the classroom teacher. Teachers are bombarded with new technology and materials from the environment that promise to improve their teaching and ease their teaching load: new texts, innovative classroom arrangements, rearrangement of students for better interaction, new technological advances.

The teachers' role in initiating change has been downplayed because their subordinate position in the structure makes this difficult. Many teachers

TABLE 12-3   Ten Indicators of Organizational Health

1. Goal focus	This is clarity and acceptance; goals are achievable with existing or available resources.
2. Communication adequacy	Communication is distortion-free—vertically and horizontally and across the system to the environment.
3. Optimal power equalization	Subordinates can influence upward. There is collaboration rather than explicit or implicit coercion.
4. Resource utilization	The system's inputs, particularly the personnel, are used effectively. There is minimal sense of strain.
5. Cohesiveness	Members feel attracted to membership in the organization.
6. Morale	There are feelings of well-being, satisfaction, pleasure in working in the organization.
7. Innovativeness	There is a tendency to invent new procedures, move toward new goals, produce new products.
8. Autonomy	The organization's response to outside demands influenced by outside inputs is neither passive nor rebellious; the organization does not treat outside responses as determinative of its actions.
9. Adaptation	When environmental demands and organization are in conflict, a problem-solving, restructuring approach evolves.
10. Problem-solving adequacy	There are well-developed structures and procedures for sensing problems, inventing and implementing solutions, and evaluating their effectiveness.

Source: From J. Victor Baldridge and Terrence E. Deal, *Managing Change in Educational Organizations.* Copyright 1975 by McCutchan Publishing Corporation, Berkeley, CA 94702. Permission granted by the publisher.

remember good ideas they had that never came to fruition because of resistance from administrators, the school board, or parents.

Change at the School Level

The "health" of the school can influence the amount of change that takes place.[17] Planned changes must take into account the "health" of the system, according to Matthew Miles. If an organization is in a healthy state, attempts at planned changes are likely to be successful. Miles gives ten indicators of organizational health (Table 12-3). The problem is that most schools do not exhibit many of these signs of "health." Therefore, change is difficult to implement. Miles suggests several strategies aimed at improving organizational health, enabling the school to cope more effectively with the change process: team training to increase communication; survey feedback to clarify goals and solve problems; role workshops to improve effectiveness; target setting between superiors and subordinates; organizational diagnosis and problem solving. Once the organization shows signs of health, a positive process of planned change is possible.

STRATEGIES FOR SCHOOL CHANGE

In order for major change to be made, the whole school system and often the community must be involved in it. First, if the community is concerned about an issue, its acceptance must be sought, since the opportunity supplies feedback and financial support. Second, there must be support from the school district, which provides money, programs, and extra personnel to assist in implementing the change. Third, the school principal must provide leadership throughout the process. Fourth, teachers must be willing to support the change. During the change process, some teachers become "early adopters"; after they are recognized as such, other teachers follow. It is not always necessary for the entire staff to support an innovation, but it seems essential to have "early adopters" who are willing to take the risk involved in the process. Finally, students affected by the change can ease its adoption or rebel against the new plans.

Types of Strategies

Educators and social scientists differ in their views concerning the strategies most effective for implementing change. Baldridge and Deal outline five key perspectives that have been commonly proposed for bringing about change, and that correspond with our levels of analysis.

Individual Perspective.   This perspective focuses on the individual and small-group approach, which is greatly influenced by psychological and social-psychological research. The individual is seen as proposing, adopting, or rejecting change. Since attitudes toward change are influenced by the individual's value system, the underlying assumption is that organizational change can occur by changing individual attitudes and thus individual actions.[18]

Implementing change depends on changing the the person(s) who will be installing and utilizing the innovation or invention. Organizational members are selected for their reliability and accountability, factors that can lead to inertia.

Behavior modification is one specific strategy being used in some institutional settings such as schools to bring about change. It involves several techniques such as punishing undesirable behaviors and rewarding desirable behaviors.[19]

The problem with conceptualizing and planning change by emphasizing individuals holding positions in schools is that it ignores the characteristics of the system within which change is to take place.

Goals and Saga Perspective.   Goals are often the focal point of educational change. Despite difficulties in clarifying vague and diffuse goals, this perspective is important because goals establish reasons for an organization's existence and a common ground from which participants can direct their efforts. A saga is a myth or belief system rooted in the organization's history. It justifies an organization's existence and reduces the time and energy needed to maintain the system. An organization with a deep-rooted saga will be difficult to change. In crisis circumstances, however, it may be possible to develop a new saga and so produce long-lasting changes. Goals and sagas are crucial elements to consider when managing organization change.

Technological Perspective.   The technology of a system or organization is the nature of the work the organization performs, and the procedures, processes, activities, and devices that assist it in accomplishing its goals and objectives. Technology changes for several reasons. Sometimes the environment places new demands on the organization, or new inventions are developed. Sometimes organizational participants themselves devise new ways of doing things. Technological changes must be assessed in terms of the demands they make on the structure. For example, implementing new individualized instructional devices might involve organizing teachers into teams and increasing their ability to deal with individual students (a structural change). Technological innovations require new roles, more coordination and problem solving, and increased interdependency, all of which involve structural changes.

Environmental Perspective.   The school environment includes not only parents, students, teachers, and the local community, but also the teachers' unions; state, local, and federal government agencies; other educational agencies; and the professional and educational climate. All educational systems depend on their environment for financial and moral support. The environment can be both a stimulator of and a barrier to educational change. It must be taken into consideration constantly when attempting to implement change.

Structural Perspective.   Structural elements include individual jobs; subunits (departments/divisions); and the organization's hierarchy, rules, goals, and plans. An organization's structure can be viewed as a consequence of change (a change in instructional devices could place new demands on the structure) or as a facilitator of innovation.

Many social scientists contend that long-lasting organization change can come about only through manipulation of *organizational* variables (authority structure, reward systems, technological and environmental relations). Though the individual and small group are necessary to implement change, structural aspects of the system must be part of planning. Basic structural reorganization is often necessary for schools to accomplish goals, monitor and influence the environment, and successfully adopt new technology.

Strategies fall into four general categories:

1. *Facilitative strategies* are the ones that make easier the implementation of changes by and/or among the target group.[20]
2. *Reeducative strategies* are used when time is not a pressing factor. The relatively objective presentation is intended to provide a rational justification for action.
3. *Persuasive strategies* try to bring about change through bias in the way in which a message is structured and presented.
4. *Power strategies* involve the use of coercion to secure the target's compliance.[21]

From our open systems perspective, a system that involves primary participants in change-oriented activities, that takes into consideration the organizational structure, and that develops an internal process to bring about change while being responsive to environmental pressures, is likely to be responsive to the many internal and external organization demands.[22]

We are all familiar with great ideas that bombed. Educational technology that was purchased but never quite integrated into the classroom is a good example. Why do such ideas fail?

Actual change in a school should involve the key participants in the planning. If the change will affect the classroom, involving teachers from the beginning of the planning can reduce resistance to the change. Training is a crucial element in the success formula; new programs are unlikely to be adopted if teachers are unclear on any details. Support from the leadership is also critical in successful implementation.[23]

The key principles are that change at one level and part of the organization will affect other levels and parts—it does not occur in a vacuum—and change is more likely to be successful if key participants are involved in the process of planning and implementing change.

Beyond that, the degree to which an innovation is implemented also depends on the extent to which certain conditions are present during implementation: clarity of goals and plans, capabilities of administrators and staff, availability of resources, compatibility of the organizational structure with the proposed changes and willingness of those involved to expend time and effort. The extent to which these conditions are met depends on the performance of the administrators during the period of implementation. Key participants—for example, teachers and students—can assure that changes proceed smoothly. However, they can also put up barriers to change.

Obstacles and Resistance to Implementation of Change

Obstacles to change often seem overwhelming to those involved in the implementation process. Vested interests in the status quo, opposing values and goals, apparent deficiencies and inadequacies in the proposed alteration, perceived intolerable consequences, and sheer human inertia can themselves limit change or allow for opposition to form and block change.

The toughest barrier to overcome is resistance from within the educational system, especially from the teachers who may have feelings of vulnerability. Their fears may stem from perceived threats of being considered inadequate in their job performance.

Teachers have their set routines and work patterns, and there must be compelling reasons for them to abandon those patterns and take a chance on new ones. They may believe the proposed change is a bad one.

Ideas, values, traditions, and beliefs are the bases of our nonmaterial culture and the institutions it comprises. While the material culture is changing rapidly, the nonmaterial culture lags behind, sometimes resisting change. Scientists developed satellite TV, which will, we are told, solve the world's literacy and basic skills problems by beaming education to stations at home and abroad. But compare the process of invention to the complexity of gaining approval and implementing the "cure-all" into the classroom; ideas change slowly.

In summary, implementation of change must take into account several factors:

1. A serious assessment of the needs of the organization must be taken.
2. The proposed change must be relevant to the organization.
3. The environment must be taken into account.
4. Both the organizational structure and individual attitudes must be considered.
5. The change must be directed at manipulable factors.
6. The change must be both politically and economically feasible.
7. The change must be effective in solving the problems that were diagnosed.[24]

Once these considerations are taken into account, change is more likely to be successfully implemented.

THE SOCIOLOGIST'S ROLE IN EDUCATIONAL CHANGE AND POLICY FORMATION

In the civil rights movement, the desegregation battles, the integration and busing controversies, and other major issues of our time, sociologists were there. They were there in a variety of capacities, filling many roles. In this final section, let us consider some of these roles and the controversy about what is an appropriate role for sociologists.

Sociologists do *basic research*. They conceptualize school systems within theoretical frameworks, collect data, and analyze aspects of the systems. They may use, as a basis, Weber's bureaucratic model, a Marxian conflict theory, or many other approaches. Studies focus on a number of aspects of schooling such as those discussed in this book.

Basic research provides knowledge about the system of education not available elsewhere. Knowledge is used by investigative committees, the legal system, school boards, administrators, and teachers to make planning decisions.[25] Some research is commissioned or funded, such as Coleman's study.

Problem research and intepretation is another major role carried out by sociologists of education. This involves the following tasks:

1. *Collecting data for a specific purpose.* A researcher may be presented with a specific question or problem, such as dropping enrollments, and be expected to collect relevant data and interpret them to shed light on the problem.
2. *Working with existing data.* The sociologist may consider existing data from one or more sources, such as the census or school testing results, and may analyze and interpret the data within a theoretical framework to see existing trends.

Teaching is a role carried out by the majority of sociologists. In this role as teachers and advisers, many faculty are aware of changing student body composition and needs, especially training students to cope with lifelong learning and solve complex problems.[26] In this capacity knowledge about educational systems is disseminated to future sociologists, educators, and citizens. Implicit in this role is the decision of what theoretical perspective to use and what information to teach.

Evaluation research is receiving increased attention because of recent pressure for accountability; evaluation can be used as strategy for producing and controlling innovations and reforms in educational systems. The purpose of evaluation is to learn how well a program or innovation is reaching its goals. In practice, evaluation is most often used to help with decisions about adopting, improving, or discontinuing a program. Evaluation can demonstrate three things:

1. the need for change,
2. whether change has taken place, and
3. the outcome of any particular change or innovation.[27]

In the past, evaluation research has been used to its full potential in supporting or discouraging educational innovations because educational systems have shown resistance to unwanted or negative information—and unwanted change. But since the importance of accurate evaluation is being recognized in the educational arena, and accountability is required by many funding agencies, it will probably be used to a greater extent and even be required as a strategy for change in the future.

Policy formation and advocacy is the most controversial role. The controversy revolves around whether sociologists should become involved in areas outside their research training, thus moving into "nonobjective" arenas. The controversy became heated in the 1950s, when C. Wright Mills[28] advocated a more active role for sociologists. He argued that sociologists cannot remain neutral and detached when they have knowledge that, if implemented into policy, could improve conditions for many people. There is a middle ground for sociologists who can make a valuable contribution to education and change.

The dynamic system of education will continue to change. We can deal with that change in a logical and consistent manner only if we have research capabilities, an understanding of the change process, and a clear conception of the educational system.

Whether you are or will be a student, a taxpayer, a parent of a school-aged child, a member of the PTA, a school board member, or an educator, an understanding of the complex elements that make up the educational system will help you deal more effectively with its problems.

SUMMARY

In this final chapter we have analyzed the pervasive process of change.

I. The Dynamics of Change

Change is a dynamic process, and an integral part of the concept of an educational system. It can occur at any level of analysis—individual, organizational, societal, or cultural—or can affect all levels if it is major change. The process originates because of stresses or strains within or outside the system.

Change comes from stresses external to the system, such as population size and composition; individuals who affect the system; material technology and the natural environment; or from strains within the system. These can come from conflicting goals of individuals or subgroups, deviant individuals or groups, or incongruencies between ideology and goals.

II. Perspectives on Change

Change can be seen from several theoretical perspectives. The structural-functional approach views the system as in equilibrium, and tending toward stability. Major change can threaten this equilibrium. Most change, however, is gradual and the system adapts to it. The conflict approach views change as inevitable and often disruptive. The open systems approach views change as a part of the system; it can be disruptive or can help the system adapt to changing environmental demands.

III. Bringing About Change

Most important in bringing about change is working with all levels of the system. For those trying to implement change, certain conditions are necessary: an understanding of the system, familiarity with strategies for bringing about change, and experience in the process. Administrators, teachers, and students serve as catalysts for change. An organization should ideally possess certain characteristics to be receptive and successful in change efforts. The health of an organization may determine whether change will be successful.

Key participants need to be informed and involved if the process is to proceed smoothly. There are, however, often obstacles that must be addressed before change can be implemented.

IV. Strategies for School Change

Strategies for change range from minor programmatic changes, to reform strategies, to total system overhaul. Most plans are for implementation of program changes. Though planned and controlled change is the ideal, in reality the process does not always work smoothly. Strategies focus on different levels and parts of the system.

Resistance to change may come from any part of the system or environment. Most important is that classroom teachers are involved in planning for the change or it cannot be successful.

The systems theme of this book suggests that no one level is enough to implement change successfully. Several cases of organizational change were used as examples. Some reasons for failure to implement change were discussed.

V. The Sociologist's Role in Educational Change and Policy Formation

Sociologists play several roles in the process of change: basic researchers, problem researchers and interpreters, teachers, evaluators, policymakers, and advocates. Each role was discussed.

PUTTING SOCIOLOGY TO WORK

1. Imagine yourself in any position in the school system: student, teacher, or administrator. Now imagine a major change in the school, let us say a change to an open classroom (school without walls) from a formal, closed classroom structure. In your imagined position, what feelings are you experiencing? Are there conflicts in your role because of this change? Why?
2. Investigate the history of a program that has been implemented at a public school or college. Find out about the stages up to implementation. What is the current status of the program?
3. Trace the history of a program or project that failed or was not implemented. Why did this happen?
4. Design a project that you would like to see implemented. What steps would you take to plan implementation?
5. Interview administrator(s) and teacher(s) about their techniques for introducing new ideas. What effect, if any, does their status have on success of the idea?

NOTES

[1] Vago, Steven, *Social Change*, 2nd ed. (Englewood Cliffs, N.J.: Prentice Hall, 1989), p. 9.

[2] Bennis, Warren G., Kenneth D. Benne, and Robert Chin (eds.), *The Planning of Change*, 4th ed. (New York: Holt, Rinehart, and Winston, 1985), p. 280.

[3] Vago, *Social Change*, p. 9.

[4] Hall, Richard H., *Organizations: Structures, Processes, and Outcomes* (Englewood Cliffs, N.J.: Prentice Hall, 1991).

[5] Toffler, Alvin, *Future Shock* (New York: Random House, 1970).

[6] Zaltman, Gerald, and Robert Duncan, *Strategies for Planned Change* (New York: Wiley, 1977), p. 11.

[7] Vago, *Social Change*, pp. 281–82.

[8] Kanter, Rosabeth, *The Challenge of Organizational Change: How People Experience and Manage It* (New York: Free Press, 1991).

[9] Kanter, Rosabeth, *The Change Masters: Innovation for Productivity in the American Coporation* (New York: Simon & Schuster, 1985).

[10] Olsen, Marvin E., *The Process of Social Organization* (New York: Holt, Rinehart and Winston, 1968), pp. 141–42.

[11] Sleeter, Christine E., and Carl A. Grant, "Race, Class, and Gender and Abandoned Dreams," *Teachers' College Record*, Spring 1988.

[12] Van den Berghe, Pierre L., "Dialectic and Functionalism: Toward a Synthesis," in Nicolas Jay Demerath and Richard A. Peterson (eds.), *System, Change and Conflict* (New York: Free Press, 1967), pp. 293–306.

[13] Eisenstadt, S. N., "Macro-societal Analysis—Background, Development and Indication," in S. N. Eisenstadt and H. J. Helle (eds.), *Macro-Sociological Theory: Perspectives on Sociological Theory*, Vol. I (London: Sage, 1985), pp. 7–24.

[14] Van den Berghe, "Dialectic and Functionalism," p. 300.

[15] Paulston, Rolland G., "Social and Educational Change: Conceptual Frameworks," *Comparative Education Review*, Vol. 21, 1977, pp. 372–73.

[16] Tominaga, Ken'ichi, "Typology in the Methodological Approach to the Study of Social Change," in S. N. Eisenstadt and H. J. Helle (eds)., *Marco-Sociological Theory*, pp. 168–96.

[17] Miles, Matthew B., "Planned Change and Organizational Health: Figure and Ground," in Baldridge, J. Victor, and Terrence E. Deal (eds.), *Managing Change in Educational Organizations* (Berkeley: McCutchan, 1975), pp. 224–47.

[18] Baldridge and Deal, *Managing Change,* pp. 25–33.

[19] Albrecht, Stan L., Bruce A. Chadwick, and Cardel K. Jacobson, *Social Psychology,* 2nd ed. (Englewood Cliffs, N.J.: Prentice Hall, 1987), p. 17.

[20] Zaltman, *Strategies for Planned Change,* p. 90.

[21] Vago, *Social Change,* pp. 289–90.

[22] Goodlad, John I., *The Dynamics of Educational Change Toward Responsive Schools* (New York: McGraw-Hill, 1975), pp. 175–84.

[23] Goodlad, John I., *A Place Called School* (New York: McGraw-Hill, 1984).

[24] Baldridge and Deal, *Managing Change,* pp. 14–18.

[25] Gross, Neal, "Some Contributions of Sociology to the Field of Education," *Harvard Education Review,* Vol. 29, 1959, pp. 275–87.

[26] Ewens, William, "Sociology and Social Change in the Coming Century," paper presented at American Sociological Association meetings, Chicago, August 1987.

[27] Ballantine, Jeanne H., "Market Needs and Program Products: The Articulation Between Undergraduate Applied Programs and the Marketplace," *Journal of Applied Sociology,* Fall 1992.

[28] Mills, C. Wright, *The Sociological Imagination* (New York: Grove Press, 1959).

Epilogue

SCHOOLS
IN THE EARLY
TWENTY-FIRST CENTURY

Planning for change assumes knowledge of educational systems and future trends. Demographers provide us with relevant information: population projections, migration patterns, and social trends. Other social scientists also study educational systems. Proposals for reform and innovation come both from within the educational organization and from its environment. In this final section we will provide examples of some trends and projections that affect education, and some policy implications.

DEMOGRAPHIC TRENDS

The rapid growth of education through the 1960s created a boom mentality: There was an expansion of teacher training programs, new facilities were built, monies became available, and innovations were implemented. With the end of the boom came the prophets of doom, loss of jobs, boarded-up schools, and dropping financial bases.

The birthrate has been dropping since the 1960s, with only temporary upswings. The low point in enrollments was 1983; since that time there has been a gradual increase each year, an increase that is projected to continue into the mid-1990s. High schools were at their low in 1990. Table E-1 shows actual and projected enrollments to the years 2000.[1]

TABLE E-1   Enrollment in Educational Institutions, by Level and Control of Institution: Fall 1980 to Fall.2000 [In thousands]

Level of instruction and type of control	Fall 1980	Fall 1985	Estimated Fall 1990	Projected Fall 1995	Projected Fall 2000
All levels	58,346	57,226	60,172	64,675	68,098
Public	50,376	48,901	51,938	55,835	58,759
Private	7,971	8,325	8,234	8,840	9,339
Elementary and secondary education[1]	46,249	44,979	46,221	50,054	52,406
Public	40,918	39,422	41,026	44,442	46,539
Private	5,331	5,557	5,195	5,612	5,867
Grades K–8[2]	31,669	31,225	33,808	36,127	37,548
Public	27,677	27,030	29,742	31,782	33,032
Private	3,992	4,195	4,066	4,345	4,516
Grades 9–12	14,581	13,754	12,413	13,927	14,858
Public	13,242	12,392	11,284	12,660	13,507
Private	1,339	1,362	1,129	1,267	1,351
Higher education[3]	12,097	12,247	13,951	14,621	15,692
Public	9,457	9,479	10,912	11,393	12,220
Undergraduate[4]	8,442	8,477	9,803	10,065	10,841
First-professional	114	112	115	136	143
Graduate[5]	901	890	994	1,192	1,236
Private	2,640	2,768	3,039	3,228	3,472
Undergraduate[4]	2,033	2,120	2,350	2,384	2,595
First-professional	163	162	158	194	205
Graduate[5]	443	486	531	650	672

[1]Includes enrollments in local public school systems and in most private schools (religiously affiliated and nonsectarian). Excludes subcollegiate departments of institutions of higher education, residential schools for exceptional children, and Federal schools. Excludes preprimary pupils in schools that do not offer first grade or above.

[2]Includes kindergarten and some nursery school pupils.

[3]Includes full-time and part-time students enrolled in degree-credit and nondegree-credit programs in universities and 2-year colleges.

[4]Includes unclassified students below the baccalaureate level.

[5]Includes unclassified postbaccalaureate students.

Note: Higher education enrollment projections based on the middle alternative projections published by the National Center for Education Statistics. Because of rounding, details may not add to totals. Some data have been revised from previously published figures.

Source: U.S. Department of Education, National Center for Education Statistics, Common Core of Data and "Fall Enrollment in Institutions of Higher Education" surveys; Integrated Postsecondary Education Data System (IPEDS), "Fall Enrollment" surveys, and *Projections of Education Statistics to 2002*. (This table was prepared April 1991.)

FAMILY AND SOCIAL TRENDS

Change in the social class composition of the school-aged population is taking place because middle- and upper-class families are having fewer children, while lower-class families are having more (see Box E-1). In 1995, 28 percent of high school students will be nonwhite. One in two black and one in three Hispanic children are estimated to be living in poverty in the early 1990s. The

1.   More children entering school from poverty households.

2.   More children entering school from single-parent households.

3.   More children from minority backgrounds.

4.   A smaller percentage of children who have had Head Start and similar programs, even though more are eligible.

5.   A larger number of children who were premature babies, including those affected by crack and Fetal Alcohol Syndrome leading to more learning difficulties in school.

6.   More children whose parents were not married.

7.   More "latch-key" children and children from "blended" families as a result of remarriage of one original parent.

8.   More children from teen-age mothers.

9.   Fewer white, middle-class, suburban children, with day care (once the province of the poor) becoming a middle-class norm as well, as more women enter the work force.

10.   A continuing decline in the level of retention to high school graduation in virtually all states, except for minorities.

11.   A continued drop in the number of minority high school graduates who apply for college.

12.   A continued drop in the number of high school graduates, concentrated most heavily in the Northeast.

13.   A continuing increase in the number of African-American middle-class students in the entire system.

14.   Increased numbers of Asian-American students, but with more from Indonesia, and with increasing language differences.

15.   Continuing high dropouts among Hispanics, currently about 40 percent of whom complete high school.

16.   Declining numbers of college graduates who pursue graduate studies in arts and sciences.

17.   Increasing part-time college students (about 25 percent are part-time).

18.   A major increase in college students who need *both* financial and academic assistance. A great liaison between the offices of student financial aid and counseling will be essential.

19.   Increasing numbers of college graduates who will get a job that requires no college degree.

20.   Continued increases in graduate enrollments in business, increased undergraduate enrollments in arts and science *courses* but not *majors*.

21.   Increasing numbers of talented minority youth choosing the military as their educational route, because of both cost and direct access to "high technology."

22.   Major increases in adult and continuing education outside of college and university settings—by business, by government, by other nonprofits such as United Way, and by for-profit "franchise" groups such as Bell and Howell Schools and The Learning Annex.

23.   Increasing percentage of workers with a college degree.

Source: adapted from Hodgkinson, Harold L., *All One System: Demographics of Education, Kindergarten Through Graduate School* (Washington, D.C.: Institute for Educational Leadership, 1985), p. 10; and National Center for Educational Statistics, *The Condition of Education, 1991,* Vol. 2, Postsecondary Education (Washington, D.C.: U.S. Department of Education, 1991).

Hispanic population, the fastest-growing ethnic group in the United States, increased from 4.6 percent in 1966 to what will be 14 percent of public school enrollment in 1996, to 20 percent in 2030.[2] Fifty percent of these children finish high school, but the dropout rate is double that of other groups.[3] These figures indicate that schools will have to teach an increasing number of children from poor backgrounds and non-native-English-speaking households.

An increasing proportion of the minority population will be Asian refugees, immigrants, and illegal aliens; this is having a great impact in some states such as California, where English as a second language is an important part of the curriculum. Because the percentage of children from poor families in urban areas is increasing, city tax bases are declining, causing increased financial problems. In addition to class and race composition, family structure is undergoing alterations; many children will live in single-parent households part of the time before their eighteenth birthday. An increasing number of mothers of school-aged children are working, causing a need for after-school care.

Many of those in poverty fail to achieve because of dropout rates and lack of access or funds to continue education. The number of service sector and skilled high-tech jobs in society is increasing, and these jobs will change every five to ten years because of new technologies, requiring reeducation.[4] However, those who have not finished high school will have problems training for these new jobs.

SCHOOLS IN THE EARLY TWENTY-FIRST CENTURY

Predictions are always problematic; technologies are changing at such a rapid rate that tomorrow is uncertain. However, a number of futurologists have attempted to draw scenarios of the schools of tomorrow using knowledge of socioeconomic conditions, predicted new technologies, recommendations from over 30 commission and task force reports, knowledge of demographics, and other sources. *Schools of the Future: Education into the 21st Century*[5] paints a picture of shorter workweeks and longer school weeks; an earlier start in education, more education, and reeducation of the total work force, for the rapidly changing work world; expansion of the school year to at least 210 days; more education in the home using new technologies; business involvement with schools; higher pay for teachers; computer software to replace some textbooks; and students placed in businesses for job training. Boxes E-2, E-3, and E-4 show the many predictions.

Futurologist Edward Cornish echoes many of the predictions in these boxes, and adds that teachers are likely to become more involved with their students, adding a human touch to education; more class time will be devoted to group discussions; field trips; demonstrations, investigative projects, and hands-on lab experiences will increase; and education will become more individualized. Lifelong learning will be a regular part of the adult experience, and will take place in many settings. Structures of schools may also change;

BOX E-2   *FUTURE STUDENTS*

Students of the twenty-first century will probably include toddlers, children, youth, adults, and older citizens. A typical school district may provide learning experiences and training for students ages 3 to 21 and for adults ages 21 to 80-plus.

Students could have many options within the extended framework of the day and year:

- Attending school seven hours a day and 210 days or more a year, depending on their needs and ability to handle tasks.
- Selecting a variety of programs, both required and elective, in academic, vocational, or enrichment programs.
- Working from an interactive computer/videodisc learning station at home or school.
- Working on a job and going to school.
- Doing apprenticeships with master teachers.
- Having opportunities for expanded time in a science laboratory, music class, art class, or vocational class.
- Having opportunities to be tutored individually or in small groups.

Source: Cetron, Marvin J., Barbara Soriano, and Margaret Gayle, *The Futurist,* August 1985.

Cornish predicts smaller schools; more private schools, especially if a system of vouchers is enacted; and more hours of operation.

Most of these plans sound plausible, but we must keep several factors in mind; first, money. Most of the suggestions for school changes require money, and at a time when many districts are struggling to hold on to the programs and teachers they have without making major cutbacks, this appears problematic. So far the public record on passage of levies for additional monies has not been promising.

In addition, some groups in American society, such as those discussed above, may not participate in the new educational and economic state. The knowledge and skill gap that exists today is likely to widen the gap between socioeconomic groups and leave an even more pronounced underclass.

REFORM AND POLICY IN EDUCATIONAL SYSTEMS

Throughout this book we have discussed issues facing education today. In some cases, such as desegregation and early childhood education, policies have been formulated and programs implemented to deal with problems. In other existing and emerging areas, such as world systems of education, problems are beginning to receive attention. The sociologist has a role to play at several stages in research, policymaking, and change process. Every organization needs to have built-in, ongoing data-collection mechanisms. Sociologists can help develop procedures for collecting and analyzing data. Specific infor-

BOX E-3 *FUTURE TEACHERS*

It may not be necessary for all of a school's staff to be trained in education. Educators will be part of the career team and will be able to provide the guidance necessary to ensure that experts from fields outside of education will present their materials effectively.

The educator of the future will have extensive experience with such topics as brain development chemistry, learning environment alternatives, cognitive and psychosomatic evaluation, and affective development.

The traditional teaching job will be divided into parts. After good computer-managed courseware has been installed in schools, the information gathered on teachers' performance in a variety of situations will determine which jobs will go to which teachers. School systems will encourage this specialization because they may make money from selling various services to business interests—or teachers may work part-time and sell the services themselves. Some of the new jobs may include the following:

- learning diagnostician,
- information gatherer for software programs,
- courseware writer,
- curriculum designer,
- mental-health diagnostician,
- evaluator of learning performances,
- evaluator of social skills,
- small-group learning facilitator,
- large-group learning facilitator,
- media-instruction producer,
- home-based instruction designer, or
- home-based instruction monitor.

Source: Cetron, Marvin J., Barbara Soriano, and Margaret Gayle, *The Futurist,* August 1985.

mation may be sought for which methodological techniques and data gathering are important. Programs often require evaluation to determine whether goals are being met, and sociologists are frequently called upon to provide these program evaluations. Data sociologists contribute to our understanding of educational systems by studying how systems work and how the parts fit together. Viewing education as a total system helps us picture the dynamic organization that is education. We have looked at some sources of tension, strain, and change from within and outside the organization that provide impetus for change; yet many reformers are pessimistic about changing the "self-preserving, inflexible" educational system in more than a superficial way. The implications of our discussions are that educational systems are vulnerable to pressures from within the system and from the environment. If those who implement change take into consideration the total context of the educational systems and their members, reform is possible—with the

BOX E-4 *FACTORS AFFECTING THE FUTURE OF SCHOOLS*

A number of current trends will affect work and schools in the twenty-first century:

- Minority populations will become the majority in most grade schools in the nation's large and middle-sized school districts.
- Computers will be available to students in prosperous districts on a 1:4 ratio. (The United States spent a total of $1 billion on textbooks in its entire 200-year history. In the next five to six years alone, the nation will spend $1 billion on computer-assisted education. Only one-third of this will be bought by and for schools; the remaining two-thirds will be provided by wealthier parents for their own children, thus creating an educational inequity far more debilitating than physical segregation. Society must do something to provide access to computers for all children.)
- Federal grants will provide a major portion of the funding for job training and equipment (including computers) in poor school districts.
- Total employment will rise by 17 percent to 25 percent as the workweek declines to 32 hours by 1990 and to 20–25 hours by 2000.
- Women, particularly married women, will enter the work force at a faster rate than any other group within the population.
- More businesses will be involved in schools, including apprenticeship training.
- Older citizens (over 55) increasingly will become students in public schools, job-training programs, and community source programs.
- A core, nine-month program will be offered in elementary and high schools, shifting electives to later in the lengthened day and to summer sessions.
- Teachers' salaries on an annual basis will be raised to within 10 percent of parity with those of other professionals who require college degrees.

Source: Cetron, Marvin J., Barbara Soriano, and Margaret Gayle, *The Futurist,* August 1985.

ever-present possibility of unanticipated consequences. To bring about reform, then, an understanding of individuals, organizations, and environment is essential.

Goals for the Year 2000

In 1991, President Bush and the nation's governors announced six national goals for education, to be achieved by the year 2000. A Gallup poll then asked the public to indicate the importance of each goal. Highest priority was assigned to ridding the schools of drugs and violence and offering a disciplined environment to students in schools.[6] Whether these goals can be achieved is a matter of debate, but most educators do not feel that current policies will turn the system around enough to see major progress, and in fact some predict that the educational statistics will only regress. A fall 1991 study indicates negative results to date.[7]

SOME THINGS WE HAVE LEARNED

It is clear that schools cannot solve societal problems. While many once held out hope that inequality in society could be reduced through equal educational opportunities, we are now more realistic about the limitations of schooling. While schooling may enhance some individuals' societal status and opportunity in societal institutions, schools can also perpetuate inequality through their structure, expectations, and other practices.

We have learned about the structure of schools, roles that individuals carry out, and dysfunctions within these structures. For instance, we know that bureaucratic structures often produce conflict for professionals, and that decision making in educational systems is complicated by bureaucracy.

We have learned how classroom and school climates affect learning. We know that the hidden curriculum plays a crucial role in the experience of students and teachers, that the value climate resulting from student backgrounds and other factors is important in student achievement, and that power relations and other interaction patterns between students and teachers in classrooms affect achievement.

We have learned that the environment can both promote and hinder or prevent educational systems from engaging in activities and decision making. Questions concerning control of school resources and decision making relate to environmental control. The home environment is a critical determinant of school success, because the child learns linguistic patterns and behavior codes that influence success in school. In addition, the type and level of community commitment and support is important in school functioning.

We have learned that educational systems differ greatly between countries of the world. We have discussed some of the variables that relate to these differences; they include economic and political systems that force countries into independent or dependent status, and colonial histories.

We have learned that educational movements come and go, that some new ideas are favorably received and integrated into the structure while others are discarded because they lack acceptance or are difficult to implement. This was exemplified by the free and alternative school movements and the back-to-basics movement. Educational systems are constantly responding to changes in the environment. Given proper conditions, change can be planned and implemented. Knowledge of the system and its environment can mean achieving planned change.

NOTES

[1] "Elementary and Secondary School Enrollment: 1975–2000," *Nation's School Report*, Vol. 16, No. 7, p. 1.

[2] *The Hispanic Population in the United States: March 1986 and 1987*, Series P-20, No. 416, Current Population Surveys (Washington, D.C.: U.S. Department of Commerce, Bureau of the Census, 1987).

[3] National Council of La Raza, "The State of Hispanic Americans, 1991: An Overview," (Washington, D.C.: National Council of La Raza, 1991).

[4] *Technology and the American Economic Transition* (Washington, D.C.: Office of Technology Assessment, 1988).

[5] Cetron, Marvin J., Barbara Soriano, and Margaret Gayle, *Schools of the Future: Education into the 21st Century* (New York: McGraw-Hill, 1985).

[6] Elam, Stanley M., *et al.,* "The 23rd Annual Gallup Poll of the Public's Attitudes Toward the Public Schools," *Phi Delta Kappan,* September 1991, pp. 43–44.

[7] "How're We Doing on the National Goals?" *The American School Board Journal,* November 1991, pp. 10–21.

INDEX

ACT (American College Testing Program), 55, 57, 109, 279

Ability grouping, 84, 87, 232, 239 (*See also* Tracking)

Absenteeism, 80–81, 95 (*See also* At-risk students; Drop-outs; Tardiness)

Academic ability, 39, 289, 296, 386
  achievement, 80, 122, 378 (*See also* Athletics)
  assistance, 417
  colonialism, 359
  control, 290
  freedom, 44, 50, 450
  requirements, 126

Access to education, 78

Accountability movement, 189, 383–85

Accrediting agencies, 290

Achievement, 80, 151, 386 (*See also* Cross-cultural; Family; Parents, styles and student achievement)
  and alcoholism, 45
  math and science, 110
  motivation, 109
  student body Composition, 223
  test scores, 39–40, 54, 57, 388 (*See also* Test)
  working mothers, 92–94

Acosta-Belen, Edna, 338

Activism, 287, 345 (*See also* Tienanmen Square)

Adler, Patricia A., et al., 287

Administration, 181, 291

Admissions:
  and the court, 280
  tests, 279

Adolescent employment, 199

Adult education, 334, 417

Adult literacy programs, 150

Advanced courses (AP), 80

Affirmative action programs, 280, 310 (*See also* Courts and affirmative action)

African-American, 78, 296 (*see also* Afrocentric curricula; Blacks; Minorities)
  achievement, 121
  enrollment, 113
  girls' enrollment, 107
  middle-class students, 417
  self-esteem, 121

Afrocentric curricula, 127

Age/ageism, 301 (*See also* Older college students)

Aggerton, Peter J., et al., 37

Agnew, Robert, 52

AIDS (Auto Immune Deficiency Syndrome), 44

Akinnaso, F. Niyi, 357

Albrecht, Stan L., et al., 407

Alcohol abuse, 45

Alexander, Karl L., et al., 80, 206, 226

All-male campuses, 294

Altbach, Philip G., et al., 287, 328–29

Alternative certification, 190

Alternative schools, 348, 375
  curriculum, 387
  movement, 380

Alumni, 210, 306

American Association of University Women, 109

American College Testing Program (*See* ACT)

American 2000: Excellence in Education Act, 81, 150, 194

Anderson, Richard C., et al., 93, 177

Andrews, Richard L., et al., 183

Angell, Robert, 13

Anomie, 343

Anrig, Gregory R., 189

Antiwar movement, 370
Anyon, Jeanne, 11, 87, 221
Apple, Michael W., et al., 27, 77, 237, 251, 265
Aptitude tests, 54
Archer, Margaret, 334, 346
Architecture of schools, 235, 387
Arnove, Robert F., 337–38
Aronson, Ronald, 117
Ashworth, Kenneth H., 283
Asian-American students, 130, 417
   girls' enrollment, 107
Aspirations, 122
Assimilation, 5
Astin, Alexander W., 313, 316
Astone, Nan Marie, et al., 91
At-home support, 38
At-risk students, 21, 31, 113–16, 136, 202–7 (*See also* Dropouts; Operation Rescue)
Athletics, 286, 316
   and academics, 198
Attendance rates, 80 (*See also* Absenteeism)
Attitudes of schools and teachers, 137
Authoritarian classroom, 51
Auto-Immune Deficiency Syndrome (*See* AIDS)
Ayres, Robert, et al., 132

Babad, Elisha, et al., 200
Babbitt, Charles E., et al., 295
Baby boom, 292, 301
Bacharach, Samuel B., et al., 195
Back-to-basics movement, 252 (*See also* Tradition-oriented education)
   and accountability, 379–80, 382, 386
Baker, David P., et al., 94, 110, 255, 344
Baldridge, J. Victor, et al., 407, 410
Ballantine, Jeanne H., 162, 273, 411
Bank, B., et al., 233
Barrett, Gill, 31
Barth, Roland S., 386
Basic education, 380–81
Bastian, Ann, 83
Beck, E.M., et al., 68, 77
Becker, Gary S., 338
Becker, Howard S., 180, 237
Beeghley, Leonard, 73
Behavior expectations, 386
   modification, 407
   problems, 387
   rewards and punishments, 407
Bell, Daniel, 339
Bell, Terrel, 38
Bellisari, Anna, 110
Ben-David, Joseph, 283
Benavot, Aaron, et al., 330, 333–34, 336, 345
Benbow, Camilla Persson, et al., 112
Bendiner, Robert, 178
Benham, Barbara J., et al., 230
Bennett, Stephanie M., 294
Bennett, William J., 42
Bennis, Warren G., et al., 396
Bergan, John R., 28
Berman, Edward H., 338
Bernard, Harold W., et al., 210
Bernstein, Basil, et al., 12–13, 91, 231, 237
Besag, Frank P., et al., 221
Bible reading, 382
Bickel, Robert, 367
Bidwell, Charles E., 13, 162
Bilingual education, 126, 130
Billson, Janet Mancini, et al., 293
Binder, Fredrick M., 159

Binet, Alfred, 55
Biological destiny, 95, 111 (*See also* Gender; Sex)
Biological learning styles, 111 (*See also* Gender)
Bjorklun, Eugene C., 49
Blacks: (*See also* African-American; Minorities)
   curriculum tracking, 86
   test performance, 86
Blake, Judith, 95
Blalock, Ginger, 209
Blanchard, John F., 373
Blase, Joseph, 180
Blau, Peter M., et al., 283
Bloom, Benjamin S., 90
Blum, Debra E., 306
Board of Education/Regents, 290, 306 (*See also* Lay board of education; State boards of education)
Boarding schools, 131
Boli, John, et al., 69
Boocock, Sarane Spence, 235
Book banning, 53 (*See also* Censorship, Textbooks)
Bossert, S.T., 229
Boulding, Kenneth E., 20
Bourdieu, Pierre, et al., 12, 237
Bowles, Samuel, et al., 11, 37, 42, 76, 174, 208, 221, 236, 277
Boyer, Ernest L., 272
Brain drain, 345
Brameld, Theodore, 374
Brenton, Myron, 194
Brickman, William W., 257
Bridgeman, Brent, et al., 293
Brint, Steven, et al., 275
British education, 349 (*See also* English primary schools; English public schools)
   control and decision making in, 348
   educational inequality, 350
   elite schools, 348, 351
   exams and credentials, 350
   faculty stratification by gender, 351
   higher education, 351
   open universities, 348, 351
   polytechnics, 351
   post–compulsory education, 348
   primary school and curricula, 349
   public schools, 348–49
   work-study plans, 348
Brodinsky, Ben, 261, 382
Brookover, Wilbur B., et al., 8, 79, 84, 224–27
Brophy, Jere, et al., 188, 233
Brown v. Board of Education, 116
Bruce, Michael G., et al., 189
Bryk, Anthony, et al., 80
Budgets, 307
Bureaucracy of schools, 154, 159
Bureaucratic model, 288
Burtles, G., 301
Busching, William A., et al., 109
Busia, K.A., 356
Business involvement in schools, 268
Busing, 4, 79, 81, 120, 410 (*See also* Desegregation)
Byrne, David, et al., 78

Calabrese, Raymond, 69
Campbell, Patricia B., 110
Campus racial/sexual incidents, 385
Capitalist societies, 237, 313
Capron, Barbara, et al., 376
Career academics, 55, 137
Caribbean girls' enrollment, 107
Carlson, Jerry S., et al., 345
Carnegie, 153

Carnoy, Martin, 76, 127, 333, 370
Caste system, 70 (*See also* Stratification)
Catholic schools, 80 (*See also* Private schools)
Catterall, James, et al., 81
Censorship, 49–50 (*See also* Book banning)
Centralized schools, 163
Cerych, Ladislav, 345
Cetron, Marvin J., et al., 418
Cha, Yun-kyung, 336
Change, 400–411 (*See also* Reform)
    barriers to, 409
    components of, 396
    conflict approach to, 401
    and innovation, 28
    and levels of analysis, 397–98
    modernization, 340
    perspectives on, 400, 407–8, 412
    and planning in educational systems, 395
    sources of, 399
    strategies for, 379, 406, 408, 412
    system approach to, 372, 404
"Channel One," 36 (*See also* Television)
Chapter I, 87
Charismatic leaders, 10 (*See also* Leadership)
Chase, Clinton I., 195
Chavers, Dean, 131
Chen, Milton, 36
Child care, 149
Child-centered curricula, 40 (*See also* Curriculum)
Children's Defense Fund, 202
Children's home environment, 2
    books/toys, 104 (*See also* Sex, role socialization)
Children's Television Workshop, 36
Chinese:
    adult literacy, 353
    Peoples' Republic of China, 352–54
    repoliticalization, 354
    school authority structures, 353
    students, 354
Choice, 81, 137, 383, 387 (*See also* Voucher)
Christian schools, 383
Chubb, John E., et al., 82, 192
Chuta, E.J., 359
Citizenship, 37, 288
Civic values, 37
Civil rights movement, 311, 370, 410
Civil Service tests, 55
Clark, Burton R., et al., 275, 289, 297
Clark, Roger, 293
Clarke-Stewart, A., et al., 34
Clarridge, Pamela Brown, 189
Class, 39
    and achievement, 72
    background, 85
    bias in teaching, 12
    clown, 221
    reproduction, 80, 87
    size, 4
    structure, 79
    system, 70
Classism, 53
Classroom:
    atmosphere, 220 (*See also* Environment)
    climate, 229–30 (*See also* Environment)
    codes, 230
    computer use, 40, 58
    decision making, 244–45
    friendships and interaction patterns, 230–32
    management strategies, 244
    noise patterns, 231
    open, 222

    power dynamics, 236
    seating arrangements, 233
    technologies, 371
Cockerham, William C., et al., 379
Coercion, 78
Cognitive development/retardation, 31
Cognitive learning and achievement, 199
Cohen, Jere, 255
Cohen, Michael D., 162
Colclough, Glenna, et al., 77, 85
Coleman, James S., et al., 21, 79, 80, 90–91, 113, 116, 136, 223, 235, 238
Collective bargaining, 194, 305 (*See also* Community colleges; Junior colleges)
College (*See* Higher education)
College-bound track, 85
Collier, Paul, et al., 278
Collins, Randall, 10, 76
Collison, Michele N-K, 295
Colonialism, 342
Communication, 406
Community colleges, 274–76
    demographics, 253
Community service, 138, 285 (*See also* Public service)
Comparative Education, 328–29, 332, 360
Comparative international studies of achievement, 330
Compensatory education, 126
Competency-based education, 384
Competitive grants (Choice), 82
Computer-assisted instruction (CAI), 388, 405
    managed instruction, 58
    technology, 58, 405
Condoms, 44 (*See also* AIDS; Sex)
Conflicting goals and functions of education, 27, 152
Conflicts over the university's functions, 286
Conflict theorists (New Left), 79
Conflict theory, 9–11, 76
Conrad, Richard, 20
Consumer fraud, 384, 417
Continuing education, 293
Cookson, Peter W., et al., 80
Cordes, Colleen, 309
Corporal punishment, 51, 53
Corporate assistance, 263, 285
Corsaro, William A., et al., 232
Corson, John J., 288, 316
Cortese, Anthony J., 130
Corwin, Ronald G., 150
Coser, Lewis A., 287
Counselors, 209–10
Counterculture movements of the 1960s, 370
Counterrevolutionaries, 354
Coursework, 80 (*See also* Advanced courses; Homework)
Courts and affirmative action, 310
Cowen, Robert, 329, 334
Cox, Harold, 301
Crack babies, 204, 417
Crain, Robert L., et al., 123, 137
Crawford, James, 257
Creation science, 257, 383 (*See also* Scientific creationism)
Credentials, 350
Cross-cultural, 110 (*See also* World cultures)
    approaches, 329, 337, 360
    curriculum issues, 328
    educational studies, 328, 360
    international tests, 328
Cross-race friends, 232
Crouse, James, 278
Cultural:
    background, 103

capital, 92, 96, 265 (*See also* Social class)
conflicts, 199
disadvantage, 133
politics, 49
reproduction, 11
stereotypes, 108
transmission, 38, 50, 380
Cummins, Jim, 130, 136
Curriculum, 4, 13, 41, 43, 78, 84–85, 328, 334, 401
hidden, 334
math and science, 39
tracking, 85
traditional, 287, 388
Cusick, Philip A., 239

Damico, Sandra Bowman, et al., 232
Dar, Yehezkel, et al., 87
Dating, 93 (*See also* Sex)
Davidson, Charles W., et al., 234
Davies, Martin R., 349
Davis, Kingsley, et al., 74
Day care, 30–35
DeLoughry, Thomas J., 292
DeRidder, Lawrence M., 203
DeYoung, Alan J., 258
Decentralization, 164
Decision making, 289, 291
Deinstitutionalization, 377
Delamont, Sara, 105
Delany, Brian, et al., 353
Delinquency, 45
Demartini, Joseph R., 345
Democracy, 37
Demographic trends, 94, 300, 415 (*See also* Migration patterns; Population dynamics)
Departmental hierarchy, 289
Desegregation, 116–22, 410 (*See also* Integration attempts)
and busing, 410
and interracial relationships, 382
Deviant individuals and groups, 400
Devins, Neal E., 81
Differential response, 233
Disabilities, 134
Disadvantaged (*See* Minorities; Stratification)
Disasters, 182 (*See* also School)
Discipline, 4, 50, 80–81, 151, 421 (*See also* Humanistic approach to discipline; Interaction theories; Non-interventionist strategies; Private schools)
Discrimination, 233, 306, 387 (*See also* Reverse discrimination)
Displacement politics, 265
Dissertation, 304
Diversity, 288
Division of labor, 69, 76
Dodge, Susan, 288
Donohue, John W., 381
Dormitory regulations, 288
Dornbusch, Sanford M., et al., 90, 92, 95
Dreeben, R., et al., 224, 236
Dronkers, Jaap, 91, 255
Dropouts, 114, 136, 202–7, 386 (*See also* At-risk students; Retaining dropout students)
African-American, 114
Asian, 114
Hispanic, 114
programs, 38, 80
rates, 93, 132, 203, 385, 418
Native Americans, 114
Drugs, 4, 44–47, 54, 421
education, 46–47

prevention, 46–47
D'Souza, Dinesh, 388
Dual hierarchies, 289
Durkheim, Émile, 6–7, 150
Dworkin, Anthony Gary, et al., 193–94

Early childhood education, 30–35, 126
Early European education, 371–72
Easton, David, 20
Eaton, Judith S., 275
Ebel, Robert L., 380, 385
Eccles, Jacquelynne S., 153
Eckhart, Penelope, 198
Economics and education, 2, 69, 258, 284, 338, 345
Eder, Donna, 232
Edmonds, Ronald R., 227–28, 386
Educational:
achievement, 90–91
climate and school effectiveness, 222
content, 78
demographics, 417
and earnings, 313–14
environment, 68, 252
formal, 372
inequality, 350 (*See also* Minorities; Stratification)
movements, 372
opportunity, 301, 344
outcome, 78
reform, 265
systems, around the world, 332, 345, 352, 355
television, 388
Educational Testing Service, 331
Education for All Handicapped Children Act, 132
Effective Schools movement, 137, 227, 386
Egerton, John, 381
Eggleston, John (ed.), 245
Eisenstadt, S.N., 401
Elam, Stanley M., et al., 3, 30, 45, 81, 189, 209, 421
Elected vs. appointed school boards, 174
Elementary and secondary school enrollment, 416
Elite universities, 278
Elite vs. public schools and colleges, 280, 348
Elitism, 278 (*See also* Stratification)
Engelking, Jeri L., 195
English primary schools, 376
English public schools, 348
English as a second language, 418
Ennis, Robert H., 84
Enrollments, 81, 107, 113, 293, 296 (*See also* Blacks; College; Ethnic group)
Environment, 19, 71, 91, 252, 259 (*See also* Classroom; Home environment; School; Technological environment)
Environmental factors, 56
and classrooms, 2
feedback and organizational change, 19, 311
influence, 57, 253–54
Epperson, Andrey I., 210
Epstein, Joyce L., et al., 41, 95, 153, 229, 255, 328
Equal Access Act, 258, 280
Equality of educational opportunity, 103
Equal opportunity, 87, 385 (*See also* Ability grouping; Stratification)
Estate system, 70
Etaugh, Claire, 34
Ethical conduct, 316
Ethnic group (*See* Multiethnic society; Race)
Ethnomethodology, 11
Etzioni, Amitai, 375
Evangelauf, Jean, 283, 285
Evans, Ellis D., 33

Evolutionary theory, 257
Ewens, Lynda Ann, 389
Ewens, William, 410
Exchange students, 345
Exchange theory, 11 (*See also* Theoretical perspectives)
Executive elite schools, 22, 86
Experimental schools, 376
Extended families, 344
Extracurricular activities, 137

Faculty, 301–6 (*see also* College; Higher education; Teachers)
    attitudes, 304, 312
    unions, 305
Fadiman, Clifton, 382
Family, 2
    background, 90–91, 117, 343
    class position, 13, 343
    educational achievement, 343
    extended, 344
    influence, 253–55
    size and achievement, 94–95 (*See also* Home environment)
    social class and education, 343
    support, 39 (*See also* Parents)
    values, 131
Faunce, William A., 224, 227
Federal aid, 81
Federal funding, 261
Fee for service, 165 (*See also* Teachers)
Female administrators, 181–83, 306
Female-dominated fields, 306
Feminization of reading, 233
Fennema, Elizabeth, et al., 111
Ferdman, Bernardo M., 126
Fernandez, Ricardo R., et al., 128
Fetal Alcohol Syndrome, 417
Fetler, Mark, 35
Financial aid, 4, 300, 417
Financial support (*See* Economics and education; Funding; Resource-dilution)
Finch, Michael O., et al., 200
Firestone, William A., 377
Fischer, Louis, 49
Fisher, George M.C., 338
Fiske, Edward B., 108
Floud, Jean, 9
Folland, Laura Enice Pickett, et al., 294
Follow-through, 126
Formal expectations, 236
Fractionalization of education, 359
Fraternities, 297
Freedman, Jonathan L., 36
Freedom of speech/press, 53, 288 (*See also* Hate speech bans; Students', rights)
Freeman, Jesse L., 175
Free schools, 376
Freire, Paulo, 344
French, Mary C., 297, 300–301
Friedman, Isaac A., 193
Fuller, Bruce, 335
Functional theory, 6–9
Functions, 152
Fundamentalist Christians (*See* Religion, Ultra-fundamentalists)
Funding, 2, 258–64, 310, 383 (*See also* Federal funding; Robin Hood plan)
    state and local, 260
Furst, Robert H., 39
Future Shock, 122, 396
"Futures," 36 (*See also* Television)

Gaddy, Gary D., 35
Gallup, Alec M., 3
Gallup poll, 30, 50, 81
Gamoran, Adam, et al., 88, 162
Gang involvement, 80
Gang violence, 206
Gardner, Howard, 390
Gardner, John W., 79
Garner, Catherine L., et al., 224, 255, 350
Garner, Richard, 50
Gaskell, Jane, 109
Gatekeeping, 277
Gender, 293
    colonization, 338
    inequality internationally 110
    issues in higher education, 288, 305, 351
    single-sex and all-male colleges, 295
    wage and occupations, 351 (*See also* Income and education)
George, Paul S., 153
Gerkas, 90
Gerth H.H., 71
Ghanaian education, 355–58
Giele, Janet Zollinger, et al., 295
Gifford, Bernard R., et al., 130
Gifted students, 134–35, 387
Gilbert, Dennis, et al., 71
Gilligan, Carol, 306
Gilmore, Michael J., et al., 230
Gipp, Gerald E., et al., 132
Glasser, Ira, 53
Glatthorn, Allan A., 377
Glenn, Charles L., 344
Glickman, C., et al., 52
Global education, 37, 332
Goals, 122, 149 (*See also* Conflicting goals and functions of education)
    for the year 2000, 421
Goldhammer, Keith, 175, 178
Goldman, Paul, 188
Goldman, Samuel, 180
Good, T.L., 88
Goodlad, John I., 150, 240, 409
Goodman, Ellen, 195
Goslin, David A., 155
Goss v. Lopez, 53
Gould, Madelyn S., 36
Gouldner, Alvin, 75
Gouldner, Helen P., 237
Gracey, Harry L., 34, 200
Graduate Record Examination, 55
Graduate students' teaching techniques, 304
Graduation standards, 41
Grant, Linda, 123
Grasha, Anthony F., 242
Graying of teachers, 297
Greeley, Andrew M., 80
Green, Robert L., et al., 121
Greenwood, Gordon E., et al., 90
Greim, Clifton, et al., 234
Grieb, Aimee, et al., 111
Griffiths, D., 14
Grindal, Bruce, 358
Gross, Neal, et al., 181, 410
Grouping, 87 (*See also* Streaming; Tracking)
Groups (*See* Business involvement in schools; Ethnic group; Peer group; Special education)
Grubb, W. Norton, 275
Guidance counseling, 126, 209
Guiton, Bonnie, 82
Gumbert, Edgar B., 363

Haberman, Martin, 189
Habermas, Jurgen, 334
Hale, Noreen, 301
Hall, Richard H., 397
Hall, W.D. (ed.), 328
Hallinan, Maureen T., et al., 86–87, 231–32
Halpern, Robert, 35, 336
Hammack, Floyd M., 138
Hammersley, Martyn, et al., 233, 240, 243, 245
Handicapped Children's Act, 132
Hardy, Roy A., 189
Hargreaves, Andy, 184
Hargreaves, D.H., 220–21, 239
Harley, Ruth, 109
Harragan, Betty, 108
Harrington-Lueker, Donna, 37, 49, 130
Hart, Harold H., 376
Hartoonian, Michael, 390
Hastings, Philip K., et al., 313
Hastings, William L., et al., 37
Hate crimes, 288
Hate speech bans, 288
Hauser, Mary, et al., 352
Hauser, Robert M., et al., 75, 122
Hawes, Hugh, 357
Haycock, Kati, et al., 128–29
Hayhoe, Ruth, 354
Head Start programs, 31, 126, 222, 417 (*See also* Preschool)
Hearn, Jeff, 50
Heber, Rich F., 57
Heberle, Rudolf, 370
Hedin, Diane, et al., 244
Henry, Jules, 207
Hentges, Joseph T., 178
Hentoff, Nat, 384
Herbert, Victor, 207
Hernstein, Richard, 56
Hertling, James, 45
Herzog, A. Regula, 109
Heterogenous grouping, 84
Heyneman, Stephen P., 336
Heyns, Barbara, et al., 94
Hidden curriculum, 105, 334
Hidden messages, 105, 219–20, 334
Hierarchical systems of authority, 156
Hierarchy, 288–89 (*See also* University
Higher education, 126, 272–317
 access to, 277
 African-American enrollment, 292
 around the world, 345
 Board of Trustees/Regents, 290, 306
 budgets, 309
 department hierarchy, 289
 elite, 278, 280
 expansion of, 277
 faculty roles in, 291, 303
 first-generation college student, 293
 freshmen characteristics, 282
 functions of, 284
 growth of, 283
 historical functions of, 273
 internationalizing of, 345
 marketing, 292
 older students, 292 (*See also* Age/ageism; Continuing education; Life-long learning programs; Senior-citizen college students)
 public confidence in, 345
 reentry women, 294 (*See also* Gender)
 roles in, 291 (*See also* Role expectations)
 sponsorship, 281
  stratification and equal opportunity in, 278
  theoretical approaches to, 277
High school, 86
 graduation, 2, 417
 single-sex, 107
High school attainment, 87, 115
High technology, 417
Hill, Paul T., et al., 165
Hillard, Asa G., 43
Hirsh, E.D., 38
Hispanic, 128–30 (*See also* Minorities)
 curriculum tracking, 86
 drop-outs, 417
 students, 83, 128
 test performance, 86
 vocational performance, 86
History of education, 355
 Colonial Africa, 355
 development of higher education, 352
Hoffer, Thomas, et al., 84
Hoge, Dean R., 312
Hollingshead, A.B., 150–51
Holloman, Susanne T., 35
Holt, John, 219, 222
Home environment, 2, 78, 90, 253–55 (*See also* Family; Parents)
Homeless children, 204
Homeroom, 157
Homework (private school), 40–41, 80–81, 92–93
Honig, Alice Sterling, 34
Hooks, Bell, et al., 109
Horton, Robin, 334
Huberman, Michael, 181
Hughes, E.C., 242
Human capital politics/theory, 255, 265, 340
Humanistic approach to discipline, 51
Humanistic education, 374–75, 380
Hurn, Christopher J., 43, 154, 313
Hutchins, Robert M., 261

Ideal type, 154
Illegal aliens, 418
Illich, Ivan, 165, 377
Illiterate, 1, 38, 335, 339, 353, 356 (*See also* Literacy; Reading)
Immigrants, 5, 130, 418
Immigration population growth, 130
Income and education, 78, 96
Indicators of school health, 406
Individual goals, 151
Industrialization, 373, 399
Inequality, 5, 76, 78–79, 117, 350, 422 (*See also* Class; Minorities; Stratification)
Infant learning, 31
Influences of home environment, 223
Informal processes, 151, 221, 236–37
Inkeles, Alex, et al., 331, 339
In loco parentis, 288
Innovative schools, 382, 415
In-service training, 137, 384
Institutional interdependence, 2, 337, 360
Institution of religion separation of church and state, 256
Integrated learning systems, 60, 410
Integration attempts, 4, 8, 118, 126, 134, 400, 410
Intelligence quotient (IQ), 54–56, 85, 95
Interaction theories, 11, 52 (*See also* Theoretical perspectives)
Intergenerational mobility, 131
Internal educational forces, 42
Internal and external systems pressures, 369

Internationalizing of higher education, 345
International tests, 328
Interventionist approach, 52
Irvine, Jacqueline Jordan, 196

Jackson, Philip, 21, 191, 218, 225, 229, 243
Jacob, Philip E., et al., 312
Jacobson, Robert L., 290
Jaffe, Donald L., 384
Janitors, 209
Jaschik, Scott, 119, 309
Jencks, Christopher, et al., 56, 90, 91, 116–17, 223, 274
Jenson, Arthur R., 56
Jocks and burnout, 198
Jones, James D., et al., 86
Junior colleges, 274
Justiz, Manuel J., et al., 196

Kalekin-Fishman, Devorah, 231
Kameen, Marilyn C., et al., 297
Kanter, Rosabeth, 398
Karabel, Jerome, 9
Karen, David, 277–78
Katz, F.E., 147
Kaufman, Bel, 158
Kellams, Samuel E., 368
Kemerer, Frank R., et al., 305
Kerckhoff, Alan C., et al., 350
Kerickson, H. Lynn, 183
Kerr, Clark, 284
Kerr, Norman D., 175
Kevin, Simon M., et al., 234
Kilgore, Sally B., 84
Kimball, Roger, 315
Kindergarten, 34, 41 (*See also* Preschool)
Kin groups, 131
King, Edith W., 43, 137, 186
King, Edmund J., 328, 339, 348
Knapp, John L., et al., 189
Kohlberg, Lawrence, 374
Konrad, Alison M., et al., 198, 306
Kozol, Jonathan, 22, 70, 203, 376
Kraft, Christine L., 297
Krauze, Tadeusz, et al., 83, 332
Kujoth, Jean S., 52
Kwong, Julia, 353–54
Kyle, R.M., 228

Labaree, David F., 159
Labeling theory, 11, 89, 134, 136
Lake, Robert, 133
Langlois, Donald E., et al., 188
Language differences, 417
Lareau, Annette, 92–93
Larkin, Maureen McCormack, 386
Latch-key children, 417
Latent processes, 16
Latin American girls' enrollment, 107
Latinos, 114–16
Lawton, Millicent, 109
Lay board of education, 163
Lazar, I., et al., 32
Leadership, 183
Learning, 2, 52 (*See also* Infant learning)
    climate, 53
    disabled, 134
LeCompte, Margaret, et al., 193
Lederman, Douglas, 286–87, 316
Lee, Seh-Ahn, 92
Lee, Valerie E., et al., 80, 108, 162, 245, 276

Legitimation of knowledge perspective, 328, 333
Leiter, Jeffrey, 162
Leveling, 69 (*See also* Tracking)
Lever, J., 108
Levine, D.U., et al., 88
Levinson, David L., 58
Levitas, Maurice, 75
Lewis, Anne C., 150
Liberation, 377
Lieberman, Janet E., 275, 297
Lieberman, Myron, 83, 164
Life adjustment movement, 374
Life-long learning programs, 293, 301
Lindsay, Paul, et al., 313
Linton, Ralph, 172
Liston, Daniel P., 11
Literacy, 131, 334, 344, 376 (*See also* Adult education; Illiterate; Technological environment)
Literacy rates, 105
Livingston, D.W., 336
Locus of control, 163
Loewenstein, Sophie Freud, 295
Lomperis, AnaMaria Turner, 306
Longitudinal research, 20–21 (*see also* Research)
Lortie, Dan, 166, 187
Lotteries, 96, 260
Louis Harris and Association, 189
Low-ability groups, 41, 87 (*see also* Achievement; Tracking)
Low achievers, 88
Low-socioeconomic group, 80
Lowy, Louis, et al., 301
Lubeck, Sally, 21, 222
Lubman, Sarah, 354
Lucas, Samuel R., 84
Lynch, James, 339
Lynd, Robert S., et al., 72

McClelland, Katherine E., et al., 297
McDill, Edward L., et al., 113, 206, 226–27
McEvoy, Alan W., 36, 45, 181, 206
McGee, Reece, 304
McGill-Franzen, Ann, et al., 38
McGiverin, Jennifer, et al., 235
McGroarty, Mary, 126
McGuffey Readers, 380–81
MacIver, Douglas J., et al., 153
McKey, Ruth Hubbell, 32
McLaren, Peter L., 221
McMillen, Liz, 306
McPartland, James M., et al., 81, 207, 379
McWilliam, H.O.A., et al., 355
Macrocosmic approaches, 11
Macro-school organization, 10
Magner, Denise K., 297
Magnet schools, 120, 387
Mainstreaming, 133–35, 265
Male-dominated academic institutions, 305
Male-female friendships, 231–33
Manifest processes, 16
Mann, Horace, 69, 373
Manski, Charles F., 387
Manual/blue collar work, 301
Marginal professionals, 165 (*See also* Professionals)
Marsh, Herbert W., 199
Marshall, Gail, 58
Marxism, 346 (*See also* Neo-Marxist theory)
Maslow, Abraham H., 374
Mason, Philip, 55–56
Mass education, 373
Maternity/paternity leave, 31

Math ability (*See also* Biological learning styles)
  achievement, 110, 235 (*See also* Cross-cultural)
Measured test performance, 86
Media, 35–36
Medley, Donald M., 235
Mehl, Robert A., 209
Meighan, Roland, 220, 236
Mental abilities, 55 (*See also* Intelligence quotient)
Mental retardation, 55, 134
Mercer, Jane R., 56
Merit pay, 192 (*See also* Teachers)
Merton, Robert, 241
Metal detectors, 51
Metz, Mary Haywood, 21, 194, 244
Meyer, John W., et al., 163
Mickelson, Roslyn Arlin, 112, 224
Micro approaches, 12
Middle-class parents, 92–93 (*See also* Parents)
Middle-class schools, 86, 221
Migration patterns, 415 (*See also* Demographic trends;
      Population dynamics)
Miles, Matthew B., 406
Miller, C.M.L., et al., 242
Miller's Analogy Test, 55
Millet, John D., 287
Mills, C. Wright, 71, 411
Milne, Ann M., et al., 94
Mingat, Alain, et al., 335
Mingle, James R., 298–99
Minorities, 40, 78, 81, 95, 296
  educational experience, 417
  high-/low-concentration communities, 85
  students, 80, 87, 199 (*See also* Ability grouping)
  teachers, 95
Mitchell, Anne W., 31, 386
Mixed classes, 108
Modernization, 339
  and change, 339, 399
  and human capital perspectives, 340
Monk-Turner, Elizabeth, 276
Mooney, Carolyn J., 388
Moore, Elsie G.J., et al., 110
Moral education, 374
Morgan, D.L., et al., 235
Morgan, William R., et al., 332
Morna, Colleen Lowe, 359
Morrow, Robert D., 131
Morse, Suzanne W., 288
Mortimore, Peter, et al., 350
Mothers (*See also* Parents)
  achievement and, 93
  working, 93–94
Motivation, 39
Mulkey, Lynn M., et al., 93
Muller, Chandra, 93
Multicultural education programs, 136–37
Multiculturalism and political correctness, 388
Multiethnic society, 86
Munitz, Barry, 288

Nagel, Joane, et al., 359
Najafizadeh, Mehrangiz, et al., 336, 339
Nason, R. Beth, 207
Natale, Jo Anna, 194, 264
National Collegiate Athletic Association, 286
National Council of La Raza, 129, 200
National Education Association, 184
National structures of educational systems and curric-
      ula, 290, 336
"A Nation Prepared," 185, 191
"A Nation At Risk," 38–39, 210

Native American, 131–33 (*See also* Dropouts; Minori-
      ties)
  tribal colleges, 274, 292
Natriello, Gary, et al., 22, 226, 255
Nebgen, Mary, 209
Negative reinforcement, 51–52
Neill, A.S., 376
Neo-Marxist theory, 76–77
Neuman, Susan B., 35
Newcomb, Theodore M., 312
Noell, Jay, 80
Non-interventionist strategies, 52 (*See also* Disci-
      pline)
Non-public schools, 257
Nontraditional-age college women, 293, 300
Novak, Michael, 268
Nuwer, Hand, 297
Nygren, Burton M., 382

Oakes, Jeannie, 84
O'Brien, Marion, et al., 104
Obscenity, 50
Obstacles and resistance to implementation to change,
      409
Occupational status and education, 313, 350
O'Connor, Sorca, 35
Off-campus sites, 300
Older college students, 300 (*See also* Age/ageism)
Olivas, Michael, 275
Olsen, Laurie, et al., 206
Olsen, Marvin E., 14, 399
Olson, Lynn, 192, 387
On-task behavior, 233
Open classrooms, 378, 382, 387
Open education, 378, 380 (*See also* Educational,
      movements)
  schools, 376, 378
  space schools, 378, 395
Open systems approach, 6, 13–20, 395, 400, 404
Operation Rescue, 210 (*See also* At-risk students)
Opportunities, 5, 344, 373
Orfield, Gary, 118, 120
Organization, 146 (*See also* Macro-school organization;
      Open systems approach; Systems model)
  deviant individuals, 400
  for profit/non-profit, 417
Organizational environment, 16, 311
  feedback, 16
  individuals, 399
  input, 17
  output, 18
  strains, 399
Ornstein, Allan C., et al., 113, 126, 261, 264, 383
Ostrander, Kenneth H., et al., 95
Otto, Jean H., 38
Outcomes of education, 78, 312
Owens, Robert G., 146

Page, Ann L., et al., 9
Pallas, Aaron M., 93
Paraprofessionals, 208–9 (*See also* Professionals)
Parelius, Ann, et al., 289
Parents, 3, 379
  accountability, 207
  education level, 83–84
  ethnicity, 94
  expectations, 92
  involvement, 4, 80, 92–95, 131, 138, 255 (*See also*
      Cross-cultural)
  Parent-Teacher Association (PTA), 82
  race, 94

Parents (*cont.*)
  single, 91–92
  support, 110
  styles and student achievement, 91–94 (*See also* Achievement)
Parsons, Talcott, 13, 199
Part-time college students, 417
Pashal, Rosanne A., et al., 226, 236
Passow, A. Harry, et al., 330, 344
Patchen, Martin, 121
Patterson, Janice H., 57
Paulson, Ronnella, 37
Paulston, Rolland G., 401
Peck, J., et al., 34
Pedagogy, 231
Peer group, 153, 232, 267, 296 (*See also* Students)
  interaction, 122
  pressures, 297
  relationships, 39
Pepper, Suzanne, 353
Perelman, Lewis J., 58
Perkins, James A. (ed.), 273, 284
Persell, Caroline Hodges, et al., 58, 80
Perspectives on roles, 173
Peters, Donald L., 30
Peters, William A., 89
Phenomenology, 11, 73
Phillips, David P., et al., 36
Pincus, Fred L., et al., 275–76
Pipho, Christopher, 266
Pitsch, Mark, 32
Political, 37 (*See also* Cultural, capital; Displacement politics)
  authority, 37
  correctness, 287, 315, 388
  indoctrination, 345, 353–54
  and legal institutions, 264
  socialization, 37
Politicization of peasantry, 376
Popularity, 232
Population dynamics, 415 (*See also* Demographic trends; Migration patterns)
Portes, Alejandro, 122
Post-compulsory education, 348
Postindustrialization and change, 399
Postman, Neil, 50
Poverty and educational opportunity, 31, 417
Powell, Brian, et al., 309
Power, 10, 71, 78 (*See also* Class, structure)
  dynamics and roles in the informal system, 236
  elite, 70–71
Prayer in school/classroom, 49, 382 (*See also* Fundamentalist Christians; Religion)
Premature babies, 417
Preparatory schools, 122
Preschool, 30–35
Prestige, 70–71 (*See also* Stratification; Social class)
Principal, 180–84
  power of, 183–84
  role of the, 180
Private schools, 80, 165, 307, 382–83, 387 (*see also* Catholic schools; Homework (private schools))
Processes (systems model), 2, 15
Professionalization of teachers, 373
Professionals, 3, 165, 299 (*See also* Marginal professionals; Paraprofessionals)
Profscam, 315
Progressive education, 374
Prohibition movement, 370
Project Raise, 207
Property ownership, 10

Property taxes, 95, 258–61
Provenzo, Eugene, 49
Psychological tests, 55
PTA (Parent-Teacher Association), 82
Public issues, 345
Public school movement, 372–73, 387
Public service, 285
Pupil interest, 4, 311
Purcell P., et al., 104

Quota systems, 280

Race, 39, 112–13, 223 (*See also* Ethnic group; Gender; Hate crimes; Minorities; SAT)
  in higher education, 293
Racial:
  bias, 53, 96
  hostility, 122
  incidents, 288, 296
  segregation, 81, 387
Racism and political correctness, 388
Radical professors, 315
Raffini, James P., 202
Rallis, Sharon F., et al., 181
Ramirez, Francisco O., et al., 337, 346
Rational-expert leadership, 10 (*See also* Leadership)
Ravitch, Diane, 38, 81, 388
Raymond, Chris, 32
Raywid, Mary Anne, 135
Raze, Nasus, 87
Reading, 38, 93, 235, 388
Reciprocal interactions, 11, 233
Recruitment programs, 293
Reentry women, 293
Reform, 370, 373, 415 (*See also* Educational, reform; Educational, movements)
  and policy in educational sytems, 419
Refugees, 127, 131, 418
Regional university accrediting associates, 290
Regressive movements, 370
Reid, Bill, et al., 186
Religion, 2, 256, 303, 343 (*See also* Anomie; Bible reading; Prayer in school/classroom; Students)
Religious clubs, 81, 256–58
Remedial education, 136
Renzetti, Claire M., et al., 104, 110
Repa, Barbara Kate, 53
Repoliticalization, 354
Reproduction theory (stratification), 76, 221
Reproduction and tracking, 77, 85
Research, 57, 307
  funding, 307
Resistance theories, 11 (*See also* Theoretical perspectives)
Reskin, Barbara, 313
Resource-dilution, 255
Retaining dropout students, 208
Retention, 299, 417
Retooling, 300
Revenues, 308
Reverse discrimination, 280
Revisionists, 77
Revolutionary movements, 370
Reyes, Pedro, et al., 291
Reynolds, Arthur J., 32
Rhoades, Gary, et al., 286
Rice, Berkeley, 55
Richmond-Abbott, Marie, 104, 109
Rich vs. poor countries, 334
Riehl, Carolyn, et al., 84
Right-to-Life movement, 370

Riordan, Cornelius, 199
Rist, Marilee C., 164, 387
Rix, S., 300
Robertson, Ian, 370
Robin Hood plan, 261
Robinson, Jean C., 352, 354
Rodgers, Harrell R., Jr., 136
Rodman, Blake, 183
Roe, Ellen, 81
Roe, William H., et al., 183
Rogers, Carl, 374
Rogers, David, 161, 172, 174, 252
Rohles, Frederick H., 234
Role expectations, 172, 174
   for teachers, 188, 405, 410
Rose, Mike, 81
Rose, Peter I., 312
Rose, Susan D., 49
Rosenholtz, Susan J., et al., 245
Rosenthal, Robert, et al., 21, 88
Rosner, Benjamin, 384
Ross, Murray, 292
Rossides, Daniel W., 72
Rothman, Robert, 83, 292
Rubin, Linda J., et al., 90, 94
Rubinson, Richard, 78
Rules, 157
Rumbaut, Ruben G., et al., 131
Rumberger, Russell W., 91
Runaways, 45 (*See also* Delinquency)
Rutter, Michael, et al., 227

Sadker, Myra Pollack, et al., 112
Sadovnick, Alan R., 13
Safe schools study, 160
Saha, Lawrence, 9, 402–3
Salaries, 156, 305, 314
Sales tax, 96
Sanchirico, Andrew, 131
Sanctions, 68 (*See also* Stratification)
Sanday, Peggy Reeves, 297
Sanders, Irwin T., 284
Sanders, Jimmy M., 310
SAT (Scholastic Aptitude Test), 55, 57, 109, 279
Sautman, Barry, 354
Say, Elaine, et al., 195
Scherer, Marge, 128
Scheurich, James, et al., 74, 76
Schiller, Kathryn S., et al., 84
Schmidt, Peter, 78, 126
Schneider, Barbara L., 92, 229
Scholarship awards, 309
School, 154, 386
   architecture, 222
   atmosphere, 39, 84 (*See also* Environment)
   budgets and national priorities, 175, 309
   classrooms, 147, 234
   climate and effective schools, 227
   community, 85, 173
   composition, 91, 399 (*See also* Women)
   curricula, 85, 149, 268
   effectiveness, 77, 227
   enrollments, 197
   environment, 52
   financing, 95, 264 (*See also* Funding)
   function, 152
   goals, 151
   health hazards, 234
   library, 48–49
   loosely coupled organizations, 162
   neighborhood environments, 224

   newspaper, 53
   overcrowding, 4
   partnerships, 263
   prayer, 257–58
   size, 4, 234
   support services, 148
   system stresses, 149, 399
   type, 85
   value climate, 223–24
School board, 174–77
   compositions and expectations, 175
   duties, 173
Schumacher, E.F., 5
Schwartz, Audrey James, 151
Schweinhart I.J., 32
Science, 334
   courses, 417
   curricula, 39
   enrollment, 110
Scientific creationism, 48
Scientific illiteracy, 38
Scopes trial, 48
Scott, W.G., 20
Scott, W. Richard, et al., 162
Scott-Jones, Diane, 206
Sealey, Leonard, 379
Seating arrangements, 233
Secondary education, 70
Secular humanism, 48
Segregated schools, 128
Segregation, 4, 88–89, 122 (*see also* Discrimination; Religion)
Semi-intransitive consciousness, 344
Sendor, Benjamin, 258
Senior-citizen college students, 293
SES (socioeconomic status), 223–24
Sewell, Nm. H., et al., 73, 223
Sex, 39, 73, 233 (*See also* Dating; Gender; Teenage pregnancies; Unsafe campuses)
   differences, 78, 110
   education, 44, 173
   and educational opportunity, 103
   role conformity, 109
   role socialization, 104
Sexism in education systems, 112
   and political correctness, 388
   in textbooks, 104
Sexual exploitation and harassment, 306
Shakeshaft, Carol, 183
Sherman, Julia, 112
Sherman, Mary, et al., 359
Shoop, Robert J., 53
Shresha, Gajendra Man, et al., 335
Sieber, Sam D., et al., 191
Sigel, R.A., et al., 37
Silberman, Charles, 374
Simon, Sidney B., 374
Sine, Barbacar, 357
Singer, Dorothy G., 36
Single-parent households, 417
Single-sex schools and colleges, 107, 293
Site-based management, 151
Sivard, Ruth Leger, 106
Sizer, Theodore R., 150
Skeels, Harold M., 57
Slavin, Robert E., 87, 138
Sleeter, Christine E., et al., 400
Slomezynski, Kalimierz M., et al., 332
Smelzer, Neil J., 311
Smith, Daryl G., 295
Smith, Mary Lee, 189

Smith, Ronald W., et al., 161
Smith, Wilma, et al., 183
Smock, Pamela J., et al., 126
Snider, William, 41, 120
Snipp, C. Matthew, 77
Snyder, Eldon E., et al., 198
So, Alvin Y., 131
Sobol, Thomas, 43
Social class, 72, 85, 103, 343 (*See also* Family, class
    position)
  background, 78
  determinants, 70–71
Socialist societies, 341
Socialization, 2, 28, 34, 304 (*See also* Early childhood
    education)
  agents, 104
  sex role, 106
Social movement typologies, 16–17, 370
Socioeconomic status (SES), 86, 91
Sociology of Education newsletter, 22
Soderman, Ann K., 31
Solmon, Lewis C., et al., 313
Sommerfeld, Meg, 138
Sororities, 297
Sorting, 68
Sources, 369
Spatial ability, 111–12
Special education, 132, 307
  interest groups, 9
Spitz, Rene A., 57
Spring, Joel, 262, 290
Stages of economic development, 339
Stages of moral development, 374
Stake, Jayne E., et al., 111
Standardized examinations, 41, 131, 157 (*See also* Test)
Standardized test scores, 58, 385
Stanford Binet IQ test, 34
State boards of education, 174, 260, 301
Status attainment, 73, 75, 171, 223, 344 (*See also* Cul-
    tural; Occupational status and education)
Steele, Claude M., 296
Steelman, Lala Carr, et al., 255
Stepparents, 91
Sternberg, Robert, 55
Stevenson, David Lee, et al., 244, 255
Stewart, David W., 130
Stipek, Deborah J., et al., 39
Stires, Lloyd, 233
Stites, Regie, et al., 353, 356, 358
Store-front schools, 376
Strang, David, 160
Stratification, 69, 72, 90, 103, 138, 284 (*See also* Disad-
    vantaged; Elitism; Family; Income and educa-
    tion; Power; Sanctions; Students; Tracking)
  conflict/functionalist ideology critiques, 70, 74–76
Streaming, 55, 239 (*See also* Tracking)
Street academics, 376
Strother, Deborah Burnett, 203
Structural and curricular changes in the schools, 386
Structural-functionalism (*See* Functional theory)
Structural politics, 264
Students, 195–208
  achievement, 4
  aid budget, 309
  alienation, 137
  aspirations, 223
  attitudes, 152, 241
  best friends, 231–33
  body composition, 282
  characteristics of, 196
  conformity, 241

coping mechanisms and failure, 201–2
credential crisis, 283–84
crime, 51
cue-consciousness, 242
culture, 87, 237, 296
deviance, 245
enrollment, 197
gender, 198
language usage, 198
learning styles, 242
motivations, 223
peer-group influence, 237–38 (*See also* Peer group)
performance, 225
protests, 311
religious and moral attitudes and values, 312
retreatism, 241
rights, 50, 53 (*See also* Corporal punishment; Free-
    dom of speech/press)
roles, 291
searches, 53 (*see also* Students, rights; Sweeps)
self-concept, 224
strategies, 240
suspensions, 78, 207–8
teacher ratio, 88
test scores, 78, 385
transfer, 275–76
values, 311, 374
working-class backgrounds, 240
Suarez-Orozco, Marcelo M., 130
Successful elementary schools, 386
Suicide (attempt), 45
Superintendent, 177–79
Supervision after school, 93 (*See also* Home
    environment)
Supreme Court, 122 (*See also* Civil rights movement;
    Desegregation)
  Abington Township v. Schempp, 256
  Engle v. Vitale, 256
  Hobson v. Hansen, 85
  Meek v. Pittenger, 257
  Milliken v. Bradley, 122
  San Antonio Independent School District v. Rodri-
      guez, 95
  Surrano v. Priest, 95
Survey feedback, 406
Survival atmosphere, 53
Suspensions, 82
Sweeps, 54 (*See also* Students, searches)
Sykes, Charles J., 315
Symbolic interaction, 11 (*See also* Theoretical
    perspectives)
Systems model, 13–15, 369 (*See also* Open systems
    approach)

Talan, Jamie, 122
Talking typewriters, 388
Tannen, Deborah, 108
Tape cassette machines, 388
Tardiness, 93 (*See also* Absenteeism; At-risk students;
    Dropouts)
Tavris, Carol, 105
Taxpayers 3, 258–64 (*See also* Funding)
Taylor, Maurice C., et al., 52
Teachers, 3, 43, 183–95, 384 (*See also* Faculty)
  attitudes, 88, 233
  autonomy, 194
  burnout, 245
  characteristics, 184–85
  demand, 187
  directed classroom, 193
  discrimination, 188

effectiveness, 189
examinations, 192
expectations, 88–89, 227 (*See also* Cross-cultural)
legitimacy, 159
licensing, 190–91 (*See also* Credentials)
pay, 4, 385
retooling, 189
salary, 4
shortage, 186
strategies, 243, 245
stress and burnout, 193–94
student relationships, 230, 233
training, 384
unions, 194
Teaching, 285
graduate student techniques of, 304
interest in, 187
team teaching, 387
Teach to the test, 385 (*See also* Faculty)
Technological environment, 388
fads, 371
gender gap, 58 (*See also* Gender; Illiterate)
literacy, 39
Teenage mothers, 417
Teenage pregnancies, 45, 206
Teenage sexual activity, 44–45
Teese, Richard, 81
Television, 92
Tenured faculty, 289, 305–6, 315
Test (*See also* Accountability movement; Admissions;
Standardized test scores)
agencies, 385
controversy, 385
and licensing, 190
scores, 160
Textbook censorship, 48–49
Textbooks, 112 (*See also* Sexism in education systems)
Theodore, Athena, 166
Theoretical perspectives, 5–12, 340 (*See also* Conflict
theory; Evolutionary theory; Exchange theory;
Functional theory; Human capital/politics
theory; Interaction theories; Labeling theory;
Open systems approach; Reproduction theory;
Resistance theories)
Thomas, Arthur E., 54
Thompson, Chalmer E., et al., 297
Tienanmen Square, 345, 354
Title IX programs, 112
Toby, Jackson, 53
Tocci, Cynthia M., et al., 110
Toch, Thomas, 81
Toffler, Alvin, 397
Tolbert, Pamela S., et al., 306
Tominaga, Kenichi, 404
Toys, 104
Tracking, 55, 69, 77, 84–87, 134, 276–77 (*See also* Abil-
ity grouping; College-bound track; Curriculum;
Minorities, Reproduction and tracking; Stream-
ing; Vocational tracking)
Tradition-oriented education, 287, 380
Training institutions, 156
Training programs, 122
Travers, E.F., 37
Tremain, Donald, 166
Trends, 415
Trent, William, 189
Tribal colleges, 274, 292
Trow, Martin, 274
Truancy, 4
Turner, Ralph H., 296, 344
Two-year colleges, 274, 283, 305

Ultra-fundamentalists, 49
Unanticipated consequences, 152
Unequal outcomes, 80 (*See also* Inequality)
University, 284
vs. big business, 286–87
single-sex, 107, 293
Unsafe campuses, 54
Uphoff, James K., et al., 256
Upper-class parent, 92–93 (*See also* Parents,
involvement)
Upward mobility, 71, 344 (*See also* Stratification)
Urbanization and change, 399
Useem, Elizabeth L., 110
U.S. international test ranking, 331
Usiskin, Zalman, 39
Utopian movements, 370

Vago, Steven, 396, 398, 408
Valenzuela, Angela, et al., 130
Values, 9
clarification, 39
climate, 222–24, 227
of college education, 313
transmission, 93 (*See also* Cultural, capital)
Van Den Berghe, Pierre L., 400, 401
VanFossen, Beth E., et al., 110
Van Laarhoven, P., et al., 81
Van Scotter, Richard D., et al., 262
Varsity sports, 287
Vassallo, Philip, 153
Vaughan, George B., 275
Velez, William, et al., 128, 275–76
Verbal ability, 111
Viadero, Debra, 37, 81
Violence, 385 (*See also* University; Unsafe campuses)
in schools, 53 (*See also* Survival atmosphere; Weapons)
Vocational education, 86, 136–37, 208, 297
Vocational tracking, 77, 85 (*See also* Tracking)
Volunteer programs, 210, 379
Von Bertalanfly, Ludwig, 14
Voucher, 80–81, 262, 387 (*See also* Choice)

Waldman, Steven, 126
Walker, David, 351–52
Walker, Reagan, 132
Waller, Willard, 11, 178, 199–200, 209, 227, 236–37
Wallerstein, Immanual, 337
Walsh, Mark, 36, 80, 119, 258
Wang, Margaret C., et al., 134
Warner, W. Lloyd, et al., 66, 72
Warren, Jennifer, 49
Washburn, Philo, 37
Weapons, 51, 53 (*See also* Metal detectors; Violence)
Weaver, Rosa Lee, 84, 87
Weber, Max, 10–11, 155
Wehling, Cindy, 204
Weick, Karl E., 162
Weinberg, Mayer, 123
Weisman, Jonathan, 387
Welch, Anthony R., 332–34
Welker, Robert, 204
Wellisch, Jean B., 183
"What Works?," 192
Wheldall, Kevin, 233
Whitaker, Kathyrn S., et al., 177
White, Burton L., 32, 93
"White flight," 123–26
Wilhelms, Fred T., 385
Wilkinson, Doris Y., 315
Williams, Robin, 150
Williamson, Bill, 337, 341, 346, 359

Willie Charles V., et al., 136
Willis, Paul, 78, 227
Wilson, Franklin D., 126
Wilson, Kenneth L., et al., 293
Wilson, Robin, 284, 292, 313
Wilson, William Julius, 114
Winfield, Idee, et al., 350
Winkler, Karen J., 114
Wiseman, Fredrick, 16
Wolf, W.C., Jr., et al., 189
Wolfthal, Maurice, 390
Women, 301
    college students, 293 (*See also* Reentry women)
    literacy, 105
    single-sex schools, 107, 293 (*See also* Gender)
Women's Liberation movement, 370
Women's status, 344
Wong, Sandra, 49
Woodhall, Maureen, 345
Woods, Peter, 237, 240–41
Working-class schools, 93, 96, 221

Working mothers, 93–94
World cultures, 288
World system analysis, 337
Wortman, Paul M., 122
Wright, Randall L., 110
Wuthnow, Robert, 303
Wynne, Edward, 52

Yock, Carla, et al., 177
Yogev, Abreham, et al., 87
Young, Michael F.D., 76, 333
Young, Robert E., 68
Young, Timothy W., 81
Youth 2000 Conference, 204

Zakharieva, Mariana, 43
Zaltman, Gerald, et al., 398, 408
Zuniga, Robin Etter, 114